Gower

HANDBOOK
of
MANAGEMENT SKILLS

SECOND EDITION

Gower

HANDBOOK
of
MANAGEMENT SKILLS

SECOND EDITION

edited by

Dorothy M. Stewart

BCA
LONDON · NEW YORK · SYDNEY · TORONTO

This edition published 1992
by BCA by arrangement with
Gower Publishing Company Limited

First published 1987 as *Handbook of Management Skills*

Second edition published 1992

CN 3759

Typeset in 11/12 Cheltenham by Poole Typesetting (Wessex) Limited and
printed in Great Britain by Billing & Sons, Worcester.

Contents

the fundamental people skills? – Are there alternative people skills? – Conclusion and Checklist – Further reading

The four principal roles of a personnel department – The six key areas of professional expertise and practice – The personnel management grid – Managing
relationships with other departments – Making a case for resources – Managing
your own department – Checklist for managing a personnel department – Further
reading

Strategic planning and the marketing process – Compiling a marketing plan – The
benefits of planning – Implementing and controlling the marketing plan – Training
and development – Motivation – Conclusion – Checklist of key points – Further
reading

How to plan the sales operation – How to organize the sales force – Training the
sales team – How to motivate the sales force – How to control the sales operation –
Summary – Checklist of key points – Further reading

How to plan the distribution operation – How to organize the distribution department – Training the distribution team – How to motivate the distribution department – How to control the distribution operation – Checklist of key points – Taking
it further – Further reading

Financial control – The role of the finance department – The finance organization –
Characteristics of the finance staff – Staffing the finance department – Recruiting
and training – Communications – Summary – Checklist of key points – Further
reading

Information needs of managers – Hardware and software – Centralization *vs.*
decentralization – The user as customer – Charging out – MIS maturity in organizations – Planning in the MIS department – Organizing the MIS department –
Project planning and control – Controlling the MIS department – Summary –
Checklist of key points – Further reading

PART IV   MANAGING THE BUSINESS

List of illustrations

Preface

This is the book I wish I'd had in my desk drawer when I was first a manager. Instead I tried to fill the gaps in my knowledge, experience and confidence with short courses, lots of other books, and an MBA course studied in the evenings for three years. The hard way to do it; but only too familiar to today's beleaguered managers.

The drawback with this approach is the gap between the learning process and your daily work. Management is a mass of different things happening, often at once, and all of them with direct repercussions on your future career. Yesterday's elegant theory expounded so convincingly by that self-assured academic just doesn't stand up to the rigours of life at the coalface.

That course on presentation skills is fine when you're there, supported by that kindly tutor and friendly bunch of co-participants. But it's very different presenting the case for your pet project in front of a sceptical board, with half-a-dozen hostile colleagues sitting round the table with knives sharpened to attack it.

So this book is the one to keep in your desk drawer, out of sight. When you need the information, you'll find a chapter to help; no fancy models or useless theories. This is a practical book for real managers, aimed at helping you manage more effectively in the real world of business today. You'll find enough background information, but no overwhelming detail. You'll find plenty of 'how-to-do-it' information, soundly based on research and years of experience and practice. This is material you can trust. It is tried and tested.

There are four sections. The first, beginning with a keynote chapter on management self-development by Mike Pedler, covers the basic personal skills no manager can survive without. Part II provides chapters on the key aspects of managing other people. Part III is a new section specially commissioned for this second edition, from experts in their field. It deals with the practicalities of managing a specialist function, taking each department in turn. Part IV contains a number of techniques chapters for the manager who wants that extra competitive edge. Inevitably there is some overlap where techniques apply in more than one area. I have tried to keep this to a minimum but since management skills tend to be multi-purpose some duplication has been unavoidable.

Of the thirty-three chapters in this edition fifteen are new; the others have been revised and up-dated. Every chapter now contains suggestions for further reading and details of relevant resources, for when you have time to pursue the subject in more detail. In addition we have added a checklist of key points at the end of each chapter, as both *aide-mémoire* and a spur to action.

We know from the sales of the first edition that this Handbook provided helpful information, in a useful form, to many thousands of managers. I hope that this second expanded edition will prove even more effective.

Dorothy M. Stewart

Notes on contributors

John Adair *(Leadership and motivation)* ex-Professor in Leadership Studies at the University of Surrey, is no armchair theorist. He has served in the Arab Legion, been a deckhand on an Arctic trawler and worked as an orderly in a hospital. For seven years he was Senior Lecturer in Military History and Adviser on Leadership Training at the Royal Military Academy, Sandhurst. During this period he led a number of expeditions, including one across the Jordanian desert by camel. At one time Assistant Director of the Industrial Society, Professor Adair has written and lectured widely on both management and military history.

Pauline Barrett *(Team building)* undertook her first team building exercise in 1970 with a group of youth and community workers, and their district officers, who were having difficulty in meeting their responsibilities against a background of seemingly irreconcilable individual and group needs. It was in that exercise that her interest in working with managers focused on the effect of group working on the success of the enterprise. Two years after this event, Pauline joined the staff at Slough College and worked on a wide variety of management development pro- grammes for both private and public sector clients. In 1981 she left the College to work as a freelance consultant and finally had the opportunity to work with teams in the way in which she had always wished. Her work with organizations and groups has taken the Learning Community approach to their development: a learner-led, tutor-supported way, to personal growth. In 1988 Pauline went to Sydney for almost a year and since her return in July 1989 has chosen to develop new skills of her own and is currently enjoying an early retirement.

Helen Beech *(Mentoring)* joined the ITEM Group two years ago and works with David Clutterbuck as a researcher/writer. They are currently working on a revised edition of *Everyone Needs a Mentor.*

Glenys Cater *(Making the most of your support staff)* is an experienced and highly-trained administrator, and an Associate Member of the Institute of Adminis- trative Management. She has worked in a wide variety of office environments in industry, commerce and the professional sector, and for a wide variety of types of bosses, including the editor of this Handbook. She is currently with the Institute for Non-destructive Testing, where she is engaged in technical committee work.

David Clutterbuck *(Mentoring)* is chairman of the ITEM Group plc, an employee communications company. He is author of the book *Everyone Needs a Mentor*, which is the basis of most mentoring programmes in the UK. David has established mentoring training programmes in a number of private and public sector companies.

John Courtis, FCA *(Recruitment; Interviewing)* has been in management search or selection for 20 years. He trained as a chartered accountant, was commissioned in the RAF and then spent five years in Ford Motor Co., before joining Reed Executive in 1967. He was then with EAL for a four-year period before setting up JC&P in 1974. He has been active in management education since 1972, for the Institute of Chartered Accountants in England and Wales and other bodies and is the author of ten books on management, profit improvement, public relations and recruitment. He is now chairman of JC&P Ltd, and a former chairman both of Deeko plc and the recruitment trade association, FRES. In his spare time he writes more books, searches for the ideal motor car of yesteryear and wonders why modern management techniques don't quite work in family life.

Alan Cowling *(Managing a personnel department)* is Reader in Personnel Management and Director of the Centre for Human Resource Management at Middlesex Polytechnic. His early industrial experience was with Cadbury Brothers and in the Gas Industry, and he has subsequently lectured and acted as a consultant. He recently completed a term of office as Honorary Vice-President of the Institute of Personnel Management. He is co-author of *Behavioural Sciences for Managers*, published by Edward Arnold in 1988.

John Garvin *(Managing an M.I.S. Department)* has wide experience of information systems and computing in industry. After gaining his BSc in Physics at Queen's University, Belfast, he began his career with Short Bros and Harland Ltd, moving to Rolls Royce Ltd in 1967 where he was first a systems analyst and then Management Systems Manager. John transferred into Production Inventory Planning and Control with Rolls Royce, an area of interest he pursued with Goodyear Ltd and Lear Fan Ltd. He currently lectures in Production and Operations Management and Information Technology at the University of Ulster, where his research interests include expert systems/knowledge-based systems and their application in industry and the public sector.

John Gregory *(Making meetings work)* is, in his early 50s, enjoying his fourth career – that of a management selection consultant. He joined the accountancy profession straight from school and later joined mechanical handling engineers, Lansing Bagnall Ltd, as a junior accountant. National Service led to a Short Service Commission in the Royal Army Pay Corps and this, indirectly, to a second career in management education because his three years in the army were spent in the RAPC Headquarter Training Unit. A developing interest in training led to John joining the Management School at Portsmouth Polytechnic where he stayed nine years taking leave in 1967 to study for an MSc in Management Control at Bath University. In 1972, he joined the Institute of Chartered Accountants in England and Wales as Assistant Director Post Qualifying Training, becoming Director, Professional Development Services in 1980. Five years later he became a partner in management selection consultants, John Courtis and Partners, and a year later opened their Milton Keynes office which he managed for four years before joining Breckenridge Consultants Ltd as Managing Director.

Feona J. Hamilton *(Managing information in the office)* has been a member of the information management profession for over 20 years. Starting as a junior library assistant at East Sussex County Library, she held progressively more senior positions in a wide variety of academic and learned society libraries. Her most recent post was as a Group Manager with Aslib. She left Aslib in April 1985, in order to complete research on which she had been working part-time since 1981. In 1985 she began operating as a freelance information consultant. She has contributed widely to the literature of her profession, and is an experienced editor of directories, current awareness bulletins, and newsletters. Her book, *Infopromotion*, was published by Gower in March 1990. She lectures widely on all aspects of information management, including presentation skills, corporate information strategy, and the marketing and promotion of information services. Feona Hamilton has a BA in Humanities from the Open University, an MPhil in Librarianship, is a member of the Institute of Information Scientists, and a Member of the British Institute of Management.

Dr Peter Honey *(People skills)* is a chartered psychologist who works as a management consultant. He worked for Ford Motor Company and British Airways before becoming a freelance in 1969. He specializes in anything to do with people's behaviour and its consequences, and divides his work between designing courses and writing. He has written widely on behavioural topics in over fifty publications. His books include *Developing Interactive Skills, Face to Face Skills, The Manual of Learning Styles, Solving People-Problems, Improve Your People Skills* and *The Manual of Learning Opportunities*. He has advised on the contents of many training films and written the accompanying booklets. He features in the Video Arts production *Talking about Behaviour*. He is an Associate Professor with the International Management Centre, a Fellow of the Institute of Management Consultants and the Institute of Training and Development. He is a chartered psychologist with the British Psychological Society and a member of the Association for Management Education and Development. He is married, has four children and lives in Berkshire.

John Lewington *(Project management)* is a faculty member of the John Simon School of Business, Maryville College in St Louis, Missouri. In addition to this he is CEO of Datafax of St Louis, a database/target marketing company. Prior to this he was Director of Management Studies at Harrow College of Higher Education. He originally trained as a production engineer with the Ever Ready Co. (GB) Ltd whilst completing his degree at City University. He spent three years working for General Motors Ltd (AC Delco) as Group Project Planning Engineer devising plans for new product proposals. In the 1970s he developed a number of short courses for executives in production planning and control techniques. His teaching experience spans the Open University, Middlesex Polytechnic and the Polytechnic of Central London undergraduate and postgraduate management programmes. In 1979 he gained an MSc in Business Administration from the City University Business School, where he specialized in market-oriented corporate planning and modelling systems. He has designed and taught management courses in the US and UK for such leading companies as Horrocks, McDonnell Douglas, Maritz and Kodak. His current interest is the development of computer-based simulation models for management training in problem solving and decision making.

John Lidstone *(Managing a marketing department)* has been acknowledged as a leader in business consultancy and training for nearly thirty years. Non-executive Director of Marketing Improvements Group plc, which he helped to build into one of Europe's foremost marketing consultancy and training companies, John's reputation is soundly based on hands-on experience in marketing and management with such organizations as ShellMex and BP Group and Vicon Agricultural Machinery Ltd, where he was Deputy Managing Director. He is the author of numerous books on marketing, sales and sales management which are all used as definitive sources of reference. Two have been made into award-winning training films by Rank and Video Arts. He has held a number of non-executive directorships, is a Fellow of the Chartered Institute of Marketing, the Institute of Management Consultants, and is a former Chairman of the Management Consultancies Association.

John Mapes *(Managing a production department)* is Senior Lecturer in Operations Management at Cranfield School of Management. After graduating in chemistry at Cambridge he joined ICI Ltd. where he worked for a number of years in the Dyestuffs Division before taking up a lectureship in the Department of Management and Business Studies at Middlesex Polytechnic. He subsequently worked as an Internal Management Consultant for Clayton Dewandre Ltd where he completed a Masters Degree in Operational Research from Brunel University. Since joining Cranfield he has lectured extensively on Production Management in Europe, Africa, the Middle East and the Far East. He also acts as management consultant to a number of companies, specializing in materials management and operating strategy.

Pauric McGowan *(Innovation and intrapreneurship)* joined the University of Ulster as a lecturer in Management in 1987. His responsibilities since then have been divided between the Department and the Northern Ireland Small Business Institute, where he has been able to work closely with managers of growth-oriented small and medium-sized companies. His experience as a counsellor and trainer to these companies has allowed him to obtain a very practical insight into the challenges and opportunities that confront growing businesses in a competitive environment, and the importance of continued entrepreneurship as one eventual response to them. He brings that experience to his chapter in this Handbook. Pauric has worked as a university administrator, a grammar school teacher, a trainee accountant, and the owner of his own small business.

Mike Megranahan *(Counselling in the workplace)* is a Director of the Employee Advisory Resource (EAR), based in Uxbridge, which is an employee assistance programme established in the UK in 1981. He has worked in personnel, consultancy and with a number of counselling agencies. A chartered psychologist and Associate Fellow of the British Psychological Society, he is also editor of *Employee Counselling Today* and past Chair of the Counselling at Work Division.

Keith Newton *(Managing distribution)* is the Director of Logistics at Amersham International Plc. His responsibilities include distribution, purchasing, information technology and operations planning. Amersham is a worldwide supplier of radio-pharmaceuticals and biological and radiological products for measurement and detection in research, industry and medicine. Amersham operates a complex, IT driven international distribution network in a highly regulated environment, providing exceptional speed and service reliability in response to medical needs for very short life products. Keith's previous career spans all aspects of logistics both as a line manager and as a consultant, including thirteen years' international experience with Unilever.

Alan W. Pearson *(Managing R&D)* having gained industrial experience with Pilkington Brothers and Simon Engineering, was appointed Lecturer in Economic Statistics at Manchester University, and later Lecturer in Operational Research at the Business School. He has been Director of the R&D Research Unit since its inception, the Management Course from 1978 to 1981 and Director of the MBA Programme from 1985–8. He is also an Adjunct Program Associate at the Center for Creative Leadership, North Carolina, and was a Visiting Professor at the University of Kiel in 1989. He is an active participant on a wide range of management and educational committees, Editor of *R&D Management*, and on the editorial board of *IEEE Transactions on Engineering Management*. He is a member of the boards of the International Association for the Study of Interdisciplinary Research, and the College of R&D of the Institute of Management Science. In 1984 he was awarded an IEEE Centennial Medal by the Institute of Electrical and Electronic Engineers, Inc. for his contributions to the field of Engineering Management. Alan has published widely in scientific and management journals and is co-author of *Mathematics for Economists* and co-editor of *Transfer Processes in Technical Change* and *Managing Interdisciplinary Research*. His major research interests are in project evaluation, selection, planning and control, and in the management of technological innovation.

Mike Pedler *(Management self-development)* is an independent management development adviser, an Associate of Transform Individual & Organisation Development Consultants and Visiting Teaching Fellow at the Department of Management Learning at Lancaster University in the UK. He is currently Chief Executive of the Sheffield Management Programme, a modular scheme to raise the quality of management in the city. His main interests are in the fields of learner-centred management development, especially self-development and action learning approaches, in learning approaches to business strategy and in the broader concept of the 'Learning Company'. Mike has a wide experience of consulting. Recent clients include British Airways, Thorn EMI Home Electronics and the UK

National Health Service. In 1987 he was in New Zealand as a keynote speaker at the National Conference of the NZ Association of Training & Development and in 1990 he was opening speaker at the 9th International Training & Development Conference at Management Centre Europe in Brussels. His most recent research (with Tom Boydell of Transform and John Burgoyne of the University of Lancaster) concerns the idea of the 'Learning Company'. This has been published as *The Learning Company Report* (1988) Training Agency, Sheffield UK. *The Learning Company* (McGraw-Hill, UK) was published in May 1991. He has published a number of other articles and books including *A Manager's Guide to Self Development*, McGraw Hill (1978; 1986) with John Burgoyne & Tom Boydell; *Action Learning in Practice*, Gower Press (1983 & 1990); and *Managing Yourself*, Fontana (1986) & Gower (1990) with Tom Boydell. He is editor of *Management Education and Development*, the journal of the Association of Management Education and Development.

William Rees *(Financial information and management)* is a lecturer in accounting in the Department of Accounting and Finance at the University of Strathclyde. His specializations are financial analysis, securities markets and international financial management. He has lectured and undertaken consultancy in these and related areas of accounting and finance. He is currently engaged in research into financial forecasting, new issues of equity, share repurchases, and international accounting differences. He has published in professional and academic journals and authored *Financial Analysis*, a comprehensive review of financial information and its uses, published in 1990. Before joining Strathclyde, Bill lectured at the University of Newcastle, and Kingston Polytechnic. Prior to his academic career he worked in the accounting profession for eight years, qualifying in 1975 whilst with Deloitte, Haskins and Sells and gained his MBA at the University of Newcastle in 1979.

Dr John W. Rogers *(Managing your time)* obtained a research degree in Materials Science from the University of Newcastle Upon Tyne in 1972. He subsequently worked with local companies in developing and applying this research. From the mid to late 1970s John worked with British Gas – Northern Region as a trainer and developer. During this period an enlightened company approach to learning enabled him to lead projects using instrumented team learning, developing internal advising skills for technical staff, assessing the effectiveness of personnel policies and management development/consultation work within departments. From 1980 John has worked with the TSB Group Management College at Solihull, West Midlands. Early work was as a trainer running traditional management courses. Currently he is developing the use of information and research in upgrading self-managed learning opportunities, managing several department development initiatives requiring no off-the-shelf approaches, evaluating training and development initiatives, researching and using appropriate psychometric testing methods, and implementing a 'local area network'. He is an active member of the Association of Management Development and Education (AMED), serving on sub-committees, and a Member of the Institute of Personnel Management. Increasingly John is interested in 'new age' approaches, and particularly balancing work/personal/family commitments, increasing our feelings of health and fitness as a natural part of our style of living, working with people to help them achieve what they want, and the wholesome integration of both scientific research and innovation/creativity in change and development.

Brian Sanders *(Effective speaking)* has been involved in maximizing the power of the spoken word all his working life. He trained as an actor and toured the British Isles, France, Belgium and Egypt with the Donald Wolfit Shakespeare Company. He left the theatre in 1954 to take up a career in education. He is a qualified teacher of speech, drama and English and for several years was head of the Speech and Drama Department of a constituent college of London University. He first broadcast in 1960 when he wrote and narrated programmes on acting, the theatre and Shakespeare. From 1970 to 1979 he wrote and presented a drama programme for BBC Schools Radio. Nowadays he broadcasts regularly on radio as an actor and narrator. He has extensive experience of teaching professional people in all aspects on communication and presentation. He runs courses on effective speaking and on speaking professionally through the media in which he deals in a practical way with interviews and talks on TV and radio, the phone-in, and discussions. He runs one-, two- and three-day practical workshop courses for the Industrial Society, the Institute of Chartered Accountants, Touche Ross, the CEGB, the Electricity Council, firms of solicitors and actuaries, and the Police Federation. Since 1985 he has devised and run courses for several UK marketing companies. He lectures to large conferences and small groups.

Bill Scott *(Negotiating)* is an independent consultant working internationally and specializing in communication. His background comprises a rare mixture of industrial and academic achievement. He conducted business research from the University of Keele and later became project director of the Centre for Business Research and eventually assistant director of Manchester Business School. His experience in industry includes six years as group training manager with Wiggins Teape and six directing management development in the 22,000-strong Carrington and Dewhurst Group. Mr Scott has lectured for Management Centre Europe, the ILO and numerous other organizations, and runs seminars regularly, in the UK and overseas, on communication and negotiation skills. He is the author of *The Skills of Negotiating* (Gower, 1981).

Colin Stamp *(Career planning)* has collaborated for the past twelve years in much of Professor Gillian Stamp's written work. Graduating from Queens' College, Cambridge in English Literature and Economics, Colin served in the Royal Navy from 1939 to 1945. Upon demobilization in 1946 he joined American Express, opening their offices in Johannesburg, Cape Town and Durban and remaining in South Africa as their senior manager until he and Gillian returned to England in 1961. Subsequent managerial and marketing posts in the Travellers Cheque Division of American Express included Regional Vice-President for Great Britain, Germany and Scandinavia, and Marketing Director for Europe and the Middle East. He retired in 1977 to set up his own audiovisual company, specializing in training and marketing productions for a wide variety of organizations, and he has lectured extensively on leadership and other social subjects in Britain and the United States. Written and audiovisual productions include *A Dream of Greece* (Johannesburg Festival Award 1953), *Abroad On Sunday Morning* (R. Beerman, 1954), *Best Course to Windward* (BISFA Silver Award 1983) and *A Gift From Doctor Schweitzer* (1984).

Gillian Stamp *(Career planning)* is Director of the Brunel Institute of Organization and Social Studies (BIOSS), a self-financing research institute within Brunel University, Uxbridge, and of the Individual and Organizational Capacity Unit within that institute. Born in London, she graduated in Psychology and Anthropology at the University of the Witwatersrand, South Africa, returning to England with her husband, Colin Stamp, in 1961. During her seventeen years in BIOSS she has been involved in consultancy work about the development of human resources and the design of organizations to take proper account of their purposes and the creativity and imagination of all their members and employees. Her clients have included multinational companies, national organizations moving to multinational scale, public service organizations, public utilities, religious organizations, military organizations in Britain and the USA, and intentional communities. She is the creator of Career Path Appreciation (CPA).

Andrew M. Stewart *(Stress at work; Making performance appraisal work)* is Managing Director of Informed Choice, an organization which applies psychology to business and industry. His activities range from diagnosing the characteristics of effective performance, conducting training needs analyses and employee attitude surveys, to personnel and management selection, performance appraisal, and the identification and development of potential managers and entrepreneurs. He also conducts stress management programmes and assists with the problems of team building. He uses many different techniques, but is probably best known for his work with repertory grid, psychological tests and, above all, assessment centres, which he has been designing and running since 1970. His most recent work includes the managed use of intuition at work, the psychology of running a business, hierarchy and organizational design, and the management of professional staff. Andrew graduated in psychology from Aberdeen University. He lectured at Surrey University for two years, and then held personnel and management development posts with IBM. He was seconded to the Institute of Manpower Studies at Sussex University, where he remained until 1977, developing the research interests which underpin his current work. He was Managing Director of Macmillan Stewart Ltd until 1986. He has published over 40 papers, eleven chapters for various handbooks, and six books, covering assessment centres, performance appraisal, management development, poor performance, and repertory grid. He is a chartered psychologist and an Associate Fellow of the British Psychological Society, a Fellow of the Royal Statistical Society, and an Associate of the Royal College of Psychiatrists.

Dorothy M. Stewart *(Effective writing)* is a writer and editor, who has spent many years in the business world. Beginning as a journalist, she worked in every aspect of book publishing, on a wide range of subjects and levels. She spent five years in Northern Nigeria, where she was involved in teaching English to east Europeans and pre-university students, and helping set up Ahmadu Bello University Press, a scholarly publishing house. After five years running McGraw-Hill's UK management book publishing programme, and gaining an MBA in finance from Middlesex Business School, she set up the Writing Consultancy, offering training and consultancy in all aspects of writing for business. As one assignment she spent almost a year as Publishing Director of the Institute of Chartered Accountants publishing wing, Chartac Books. She now lives in Somerset, concentrating on writing, tutoring writers, and gardening.

Cathy Stoddart *(Developing your people)* graduated in economics and government but chose to go into industrial relations working for a major employers' association. After initially dealing with day-to-day queries arising from the intricacies of a 26-clause national agreement, she was soon dealing with national officials of the major trade unions with which the association negotiated. In this period, she also developed an interest and skills in job evaluation. In 1978 she was appointed job evaluation co-ordinator (in addition to her IR responsibilities) with an independent seat on the National Joint Council for the Environmental Engineering Industry. In her next job as a personnel manager for Lucas CAV she became interested in training and development and later joined a relatively new consultancy company, the Prospect Centre, which specializes in developing strategic manpower development policies and practices for organizations. Cathy's personal experiences as a woman and now a mother of two small children who also wants to work have sparked an interest in the whole field of equal opportunities. After a year combining consultancy with two small sons, Cathy decided to have another child and concentrate on parenting. She now uses her management and negotiating experience mainly in that role, but also in working with voluntary bodies with which she is involved.

Charles Verrall *(Managing a finance department)* has spent 31 years in senior financial positions with major industrial, trading and financial organizations including ITT, British Leyland, BICC, Midland Bank and the Westland Group, in the USA and UK. He began his career in professional accounting mainly with well-known accounting firms which also provided the opportunity to live and work in the USA, Spain, Portugal and Belgium. Although he claims to have semi-retired in 1985, he has found his working life even busier and more exciting, as Finance Director of Westland Group plc and Director of Financial Control at Guinness plc.

Peter Walker *(Decision making and problem solving)* Peter Walker is Senior Consultant at Walker Associates. He has previously held posts of European Training Manager at Texas Instruments, and Manager Organization Development at Rank Xerox. He specialises in providing training and consultancy to organizations in Problem Solving approaches, the Management of Change, People Development, and the Introduction of Total Quality Management. Much of Peter's work has been with multi-national companies, helping country managers and the training function put in place Quality Improvement Strategies, train in-company staff as Instructors, and develop internal Consultants capable of providing on-going support to the organization. As a Chartered Engineer he brings management and business experience to the training function in fields such as Technical Sales, Product Support, and Services Management.

Krystyna Weinstein (Managing communications) is a freelance trainer and consultant specializing in issues around non-communication. She has an extensive background as a writer and editor, and has worked in business and other fields. She combines this experience with a knowledge of organizational issues gained while on the staff of Manchester Business School, and an interest in action learning and learner-centred development. Her current work includes editing, writing and compiling material for a variety of organizations on many subjects – from recruitment and personnel to marketing – and running communications skills workshops.

M. T. Wilson is Chairman of Marketing Improvements Group plc, the leading marketing consultancy, research and training organization, and a visiting Professor at Cranfield School of Management. Marketing Improvements was formed in 1964 by Mike Wilson following experience in the Institute of Marketing and Ford Motor Company, which he joined on graduating from Manchester University. Mike Wilson is widely known for hundreds of seminars and courses on all aspects of marketing which he has run in all five continents. He is perhaps even better known within industry for the highly creative and perceptive consultancy advice given to companies throughout Europe, both multinational and national. He is particularly involved in helping clients improve their strategic marketing processes and activities in such industries as banking, hotels, computers and healthcare as well as in a broad spectrum of consumer and industrial organizations. His books *Managing a Sales Force* and *The Management of Marketing* are standard texts within many companies and his articles on marketing appear regularly in business publications.

Dr H. Beric Wright *(Managing your health)* retired from his executive role in BUPA in 1983 where he had been Chairman of their Medical Centre and Hospital companies, and a Governor. He retained a non-executive role for a further three years. In 1958, Dr Wright had joined the Institute of Directors to start their medical research unit and in 1964 this became the first specialized executive health centre in Europe. It merged with BUPA in 1970 and has grown steadily ever since. Dr Wright qualified in 1941 from University College and Hospital and spent his RAMC years doing operational research as an applied physiologist. He then trained as a surgeon and worked overseas for Shell International. The early work at the IOD taught him that the diseases people get are largely related to the lives they lead and that a holistic or psychosomatic approach is essential. Dr Wright is a Fellow of University College, London, and for many years was involved in the problems of housing the elderly through the Abbeyfield Society. He was also a founder member of the Pre-Retirement Association and still lectures about retirement. Since 1960 he has been in the forefront of informing the public about medical problems through the media.

Part I

MANAGING YOURSELF

Introduction: understanding yourself and your skills needs as a manager

Among the most bewildering causes of unemployment are shortages of skills. There are plenty of people who want to work and there are people who want to employ workers. But the posts and the people do not match – because the people do not have the skills the employers want.

As business moves on into the twenty-first century, the skills that managers need are changing too. A mismatch between posts and people is increasingly likely, especially for people in a post which changes when they do not. In the all too common case of companies that offer no management training, your future is indeed in your own hands.

A personal inventory of your current skills, their strengths and weaknesses, and of the skills demanded currently by your job, will provide a start. But do look ahead to where you think you and your job may be going, and assess your skills needs for the future. Then it is time to get to work on plugging the gaps you see, and polishing up your poorer skills.

Part I of this Handbook focuses on your personal skills. Chapter 1 is a key chapter on management self-development – what it is and why it has evolved into mainstream importance today. It also offers a primer on getting started in your own development as a manager. Do read this chapter first, before dipping into the rest of the book.

The other chapters in Part I offer guidance on fundamental skills for the manager: managing your time, which provides a review of the main time management systems and methods; managing the information that threatens to overwhelm us all, with guidance on assessing your own information needs and how to control the information when you've got it – highlighted by Hamilton's wry 'laws'; and two chapters on the other side of the coin: managing the production of information – effective writing, which aims to help you save time and effort in producing effective written material, and effective speaking, which treats not only the planning and preparation of the material of your presentation but also the technical details of delivery and presentation.

Management is a demanding profession and many managers find that the lifestyle can be damaging in many ways. Dr Beric Wright in Chapter 6 maintains that it is not only possible but necessary that managers manage their own health to achieve a high level of wellbeing, and points out both the dangers and some ways to survive them. Dr Andrew Stewart in Chapter 7 focuses on the effects of stress, its various symptoms and causes, and provides guidelines for its management, both by the individual and by the organization.

Part I concludes with a chapter on career planning which is derived from Professor Gillian Stamp's work on Career Path Appreciation. This considers career in the organizational context, and the chapter offers some useful exercises in self-diagnosis.

1 Management self-development

Mike Pedler

The editor of this book, having given me the honour of opening the batting, has asked for something 'practical and pragmatic, which will help real people become capable managers'. In putting self-development first, I presume she wants you to get the message that becoming a capable manager is first and foremost a self-developmental process.

I would agree (you might expect that), but what does it mean to say that becoming a capable manager is primarily a self-development process? I'll try to explain what I understand by this and provide some ideas of how to get started on self-development. (Although if you're reading this you must be well along the road already.) Before coming to the ideas however, let's begin with a story . . .

MARTIN AND MARINA

Martin and Marina met in 1990. Neither was the sort of person to whom the other would gravitate naturally. At first sight they did not have much in common.

Martin's family had lived in Sheffield's Rivelin Valley for at least 400 years. Some of his ancestors are buried in the little Quaker graveyard nearby. Unlike them, Martin had never thought of himself as different; he was just an ordinary bloke. Over 35 years with the same firm he had joined on leaving school, he has worked his way up to the post of commercial sales manager. Apart from the occasional sales conference he has never had any management training or development.

Marina has always known she was different. Born in Sheffield 10 years after Martin started work, her parents came from Trinidad and her forebears came from what is now Nigeria. Unlike Martin, she's had considerable training and education – 'O' levels and 'A's, which led to a degree, and now, job training as a nurse manager with the Health Authority.

Marina and Martin met on the Sheffield Management Programme – a management development scheme aimed at all Sheffield's estimated 27 000 managers. SMP is open to everyone and there are no barriers to entry apart from the fees. Everyone starts with the 'Diagnostic Day' on which they assess themselves against a list of the managerial qualities or competencies which make up the effective manager. People do this self-assessment with lots of help and feedback – not only from other participants on the day – but also from their colleagues back at work. Having diagnosed their strengths and weaknesses, they then go on to select from a 'menu' of one-day modules ranging from 'Using Money in the Business' to 'Assertiveness', from 'Managing Groups and Meetings' to 'The International Manager'.

As learning partners for part of the Diagnostic Day, Martin and Marina discovered that despite the differences of age, experience, 'industry' and cultural background, there was much that they shared. For a start, both were feeling pressurized at work. Things were changing. Martin's firm was finding it hard to keep up with the competition; even old, local accounts were being lost to the invaders. Marina's hospital is struggling to come to terms with the 'market economy' which the Government is seeking to introduce into the Health Service. For both of them, the old ways – that they had been taught as part of learning the job – are disappearing. Marina was quite optimistic about some of this. If the Health Service was under pressure to be more 'customer oriented', there also seemed to be possibilities opening up. Maybe she wouldn't be a nurse manager in five years time; maybe she'd have acquired some management qualifications and be working in a completely different setting – perhaps even in an engineering company like Martin's?

Martin was less optimistic. It was hard to see how change could be for the better. Too many of his old friends and colleagues had lost their jobs in the 1980s. Too many of them still hadn't found anything else and felt abandoned, with no prospects at 50 or 55. Martin's boss had had to give him a bit of a push to join SMP, but now that he'd arrived he was quite enjoying it. He'd never sat down before to think about what he'd learned in all those years; about what he was good at; about what he didn't do very well; and what he wanted to do in the future. He discovered that he had things he wanted to learn about . . . Total Quality Management for example. He'd heard his boss going on about it but had not really been able to see it himself. He was surprised to find out that Marina knew all about TQM and was even on a Nursing Quality Enhancement Task Force in her hospital. It hadn't occurred to either of them that hospitals and engineering companies had anything in common at all.

SO, WHAT IS MANAGEMENT SELF-DEVELOPMENT?

The story of Martin and Marina is an ordinary, everyday one. What does it tell us about management self-development?

Some managers – perhaps as many as half – have had no formal management education or training. In Martin's case, therefore, we might argue that anything he has learned about being a manager in the last 35 years has been self-development – in the sense that it has been done by himself without outside help. In fact most management development is self-development in this 'naturally occurring', non-contrived sense. The idea of self-development puts the learner and the learning process at the centre of its concerns. Over the last few years a learning model – often known as the Kolb model after one of its popularizers – has become the badge of people who want to work in this way and who show this to managers to demonstrate that it is the idea of learning they want to focus on (see Figure 1.1). From the self-development perspective, there is a great deal of management

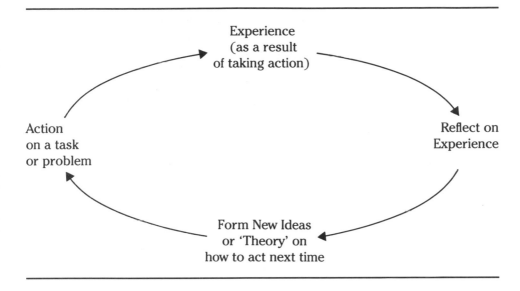

Figure 1.1   The Kolb model of learning

development going on all the time, but there is so much more that could happen, if we decided to help with these 'naturally occurring' processes, instead of interfering with them as we often do. One consequence of focusing upon this learning cycle is that the manager's everyday work is seen as the most potent source of action and experience which can then be reflected upon, conceptualized and learned from. This means we don't need courses to provide the 'input'. Work itself provides as much of this as we manage to convert into learning. This is in contrast to what we might call the management training tradition which focuses upon the course, trainer, and the content of the training materials.

In contrast to Martin's experience, Marina has received considerable education and training from others. Is this self-development? Did she really choose what she wanted to learn or did others choose it for her – 'elders who know better'?

The first meaning of self-development – what I call the 'by self' element – management self-development means the learner (and not the boss, teacher or any other outside person) taking the primary responsibility for what they learn. Most management development still isn't like this, despite the fact that the ideas of self-development have been around for the last 15 years or so. Most people still get sent on courses, or are expected to undertake training, rather than choosing for themselves.

It may sound a small thing – giving people the right to choose what to learn, when to learn, at what pace to learn, when to stop learning and so on – but it is actually a revolutionary principle in the world of work where we are still largely expected to do as we are told. A self-development approach to learning how to manage means taking the responsibility for choosing ourselves.

This leads to the second principle of self-development – what I call the 'of self' element. When we choose for ourselves and take responsibility for what may be a wrong decision (after all we're learners and we make mistakes), it affects us as whole persons and not just in our manager role. This 'whole person' aspect of self-development is the other major way in which this approach differs from more traditional approaches to management development, where the focus is on learning new skills and abilities in the role of manager. Self-development holds that what we choose to learn affects the whole person and that if we learn something useful as a manager we will also use that in other settings – at home, with our children, in the community. The corollary is also true: that we learn useful things from our children – about how important it is to recognize and reward their efforts to learn to read for example – which we then use in our managerial lives.

So whether a management development process is self-developmental or not can be measured against the extent to which the learner freely chooses it (byself), and to the extent they learn or grow as whole persons (of self). We can also see from Martin's story that he needed encouragement to make his choice. Sometimes we need a little help from our friends – as long as they leave the choice with us.

What we can also see from a glance at the story is that Martin and Marina are very different – separated by age, experience, the type of business they are in, cultural background and so on. Marina and Martin are not going to learn the same things, they are not going to learn in the same way, they are not going to learn at the same pace. They can sit in the 'same' seminar, take part in the 'same' project and learn uniquely. Marina is a young, well-educated, black, female, professional working in Health Care. Martin is a middle-aged person from Yorkshire, who is also male and white – although, in a very real sense, he hadn't noticed this until now.

Given these differences, and like the rest of us who are different, Marina and Martin can never do the job in the same way. Of course, we want all managers to do some of the same things – to be good at motivating people, competent in managing budgets and so on. There are also similar things to do with the era or time which all managers have to take account of wherever they work. Martin and Marina found they had some things in common – pressure to be more customer-oriented, an interest in Total Quality Management and so on, which are currently part of what many people in widely varying fields of endeavour are trying to do.

One way to deal with these 'required competencies' is to specify them and then put everyone on courses to learn them. This is the old – and non-self-developmental – way of doing things which deals with managers in cohorts with generalized needs rather than as individuals with unique starting points.

One last thing from the story. Some form of self-diagnosis is essential to start a self-development process. Martin and Marina were offered a structured form of this, but diagnostic information can come from many places – from the job, from colleagues, friends, 'role models', or inner questions that arise in us from time to time about what we're doing and where we're going and to which we often don't listen well enough. It is at this point of diagnosis that one of the apparent paradoxes of self-development comes to light – that to really take responsibility for our own choices about what we need to learn, we find we are dependent upon the insight, feedback and ideas of others. Far from self-development being a wholly DIY process, it is in this approach to management development that we most need the help of others – to give us honest feedback and constructive advice to overcome our blocks and blind spots.

The main aim of self-development is not to help a person learn this or that, but to help the learner understand and master the learning process itself. This can help us 'learn how to learn' in that we begin to recognize what to do in order to act and learn in unfamiliar situations. The ability to learn how to learn is a key component of self-starters and is perhaps the best insurance in a changing world against the inevitable redundancy of our existing stock of knowledge and skills.

The ability to learn how to learn is the real payoff from the self-development process. Why bother to learn about, say, budgeting or a new technical skill in a self-developmental way when I can be easily instructed to 'operate by numbers'? Because only when you set out to learn because you want to, and in a self-responsible way, can you become aware of the actual processes involved in learning. Internalize these processes, make them part of your practice and, like riding a bicycle, you'll never forget them. That is the key purpose of the self-development approach – not just to get this or that skill developed, but to help people to acquire the learning habit.

GETTING STARTED: A PRIMER

What are the implications for the person, younger or older, well-trained or inexperienced, who wants to develop themselves as a manager?
1 Self-development starts with you and with your desire to learn – learn a job, understand an organization, master a current difficulty, advance in your career, be different. Without this desire, self-development cannot start. For example, you don't have to know in precise terms what you want to learn. Most of us don't really know what we need to learn (which is why we so often surrender to 'experts' who will 'diagnose our needs' for us) but you do have to be dissatisfied or feel some discomfort with your present state. Without this you can't start – you might as well ask someone to send you on a course on something or other.
2 You need to understand why you are currently dissatisfied and how you can move forwards from this state. This is called self-diagnosis. You always have four choices when you are dissatisfied: to put up with things, to leave, to get others to change, or to change yourself. Only if you choose the last option do you need a self-development programme.

There are various ways to get help with self-diagnosis. You can buy a book (some are given in the list of Further Reading at the end of this chapter) which provides a structure and a model of managerial qualities to measure yourself against. You can interview your colleagues, your partner and your customers and ask them how you could improve your service to them. If you're a reflective sort of person, you probably only need to sit and think. You can go and see an expert – a management development person or a chartered psychologist who specializes in psychometric tests – and get their opinion. You can choose a course like the Sheffield Management Programme which offers you some sort of self-diagnostic process as part of the package. There are lots of different ways of going about it and you'll find many more listed in the various recommended books. The main thing is that it is self-diagnosis – you are making the decisions and the choices – usually with a little help from your friends.
3 Having diagnosed yourself, you can set yourself some goals for self-development. How would you like the current state to be different? What would the ideal state look like? Write down your goal in a measurable form if you can and give

yourself a deadline. 'I will get better at asserting myself' is pretty useless (and not very assertive by the way) as a goal, but 'I will ask Jenny to share the cleaning with me by Friday' is much more direct. If I knew about it, I could ask you how you got on, and we could probably agree a) how successful you'd been and b) what else you should try to make yourself more assertive.

There are lots of frameworks for helping you set goals and most of the self-development books have them. 'Domain Mapping' in *Managing Yourself* is one example.

4   Armed with some goals, you can set about designing yourself a learning programme and finding the appropriate resources. Obviously, this depends on what you want to learn. In the assertiveness example above, part of the learning programme follows obviously from the goal – a try out on Jenny. However, as preparation you might decide to ask someone or read a book to discover the right form of words in which to put your request. Next you might decide on a rehearsal – with a friend, or in front of the mirror, or in your head whilst you're going to meet Jenny. 'By March, I will learn to do my accounts on a spreadsheet' is a longer term goal but the same principles apply. Who can teach you keyboard skills if you don't have them? Could you learn from a book with bits of consultancy from an experienced friend? How much time will you need to practise? Where can you get hold of the machine and the software to practise with? With a long learning programme you need an overall goal, and also sub-goals to provide staging posts and keep you going.

(I mentioned earlier that 'learning to learn' is the key payoff from self-development. Part of learning to learn is understanding and internalizing – so that it becomes a part of your professional practice – the process I'm spelling out here. For example, you'll notice what's involved with developing a learning programme – a goal; some resources, for example, time for learning; friends or 'learning consultants' to help you; a practice regime; commitment and determination etc. Knowing this – and being able to do it each time you need it – is a key part of what it means to be able to learn.)

5   As part of this learning to learn process are you noticing how often friends crop up? For most of us learning is a social affair – we need feedback, encouragement and the help of friends to pinpoint our goals, devise our learning programmes and to keep us going. Equally if we have friends like this, we're probably helping them with their self-development too.

An important part of self-development is the recruiting of other people to help you with your efforts. I call these friends, but they can be all sorts of people – your colleagues, your actual friends, people with particular skills or resources, members of a professional association. And you need to learn to recognize how other people can help you and to build up networks of such people. The reason I call them friends is that I think of them as people who take an interest in your development, people who want you to succeed, and not people who want to put you down, impress you with their knowledge etc etc. Take people like this off your 'Friends & Helpers' file.

You can say with confidence that anyone who is good at developing themselves has a wide range of contacts and friends with whom they network and stay in touch. Some of the learning methods associated with self-development – especially action learning and self-development groups – make this process of working with a small group of people of central importance. You can find out about these methods from the books in the list of Further Reading.

6   Keeping on with your learning programme, stickability and perseverance – whatever you want to call it. You won't get far without this. If spotting your current dissatisfaction is your five per cent inspiration, this number 6 will take up 95% of your time and energy. Go back to the previous point again – self-development has a lot in common with weight watchers – you're more likely to keep going and succeed if you've got other people with you.

7   Lastly, you need to assess yourself against your goals. How well are you doing? If you set lots of learning sub-goals then these make good points at which to test yourself. It is a little like being tested at school, but only a little; here *you* set the goals and decide when to test; you interpret the test scores and they're your property. Testing is a healthy process when you're in charge. You need test results to tell you whether you're on track, whether you need to revise future goals and so on.

This seventh point takes you back to the first. Testing yourself leaves you feeling satisfied – in which case you stop learning – or dissatisfied – in which case you carry on, heading for the next target. In the light of this here's an important health warning, which, perhaps, I should have started with:

IMPORTANT HEALTH WARNING

Self-development can seriously change you and how you think, feel and behave. It should not be undertaken without thought and adequate preparation. For example, your partner, children and colleagues may want you to stay the same. It should not be undertaken lightly by people who have not done any learning for the last decade or two. Self-development can be addictive; people report that learning something 'gives them a buzz' and find they go on to learn more. If this happens on a wide scale it will threaten the fabric of our companies and public service organizations as we know them. You have been warned.

However there are some other reasons why you should have a go despite the dangers. To explain this needs a bit of history and a bit of the future for organizations.

WHERE DOES SELF-DEVELOPMENT COME FROM?

Over the past 10 or 15 years, self-development has moved from being a fringe pursuit to a position in the mainstream of management and business development. There can be few training and development programmes in the 1990s which do not include at least a self-development element in their design and delivery. Self-development emerged, or perhaps re-emerged, as an idea in training and development in the 1970s and 80s as a response to the limitations of the earlier idea of 'systematic training'.

Systematic training was an answer to the skills shortages experienced in industrialized countries in the post-war boom years. When industries and economies tried to respond to the massive demands placed on them, they simply did not have the skilled people to produce the goods. In Britain the 1964 Industrial Training Act

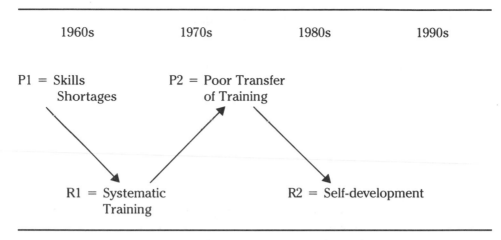

Figure 1.2   The learning process as a historical sequence of Problems (P) and Responses (R).

set up Industry Training Boards to create an adequate supply of skilled 'manpower' especially in craft and operator grades. Systematic training was just that: the approach was scientific/analytic based upon detailed job descriptions, followed by even more detailed task, skill and needs analyses. This work study process was carried out by qualified training officers who specified training objectives for 'target populations' which followed standard syllabi on highly structured training programmes which were thoroughly evaluated. Systematic training was often very successful in cutting down the time needed to bring people to the required skill levels.

When applied to supervisory or managerial work in industry or to less definable or 'people-centred' jobs however, the systematic approach did not work so well. Faced with complexity, variety and general 'unprogrammability', systematic training is far too prescriptive. Whilst the programmes were well designed and delivered and the returning participants often evaluated them as enjoyable, very little seemed applicable in the messy world of practice.

It is this 'transfer of training' problem, as it became known, which led to a change of focus – to the learner and the learning process rather than the trainer and the training process. Learner-centred designs such as action learning, self-development and self-managed learning in which the learner's work and life tasks become the primary vehicles for learning and development began to gain in popularity.

We can map this process as a historical sequence of problems and responses (see Figure 1.2). Self-development can also be seen as a re-emergence of an old idea. In 1938 Dale Carnegie influenced a generation on both sides of the Atlantic with his book, *How to Win Friends and Influence People*, which urged people to self-improve and not to rely upon external help, in much the same way that Samuel Smiles had done in 1859 with his book, *Self Help*. In this perspective, the idea of self-development as currently applied to training and development activities reflects a concern to empower the learner, to urge him/her to stand on his/her own two feet, to take charge and seek out the training and development needed. We are now again at a point on the historical wave which weights individual choice and agency as well as social or organizational definitions of what is needed. This is what makes self-development such a powerful and appropriate idea for now.

Because self-development means learners taking the primary responsibility for choosing what, when and how to learn, this implies the freedom of the individual to choose *not* to develop particular skills, knowledge or career directions at the behest of others. Such freedom, of course, carries with it the responsibility for the consequences of such choices.

WHY ARE ORGANIZATIONS SUPPORTING THE SELF-DEVELOPMENT OF THEIR PEOPLE?

Why should people in organizations be given this sort of freedom when they may make choices which are not in the interests of the organization? One answer to this good question is that the world of work is changing so rapidly with people being asked to change roles, develop serial careers and swap outdated skills for new ones, that it is increasingly difficult for one person to prescribe for others what they should learn next.

To put it another way, the consequences for the organization of taking one path and getting it wrong are dire. There is a move towards higher trust employment relations and a realization that the topical cliche 'Our people are our most valuable asset', needs action as well as fine words.

Secondly, we no longer use the term 'the organization' with the old taken-for-granted certainty. Systematic training is about meeting organizational needs and requirements. But *who* is the organization and what are its needs? It often turns out that the senior managers define these things. But in these new days of skills shortages to what extent do senior managers have the power to decide in what direction you or I should develop? Self-development is, in part, an approach which recognizes the increasing power of the 'knowledge worker' who may often have a professional career loyalty first and an organizational loyalty second.

A third answer to the question of why learners should be empowered is that people who choose to develop themselves have much more motivation to learn and succeed than those who are instructed to learn something for the good of the organization. To the extent that the learner chooses directions which benefit the organization, and most of us are highly aware of the context in which we are developing and the trade-offs involved, then you have a self-motivated, self-starter who can be relied upon to respond with initiative in a wide variety of circumstances.

It is this self-starting capacity which we are coming to value most highly in people. Recently we have begun to talk about the Learning Company or Learning Organization as a model for the future. This is an organization which creates learning opportunities for all of its members and which also is capable of learning and of transforming itself as a collective. Learning Companies cannot operate with people who wait to be instructed, who must have permission before they can act, who fear the consequences of taking initiatives. In other words, Learning Companies are organizations which are both fitted for self-developers to work in and require their people to be self-developing in order to maintain and enhance individual and collective learning capacity. Flexibility and adaptability in both the organization as a whole and in individual members is seen as a critical factor for the future well-being of the enterprise. Self-development as a process offers a way of developing this learning habit:

> . . . any effective system for development must increase the learner's capacity and willingness to take control over, and responsibility for, events and particularly for themselves and their own learning.
>
> (Pedler, Burgoyne and Boydell 1986: 1)

CONCLUSIONS

This chapter sets out to define management self-development and explain why it evolved to the mainstream from a peripheral position some years ago. Key points are:

1 Most management development is self-development in the sense that it is 'naturally occurring' on the job. However, what happens naturally is only a small fraction of what is possible and what is increasingly necessary. Some people learn some things but could learn more; others just get stuck.

2 Encouraging self-development consists of trying to understand and strengthen the learning rather than the training process.

3 Self-development is a by-self process which puts the learner at the centre in terms of being the person with the primary responsibility for choosing what, when and how to learn.

4 It is also an of-self process which involves the whole person and not just some particular aspect of that person.

5 Self-development starts with a desire to learn and self-diagnosis. Other people – other learners who also act as informal teachers – are crucial to the process of helping us diagnose ourselves and in helping us achieve our learning goals.

6 The primary purpose of self-development is to help people understand and develop their learning processes and to acquire the 'learning habit'.

7 The proper home for the self-developer is the Learning Company which creates lots of learning opportunities for all its members and is able to transform itself as a whole.

The reading list which follows offers some books which the reader might find useful in furthering their own development.

FURTHER READING

Back, K. and Back, K., *Assertiveness at Work*, McGraw Hill, 1982. A book which focuses upon one of the key 'skills' in self-development.

Francis, D., *Managing Your Own Career*, Fontana, 1985. A good self-diagnostic book which focuses on how to develop your career by analysing what drives you, what talents you have, what organization suits you and so on. This book is part of a series for the 'thinking manager'. Dave Francis has written other books relevant to self-development.

Hopson, B. and Scally, M., *Build Your Own Rainbow*, Lifeskills Associates, 1984. A workbook for career and life management which includes a number of ideas, exercises and questionnaires.

Megginson, D. F. and Pedler, M. J., *Self-development: A Facilitator's Guide* McGraw Hill, 1991. A book for managers as developers to help them encourage self-development at work. Lots of ideas and exercises for working with individuals, groups and the whole company.

Mumford, A., *Making Experience Pay*, McGraw Hill, 1980. A book which discusses how to learn from experience at work. The author focuses on the work setting and sees self-development mainly in the service of achieving job requirements and to satisfy organizational purposes.

Pedler, M. J. (Ed.), *Action Learning in Practice* 2nd Edn, Gower, 1991. Case studies, accounts and contributions from the best known practitioners of action learning in the UK as well as some from round the world.

Pedler, M. J. & Boydell, T. H., *Managing Yourself,* Gower, 1990. Based on the assumption that you must manage yourself before you can organize others, this book helps you develop yourself in 4 main areas – health, skills, action and identity, and includes lots of worked examples and activities as well as ideas.

Pedler, M. J., Burgoyne, J. G. and Boydell, T. H., *A Manager's Guide to Self-development* 2nd. Ed., McGraw-Hill, 1986. This book is a self-development package with a self-diagnostic questionnaire based on the 11 qualities of an effective manager together with 42 activities for developing the qualities.

Pedler, M. J., Burgoyne, J. G. and Boydell, T. H., *The Learning Company: A Strategy for Sustainable Development*, McGraw-Hill, 1991. Defines the idea of the Learning Company and offers some ways of diagnosing the reader's organization against the model offered. Also contains 101 glimpses of the Learning Company in practice.

Pedler, M. J., Burgoyne, J. G., Boydell, T. H. and Welshman, G. (Eds), *Self-development in Organisations*, McGraw Hill, 1990. A sourcebook with case studies and contributions from practitioners about the use of self-development ideas in organizations, particularly in how they relate to wider organizational issues and systems.

Revans, R. W., *The ABC of Action Learning*, Chartwell Bratt, 1983. The primer on action learning from its founder. Action learning is one of the most powerful philosophies and methods for self-development and has been widely adopted.

2 Managing your time

John Rogers

This chapter presents guidelines that will help you manage your time better. Six proven approaches are described – objectives and key task areas, diaries and planning, time logs, personal behaviour, managerial style and visual reminders. A discussion on the thinking behind each approach is accompanied by suggestions and self-assessment exercises. Your strategy in managing your time better is likely to involve a combination of several approaches, dependent upon your circumstances and preferred style.

INTRODUCTION

This morning different people have exclaimed to me:

- 'Yet more paperwork in the post, no wonder I can't get my *proper* job done.'
- 'I'm going to send the telephone on holiday, and lock myself away in a quiet room.'
- 'If I've told him once, I've told him a dozen times.'
- 'She wants me to re-write it yet again. Why can't she tell me what she wants in the first place; another evening spent working.'

Have you heard similar comments today? What do they all have in common? And why do we feel so powerless to respond constructively? It occurs to me that all these basic statements relate to how we organize and manage our time. It seems such common sense; after all, it's simply a matter of setting objectives, determining priorities and carrying out tasks. Or is it? If common sense was so common we would all be experts at managing our time, with the above exclamations becoming extinct.

Time as a resource

First, we need to recognize that time is a remarkable resource. Whatever your requirements, race, class, sex and age, time is the limiting factor in achieving anything. You cannot hire it, buy it or rent it (although octogenarians may disagree), and you cannot obtain more than your allocation of 24 hours per day. In economic terms you cannot construct a marginal utility curve for time, and its supply is totally inelastic – no matter how high the demand, the supply will not and cannot be increased. Time is totally perishable; it cannot be stored in freezers, tins or deposit accounts, or slowed down like coastal erosion. Time is totally irreplaceable, unlike plastics (for steels), bread for potatoes and automation for human labour.

Biologically we appear to be ill equipped to manage time. In an isolated darkened room, deprived of our main senses, we soon lose track of time passing. Similarly boredom apparently extends time, whilst excitement and deadlines compress it. Paradoxically, with unemployment levels comparatively high and the promise of an age of leisure, many managers still work long hours, suffering the consequences in the relentless battle 'to get things done'.

The changing world and time

The context of managerial work is changing rapidly. So in addition to managing our time well to carry out our existing roles, we need to adapt, learn and unlearn to cope successfully with our 'brave new world'. A branch manager of a bank, for example, is now responsible for selling up to 150 services to more sophisticated personal and commercial customers in an increasingly competitive market, whilst adapting to complex technological innovations. Such change is not unique – your context is likely to be changing just as dramatically. But in the last analysis, it is your responsibility to commit yourself to using time well to manage these changes and achieve success.

Think of three managers you know well. Using the matrix shown in Figure 2.1 write down four areas of improvement for each manager that you believe would enable them to operate more effectively. It is highly likely that you have included items related to time management – organizing paperwork, running meetings, putting things off, consulting others etc.

A survey of over 1300 managers reported that poor priority setting is common. Despite the long hours worked, only 47 per cent of actual working time was taken up with managerial activities. Most of the remaining time was spent doing their subordinates' jobs; that is, doing the familiar and less threatening non-managerial activities they themselves *used* to do. Consider a salary of £20,000 per year. This can be translated as about £85.00 per day or £11.00 per hour (excluding employment costs). The cost of this time wasting can be rapidly computed into a fixed overhead, highlighting the need for good time use and behaviour to change. And remember that there is *always* time to complete the most important matters.

This chapter looks at six approaches that will help you become aware of how you use your time, and then do something about it.

OBJECTIVES AND KEY TASK AREAS

Goals

What are your lifetime goals? Lakein claims that you should be clear about them. By writing them down you discover what you really want to do, generate motivation

Areas for improvement	Manager 1	Manager 2	Manager 3
1			
2			
3			
4			

Figure 2.1   Areas of improvement for three managers you know well

to do it and give meaning to your minute-by-minute use of time. Lifetime goals are linked to visions, purposes, missions and basic beliefs. Vital questions suggested by Lakein as focusing our use of time are:

- How would you *like* to spend the next three years?
- If you knew *now* you would be struck by lightning six months from today, how would you *live* until then?

Remember that goal setting is an ongoing activity which needs regular updating, recording, prioritizing and reviewing for both long and short term goals. Do it at least every six months. And write it down.

When developing your goals, objectives or key task areas try to be aware of any inconsistencies or paradoxes: for example, becoming managing director is not usually compatible with having unlimited time with your family. Similarly to be liked by everyone is usually incompatible with having strong opinions which you voice regularly. Look at your own lifetime goals for such incompatibilities, but do not stop yourself from starting to achieve lifetime ambitions.

Key task areas

So how do you establish your own key task areas? First you need some data about what you do and how you do it. This can come from a time log (see page 28). An alternative approach often favoured is to generate your own key task areas. The latter is more future orientated and likely to lead to more immediate results. Data to develop your key areas may come from considering the following checklist of business objectives:

- Why is the company in business?
- What is it in business for?
- What do we need to do to remain in business?
- Where do we need to be in two, five years' time?
- How can we get there?
- What parts do I have a direct influence upon?
- What are my department's objectives?
- What are my objectives?
- What must I contribute to achieve them?
- What powers do I have?
- Who else must play a part?
- What do I expect of them?
- What do they expect of me?
- How can I improve my performance?

You may also have more personal sources, such as:

- job descriptions, but beware that these may be out of date or static and in any case will not usually tell you much about priorities;
- appraisals and assessment interviews, which indicate potential strengths and weaknesses in attaining goals;
- colleagues, who will help you to understand how you use your time, and how they think you *should* use your time;
- company goals, from notice boards, house journals etc.;
- professional journals and databases, which contain factual information about companies and managers in similar fields to yourself;
- your own life plans, what you really want to achieve with your life.

Examples of key task areas

As with your time log categories, key task areas should be of a manageable number, action orientated, cover *all* the tasks you do (or should do) and be vividly and concisely expressed. As an example consider a branch manager or assistant manager of a financial institution. Typical key areas in this job could be based upon:

- staff relations/effectiveness/training and development/motivation/delegation;
- finance/administration (budgets, credit controls, statistics, routines);

	Before course (%)	After course (proposed %)	After course (actual %)
Lending	20	35	20
Marketing	15	20	25
Planning	5	10	15
Improving profitability of existing services	5	10	15
Staff training	5	15	10
Administration	20	5	10
Achieving targets	30	5	5

Figure 2.2   Percentages of time spent in key task areas

(The key figure shows the percentage of time spent by a manager in seven key areas before attending a time planning course, as proposed for the next six months and as actually achieved six months later.)

- clients/customers/accounts (large–small, maintain–develop);
- new business (societies, directors, business clubs);
- local market information (competitors, potential clients);
- premises (building maintenance, equipment, security);
- internal coordination/communications (head office, boss, other branches);
- external relations (accountants, solicitors, business people, estate agents);
- special projects/large one-off tasks;
- professional updating;
- personal development.

Planning time allocation

One assistant manager in a large border county branch identified seven distinct areas of activity, estimating the percentage of time spent in each category:

- before a time planning course;
- as proposed for the next six months whilst on the course;
- actual achievement as assessed six months later.

See Figure 2.2.

Exercise

Insert your own key areas, then complete the past and proposed columns of the table shown in Figure 2.3. The differences between past and proposed percentages form the basis of an action plan that can be reviewed at a later date by completing the actual columns as in our example (Figure 2.2). Obviously your own key task areas will be different.

Key task area	Past	Proposed (state time deadline)	Actual

Figure 2.3   Percentage of time spent in key task areas (your own)

DIARIES AND PLANNING

The need for information

You need some way of capturing and having ready access to important information. Apart from a sensible working environment with well labelled filing systems for static information, you will need some form of diary/notebook that is designed with good time management principles in mind. Most diaries bought at the start of a new year from stationers are inadequate for anything but appointments.

Ask yourself, what kinds of information do I need to refer to on a regular and often unprepared basis? This might include:

- appointments and other dated deadlines;
- tasks – to do, in progress and completed;
- ideas and other notes;
- key task areas – keep them 'in sight and in mind';
- birthdays, school terms and household/garden tasks;

- maps and timetables;
- books to read, films to see and places to visit;
- expenses, budgets and other financial matters;
- delegation, crises and interruption logs.

Choosing a diary

When choosing a diary ask yourself:

- What size do I want? Sizes range from large wall charts and planners via desk diaries (about 20 × 25 cm) to pocket diaries (about 10 × 15 cm) – but beware of running two or more diaries! Formats include one or seven days per page and one month per page. The increasing use of specially designed loose-leaf time management diaries helps you to create a system that works for you: some typical designs I find useful are shown in Figure 2.4. A modern photocopier enables you to find the right size for your planner.
- What information do I need a diary or time planner to contain? Traditional diaries usually contain standard information that may or may not be useful – a map of the London Underground system or the address of airports in Asia will be of little use to someone who never leaves Scotland. Diaries designed with time management principles in mind offer a wealth of information that you can choose from as it suits you – maybe even a road map of Glasgow and Edinburgh.

Suppliers of useful time planning systems are listed at the end of this chapter; but design your own as well.

At this stage you should stop and consider what diary planning systems you use and whether they are adequate. If you find yourself hunting through scraps of paper, missing appointments, losing track of ideas and generally unaware of what you are really trying to achieve you should consider changing to something more suitable. But beware! If you are a perfectionist you may spend far too much time keeping the perfect neat time planner, without actually achieving anything other than administrivia.

Determining priorities

Whatever system you choose it is essential to list all the activities that you need to do. For many line managers this is best done daily, either immediately on arriving at work or just before leaving the previous evening. If necessary you can find the mental space by arriving 10 minutes earlier, or leaving 10 minutes later. Where life is less hectic, a Project Manager for example, the list can be made weekly or monthly. But whatever your role do it when it suits you. What you will end up with is more activities than time available. Don't be overwhelmed at this stage: you need to prioritise. Go through your list and pick out priorities using the ABC system: 'A's, are priority jobs, 'B's less so and 'C's not so important. 'A's are usually the hardest, most complex and difficult – and the most important! 'C's are often trivial, easy to do, look impressive when crossed off a list, but don't get you anywhere. So start with 'A's, not with 'C's or 'Z's.

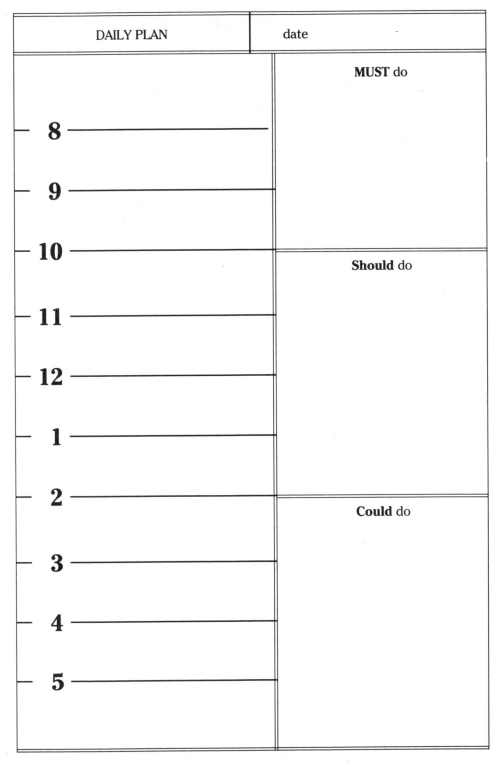

Figure 2.4   Typical planning forms for managing your time

				Date		
	JOHN	GAIL	COLIN	HELEN	BARRY	DANIEL
MON						
TUES						
WED						
THURS						
FRI						
SAT						
SUN						

Figure 2.4   (continued)

WEEKLY PLAN	WK NO:
	DATE:

	MUST DO:
MON	
TUES	SHOULD DO:
WED	
THURS	
FRI	COULD DO:
SAT	
SUN	

Figure 2.4   (continued)

	Wk no: period
Objectives of the week	1. _____ 2. _____ 3. _____ 4. _____

MON				
TUES				
WED				
THURS				
FRI				

Figure 2.4   (continued)

	month

Objectives of the month	1.	
	2.	
	3.	
	4.	
	5.	
	6.	
	7.	

1		17		
2		18		
3		19		
4		20		
5		21		
6		22		
7		23		
8		24		
9		25		
10		26		
11		27		
12		28		
13		29		
14		30		
15		31		
16				

Figure 2.4   (concluded)

Look at the 'A's. You may like to prioritise again (A1, A2, A3 . . .) and then begin to see connections between tasks. By now you should be crossing off tasks and interlinking them: it may look a bit messy, but your left and right brains will be working away on speedy and effective methods of getting things done. If 'ABC's fail to appeal try prioritising using 'MSC's:

- tasks that *must* be completed;
- tasks that *should* be completed;
- tasks that *could* be completed (if only I had the time).

Avoid generating multiple lists, unmanageable numbers of priority jobs, items duplicated on several lists and constantly changing priorities.

Using a diary or planner

If you use a traditional diary make sure you transfer tasks and times into it in addition to the usual appointments. Do this by blocking out chunks of time. Be aware of the amount of time needed for project work, such as board reports and marketing programmes, and plan it into the diary. The alternative is a bulging briefcase to accompany the trek home and needlessly burning the midnight oil.

Similarly be aware of your continuing daily tasks and how long they take, and the average time that must be left unplanned to deal with crises, the unexpected and the unreasonable. An overall picture of your total work requirements can be built up which enables you to be clearer on when to say 'yes' and 'no' to the demands of others.

TIME LOGS

Why bother?

Many managers have at some stage in their working lives logged their time as it is actually being used, and analysed it later. But why bother? The answer is simply because you are probably unsure about how much time you spend on various activities. All right, you have some general ideas; but to effect *real* improvement a constructive survey and analysis is critical. Sometimes a manager will find that his time use is even more haphazard and fragmented than he previously believed! This realisation is a poignant lesson about the need to make changes. If a manager delegates more effectively, closes the door occasionally to plan and says 'no' and 'yes' as appropriate, a second time log can be completed for two weeks at a later date to determine his relative success in changing.

The main advantages of the time log approach are:

- the self-development opportunities, in that the results can be used by you personally and revealed only to those you wish to see it; thus you can be honest with yourself;
- it deals with real indisputable *facts* about how you spent your time;
- you learn from the actual process of doing it; for example, a salesperson may be surprised at how much time is spent chasing low-yield prospects; managers may learn just how much discretionary time is available to them.

However, it can be tedious to commit yourself to two to four weeks of logging, especially if your design is complex or you are too busy. If the latter is the case you would be strongly advised to find time to do a time log!

Designing and using time logs

In its most straightforward mode you will need to divide your working day into six–eight main categories of activities. These will normally be linked to your objectives or key task areas. You will need to note during the course of your day the amount of time spent in each category; activities outside these key task areas may be recorded in an extra catch-all category.

All time spent must be allocated. Ideally the noting should take place on changing activities or tasks; in practice, this may be impossible. In the turmoil of managing, a sensible compromise enabling the log to be useful and accurate without being laboriously detailed, is to complete your prepared sheets as convenient. But this should be a minimum of hourly – use the bleep on a digital watch, the memory being notoriously unreliable.

Other useful guidelines

In carrying out a time log analysis you should also bear in mind that:

- The log should be kept for a *typical* two to four-week period. You may find that there is no 'typical' period: indeed if you sense such a luxury on the horizon, you can guarantee some emergency or crisis will evolve. This will not invalidate your log. It will in effect enhance it with data about how you coped with unexpected events! Remember that the main purpose of the log is to excite you into wanting to improve your use of time, and not to define the mythical normal week.
- Your designed time log should be easy to understand and complete, so that revealing data will unfold. Do not make it so intricate that completing it every few minutes supercedes your role as a manager.
- Using symbols and abbreviations where you can is helpful, particularly in the notes column.
- You should acknowledge your log as soon as you get to work by getting it out and confirming your priority objectives or tasks for the day.
- Time spent travelling, working outside normal hours and meals should be included if relevant.

Sharing your time log with others

Whilst your time log is personal to you, it is useful if a group of managers performing similar roles get together to discuss their logs. A procedure that works is that each manager takes about 30 minutes of group time to give an informal chronological presentation of the time log data. The remainder of the group should act as devil's advocates and question the manager's explanation of the time use. The presenter's role is rotated until all managers in the group have experienced the 'hot seat'. Managers should identify and commit themselves to at least one specific aspect of improvement in their use of time at the end of their 30 minutes.

Some questions that may enable the group members to help in this process are:

- Where has time been used effectively? Why?
- What could/should have been delegated? Up, down, or sideways?
- Could some tasks (meetings, paperwork, interviews etc) have been carried out more quickly? How?
- Should 'no' have been said politely but firmly to some jobs? Why wasn't it? How could it be in the future?
- Are there any tasks not done that should have been done? What has prevented them from being done? How may this be avoided in the future?
- What kinds of decisions are taken? Alone or with others? Who? How often?
- What are the main similarities/differences between the time logs in the group? Why?
- What do you like/dislike about what you have decided or been told about your own use of time?
- What might/are you going to do about it? How can we help you make those changes?

Examples of time logs

During a development programme a group of managers jotted down all the activities they spent time on over a period of several weeks. Over 50 activities were identified which were subsequently divided into 22 main activities and seven categories of activities, as shown in Figure 2.5.

A daily time log was used which included an assessment of achieving specified priority objectives. As can be seen in Figure 2.6 the categories of activities are listed horizontally, with vertical sub-divisions representing time bands. The notes column was used for comments by the manager on levels of effectiveness, thoughts, feelings etc. For each daily sheet the columns were totalled and transferred to a summary sheet (see Figure 2.7).

Variations in time spent in key task areas

The minimum, maximum and percentage range of time spent in each key task area for each manager was summarized and is shown in Figure 2.8. The differences were explained in terms of unit size and geographical location, experience of staff, managerial styles, priorities and business mix – *and the manager's ability to use time effectively!*

In one unit the manager and assistant defined four main areas of responsibility and the time log approach in developing their effectiveness in working together.

TIME LOG – CATEGORY SUMMARY

A   PLANNING, PREPARATION AND UPDATING

A1   Planning ahead
A2   Preparation for interviews/visits etc.
A3   Keeping your knowledge up to date

B   CUSTOMER INTERVIEWS (IN BRANCH)

B1   Lending interviews – personal and commercial
B2   Other interviews with customers arranged to increase business etc.
B3   Non-lending/non-business development interviews

C   CUSTOMER CONTACT – INFORMAL (IN BRANCH)

C1   Working at an enquiry desk
C2   Meeting customers informally in the banking hall/casual meetings
C3   Working at a customer point

D   STAFF CONTACT

D1   Checking/advising on the work of others
D2   Briefing staff about changes in working routines/products etc.
D3   Training staff/discussing progress/coaching others

E   OFFICE – ROUTINES AND PROCEDURES

E1   Dealing with correspondence/telephone calls etc.
E2   Attending to faults, problems, priorities, administration etc.
E3   Interpreting/issuing HO advices/procedures

F   ATTENDING MEETINGS

F1   Meetings with Area Manager or equivalent
F2   Attending non-business professional meetings
F3   Meetings with other departments (e.g. Marketing, Personnel)

G   WORKING OUTSIDE THE BRANCH

G1   Seeing customers at their premises
G2   Visiting existing/prospective business clients
G3   Meeting/lunching with professional contacts
G4   Visits/talks/film shows outside the branch

H   OTHER CATEGORIES

H1
H2
H3

Figure 2.5   The 22 main activities and seven categories of activities for a managerial type job

There was a strong need to know what each other was doing over a period of time. In addition to achieving certain key objectives the percentage time spectrum shown in Figure 2.9 was seen as an appropriate goal.

These examples are described primarily to stimulate you to design a time log for yourself and to show you how it can be used, especially in discussion with other managers.

31

Time Log

Priority Objectives   Achieved?

1 _____

Day No.

2 _____

Date

3 _____

Time	Plan/ Prepare Update			Customer Interviews			Informal Customer Contact (in-branch)			Staff Contact			Office Routines & Procedures			Attend Meetings			Work outside the Office				Other :-			Comments
	A			B			C			D			E			F			G				H			
	1	2	3	1	2	3	1	2	3	1	2	3	1	2	3	1	2	3	1	2	3	4	1	2	3	
9.00																										
10.00																										
11.00																										
12.00																										
1.00																										
2.00																										
3.00																										
4.00																										
5.00																										
6.00																										
Sub-total																										
Total																										

Figure 2.6   A daily time log for a managerial type job

INDIVIDUAL BEHAVIOUR – PROBLEMS AND SOLUTIONS

The need to have objectives, develop priorities and measure success in time management is well known and on occasions usefully practised. But what about all those behaviours we exhibit, often out of our awareness, that influence our ability

Time Log Summary

Date	Plan/ Prepare Update			Customer Interviews			Informal Customer Contact (in-branch)			Staff Contact			Office Routines & Procedures			Attend Meetings			Work outside the Office				Other -			Comments
	A			B			C			D			E			F			G				H			
	1	2	3	1	2	3	1	2	3	1	2	3	1	2	3	1	2	3	1	2	3	4	1	2	3	
Sub-total																										
Total																										

Figure 2.7   A summary sheet for collating daily time log data

to manage time? Some commonly recurring individual problems managers have, and their solutions, are considered below.

Don't procrastinate

Do you have a house full of leaking taps, faulty electrical connections and loose doorhandles that you've often faithfully promised to put right? Do you *still* have

	Min (%)	Max (%)	Range (%)
Planning-preparing-keeping up to date	3	15	12
Customer interviews (in branch)	14	26	12
Informal customer contact/approaches (in branch)	0	20	20
Staff contact	4	14	10
Office routines and procedures	18	48	30
Working outside the branch	0	27	27
Attending meetings etc	0	16	16

Figure 2.8   Percentage minimum, maximum and range of time spent in each key task area for managers doing similar jobs

	Manager (%)	Assistant Manager (%)
Business development (outside contacts)	30	5
Staff (training/development/motivation)	20	40
Administration	10	20
Customer interviews (lending/investment/tax)	40	35

Figure 2.9   The overlap in key task areas and time spent in those areas by a manager and assistant

that difficult customer who you really must contact, or is that urgent sales report nagging away to be completed rather than gathering dust in your in tray, or that awkward appraisal interview needing to be done before the end of the month, or that overdue apology? The gentle art of putting things off, procrastination, is an enormous time stealer.

Procrastination is a deep rooted habit that must be tackled while you are motivated to change. Take the first steps straight away using the following guidelines:

- Decide you are going to change as soon as you can – maybe *now*!
- List all those tasks you have been putting off. Make no exceptions; everything must be on your list.
- Remove one or two items on the list immediately by doing them. Doing them is often quicker than writing them out again.
- Plan how you will deal with the others, maybe relieving yourself of three each day. Try this first thing in the morning as it sets a positive tone for the rest of the day. You can tell yourself 'Great, the day's only 20 minutes old and I have already accomplished the most irritating tasks of the day.'

- If you stick to your plan reward yourself. If you don't, punish yourself in a way that makes it work in future.

Don't be a perfectionist

Do you have to retype letters because of a minor error, expect *no* customer complaints, or interruptions never to occur at work? Do you expect your pre-school children to have impeccable table manners, the garden to be perfect, or every day to be like Christmas?

Perfection is paralyzing. There seems to be a fundamental difference between striving for excellence and striving for perfection. The former is achievable, realistic, healthy and personally satisfying; the latter leads to frustrations and neurotic behaviour. You will need to recognize in what areas of your life you really need to 'be perfect', and ensure such compulsions do not trap you into missing opportunities and achieving excellence elsewhere.

Set challenging objectives

Do you find yourself consistently failing to meet your objectives and being disappointed, annoyed or frustrated? Do you find yourself regularly underachieving, meeting all objectives without too much physical or emotional effort?

Imagine spending an hour throwing tennis balls into a bucket, with success defined as a product of distance from which you choose to throw from and the percentage of balls actually going into the bucket. If you set your objectives (i.e. distance) very low, say position 'A' in Figure 2.10, you will achieve some initial low level success. After a few minutes you will recognize a lack of sense of achievement, an absence of risk, and experience increasing frustration and annoyance. Conversely if you set your objective (i.e. distance) very high, say position 'B', you may achieve some limited initial success in this high risk situation. Again motivation and achievement are likely to fall as frustration and lack of success become apparent. Position 'C' is a potentially healthy development position resulting in optimum success. With coaching, positive recognition, support and a few allowable mistakes C1 can be reached; with isolation, negative recognition and lack of support only C2 may be possible.

Have a look at your own objectives. How realistic are they? What happens to you personally if they are too difficult or too easy to achieve? And how realistic are your staff's objectives?

Learn how to learn

How children learn is well researched and understood; adult learning less so. Learning, un-learning and re-learning are key issues for good time management. You cannot rely on the occasional course or epistles from on high for your learning. In any case there is increasing evidence that mature adults have a strong need to be self-directing in their learning. However you must be aware of:

- the barriers you place in the way that hinder your learning;
- your preferred manner of learning for such situations;

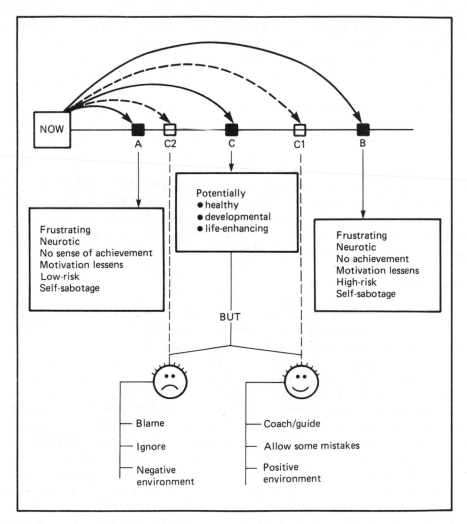

Figure 2.10 Setting challenging objectives

(The figure shows the value of challenging but realistic objectives in achievement – A is too low, B too high, with C about right in normal circumstances and C1 where managerial support happens.)

- and what you did that enabled you to learn successfully in the past.

Modern learning methods such as distance learning, action learning and computer based training (CBT) help you learn at paces, styles and times of your choice; thus you can manage your learning time effectively.

Fight recurring crises

There's nothing wrong with the occasional crisis; but if it is the same one that occurred last week, the week before and the week before that, you may not be learning from them. Good practices in a crisis are:

- to use your energies to find solutions (not for shouting or finding scape-goats);
- to focus upon the problem (not your performance or how it will look);
- to relax momentarily before considering options and then controlling that crisis;
- to turn the crisis into an opportunity for new ideas and methods. Contingency plans that help avoid future identical crises can be devised.

Other individual time problems

Five of the biggest personal time wasters have been described together with ways of resolving them. To manage your individual behaviour and time you also need:

- to plan (both short and long term);
- to concentrate and not be distracted by interruptions;
- to take breaks;
- to avoid clutter (physical and mental);
- to beware of becoming a workaholic;
- to learn to say 'no' firmly but graciously when appropriate;
- to access and use information well;
- to read and write accurately and quickly;
- to relax and reduce tensions.

MANAGERIAL STYLE

Think about the way people manage in your organization. Time spent working is not usually a measure of effectiveness at work. Who is more highly regarded:

- The manager who explains over and over in detail why a problem cannot be solved or the manager who solves the problem and then quickly and quietly moves on to other tasks?
- The supervisor who makes few decisions of any kind, even when decisions are urgently needed, or the supervisor who makes the required decisions but occasionally makes a mistake?
- The boss who frantically dashes around solving subordinates' problems again and again or the boss who develops subordinates so that crises are avoided or that they can solve their own problems.

Managerial style and time

One popular model of management describes five styles of managing as follows:

Telling: An authoritarian style where managers make decisions themselves, announce them and command that they be carried out.
Selling: A style where managers make the decisions with some limited discussion and explain or convince their subordinates.
Consulting: A style where managers get suggestions by inviting questions, making suggestions themselves, and consulting subordinates before making decisions.

Style	Time management		% of time spent	
	Advantages	Disadvantages	Actual	Ideal
Telling				
Selling				
Consulting				
Sharing				
Delegating				

Figure 2.11   Managerial styles and managing time

(The figure shows a matrix where you consider the advantages and disadvantages of several managerial styles in time management terms, before allocating your actual and ideal percentages of time spent in each style.)

Sharing: A style where managers present the problem, define the limits of any solution, and decisions are made jointly.

Delegating: A style where managers allow subordinates to function within defined limits by defining constraints and by conforming to subordinates' requirements.

On going down the five styles the area of freedom for subordinates to make decisions increases, whilst the use of authority by managers decreases.

Your own predominant style will influence the amount of time you spend with subordinates and others, and how you spend that time. The telling style will save time in the short term – it's easy to tell people what to do if they are willing to do anything you tell them. But it could mean extra time eventually being spent dealing with the dissatisfactions and mistakes that occur as the culture matures or individuals give up. The consulting style will mean more time spent meeting subordinates, often at their request, to deal with the many ideas and options around; but good time management principles still apply.

Exercise

You should recognise your own predominant managerial styles and the advantages and limitations in time management terms using a grid shown in Figure 2.11. The actual and ideal percentages of time spent in each style should be completed, together with a statement about how you will make the changes occur.

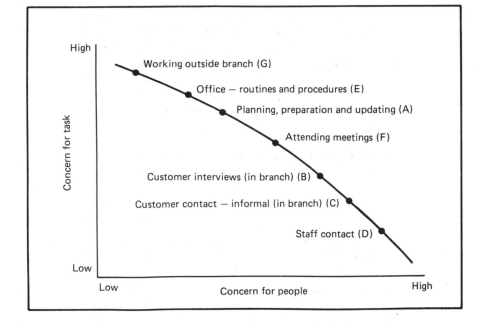

Figure 2.12   Key task areas and managerial concern for task and people

(The figure shows how key task areas are related to the popular concept of a manager's concern for task and concern for people. Time spent in our key task areas reflects our managerial styles.)

Key task areas and management style

Many models of management express success in terms of our ability to get things done and our relationships with people. Graphically a vertical axis represents concern for completing tasks, the horizontal axis concern for people. We can relate key task areas to this concept. Consider for example the seven key task areas (A to G) listed in Figure 2.5. Office routines and procedures (E) and Working outside the branch (G) are primarily task functions, whilst Staff contact (D) and Customer contact, informal (in branch) (C), are primarily people functions. A spectrum of key task areas in terms of task and people orientations is shown in Figure 2.12.

Exercise

You should now look at your own key task areas in a similar way by representing them on a task/people plot. Study the emergent picture carefully and identify what balance you need for success in your environment. You may need to develop some strategies to change the balance.

Functions of management

Other models of management look at the functions of management. One such function is delegation. 'Why should I be concerned with delegation?' I was recently asked. It is not easy to admit to doing too much yourself. It is often simpler to do a task yourself than to arrange to meet, explain, watch, and critically assess a subordinate doing it, but the freedoms gained in delegation for the manager are enormous.

Delegation means giving responsibility, authority and sharing accountability rather than 'dishing out work'. Delegation can be difficult and it can go wrong, but it can be planned to work and be managed properly. Listing the advantages/disadvantages of delegation and the examination of how time is spent at work, often commit a colleague to the principles and practice of good delegation. One manager I met operates on the principle of 'never doing anything he can get someone else to do' – what's more, he is highly respected and extremely effective!

Other managerial time problems

In relation to our managerial style other common time wasters include meetings (as a leader or participant), dealing with crises, communicating through a hierarchy, unwieldy control systems, using technology (including the computer and telephone), decision making, working with a secretary and finding thinking time. You will find a number of these subjects dealt with in other chapters in this book.

VISUAL REMINDERS

Quotations and slogans

Despite all your good intentions and plans too much time still gets wasted. It seems as if there are mental blockages that allow you to default when the going gets tough and crises or the unexpected happen. To remind yourself of good time management principles on such occasions you really need an immediate stimulus.

Now, we have all heard quotations and slogans like 'time and tide wait for no man', 'master your time and you master your life', 'get a round to it', 'to thine own self be true', and they make sense. One I particularly like is 'illegitimi non carborundum'. You will need to design or find slogans that work for you, and think about where to put them for maximum effect. A 'slogan of the week' is sometimes preferred.

Your own quotations

You can of course keep your 'slogans' in your head, repeating them like mantras until they reach an almost spiritual significance. Better locations could include your wall chart, inside your desk blotter, on a stand on your desk, in your time planner in bold letters where they will be seen, and on the telephone, especially if the telephone is your favourite time management problem. You may prefer initials DIBS ('Do it before sunset') or foreign phrases ('tempus fugit'); they are certainly more private and mysterious. Remember, if it works for you it works for you!

An organized office

More naturally recurring visual reminders will abound in your office anyway. Whatever the slogans you use, if your office looks a mess, your time management may be a mess. Bear the following general visual points in mind:

- Keep paperwork under control; where you can, handle each piece of paper only once. Decide whether to take action at the time (and pass it to the out tray), start some action (and place it in a pending tray), or read and store or GROAN ('get rid of it anyway – *now!*'). Chapter 3, Managing information in the office, will help you manage the paperwork.
- Choose and site your office furniture as appropriate for good time management. Filing cabinets should be well organized and work for you, especially if you have a secretary to help. Your files should not involve an exploration or paper safari every time you encounter them – nor should they challenge the exhibits in the local museum or company archives. Desks and chairs should be ergonomically matched and sited in a position to give you privacy when you need it – don't be your own worst interrupter and catch the eye of every passer-by.

SUMMARY AND CHECKLIST

The main purpose and reward for managing your time well is the feeling of being in control that results. Having considered six successful approaches you should answer the following questions:

- Am I unclear about and out of date with my lifetime goals, objectives and/or key task areas?
- Do my time planning systems (diaries, ABC priorities etc) need revising?
- Would completing a time log help me understand where my time is being used, and for me to plan for improvement?
- Is there anything about my individual behaviour (procrastination, 'being perfect' etc) that limits my effective use of time?
- Is there anything about my style of managing (concerns for task/people, delegation etc) that limits my effective use of time?
- Does my work place look an administrative mess? Would revised systems and visual reminders help me?

If you answer an honest *no* to all questions, you can move on to the next chapter. Otherwise a final action plan exercise (Figure 2.13) should be completed. You will need to identify your strengths and weaknesses, before deciding on general improvement areas. Determine specific objectives and achievement dates, and write down the steps involved and possible problems that might occur on the way.

Will you complete the action plan? Or has that alternative and vital A1 loomed up from the nether reaches of your mind? Or are you procrastinating? As Lakein says – *what is the best use of your time right now?*

Improvement areas	Objectives	Stages toward objectives	Possible problems	Achievement date

Figure 2.13   Action plan for managing your time

(The figure leads into developing an action plan that you can use to monitor your improvement in managing your time.)

FURTHER READING

Bliss, E. C., *Doing it Now*, Macdonald, 1983. The author claims that successful people never procrastinate – they always do things now. The book is in a very readable question-and-answer format, with good advice from the author's anti-procrastination seminars. A top 40 most commonly used reasons for putting things off are listed.

Garratt, S., *Manage Your Time*, Fontana/Collins, 1985. An excellent book from a series published in conjunction with the Association of Management Education and Development. It contains practical, realistic examples likely to prove popular with younger and more recent managers, and also supervisors and secretaries.

Lakein, A., *How to Get Control of Your Time and Your Life*, Gower, 1984. This classic book spawned several excellent training films and describes the author's system of time management, which includes simple but powerful techniques that succeed in life, work and in leisure. Unreservedly recommended.

Mackenzie, R. A., *The Time Trap*, McGraw-Hill, 1975. From studying people's work habits, the author presents practical, easy-to-apply tips and techniques for good time management. Particularly useful is a list of time wasters with their possible causes and solutions.

Oncken, W. Jr, *Managing Management Time – Who's Got the Monkey?*, Prentice-Hall, 1984. A book that deals in a unique way with using your time to achieve more visible, far-reaching results. Using 'organizational leverage' to concentrate efforts appropriately at the right time, capitalizing upon intrusions and extending your influence are some of the more complex time management topics to think about and practise that are included.

Pernet, R., *Effective use of Time* (Notes for Managers number 31), Industrial Society, 1978. A short neat booklet covering a broad band of time management items such as meetings, telephones and delegation plus some useful checklists.

Reynolds, H. and Tramel, M. E., *Executive Time Management – Getting 12 hours work out of an 8 hour day*, Gower, 1979. The sections on writing clearly, conducting productive meetings and organizing paperwork are particularly helpful.

Stewart, R., *Managers and Their Jobs*, Macmillan, 1967. A study of the similarities and differences in the ways managers spend their time, using a detailed research diary. The author presents the information and conclusions in a readily accessible way that has as much validity today as it did when published.

Diaries and planning systems can be purchased from many outlets but two very useful sources are:

Filofax plc
Filofax House
Forest Road
Ilford
Essex IG6 3HP
081-501-3911

TMI
50 High Street
Henley-in-Arden
Solihull
West Midlands B95 5AN
0564 794100

3 Managing information in the office

Feona J. Hamilton

When you walk into your office for the first time, have a good look round. Whether it is a new office, or one just vacated by someone else, the first impression will probably be the same. It will be empty and *tidy*. Maybe there are a few drawing pins left in the wall/notice board, or a scribble or two on the calendar, but that's all. The desk will be pristine – no overflowing trays (maybe no trays at all), lots of lovely space, pen tidy gaping open-mouthed back at you, perhaps a blotter with nothing in it but a clean piece of blotting paper. When all this neatness is imprinted on your memory, here's what you do: open your diary, and make a note to look again in a month's time.

You will probably see something very different. The trays will certainly be there, but they will be buried under piles of paper. There will be dog-eared and outdated memos on the notice board, and the phone will be ringing somewhere, under another pile of rubbish – sorry, information. Sounds familiar? I thought it might, but don't just nod despairing agreement, and turn the page.

This chapter is for you to read as a step in the direction of managing the information that comes into, and goes out of your office, and across the desk. It considers what you need to see and what doesn't matter, plus what you need to keep, and what you can discard. It will also indicate what you positively shouldn't see, and what you can have a look at outside the office, so that it need never come in and clutter up the place. Finally, there will be a quick glance at computers, since they certainly have their uses when it comes to controlling information.

WHAT IS INFORMATION?

Everything that comes into the office is information of some kind. It may come in many forms, such as:

- minutes of committee and other meetings;
- scribbled memos from colleagues;
- messages left by your staff;
- reminders to yourself;

- house magazine;
- other published material – books, journals and so on;
- correspondence;
- reports written by you;
- reports written to you;
- telephone calls;
- face to face conversations;
- computer printout;
- messages via the computer, if you have one.

YOUR DESKTOP

The top of your desk is the starting point from which you will control (or manage) the information which comes into your office. Any written or printed material is bound to land there, and spoken information you will either get through the telephone, or from someone speaking to you, when you will no doubt make notes as memory aids. If you don't do this, you should – it's a useful habit to get into.

One of the most basic things which you can do is to have two diaries – a large one for your desk, and a small one for your person. It is important to keep them both bang up to date. This means having to remember to put engagements in both of them, which is easy if you make an appointment over the phone, or face to face with someone in the office, but not so simple if you make it on the golf course, or during a working lunch. However, it really is not an onerous task, and both you and your secretary will be better informed about your movements as a result.

The diary and the telephone are not the only items which you should have on your desktop, useful though they are. Those filing trays which have already been mentioned do have their uses, if managed properly. A set of three – in, out, and pending – is usually sufficient, unless you're in charge of the post-room! Although it is possible, and very tempting, to spend an entire morning shuffling everything round from one tray to another, without actually achieving anything, you should try to resist. Nor, on the other hand, should you rely on the false premise that if you leave something in the in tray long enough, eventually you'll be able to throw it away. Some of the information sent to you will arrive because you are on a circulation list, and it is selfish, as well as inefficient, to delay sending it on its way to the next person, simply because you're too lazy – or too disorganized – to sort through the in-tray regularly. Do it once a day, and you'll find that you can scan much of what should be passed on quickly in the time it takes to have a cuppa. You can then put it in the out tray and forget about it.

That 'out' tray can be one of the least used items in the office, if you're not careful. Some wits have been known to refer to the wastepaper bin as the out tray, and it *is* in a sense, but it cannot replace the real thing. An out tray, properly used, tells whoever else comes into the office to work with or for you precisely what they may remove without a qualm. Your secretary will be pleased to see an obvious pile of things to be removed, and any colleagues who wander in during your absence can succumb to the urge to see what other people are looking at without a twinge of conscience. After all, if it's in the out tray, and not in a sealed envelope, then you've finished with it and it's not confidential is it? Which brings me neatly to:

Hamilton's Law 1:   *There is nothing outré about an out tray*

The only tray not mentioned so far is the pending tray. Some people use the entire desktop as a pending tray, and leave little piles all over it, in some mysterious and unspecified order, which they understand at the time, but have completely forgotten by the next morning. This is another indication of lack of organization, as well as being very difficult to cope with when searching for a specific, single sheet of paper with the information which you need for the meeting you should have been in twenty minutes ago. There is also the matter of having to find some space to make notes the next time the phone rings, as well as somewhere to put the next cuppa. It's better to have just one pile on the desk in front of you, work through that, place in appropriate trays, take the next handful from the in tray and so on. Remember:

Hamilton's Law 2:   *Piles on the desk are also uncomfortable*

EDITING YOUR INFORMATION NEEDS

However hard you try, you cannot possibly see everything of relevance – there is simply too much of it. The 'information explosion' is one of the more apposite phrases used today. Try stuffing too much into your brain, and it will have a pretty explosive effect on you, as well. If you suffer from the following symptoms: difficulty focusing on the page without the words jumping up and down; slight headache and dizziness; nausea; trembling hands; bursting feeling between the ears; you're either trying to absorb too much information, or you have just absorbed too much alcohol. If it's definitely the former – and be honest about this – there is a remedy: Divide the information you see into the following four categories:

1   *What you must see.* This will include minutes of any meetings which you have – or should have – attended recently; memos from the boss; relevant press cuttings; whatever the post has brought *that day* as far as possible (if you're on holiday, or out of the office on business, this cannot be strictly applied); telephone messages.

2.   *What you like to see.* This means items for information which, while not vital to your work, are useful additions to those things which are included in 1 above. They will include minutes of meetings in related areas of work; general office memos; items of peripheral interest from journals or newspapers coming into the building; and items of interest which you are told about by a colleague, or friend, such as special supplements in newspapers – *The Times* often has some very useful inserts, on anything from Sussex University to Saudi Arabia. The relevance of such material depends, of course, on your job. Only you can make the decision.

3.   *What you want to impress others by seeing.* This is usually a complete waste of time, as what you are looking at may well be of little or no relevance to what you are actually supposed to be doing. It can also be painfully obvious to whomever you're trying to impress that you don't actually understand much of what you're trying to read. Having said that, there can be times when something which you're reading for this reason turns out to be so fascinating

that you decide to change careers, and go and find yourself a marvellous new job – but it is very rare.

4. *What you don't need to see.* You don't need to see all the bits and pieces connected with tasks that you've already delegated to somebody else. Delegation is an art which very few managers do really well. If they manage to pass on a task, they either check up so constantly that they might just as well do it themselves, or they take absolutely no further interest. The happy medium is to delegate, and ask for a progress report at properly spaced intervals. The information received thus is all you should want to see. Neither do you need to read every piece of advertising bumf that lands on your desk. Mail shots can be a good source of information on what the competition's up to, but you simply don't have time to scan it all. A quick look now and then is sufficient.

If you ignore the warnings, and try to read everything, you will find that you have no time to do any of the other tasks which make up your total job – i.e. you will be acting inefficiently. You will certainly find yourself becoming ever more muddled and confused, as you will be trying to stuff so much information into your mind that you will be unable to sort out the wheat from the chaff, and all you will have is a great lump of indigestible material, which you are unable to break down into its component parts. This means that, in turn, you will be unable to apply what you have read to the task in hand, and this will also lead to inefficiency.

Hamilton's Law 3:   *Too much information gives you mental indigestion*

KEEPING IT IN ORDER (SOMEWHERE)

As well as reading, or scanning, the material as it comes into your office, you will want to keep some of it. How you store it will depend on the reasons why you need to hold on to it, and the methods of storage available to you. Those most commonly used are:

- typed, printed, or handwritten: cards, files, filing cabinets or folders
- tapes: cassettes or reels;
- computerized: disks or magnetic tapes.

Some of these are interchangeable, e.g. you may have stored some information from a computer as printout, in which case it may be stored in a hanging file; or you may decide that something which is currently typed will be better stored on computer.

You will also wish to divide your material into that which is available to others, and that which you feel should be confidential. The most obvious candidates for the second category are personnel records, and business or development plans which you may be working on. If you are responsible for matters such as projects and contracts with other organizations, material relating to those will also be confidential. All these should be stored in a safe place – a locked filing cabinet or cupboard, to which only you and, perhaps, your secretary have keys, should give sufficient security. (Any members of the Civil Service or Armed Forces reading this will already know of the security arrangements connected with their positions.)

```
┌─────────────────────────────┐        ┌──────────────────────────────────────┐
│   WOOL – see YARN           │        │   ANGORA – see also CASHMERE          │
│                             │        │                    MOHAIR              │
│                             │        │                    WORSTED             │
│                             │        │                                        │
│                             │        │                                        │
│                             │        │                                        │
└                             │        └                                        │
```

Figure 3.1   Reference   Figure 3.2   Cross-reference

Once you've divided by format, and by confidentiality, it's up to you to decide on arrangement. This is one of those tasks which is often best delegated to the person likely to need access to the information most frequently. This is generally a secretary or an assistant rather than the manager in person. It is important for you to know how the system works, of course, so that you can get at the material yourself if necessary, but it's a waste of time and senior staff for you to do the setting up. Just remember, the simpler the system, the better, and alphabetically by subject is usually the best for the majority of filing systems. You should also have a very careful index to the files, so that you can trace material that is not where you thought, and find material on related subjects more easily. You do this by means of references and cross-references (see Figures 3.1 and 3.2). Make sure that the person in charge understands what you're asking for, and then leave them to get on with it. Once the system is operational, all that's needed is to check that it's kept up to date.

Initially, your information bank will grow rapidly, and this is fine until you come to the perennial problem of lack of space. It's bound to happen before you anticipated, and the only way to solve it is to have rules for how long you hang on to material. It's impossible to draw up a rigid framework for this, as different types of information are important for different reasons, depending on the kind of manager you are.

There are some obvious rules you can set: the personnel records already mentioned will have to be kept for at least as long as the individual is employed by your organization. In the same way, any notes or reports you may have concerning projects in which you are involved will also have to be retained at least for the duration of the contract. What about the rest – the memos and the press cuttings, the committee minutes and the journal articles?

If there is some kind of central archive held somewhere in the organization, much of the decision making about what to keep and what to discard is solved for you. You will simply have the files weeded at regular intervals, and have whatever is older than a fixed length of time – a year, perhaps – sent for storage in the archive. If there is no central archive, then it becomes a bit more difficult, and you'll have to set your own rules. You can always suggest setting up an archive – it may be simply that no one thought of doing so before. Otherwise, you might decide to do this:

- Keep everything that you decide to retain for at least one year.
- Keep committee minutes and project reports for three years.
- Keep personnel records for one year after the employee has left the company.

- Keep all financial records for five years.
- Keep one copy of everything you write yourself forever.

Hamilton's Law 4:   *Nobody needs two copies forever*

It will probably be safe to discard the rest of the material – but this does not simply mean junking it. Someone else in the organization may find it useful. If you have an information unit or library, offer the staff your press cuttings and back journals, at least. Check them carefully first; you may discover that your copy of a journal was actually the library's originally, and that can be very embarrassing! When you've done all that, there should still be something to put in the wastebin, which is always satisfying. Sure as fate, there will be at least one thing which you will need tomorrow, but that's another law, already attributed to someone else.

INFORMATION SOURCES OUTSIDE YOUR OFFICE

As well as all the material that comes into your office, there will be other information available to you. This may be inside your organization, or outside it. (I am excluding the results of industrial espionage and other illegal ways of getting hold of the stuff.) Apart from conversation with colleagues and others over lunch, there is another source, which may well be under-used by you. This is the library, or information unit, which may be housed right in the building with you. A few years ago many organizations closed down their information units, but most places have now realised the importance of such units, and either set one up, or reopened one.

If there is such a place in your organization, when did you last visit it? Many middle and senior managers claim to have no time to do so, little realising what a useful place it can be. As well as its obvious function, a library/information unit can be a good place to retire to if you need somewhere quiet to sit and do a spot of writing, or thinking, without constant interruptions. This assumes that it is large enough to have room for a few desks and chairs, of course; some information units are so small that there is barely enough room for the stock and the staff, let alone people from other parts of the building!

It is a good idea to make yourself known to the librarian/information officer, or whatever title is used. He or she can be a valuable friend. Well run units of this type keep profiles of all senior staff (at least), giving details of their interests and information needs. This helps them to feed you the right information, as it arrives, so that you are kept up to date with the latest developments. You will be a favourite if you pass on circulated journals as quickly as possible, and return borrowed material rapidly. The information staff will make an extra effort for you, and will do their best to get the information you require as soon as they can. Remember that it is often possible to order material which is not available in your own organization via a national and international system of inter-library loans.

Computers play a large part in the information profession nowadays, and most library and information staff are trained to use them. Tell them your needs, and leave them to it, but be reasonable, and don't always expect immediate results. Looking for a specific item can take some time, especially when you have not been able to give full details of your request. If you can give a title, author, and date, plus (in the case of a journal article) some idea of the name of the journal, it will be

Author					Office use
A EWING					
Title (Book/Journal)					
CHEESE PLEASE : OR FETTA IS BETTER					
Publisher	Date	Edition	Vol.	Part	
CHURN PRESS	1986	1	—	—	
Your name and department					
ANN ONYMOUS — MICROBIOLOGY					

Figure 3.3   Loan request form

found much more quickly than if you mutter vaguely about books with green covers that you saw last time you came in.

Hamilton's Law 5:   *Even a librarian can't get it for you yesterday*

THE BLINKING CURSOR

There was a time, not long ago, when it was possible for managers to more or less ignore the presence of computers in an organization. Some trendy people had them in the office, fewer had them switched on, and fewer still actually used them for anything other than show. Most managers had studiously avoided learning to type, since it was perceived as a clerical or secretarial skill and they weren't going to block their careers by going down that route.

Well, what a mistake that turned out to be, especially for anyone over forty and under retirement age as I write. Typing (now called a keyboard skill) is a must, if you are to show that you are computer-literate – i.e. able to use a computer for at least basic tasks – and therefore fit to have a job in an office.

The basic tasks referred to are: word-processing, using a spreadsheet, and using a database management system. All three are useful for handling information in the office.

Word-processing

Word-processing is probably the first skill that anyone learns on a computer, after finding out how to play daft games which involve shooting things by pressing the appropriate key. It is a refined form of typing and it is a comfort to realise that a keyboard on a computer bears a marked resemblance to a typewriter. The letters are laid out in the familiar 'QWERTY' order, and the numbers and punctuation symbols may also appear in a familiar format. The difference comes with all the extra keys surrounding them.

Since this is not the place to go into great detail, suffice to say that the ease with which you can learn to use a computer for word-processing is stunning, given average intelligence. Once learned, you will wonder how you managed without the skill and vow never to return to writing with a pen and paper again. Not only will you produce memos, letters and reports with consummate ease, you will also have a record of everything you have done stored for you on a disk, which you can recall instantly.

Spreadsheets

Spreadsheets can vary greatly in complexity, but they all basically fulfil the same function. The most common use in the office is for budget forecasting and budget control. They have the advantage of carrying out all the calculations for you, so you don't have to be too numerate in order to use one. Using a spreadsheet is more difficult to get to grips with than using a word-processor, but, again, a skill well worth acquiring. And, of course, you are once again in the fortunate position of being able to keep records of previous annual budgets/statements of expenditture et al on disk, which takes up very little space.

Database Management Systems (DBMS)

This particular form of software is the one which is most used in any form of information management, whether it's in your office, or in the biggest library you can imagine. Again, there is a wide range of complexity, going from a simple one which you can run on a home computer, allowing you to set up separate files and search them according to fairly basic criteria, to the all-singing, all-dancing, linked-to-everything-else-on-the-computer type.

It has become common to find the latter sort in a 'bundle', i.e. word-processor, spreadsheet and database management system all in one piece of software. The most recent ones allow you to pop in and out of all your files, merge something from here with something from there, include charts and text in one new file and so on.

The files that you need to set up on your DBMS depend on the contents of the manual files which you have in your office, which I have already mentioned above. You may find that you can now put some of the material which is currently held as a card index on to a computer file. This is a good way to start, because you have already worked out the format of the file – i.e. you have decided what information you wish to keep on each card, and the headings under which they will be entered.

When using a DBMS, each card becomes a record and each heading on the card is called a field. What you do is set up a blank record, which just contains the field names, store that, then call it up each time you want to add a new record. Once you have a good number of records, you can search them in all kinds of ways. For example, a name and address file can be searched thus:

- by name;
- by street;
- by town;
- by postcode;
- by county;

- by telephone number.

This requires only that you have made allowances for all those fields to appear on the record in the first place. Instead of you having to sort all through, the computer does it in the blink of an eye. This is a very simple example, but you can see where it might lead. You can set up files for stock, customers, invoices, index press cuttings, memos, archive materials – anything where you have to search out specific items of information.

GETTING YOUR BACK-UP

Life with a computer is not all sweetness and light. Although it is quite difficult to actually damage the hardware by dropping it, it is all too easy to find that the contents of disks, both hard and floppy, have been damaged by the dreaded power surge. This happens because the electrical current which pulses silently through your building does not always do so in a regular fashion. Everyone comes into the office and switches on their machines, and the current wiggles slightly, first dropping, then surging to compensate. Alarming strings of absolute rubbish can appear on the screen, especially if you were in the middle of doing something on it. Sometimes a floppy disk gets scratched and the computer can no longer read it when you place it in the disk drive. Occasionally, an even greater tragedy happens, and some bright spark hits the wrong key at the wrong time and 'crashes' the hard disk – i.e. wipes all the information off it.

Everybody does this at least once in their computing lives, so if you happen to be around one of your staff when they do it, don't yell at them. Remember how awful you felt when you did it, and don't add to their pain and embarrassment. If the information is lost, or damage caused, by a power surge, then that could have been avoided by taking the trouble to purchase special equipment such as 'spike breakers', which look like fancy plugs and fit the socket in the same way. In any case, if you've 'backed-up' (copied) everything regularly (as you should have done), it's more of a nuisance than a tragedy. Backing-up simply involves taking a copy of every file you produce on the computer and keeping it somewhere else. If you're backing-up a floppy disk, do it to another floppy disk: if it's the contents of a hard disk, you will use something called a tapestreamer.

Since there isn't room to give you more than the bare bones of computer use in information management in these pages, why not have a look at some of the books listed at the end, if you're interested in finding out more for yourself? You could find yourself going on courses and really getting proficient at using a computer, but however much or little you learn, just remember one thing, if you want to get the best out of your computer:

Hamilton's Law 6:   *Information needs data day handling*

Never, never go home without getting your back-up.

THE NETWORK

Many organizations now have their own internal computer network. This means that your computer can be used to link you to any other computer in the place, or to all the branch offices, wherever they may be in the world. It works like the telephone, in fact, except that you communicate by typing words at your end, instead of speaking into a handset – as at present. There are developments afoot, and research underway, which could well lead to you speaking to the computer (not in the way you do now when things go wrong) and the message being accepted that way.

Whichever means you use, the fact is that you can have instant access to information which other people have stored on their computers, or which is kept on a central computer, simply by keying in the correct passwords and commands. The passwords are used as a means of protecting information which is confidential from prying. The 'hackers' about whom you read in the newspapers are nosy individuals, who like to have a look at your private information, and do so by guessing what the passwords might be. For this reason, always try to use the less obvious ones – i.e. not your name, or a word connected with the file, such as a client name. If you do need to keep something confidential, remember that other people can access your files, as well as vice versa. It is common to have different levels of access available, depending on the password used. As an example, a personnel file may be available simply for names and salary levels to accounts personnel, and another password would be necessary for access to appraisal files, which only managers are given.

Networks are also used simply for passing messages round, so that you can alert other members of staff, perhaps in your department, that there will be a meeting, or that some event has happened. This type of function can also be used by the library to send you notification of items in the press which you should see, so that you don't even have to open the newspaper to see what's going on, if you don't feel like it.

So, in a few years, computers have become indispensable for the effective management of information. Having a computer means that you can organize your own information much more effectively, and you will also open up access to information on a global scale. The problem can be deciding where to start looking, when there's so much information available. I can give you one final law, which will help you to decide where to begin, and also whether you should even be there behind your desk. It is most effective after lunch, when it operates on both levels. It will bring you comfort and, if you can say it, indicate that you are in control. If you can't say it, you should be drinking black coffee somewhere quiet and avoiding all decision making.

Hamilton's Law 7: *Serendipity is a valid search strategy.*

CONCLUSION AND SUMMARY

Whatever kind of manager you are, and wherever you work, you will be an information user as well. If you try to see everything there is on your subject, and also try to keep it forever, you will rapidly become an inefficient manager, who is being pushed out into the corridor by the great mass of unsorted material lying around inside the office. You will also damage the efficiency of your colleagues and, eventually, the whole organization.

If, on the other hand, you manage the information which comes into the office by the methods outlined above, you should be more efficient, because you will have it all under control, all of the time. So remember:

- Decide what you need to see, and what you would like to see.
- Forget about the rest.
- Pass on circulated material quickly.
- Make sure you understand your own filing system.
- Keep it up to date.
- Weed out the old stuff regularly.
- Use the library/information unit.
- Learn to use the computer if you can't already.
- Acknowledge copyright when quoting Hamilton's Laws.
- Read this chapter when you're stuck/depressed/bored.
- Enjoy your job.

FURTHER READING

Bakewell, K. G. B., *How to organize information*, Gower, 1984

Dare, G. A. and Bakewell, K. G. B., *Manager's guide to getting the answers*, Library Association, 2nd edition 1983

Drucker, P. F., *Changing world of the executive*, Heinemann, 1982

Sox, C. W., *Introduction to office automation*, Prentice-Hall, 1990

Torrington, D. et al., *Management methods*, Institute of Personnel Management, 1986

Webb, S. *Creating an information service*, 2nd edition Aslib, 1989

Journals

Management Computing

Management Today

Both have articles on information management.

4   Effective writing

Dorothy M. Stewart

Management, it has been said, is the art of getting things done through and by other people. Much of the instruction (or persuasion) is done face to face, on the shop- or office-floor, day by day. But much also is done in writing – memos, telexes, letters, proposals, and reports.

Most people find business writing a chore, and many find it difficult. No wonder, as Figure 4.1 shows. When you meet face to face, you and your 'recipient' have three means of communicating – words, voice and body language. The figure shows the relative importance of each of these three as sources of information

Words	10%
Voice	35%
Body language	55%
Total	100%

Figure   4.1   Relative   importance   of   the   three   components   of   face   to   face communication as sources of information

(Derived from J Townsend, 'Paralinguistics: how the non-verbal aspects of speech affect our ability to communicate', *Journal of European Industrial Training*, 1985, vol. 9:3, pp. 27–31.)

Body language and voice are shown as the main sources of information. If you hesitate to accept this, try saying 'You will enjoy this' in different tones of voice, stressing different words each time, leaning back in a relaxed manner, leaning forward threateningly etc. The words contribute to meaning, but the other factors are clearly influential.

Writing consists of words alone. With writing, you must convey 100 per cent of the information through a medium which in everyday face to face interaction contributes only 10 per cent of the data. Body language and tone of voice are denied to you. In writing, you are communicating under a severe handicap. No wonder many people find writing difficult!

The handicap, however, can be overcome. This chapter sets out to provide you with guidelines on how to do just that in your business writing. You will find that the ideas will also apply to other kinds of writing that you do, since the principles are the same.

WHY ARE YOU WRITING?

The first thing you need to know is your purpose in writing to someone. What do you want to happen as a result? If you are unclear about this, your writing will be unclear, and your recipient will be unclear about how he is meant to respond.

Consider the following extract from a letter:

> In case of any mistake on our part or your own, we felt that you would wish to be informed that at the close of business tonight your account appears in our books as £397.96 overdrawn.

The letter suggests that it is simply keeping you informed 'in case of any mistake on our part or your own'. The information being provided, however, is that you are overdrawn. This is being stated in a low-key, face-saving way which gives you the opportunity to put it right – if you wish. The bank are perfectly clear about their purpose, and so they have created an effective letter.

Not so, however, the writer of the next letter:

> Dear Sir,
>
> Many thanks for your application for a credit account at our store. As Credit Control Manager, it is my responsibility to check all applications and take credit decisions. I have found your application particularly interesting.
>
> You will remember we asked for information about other credit accounts you hold. You correctly mentioned those at Ace Sports Stores and Music Unlimited; your information on the amounts involved, however, was higher than supplied by these stores. Ace Sports Stores also informed me that you no longer work for Meltec Machinery Ltd. Meltec provided me with the name and address of your current employer, Fraisons Plant Ltd, from whom I obtained necessary employment/salary details.
>
> In the light of the above, I am happy to open a credit account for you with our store. I have carefully considered your circumstances and have decided that your credit should be £1000 per annum, not the £2000 you have requested. If you feel that there is sufficient change in your circumstances to warrant raising the limit, then I will be prepared to reconsider this in one year's time.
>
> Many thanks for applying for a credit facility. If we can be of further assistance, please do not hesitate to contact us.
>
> Yours faithfully,
>
> Credit Control Manager

Here we have someone, perhaps new to their job or delighting in the power it gives them, forgetting that the purpose of their business writing is to improve their company's business. Instead, they use the opportunity as an ego trip and as a result alienate the customer, and lose the business on which their salary depends.

'Business writing' means that you are writing on behalf of the organization that employs you. Your primary purpose in writing is therefore your company's purpose, and that is always a business purpose.

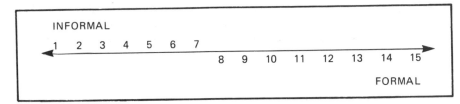

Figure 4.2   Organizational culture continuum

Part of the purpose is one of public relations. This includes not only making a good impression on your recipient, but making the *right* impression.

Consider your organization. What kind of image do you think it has in the minds of people outside, e.g. bankers, customers, financiers etc? Try to pin this down by giving it a place on the organizational culture continuum in Figure 4.2. Number 1 is the most informal (found in advertising agencies, the pop record business), and 15 is the most formal (old-fashioned, traditional lawyers and accountants, for example).

Now think about your own business writing style and the general style of written communication in your organization. Are you on first name terms with colleagues and superiors and with outside correspondents? Or do you use the formality of Mr/Miss, or even the very formal 'J. Brown Esq.'? Place the 'written culture' of your organization on the continuum also.

You may find that the two scores match. This is a considerable measure of success in making the right impression. It may be, however, that old-fashioned writing styles are damaging your company's otherwise modern image.

This is very common nowadays especially in the traditional businesses, e.g. banks, insurance, shipping, where a strong lead from the top is transforming the business but at the lower levels the traditions hold firm, especially where writing is concerned. This presents a very confusing face to the outside world. Is the company really part of the twentieth century as top management insist – or is that merely a shallow façade behind which the business goes on unchanged from the Dickensian era of clerks scratching out their copperplate letters at high desks with quill pens?

These impressions are important to customers and financiers, who both need to have confidence in your organization.

WHO ARE YOU WRITING TO?

The next step is to motivate your recipient to reply in such a way as to satisfy your purpose. This is not manipulation; it is more like good manners. There are ways of asking for another piece of cake!

First, you need to understand something of your recipient. Why should they read your letter or report, let alone agree with your request, send the information, promote you etc.?

Too many letters or memos begin, in effect, 'I have a problem . . . I want . . . I need . . .' To persuade your reader to read, you must capture his attention. To do this, you need to capture his interest. And everyone is most interested in how things apply to *them*.

- Catch and hold your reader's attention

- Show your reader why your message is important to *them*

- Show your reader the benefits to *them* from agreeing/replying etc.

- Aim for one page only for letters and memos

- Make it easy to read, understand and *act on* at one reading!

Figure 4.3 Checklist – writing for your reader's needs

Think back over the people you have written to in the last week, and the nature of the correspondence. Think about the correspondence from *their* point of view. Can you identify the ways in which each was important to the recipient?

Now consider why your recipient should agree to your request, approve your report etc. Step inside his shoes and think about each from his viewpoint. How does it affect him? What benefits are there to him from agreeing/disagreeing?

Remembering what you actually wrote, you may find it revealing to ask yourself if you mentioned these things. Do you in fact know enough about your recipients to know how the contents were important to them, or what the benefits were to them?

There are a million claims on a manager's time. You need to give your readers good reasons for taking time to read your memos and reports, and good reasons for asking them to help you achieve your objectives. If you write with your *reader's* needs in mind rather than your own, you will find your success rate soars! See checklist in Figure 4.3.

HOW SHOULD YOU WRITE IT?

This is what most people would assume is the meat of this chapter. It is my contention that the most elegant style and structure will not compensate for lack of consideration of the earlier points. This understanding provides you with the basis for your strategy. Structure and style are your tactics.

Structure

Clear thinking leads to clear writing, and much of that clarity comes from good organization. It is the poorly thought out letter or report which weaves uneasily through arguments and counter-arguments resulting in total confusion for the reader.

Whether you are writing a telex, a memo, a letter or a long report, time spent thinking and planning *before* you put pen to paper (or finger to key) is time well spent.

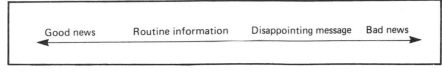

Figure 4.4   The information continuum

Structuring letters, memos and telexes

Begin by identifying your purpose. Are you providing information? You may like to think about the effect of the information on your reader along a continuum from good news to bad news. See Figure 4.4.

A successful good news letter (memo or telex) will require a different structure from that of a bad news letter. Good news or routine information, for example, has efficiency of communication as its goal. There is nothing to be gained from beating about the bush or wasting the reader's time with your warm-up sentence, so you can open directly with your main idea or central point, i.e. what it is about.

The bad or disappointing news letter needs to bring your reader in gently so that they are at least in a neutral frame of mind. This means starting with a buffer – neutral or positive information that the reader is not likely to disagree with. Then present your reasoning for the bad news. This should be in terms the reader will understand and agree with. Avoid the so-familiar over-complicated explanations and negative language. Aim for logic and clarity. Then, end on an optimistic note, offering a lesser alternative if that is appropriate and possible.

If your purpose is persuasion, you will need to get your reader's attention straight away. Do this by explaining your proposal in terms of the benefits to the reader. Do this crisply. Don't waste any words – you are already imposing on your reader's time! It is more courteous to state clearly the action you want rather than waste time with coyness. State the deadline and, if you can, suggest an incentive to act soon. It is useful to remind the reader at the end of the letter of the action you want and why they should agree.

Of all the three types, this is the most 'you-centred', focusing strongly on 'what's in it' for the reader. The pattern is probably very familiar from various mail shots you receive. These go on being sent out because of their proven effectiveness. Try the formula and see!

A general point about letters: do try to make letters look attractive. They are your letters; you sign them with your name, not your secretary's, therefore it is important that your letters convey the visual impression you want. This means that you must control layout. Many secretaries despair of vague bosses who provide no instructions on this and then complain about the results. If you do not have strong feelings or clear ideas on this, you may find it useful to look through your incoming mail and compare it with your usual layout style to see which you prefer.

Structuring reports and proposals

As before, your first step is to consider your purpose since this has implications for the structure. If you are writing to provide information, the good news/bad

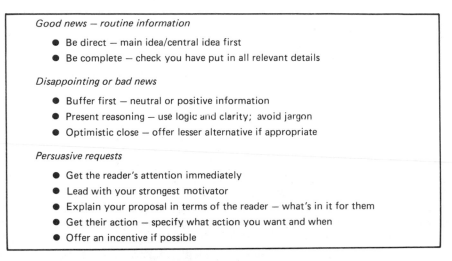

Figure 4.5   Checklist – purpose and structure of writing

news formula may help. See Figure 4.5. In any case, your readers will be expecting an emphasis on data, hopefully well organized, and possibly ending with a summary. If, however, you are offering a proposal, you will be expected to provide a description of the current situation, with a reasoned account of the steps leading to your conclusion, i.e. your proposal. If your report aims to solve a problem, your readers will want to see a clear analysis of the problem and recommendations for dealing with it.

Where a conclusion is required, there are three choices for the organization of the report:

Choice 1	*Choice 2*	*Choice 3*
Introduction	Introduction	Conclusion
Body of the report	Conclusion	Introduction
Conclusion	Body of the report	Body of the report

Choice 1 is particularly useful where your recipient might tend to resist your conclusions, e.g. where the report contains bad news, or be contrary to your reader's opinions. It is also a good choice where your recipient may not be able to understand the conclusions until he/she has read the rest of the report. However, the main drawback of this choice is that busy people tend to flip to the end and read the conclusions first, thus defeating your strategy.

Choices 2 and *3* are the more modern ways of presenting reports. Introduced first in America, these patterns are preferred by most American companies and by senior managers who have worked for American companies or been educated at business school.

They are particularly appropriate when the report contains good news for the reader, or where the reader has enough background to understand the conclusions without further explanation. Readers may find the report easier to read since the conclusions provide a framework around which to interpret the detailed information.

The main benefit of these two structures is that they save the busy executive

> 1   What is your purpose:
>   ● provide information?
>   ● write a proposal?
>   ● solve a problem?
>
> 2   About your recipient:
>   ● who is your recipient?
>   ● what do you know about your recipient in relation to:
>
>   expertise — how much do your recipients know about the topic?
>   — will they understand the technical jargon you might use?
>
>   interests — is there a preferred format you must use?
>   — do they like tables, charts, pictures, statistics?
>   — how much detail do your recipients want?
>
>   opinions — will your recipients be for or against your recommendations?
>   — do they think the topic is important?
>   — what do they think of you, e.g. expert authority, scribe,
>   junior?

Figure 4.6   Checklist before writing a report

time. If you prefer (or your organization insists that you use) the more traditional *Choice 1*, you may find that putting in a one-page 'Management/Executive summary' at the beginning will provide you with the best of both worlds. This should summarize your conclusions and recommendations, and how you got there, referenced to the main body of your report so that readers can follow up any points they wish.

This is a particularly useful style for reports presented to a committee. The management summary offers an overview and a ready-made agenda for discussion of the report, without the problems of getting bogged down in unnecessary detail.

See Figure 4.6 for a checklist before writing a report.

Organizing the data

Once you have decided the general structure, you must marshal your data to best advantage within that structure. A prioritizing system is a useful aid in this.

First list the main points on a piece of paper. Then think about each idea in turn and list the facts and ideas that go with each main point.

If the material is very detailed or complex, you may need a third stage where you add a further category of subordinate items. Figure 4.7 gives an example.

Now re-read your list to check that it is complete and you have missed nothing out. When you are confident that it is complete, take a few moments to consider your purpose and your recipient. What will motivate them best? What data will be most convincing or most interesting to them? Now look back over your main points and arrange them in the best sequence for your purpose, numbering them in order. Do the same for each set of subordinate points, using a decimal system as shown in Figure 4.8, until you have numbered each item. You may now want to rewrite your outline in order.

This provides you with a clear and well organized structure for your writing. You will find that it gets you started on your project and deals very effectively

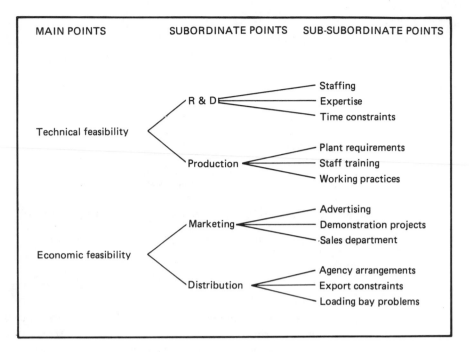

Figure 4.7   Example of a report outline

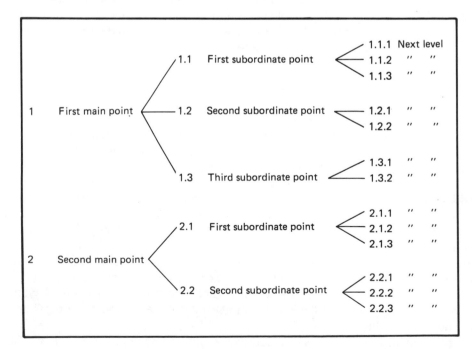

Figure 4.8   Numbered outline for a report

with any 'writer's blocks'. It cuts down substantially on writing time since all you need to do is follow the route map your outline provides. And for long reports, your first and second categories of points provide headings and sub-headings.

REPORTS GUIDELINES

- Plan carefully – think through the entire situation before you start to write.
- Gather all the facts and double-check them for accuracy and relevance.
- Choose an appropriate structure.
- Prepare a detailed outline.
- Anticipate objections and jot down ideas in response to work into your writing.
- Put yourself in the reader's place and try to imagine what materials would be most convincing.
- Beware of exaggerating, stating opinions as facts, or using biased statements.
- Edit every sentence and paragraph to make sure your meaning is clear.

Style

Style is a rather vague, literary term for the way you use words. To put it in more concrete terms, your chosen structure is your blueprint; words are the building blocks. Your vocabulary is your personal stock of bricks.

Some are everyday common-or-garden bricks; others are for special purposes. Many of the words you take for granted may be jargon to someone not in your industry or profession. Some of these words may be justifiable technical terms; others may be incomprehensible jargon to the outsider. The key to deciding which is which is your reader. What would he/she understand?

As well as jargon, there are a number of insidious 'weeds' which creep into our writing. These are the words and phrases we would never use in conversation; they are pompous, old-fashioned, and long-winded, e.g.

approximately	effected
assistance	terminate
commence	endeavour to ascertain
with all due despatch	concerning
in the event that	commendation
customary channels	

These are only a sample. I am sure you can think of many more. Can you find everyday, shorter ways of saying the same thing?

Clear English is the lifeblood of business communication. It can also make the difference between life and death as the following quotation shows:

> Of course, there were warnings about the fire risk at Bradford. I wish that they had been written in plain English, but they were written in the doughy, ponderous style that officials fall into, clearly under the impression that to use ordinary language is unworthy of their position. Anyone wanting to make the point would have written, 'people must be able to get away from the stand in two to three minutes. At present

they cannot.' What the football club received was, 'Egress from the grandstand should be achievable in 2.5 minutes.' It was told that 'an appraisal of structural adequacy' was 'desirable'. Even the question of litter was put into terms that remove it a stage from reality '. . . there is a build-up of combustible materials in the voids beneath the seats. A carelessly discarded cigarette could give rise to a fire risk.'

Was it beyond anyone to write, 'There are piles of rubbish under the seats. If someone drops a lighted cigarette into this lot, the whole stand could go up in flames in minutes'?

(This first appeared in *New Scientist*, a weekly review of science and technology.)

Grammar and spelling

A few words about two other bugbears: grammar and spelling. You need to be ruthlessly honest with yourself about these. Are you 'good at' grammar and spelling? If you are, no need to worry about them. If you are not, there is still no need to worry.

Grammar is something taught to children at school *after* the children have been communicating successfully for five or six years. Imagine learning Russian or Spanish, living in Russia or Spain for five or six years, speaking the language every day, and only then being taught the grammar. It's a crazy idea. Grammar is *part* of the language, not something complicated which is imposed on top of it. Grammar is something you know about; you use it every day speaking to people. The objective test for grammar is: do people understand you? If they do, and nobody complains about your use of English, then you are good enough at grammar. If, however, people complain about your use of English, help is required. Do *not* try to do this for yourself! Call in the experts, the people who complain, your secretary. State your problem: 'Never did get to grips with the finer points of grammar. I'd really appreciate it if you'd cast your eye over this and tidy it up for me.' The experts, especially those who complain, love to be asked to display their expertise. Don't get drawn into discussions (arguments) simply hand it over and let them get on with it. (If you do want to brush up grammar for yourself, you will find some ideas for this in the list of further reading at the end of this chapter.)

I believe that as far as spelling is concerned, there are only two types of people in the universe: those who can spell and those who cannot. It's rather like an ear for music. Either you have, or you haven't. If you have, rejoice. If you haven't, do not worry about it.

Have a good dictionary in your desk drawer and look things up. Don't be embarrassed about this. It's not a sign of failure. The secret of the perfect spellers is that they know their way round a dictionary. Not all dictionaries are the same in layout, presentation etc. Browse in a good bookshop and test out a few until you find one you really like. Then guard it with your life.

Again, do ask people for help, friends, colleagues, spouse, secretary – if they can spell. A simple request to 'check the spelling for me' will do the trick. It is very important for the manager who knows he/she is not good at grammar and spelling to ensure that their secretary is. Do include some test of these abilities in any selection process, then inform your secretary that she is responsible for the standard of grammar and spelling in anything she types for you. This should solve your problem, and end your worries on this.

CONCLUSION

Business writing is writing with a purpose. There is the PR purpose, representing your organization and yourself in an appropriate way. And there is the result you wish to achieve from the communication, ranging from the swift return of required information to the final blessed silence of a long term complainer. Knowing your purpose is the first step to effective writing. This chapter has offered guidelines and ideas for achieving that purpose through the choice of structure, organization of your ideas, and the use of language.

CHECKLIST

Key questions to be considered before you start writing are:

1 What is my PURPOSE? Why am I writing? What result do I want to achieve?
2 Who is my RECIPIENT? Who will receive and read this? Can I picture them in my mind?
3 What is my MESSAGE? What am I actually trying to say?
4 What is my ROLE? Am I friend or foe, subordinate or superior, expert or student, in relation to my recipient in this communication?
5 What are my RECIPIENT'S MOTIVATORS? How is this matter relevant to him/her? What do they need to know to be able to respond appropriately? Are there any benefits for them in doing so?

FURTHER READING

Howard, Godfrey, *Getting Through! How to make words work for you*, David & Charles, 1980
Sussams, John E. *How to Write Effective Reports*, Gower, 2nd edition 1991.

Dictionaries

The Concise Oxford Dictionary, Clarendon Press

The Oxford Dictionary for Writers and Editors, Clarendon Press (Try to get the most up-to-date edition of the dictionary of your choice.)

Moseley, D. and Nicol, C., *The ACE Spelling Dictionary*, Learning Development Aids, 1986. This is *the* dictionary for the hopeless speller. The ACE stands for Aurally Coded English and offers a simple and effective method to find the words you can't spell (by the sound of the words) and see how to spell them correctly. Highly recommended.

Grammar and usage

Roberts, P. D., *Plain English: A user's guide*, Penguin, 1987.

5 Effective speaking

Brian Sanders

We are all capable of speaking effectively to an audience large or small but many of us are woefully out of practice, some of us have never had any practice, and the vast majority have had no tuition in the skills involved.

This chapter provides a practical and basic introduction for the busy manager who has to talk to a group of people. The chapter is divided into four parts:

- The spoken word.
- How to make the best use of oneself.
- How to prepare the material.
- Extending the vocal range.

The word 'talk' has been used throughout and is intended to cover presentation, speech, address, lecture and synonymous expressions. The word 'audience' is used to include listeners, conference, meeting, assembly and similar expressions.

THE SPOKEN WORD

The art of speaking has been neglected in favour of writing. Few schools teach it. On a recent course a man of 45 said that the last time he spoke to an audience was at a primary school assembly!

Because of this neglect, confidence is lacking and the results may be disastrous. But with effort and practice much can be achieved. Preparation and practice are essential.

Effective speaking

The term 'effective speaking' has replaced the older 'public speaking'. The latter suggests a formal gathering with a platform and a large audience. Much work today is done in an informal situation and with an audience of only three or four.

But one must be effective. Do not underestimate the amount of effort required to talk to a small group. The world is full of mutterers. Do not be one of these. If you are to sound enthusiastic and convincing, vocal vitality is essential.

Whether you talk to three, 30 or 300 the basic approach is the same. You need a conversational style. But both your physical self and your voice need enlarging and projecting to meet the needs of the larger audience.

Lord Curzon (1859–1925) was recognized as one of the finest orators of his time. He made a perceptive statement about talking to audiences. He said that the three most important things to remember, in their order of importance, are:

- Who you are
- How you say it
- What you say.

At first sight the second and third statements may appear to be the wrong way round. But no matter how excellent your material, if you cannot present it in an interesting and entertaining way, if you cannot make it palatable, then you might as well not bother.

Who you are is your personality, relevant knowledge and experience. You must engage the whole of yourself – voice, eyes, face, hands, arms – the whole of your physical self to assist communication.

If you are extrovert then discipline yourself as necessary; don't completely overwhelm the audience. If you are a quiet and shy person, use these attributes to draw your audience towards you. Shyness does not prevent voice projection or vitality.

Don't be over-modest. Use relevant experience whenever you can. Anecdotes always stick in the mind.

How you say it demands the best use of your voice, the best possible presentation of your whole self and of the material.

Every effort should be made to increase and enlarge the vocal range and to keep the voice in trim with constant exercising. (Refer to the final section 'Extending the vocal range'.)

You must create the right atmosphere. Jargon and technical terms must be avoided if they will not be understood.

What you say requires careful selection and ordering. Everything must be relevant to the particular occasion.

Personality

You will be effective only if you are willing to disclose your personality. The actor hides behind the character he portrays. You must be yourself. You must be prepared to put yourself at risk.

But the element of risk causes nervous tension which will inhibit your performance. Relaxation will prevent this. Until you are relaxed you will never give of your best.

To learn relaxation takes some weeks of practice. But it can be done. Once relaxed you will enjoy the experience of talking to audiences.

HOW TO MAKE THE BEST USE OF ONESELF

Speakers sometimes fancy that if they take refuge behind an overhead projector or some sophisticated aid their lack of skills or nervous tension will go unnoticed. It is not so. In fact the more sophisticated the aids the more the weaknesses of a poor speaker are highlighted. A multiple projector presentation has often been followed by a disastrous question time because the speaker was tense, looked desperate and mumbled the answers. And this is what the audience remembered.

Relaxation will solve all the problems caused by tension. Practice will improve the speaker's performance.

Nerves and tension

It is important to distinguish between nerves and tension. Nerves are essential to set the adrenalin flowing into the blood stream. This has a stimulating effect on the system and gives the necessary 'edge' to our performance.

Some think, quite incorrectly, that eventually a person 'grows out' of nerves with the benefit of experience. This is not so. The time to worry is when you don't feel nervous!

Watch actors pacing, coughing and fidgeting backstage before a first entrance. See the effect of the red light in a BBC radio studio on the most experienced actors. But they have learned to control their nerves and so prevent the assault of tension.

Tension is a wrecker. It constricts the voice, prevents breath control, and makes the speaker look anywhere but at the audience. Clinging to a lectern or a piece of furniture, swaying, fidgeting and other distracting mannerisms are further manifestations.

Controlling nerves and eliminating tension

Useful exercises practised for a few minutes each day will eventually enable a person to relax at will. It is simply a question of mind over matter. Once relaxation is achieved speaking engagements become a positive pleasure. The speaker knows that self-control through relaxation will give an appearance of relaxed authority.

Some exercises for relaxation

1   On tiptoe, stretch arms upwards, fully extended; stretch fingers on hands. Stretch calves and thighs. Stretch the abdomen. Imagine yourself on a vertical rack with toes nailed to the floor and fingers pulled by unseen wires towards the ceiling.

    Feel the discomfort of it. Hold the position for a few moments and then relax. Feel the pleasure of relaxation. Repeat this exercise three times.
2   Tense the arms from shoulders to fingertips. Feel the discomfort. Relax and feel the pleasure of relaxation. Repeat three times.
3   Keeping the soles of the feet on the floor, stretch the legs from thighs to tips of toes. (Keep the arms relaxed during this exercise.) Feel the discomfort. Relax

and feel the pleasure of relaxation. When you relax keep both knees braced but not rigid. Repeat three times.

4   Stretch arms and legs together (as in 2 and 3). Feel the discomfort. Relax and feel the pleasure of relaxation. Repeat three times.

The shoulders and neck are most prone to tension. Breathing becomes difficult, the voice is stifled in the throat and the speaker is extra-ordinarily aware of hands and arms.

The following exercises are designed to help remove tension from these vital areas.

5   Shake the fingers loose on limp wrists and try to throw them on to the floor. Next shake the fingers and lower arms from the elbows. Finally throw the arms from the shoulders. Feel all tension in the arms being flung out of the finger-tips.

6   Roll the right shoulder forwards and then backwards several times in vigorous circles. Repeat with the left shoulder. Then exercise both shoulders together.

7   Relax the muscles in the neck and allow the head to fall forward. Roll the head round *slowly* three times, bending from the waist so that the weight of the head takes it round. Stop and rotate slowly in the opposite direction three times. Stop with the chin resting on the chest. Lift the head level. *Note*: This exercise must be undertaken slowly.

CREATING A FEELING OF CONFIDENCE

Standing or sitting well creates a feeling of confidence in both speaker and audience.

For the speaker it aids relaxation, enables ease of movement, assists breath control and helps to free the voice.

The audience see someone authoritative, knowledgeable, confident and delighted to talk to them.

If the audience exceeds 15 or 20 in number, it may be necessary to stand, however informal the occasion. If when seated, you cannot see all the faces, they cannot see you.

Standing well

The feet should be slightly apart. This gives a good grip on the floor. Never stand with your feet together. Brace both knees firmly but without tension. Bring the stomach wall under control so that it is firmly held but not pulled in.

Hold the chest freely without pushing it forward and settle the shoulders on the chest with two or three easy movements up and down. They should be very slightly braced.

Look comfortably straight ahead. The position should be 'head in the air' and not 'nose (or chin) in the air'.

Have the weight of the body on the soles of the feet and not the heels. If you stand on your heels the blood flow is restricted and this will make you tense and tired. Stand in your footprints.

Keep the feet anchored and swing the trunk left to the back and then right to the

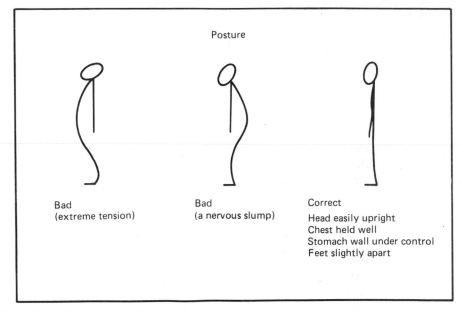

Figure 5.1   Posture: standing

back. This will prevent any stiffness creeping in. See Figure 5.1 for examples of correct and bad posture.

Sitting well

Choose a chair in which the seat and the back form a right angle. Place your bottom as far back as possible. When you sit up the back of the chair supports you. You can both sit comfortably and in a position which allows maximum freedom for movement from the waist upwards. It also allows freedom for breath control and voice projection.

If you are condemned to a badly designed chair sit forward on the seat and lean very slightly forward as well. See Figure 5.2 for examples.

Eye contact

Standing or sitting well enables an ease of eye contact with the audience. The top half of the body can move freely and, so long as the neck muscles are relaxed, the head will turn freely in every direction.

Eye contact with a large group is easier than with a small one. When talking to an audience of less than 20 people the speaker's eye must light occasionally on each person. But don't 'searchlight' the group from side to side. This can be very wearisome all round!

With a large group the speaker should look for the most part about two-thirds of the way back. Occasional glances should be made to left and right of the front rows.

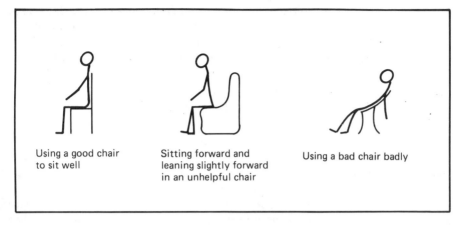

Using a good chair to sit well

Sitting forward and leaning slightly forward in an unhelpful chair

Using a bad chair badly

Figure 5.2   Posture: sitting

Gesture

Good gesture helps to underline what is said. All movement of the arm should be hinged at the shoulder and not the elbow.

The elbows give strength to gesture, the wrists enable precision and the hands contain power and control.

Bad gesture distracts. Twitches, fidgets and repetitive movements are fatal. The audience spots them and attention is diverted from what is said.

USING A MICROPHONE

There are times in a large hall or a room where acoustics are bad when a microphone becomes necessary. Neck microphones are preferable to stand microphones particularly if your talk requires movement. The neck instrument remains at a uniform distance from the larynx and allows you the necessary freedom to move about.

There are many types of stand microphone. Rehearse well before the event to discover what the instrument will and will not do. Take the advice of a technician if one is available. But remember that even technology cannot provide all the answers.

You must bring vitality to the microphone. There must be something irresistible about your performance. If you project both subtlety and vitality then the micro-phone will be most effective in transmitting them.

PREPARING THE MATERIAL

Pre-preparation

Before attempting notes or jottings for the talk ask yourself the following five questions. Answer each as thoroughly as possible. This will help you to concentrate on material relevant to the specific occasion, will ensure that you pitch the talk at the correct level, will prevent last minute panics and will also save you time.

1   *What is my aim?* You may wish to inform, persuade, teach or stimulate. You will certainly always wish to entertain.

To entertain does not simply mean telling jokes. It is a combination of 'who you are' and 'how you say it' together with the eventual selection and ordering of your material. It also includes relevant jokes and anecdotes. But if you are no good at telling jokes, don't.

Remember too that you cannot talk on technical matters or specialized knowledge for long without giving your audience a chance to relax a little.

Within your general aims consider your specific aim. What is it that you most wish your audience to remember, or what action do you wish them to take? This gives you a 'cutting edge'. It is worth noting now that your specific aim may change during the course of the preparation.

2   *Who am I talking to?* Find out all you can about the audience. Detailed research may be necessary but it is worth it in the long run. You must gear your talk as closely as possible to the listeners. Avoid jargon and technical terms if they will not be comprehensible. Find out what your audience wants to know, needs to know and doesn't need to know.

3   *Where am I giving the talk?* Know the size and shape of the room, the height of the ceiling, whether there are heavy curtains and a thick piled carpet. The room may resemble a concrete box. These things will affect the acoustics. A microphone may be necessary but don't use one unless you have to.

Decide where you will stand or sit. You must be seen easily by everyone. You should be in a dominating position though almost certainly not on a platform unless the audience is very big.

The natural light should always come from the side of the room unless the artificial lighting is excellent. If you are using electrical apparatus make sure that the sockets are conveniently placed.

Knowledge of these matters will help relaxation when the time comes.

4   *What time of day am I talking?* This may affect the arrangement of your material and will certainly shape your opening remarks.

After morning coffee is a good time to speak – probably the best. The audience are fully awake and ready for you.

After lunch – the siesta session – is a bad time. You will need to entertain to your utmost.

If it's an evening talk discover how your audience have been occupied during the day.

This information will enable you to gear the talk correctly from the start of your preparation.

5   *How shall I organize the time available?* Forty-five minutes is the longest time one person can sustain. If you have over an hour, you must organize the time carefully. After your introduction you might divide the audience into groups. Each group would retire, appoint a leader/secretary, and discuss some particular point(s). After a given time the groups reassemble, each secretary reports back to the whole audience and a general discussion takes place. It would then be the speaker's task to pull the threads together, summarize and point the way ahead. All this takes a great deal of preparation.

Decide how you will organize question time. And consider whether visual aids will be helpful.

Even when refurbishing an old talk it is still essential to answer these five questions.

Preparation time and the shape of the talk

The ideal time for preparing a talk is two or three weeks. Many have only two or three days, or even hours. The notes on assembling and selecting the material have therefore been divided into sections according to the time available.

All talks should have an introduction, a main part and a conclusion. Where should you begin? The principal facts or arguments go into the main section and this should be your starting point in the preparation. This section will comprise all but four to eight minutes of the total talking time.

Assembling and selecting material for the main part

Two weeks or more to prepare   Write down on a large sheet of paper, notes, key words and headings. These may eventually form the basis of your notes. Don't write sentences, and don't worry about the order at this stage. Check dates, figures, statistics; do necessary research.

Work at this in bursts of 15 or 20 minutes and then turn to something else. Return a while later and do some more. Your subconscious will work for you during the break and thoughts and ideas will flow more freely. Work again for only a short time and return again later or on the next day.

After five or six days, perhaps sooner, you will have a sheet or more of paper filled with a mass of material. There will be far more than you can possibly use in one talk.

Analysis on audience retention carried out some years ago produced most interesting figures. In a series of 40-minute talks it was found that an intelligent audience (an audience knowledgeable about and interested in the subject) could remember seven facts. An average audience could remember three facts. These figures are not sacrosanct but they are a positive guide.

Leave your jottings for a couple of days and allow your subconscious time to get to work again. Stored in your brain you have the answers to the five pre-preparation questions and all the rough headings and notes.

A burst of insight will tell you the theme you wish to pursue on this occasion because you are talking to that particular audience, in that place and at that time.

Now comes the vital moment of selection when you know what in your jottings is relevant and what is not. Strike out what is not relevant. Be ruthless. Take no matter you can dispense with. Better to say too little than too much.

Two days to prepare   Notes and headings concerning the subject should be jotted down on a large sheet of paper. Don't worry about the order. Check facts and figures. This work should be done in 'bursts' and should be completed in one day.

You will probably have too much material for one talk. Realise your specific aim for talking to this particular audience. Then remove any material not wholly relevant.

Two hours to prepare   Jot down all the headings which seem relevant. Leave the jottings for about half an hour. Return and delete irrelevant material. If you must add to the list then do so.

Two or three minutes to prepare Should you wish to speak at a meeting and without prior preparation write down half a dozen key words on a sheet of paper. Then get them in a useful order. Speak for no more than three minutes and you may find yourself popular!

The main part of the talk

The skeleton of the main part is now to hand in what remains of your headings and jottings.

Get your headings in the correct order. If you are following a procedure or the way a piece of machinery works, then the order may be dictated by this. If there is no obvious order then arrange your points in order of importance.

Suppose you have six main headings. Arrange these in order of merit: 1 is your least important; 6 is your most important. Follow the Greeks who were masters of oratory. Begin your main section with point 5, your next-to-best; it will commend your whole case. Then proceed with 1, 2, 3, 4, and finish with 6.

You must work up towards a climax and not down. If you begin with your most important point ('They'll doze off after five or six minutes') then subconsciously you will know you have made the vital statement and you will 'run down' whether you like it or not. And they will doze off! Always work up to the point of greatest interest or intensity.

Next you must put the flesh on the skeleton of your talk. Write each heading on a separate large sheet of paper. Jot down your thoughts on how you may illuminate or develop that section. When you have completed the section in note form reshape your jottings to produce the right order. If you have stuck to notes and headings you will almost certainly find that the essential key words and phrases have emerged. Transfer these to the cards you will use for notes.

Pattern your notes in the way that suits you. Once you have found a satisfactory method of note making stick to it.

Having completed one section of your talk work on the others in a similar fashion.

The conclusion

This is a reiteration of the main points. Gather all the threads together and end on a conclusive or challenging note according to the purpose. Point the way ahead. Leave the audience with something to consider.

Introduction

This is the last section to be prepared and falls into two parts: the general introduction and the introduction of the subject matter.

The general introduction It is essential for the audience and yourself to 'tune in' to each other. They may never have seen you before. If so they will size you up visually before they are fully prepared to listen to you. If you begin with some vital matter most of them will miss it.

If you are a stranger they need to be told who you are, your relevant experience and background. Your host may do this but it is often helpful to reserve some of this information for yourself.

If possible compliment your audience. Find out something about their organization. Show you are interested in them outside the specific subject matter. Make them feel you are delighted to talk to them. If this is sincerely done the effect will be positive and helpful.

This general introduction can be done without reference to notes. This enables you to make eye contact with everyone and allows you to hear your voice projected to the back rows. If you can manage a smile as well – so much the better!

You may be addressing the firm's board of management or colleagues at a weekly meeting. Then much of the general introduction will be inappropriate. They may already know far too much about you! But an audience of colleagues still requires about a minute's 'settling time'. An appropriate observation or two will induce all eyes and ears in your direction.

Introduction of the subject matter Your subject and objectives must be made abundantly clear. Avoid startling and striking openings. A clear, quietly stated opening is best. Tell them succinctly the ground you are about to cover and your aims.

NOTES

Cards (6" × 4") are best for making notes. Find a pattern for note-making which suits you and stick to it. When these are completed number each card in the top right-hand corner. Then punch a hole in the top left-hand corner and tag the cards together. This makes it easy to turn them over and, should you drop them, they will remain in the right order!

Always carry your notes with you. There is no one to prompt you if your mind goes suddenly blank. And it is easy to miss something out. Discipline yourself to glance at the notes from time to time even if you are familiar with the subject matter.

A GENERAL OBSERVATION

Remember that the people being addressed are receiving the information for the first time. Facts and ideas must be presented simply and logically. Precise English is essential.

Always proceed from the known to the unknown. Build bridges from one point to the next. Do not elaborate the obvious.

Support statements with examples and anecdotes; tell jokes if you can and if they are relevant. Keep to the point.

USING VISUAL AIDS

Visual aids are used to assist communication and to present information so that it will be quickly grasped. They convey what words cannot get across.

Always let the subject matter speak for itself. Words are not visual aids. If using words keep them short and simple; make them forceful.

When showing a visual aid keep quiet for a little to allow the audience time to take it in. It is difficult, if not impossible, to read and listen at the same time. Remove the visual when you have finished with it.

Don't lose eye contact with the audience by talking to the flip chart or screen. Use a pointer or pencil and talk to the audience. But don't be afraid to write or draw on a flip chart or blackboard and talk a little at the same time, provided of course that you are talking about the matter on the board. Project your voice a little more at the same time.

The projector is better than other means for maps, charts, graphs and diagrams.

Visual aids should never be used merely as a concentration break or as a cue for the speaker.

Never display all headings at once. Use an overlay and limit strictly what is being looked at – that is what is being talked about.

Take care with colours. Blue and green together appear the same to the partially colour blind. Some colours are weak when projected.

Do not use too many visual aids. This confuses the audience and often confounds the speaker.

Prepare carefully and rehearse assiduously. Check equipment and always carry spare bulbs and extension leads.

Know beforehand what you will do if for any reason you are unable to use your visual aids.

ANSWERING QUESTIONS

In most cases a question session is essential unless you are satisfied you have given a complete performance. It is a matter of getting nearer to the whole truth and of meeting the needs of the audience.

Unless the talk is 'in house' it may be necessary to have a short interval when you have finished your talk. An audience cannot go into reverse at once. Tell them that questions will follow in two or three minutes. This will give them time to consider.

Answer as shortly as you can. Having answered the question don't go on answering it beyond the point of satisfaction.

If you do not know the answer say so. Call on somebody in the audience or offer to find out and write. Or suggest sources. Never invent an answer.

If you should know the answer but don't the fault is probably in your lack of preparation.

Rephrase a bad question before you answer it to avoid possible misunderstanding and embarrassment.

Repeat each question so that the back rows know what is being answered.

In the face of hostility remain courteous and keep your sense of humour. If a heckler persists and if there is no one in the chair to intervene offer to discuss the matter at the end as time is short and others wish to be answered.

When time is running out say, 'There's just time for three more questions', and hope to finish on a high note.

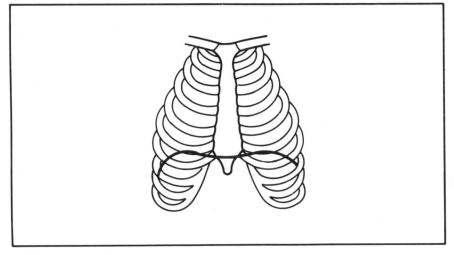

Figure 5.3 The chest from the front

(The thick black line indicates the position of the diaphragm before inhalation.)

EXTENDING THE VOCAL RANGE

The human voice is a unique instrument. Unless physically impaired we each possess the necessary equipment and may do wonderful things with the voice. But we must learn to use it properly and to realise its full range. Relaxation and good posture help to free the voice.

Breathing

Correct breathing assists projection, helps avoid strain, gives the voice the necessary vitality and helps the speaker to sound enthusiastic.

For any form of public speaking we need to inhale quickly and deeply. In normal conversation we breathe through a slightly open mouth. This enables speedy and silent inhalation.

To breathe more deeply we must learn to expand the chest cavity. In normal breathing the rib cage moves upwards and outwards, and the diaphragm (a powerful muscle separating the chest from the abdomen) contracts and descends. These movements increase the volume of the chest cavity, a partial vacuum is created and air is sucked into the lungs (see Figure 5.3).

The more movement of the ribs and diaphragm the more air is drawn into the lungs. The more air in the lungs the better our voice control.

Exercises for expansion and control

These exercises are best done near an open window or in a room with plenty of fresh air. (Outside is best of all – if you dare!)

Spend only two or three minutes at a time on breathing exercises. Should you feel dizzy then stop immediately. Overdoing things may result in hyperventilation.

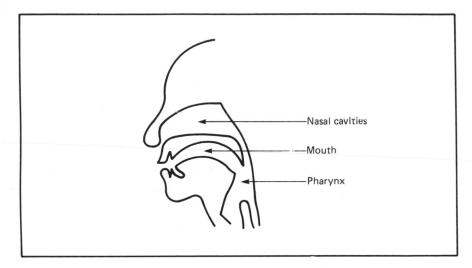

Figure 5.4   Cross-section of the head showing the resonating chambers

(*Note:* The term 'nasal cavities' is intended to cover the nose and the various tubes and chambers associated with it.)

1   Practise heavy sighs. This is a natural way of relieving tension. Sigh heavily and feel the rib cage collapse. Sigh several times. As you draw breath before the sigh feel the upward and outward expansion of the rib cage.
　　Note that the shoulders play no part in breathing. They should be slightly braced (as for good stance), relaxed and still. On no account should they hunch at the time of inhalation.
2   Stand at one end of a large room. Inhale deeply and whisper 'One, two, three, four, five' using all the breath. Send the whisper on the stream of breath to the far end of the room.
3   Hum quietly. On the same note intone (or chant) 'One'.
4   Fill the lungs and intone 'One, two, three, four, five'. Repeat two or three times.
5   Once able to complete exercise 4 with ease and with 'five' fully projected repeat the exercise to 'ten'.
6   When you can complete exercise 5 with ease gradually extend the counting to 'fifteen'. The final number intoned should always sound as resonant as the first. When you run out of sufficient breath then stop.

The exercises are to employ the rib cage and diaphragm so that they may work fully and easily: they are not voice exercises. Constant practice (a little at a time) will help to ensure an ease of deep breathing.

Resonance or the human amplification system

We should strive to make the best use of our vocal tone by ensuring that we are fully resonant.

　　All hollow chambers above the voice box (larynx) act as resonators. These are the pharynx (the back of the throat), the nose and all the cavities and chambers connected to it, and the mouth (see Figure 5.4).

The key exercise is humming.

1 Moisten the lips with the tongue and hum gently on an 'm' sound.
  The lips should be lightly together and the teeth slightly apart. When you hum a tingling sensation should be felt on the lips.
    If no sensation is felt part the lips slightly and make a sound like a foghorn by blowing through them. Repeat this but after three seconds bring the lips together for the hum.
    The tingling should resemble that when playing the comb and tissue paper. Quality of humming is more important than volume.
2 Hum, feel the tingle, open the mouth slowly and as wide as possible and sing 'ah'.
3 Intone 'Mary had a little lamb' feeling the tingle at the beginning and end of the line.
4 Speak this sentence with conviction, 'I must keep my voice in the front of my mouth'.
5 Do 3 and 4 together. Attempt to speak the words of 4 in the same place that you intoned 3.
6 Hum up and down the scale with a slow, smooth beat. Think and feel the sound on the mask of the face.
7 Hum any tune you know and keep the sound forward.

These exercises help to produce a forward voice and a well balanced resonant tone.

Clarity

Good articulation helps to make speech clear and distinct. The key instruments are the tongue, the teeth and the lips.

1 Say 'Articulation is a form of gymnastics between the tip of the tongue, the teeth and the lips'.
2 Say 'the tip of the tongue, the teeth and the lips' three times as nimbly as you can but without gabbling. The letter 't' is made by the explosion of teeth and lips parting.
3 Say *ttt ttt ttt ttt* (don't say *tee tee tee*).
4 Practise '*t-say*', '*t-sow*', '*t-sigh*' and then try '*t-snake*' '*t-slave*' '*t-star*'.
5 Practise precision of consonants:
    ppp ppp ppp ppp (lips)
    bbb bbb bbb bbb (lips)
    ttt ttt ttt ttt (teeth and tongue)
    ddd ddd ddd ddd (teeth and tongue)
    kkk kkk kkk kkk (body of tongue and soft palate)
    ggg ggg ggg ggg (body of tongue and soft palate)
6 Practise tongue twisters.

Modulation

To modulate means to vary or to change. Vocal modulation helps to highlight important words and phrases and makes it easier for the listener to comprehend the meaning.

The communication of technical information is particularly dependent on a well modulated voice.

Vocal modulation depends on inflexion (glides or kicks up or down on one word), changes of pitch (usually on a phrase), the use of pause, and pace (here defined as a slight speeding up or slowing down of the rate of speech in reaction to the matter). A voice that is not modulated is monotonous.

1   Use inflexion to change the meaning of the following words:
    goodbye; hello; yes; what; please; fancy;
    e.g. goodbye
    • to a friend you will see tomorrow;
    • exit in fury, slamming the door;
    • Romeo/Juliet leaving Juliet/Romeo.
2   Vary the meaning of the following groups of words by changing pitch (steps up or down) and using inflexion:
    what is that; if I must; why me; yes sir.
3   Using inflexion, pitch, pause and pace, how many ways can you say:
    You are coming home with me tonight.

Phrasing

A phrase is a group of words which makes sense. Phrasing is the grouping of words in a way which is calculated to bring out the meaning. All words forming a phrase belong closely together and nothing should spoil or break this sequence. A phrase therefore should be spoken on one breath.

Exercise: Practise reading aloud from good prose. Stories for children provide excellent material.

The voice

The voice is our main and easiest means of communication. It can also be the most effective. But we must learn how best to use it, and to keep it in trim.

Athletes, singers, boxers, golfers, rugger and tennis players and people in many other professions practise daily. So should we if we have a professional approach.

KEY POINTS

1   Make the best of yourself:

    • control nerves and eliminate tension;
    • share your personality;
    • stand and sit to advantage.
    • make eye contact with your audience.

2 Prepare thoroughly:

- realise your aim;
- know your audience;
- select and organize your material;
- shape your talk.

3 Explore the full potential of your voice:

- practise breath control;
- achieve full resonance;
- articulate;
- modulate.

FURTHER READING

Cole, Wilton, *Sound and Sense: a handbook on Elocution*, Allen & Unwin, 14th impression 1976

Kapp, R. O., *The Presentation of Technical Information*, 2nd edn revised by Alan Isaacs, Constable, 1973

Burchfield, R. *The Spoken Word* – A BBC guide, BBC 1981

Gowers, Sir Ernest, *Complete Plain Words*, Penguin, revised by Sir Bruce Fraser, 1973

Partridge, Eric, *Usage and Abusage*, Penguin, 1963

6 Managing your health

Dr H. Beric Wright, MB FRCS MFOM

HEALTH AND WELLBEING

To the extent that management is about taking decisions concerned with the allocation of resources and the settlement of priorities, an individual's health – your health – can increasingly be viewed against a similar grid. Starting with genetic inheritance and the degree to which one has learnt from experience, health is, in my view, very much a reflection of general wellbeing and adjustment.

On the whole, well adjusted people, enjoying what they have set out to do and not being continually stretched beyond their capabilities, and involved in good relationships, are unlikely to be ill. Illness is largely dis-ease, and wellness, as I have said, is a function of general wellbeing. As the World Health Organization said shortly after the war, 'health is a state of physical, mental and social wellbeing'.

This somewhat pompous definition implies that to be well, one must be reasonably in tune with the physical, mental (emotional) and social parameters of one's life. In other words, the avoidance of too much dis-ease in one's lifestyle is likely to influence mortality and morbidity.

Lifestyle is very much a matter of choice and discipline. Diet, and more particularly calorie intake, largely determines weight. Animal fat consumption against a genetic background determining metabolism (the way in which the body deals with nutritional essentials) plays a part in coronary risk rating. Smoking, drinking and exercise are well within the control of a reasonably motivated and knowledgeable person.

As will become apparent, in the present state of our understanding of the common killer diseases, lifestyle, which is very much open to choice, is a significant determinant of disease risk. And conditions like coronary thrombosis (CHD) which still kills at least a fifth of all men in the UK, can be usefully 'risk rated'.

Such an assessment of the odds, which can be made from the results of a detailed health check, will give you the probability of suffering a coronary. It does not necessarily mean that you will get one, or even avoid one entirely, but it does measure the likelihood and you can make your own choice as to what you do about it.

To make such a choice, it is necessary first to understand the various risk factors and the causes and incidence of common diseases; also to know about yourself, your aspirations, attributes and a few other basic facts. For instance, you cannot know what your blood pressure is, or the balance of lipids (blood fats) in your blood unless these are measured periodically.

We know that what becomes an overt disease, like CHD, is the end result of a process that in its early stages produces no symptoms and that the process can often be halted and reversed if caught early enough and dealt with vigorously.

To give another example, breast cancer kills about one in every 13 women. Breast and lung cancer are the commonest cancers in women; the former is increasingly treatable if detected early and the latter is very much smoking-related. Thus it is sensible for a woman to attend a breast screening clinic and practise regular self-examination to maximize the chances of early diagnosis and treatment by minimal surgery. Similarly anyone who chooses to smoke cigarettes must do so in the sure knowledge that they are reducing their life expectancy. This is then their free choice, based on the facts as they know them.

Management, as I have said, is about taking decisions in the light of the best information available to obtain a desired objective: in this case optimum health and functional efficiency. As I hope to be able to explain, your life is largely in your hands because you *can* decide how you live and what your priorities in living are. Traditionally, doctors treat established disease. This doctor wants to keep you out of the hands of his colleagues!

Health is probably our most precious asset and good managers are a company's least replaceable one. Thus, as I see it, there is both a joint responsibility and mutual benefit in contriving a situation in which both flourish. Some companies, which in my view are badly run, have a propensity to consume people by driving them too hard. Managers, on the other hand, can be bribed or seduced into becoming full-time workaholics to the neglect of their other relationships and the needs of a compensatingly reasonable physical and emotional 'other life'.

These again are matters of conscious choice and not necessarily the inevitable rat race that they might seem. Living successfully is very much a matter of facing realities and making the right choices. Although it is difficult to prove statistically because there are always exceptions in all things biological, reasonably fit people are on the whole more lively and effective. As is often apparent, disciplined people are more effective because they know what they are trying to do and have the right priorities.

What I am trying to say is that health is very much a matter of choice and that the overall ground rules for making these choices do exist. As we tend to work in one group and live in a family unit, it is the 'climate' in these and the rules that are set up for them, that largely determine our wellbeing. Exercising the right options and understanding the odds are what is critical, plus a willingness to change if the equations don't balance.

WHAT YOU HAVE TO SURVIVE

If management is about understanding and choosing priorities and backing probability, management of your health should follow a similar path. Although you may inherit good, long lived genes or bad, short lived ones, because of genetically determined diseases or predispositions, it is useful to know something about the commoner hazards to your survival.

Two short examples will help to make this point. Coronary heart disease (CHD) still kills at least a fifth of all men in this country before retiring age, and this amongst other things creates a lot of widows. The incidence of CHD in developed countries increased rapidly after the war and has been rightly regarded as an epidemic. In America the incidence has fallen significantly over the last few years. In Scandinavia it is under control and falling as it is also at last beginning to here. Most of the predisposing or 'risk factors' for CHD are lifestyle related, i.e. they are well within an individual's or community's control and can thus be considered as a management problem.

Cigarette smoking, or the inhalation of tobacco smoke, increases the chances of a man getting a coronary by three or four times. It is the largest cause of lung cancer, the commonest cancer in men, and through chronic bronchitis, often euphemistically disguised as 'the smoker's cough', is responsible for a great deal of lost time and serious disability during the working life, as well as seriously clouding the retirement years through breathlessness and a weak chest.

Similarly, breast and lung cancer are the commonest killers in middle-aged women. The latter can be avoided by not smoking and the former to an increasing degree mitigated by early diagnosis and early removal of small lesions by minimal surgery. This depends, as does the more acceptable cervical smear for cervical cancer (which has about one quarter the incidence of breast cancer), on the woman's willingness to attend a specialized Well Woman clinic.

These then are some high priority areas which are very much a matter for individual decisions, but decisions which significantly determine life expectancy.

Going back to probabilities, all this can be regarded as a relatively simple equation in which the overall odds are made up of the incidence and risk factors for various common diseases and the denominator provided by genetic inheritance and personality factors. Thus, if there is a family history of heart disease, it does not mean that all the sons of a coronary mother will be so afflicted but it does make it more likely that they will be. Thus, it is prudent for them and indeed for all of us, to know what the odds are and then to proceed more wisely through life, to minimize the overall risks.

Equally, someone with long lived parents can more safely risk being mildly overweight and perhaps eating more animal fats because they may well have a less vulnerable metabolic system. Obviously to make such decisions the facts must be known: hence the prudence of regular health checks so that you know what your blood pressure is and how your lipid and blood fat levels are behaving. If you like, this personal data is as important to health management as is regular information about your company's cash flow and sales ledger.

What this means is that having your staff, yourself and your family regularly serviced should be seen in the same light and with the same priority as servicing your car, plant and machinery. These are serviced to minimize breakdown and it is, I suggest, merely a matter of wise asset protection and a legitimate and tax deductible cost for a company, to encourage health servicing of staff.

Another and sadder denominator, about which space precludes detailed consideration, is the factor of social class or occupation. Although the incidence of the common diseases has been falling in the professional and managerial classes over

Age	Men				Women			
15–34	Accidents (1) 614	Cancer 113	Circulatory 70	Respiratory 34	Accidents 370	Cancer 251	Circulatory 83	Respiratory 48
35–44	Circulatory 299	Accidents 265	Cancer 223	Respiratory 40	Cancer 537	Circulatory 145	Accidents 122	Respiratory 32
45–64	Circulatory 469	Cancer 334	Respiratory 61	Accidents 47	Cancer 534	Circulatory 244	Respiratory 58	Accidents 45
65+	Circulatory 478	Cancer 258	Respiratory 142	Accidents 13	Circulatory 495	Cancer 212	Respiratory 124	Accidents 16

Figure 6.1   Selected causes of death by age and sex in 1989 as rates per 1,000 deaths.
(1) Accidents include suicide and violence.

Source: HMSO 1991 Social Trends

recent years, the gap between them and the semi-skilled and unskilled workers has been widening. Thus the incidence of CHD, hypertension (high blood pressure), and lung disease is several times higher in these groups. This is partly for socio-economic reasons and partly because the 'lifestyle message' has not got through to these groups. Smoking, for instance, obesity, alcohol consumption and so on, have a higher incidence in social classes IV and V than in classes I and II. Sadly, this reflects a major failure of the NHS to really improve the health of the nation and does provide management with a chance to improve the health of its own work force.

Seven or eight years ago, the Electrical Contractors' Association and their division of the ETU put in a health screening scheme with BUPA. More recently, IBM in the UK have made a similar facility available to all their staff on a country-wide basis. In both cases the screening activity revealed a significant amount of untreated disease and provided an opportunity and the motivation for lifestyle counselling.

As this is so obviously important and valuable, employers are now under increasing pressure to provide 'on site' screening facilities for shop floor and office workers and this is becoming more widely available through organizations like the BUPA Medical Centre. Marks & Spencer in the UK pioneered the provision of cervical screening for all women employees and soon extended this to include breast screening. Many larger companies have in-house medical departments which will play a growing role in health promotion as well as the more traditional one of monitoring for toxic hazards and the provision of a 'works' surgery' for rapid treatment.

New regulations regarding toxic exposure to potentially harmful agents will make such monitoring obligatory and it should be easy to combine it with a simple health check at the work place.

Incidence of common diseases

Figure 6.1 shows the commonest causes of death in men and women at various ages in the UK. Although the numbers are small in the younger age groups, it is for instance significant that accidents (which include suicide) do figure for those up

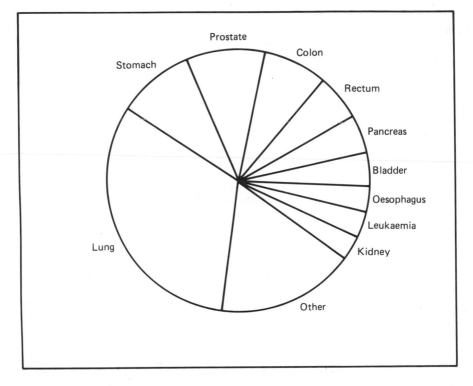

Figure 6.2   Frequency of cancer deaths in the UK (men)

Source: OPCS Monitor DH2

to age 44 and must be regarded as to a degree preventable. But the most significant figure in this table is, of course, the incidence of circulatory causes. Cancer begins to figure from middle life onwards and the individual cancers are shown in Figures 6.2 and 6.3. This shows, as I have already said, that cancer of the lung and breast in women are top of the league and to a degree are either avoidable or treatable. There is also now a growing conviction that there is an environmental element in many cancers due to diet, pollution and so on. These again represent management and personal decisions about which more will be heard. Recent tragedies and near misses in the nuclear industry make such decisions more pressing.

One particular factor of survival, with considerable social consequences which cannot be discussed in detail, is the fact that at all ages women live longer than men. In spite of what I have said about the incidence of conditions like CHD, we are in the UK an ageing population and the biggest bulge will be, between now and the end of the century, in the over 80 age group, scheduled to increase by about 10 per cent. Most of these will be women living alone and perhaps on reduced means. The problem of the frail elderly is, in my view, the biggest social challenge of the next decades and requires individual consideration in the planning of one's later years. It will also require much more 'management' in terms of providing social, financial and medical support.

In summary, it is worth making the point that there is a virtue in managing your

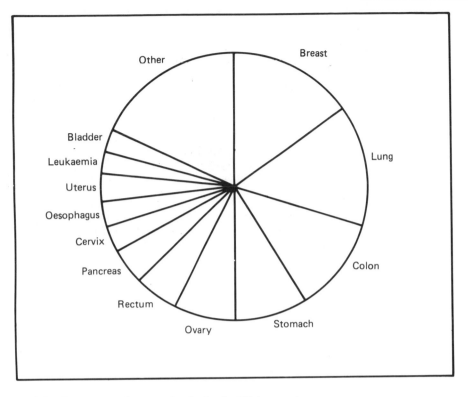

Figure 6.3   Frequency of cancer deaths in the UK (women)

Source: OPCS Monitor DH2

health sensibly but it is an advantage first to have good genes, second to be a woman and third to be in social classes I or II.

A much more detailed description of these critical underlying factors determining mortality, morbidity and their demographic implications, will be found in the author's *Are You Managing Your Health*, (Industrial Society, 1990).

Coronary risk factors

As many of the keys to living sensibly, particularly for men, relate to avoiding CHD, it is worth describing briefly the factors which predispose to this still too prevalent killing disease.

Genetic factors

Reference has already been made to the fact that CHD can run in families. As will be apparent from the risk factors to be described, CHD is a multi-factorial disease, i.e. it has no single cause but results from an amalgam of factors which perm differently in different people. Similarly there is no single gene responsible for, say, blood pressure, lipid metabolism or personality. But we do know that a serious condition called hypercholesterolaemia, in which blood fats are raised, is genetically determined. And there is reason to believe that some aspects of the way in which the body deals with fats, either well or badly, lies within the genes. Thus, it could be that in the years to come, genetic engineering will become a factor in coronary control. At the moment, however, this is highly speculative.

You will, I hope, remember that the genetic set-up, good or bad, is the main denominator of the coronary and other equations.

Blood fats – cholesterol

When I started being interested in the prevention of CHD in about 1960, it began to be apparent that men with high cholesterol levels in their blood were at greater coronary risk. This started the interest in low cholesterol diets by reduction of animal fats and established cholesterol as a risk factor.

But it did not explain why some thin men with low cholesterols got CHD and conversely why some fat men with high levels avoided it. We now know much more about the 'cholesterol package' and have refined ways of measuring its individual components. From this, it has been found that the two main factors are called High (HDL) and Low (LDL) Density Lipoproteins.

Very briefly HDL is metabolically good and the main way in which usable fats, for energy, are transported round the body. LDL on the other hand is more unfriendly and is the substance that gets deposited in the walls of blood vessels to narrow them and predispose to blockage. A coronary thrombosis is a blockage of the coronary arteries which supply the heart muscle, which if severe enough destroys the muscle itself and the heart's capacity to function as a co-ordinated pump.

What we now know is that it is the ratio, within the cholesterol package, between HDL and LDL which largely sets the coronary governor, high HDL levels being much less important than raised LDL which is largely in animal fats and dairy products.

Two things seem to govern the way in which an individual deals with his or her cholesterol. The first is, fairly obviously, the amount and nature of the fats eaten, and the other is the genetically determined governor that deals with these fats. The latter is more important than the former but a strict low cholesterol diet will reduce cholesterol levels and bring the ratio back into better and less harmful balance. It will also remove at least some of the LDL out of the vessel walls.

Diet

We are now, in developed countries, on the verge of a dietary revolution. There is a growing move away from a high protein, high animal fat diet, towards a more vegetarian – fruit, fibre, vegetable – one. Since the war the consumption of meat, dairy products and sugar has gone up significantly, and so has the incidence of CHD.

In America, Norway and Finland, careful long term studies have shown that by changing diet not only do cholesterol levels alter for the better but the coronary rate falls. Obesity is said to be the commonest 'disease' in developed countries, particularly America and Germany. That thin people live longer than fat people has been known for years by life insurance companies. This is largely but not entirely through the relationship between weight and blood pressure but there are other considerations as well.

Lack of exercise, as will be seen next, is also a risk factor and it is obviously more difficult for an overweight person to be physically active without putting undue and dangerous strain on his bones, joints and muscles.

Obesity again is genetically determined through body build but essentially if you eat more calories (energy) than you need for daily living, these will be banked within your body as fat. A calorie overdraft is in fact starvation. We do all mostly eat far more than we need and hence have a podgy credit account.

Sugar and fats account for most of this and their over-consumption has become a serious reflection of postwar life now being reversed by health re-education.

Eating is very much a culturally based habit pattern. We like what we are used to and have been brought up with. Being human, we resent change and are reluctant to experiment. This is very true of salt consumption. We eat salt in most prepared foods without knowing it is there but would miss it if the level was reduced. Some of us also add extra salt.

High blood pressure is again a complicated multi-factorial condition. It relates to arteriosclerosis which is part of the coronary picture. Hypertensive people are more coronary prone but also get strokes, heart failure and blood vessel disease. Salt is very much one of the factors relating at least to some forms of hypertension. There are thus good grounds for reducing direct and indirect salt consumption and at least demanding that food manufacturers state the salt content of their products.

Exercise

The body is a machine designed for constant use. Joints need to be put through their range of movement and muscle strength, including that of the heart itself, can only be maintained by constant load carrying. Your heart muscle is as flabby and as fat as the rest of you.

In addition to living longer, because thin people have a lower coronary rate, physically active people largely feel better, sleep better and are more mentally and physically lively. Reasonable fitness puts up HDL and lowers LDL in the blood. Taking enough exercise is again a family and personal discipline which has an obvious reward, hence the current interest in jogging and other outdoor activity.

Smoking

Inhaling tobacco smoke is an addiction which has a higher mortality and morbidity rate (death and disability) than all the other 'drugs' like alcohol, heroin, etc. Until very recently it was socially acceptable and of course the government obtains a large slice of revenue from tobacco tax. Additionally money spent on advertising and sponsorship oils many of the wheels of our social life.

Tobacco smoke is chemically complicated but nicotine, a substance with a direct effect on the autonomic nervous system and a depressant or tranquillizing effect on mood, is the addictive element.

The tars in the smoke are irritant and the lungs, being an efficient filter, absorb substances from it which are both locally irritant and chemically harmful. Efficient inhalers, that is those with relatively undamaged lungs, can raise the level of carbon monoxide in their blood significantly above that allowed under industrial legislation. This carbon monoxide damages the lining of blood vessels, which in turn facilitates the deposition of cholesterol and the narrowing of the vessels, reducing blood flow and increasing the chances of blockage by thrombosis.

Smoking is also harmful because it raises the level of LDL and smokers are three or four times more likely to suffer a coronary thrombosis. As has been said, lung cancer is uncommon in non-smokers. Chronic bronchitis and emphysema cause a great deal of respiratory disability and ultimate death.

The incidence of smoking has been declining significantly over the last ten years, so that in social classes I and II smokers are in a growing minority. The problem now is to reduce smoking in social classes IV and V and to stop young-sters getting hooked at an early age.

It is never too late to stop and some of the benefits are immediate. Physically active smokers appear to be better off than their less athletic brethren but still a lot worse off than abstainers. Pipes and cigars which are not inhaled appear to be relatively safe.

Companies are now taking action to restrict smoking at work, because of fears about the dangers to non-smokers from 'passive smoking'. More than 4 out of 5 large companies impose restrictions on smoking while total bans are becoming more common. Some companies too give preference in recruitment to non-smokers because of their lower absentee rate.

Alcohol

Alcohol is not a direct coronary risk factor. Indeed, modest drinkers, particularly of wine, have a lower CHD rate. This may be because alcohol raises HDL. Neverthe-less alcohol, which is socially acceptable and encouraged, i.e. a drink is offered at all social occasions, remains a dangerous addiction with social and directly medi-cal ill effects.

We do not really know why a few people become uncontrolled or truly depen-dent drinkers but the probability is that there are both biochemical and persona-lity related factors which predispose. Individuals have to be careful about how much they drink because unlike smoking there is a tendency, as tolerance deve-lops, to drink more, rather than to stay at the same level. Individuals and organiza-tions thus have, in my view, a responsibility to set modest personal and corporate standards and to demonstrate appropriate examples.

Alcohol is a useful social lubricant and enjoyed by many people. It is now vital that we try to control consumption to avoid penal taxation and legislation. This is, I suggest, a legitimate area for management intervention by both setting standards and providing counselling and discipline for their staff who drink too much and perform badly.

Alcohol has two quite different harmful effects. The first is to damage the liver, which is responsible for most of its metabolism. This damage is called cirrhosis and unless caught early will lead to death from liver failure. This effect can be measured by blood tests done as part of a health check. As a result it is possible to tell a patient that he is drinking more than his liver can deal with and that he ought to stop for three months and then proceed at a lower level.

The second effect is the behavioural decline of the alcohol dependent. This reduced performance disrupts families and will end either in Skid Row or with cirrhosis.

Experience has shown that what the Americans called 'job jeopardy' is the strongest weapon for dealing with an alcohol dependent employee, hence the value of a firm company policy. Everyone in the organization knows who the drinkers are and they must be seen to be discouraged.

Stress and relationships

Stress is discussed in detail in the next chapter but as it is a variously interpreted phrase, I must make my position about it clear. All living things, including man, require challenge from the environment to keep them alert. Indeed it is by meeting challenge in a variety of ways and at various levels that we get most of our satisfactions in life. Conversely failure or inability to cope causes conflict and frustration.

Stress is a term borrowed from engineering where it implies an ability to withstand strain. If the strength of the substance is exceeded by the load, it will distort and collapse. Thus, in my definition, stress is *not* challenge but is what happens to an individual when he or she cannot cope with the challenge. It is a biological defence reaction to get them off a hook, or solve a conflict.

This may sound simple but in fact it is a very complicated and subconscious or 'automatic' reaction, without necessarily obvious relation to the cause of the stress. The reaction can be physical, in terms of pain, a skin eruption or a peptic ulcer, or purely behavioural in emotional or performance terms. Thus, anxiety, insomnia, irritability etc., are just as much diseases as are more traditional physical disorders.

Another complication is that stress thresholds vary for different types of challenge and relate to personality and past experience. Calm, extroverted people react differently to tense, anxious, introverted ones. It is also essential to realise that stress can arise from too much challenge or conflict in any aspect of life. It can be work or home based or to a degree due to lack of alternative relaxational satisfactions balancing out the other pressures.

This concept of stress and its relationship to wellbeing is obviously the basis of the whole man or holistic approach to disease. Why someone is ill – or out of balance – is just as important as what is wrong with them. Symptoms may be treatable by drugs but it is better to deal with the cause. This involves understanding and insight or objective knowledge about oneself.

In my very general terms, even busy people who are succeeding are not necessarily stressed but managing to carry a heavy load of challenge. They may be tired but they are on top, particularly so if they have good relationships at home.

One of the skills of survival, then, is both to know your own aspirations and attributes and to pick, as far as possible, the right challenges for you. There are horses for courses and no one person has all the skills. Under-employment or being in a dead end is just as stressful as having too great a load.

Management must organize the enterprise so that unnecessary stress is minimized and energies directed in productive rather than frustrating directions. Jobs must have a discernible end point within the skills and experience of the individual.

Across the biological spectrum most of the challenge to living things comes from the physical environment: the need and competition for space, nutrition, warmth, water and so on. Species that live in social groups, like monkeys, elephants and many others, have evolved a series of harmless rituals to settle the problems of aggression and competition with minimal trauma to the participants. Very seldom does a species prey on its own members as we do.

In developed countries, however, a reasonable physical environment is largely available and the majority of challenge – and stress – comes from the psychosocial and interpersonal environment. Our successes and failures tend to relate to people rather than things. It is our ability to deal, in biological terms, with our own species at work, at home, in our social groups and then in the world as a whole, that provides the stress and the conflict. At personal, national and international levels, we do not seem to be very good at it.

A last point in this brief overview of the stress field, is that there is nothing new about stress or being stressed. Each generation tends to pride itself that its life is more complicated and difficult than it was for its parents, so that ergo, they/we are the most stressed. This is nonsense because, as I have said, challenge is essential and there have always been individuals and 'tribes' who cannot cope without it. All that alters is the nature of the stress and as we learn to cope in the here and now, society evolves to throw up new problems.

It worries me at the moment that because of lack of understanding about the difference between stress and challenge, being stressed has become a bit of a status symbol. Busy people tend to think that they cannot be flat out unless they are stressed but in fact if they are keeping on top they are largely winning and coping well. In very general terms stress is a manifestation of failure rather than success.

But essentially it is our ability to deal with interpersonal relationships and get ourselves into positions in which our aspirations and attributes largely match, that determines our stress.

It may, in these terms, be better to change a job, a marriage partner or a place of residence, than to be perpetually torn by conflict which cannot be resolved. At work, particularly, interpersonal relations tend to be hierarchical so that it is difficult for an individual to deal with incompatibility from above, unless the organization is sensitively structured so that these things can be discussed openly and objectively. For most of us, however, it may be better to be brave enough to do our own thing in a smaller pond than to be continuously buffeted by an uncongenial system. But remember too that work is only one source of stress. It comes from all aspects of life and impinges on our whole personality and not just a bit of us. Work, home and play do interrelate with the 'whole of us' to determine who we are and how we react.

MANAGING HEALTH

Two points, I hope, are now clear about the management of health. The first is that it is manageable and that the odds are both worth playing for and reasonably understood. The second is that in the medium and longer term there are considerable benefits, in terms of both survival and effectiveness, to be obtained from successful management.

To this I would add two further points. First, that in spite of the hazards I have listed, living prudently is in no way living miserably. Good or sensible habits are just as enjoyable as over-indulgence. Prudence and survival are very much a matter of getting into a sensible habit pattern and sticking to it. The second is that in terms of at least the larger working groups, the management of health is also very much the joint responsibility of the individual and the organization. Their interests should be mutually devoted to health and survival.

Thus, the individual should set himself the right priorities and have the requisite understanding of the pitfalls. As part of management, particularly at a senior level, he should insist on providing a 'healthy' environment; not so much in physical but in psychosocial or dynamic terms.

Companies should be organized so that the challenges of individual jobs are appropriate, communications are good, end products obvious and satisfying, with minimal frustrations. It is also sensible to create an atmosphere in which problems and frustrations can be brought into the open and discussed objectively. I think too that regular assessments of performance against defined targets are helpful, and so is the availability of counselling and career guidance, particularly on promotion. When an interpersonal problem or a failure becomes overt and may even lead to possible job loss, the individual may often complain that 'nobody ever told me about this weakness'.

It is assumed that because a person is deemed to be good enough to promote, he or she will be *ipso facto*, capable of doing a more demanding job without training or indoctrination. I often used to see rapidly promoted youngsters stressed by having to run to stand still. This is particularly true when a technically trained person, good at doing things himself, is promoted into a role where he has to deal with people, ideas and hierarchies.

Neither individuals nor organizations themselves realise clearly enough that there are inevitably and necessarily management styles into which individuals have to fit. Within this framework there are senior people with whom subordinates have to be reasonably compatible if they are to flourish. Thus, in choosing a job or appointing a person, there must be a large degree of congruence between the individual and the overall climate, which means that individuals should be prepared to change their jobs, even to ones of lesser status and income, rather than be driven to a coronary by perpetual frustration or boredom. Doing one's own thing, even in a small way, may be more fulfilling than being a small cog in a vast but safe bureaucracy.

In these terms, then, management can control the environment in which their staff can be healthier. I think that regular health checks are part of this because they provide both a database, an early warning and a counselling service. But at a more mundane but nevertheless useful level, should management actively discourage smoking at work? Many now do. Should they employ non-smokers who are known to have a better health record, in preference to smokers? Should they take more interest in what their canteens serve? Do they have sensible standards about alcohol consumption both in house and in relation to expense accounts? Along these lines the list is endless but the issues are important. The standards they set must feed back into the individual's lifestyle and the company 'climate'.

In more positive terms, should management encourage staff to take exercise and even provide facilities for this? A number of companies are beginning to provide their own fitness centres. (Fitness for Industry, 116 Pall Mall, London SW1, will advise on this.) Similarly, it is sensible to see that people take their holidays, do not overwork for prolonged periods and look out for signs of stress, like a fall-off in performance, irritability, increased drinking and work taken home but not done effectively.

It is wise to monitor sickness records because it is certain that an individual who has previously had a good record and suddenly 'goes bad', has a lifestyle related problem which needs sorting out. If one group has a worse record than another, something could have gone wrong with the motivation and supervision within the group. The probability is that there are personality clashes or frustrations that need attention. Although it may be superficially expensive, attention to the welfare of staff and help with personal problems will raise morale and increase productivity.

What then for the individual? He or she needs to realise the ground rules for their own health maintenance and be prepared to adopt the disciplines. These are relatively simple and to a degree have their own reward. Smoking, drinking and weight must be controlled within reasonable limits. Diet should be sensible and 'modern', in terms of less animal and dairy products, and more fresh food and fibre. Regular exercise of any sort is a must and will promote a sense of fitness.

But most important is the matter of relationships, both at work and at home. In my view, couples still get married too young and without thinking through why they want to get married and what is in it for both of them. These targets change with age and status and need occasional renegotiation. The conflicts of career development and home life are considerable and unless faced and agreed lead to a lot of unhappiness, particularly for the isolated wife. The needs, for instance, of job mobility and business travel can cause considerable conflict and merit open discussion.

The vital thing about dealing with relationships is to be honest and open enough to discuss the problems and differences, rather than to bury them as a smouldering grievance which may surface as total incompatibility years later. There must at all times be enough in it for both partners. Children as they grow up must be established as independent adults and not expected to be obedient and grateful dependants.

Relationships are difficult, complicated and require constant attention but for most people they provide life's greatest single satisfaction. They need more work and attention than they mostly get, both at home and in the work place.

I would suggest that periodically you do three things: first, ask yourself what you are like to work for, how you are perceived by your peers and whether you are giving them a square deal in terms of delegation, supervision and encouragement. Second, ask yourself what job satisfaction you think that your spouse gets out of being married to you. A useful extension of this would also be to try and assess yourself as an effective parent.

The third and more complicated point is to be brave enough, particularly in middle age, to review your self-image. Look, as it were, at yourself in the mirror and try to see yourself as others see you. Are you brisk, alert and reasonably well dressed? What do the whiskers all over your face convey to others? More important, are you reasonably happy and fulfilled or are you frustrated and miserable? If the latter, what are the real options and what are you going to do about them?

Much of stress and frustration stems from the feeling of being caught helplessly in some interpersonal trap. It is useful to try to analyse the situation by listing the things that bug you and the various options. It may be that you are caught and cannot move, in which case live with it, find other outlets and stop worrying.

If you are a tense, nervous and rather stressed person, it is also worth remembering that relaxation can be learnt and that there are techniques and teachers about. In a similar way, there are coping skills that can be acquired for dealing with stress from work or home and by learning these you can reduce the heat in the kitchen. But if at a moment in time this does get too hot, be brave enough to hop out of the frying pan before you get burnt. Life is for living rather than mere endurance. A smaller house on a lower income, doing simple things, can be far more satisfying then endlessly commuting to a boring or uncongenial job.

What all this adds up to is that there are two keys to 'health'. The first is to know the main hazards to survival and how to avoid them. The second and more important is to understand that health is a reflection of general wellbeing which can be cultivated by understanding, insight and discipline. If you achieve this you should join the 80-year-old bulge, and this will present other problems! But it is important to maintain your wellbeing as long as you live. The more successful you are at this, the longer you *will* live.

KEY POINTS

Your life is in your hands

1 *Management* is about making informed decisions, based on hard data and defined objectives.
2 *Exercising personal responsibility*: the same principles should be applied to decisions about personal and family health.
3 *Health* is synonymous with wellbeing, which is a function of the relationship between the individual (personality, skills and experience) and the environment (psychosocial and physical).
4 *Hard data on survival* comprise two main elements:

- understanding the hazards to be avoided in terms of the incidence of the main killer diseases for men and women of specified ages and social-economic class;
- knowing the individual risk factors (diet, exercise, cholesterol, stress etc.) which predispose against this background. After a detailed health check or 'medical servicing', a personal risk rating can be calculated. You need to know the facts about yourself.

Armed with these hard data and with as much objectivity as can be mustered about your strengths, weaknesses, aspirations and attributes, wellbeing and health should be largely and beneficially controllable.

Caring and successful managers should contribute to personal, family and company health in this way.

FURTHER READING

Relaxation for Living – for advice on relaxation and coping, from 29 Burwood Park Road, Walton-on-Thames, Surrey KT12 5LH

Wright, Dr H. B. *Ease and Dis-Ease*, Longman Professional, 1986

Wright, Dr H. B. *Managing Your Health*, Industrial Society and Allied Dunbar, 1991

Wright, Dr H. B. et al., *Allied Dunbar Retirement Planning Guide*, Longman Professional, 1985

7 Stress at work

Andrew M. Stewart

The subject of stress, and the way it affects people at work, has been receiving a great deal of attention recently. There have been radio and television programmes about it, and there is a wide range of published work available. This work tends to be at one of two extremes. It is either academic and rather heavily research based, or it is popular and inspirational but based only loosely on fact. This chapter aims for the middle ground, and poses the following questions:

- What is stress?
- What does it cost?
- What causes it?
- What are the signs?
- What can the individual do about it?
- What can organizations do about it?

After reading this chapter you should have some answers to those questions.

This chapter concentrates on stress at work, but people are not divided up into watertight compartments. What happens to you at work will affect you at home, and vice versa. Because the home or leisure environment can affect your performance at work, this chapter will also look briefly at a few of the main domestic considerations. This is not a medical chapter, so clinical problems are mostly avoided. People who find themselves in difficulty at work are usually normal, healthy, sane individuals who find themselves for the time being in an environment which is, for them, abnormal, unhealthy or insane.

People sometimes use stress as an excuse for not performing as well as they should, or for failing to do what they said they would. It is true that many people do experience levels of stress which are too high, but others might be helped by increasing their level of stress. The aim should be to help people find the best level of stress for them in their particular circumstances, and to help them to maintain it and adjust it to change. This will sometimes mean increasing it rather than necessarily reducing it. Stress management is about *managing* stress, not about making people so relaxed that they forget to *do* anything.

WHAT IS STRESS?

You are likely to experience stress when you face a challenge or when you perceive a threat, and you see that there may be an imbalance between the demands being made on you and your resources. Stress arises, therefore, in a specific kind of interaction between you and your environment:

- You perceive a situation of challenge, threat, or harm.
- You consider the outcome important to your welfare.
- You are uncertain whether you will be able to meet the challenge successfully, or avoid the threat.

People vary enormously in the amount, intensity, type, and duration of stress that they can cope with.

It is important to realise that stress is not something strange and separate, unrelated to normal things that happen to normal people, but that it sits firmly on a continuum. This continuum runs from having too little to do, through normal healthy levels of activity, to rushing around trying to do too much too fast. Either too much or too little to do will trigger changes in your physiology. People are quite good at detecting some of these changes, but it is often more difficult to do anything about them.

The motivation connection

To understand stress you need to understand a little about motivation. Motivation is not a single-shot event, but a cyclical process. One of the more stressful aspects of managers' lives is that the task of motivating their subordinates is truly never-ending.

The cycle begins with a motive, drive, or need. You want to do something (motive). You do something as a result. If what you do takes you closer to your desired goal, then you will experience relief. If what you do is unsuccessful, then you will feel no relief, and there may be an increase in the drive or need. In either event, the cycle does not end, since you are now merely in a new motivational state, and ready to do the next thing on the way to attaining the next goal. Put briefly, people are never satisfied for long. This is an ample source of stress for managers, since it implies that they can never win.

It may be possible for managers to reduce the stress they put on themselves when thinking about how to motivate their staff. Perhaps it is not possible to motivate other people at all, at least in the sense of doing something to them directly which will make them 'motivated'. It may be possible, however, to create the conditions under which people are more likely to motivate themselves. This is both an easier task for the manager, and more likely to bear fruit.

There is an old-fashioned view about motivation which can be expressed as: the more you push people, the more they will do for you. This theory of motivation is wrong – or at least inadequate.

The truth is more complicated. Up to a point it is true that people will do more for you if you push them harder. After that point their performance will level off. If you try to start them on the upward path again after that, you are likely to achieve the opposite of what you want. You may actually impair their performance.

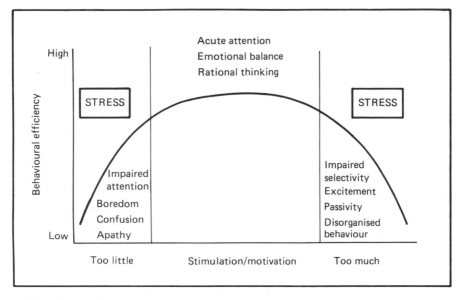

Figure 7.1   Motivation, performance and stress

This curious state of affairs was first demonstrated by two psychologists called Yerkes and Dodson. In 1908 they found that motivation works in this way over a wide range of circumstances. They also found that it did not matter much whether the motivation was self-generated or created by someone else. Two factors will modify the picture, however. First, the simpler the task, the higher the level of motivation it can tolerate. Second, the shorter the task, the higher the level of motivation it can tolerate. Thus, if you are digging the garden and someone shouts that lunch is nearly ready, you can probably get that last row dug in double-quick time. It is a simple job and you know it will be over in three or four minutes. On the other hand, if you are sitting at your desk trying to work out next year's budget you are unlikely to respond well either to being shouted at or being hurried up. That is a complicated job and needs unhurried consideration to make it more likely that you will get it right.

The relationship between motivation, performance and stress is shown in Figure 7.1, where it becomes clear that either too much or too little motivation can lead to stress related behaviour. The most important point to note, however, is that for most people, stress is not something peculiar which means that they are losing control or actually ill. Stress is just what happens to motivation when there is a bad match between the person, what they are being asked to do, and the way they are being asked to do it. Stress is, if you like, motivation gone bad.

Fear and anxiety

Fear is a special kind of stress. Fear experienced during an event or, more usually, fear experienced before the event, will cause the same changes in your physiology as stress. Not many of us meet real fear very often, but most of us experience anxiety. Anxiety might be described as the fear of something which has not happened yet or which may never happen. You may experience fear half-way up a rock face, but your anxiety beforehand may prevent you from even starting the climb. Many outdoor development programmes have special techniques for helping people meet and cope with this sort of situation. The idea is that you are then better equipped to deal with less obvious sources of fear or anxiety at work.

Free-floating anxiety occurs when you have acquired the habit of being anxious, whether or not there is actually anything to be anxious about. If you cannot think of anything to worry about, you will worry about that! This kind of anxiety is quite difficult to deal with because there is no obvious or concrete source, so it can be hard to find anything to do to fix the problem. Because free-floating anxiety is often about things that may never happen, sufferers sometimes get rough treatment – 'Pull yourself together. It's all in your imagination.' If you could pull yourself together, you would. The fact that it is irrational does not make it any less real for the sufferer.

Type A behaviour

In 1960, two American cardiologists, Friedman and Rosenman, began a study of over 3000 people – the Western Collaborative Group Study (WCGS). They found that those who showed one particular pattern of behaviour were more than twice as likely to experience coronary heart disease than others. They called the high-risk pattern Type A, and the low risk Type B. The chief characteristics of Type A behaviour were said to be:

- insecurity about status;
- hyperaggressiveness;
- free-floating hostility;
- sense of time urgency (hurry sickness);
- drive to self-destruction.

Type As have a clearly identifiable response to stress. They are already highly vulnerable before the event because of their high expectations of themselves and others, combined with their physical hyper-reactivity. They live on the edge. The trigger for the stress episode can be anything and everything, since Type As treat even minor obstacles as major provocations. Their reaction to the event itself is usually out of proportion, since Type As have no brakes to dampen or slow down their response. All wars are nuclear wars! Arousal is too strong, takes too long, and may even interfere with efficient performance. Finally, people without the Type A behaviour pattern will take time after a stressful event to re-group, to review what happened, to replenish their energy, and to prepare for the next event. Type As do not take the time for any of that. Their idea of recuperation is to look immediately for the next battle until they are finally felled by exhaustion or ill health.

This presentation of Type As led to the conclusion that Type A behaviour was 'bad', and that stress management programmes should aim at encouraging the opposite – Type B. This was probably a mistake. Friedman and Rosenman did not suggest it in the first place. Second, the analysis is too simple.

It is possible to be a healthy and effective Type A. The Type A characteristics listed earlier are those of the ineffective, unhealthy, vulnerable Type A. In the original study, over 11% of Type As experienced some form of coronary heart disease, as against less than 6% of the more laid-back Type Bs. But that also means that over 88% of Type As in the study did *not* experience problems. So it is entirely possible for a Type A to get it right. This is just as well, since organizations need effective Type As to make things happen fast and efficiently.

The ineffective Type As are too quick on the trigger, indiscriminate in the strength of their mobilization, and too slow to recover. As a result, they get the job done, but with a wastefully and unnecessarily high use of energy. The effective Type As are alert but not over-reactive, mobilize quickly to the level of response which they judge to meet the nature of the problem, and review the event afterwards, so that they can learn from any mistakes and store any successful solutions for future use. The job is done swiftly and with economy, with an eye to improving the response to anything similar.

Finally, the initial definition of the unhealthy Type A may have been too broad. The significant components appear to be hostility and cynicism, leading to what has been called 'joyless striving'. This kind of behaviour is both ineffective and a good predictor of coronary heart disease. Impatience and irritability are bad signs. There appears to be nothing wrong with vigorous achievement striving – indeed, it should be encouraged.

The physiology of stress

To understand and cope with stress, it is useful to know what is going on in your body when you experience fear, stress or anxiety. It all starts when you perceive some kind of threat. This could be a bump in the night, someone stepping out suddenly in front of your car, or a sharp comment from your boss. Whatever the source, as soon as the message reaches your brain and is perceived as actually or potentially threatening, a number of changes take place (shown in diagrammatic form in Figure 7.2).

Information about external stressors will enter your system through one or more of your senses, and will be received in your cortex (grey cells, which make up the outer layers of your brain). Internal stressors, generated by your own memories, thoughts, and fantasies, are already there. In either event, signals now pass to your hypothalamus, a pea-sized organ in the middle of your brain, which triggers action via two separate routes.

The first route goes to the pituitary gland (about one inch in from the bridge of your nose) to stimulate the production of a hormone called the adreno-cortico-tropic hormone (ACTH), which is released into your blood stream to bring your adrenal cortex into play. Your adrenal glands sit like small hats in the small of your back, one over each kidney. The adrenal cortex (outer part) produces cortisol, which influences your immune system, counteracts inflammation, and affects the metabolism of carbohydrates, lipids, and proteins in all body tissues to produce energy.

The second route runs from the hypothalmus to your sympathetic nervous system, which is responsible for most of your normal automatic physical responses. The sympathetic nervous system in turn stimulates the adrenal medulla (middle part), which produces adrenalin and noradrenalin (also known as epinephrine and norepinephrine). Adrenalin increases your heart rate and re-directs

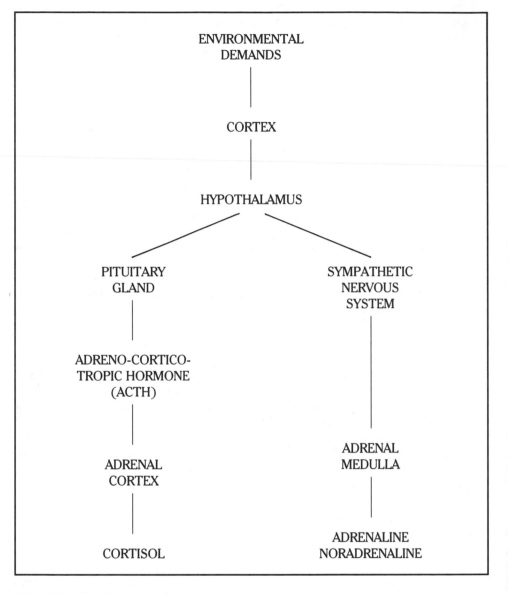

Figure 7.2   The physiology of the stress response

your blood from inner organs to muscles. Noradrenalin causes blood pressure to rise by contracting your blood vessels. So far you will not have been aware of any changes, but from now on they become apparent.

The main changes are listed below, together with the reasons for them. None of these changes is without one major purpose: to help you survive.

- The pupils of your eyes will get larger. More light will enter your eyes so that you can see any potential source of danger earlier and better.
- Your hearing may become more acute, again so that you can detect danger

further away and give yourself more time to think of something to do about it.

- You will breathe faster. This increases the amount of oxygen in the blood, which is your fuel for action.
- Your heart will pump faster and harder, so that the flow of fuel is speeded up, and also so that any waste products caused by the burning of the fuel are quickly carried away.
- You may go pale. This is because blood has been taken away from the outside of your body, so you will bleed less if wounded. Another agent ensures that your blood will clot quicker, reducing blood loss if you are cut.
- You may feel sick or have upset bowels. This is because blood has been removed from your digestive system as well, and, in extremes, you will empty yourself either by vomiting or diarrhoea. This is to get rid of surplus weight if you have to run fast.
- The fuel-rich blood is sent instead to the muscles you may need to use in a hurry if the threat is real.
- You may sweat more. This is because physical effort generates heat. You only work efficiently over a quite small internal temperature range, so your cooling system is switched on. You lose heat by evaporating fluids from the surface of your skin – sweating.
- You may shake or tremble. This is partly because your muscles have tensed up generally. It may also be to warm you up if the cooling system has come on but you have *not* done anything physical to actually generate any heat.

These changes are all normal, healthy and aimed at ensuring your survival in an emergency. They were extremely useful when we lived in caves. They can be a real nuisance in the office or at home.

What has happened is that your body has been prepared for *fight or flight*. You may be in no position to do either. Many of the problems of coping with stress have to do with finding some way of discharging all this potential energy in a harmless or constructive way. If the energy is not discharged it will eventually cause damage. You will find that you have been pushed over the top of the curve in Figure 7.1, and your performance will suffer. At home or at work the problems may become worse. An anxiety spiral has been started.

THE COSTS OF STRESS

Managers usually prefer to spend money in ways which show some measurable return. There is no point, commercially speaking, spending money managing stress unless it is costing more money to ignore it.

In the days when you had to have a certificate for any spell of absence from work through sickness of more than three days, it was easier to estimate the commercial damage caused by stress related disease. Even then, the bulk of absences were not covered because they were for only half a day or a day, and therefore did not appear in the official figures. Even working on those reduced figures, the number of working days lost through psychosis, psycho-neurosis, nervousness, debility and headaches was well over double the days lost through industrial accidents. Other forms of sickness thought to have a psychological component, such as indigestion, skin complaints, muscular aches and pains, back problems, ulcers and heart disease, are *not* included in those figures. A fairly modest estimate of the working days lost through stress related problems each year is around 120 million. That is expensive.

Worrying though that figure undoubtedly is, it still does not address the whole of the problem. There is no estimate of the cost of mistakes made by people who remain at work while under stress. The figure relates largely to losses at shop floor level, where you can measure losses in production, orders not sent on time, poor quality products and paperwork errors fairly easily. But how do you assess the costs of lost management days? It is even more difficult to assess the costs of wrong decisions, wasted time, over-long lunch hours, together with too much alcohol and tobacco, and poor or inaccurate monitoring of performance. Evidence of the cost of poor decision making is all around us.

Industrial unrest may well have some of its roots in stress. The boredom (under-motivation) of routine production line work probably contributes to the readiness of some production workers to strike, even if only to generate some variety! The girl working on the supermarket till who would much rather talk to her friend than serve you is quite likely to be thoroughly bored. Even worse, the only feedback she may get on her performance is the occasional and unpredictable ticking-off from her supervisor when she happens to be spotted doing something wrong. How often is she rewarded specifically for good customer work? Can she predict which actions will get her into trouble and those which will lead to some form of reward? If not, why should she bother?

At management and shop floor levels, stress in its various forms is squandering resources we can ill afford. The cost of cure is a very small fraction of the total bill. Prevention would be even better. The whole cost might even be recovered simply from reduced labour turnover costs.

THE CAUSES OF STRESS

Different people react in different ways to the same situation. What you find merely stimulating might be uncomfortably heavy pressure to someone else. With that reservation in mind, some of the common causes of stress at work are now reviewed.

Physical causes

Noise is a source of stress for many people, and its occurrence is the most usual source. This has now been recognized in legislation about maximum noise levels. Many workers have now been persuaded to wear ear protection who might have scorned to do so before: tractor drivers, road drill operators, boiler makers and chain saw users, for example. Attention is also being turned to domestic noise generators, such as vacuum cleaners, washing machines, food processors and the nuisance of other people's radios. The damage that is being inflicted by discos is also well understood.

It is less well known that things can also be too quiet! British Rail met this problem when building new modern coaches. The level of soundproofing was originally so high that the quiet interior made it too easy to hear other people's conversations. It was necessary to reintroduce some noise to mask the distraction from other passengers, and to allow relatively undisturbed reading, conversation or thinking. The level of quiet in a jumbo jet is very near to this disturbance level.

Tiredness causes stress as your ability to perform decreases. Worse, at the early stages of tiredness, you may not know that your performance is declining, and therefore you may assume that all is well and go on to make expensive errors or omissions. On top of that, because you are tired, you will be less willing to hear warnings about your performance from anyone else. The ability to assess your own performance accurately is one of the earliest things to go when you are tired, coupled with your emotional resilience.

Shift work patterns sometimes allow or encourage people to do other jobs during their off-periods. Split-shift patterns for bus crews often lead to this problem. As a result neither the official nor the side job is done well. In the case of drivers of any kind this has immediate and obvious dangers. Few managers in the UK work shifts, but some of them put in very long hours. Not all those hours are productive because of fatigue. Midnight oil burners can make bad mistakes. Frequent changes of shift pattern are also disruptive. It is better to have a long stint on nights, then a good break, followed by a long period on days, rather than changing every two weeks or so.

Jet lag is a special sort of tiredness, made worse by changing time zones and upset body rhythms. It is most unwise to make important decisions immediately after a long flight, especially if you have travelled from west to east. Few organizations seriously advise their people to rest for at least 24 hours before doing anything that matters, however.

Temperature and humidity also need to be controlled. Legislation lays down working limits, but greater extremes of temperature can be tolerated at lower levels of humidity. There are suggestions that increasing the level of negative ions in the air is beneficial, but this is quite hard to do on a large scale and the results are not yet certain.

Amount of work

Too much to do is a familiar idea, although it is often claimed before it is a fact. There are three different types of overload:

- the skill level demanded may be too high for the person;
- the speed may be too high for them;
- the volume may be too much;

or some combination of these.

Too little to do is also possible, but less often talked about. Again, there are three kinds of underload:

- the skill level may be too low (asking a graduate to do a school-leaver type of job);

- the speed may be too slow (when a meeting takes all day to decide some-thing you could have done on your own in ten seconds);
- the volume can be too small (when a bright secretary is asked to do two letters and some filing in a whole day);

or some combination of these.

A sure sign of underloading at work is when the level of office politics starts to rise. People who have too little to do may fill the time with politics. The long term unemployed have met the underload problem. They often find it difficult to get out of bed and go out at all. The level of stimulus in their environment has dropped to the point where they actually need help to get going again. This is not deliberate idling at all, but a genuine psychological problem induced by boredom, loneliness and a sense of defeat.

Nature of work

New or unfamiliar situations, such as your first day in a new job or organization, will be stressful because they are full of uncertainty.

Personal threat may be felt if your personal space is invaded by crowded con-ditions or by your boss standing too close when talking to you. If you feel that you are the victim of unreasonable control or arbitrary decisions about personal matters, such as going to the lavatory, your stress level will rise. Too little personal threat can also create problems. If nothing much happens when you fail to meet standards, then your standards of performance are likely to fall.

Pacing. The inability to pace your own work is highly stressful, as many production line workers will tell you. Likewise, if you happen to work in an office where your colleagues, your manager or your customers make frequent and unpredictable claims on your time, your performance will suffer.

Ambiguity. People vary a great deal in the amount of ambiguity or lack of clarity which they prefer. Some salesmen like very little uncertainty and prefer to work in the short term. They like to know at the end of each day how much they have sold and how much they have earned. On the other hand, a salesman dealing with large computing systems may have a long wait and a lot of work before he knows whether he has the order, and the nature of the installation may change during the course of implementation. It is much more difficult to establish a direct link between sale and reward; nor would that kind of salesman seek it. If you are a manager, the relationship between performance and reward can seem very indir-ect and uncertain indeed.

Feedback needs to be reliable and undistorted, frequent, and based on clear standards. Unclear standards and unreliable, distorted or non-existent feedback are the surest way to stress employees. They often lead to the use of some form of punishment as the only feedback offered, with no obvious connection to perfor-mance.

Fear of freedom

Most of us kick against rules and regulations. 'If only "they" would get off my back
...' is the frequent cry. When the restrictions are removed, the reaction often
surprises. While it is a true liberation for some, for many it leads to great
uncertainty, stress and even complete inability to act. We seem to need rules to
react against. They provide a map which lets us know where we are and how to get
somewhere else. If there are no rules and no map, many people simply feel lost and
unable to move. Many managers, who have been excellent performers on their way
up the organization, disappoint when they finally reach the top seat because they
suddenly find that there is no one to tell them what to do and no one to react
against. They are fine as subordinates, and their impatience to succeed may have
driven them on well, but now they have 'made it' they are no longer sure what their
target should be. Their reaction can be to sit very still and to do the bare minimum
necessary to keep out of trouble.

Domestic troubles

Stressors are also found at home. Domestic troubles, ranging from bereavement
to marital discord, often coupled with financial problems, can severely affect
performance in all spheres of your life.

Communication is a common problem amongst married couples. Imagine you
have come home after a bad or boring day. The last thing you want to do is talk
about it. You have just lived it. You do not want to go over it all again. Your partner,
on the other hand, has just spent the day in the company of your three-year-old
offspring of apparently manic and suicidal bent, is desperate for someone adult to
talk to, and wants to know what you are doing so that some sharing of your life is
possible. You are both right. Here lie real problems which can lead to marital
breakdown. Worse still is the case where both partners work and may wish to
discharge some of their day's problems. A perfectly reasonable response might
be. 'Don't tell me. You want to try my job!'

Relocation is an increasingly frequent source of difficulty for families. When one
partner is promoted, or finds a new and better job which involves moving house,
who has priority? The male? The higher earner? The one who stayed put last time?
The children's education? Will 'week ending' offer any solution, or will that simply
lead gently to total and permanent separation? Pressure on the family will be
heavy, and the solution may well affect the career prospects of one or both
partners, quite aside from any personal damage that may occur.

THE SIGNS OF STRESS

The signs become easier to detect if you recall the fight or flight reaction mentioned earlier in the chapter. Under short term stress the fight or flight nature of
the reactions is quite clear. Under long term stress it is not always so obvious.

Short term stress

The fight reaction when escape is possible is usually to have a short, sharp row on the spot with whomever is seen as causing the problem. The form of the row can vary from verbal abuse to a punch on the nose.

The fight reaction when escape is not possible, which is what most of us experience, is either to take it out on others or to punish yourself. If you take it out on others, then your staff may suffer because you have had a difficult meeting elsewhere. If you take it out on yourself then you may spend the rest of the day sunk in gloom.

The flight reaction when escape is possible is to go sick, take long lunch breaks, resign, or retire early. The main point is to remove yourself from the situation.

The flight reaction when escape is not possible may involve slowing down, withdrawing commitment to the business, delaying, acting with extreme caution, withdrawing from involvement with the business, or simply sleeping a lot more than before.

Long term stress

Psychosomatic illness may occur where there is no obvious physical cause for a physical ailment. It is arguable that ulcers, some heart attacks, strokes, indigestion, headaches, migraines, skin irritation, acne, over- and under-sleeping are all associated to some degree with stress.

Predisposition to illness can be caused by stress. You become vulnerable to illnesses that otherwise you would have brushed off, and your recovery is slower. The self-employed tend not to get colds!

Absenteeism may occur, ranging from lateness, through continuing small bouts of illness, to complete withdrawal by striking or leaving.

Indecision may increase to the point where it is difficult to get anything done at all without setting up a committee.

Capriciousness in decision making may appear. There is little hesitation, but there is equally little reason underlying the decisions. You may also see surprisingly light-hearted behaviour from the normally serious, or sexual promiscuity from the previously well behaved. You will find it increasingly hard to predict their behaviour.

Excessive consumption of food, drink and tobacco are fairly sure signs. No one should smoke anyway. Alcohol taken in more than moderation is damaging, and may be lethal if combined with driving. Too much food leads to obesity and all its associated health problems. It is also possible to consume material possessions to excess (cars, furs, jewels, and so forth). Excessive consumption of the opposite sex is often a sign of serious, unresolved stress.

Theft may increase under stress. When a factory is about to be closed, security should be tightened because anything not actually bolted to the floor may be considered fair game. On a smaller and more day-to-day scale, stationery, personal phone calls on company time, over-long lunch breaks, and a decision not to return to the office after an appointment that ended at three o'clock, are all forms of theft. Theft of goods is readily detectable. Theft of time, which may be more costly, is harder to see and control.

Workaholism. It is sometimes necessary to put in unusual hours to get a job done. If it becomes a habit, your job needs reorganizing or you are running away from something.

Displacement activity. You find yourself doing all kinds of things except the really important one that is actually causing the problem.

Identification with the aggressor. Your boss is difficult with you. You cope by being unpleasant with your staff. They pass it on down the line. Soon everyone is having a terrible time.

Over-reaction to normal events. The phone rings and you leap out of your chair to answer it, rather than taking things in a more measured fashion. Your boss calls to say you are to meet at five o'clock. You assume that you are being fired, or promoted, instead of assuming that this is the only available time for a routine discussion of something.

Change is the key to detecting stress. Whatever your normal pattern of behaviour, any sudden change should be looked at briefly, in case it indicates some unsuitable level of stress. If someone you work with is always miserable, that may not be a sign of stress. That is just how they are. But if they suddenly become amazingly cheerful, something has obviously changed for them. It may well be perfectly pleasant and understandable. On the other hand, they may have decided to jump!

WHAT CAN THE INDIVIDUAL DO ABOUT STRESS?

There seem to be four main groups of techniques that can make long-lasting beneficial changes to your ability to manage stress.

Exercise. Walk until you sweat slightly. Try swimming. Find something you can enjoy doing that makes your heart and lungs work a little harder than usual. Try to do it three times a week. *Warning:* if you have spent twenty-five years getting out of condition, do not try to fix it all in half an hour on the squash court. You could damage yourself seriously. Build gradually into physical exercise; do not slam into it.

Biofeedback. Biofeedback teaches you how to control consciously some of the physical stress reactions that are normally automatic. By linking yourself to heart rate or skin resistance monitors, you can quickly see variations in the readings. Heart rate will rise and skin resistance will fall as you become more stressed. You can learn what you have to do to lower your heart rate or to increase your skin resistance, getting feedback on your success from the monitors. After a number of training sessions you will no longer need the monitors, but will be able to control a number of stress symptoms directly and consciously.

Cognitive techniques. Much of what we call stress we do to ourselves. You can be helped to recognize when a particular stress reaction started – usually an event when you were quite young. You can then review your actions at that time, and acknowledge that there was probably not much else you could have done about it at the time. You can then be guided to question whether the coping technique which was appropriate or necessary at, say, six years old is still appropriate or necessary now that you are, say, thirty-six. Probably not. What else would you like to do if you were in that situation again, but as you are *now*? Gradually you are enabled to recall past events, recognize and evaluate realistically your reactions to them then, assess their suitability to present events, and think through new and more appropriate actions to replace the old reactions. This process has a strong appeal to the highly rational individual, but can be effective with a wide range of people.

Relaxation techniques. Breathing exercises and some forms of meditation have been shown to produce enduring physiological and psychological benefits for individuals. However, this is one set of techniques which needs careful introduction to Type As. If the purpose is clear, and the expectation is set that the Type A will emerge from the process more vigorous and alert, and better equipped to tackle whatever problems come their way, then they will accept relaxation techniques readily and obtain great benefit from them. If Type As gain the impression that these techniques are designed to slow them down and make them somehow dreamy and detached, then they will resist and may respond with increased stress levels.

In addition to the above four main groups of activities, you might want to see if any of the following techniques interests you enough to try them. They have all worked for someone.

Physiological and physical action

Control eating. Surplus is surplus. You do not need to consume it. You do not need to carry it around. It is a waste of time and energy.

Control alcohol intake. There is some medical evidence to suggest that a little wine may be positively beneficial, but treat alcohol with care. If you drink a bottle of brandy in one go it will probably kill you. Alcohol is high in calories and will allow your other food intake to go into store as fat.

Abolish smoking. Smoking kills about 100 000 people a year in the UK.

Control posture. Sit up so that your lungs can breathe properly and your digestive system has room to function. Walk as if your pelvis were a bowl full of water which you must not spill. Keep the spine stretched and head erect. Make sure you get up and move about during the day.

Control breathing. Sit somewhere comfortable. Take a normal breath. Hold it for a slow count of three. Let it out with a slight huff. You may find it helpful to have your eyes shut while you are doing this. Do this twice a day for three weeks. See how you feel.

By controlling your breathing in this way you are breaking into the alarm reaction that you read about earlier. When your system picks up that your breathing rate has dropped, it will assume that the threat has gone or at least lessened, and will automatically run down the rest of the alarm system. Do not try to interfere with this process. You have a perfectly effective automatic system for doing all this, which you can trigger with the pause breath. Over a period of three weeks you are likely to find that you have become generally calmer and more alert, as well as being better able to cope with stress when it occurs.

Aim for contrast. Whatever you do during the day, try to find something different to do in the evening or at weekends. Try to find ways of varying what you do during the day. Vary the pace. Vary the intensity. Vary the importance. Do some things alone and some with other people. We thrive on variety, provided we feel that it is of our choosing and under our control to some degree.

Action against stress at work

Recognize that you can be a victim of stress. You are not invulnerable. If a problem does occur for you, you can waste a lot of time denying that it exists when you should be getting on and fixing it.

Analyse the probable causes. Keep this simple. They are not usually hard to find. They may be harder to admit.

Can you leave the situation? This is not a cop-out, but simply a quick check to establish whether you really do have to put up with the interview, training course, car journey, meeting, conversation or social gathering in which you find yourself. What is the price of leaving? What is the price of staying? Do your arithmetic. Then act.

Decide when to cut your losses. Make a date with yourself. By then, the situation will have changed, you will have resolved the situation, or you will take more emphatic action (leave, go over your boss's head, fire your subordinate, dump the customer etc). Once you have made this kind of deal with yourself, stick to it. If you break your word to yourself, you will never quite trust yourself again to do what you set out to do. This can be very destructive, so think over your bargain carefully before you commit yourself.

Control the pace. Good tennis players do not spend all their time up at the net. Sometimes they need to get to the back of the court so they can see what is going on in time to plan what to do next. Someone may be firing questions at you very fast and hard. You do not have to let them control the speed of your response. Play it your way. They have no control over your choice in this matter. If things seem to be slipping away from you, make sure that, whatever your answer, your final sentence is a question. This puts you in control of the conversation. You can even induce stress in others by delaying your replies just a fraction longer than they are comfortable with.

Discharge. Make sure you have something explosive to do to wash out any unresolved anger or frustration at the end of the day. If you play a high activity sport, that will help. If not, try digging a hole in the garden, thumping something inanimate, or just shouting loudly, once. Be careful who is around when you are doing any of these! Again, you are fooling your physiology into believing that the violent physical activity for which it has been preparing itself (fight or flight, again) has actually happened, and it can now relax.

Set your own objectives and life goals. Decide what you want to do, then go for it. This goes broader than merely work, and extends beyond retirement.

Medical aid. If you are in trouble, ask for help. This is not weak, but sensible self-management. Drugs will not solve your problem, but they can sometimes help you temporarily to a frame of mind in which you *can* solve your problem. Tell your doctor the moment you are not happy with what you feel the treatment is doing to you. There may be another way of dealing with the problem.

Review before relaxing after you have coped with the problem. Celebrate when you know *why* what you did worked. That way you know what to do if the problem ever occurs again.

Action against stress at home

Recognize that it can happen to you and yours. No household is immune.

Analyse the probable causes.

Discuss the problems openly and early, before they become too difficult to talk about.

Recognition mechanisms exist for most people. Offer the signs that you are getting upset to your partner. Accept their signs in return. This way you can both spot when trouble is looming before it gets too developed.

Share some planned time and activities together. Do not spend all your home time in retreat.

Communicate with your partner and family. They need information from you and you need information from them so that difficulties can be dealt with early and opportunities for pleasure and reward can be developed.

Financial information needs to be shared. Many wives have been blamed by their husbands for spending the family into debt, when their husbands had never let them know what was happening and how much money was on hand. There are large cultural differences within the UK on this point, so check your family's expectations before acting on financial matters.

Consult on domestic arrangements. It is not a good idea to bring three colleagues home from work unannounced on a Friday night for a meal. Similarly, it is not helpful to announce as your partner comes in the door that Uncle Joe and Auntie Ethel have moved into the spare bedroom and are here for a week, especially if you have known for some time that they were coming.

Territory. Everyone needs somewhere that is their own. It need not be large. A desk; a dressing table; a small patch in the vegetable plot will often be enough. But that territory should be unique to the individual 'owning' it, and other people should only enter by invitation.

Solitude. Even in the most affectionate families, people sometimes need to be alone. This should be respected. It is not rejection. It may even be a statement of confidence that the relationships are so good that it never occurs to the person concerned that it would be seen as rejection. It can be difficult to find a moment of quiet in a busy family, but it is important to have the freedom to try.

COPING AT THE TOP

Figure 7.3 represents a very simple picture of the essential differences between healthy and unhealthy coping.

The healthy Type A is active and satisfied. Adrenalin levels are raised, cortisol levels are lowered. High demand has combined with autonomy and influence, requiring the mobilization of considerable effort. But Type As enjoy working in this kind of situation. This is 'happy stress'. The unhealthy Type A is active and distressed. High demands are coupled with lack of control and influence, leading to both effort and discomfort. This state is associated with sharply increased adrenalin levels, combined with increased cortisol levels. Taken to extremes, the Type A will take refuge in learned helplessness, in which nothing is done but the frustration and anger levels soar.

The healthy Type B is passive and satisfied. Adrenalin and cortisol levels are both lowered. A pleasant and undemanding environment offers the Type B relaxation of both body and mind, with no feelings of either effort or distress. This does not mean that they do nothing, however. The healthy Type B can be creative and imaginative, or at least will do what needs to be done at a steady pace and without fuss and bother. An unhealthy Type B is passive and distressed. Adrenalin levels are slightly raised and cortisol levels are considerably raised. The unhealthy Type B exhibits distress without effort, appearing unwilling or unable to do anything about the situation. It is easy to confuse the learned helplessness of the unhealthy

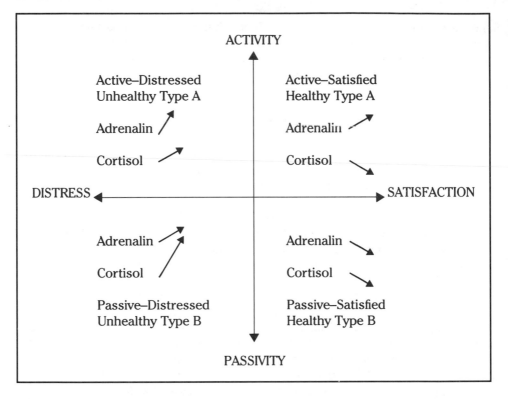

Figure 7.3   Healthy and unhealthy coping

Type A with this passivity in a damaged Type B, but the Type B is unlikely to be angry about it.

A survey of a large number of Type A chief executives, from a wide range of industries and professions, yielded the following stress management techniques held in common. Note that they are all preventive, the very area into which individuals and organizations seem least willing to put effort.

- Be intellectually curious. Intellectual curiosity and education (formal or informal) expand a person's understanding of the world, providing perspective as well as knowledge for problem solving.
- Be physically active. People who are physically active dissipate stress induced energy while at the same time developing a stronger and more efficient cardio-vascular system.
- Balance work with non-work. People who balance work with non-work activities place their work in a larger, broader context which gives perspective and reduces psychological dependence on work.
- Seek social support. Supportive relationships satisfy a variety of informational, evaluative and emotional needs essential to healthy functioning.
- Create systemic change. The people at the top need to be able to create a work environment that is challenging, productive, creative, and at the same time emotionally healthy.

WHAT CAN ORGANIZATIONS DO ABOUT STRESS?

Organizations, as such, can do nothing. If you are a manager, you may be able to, however. What you and your colleagues choose to do can be understood as the organization doing something.

Remedial action

A problem has occurred. You now have to try to cope.

Recognize that it has happened. Do not ignore it or hope it will go away by itself.

Removal. Does the person concerned have to stay in that situation? If not, move them. If so, plan with them how they can cope better.

Expert help. If the person has had a serious problem, and especially if they do not seem to be improving now that the apparent cause has been removed, get help. This is probably beyond you as a manager, and you possibly should not be spending that much time on it, even if you could do something about it. This is not your only subordinate. You could be adding significantly to the stress of others by over-concentration on this one problem.

Frequent feedback on performance will help restore confidence and ability. Give the person a lot of short term tasks which are well within their capability. Make sure they know they have done them well. Gradually increase the difficulty and length of the tasks, giving positive feedback all the way, until they are back to strength again. Do not make a big deal if they fail on some of the tasks. Just go back a step and try again. Do not expect or seek thanks for your help. They need to feel that they are standing on their own feet, and acknowledging any kind of dependency may make this difficult for them. This is part of your job as a manager.

Preventive action

It is far better to stop undue stress occurring in the first place than it is to cure it once it has arrived. You may never know if your efforts have worked. That is why prevention is not popular. Cure is much more obvious and dramatic. There are some measures which you can take as a manager which are highly likely to pay off by leading to a better managed organization anyway.

Recognize that stress can occur.

Collect stress related data. This includes labour turnover, absenteeism, lateness, pilferage, accidents, performance appraisal ratings, and employee attitude surveys. Be especially alert for sudden change.

Cut out deliberate stress. This includes lack of feedback and poor communications generally; sudden and unannounced moves of people and offices; and making people wait unnecessarily.

Working conditions may be at fault. Check lighting, heating, ventilation, humidity, noise, smoking, shift patterns, and the possibility of flexible hours at work.

Selection. There are few organizations that could not improve their initial selection methods. Having the wrong person in the wrong job is bound to cause problems.

Induction. Having got good people on board, make sure they know what they are supposed to do and help them form the connections and gather the information which will help them do it.

Training. We all need training and retraining to cope with the changing demands of work. The UK has a bad record of inadequate educational preparation for work, followed up by poor or non-existent training and development at work. You will become stressed if you are being blamed for poor performance but no one is helping you in any concrete way to do it better.

Potential assessment needs careful attention if you are to avoid appointing people to more senior posts who then fail to produce results. It is bad for them and bad for the organization to promote people to positions which they cannot cope with.

Feedback. Give frequent, reliable feedback on performance.

Performance appraisal. Check that the formal annual appraisal is doing what it is supposed to do. Has it become an administrative chore? Is it too formal or too complex?

Job design. How well matched are people's capacities and what they are being asked to do? Do they have too much or too little to do? Is it too fast or too slow for them? How much control do they have or want over what they do?

Face up to bad news early, and then take action before the problem gets out of hand.

Avoid indecision. You will hardly ever have all the information you would like to help you make your decision. Do not take rash risks, but do not hesitate over-long either. Do not create indecision in others by your own unwillingness to make decisions or to let them do so.

Use stress positively. Remember stress and motivation are part of the same continuum. There is a large healthy area under the middle of the curve in Figure 7.1. People can take a surprising amount without burning out if they know what is going on.

Counselling. Have a confidential counselling service available. People need someone to whom they can go to talk freely about their problems, of whatever scale. Companies which run such programmes claim that they make a major contribution to the health of the organization and the people within it, but the confidentiality must be absolute.

Medical/psychological help should be available at short notice. When you hit a crisis, or one of your employees does, you cannot wait three weeks for an appointment. Something needs doing *now*. You might want to consider routine health checks for all employees as part of your action to prevent stress building up in the first place.

You can manage stress – both your own and others'. Your objective should be to achieve that level of stress which best matches the person, what they are being asked to do, and the circumstances under which they are working. Sometimes this may mean increasing their stress level to help them achieve more, but never to the point of asking them to risk damaging themselves.

It might be as well to conclude with a warning. Do not overdo your concern with stress. Not every problem is stress related, and attempts at do-it-yourself psychiatry for trivial upsets are likely to be a waste of time, and may do more harm than good. But managing yourself and others to avoid inappropriate stress is a highly profitable venture.

CHECKLIST

1   *Take stock.* What is your physical state? What is your psychological state? How are things at work? How are things at home? How are you doing as a manager (if appropriate)?
2   *Do a gap analysis.* Where are you now in your stress management? Where do you want to be? Make the clearest list you can of achievable changes, together with measures which will let you know that you have done what you set out to do.
3   *List the resources* you have available, or that you could obtain or create.
4   *List the limitations* on what you are trying to do.
5   *Create an action plan*, which says what you are going to do, by when, given your resources and limitations.
6   *Carry out your plan*, one item at a time. Make sure that you get accurate feedback on the results of your efforts, especially if you have to give it to yourself.
7   *Revise your targets*, and select new ones, in the light of your progress.

There is no end to this checklist. It is a continuous process.

FURTHER READING

Booth, A. L., *Stressmanship*, Severn House Publishers, 1985

British Medical Association, *The BMA Book of Executive Health*, Times Books Ltd, 1979

Quick, J. C., Nelson, D. L. and Quick, J. D., *Stress and Challenge at the Top – the paradox of the successful executive*, Wiley, 1990

Roskies, E., *Stress Management for the Healthy Type A – theory and practice*, Guilford, 1987

Rudinger, E., *Living with Stress*, Consumers Association, 1982

Selye, H., *Stress without Distress*, Corgi, 1987

Wood, C., *Living in Overdrive*, Fontana Paperbacks, 1984

8 Career planning

Gillian Stamp and Colin Stamp

Are you feeling uneasy about your present job? Bored, anxious or frustrated? If so, Mike Pedler's keynote chapter on 'Management self-development' offers you a valuable primer on carrying out what could be one of the most important resolves that you ever make – to take the development of your career into your own hands. In this chapter we want to add the organizational dimension in which we all operate. For to be fully effective, management self-development has to be seen in the context of an inescapable fact of life – corporate policy.

Of course it is up to us to assume responsibility for planning our own careers. By deliberately setting out to develop new skills and to take care of our own working lives, we can all improve our career prospects, at least in the short term. In the long term, too, as our knowledge and experience grows and while things go well.

But, despite our best efforts, things do not always go well. For unless we are already working at senior management level we will rarely be in a position to influence corporate policy directly. However carefully and energetically we try to plan our own careers, they are also in the hands of others whose decisions and actions – or lack of them – may not always be in our best interests. If they are, we are indeed fortunate. But most of us are adversely affected, at some point in our careers, by decisions based on far wider issues than *our* skills or capabilities. At such times a wider perspective than that of 'self-development' may be needed if we are to escape a tendency to blame ourselves for what has gone wrong.

Hence the question with which we began. For even after a long period of conscientious self-development you may still be left feeling uneasy about your present job; bored, anxious or frustrated. Possibly you may feel guilty too, because you suspect it must have been *your* fault that it didn't work out. Taking responsibility for our own development is a taxing enough business without burdening ourselves with self-doubt, or with guilt for a problem whose causes lie elsewhere. The following exercise might help you to begin setting some boundaries.

The thoughts reported in each case were expressed by five different people as they participated in a guided conversation about their career. The conversations were strictly confidential, and they all formed part of a tested and widely applied appraisal procedure known as Career Path Appreciation (CPA), which will be described later in this chapter. Needless to say the people who revealed these intimate thoughts were not talking to their boss. In many companies it would be a risky business to discuss your frustrations and anxieties so frankly. But suppose, for the purposes of the following exercise, that they had done so.

Case 1. They're pushing me too far, too fast. I never seem to have time to sit back for a moment and think things through, so I have to guess at what they're looking for. Frankly I think I'm out of my depth, and I think I'm getting an ulcer.

Case 2. I can see quite clearly what changes I ought to be making in my new department, but somehow I keep putting it aside and falling back on things I know I can do well. It's beginning to get me really worried.

Case 3. There doesn't seem to be any point in my job. Certainly there's no challenge in it. But if it's so easy, why am I doing it so badly?

Case 4. I think I'd go mad with boredom if I didn't have my amateur dramatics to come home to, and a nice juicy part to learn, tucked away on my desk under last month's sales figures.

Case 5. It's all slipped. I might as well chuck it in.

Exercise 1

Select from the following alternatives the comment that would have been most likely to appear on each individual's file.

Case 1.
(a) A clear inability to perform under pressure. Overpromoted.
(b) Should be given a job in which he can catch his breath for two or three years and recover the capability that clearly still exists.

Case 2.
(a) A tendency to procrastinate, of which she is fully aware.
(b) Needs to be given space in which she can reflect and master the scope of her new role.

Case 3.
(a) A lack of motivation and a failure to understand the importance of her job are affecting her morale and hindering the work of her department.
(b) The challenge offered by her present level of employment no longer matches her growing capability, with the result that she has 'gone stale'. She is ready for promotion to department manager.

Case 4.
(a) Pursuing a hobby during working hours indicates a serious lack of commitment to the company.

(b) His creative leanings might possibly be put to better use in a more challenging role.

Case 5.

(a) He is evidently approaching a serious mid-career crisis and has probably nothing further to offer the company.

(b) His capability is clearly being neglected and a review of the challenges now being offered him is urgently necessary.

MATCH AND MISMATCH

It will be evident that two common threads run through the case stories. In each case there is a *mismatch* between the person's capability and the challenges that they are currently being offered. In each case the first assessment places the problem firmly at the door of the respondent. The second acknowledges the existence of a mismatch and makes an appropriate, if slightly simplistic, recommendation for managerial intervention.

In practice such intervention should always take account of conditions within the company that may have caused the mismatch. The temporary overpromotion evident in *Case 1* could have arisen as a result of a shortage of suitable candidates for the next level, while in *Case 3* the respondent could be 'going off the boil' because there are too many managers immediately above her. Either case would suggest a need to address the imbalance between the structure and objectives of the company and potentially available human resources. In a word, a need to replace the mismatch with a *match* between capabilities and challenges.

Mismatch can take two forms: *misuse*, when a person's present capability is not equal or appropriate to the challenges presented by their present job, and *disuse*, when it exceeds those challenges. Misuse is experienced as a feeling of being overstretched or overwhelmed; disuse as a feeling of being underused or 'underwhelmed'. Either condition is damaging to the individual experiencing it, and costly to the organization.

IN FLOW

The thought that follows was also expressed in the course of a Career Path Appreciation, and may provide a welcome relief after the rather depressing examples of mismatch already quoted.

> Right at this moment I'm in my element! They're letting me use my own judgement; I know exactly what the job is, and where my own contribution fits in with the whole plan. It gets a bit hairy at times, and sometimes I feel I'm being stretched to the limit. But that's when the adrenalin really flows, and I wouldn't want it any other way.

Here there is obviously a *match* between capabilities and challenges, which underlines the vital importance of recognizing and fostering a human attribute of even greater long-term value than technical, professional or communication skills.

The person who expressed his feelings so enthusiastically was 'in flow'. He was neither overwhelmed nor 'underwhelmed'; his present capability exactly matched the challenges with which he was presented. *And they were letting him use his own judgement.*

Put yourself in his place. Allow yourself to dream for a moment about a career where you were always 'in your element', facing challenges that were just right – neither so big that they overwhelmed your judgement nor so feeble that they provided no test for it. And where, as your capabilities grew, the appropriate challenges would continue to come your way.

Does this sound like an impossible dream? Or a luxury only available to the lucky few? Is any organization going to be prepared to make that kind of commitment to its staff? To enable them to pace challenges and capabilities, and thus do their job with enthusiasm and fresh imagination throughout their working lives?

For organizations faced with a world-scene of unprecedented turbulence, this is neither dream nor luxury, but stark necessity: the very survival of their business may depend on it. To cope with high-pressure markets, increasingly sophisticated customers and competitors, new demographic trends and a growing need for flexible working arrangements, they must pay serious attention to staff expectations for job satisfaction, continuous education and updating, development and quality of life.

So, it is not an impossible dream but a reality. Today, as you think about your career, you no longer have to accept soul-destroying working conditions or pretend that you are not really interested in using your own judgement.

WHAT IS JUDGEMENT?

While judgement-making is not the only skill or competence needed for work, it lies at the heart of what people talk about when they really sit down and think about 'job satisfaction.' We all want to be allowed to use our judgement: to cope with uncertainty, to analyse a flood of information, mull it over, play with it, 'put it on the back burner', re-shape it and eventually arrive at a decision. We all have our own ways of describing what happens when we use our judgement: we call it 'following our intuition', we reach into an inner resource to 'get a feel' for what should be done, we 'gather our thoughts' and 'sense the right thing to do'.

But one of the exciting and disturbing things about judgement is that it is a process that cannot be precisely put into words. The difference between what can and can't be put into words is important in understanding what work is about, and how we obtain satisfaction from it. If you can set down all the reasons why you made a certain decision, it wasn't a decision but a calculation. Using your judgement is what you do when you don't know what to do. And the exercise of judgement lies at the heart of job satisfaction.

You use your judgement when you turn inwards to something intrinsically 'unreliable', in the sense that you can neither summon it to order nor put it into words. Unlike the acquisition of skills, the development of judgement is what enables you to make your own unique contribution – to do what only you can do. And this is why it is important for you to be 'in flow', for the challenge to be 'just right', for there to be enough to call for your judgement but not so much that you are overwhelmed and cannot answer the call. People 'in flow' are effective decision-makers, at ease with their responsibilities and therefore able to act as good stewards of the resources for which they are responsible.

The manager of an information services department put it like this:

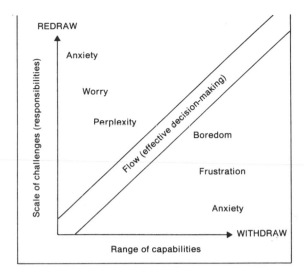

Figure 8.1 The individual decision-maker (Adapted from M. Csikszentmihaliy, *Optimal Experience*, Cambridge University Press, 1988)

> I was in tune with myself and the world. It was great . . . judgements just seemed to come of their own accord, they were always there when I really needed them. Everything that happened went with the grain.

Once you begin to think honestly about your career, this is obviously the way you would want it to be all the time. It is equally obvious that you would want to avoid being overwhelmed or 'underwhelmed' by your challenges. But while this is obvious, it is not easy to bring about.

OUT OF FLOW

It is all too easy for the balance between capabilities and challenges to slip. Perhaps you have grown and your job has not. Perhaps you have gone into a new job and it is turning out to be bigger than you realized. Perhaps the organization is changing very fast and you are reacting to a general anxiety and uncertainty.

When any of these things happen, you may feel that you have 'lost your touch', that it's suddenly no longer fun, even frightening, to use your judgement. You start to behave differently, and others blame and criticize you.

> You'd think he'd be delighted with his promotion. More money, a new car, plenty more people working under him. But no, not him. He always was a bit irritable but now he's a really difficult personality.

Figures 8.1 and 8.2 are based on the proven hypothesis that our capability to exercise judgement grows over time. By plotting the scale of challenges offered to the individual against his or her range of capabilities at a given moment, Figure 8.1 helps us to understand what is happening to the individual as a result of a mismatch between challenges and capabilities. When the former exceed the latter,

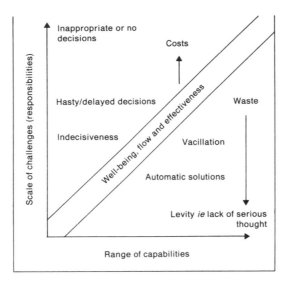

Figure 8.2   Decision-making capability and organizational well-being

initial perplexity may pass into deep anxiety and, in the severest cases, a tendency to *redraw* one's role in a desperate attempt to recover some balance with what one feels able to do.

When capabilities exceed challenges, initial boredom may develop via increasing frustration into a no less damaging state of anxiety, followed eventually by a tendency to *withdraw* commitment to the organization. Figure 8.2 gives a complementary picture of the possible effects on the organization of actions and/or behaviour caused by mismatch.

There is no end to the possible permutations of distress and anxiety that may confront us as a result of being disused/overwhelmed or misused/'underwhelmed'. A few of them have already emerged from thoughts expressed in the course of actual Career Path Appreciations and mentioned earlier in this chapter.

The following exercise offers a further range of thoughts which you may find it helpful to match against your own experience.

Exercise 2

Rate the state of mind suggested by each of the quoted thoughts on one of the following scales and pencil your rating in on the right. Scale from M1 (perplexity caused by mild misuse) to M3 (deep anxiety caused by severe misuse) or from D1 (boredom caused by mild disuse) to D3 (deep anxiety caused by severe disuse). Consider whether the thought expressed matches your own state of mind, either now or at some previous point in your career. If it does, or did, tick under 'Rating applicable?' and jot down brief details on a piece of paper. Then add to those details any instances that you may have experienced of feeling 'in flow' during your career to date.

	Rating applicable?
1 'Something seems to have gone a bit wrong with my judgement. Things aren't quite falling into place the way they should.'	
2 'This is so easy. So why am I doing it so badly?'	
3 'I feel as if I'm being forced to break a journey just when I'm all set to get going.'	
4 'How am I doing? Am I doing it right? Should I be doing it at all?'	
5 'Whatever it was I thought I had, it's certainly gone by now. And I can't see how I'm ever going to get it back again.'	
6 'There's no point, no challenge. It's not getting me anywhere.'	
7 'I'm completely out of my depth – with weights tied to both feet.'	
(Suggested ratings in order: M1, D1, D1, M2, D3, D2, M3)	

When made with total honesty this simple analysis may help you to establish links between hitherto unperceived patterns in your past and present career which can only be helpful to the task of self-development. It does not encourage you to 'pass the buck', or to shirk responsibility for obvious personal faults or failures that may have got you into difficulties. Moreover it is most important that the times when you were 'in flow' as a result of perceptive management should stand there alongside those times when you were stressed by the organization's failure to present you with challenges that matched your capability to exercise judgement.

One further exercise may help you towards some helpful and – we hope – encouraging conclusions. Others may very possibly come to your mind as you gain confidence by contemplating your own work experience, and especially those points when you have felt happy and fulfilled/overwhelmed/underwhelmed.

Exercise Three: Twenty-one Questions

Jot down the answers to the following questions.
1 When I received my last promotion was I (tick one)
        pleased/puzzled/uneasy/apprehensive/panic-stricken?

2 Is my job description clear, complete and unequivocal?
3 In particular have I been given clear guidance about the exact limit of my responsibilities?

4 Does my present role call for specialized skills and/or training which I was known not to possess when I was offered it?

5 If so, has any provision been made for me to acquire them?

6 If not, is this because there is a shortage of managers at the level to which I have been promoted?

7 Or because the organization is unable to cope quickly with an abnormally high pace of change and is consequently relying on ad hoc decisions?

8 Do I have a feeling of having been 'left to get on with it'?

9 If the answer is 'yes', does this give me the feeling that I am being trusted to use my judgement?

10 Or that my judgement is of no interest to the organization?

11 Is it now a considerable time (two or more years) since I was offered an extension to the range of my responsibilities?

12 If so, is this because there are too many managers at the level immediately above mine?

13 Or because nobody 'up there' pays much attention to that kind of thing?

14 Or because the organization is stagnant?

15 Does my immediate boss interfere with my right to make my own decisions and be accountable for them?

16 Am I at ease with the criteria by which my job performance is being judged – e.g. number of 'calls' made annually as the principal or sole criterion of effectiveness as a sales manager?

17 Has my performance been affected by private concerns – e.g. a partner's career needs, children's schooling?

18 Is there a channel by which I could frankly discuss with management my perception of any of the above problems?

19 If so, can I say from experience that I believe I would be listened to sympathetically and perceptively?   .

20 If not, have I given enough thought to other possible roles within the organization that I might find more fulfilling?

21 If no such roles appear to exist, what opportunities might be available to me outside the organization, possibly in some completely different field to which I may now be drawn by my 'do it yourself' review of match and mismatch?

Those questions, not entirely chosen at random, may help point you towards a form of simple self-analysis that has little to do with your technical, professional or social skills and much to do with your self-confidence and your growing capability to exercise judgement. Let's try to recapitulate one or two ideas that place those two attributes right where they belong: at the top of your own – and your organization's – agenda.

The feeling of unease or 'mismatch' which almost all of us face at one time or another in our careers may well have its roots in some personal inadequacy. An honest and courageous look at the gaps in our own armoury can increase our chance of being able to come up with the necessary skills when they are needed.

But conventional measurement of 'skills', with its emphasis on 'aptitude tests', technical qualifications etc, tends to ignore two very important things about people. First – while their capacity to draw on that inner resource that we call 'using our judgement' cannot be precisely measured, it is the one resource they possess that actually appreciates over time.

Second, 'human resources' no longer belong to the comfortable world of the glossy annual report with its threadbare clichés about 'the caring organization'. Paying attention to everyone's inner need for 'job satisfaction' is no longer merely a soft option about 'being kind to people'. The ability to identify and consistently cultivate judgement-making capability – and thus ensure that people are happy and fulfilled throughout their working careers – may now represent the stark difference between corporate success and failure.

An organization's ability to take on board this unequivocal message depends on the degree to which it accepts its own responsibility for the unending work involved in providing job satisfaction. This responsibility has two elements. First, it involves responding appropriately when employees demonstrate by their performance that things are 'just right' for them. And second, it involves respecting its employee's ability to recognize quite clearly that things are going wrong, and why, and to speak up without inhibition. If these responsibilities became a general part of corporate ethos we would hear more about people being 'in flow' and less about 'mid-life crisis' and (odious invention) 'middlescence'.

A FINAL CHECKLIST

1   Are you 'in flow', with a match between challenge and capability?
If not, does your personal mismatch between challenge and capability involve:
2   Misuse (Demands on your judgement-making capability that you are not at the moment able to respond to, perhaps leading to an attempt to redraw your role?)
3   Disuse (Lack of challenge and a feeling of 'going stale' leading to withdrawal?)
4   Write down two positive actions by your organization that you feel would be most likely to restore your feeling of being 'in flow'.

NOTE ON CAREER PATH APPRECIATION

It might be helpful if we were to close this Chapter with a brief introduction to the nature and practice of Career Path Appreciation.

Over twenty years research into individual differences in the rate of growth of decision-making capability has shown that it is possible to evaluate current capability, and predict future capability, with considerable accuracy. The predictive tool used is called Career Path Appreciation. It is based on the theory of time-span introduced by Elliott Jaques which postulates that levels of work can be measured on a scale from 1 to 7, based on the length of time that will elapse before the outcomes of decision-making can be properly understood and fully evaluated.

Career Path Appreciation (CPA) postulates that our capability to exercise sound judgement is broadly measurable by the maximum amount of time we are able to tolerate and cope with uncertainty about the outcome of our decision-making, ranging from periods of from one day to three months (level 1) to twenty-five years or more (level 7).

There are important implications both for the individual and the organization in the further postulation that growth in capability to exercise sound judgement, and thus successfully accept wider challenges, progresses at different rates and can be reliably predicted.

For the individual it opens up the possibility of career planning based on the optimum condition of being 'in flow'. For the organization, CPA offers a proven means of succession planning over a long period of time, ensuring that the necessary judgement-making capabilities will be in place at the exact place and moment they are needed – often many years into the future.

A Career Path Appreciation lasts from two to three hours and consists of four parts. The first part is designed to guide conversation about the respondent's approach to work. The second part offers insight into his or her capacity to create order out of disorder. Neither is intended to elicit information about ability to handle specific jobs. The third part consists of a free discussion focused on the respondent's career. Discussion of technical skills and competence is not sought, but the respondent is encouraged to talk about times when there were feelings of being overwhelmed, 'underwhelmed' or 'in flow'. The discussion is totally non-judgemental, and often represents the first occasion on which respondents have ever been encouraged to talk frankly about their work, their achievements, excitements, anxieties and disappointments. The fourth and final part is the feedback.

Certain words have been deliberately adopted to underline a sense of respect, commonality and sharing. We do not 'undergo' still less 'submit to' an Appreciation: we are 'offered' it and we 'work through it'. The word 'appreciation' itself, with its connotations of mutual respect, was chosen because it epitomizes the two-way nature of the process, the immediate establishment of a trusting relationship between the respondent and the practitioner, the long-term cultivation of a trusting and mutually beneficial relationship between the respondent and the organization. Above all the practitioner's role is to help people understand and *appreciate* their current capability and career potential, and to see their own work experience, good and bad, as at the same time unique yet linked by a vast body of accumulated knowledge to the experience of others.

When a group of Japanese managers visited an American institute at which Career Path Appreciation is regularly used, the interpreter translated the word 'appreciation' with the Japanese word for 'gift'. That was entirely appropriate, for the experience is often described as an intensely liberating one. As one manager said 'This has offered me a completely new way of looking at myself.'

These notes are offered to you in that same spirit and in that same hope.

FURTHER READING

The ideas explored in this chapter are rooted in the appraisal method known as Career Path Appreciation. The following is a list of relevant publications available from:

The Individual and Organizational Capability Unit
Brunel Institute of Organization Studies
Brunel, The University of West London
Uxbridge
Middlesex
UB8 3PH

Jaques, E., *Requisite Organisation*, Gower, 1989

Stamp, G., 'Levels and Types of Managerial Capability' in *The Journal of Management Studies* **18**, (3), 1981

Stamp, G., 'Management Styles' in *The Leadership and Organisation Journal*, **7**, (2), 1986

Stamp, G., 'Some Observations on the Career Paths of Women' in the *Journal of Applied Behavioural Science*, **22** (4), 1986

Stamp, G., 'Career Paths in Tomorrow's Organisation' in *Industrial and Commercial Training*, March/April, 1986

Stamp, G., 'Pacing Capability and Responsibility' in *Training and Management Development Methods*, **1**, (2), 1988

Stamp, G. 'Well-Being and Stress at Work' in *ICIS Forum*, **19**, (1), 1988

Stamp, G. 'Tokens and Glass Ceilings: the Real Issues of 'Minorities' in Organizations' in *The International Journal of Career Management*, **1**, (2), 1989

Stamp, G. 'The Individual, the Organization and the Path to Mutual Appreciation' in *Personnel Management*, July, 1989

Baker, J. and Stamp, G. 'Identifying Individual Potential: Career Path Appreciation as a cost-effective alternative to Assessment Centres' in *Guidance and Assessment Review*, **6**, (3), 1990

Stamp, G. *Longitudinal Research into Methods of Assessing Managerial Potential*, US Army Research Institute for the Behavioral and Social Sciences, Washington DC, USA, 1989

NOTE:

During a period of economic recession, countless skilled and competent people face the threat or the reality of compulsory redundancy. This chapter is addressed no less to them than to those who are in employment. For an honest assessment of past experience is never more needed than when a change of direction is called for.

Part II
MANAGING OTHER PEOPLE

Introduction: understanding other people

Management involves getting things done through or by other people. Here is where most managers make their first mistake. 'It's quicker to do it myself', they say. 'The only way to make sure something is done correctly is to do it yourself.' And so on. This is not what management is about.

If you insist on doing things yourself, instead of getting them done by or through other people, a number of things happen:

- You fill your days doing things that should be done by other people.
- You waste your organization's money: calculate the rate per hour your organization is paying you and the rate per hour for those subordinate to you who should be doing what you're insisting on doing yourself. Subtract the difference. That is what your organization is losing.
- You have less time available to do the things you are actually paid to do. This may be deliberate – you're too unsure of your ability to operate at the level you've been promoted to so you spend your time doing things you know you *can* do.
- Your subordinates do not have enough work to do and have to find other things to do, e.g. office politics, rumour mongering, industrial relations.
- Your subordinates do not have the opportunity to learn new skills.
- Morale and motivation drop.
- Your stress levels rise.

The answer, of course, is management through people: achieving *your* targets through *their* contribution, *their* work.

First, you need to be clear about what your targets are: what are you meant to achieve? Next, who are 'your' people? What are their skills, their strengths and weaknesses? A brief review of these points will provide a valuable basis for assessing current performance and planning for the future.

But it does not touch upon the heart of the matter. How do you marry 'your' people and their skills with the tasks and targets you need to achieve? In this section, we cover a range of skills you may need to help you: the people skills you may find useful; leadership and motivation; developing your people and using your support staff to best advantage; team building; mentoring; performance appraisal and counselling; selection and interviewing; the skills of communication with staff, and making meetings work.

FURTHER READING

Handy, Charles B., *Understanding Organizations*, 3rd edition, Penguin, 1987. Detailed yet very readable introduction to organizations and the people who 'are' those organizations. An illuminating and useful overview of organizational theory, designed to be of practical use for the intelligent manager who wants to understand as well as manage.

9 Leadership and motivation

John Adair

Ideas about leadership have changed considerably in recent times. People today are better educated and more articulate. They can no longer be commanded in the same way as before. In industry trade unions are certainly more vigilant and often more militant. There needs to be much more involvement and participation at work – everyone recognizes that fact. But to achieve these ends industry has to see its managers more as leaders. Indeed, every kind of working enterprise has acknowledged that it needs more and better leadership at all levels. How can it be developed?

The aim of this chapter is to help you to improve your own abilities as a leader. I am assuming that you have a direct personal interest in leadership. You may be in a position which you suspect – or have been told – requires leadership. You may already be an experienced leader, or you may be on the threshold of a career in management which will expect you to become a leader. In each case leadership matters to you. So how can you improve your leadership ability?

- You need to stimulate your own *awareness* of leadership in all its aspects. That means being aware when it is required in a given situation and aware when it is lacking. It also entails an awareness of the changing values of society (and industry which reflects those values) which will deepen your awareness of the importance of good leadership if free men and women are to cooperate effectively.
- You need to establish your *understanding* of the principles, requirements or functions of leadership. The poor leadership of many managers can be attributed, in part, to ignorance. No one ever told them the functions of leadership. So they miss out some vital factor. A good leader understands the whole spectrum of leadership behaviour, and knows when a given function is required.
- You need to develop your *skills* in providing the necessary functions, not only *when* to do a particular action, and *why* it should be done, but also *how* it should be done.

WHAT YOU HAVE TO BE

'It is a fact that some men possess an inbred superiority which gives them a dominating influence over their contemporaries, and marks them out unmistakably for leadership.' So declared an eminent lecturer on leadership before the University of St Andrews in 1934. Since time immemorial people have sought to understand this natural phenomenon of leadership. What is it that gives a person this influence over his fellows?

The traditional or *qualities approach* to leadership suggests that the person who emerges as a leader in a group does so because he possesses certain traits. This view has been rejected by academics. They emphasize the lack of agreement among researchers on what constitutes these distinctive leadership qualities. Such a notion of leadership also seems to run counter to their assumptions about democracy.

Some researchers concede that leaders do possess the qualities expected or required in their working groups – the coxswain of the lifeboat, for example, clearly needs to exemplify the qualities of a good lifeboatman. But are there more general or universal qualities of leadership? Most people accept that leadership implies *personality*. Enthusiasm and warmth are often deemed to be especially important. There is also an impressive testimony in history that *character*, incorporating moral courage and integrity, matters enormously.

The following is a ranking of attributes rated most valuable at top level of management by a cross-section of successful chief executives:

1	Ability to take decisions	14	Capacity to speak lucidly
2	Leadership	15	Astuteness
3	Integrity	16	Ability to administer efficiently
4	Enthusiasm	17	Open-mindedness
5	Imagination	18	Ability to 'stick to it'
6	Willingness to work hard	19	Willingness to work long hours
7	Analytical ability	20	Ambition
8	Understanding of others	21	Single-mindedness
9	Ability to spot opportunities	22	Capacity for lucid writing
10	Ability to meet unpleasant situations	23	Curiosity
11	Ability to adapt quickly to change	24	Skill with numbers
12	Willingness to take risks	25	Capacity for abstract thought
13	Enterprise		

You may find it useful to complete the checklist in Figure 9.1 and consider what it reveals about your leadership qualities.

An understanding of leadership in terms of the qualities of personality and character which one person has to a greater degree than his fellows *is* relevant, but it is far from being the whole story.

WHAT YOU HAVE TO KNOW

The second major approach to understanding leadership focuses upon the situation. Taken to extremes this school declares there is no such thing as a born leader: it all depends upon the situation. Some situations will evoke leadership

List the five key characteristics or personal qualities which are expected or required in workers in your field:

	Good	Average	Weak
_____			
_____			
_____			
_____			

Now rate yourself in terms of each of them — Good, Average or Weak
Circle the number where you would place yourself on the following continuum:

Very introvert   Very extrovert

5   4 3 2 1 2 3 4   5

(Leaders tend to be slightly more extrovert than introvert on this scale, i.e. they are ambiverts — mixtures of both)

	Yes	No
Have you shown yourself to be a responsible person?	☐	☐
Do you like the responsibility as well as the rewards of leadership?	☐	☐
Are you self-sufficient enough to withstand criticism, indifference or unpopularity from others and to work effectively with others without constant supervision?	☐	☐
Are you an active and socially participative person?	☐	☐
Can you control your emotions and moods — or do they control you?	☐	☐
Have you any evidence to suppose that other people think of you as essentially a warm person?	☐	☐
Can you give instances over the past three months where you have been deliberately dishonest or less than straight with the people that work for you?	☐	☐
Are you noted for your enthusiasm at work?	☐	☐
Has anyone ever used the word 'integrity' in relation to you?	☐	☐

Figure 9.1   Checklist – do you have some basic leadership qualities?

from one person – other situations from another. Therefore it is useless discussing leadership any longer in general terms. This *situational approach*, as it is called, holds that it is always the situation which determines who emerges as the leader and what 'style of leadership' he has to adopt.

This 'horses-for-courses' approach has some obvious advantages. It emphasises the importance of *knowledge* relevant to a specific problem – 'Authority flows to the man who knows', as one writer put it. There are broadly three kinds of authority at work:

- the authority of *position* – job title, badges of rank, appointment;
- the authority of *personality* – the natural qualities of influence;

		Yes	No
Do you feel that your interests, aptitudes (e.g. mechanical, verbal) and temperament are suited to the field you are in?		☐	☐
Can you identify a field where you would be more likely to emerge as a leader?		☐	☐
How have you developed the 'the authority of knowledge'? Have you done all you can at this stage in your career to acquire the necessary professional or specialist training available?		☐	☐
Have you experience in more than one field or more than one industry or more than one function?		☐	☐

Do you take an interest in fields adjacent
to your own and potentially relevant?

        sometimes ☐
        never ☐
        always ☐

How flexible are you within your field? Are you:

Good	You have responded to situational changes with marked flexibility of approach; you read situations well, think about them and respond with the appropriate kind of leadership	☐
Adequate	You have proved yourself in two situations, but you fear some situations; you are happiest only when the situation is normal and predictable	☐
Weak	You are highly adapted to one particular work environment and cannot stand change. You are often called rigid or inflexible	☐

Figure 9.2   Checklist – are you right for the situation?

- the authority of *knowledge* – technical, professional.

Whereas leaders in the past tended to rely upon the first kind of authority – that is, they exercised mastery as the appointed boss – today leaders have to draw much more upon the second and third kinds of authority.

Technical competence or professional knowledge is a key strand in your authority. Yet expertise in a particular job is not enough; other more general skills are also required. These focus upon leadership, decision making and communication. These can be *transferred* as you move into a different situation in your field or change to a new sphere of work. Within your field you should aim to widen your knowledge of the work and develop the general abilities of leading others. That will increase your *flexibility*.

Even within the broad continuities of a particular industry or business the situation will change. Social, technical or economic developments will see to that. Are you ready?

The checklist in Figure 9.2 reviews the situational approach, and offers an opportunity for assessing your flexibility.

WHAT YOU HAVE TO DO

A third line of research and thinking about leadership has focused on the group. This *group approach*, as it may be called, has tended to see leadership in terms of functions which meet group needs: what has to be *done*. In fact, if you look closely at matters involving leadership, there are always three elements or variables:

- The leader – qualities of personality and character.
- The situation – partly constant; partly varying.
- The group – the followers: their needs and values.

The most useful theory about groups for the practical leader is that they are rather like individuals – all unique and yet all having things in common. What they share, according to this theory, is *needs*, just as every individual does. These needs are related to the *task, group maintenance* and the *individual*.

Task

One of the reasons why a group comes together is that there is a task which one person cannot do on his own. But does the group as a whole experience the need to complete the task within the natural time limits for it? Now a man is not very aware of his need for food if he is well fed, and so one would expect a group to be relatively oblivious of any sense of need if its task is being successfully performed. In this case the only sign of a need having been met is the satisfaction or elation which overtakes the group in its moments of triumph, a happiness which social man may count among his deepest joys.

Before such a fulfilment, however, many groups pass through a 'black night of despair' when it may appear that the group will be compelled to disperse without achieving what it set out to do. If the members are not committed to the common goal this will be a comparatively painless event; but if they are, the group will exhibit various degrees of anxiety and frustration. Scapegoats for the corporate failure may be chosen and punished; reorganizations might take place and new leaders emerge. Thus, adversity reveals the nature of group life more clearly than prosperity. In it we may see signs or symptoms of the need to get on effectively with whatever the group has come together to do.

Group maintenance

This is not so easy to perceive as the task need; as with an iceberg, much of the life of any group lies below the surface. The distinction that the task need concerns things and the second need involves people does not help overmuch. Again, it is best to think of groups which are threatened from without by forces aimed at their disintegration or from within by disruptive people or ideas. We can then see how they give priority to maintaining themselves against these external or internal pressures, sometimes showing great ingenuity in the process. Many of the written or unwritten rules of the group are designed to promote this unity and to maintain cohesiveness at all costs. Those who rock the boat, or infringe group standards and corporate balance, may expect reactions varying from friendly indulgence to

137

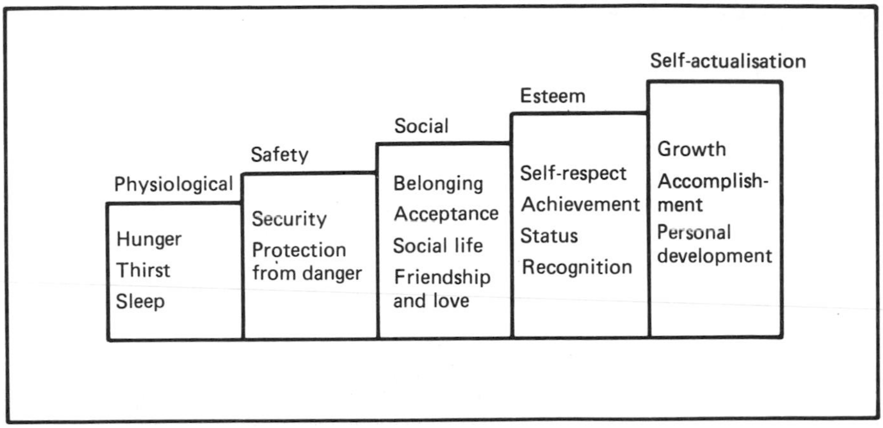

Figure 9.3   The hierarchy of needs

downright anger. Instinctively a common feeling exists that 'united we stand, divided we fall', that good relationships, desirable in themselves, are also essential means toward the shared end. This need to create and promote group cohesiveness I have called maintenance need.

Individual needs

Third, individuals bring into the group their own needs; not just the physical ones for food and shelter, which are largely catered for by the payment of wages these days, but also their psychological needs: recognition; a sense of doing something worthwhile; status; the deeper needs to give to and receive from other people in a working situation. These personal needs are perhaps more profound than we sometimes realise.

These needs spring from the depths of our common life as human beings. They may attract us to, or repel us from, any given group. Underlying them all is the fact that people need each other, not just to survive but to achieve and develop personality. This growth occurs in a whole range of social activities – friendship, marriage, neighbourhood – but inevitably work groups are extremely important because so many people spend so much of their waking time in them.

The work of A. H. Maslow forms a useful springboard into the deep water of understanding 'what makes people tick'. He suggested that individual needs are arranged in order of prepotence – the stronger at the bottom and the weaker (but more distinctively human) at the top (see Figure 9.3).

Physiological. These are man's physical needs for food, shelter, warmth, sexual gratification and other bodily functions.

Safety. These include the need to feel safe from physical danger and the need for physical, mental and emotional security.

Social. This covers the need for belonging and love, the need to feel part of a group or organization, to belong to or be with someone else. Implicit in it is the need to give and receive love, to share and to be part of a family.

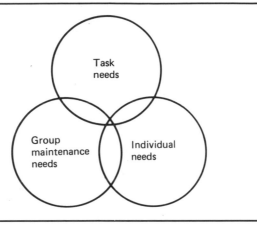

Figure 9.4   The three-circles model

Esteem. These needs fall into two closely related categories – self-esteem and the esteem of others. The first includes our need to respect ourselves, to feel personal worth, adequacy and competence. The second combines our need for respect, praise, recognition and status in the eyes of others.

Self-actualization. The need to achieve as much as possible, to develop one's gifts or potential to the full.

Maslow makes two interesting points about these needs. First, if one of our stronger needs is threatened we jump down the steps to defend it. You do not worry about status, for example, if you are starving. Therefore if you appear to threaten people's security by your proposed changes as a leader you should expect a stoutly defended response.

Second, a satisfied need ceases to motivate. When one area of need is met, the person concerned becomes aware of another set of needs within him. These in turn now begin to motivate him.

THE INTERACTION OF NEEDS

The three-circles diagram (Figure 9.4) suggests that the task, group and individual needs are always interacting with each other. The circles overlap but they do not sit on top of each other. In other words, there is always some degree of tension between them. Many of an individual's needs – such as the need to achieve and the social need for human companionship – are met in part by participating in working groups. But he can also run the danger of being exploited in the interests of the task and dominated by the group in ways that trespass upon his personal freedom and integrity.

It is fundamental that each of the circles must always be seen in relation to the other two. As a leader you need to be constantly aware of what is happening in your group in terms of the three circles. You can imagine one circle as a balloon getting bigger and another shrinking, or you can visualise the situation as if one circle is completely blacked out. Cut out a disc or use a cup to cover one circle

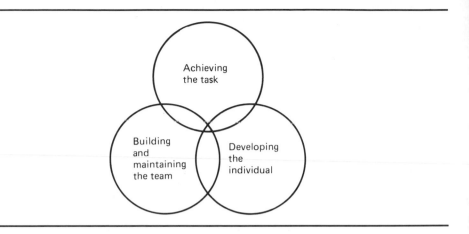

Figure 9.5   What a leader has to do

now. At once segments of the other two circles are covered also. Using the disc and doing the following exercise you can begin to develop this awareness yourself.

Contrary to assumptions in the group dynamics movement, the roles of leader and members should not be entirely confused. Leaders in real situations, as opposed to artificial 'laboratory' ones, are appointed or elected or they emerge – usually a combination of two of these methods. All group members share responsibility for the three areas but the appointed or elected leader is *accountable* for all three. By performing the functions of leadership he guides the group to:

- achieve the common task;
- work as a team;
- respect and develop its individual members.

See Figure 9.5 which shows these applied to the three circles.

Understanding your position as the leader in relation to the three circles is vitally important. You should see yourself as half-in and half-out. There should be some social distance between you and the group, but not too much. The reason for maintaining this element of distance is not to enhance your mystique; it is because you may have to take decisions or act toughly in the task area which will cause reactions to be directed at you from the group and the individuals who face, in consequence, some unwelcome change. You have weakened yourself if you are on too friendly terms, or rather you have exposed yourself to pressures – 'we didn't expect that from *you*' – which you may not be able to handle.

There is an especial problem for leaders who are elected or appointed from among their workmates and remain with the same group. To exchange the close friendly relationship of colleagues for that of a leader and subordinates is not easy.

You can begin to see why a degree of self-sufficiency is important for a leader. Leadership is not about popularity, though it would be inhuman not to enjoy being liked. Because leaders tend to have social, even gregarious, natures they can find the inevitable brickbats that come their way hard to endure. But what matters in the long run is not how many rounds of applause a leader receives but how much *respect* he gains, and that is never achieved by being 'soft' or 'weak' in the task,

BEHAVIOUR	USEFUL	NOT USEFUL
Leader emphasises distance	Where group knows him well before he became a leader. When group seems to want over-familiarity. When unpopular decisions are in the offing. When taking charge initially of a new group.	Where group already has a strong traditional sense of distance from its leaders. When people can be fully trusted not to become too familiar anyway.
Leader minimises distance	When there is lack of communication and trust between management and employees. Where all are roughly equal in knowledge and experience	Where the distance is already fairly minimal owing to the predecessor's style. Where it can be misinterpreted as familiarity
Leader strikes balance between closeness and distance	Most working situations.	Where the group needs corrective treatment after either too remote or too friendly leadership.

Figure 9.6   Position of leader in relation to group

team or individual circles. See Figure 9.6 for some relationships between leader and group.

The leader's social needs can be met partly by relations with his team, but it is always lonely at the top. He can never fully share the burden with those who work for him, or open his heart about his own doubts, fears and anxieties: that is best done with other leaders on his own level. If the leader's superior is doing his job he will help to make such meetings possible (they are often called management training courses!). Even more important, the leader's superior will himself be a resource; a pillar of strength and – at times – a shoulder to weep upon, should the leader require it.

Until you can do the essential work illustrated in Figure 9.5 your appointment as a leader will not be ratified in the hearts and minds of the group. Try out the checklist (Figure 9.7) to help you assess your performance.

MOTIVATION

Individual needs are especially important in relation to motivation, which is closely connected with leadership. One of the things that leaders are supposed to do is to motivate people by a combination of rewards and threats – the carrot and stick approach. More recent thought and some research suggests that you and I motivate ourselves to a large extent by responding to inner needs. As a leader you must understand these needs in individuals and how they operate, so that you can work with the grain of human nature and not against it.

Douglas McGregor has pointed out that managers often operated mainly under one of two sets of contrasting explicit or implicit assumptions about people, which he labelled theory X and theory Y (see Figure 9.8).

McGregor made the point that what we believe about a person can help that

	Yes	No
Have you been able to give specific examples from your own experience on how the three circles or areas of need — task, group and individual — interact upon each other?	☐	☐
Can you identify your natural bias:		
You tend to put the *task* first, and are low on group and individual	☐	☐
For you the *group* seems most important; you value happy relationships more than productivity or individual job satisfaction	☐	☐
Individuals are supremely important to you; you always put the *individual* before the task or the group for that matter. You tend to over-identify with the individual	☐	☐
You can honestly say you maintain a balance, and have feedback from superiors, colleagues, and subordinates to prove it	☐	☐
Do you vary your social distance from the group according to a realistic appreciation of the factors in the situation?	☐	☐
Can you illustrate that from experience?	☐	☐

Figure 9.7   Checklist – the three circles

Theory X	Theory Y
People dislike work and will avoid it if they can	Work is necessary to human psychological growth. People want to be interested in their work and, under the right conditions, they can enjoy it
People must be forced or bribed to put out the right effort	People will direct themselves towards an accepted target
People would rather be directed than accept responsibility, which they avoid	People will seek, and accept responsibility under the right conditions. The discipline people impose on themselves is more effective, and can be more severe, than any imposed on them
People are motivated mainly by money People are motivated by anxiety about their security	Under the right conditions people are motivated by the desire to realise their own potential
Most people have little creativity — except when it comes to getting round management rules!	Creativity and ingenuity are widely distributed and grossly underused

Figure 9.8   Assumptions about people

person to behave in that way (*the self-fulfilling prophecy*). If you tell someone you believe that they are bone idle, for example, they will tend to live up to your prediction. If you have a high regard for them, although that is not strictly justified by the facts, they may well rise to meet your expectations.

Another approach was taken by Frederick Herzberg. In the mid-1950s Herzberg and his associates interviewed 203 engineers and accountants in Pittsburg to find out why they found some events in their working lives highly satisfying and others highly dissatisfying. Herzberg divided the factors involved into two factors, which he called 'motivators' and 'hygiene factors' (see Figure 9.9). The motivators provided longer lasting satisfaction to individuals. The hygiene factors cause us dissatisfaction if they are wrong. But if you give a person more of a hygiene factor you will only either reduce their dissatisfaction or else give them a short lived sense of satisfaction.

Herzberg's 'two-factor' theory has been the cause of much controversial debate. Like most black and white, 'either–or' pieces of analysis, binary interpretation achieves the appearance of simplicity but only at the cost of sacrificing elements of the more complex truth. Money, for example, cannot be regarded only as a hygiene factor: it can serve as a tangible and necessary expression of recognition in some spheres. Nonetheless, Herzberg has had a powerful influence on the movement to increase job satisfaction in industry, a practical application of the wider understanding of individual needs.

Although Herzberg includes 'supervision' in his set of hygiene factors – those which cause great dissatisfaction when they are not met or are 'wrong' – he is clearly mistaken on this point. Leadership, a word he did not use, is more than just part of someone's job context; in many instances it is integral to the job itself. You only have to look at the list in Figure 9.9 to see that leaders can play a large part in the 'motivators'. Here are some of the ways.

Achievement

The function of evaluating means that the leader will give both the group and the individual feedback when the task is achieved. Sometimes there is direct feedback to the group or individual not involving the leader, as when a football team scores the winning goal in a cup final or a construction crew contemplates a finished suspension bridge. In other situations the feedback may come via the leader, who then needs to communicate success to the group.

Recognition

Managers are sometimes tempted to claim the credit for themselves after a success. If so, they are thinking of their own advancement. As a leader, however, you should seize every opportunity to motivate people by recognizing their worth, services or contribution. Credit has to be shared, while you take the blame for yourself. At the first level of leadership, good leaders naturally meet recognition needs by acknowledging the contributions of individuals or of their team as a whole. If they receive some symbolic reward, such as a medal or citation, they interpret it as a recognition of the group's achievements as a whole. Equally, at a higher level, the leader may show recognition of the contributions of groups,

HYGIENE FACTORS	DEFINITION/EXAMPLE
Company policy and administration	Availability of clearly defined policies; degree of 'red tape', adequacy of communication; efficiency of organisation
Supervision	Accessibility, competence and personality of the boss
Interpersonal relations	The relations with supervisors, subordinates and colleagues; the quality of social life at work
Salary	The total rewards package, such as salary, pension, company car and other 'perks'
Status	A person's position or rank in relation to others, symbolised by title, parking space, car, size of office, furnishings etc.
Job security	Freedom from insecurity, such as loss of position or loss of employment altogether
Personal life	The effect of a person's work on family life e.g. stress, unsocial hours or moving house
Working conditions	The physical environment in which work is done; the degree of discomfort it causes

MOTIVATORS	DEFINITION
Achievement	Sense of bringing something to a successful conclusion, completing a job, solving a problem, making a successful sale. The sense of achievement is in proportion to the size of the challenge
Recognition	Acknowledgement of a person's contribution; appreciation of work by company or colleagues; rewards for merit
Job interest	Intrinsic appeal of job; variety rather than repetition; holds interest and is not monotonous or boring
Responsibility	Being allowed to use discretion at work, shown trust by company, having authority to make decisions; accountable for the work of others
Advancement	Promotion in status or job, or the prospect of it

Figure 9.9   Herzberg's two-factor theory

departments or units to the success or prospects of success of the whole organization.

The individuals or groups with high prestige or obviously vital functions tend to get all the recognition. A wise and able leader, however, will make sure that the apparently weak and insignificant individuals or groups also get their fair share of recognition. This equalizing work both promotes or builds up a sense of being a team and also meets the needs of some individuals (or groups) who would otherwise receive no recognition in the world's market place, where such rewards go naturally to the most powerful, best looking, most active or simply the most apt at edging themselves into the limelight.

Job interest

If work is to be restructured in order to allow more job satisfaction someone has to have the vision to undertake it and the consultative skills to bring about the change. That means leadership. In particular it calls upon the leader's organizing ability.

Responsibility

The leader is accountable for the results of his group. Marshal Pétain, when asked after the First World War, 'Marshal, did you personally win the Battle of Verdun?' replied, 'I've no idea, but I know very well who would have lost it'. But as a leader you should share the sense of responsibility as widely as possible.

The clue to developing responsibility is to extend the boundaries of trust. There can be an element of risk in this process, but there is no other practical alternative. Delegation, the entrusting of authority to someone to act as your deputy, is a major expression of trust and a means of creating responsibility. But delegation has some inherent risks that make otherwise excellent leaders reluctant to do it.

Advancement

Leaders play a vital part in promoting people. That gives them a certain power to motivate ambitious and able subordinates. They may not have the necessary jobs in their gift directly, but their word is often influential if not decisive. You can often motivate such an individual by reminding him that the prospects for advancement in position or status do exist.

Of course promotion is not a motivating force if it is not related to merit and performance. No one is going to work harder if advancement is reserved for the company's 'blue-eyed boys'. By stressing that ability and results are the necessary condition for promotion, you can create the right bracing atmosphere to motivate people to give their best.

Therefore, if you examine closely all the factors which positively motivate people at work, you can see that good leadership plays an important part in all of them. Consider your reactions to Herzberg's hygiene factors (see Figure 9.9), those elements that have the power to dissatisfy you if they are inadequate, but do not provide more than modest or short term satisfactions.

Leadership enters into all these factors whether we wish it to or not. If poor organization and an apparently unfair rewards system leaves people dissatisfied, someone has to organize things properly, and that 'someone' is usually a leader. Good leadership resolves most of the dissatisfying factors implicit in being supervised and working with others: much of this chapter has been concerned with just those interpersonal relations. Your leadership should also contribute to reducing insecurity.

Status as one's position or rank in relation to others is an inescapable fact of life in working groups and organizations. Roughly speaking, higher status goes to those individuals who contribute more or hold the more responsible jobs. Most dissatisfaction over status is caused by apparently petty grievances over status symbols, such as parking space, offices or job titles. These often are symptoms of a deeper disease. For example, a very competitive person may make an issue of not having an office of his own because he sees that a potential rival has one, and he fears that he is being left behind in the race for promotion. Here the cause – insecurity – must be treated, not the symptom.

Personal problems may be caused by the effect of work on family life or the reverse process – some unhappiness at home which is causing difficulties at work. A good leader is sensitive to the individual: he can detect changes in norms of behaviour. As a leader it is important for you to demonstrate in some way or other that you are aware and that you do care. Even if you can do little or nothing, as in the case of a bereavement, the very fact of showing your sympathy does matter. In many instances, however, you can do something yourself to remove the obstacle which is damming and diverting natural motivation.

To assess your skills and attitudes, consider the checklist in Figure 9.10.

A FUNCTIONAL APPROACH TO LEADERSHIP

The three approaches – qualities, situational and group – in the foregoing sections can be visualized as paths leading up to the summit of a mountain. If you go up one path you will be led nearer to the other two. In other words, rather than seeing them *as alternative* theories you should look upon them as *complementary* to each other. You may be content to hold all three approaches as distinct entities or 'paths' in your mind, or you may want some closer integration of them, a 'general theory' that will reconcile their differences.

In some respects I believe that the general approach that I have evolved over the last 20 years does serve to integrate or pull together those three threads. The functional leadership approach sees the functions as touching upon *all three circles*, either directly or indirectly. Moreover, it adds other functions to supplement the traditional list, especially in the team maintenance area. Functional leadership draws upon a number of traditions but subtly changes their offerings. The well established lists of management functions, for example, are applied to all three circles. Qualities can be interpreted in functional terms as well. Do they help you to achieve the task? Do they contribute to unity or are they disruptive? See Figure 9.11 for some examples.

Some qualities are especially important because they apply to all three circles – *enthusiasm* is an excellent example. Some enthusiasts are not leaders, but if you have the gift of enthusiasm you almost always will spark it off in other people. It

	Yes	No
Have you agreed with each of your subordinates his main targets and continuing responsibilities, together with standards of performance, so that you can both recognise achievement?	☐	☐
Do you recognise the contribution of each member of the group and encourage other team members to do the same?	☐	☐
In the event of success, do you acknowledge it and build on it? In the event of setbacks, do you identify what went well and give constructive guidance for improving future performance?	☐	☐
Can you delegate more? Can you give more discretion over decisions and more accountability to a sub-group or individual?	☐	☐
Do you show to those that work with you that you trust them, or do you hedge them around with unnecessary controls?	☐	☐
Are there adequate opportunities for training and (where necessary) retraining?	☐	☐
Do you encourage each individual to develop his capacities to the full?	☐	☐
Is the overall performance of each individual regularly reviewed in face to face discussion?	☐	☐
Does financial reward match contribution?	☐	☐
Do you make sufficient time to talk and listen, so that you understand the unique (and changing) profile of needs and wants in each person, so that you can work with the grain of nature rather than against it?	☐	☐
Do you encourage able people with the prospect of promotion within the organisation, or — if that is impossible — counsel them to look elsewhere for the next position fitting their merit?	☐	☐

Can you think of a manager by name who (a) delegates more effectively (b) less effectively than you do? What are the results in each case?

(a)

(b)

Figure 9.10   Checklist – motivating

Leadership characteristics	
Quality	Functional value
Task *Initiative*	A quality which appears in many research lists. It means the aptitude for initiating or beginning action; the ability to get the group moving
Perseverance	The ability to endure; tenacity. Obviously functional in many situations where the group is inclined to give up or is prey to frustration
Team *Integrity*	The capacity to integrate; to see the wood for the trees; to bind up parts into a working whole; the attribute that creates a group climate of trust
Humour	Invaluable for relieving tension in group or individual, or, for that matter, in the leader himself. Closely related to a sense of proportion, a useful asset in anything involving people!
Individual *Tact*	It expresses itself in action by showing sensitive perception of what is fit or considerate in dealing with others
Compassion	Individuals may develop personal problems both at home and work. The leader can show sympathetic awareness of this distress together with a desire to alleviate it

Figure 9.11   The functional approach to leadership qualities

produces greater commitment to the task, creates team spirit and enthuses the individual.

Other qualities are more latent. They can be called out and express themselves in behaviour in any of the three areas.

THE DIFFERENT LEVELS OF LEADERSHIP

Leadership happens on different levels. Originally work on leadership focused upon the small group. Recently my own work has extended the functional leadership concept to leaders at all levels within the sphere of work, including the chairmen and chief executives of organizations employing more than 100 000 people.

According to the well known 'Peter Principle', people tend to be promoted to the level of their incompetence. Some people are perfectly good leaders at one level, but they are less able to cope at the next level up. What can help you to determine your own level is your ability to appreciate the subtle changes which take place in the task, the team and the individual as you go higher up the mountain.

The three circles still apply. In the task area the top leader is concerned more with longer term and broader aims. In the team area he has the double job of building and maintaining his immediate team of senior executives, and promoting a sense of unity among the diverse parts of the organization. These two jobs are clearly interrelated. Again, the individual for him is both a senior leader – a known person in the senior team – and also each individual in the organization. The latter will not be known personally or even by name in organizations of more than 500 people, but the top leader still needs to think constantly about that individual – and talk to him whenever possible.

At whatever level of leadership you are fitted for, by nature, training and experience, you should encourage thought about the task in terms of values as well as needs. Then the common purpose will overlap with the values of the groups and individuals in the organization – including your own.

PRACTICAL LEADERSHIP CHECKLIST

The following checklist is a practical one, which you should apply to a situation you have recently experienced. It is derived from the Sandhurst List of Assessment Definitions. When you have completed it, count up your good, adequate and weak scores. If you have more than three adequate or weak ticks, you should take seriously the idea of getting some further leadership training.

GROUP INFLUENCE
The ability which enables an individual to bring about a willing effort on the part of the group towards achieving a desired objective/goal

Good	*Adequate*	*Weak*
as a leader, you were impressive throughout, obtaining a high degree of commitment from the group by an excellent personal example	you managed to convince the group to work to the achievement of the objective with adequate personal example	had little influence on the group to the extent that they ignored you

COMMAND
The ability to make up one's mind as quickly as the situation demands and carry through a course of action with firmness and strength of purpose

Good	*Adequate*	*Weak*
came to a decision quickly and effectively and was positive in implementing it	eventually came to a decision but displayed a certain lack of firmness in implementing it	unable to make up mind, got confused with conflicting information and hesitant in carrying through action

---

COOLNESS
The extent to which the leader remains cool and unperturbed under testing or trying conditions

Good	*Adequate*	*Weak*
calm, unruffled and in control of self; justifiably self confident	a reasonable and balanced confidence; comfortable in front of a group	under/over-confidence seriously impaired effectiveness and credibility as a leader

JUDGEMENT
Ability to arrange available resources and information in a systematic and commonsense way so as to produce effective results

Good	*Adequate*	*Weak*
shrewd and discerning, the leader saw his way through all complexities and was effective	showed commonsense and judged the task appropriately producing a satisfactory result	lack of commonsense and poor judgement gave rise to difficulties; lost credibility as a result

APPLICATION/RESPONSIBILITY
The demonstration of sustained effort combined with the degree of dependability in order to complete a task or achieve an objective

Good	*Adequate*	*Weak*
applied self thoroughly and energetically to the task showing determination and persistence	satisfactory industry and general determination to succeed	did not accept responsibility and was overwhelmed by the difficulties faced; showed little or no determination

FURTHER READING

Adair, John, *Effective Leadership: a self-development manual*, Gower, 1983.

Cribben, James J., *Effective Managerial Leadership*, American Management Association, 1977. A readable, research-based guide to the subject.

Hunt, John W., *Managing People at Work*, McGraw-Hill, 1979. A readable introductory guide to the fields of organizational behaviour – motivations, perception, communication, groups, roles, power, organizations, structures, managers, leaders, participation. Besides distilling some of the more enduring concepts and theories, the author does offer some interesting ideas of his own.

Garnett, John, *The Work Challenge*, The Industrial Society, 1973. Gives the Industrial Society's practical and down-to-earth approach to 'the human side of enterprise' with plenty of examples of good practice.

Prior, Peter J., *Leadership is not a Bowler Hat*, David and Charles, 1977. A rare example of a chief executive in industry giving his personal philosophy of leadership.

Gibb, C. A. (ed.), *Leadership: Selected Readings*, Penguin, 1969. An introduction to academic research on the subject. Some classic articles – and some opaque ones.

Stogdill, R. M., *Handbook of Leadership*, Free Press, 1974. This weighty book sets out to be a systematic analysis and review of the literature on leadership, and is undeniably a useful collation of the published evidence on this subject, but practical leaders are likely to find it of limited value. The 'Summary and discussion' in Chapter 40 may, however, be found useful.

Herzberg, F., et al., *The Motivation to Work*, Wiley, 1959, and *Work and the Nature of Man*, World Publishing Co., 1966.

McGregor, Douglas, *The Human Side of Enterprise*, McGraw-Hill, 1961.

Maslow, A. H., *Motivation and Personality*, Harper, 1954.

10 People skills

Dr Peter Honey

People come in all sorts of shapes and sizes, which is another way of saying that people are complex and infinitely variable. Remarkably, however, there are some fundamental skills for handling people that are not dauntingly complex. This chapter will introduce you to those fundamentals and give sufficient practical advice to help you become even more skilful with people.

The chapter is written on the assumption that you have already acquired some people skills through an ad hoc process of learning from experience. There will undoubtedly be things you already do well, that no longer require any conscious effort on your part. The problem is that, quite understandably, we all tend to stick to the tried and tested and therefore repeat over and over again the same skills. In effect, therefore, we stop acquiring any new skills and this may mean we risk having too narrow a repertoire of skills to equip us adequately for the variety of people situations we are likely to encounter. This chapter will encourage you to experiment and broaden your repertoire of people skills.

WHAT ARE PEOPLE SKILLS?

People skills are behaviours, used face to face, that succeed in helping progress towards a useful outcome. Let's separate these ingredients and examine them more carefully. *Behaviours* are everything you say and do. As we shall see they are important because they are so immediately apparent to everyone you come face to face with and therefore have a direct effect on other people. *Face to face* covers a whole multitude of different interactions between people. It might be an informal chat with someone or it might be a formal meeting with a group of people. The point is that it is only during face to face encounters that your behaviour is totally evident. During phone calls, by contrast, only what you *say* counts. Written communications are different because whilst what you write represents your behaviour even though you are not present, it isn't happening 'in flight' as is the case with face to face behaviours. A *useful outcome* is the third ingredient, for what would be the point of skills that led you to a useless outcome? The proof of the

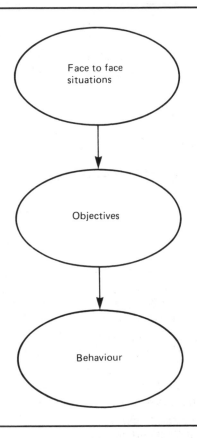

Figure 10.1   Behaviour is the means to achieving your objectives in face to face situations

pudding is in the eating and the proof of people skills is that they make it as likely as possible that we achieve our objectives with people.

The trick is to get all three ingredients to come together in a smooth and easy symmetry. Face to face situations provide the context, objectives spell out the desirable end and behaviours are the means (see Figure 10.1).

WHY THE EMPHASIS ON BEHAVIOUR?

Quite simply because your behaviour is the only part of you that other people can observe. So far as other people are concerned, you are your behaviour for they cannot observe your underlying thoughts, motives, attitudes or feelings (see Figure 10.2). It follows, therefore, that your behaviour influences:

- other people's perceptions of you (i.e. whether they like or dislike you, trust or mistrust you and so on);
- other people's reactions to you (i.e. whether they behave helpfully or unhelpfully towards you).

The only people skills that matter, therefore, are encapsulated in the things you say and do when face to face with other people: in a word your *behaviour*.

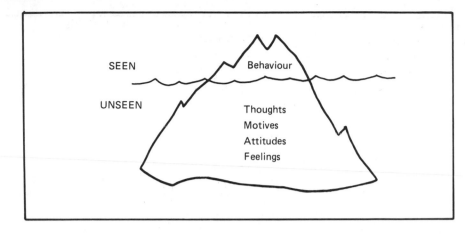

Figure 10.2   Your behaviour is the only part of you that other people can observe

WHAT ARE THE ADVANTAGES OF IMPROVED PEOPLE SKILLS?

There is no doubt that improving your people skills by extending your repertoire of behaviours is not easy. As with the acquisition of any skill it requires conscious effort as each skill is practised to the point where it becomes effortless. Since an investment of time and effort is required it is important to be sure that it will all be worthwhile. Some of the advantages of improved people skills are that you will be better at:

- Assessing and understanding face to face situations. You will thus benefit from fewer misunderstandings.
- Setting specific and realistic objectives for face to face encounters with people. You will thus benefit from being clear about what you are aiming at and successfully achieving it more often than not.
- Choosing and using behaviours that complement the circumstances and are appropriate to the objective. You will thus benefit by having an easier, and pleasanter, interaction en route to achieving your objective.
- Being aware of other people's behaviour and influencing it. You will thus benefit from being able to use your own behaviour as a powerful influence.

These are just some of the potential benefits of enhanced people skills. There are others which will emerge as the chapter pinpoints the skills more precisely.

CAN PEOPLE SKILLS BE IMPROVED?

The straight answer is yes, of course they can. You learned to behave the way you do now and there is nothing to stop you learning new behaviours. The secret of success is to learn from experience by:

- experimenting with new and different ways of behaving;
- reviewing what happened;
- concluding from the experience;
- planning what to do next (i.e. continue with the experiment, modify it to make it more successful, or try something quite different).

Unfortunately, people are often reluctant to embark on this learning process. There are all sorts of excuses to stay exactly the way you are now. 'You can't teach an old dog new tricks', 'leave well alone'. 'a leopard cannot change its spots'. Pessimism abounds. There is, however, nothing to prevent you from improving your people skills except yourself. If you don't want to enhance your skills, then no one or anything can force you to do so. The door to development is locked with the key on the inside. Other people can hammer on the door imploring you to open it; they can even entice you with attractive learning opportunities, but you and you alone hold the key. The choice is yours.

WHAT ARE THE FUNDAMENTAL PEOPLE SKILLS?

The fundamental skills are those which give us a process that is equally applicable in all situations. This is preferable to having a 'shopping list' of skills where the items on the list will inevitably vary in importance depending upon the situation. If, for example, you were in a foreign country where the water is suspect, then bottled water would be high on your shopping list. It would not, however, feature as a necessity on a shopping list in the UK. It is the same with people skills. If you are discussing how to solve a problem with a person who has more experience than you, then listening would be high on your list. If, on the other hand, you knew much more about what had to be done to solve the problem than the other person, then communicating clearly and testing the other person's understanding would be higher priorities.

We avoid this 'it all depends' qualification if we have a few fundamental skills on our list that apply in *all* situations. Just six are sufficient:

1 Analysing the situation.
2 Establishing a realistic objective.
3 Selecting appropriate ways of behaving.
4 Controlling our behaviour.
5 Shaping other people's behaviour.
6 Monitoring our own and others' behaviour.

The first three skills are essentially about thinking; the last three are about doing. It is the combination of both that is vital for there is no point in thinking without doing, nor in doing without thinking.

Notice also how these skills provide us with a timeless wisdom, applicable to all 'people situations' anywhere. Analysing the situation helps us to detect the circumstances that need to be heeded when setting a realistic objective. The objective, in turn, provides a backcloth against which to make choices about how best to behave. Each thinking skill cascades into the next and the three combined help us to be aware of the situation and to have worked out what to do about it. By consciously controlling our behaviour we are more likely to do the things that need to be done to achieve the objective. In so doing we influence other people's behaviour in the only way possible, via our own behaviour. And all the while we monitor, to keep tabs on what is happening and to get the feedback we need to make in-flight adjustments.

Let us look more carefully at each of these skills.

How to analyse situations

Remember that in the context of people skills we are concerned only with face to face situations. There are six key questions to ask of any situation you encounter:

1 Is the task/problem/subject matter to be discussed complex or routine?
2 On balance, who has the most know-how, you or the other people involved in the face to face discussion?
3 Is time very tight (as in a crisis) or is there sufficient time to discuss all aspects thoroughly before reaching a decision?
4 Is commitment from everyone essential or merely desirable?
5 Are the risks of making a mistake unacceptably high (financially and/or physically and/or from a credibility point of view) or are the risks within acceptable limits?
6 How many people will be present at the face to face discussion: just one other person, or a small group of say 6–8, or a medium sized group of 9–15, or a large group of 15 plus?

The answers to these key questions render enough data to move you on to the next skill.

How to set objectives for face to face interactions

An objective (for any activity, not just for face to face interactions) is a forecast of what you want to achieve at some point in the future. It might be a long term, medium term, or short term objective.

An immediate objective forecasts what you want to achieve by the end of the interaction.

Here is a recommended procedure for setting an immediate objective: First set yourself an *end result*. Do this by answering the question 'What do I want to achieve by the end of the interaction?' Second, work out some *indicators of success*. Do this by answering the question 'How shall I know that I have successfully achieved my end result?'

Here is an example of an objective set this way. Imagine you are going to meet someone (let's call him Bill) for the first time and you want to get off to a good start with him.

End result

• By the end of the meeting I will have established rapport with Bill.

Indicators of success

• Bill has asked at least six questions about me/my work.
• Bill has 'opened up' to me about a significant current problem.
• Bill has relaxed sufficiently to volunteer at least a couple of personal details (about outside interests, family, etc.).
• We have booked a date, time and place for our next meeting.

- Bill has specifically asked me to provide some additional data for our next meeting.

All achieved within 1½ hours (longer than Bill originally scheduled, i.e. he was 'happy' to overrun).

How to select appropriate behaviour

The secret is to limit the choices so that the vast spectrum of different behaviours is reduced to something manageable. It is best to think of your behaviour as a mixture of verbal (i.e. the things you say) and visual (i.e. the non-verbal things you do such as facial expressions, gestures with hands and arms and so on). Both verbal and visual aspects need attention. Let us look at verbal behaviour first.

Verbal behaviour

Limit yourself, at least initially until you become practised at using this method, to nine alternative behaviours:

1 *Seeking ideas.* Asking other people for their ideas.
2 *Proposing.* Putting forward ideas (possible courses of action) as statements.
3 *Suggesting.* Putting forward ideas as questions (i.e. 'How about doing so and so?').
4 *Building.* Developing someone else's idea.
5 *Disagreeing.* Explicitly disagreeing with something someone else has said.
6 *Supporting.* Agreeing with something someone else has said.
7 *Difficulty stating.* Pointing out the snags or difficulties with something someone else has said.
8 *Seeking clarification/information.* Asking other people for further clarification or information.
9 *Clarifying/explaining/informing.* Giving information, opinions and explanations.

These nine behaviours are not an exhaustive list but you will find they give you adequate scope. When it comes to selecting the most appropriate behavioural recipe, think of the behaviours as offering you a series of alternatives in the following way.

In a face to face interaction you could either:

seek ideas	or	give ideas (proposing or suggesting)
build	or	disagree
support	or	state difficulty
seek clarification/ information	or	give clarification/ explanation or information

You will quickly see that the left hand side is a recipe for being participative and supportive towards other people. By contrast the right hand side is a recipe for being more directive and challenging towards other people. In the case of meeting Bill for the first time (see page 157) with the objective of establishing rapport with him, clearly the left hand behaviours are going to be more appropriate than the right hand ones. This will not always be so. With a different objective, an alternative mix of behaviours would be necessary. This illustrates the importance of first being clear about the objective, and second, thinking about which behaviours are appropriate to achieve it. As the objective alters so will the recipe of appropriate behaviours.

Visual behaviour

Visual or non-verbal behaviour covers a wide range of different aspects including:

- facial expressions;
- eyes;
- hand movements;
- gestures with hands and arms;
- leg movements;
- body posture;
- spatial distance and orientation.

In addition, there are some fringe areas such as clothes, physique and general appearance.

There is overwhelming evidence that visual behaviours play a larger part in communications between people than is usually supposed.

It seems that, without necessarily being able to describe how they do it, people make judgements and form impressions based on the visual behaviours they see other people using. Perhaps the most dramatic example of this is when people meet for the first time. Within seconds visual behaviours are sending signals which create a favourable or an unfavourable impression. Initial judgements are formed about whether the other person is friendly or unfriendly, confident or timid, trustworthy or untrustworthy, nice or nasty. Sometimes these first impressions are so strong that they linger stubbornly and defy revision even when different signals are being transmitted by subsequent visual behaviours.

Clearly the great advantage of thinking about your visual as well as your verbal behaviour is that you can choose visual behaviours that help rather than hinder progress towards your objective. You may be in the habit of using some visual behaviours that run the risk of giving the other person a poor impression of you. The secret of success is to concentrate on some simple combinations. If you do just one thing in isolation it probably will not have the desired effect because people gain a general, overall impression from a combination of:

- your facial expression and head movements;
- gestures with your hands and arms;
- the rest of your body including your legs.

All three aspects need to be practised so that they all come together to give the right impression.

Here are some combinations of visual behaviours. Practise doing less of the left hand ones and more of the right hand ones.

People will tend to see you as **defensive** if you:	If you want to come across as **friendly and cooperative** adopt the following combinations:
Face and head Don't look at the other person. Avoid eye contact or immediately look away when it happens.	*Face and head* Look at the other person's face. Smile. Nod your head as the other person is talking.
Hands and arms Clench your hands. Cross your arms. Constantly rub an eye, nose or ear.	*Hands and arms* Have open hands. Hand to face occasionally. Uncross arms.
Body Lean away from the other person. Cross your legs. Swivel your feet towards the door.	*Body* Uncross legs. Lean forward slightly. Move closer to the other person.
People will tend to see you as **anxious** if you:	If you want to appear **confident** adopt the following combinations:
Face and head Blink your eyes frequently. Lick your lips. Keep clearing your throat.	*Face and head* Look into the other person's eyes. Don't blink your eyes. Thrust your chin forward.
Hands and arms. Open and close your hands frequently. Put your hand over your mouth while speaking. Tug at an ear.	*Hands and arms* Keep hands away from your face. 'Steeple' your finger tips together. If standing, have hands together behind you in an 'at ease' position.
Body Fidget in your chair. Jig your feet up and down.	*Body* If seated, lean back with legs out in front of you. If standing, keep straight. Stay still, no sudden movements, no wriggling.

People will tend to see you as **overbearing** and **aggressive** if you:	If you want to appear **thoughtful** try the following combinations:
Face and head Stare at the other person. Have a wry 'I've heard it all before' type smile. Raise your eyebrows in exaggerated amazement or disbelief. Look over the top of spectacles. *Hands and arms* Point your finger at the other person. Thump your fist on the table. Rub the back of your neck. *Body* Stand while the other person remains seated. Stride around. If seated, lean right back with both hands behind your head and legs splayed.	*Face and head* When listening, look at the other person for about three quarters of the time. Tilt your head to one side slightly. *Hands and arms* Hand to cheek. Slowly stroke your chin or pinch the bridge of your nose. If you wear spectacles, take them off and put an earframe in your mouth. *Body* Lean forward to speak. Lean back to listen. Keep your legs still (no jiggling).

How to control your behaviour

Obviously there is little point in using the first three skills (analysing the situation, setting objectives and selecting appropriate behaviours) if, come the important face to face interaction, you fail to keep your behaviour under control. The whole point of controlling your behaviour is to avoid doing things that will be detrimental to achieving your objective and to force yourself to do sufficiently the things that will aid and abet its achievement. The word 'force' is used deliberately since you will undoubtedly find that, initially at any rate, you will need to stick consciously to a behaviour plan. You are more likely to be able to do this if your plan is:

- specific in spelling out precisely which verbal and visual behaviours to use;
- realistic in pinpointing a few key behaviours to use or avoid, rather than being over-ambitious by listing too much.

The other important aid to good control is to be selective about when you will consciously practise using your people skills. Initially, it may be sensible to choose face to face interactions where the risks of making mistakes or being more hesitant than usual are not too great. It also helps to practise on people who are likely to be supportive of your efforts rather than apathetic or hostile.

How to shape other people's behaviour

This is the key to the whole business. Clearly if your behaviour made no difference to the reactions of the people you dealt with then people skills would be of no

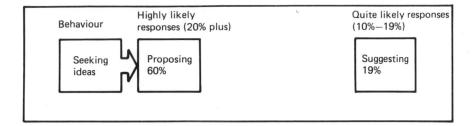

Figure 10.3   Responses to seeking ideas

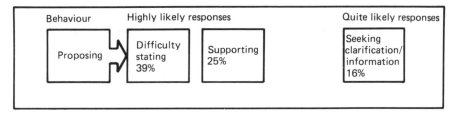

Figure 10.4   Responses to proposing

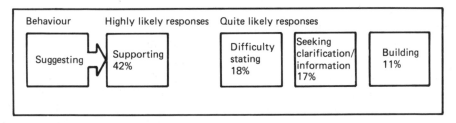

Figure 10.5   Responses to suggesting

consequence and this chapter would never have been included in this Handbook. The plain fact is, however, that the way you behave has a considerable influence on the way other people behave in face to face situations. The precise effects of the verbal behaviours have been more thoroughly investigated than those of the visual behaviours. Let us look at each behaviour in turn and see their shaping abilities.

Seeking ideas is a powerful behaviour. Nine times out of ten it is successful in provoking some ideas from the other person (Figure 10.3). It is a helpful behaviour to use whenever you need to pick someone else's brains.

Proposing ideas unfortunately provokes difficulties or objections more often than it wins support (Figure 10.4). If you want to 'flush out' people's reservations then proposing is a good behaviour to use. If, on the other hand, you want to make it more likely that there will be agreement to your idea then the next behaviour is a safer bet.

Suggesting ideas is a more effective way of gaining agreement than proposing ideas (Figure 10.5). There are, of course, no guarantees that it will succeed because your idea may be such a rotten one that even though it is suggested it

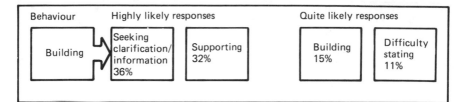

Figure 10.6   Responses to building

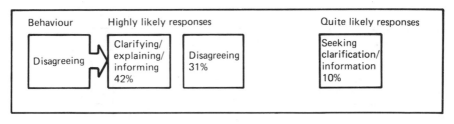

Figure 10.7   Responses to disagreeing

runs into difficulties. The actual statistics reveal that four times out of ten a suggestion is followed by an agreement and that isn't a bad rate.

Building on someone else's idea is a powerful way to get their wholehearted support. Despite this, building is a fairly rare behaviour. It seems that people find it easier to find fault with ideas than to build them up into something better (Figure 10.6). This is a good example of having a choice. People who think about their behaviour are more likely to try building than people who are in the habit of immediately criticizing ideas. The fact that seeking clarification is so prevalent reminds us what a potentially confusing behaviour building can be. The lesson is to 'flag' building so that people are in no doubt, and then supporting and more building are the most likely reactions.

Disagreeing on seven out of ten occasions triggers a defensive reaction or even further disagreements (Figure 10.7). It is interesting how often people get locked into a disagreeing 'spiral' where one disagreement breeds another which, in turn, breeds another and so on. Disagreeing is very much a last resort. It is best to try some of the more constructive options first.

Agreeing with something someone else has said is a powerful way to encourage them to go on and say more. Eight times out of ten this will be the effect (Figure 10.8). Agreeing is therefore a useful behaviour if you want to gain more information from the other person. It isn't an appropriate behaviour if you want them to shut up.

Pointing out difficulties is a very common behaviour but it is one of the riskier ones because research shows that it is far from certain how people will take it (Figure 10.9). Marginally, the most likely reaction is to offer some clarification or explanation. However, people often take umbrage and start disagreeing or, if you persist with difficulties, they may give up and go and find someone more positive to talk to. You need to watch carefully to see whether pointing out difficulties is hindering or helping the proceedings.

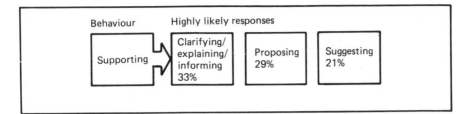

Figure 10.8   Responses to supporting behaviour

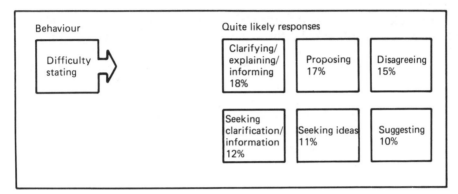

Figure 10.9   Responses to difficulty stating

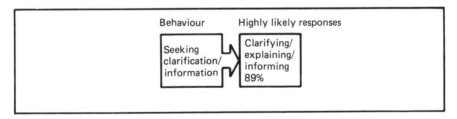

Figure 10.10   Responses to seeking clarification/information

No suprises with the next category (Figure 10.10). If you ask for clarification then nine times out of ten you will get it. Seeking clarification is a frequent behaviour that exerts a powerful influence over the behaviour of the other person. This is very useful behaviour when trying to get to the bottom of things and when you need to tease information out of the other person.

Informing is the behaviour that happens more often than any other in conversation between people. This isn't surprising, of course, since the overall purpose of talking with someone is to impart information of some kind. The most interesting aspect is how informing breeds informing, which breeds informing and so on in what can be a time-consuming loop (Figure 10.11). Sometimes this is appropriate and necessary. At other times the loop amounts to going round in circles and not getting anywhere fast enough.

The reason why people often prolong the informing loop is because it is a

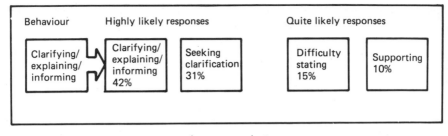

Figure 10.11   Responses to clarifying/explaining/informing

relatively 'safe' way to pass the time. When you offer a piece of information, you don't commit yourself in quite the same way that you do when you propose or suggest an idea.

The lesson from all this? Simply that the behaviours you use have known shaping effects on the behaviours you get back from other people. The data underline the fact that you are more likely to succeed with people if you think about your behaviour and select and use behaviours that help rather than hinder progress towards your objective. This process is enhanced still further if you adopt visual behaviours that reinforce what you are saying. It is the combination of verbal and visual that has the desired effect.

How to monitor your own and others' behaviour

This is purely a matter of practice. Since all behaviour, whether verbal or visual, is observable in a straightforward way there is no reason why you shouldn't develop your powers of observation. When you next attend a 'boring' meeting where some of the agenda items do not directly involve you, try monitoring the behaviour of the participants. See if you can spot the differences between proposing and suggesting, disagreeing and difficulty stating. Count how many times clarification is sought and given. Study people's attempts to build on one another's ideas. Scrutinize each person in turn to see what non-verbal characteristics they display when they are speaking as opposed to when they are listening. Watch to see when people lean forward in their chairs and when they lean back. Monitor who speaks to whom. Are any patterns that emerge associated with where people are seated round the table? There is no end to it, and certainly there is no excuse for being bored at a meeting ever again! Another obvious source of practice is when watching television, especially debating programmes such as *Question Time*. To study visual behaviour, just turn the sound down.

The whole idea of gaining practice in these ways is so that monitoring behaviour becomes second nature. When you yourself are a busy participant in an interaction it is best to monitor behaviour on an exception basis rather than try to cope with everything. So, for example, concentrate on the unexpected behaviours. If you were hoping that someone would be positive and develop your ideas, be especially alert to their disagreeing and difficulty stating and think hard about how best to respond to nudge their behaviour towards building and supporting. (Do this by being careful to suggest rather than propose and by seeking ideas from them and proceeding to build on them yourself. There are always hopeful things you can do *if* you use your people skills).

ARE THERE ALTERNATIVE PEOPLE SKILLS?

That concludes our examination of the six fundamental people skills. Acquiring them is not easy but the advantages of doing so are considerable and the skills are both sensible and pragmatic.

There are, of course, many different ways of describing people skills. We have focused purely on verbal and visual behaviours. Once you have mastered the fundamentals, what other skills could you practise? For the sake of brevity we will finish the chapter by looking at three interesting possibilities.

Management styles

You might find it useful to think about your characteristic style of management, when it is appropriate and when it isn't, and when to adopt consciously a different style from your usual one. One of the simplest ways to classify alternative management styles is shown in Figure 10.12.

Since most managers seem to find it easier to be directive than to use the other styles it is good advice to:

- think delegative first;
- if delegative is inappropriate in the circumstances then next think collaborative;
- if collaborative is inappropriate in the circumstances then next think consultative;
- if consultative is inappropriate then go ahead and be directive.

This plan ensures that you consider all the alternatives. All four styles are appropriate at some time. The skills we looked at earlier of analysing situations and establishing objectives are the key to deciding when to use which management style.

Ego states

You might have come across an approach to people skills called transactional analysis. It originated from the bestseller *Games People Play* by Dr Eric Berne. A core concept in transactional analysis is a framework for describing three different ways of behaving.

The three behaviour categories, or ego states, are called Parent, Adult and Child. In TA they are distinguished from *real* parents, adults and children by the use of capital letters.

Parent behaviour stems from feelings about what is proper, right and wrong. This provides discipline and protection. The Parent speaks in dogmatic, autocratic terms with a heavy emphasis on controlling. Parent behaviour is subdivided into:

- Critical Parent behaviour: critical, prejudicial, moralizing or punitive. Typical non-verbal clues are the pointed finger, shaking head, handwringing, arms folded, foot tapping, wrinkled brow, sighing, impatient snorts and grunts.

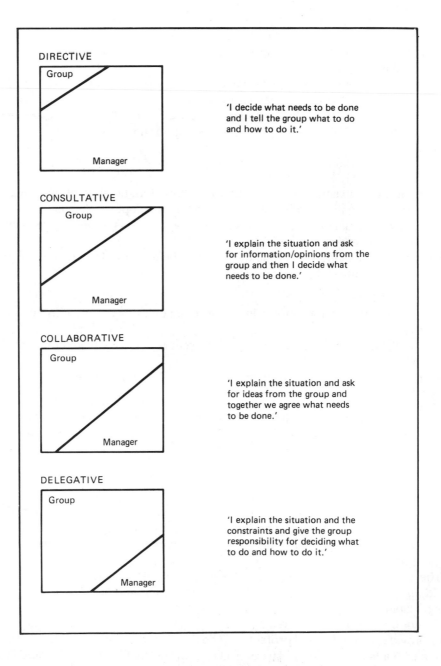

Figure 10.12   Alternative management styles

Typical verbal clues are 'always, never, remember, you ought to know better, you should do better, don't do that, you should never do that, that's wrong, stupid, ridiculous, absurd, how dare you'.

- Nurturing Parent behaviour: nurturing, protective, sympathetic and comforting. Non-verbal examples are: a comforting touch, patting a person on the shoulder, consoling sounds. Verbal examples are: 'there, there, you poor thing, try again, don't worry'.

Adult behaviour involves gathering information, evaluating it and using it to make, and implement decisions. The Adult has the capacity to monitor and, if necessary, update Parent and Child tapes. Adult behaviour stems from thinking rather than feeling. Non-verbal examples are: postures indicating interest, listening, thinking and generally being 'with it'. Verbal examples are: 'why, what, where, when, who, how, alternatives, possible, probably, relatively, practical, feasible'.

Child behaviour stems from feelings, either of joy or of sorrow, and, therefore, tends to be spontaneous. Child behaviour is subdivided into:

- Natural Child behaviour is entirely dictated by feelings; it includes being impulsive, inquisitive, curious, affectionate and playful. NC is also fearful, self-indulgent, self-centred, rebellious and aggressive. Non-verbal examples are: tears, temper tantrums, no answer, biting lower lip, downcast eyes, shoulder shrugging. Verbal examples are: 'look at me!, Nobody loves me. That's mine, can't, won't, that's fun, I love you, whoopee!'
- Adapted Child behaviour is a toned down version of Natural Child: it is literally an adaptation of completely natural impulses so that they are more acceptable to other people. Non-verbal examples are: giggling, teasing, flirting, pouting and whining. Verbal examples are: 'please, thank you, I wish, I'll try, please help me, I don't care, I don't know'.

The whole idea of this classification system is to have a practical method of monitoring different modes of behaviour in ourselves and in others we encounter. A main tenet in transactional analysis is to practise using our Adult ego states to weigh up situations and decide whether Parent, Child or Adult behaviour would best suit. In other words, the Adult is encouraged to use the six basic skills that we examined earlier in this chapter. Many people have found the ego states a helpful way of looking at behaviour and bringing it under conscious control.

Assertiveness

Finally, you might find the assertiveness approach a useful way to enhance your people skills. This approach tends to specialize on behaviour in tricky situations where your needs are in conflict with the needs of other people. Such situations are made worse or better depending on how you handle them. Broadly you have three choices. You can be assertive, submissive, or aggressive.

Assertive behaviour involves standing up for your own rights in such a way that you do not violate another person's rights and expressing thoughts, feelings and beliefs in direct, honest and appropriate ways.

For example, someone keeps disagreeing with your ideas. An assertive response would be:

I appreciate that you want to see improvements as much as I do, and yet you keep finding fault with my ideas. What can I suggest that would be more acceptable to you?

So assertiveness is based on the beliefs that we have needs to be met, others have needs to be met; we have something to contribute, others have something to contribute. It is characterized by statements that value ourselves and also value others.

Submissive behaviour – you are being submissive when you:

- fail to stand up for your rights or do so in such a way that others can easily disregard them;
- express your thoughts, feelings and beliefs in apologetic, diffident or self-effacing ways;
- fail to express honest thoughts, feelings or beliefs.

For example, someone keeps disagreeing with your ideas. A submissive response would be:

Well, I suppose you've got a point. My ideas probably wouldn't have worked out in practice.

So submission is based on the belief that our own needs and wants are less important than those of other people. It is characterized by long, justifying explanations, often putting ourselves down whilst accommodating others.

Aggressive behaviour. You are being aggressive when you:

- stand up for your own rights in such a way that you violate the rights of another person;
- express thoughts, feelings and beliefs which may be honest or dishonest, but in inappropriate ways.

For example, someone keeps disagreeing with your ideas. An aggressive response would be:

To hell with all your objections. Just listen to me and I'll spell out what I want to happen.

So aggression enhances ourselves at other people's expense; it puts the other person down. It is based on a belief that our opinions are more important than other people's. It is characterized by blaming other people, blaming outside factors, by showing contempt and by being hostile/attacking or by being patronizing.

The assertiveness approach urges us, when faced with a conflict situation, to hang on to assertive behaviour rather than succumbing to our emotions and either being submissive or aggressive. Once again this is only possible if we think about our behaviour *vis-à-vis* the situation we are in and the objectives we wish to achieve.

CONCLUSION AND CHECKLIST

Here, finally, is a checklist (Figure 10.13) of behaviours that hinder and behaviours that help. It is not an exhaustive list but you will find more than enough to

HINDERING BEHAVIOURS	HELPING BEHAVIOURS
Lean away with hands clenched, arms crossed and legs crossed	Lean forward with hands open, arms uncrossed and legs uncrossed
Look at the other person for less than 50% of the time	Look at the other person for approximately 60% of the time
Listen silently with no continuity noises and/or interrupt before the other person has had their say	When listening nod and make 'I'm listening' noises such as 'um' 'yes' 'really'
Have a blank expression	Smile
Sit opposite the other person	Sit beside the other person or if this isn't possible, at a 90° angle to them
Don't use the other person's name or use it artificially so that it jars	Use the other person's name early on in the transaction
Don't ask questions or ask closed questions	Ask the other person open questions
Offer no summaries and don't check your understanding	Summarise back to the other person what you think they have said
Stick rigidly to saying things that are routine and standard	Say things that refer back to what the other person has said
Don't acknowledge the other person's expressed feelings or point of view	Show empathy by saying you understand how the other person feels and can see things from their point of view
Acquiesce or never explicitly agree with the other person	When in agreement with the other person, openly say so and say why
Pick holes in the other person's ideas	Build on the other person's ideas
Criticise the other person	Be non-judgemental towards the other person
Disagree first then say why	If you have to disagree with the other person, give the reason first then say you disagree
Be defensive and never admit to any inadequacy	Admit it when you don't know the answer or have made a mistake
Be secretive and withhold information from the other person even though it affects them	Openly explain what you are doing, or intending to do, for the other person
Have visual and verbal behaviours out of step with each other	Be genuine, with visual and verbal behaviours telling the same story
Remain aloof and don't touch the other person	Whenever possible, touch the other person
Don't give the other person anything	Give the other person something even if it is only a name card, or piece of paper with notes on it

Figure 10.13   Checklist – hindering and helping behaviours

start you off. To succeed, practise doing less of the hindering behaviours and more of the helpful behaviours.

Remember the choice is yours and, so far as other people are concerned, *you are your behaviour.*

FURTHER READING

If Looks could Kill: The Power of Behaviour, Video Arts, 1986

Honey, Peter, *Face to Face: A Practical guide to Interactive Skills,* Gower, 2nd edition 1988

Back, Ken and Back, Kate, *Assertiveness at Work: A practical guide,* McGraw-Hill, 1982

Morrison, James H. and Hearne, J. J., *Practical Transactional Analysis in Management,* Addison-Wesley, 1977

11 Recruitment

John Courtis

People are a major resource common to all organizations. Money is the other and you need the people to obtain and use the money properly, even in a non-profit-making environment.

It follows that obtaining and using the people properly is also important. Most employees are 'obtained' by a process known as recruitment. This has parallels with the procurement process, in that you aim to get the right people in the right place at the right time, for the right price.

Purchasing (or buying or procurement) is generally done by professionals. Recruitment is generally done by amateurs, unprofessionally. There are parallels with child rearing. Most people only have their parents' example to guide them when they in turn try to raise the next generation. Previous faults are repeated. So it is with recruitment. Everyone believes they know something about recruitment because they have themselves been recruited. It is not wholly surprising that simple errors are repeated and even presented as good practice. This is bad news for the victims (and in these cases everyone is damaged by bad recruitment – the candidates, peers, bosses and the organization itself) but good news for anyone who is prepared to take a fresh look at recruitment policy and practice.

This chapter offers a menu for such a review. It cannot be encyclopaedic but it should make it possible for you to improve most aspects of the process. There is an added bonus. Recruitment divides naturally into seven stages and being only 10% better at each stage multiplies up to an improvement approaching 95%. If the 1990s have their fair share of skills shortages, such an improvement must give you a head start over the competition, i.e. the Unprofessionals.

First, the seven stages from which we shall build our menu:

- Is there really a vacancy and for what?
- How are we to find the candidates?
- How do we process the results through to interview?
- Interviews (see Chapter 12).
- The selection decision and relevant tools.
- Offer and contract.

- Induction.

All of these are important and in each phase it is well to remember a very old piece of advice: 'Do unto others as you would be done by'. Candidates are people. They are also potential customers. On both levels, good practice pays dividends.

Good practice, as in many areas, starts with the basic advice – Read the instructions. This chapter is only part of the instructions. Other books and management media are worth attention too. Even the national daily and Sunday papers are printing some sound advice as part of their continuing efforts to enhance their credibility as recruitment media.

One thing the media may forget to tell you is that the comparison with the purchasing function is only part of the context. Good recruitment is also a marketing exercise. The employer is not allowed to turn the open door into an obstacle course or a high security minimum disclosure ego trip. The best candidates will only be attracted by open and interesting advertisements, letters or other approaches – in short, a direct marketing programme. Helping your colleagues to think like this about recruitment may be one of the most helpful things anyone can do for them. Reminding them of the level of disclosure and attention they might welcome if they were in the job market may also help. Or asking 'How would you want your husband/wife/children to be treated?' may be necessary if it becomes obvious that they are masochists about the obstacles.

Conditioning is important. There is little point in practising properly if your colleagues are dedicated to mediocrity or, worse but not unusually, are working against what you are trying to achieve. Nowhere is this more apparent than in the politics and practice of defining the vacancy and the candidate – the first phase of the seven.

IS THERE A JOB? AND WHAT IS THE CANDIDATE SPECIFICATION?

The first query is very important. Busy managers tend to assume that resignations create vacancies; or that too much work implies a need for more employees. Neither is the correct starting point. In both cases the initial reaction should be to analyse the work involved and to ask:

- What are the tasks, objectives and benefits?
- Is the work really necessary?
- Could we avoid, reduce, reallocate, mechanise or sub-contract it?
- What would happen if we did not do it?

The same ruthless attitude should be applied to defining the minimum candidate. Not the ideal, the minimum. Both are important but the ideal is a luxury, whereas the minimum is the more realistic yardstick, particularly if someone is looking for a clone of the departed job-holder or for someone who has done the job before somewhere else.

In the former case, it is important to point out that even if the lost paragon was good, he or she came into the job with much less experience, and it may be correct to go back to their entry standards as the baseline. Equally, good people who have done the job before seldom want to do a replica thereof, unless there is something new and exciting about the environment or the problems. Specify again, from a clean sheet of paper. Accountants love zero-based budgeting. Make them practise zero-based candidate specifications or all the marginal jobs in the accounts department will be filled by qualified accountants and, elsewhere, jobs that A level entrants could do will be filled by graduates. If they are so filled, it won't be for long. The best people will realize they are under-employed. Only the mediocre will stay.

The worst political problem is usually the manager who needs support staff to support his or her (usually his) ego. Empire building is common. Fortunately, most managers are assessed on financial and headcount budgets. Reminding the culprits of the performance benefits of running a tight ship should be an adequate counter argument. If a new job is involved, the nuisance of getting budget approval should be an adequate deterrent. If a replacement, the reflected glory of making 'headcount savings' may be an adequate carrot unless the culprit is very backward. In which case a different headcount saving may be worth considering.

HOW DO WE FIND THE RIGHT PEOPLE?

The sourcing decision is not just about the sources you choose. It is also about timing. Proper attention to the questions posed in the previous phase should have identified that the performance of the job will increase revenues, reduce costs or otherwise pay for itself, preferably several times over. If this is not so, have another think about the rationale for recruiting.

If the job is worth doing, it is worth doing *now*, unless your people planning is so good that you are recruiting at leisure for a forecast future need. It follows that the choice of source(s) must recognize a degree of urgency. 'Saving' money by choosing a cheap, slow or unreliable sourcing programme will actually cost money because the job is not being done fully or at all.

It is important to remember this as we review the sources, some of which cost thousands of pounds, some of which are free. These include:

- people you already know, including ex-employees and past applicants;
- direct advertising, supported by a sound advertising agency;
- employment agencies and registers;
- selection consultants, plus advertising;
- search consultants (headhunters);
- DIY search, using your own network;
- contact with local or specialist redundancy situations, direct or via outplacement consultancies.

The first one is seldom mentioned, but is often a significant ingredient, particularly if there is a policy of retaining past applications; if there is not, start one. And do not be afraid to talk to past employees who have the massive advantage that you know their merits better than any interview and many tests can show.

As with direct advertising, DIY headhunting and trawls of redundancies you remain in control of the programme. The key question is whether the chances of a successful appointment justify sticking to these sources. In many cases, unless you are looking for scarce skills, you can avoid agency and consultancy fees, but probably not some advertising costs.

Advertising, properly written and placed in the right medium, on the advice of a competent agency, can be successful and cost-effective. The difficulty is to ensure that the professional route is followed without amateur interference. In brief, the advertising copy should achieve a high level of disclosure about the organization, the job, rewards, problems, opportunities, location and reply method sought. Non-disclosure, tricky copy, poor typography, wasted space, verbiage and onerous reply instructions all erode response. Poor disclosure of the candidate requirement and rewards also ensures a high level of junk replies and a reduced level of good ones – or none at all.

The only problem with advertising agencies is that they get paid by the media, in the form of a discount on the space cost, so there is a tendency for them to write longer copy than is strictly necessary and to use more space in more expensive media. Good ones don't fall into this trap, because they know that in the long run the client does notice the balance between costs and results. If you want to eliminate the temptation you could negotiate a fee-based reward system, with all the media discount credited to the organization and a further incentive for reducing average costs per hiring.

The use of agencies and consultants is more complicated. They exist because they satisfy employers' needs and you have to decide for yourselves which of the many firms satisfy yours. The services on offer can be summarized crudely as follows:

- No-sale, no-fee access to a database of relevant candidates;
- Genuine consulting advice on all aspects of the job and related variables, plus advertising support;
- Search competence;
- Selection competence, i.e. an ability to relieve you of most of the processing burden and deliver a shortlist which has been objectively assembled as well as you could do it, or better;
- The time to concentrate on the recruitment task as a priority;
- Test administration, reference checking, etc;
- And of course a mixture of any or all of the above.

Other things being equal, the quality of the service will vary with the quality of your organization's input. Proper disclosure by the client company is a key factor in getting results out of the agent.

PROCESSING THE RESULTS

The same principles apply whether you are reviewing the results of an advertising campaign, a bundle of CVs from an agency or more informal data from the other possible sources. From the moment you establish contact with the potential employee, you are involved in a marketing exercise in parallel with the selection process. As indicated above, the same applies to your contacts with consultants and agencies. Bad behaviour by your staff will be noticed and cost you goodwill, service, good candidates and money in the future. It can also make your organization a laughing stock or drag you to an industrial tribunal. This applies to everything from discourtesy, through incompetence, to accidental or deliberate discrimination against minority groups.

The IPM Recruitment Code is an excellent starting point on this front. It is too long to reproduce here but single copies are obtainable direct from the IPM (see Further Reading for details).

The recruitment trade association, FRES, also produces a pragmatic leaflet entitled *Opportunities For All* which makes the commercial case for avoiding discrimination and is therefore a useful tool for convincing colleagues who don't care much about good practice or the niceties of employment law.

Good practice is good marketing; and vice-versa. The quality of ad replies and their relevance will increase in direct proportion to the level of disclosure you achieve and the quality of the reply instructions. The warmth and practicality of those instructions also help. Make the process easier and people are more likely to think well of you. People with rare skills are often the most demanding of candidates. Good practice can solve skills shortages, providing much more than the modest 10% improvement suggested earlier if the rare bird is attracted to your presentation and rejects the competition.

The effect will be enhanced if you generate enough information to permit interview decisions without the necessity for candidates to complete application forms. Sending candidates a brief about the organization, job and candidate specification also helps retain their interest and lets them help you in the selection process in that if there is no real match they can cry off without a meeting.

The same applies to flexibility over interview timing, which can make you look more professional and more sympathetic. And there is another side to the coin. If you achieve high standards in the pre-interview process you are in a better position to look at the candidates' actions and decide whether they meet your standards. If you have been unhelpful or cavalier in your corporate behaviour, it is not a fair test to expect impeccable reactions, whereas poor reactions to good behaviour are in some ways a work sample – and one to beware of.

Finally, the other under-recognized area in the pre-interview process is the difficulty of comparing the different results from the various sources. A CV prepared by a candidate may be less over-written than one prepared by an agency, but more so than a report from a good consultant. Similarly, the limited amount of data volunteered by a search target or someone whom you have found through your network may do less than justice to the individual. And the ex-employees' records may be on a warts and all basis. It is vital to allow for these differences or you may end up with an interview programme which is totally unbalanced, toward the incorrigible optimists. And people are seldom better than their track records, provided that you have the full record!

Interviews

Most of this subject is covered in the wider chapter on pages 181 but there is one point about attitudes which must be applied by everyone in the interview pro-gramme. It is simple. Interviews are designed to help you gather information, so that you can determine how well the candidates would perform in your environ-ment, usually in a specific job. They are not supposed to lead only to the first (subjective) reason why the candidate will not fit. If your colleagues interview on the latter basis, they will not accumulate enough data to make an intelligent comparison between candidates at the later stage when you find that between you you have vetoed ALL the candidates and must think again!

As a minimum discipline I would now recommend that all notes of interviews indicate clearly the extent to which each candidate meets or approaches the specification, with objective reasons for rejection. If the interviewers cannot understand this instruction, perhaps they should not be interviewing. One useful guide is to insist that all interviewers have agreed the candidate specification before the start of the exercise and that later rejections relate to matters covered by the specification. Introducing new criteria later is not on.

DECISIONS, DECISIONS

Well, you've done the interviews and perhaps the tests, reviewed the track records and taken up those references which can be sought without damaging the candidates' current employment or position in his or her incestuous little world. If you have not done all these you are not yet in a position to make a valid comparison between the candidates, not least because the interview has a poor record as a predictor of work performance. It can be made better, if properly structured, but formal tests are significantly better. So are work samples and, if referees are given the right context and questions, so are informal references (face-to-face or by telephone, please; the written reference is usually just a parlour game about euphemisms).

There is no space here to explore the shades of grey which usually have to be compared in making the selection decision. Too many variables, little weighting and no way of knowing how your colleagues think. Nevertheless, some of the guidelines above may help. It will also help if someone has confirmed that each candidate is actively interested and has gained some idea of what the organization has to do to attract each of them. There is no point in choosing the one whom you cannot afford, or cannot interest.

ACCEPTANCE

This section is about getting a contractual acceptance. This word is stressed because the objective is that the parties make an agreement which they can keep. The offer is only a part of that process and, although important, should not be considered in isolation. In particular, there is a dangerous temptation to produce an offer which is acceptable and gets accepted, thereby distracting attention from the need to produce documents which satisfy the statutory requirement for contracts of service. Two different aspects of good practice clash here. The warm, welcoming offer letter is important, so is the formal contract. It is very difficult to merge the two, but some effort must be applied to making the contract simple and intelligible so that it does not destroy the effect of the upbeat offer by its length, legality or petty content.

Also, following the direct marketing theme, create an opening for the candidate to query anything anomalous. Ideally the offer should not be a *fait accompli*, but the result of a discussion about the likely content of the package, which could even lead to the question 'If we were to construct an offer along these lines, would it be acceptable to you?' This preliminary spadework, plus an indication in the letter that the candidate must feel free to telephone you about anything which needs clarification. (This must be carefully worded. Do not accidentally invite bargaining!) should produce an acceptance or a convertible response. If it does not, you should have left the door open with the runners-up so that they are not affronted by the delay. In this context, telling them earlier that you all like him/her, but there is one other candidate who is slightly closer to the technical or functional specification (usually true) is a useful insurance. Leaving them in the dark for weeks is not a valid alternative.

INDUCTION

This is a crucial part of the process. Errors and omissions in the induction process cost time and money, both if you lose the candidates and if you brief them incorrectly.

Inadequate induction demotivates people, increases staff and labour turnover, causes disputes, makes work for industrial tribunals, and/or generates litigation, damages corporate reputations and in extreme cases injures or kills people. Hence good induction pays for itself. It is just as important to have a formal induction plan at senior level as at blue collar. Employees at every level are entitled to be properly briefed and in the absence of positive information people may make assumptions or ask the wrong person and get information which is at best incomplete and at worst totally wrong.

This message is not just for personnel staff. Everyone involved in recruiting and settling in a new employee should be aware of the principles and the organization's practice.

Create an induction checklist, or adapt the Recruitment Society's standard example which is slightly too long to be repeated here. Constructive things which are often missed in a traditional induction programme include:

- Using the telephone reference check for guidance on how to get the best out of the employee. This has two advantages. It sounds and is constructive and it also encourages disclosure of weak points.
- Making sure new employees hear about events in the organization before they read about it in the papers. Perhaps put them, temporarily, on the PR department mailing list?
- Keep in touch during long notice periods to make people feel wanted. The more important they are, the longer the notice to be worked out at the previous place and they can be diverted in many ways. Don't let them be!
- Make sure you honour all promises on time or early! This applies to everything from removing the previous incumbent, through car availability, to review dates for rewards packages.
- The above also involves recording all the promises made or implied at interview. In other words, the induction process starts at the beginning of the first interview, a point which needs to be registered with every interviewer.
- Make time to talk about first impressions, by appointment, after the first week or so. This exchange can eliminate a lot of misunderstandings.

Finally, remember that the effort applied to the induction process needs to be

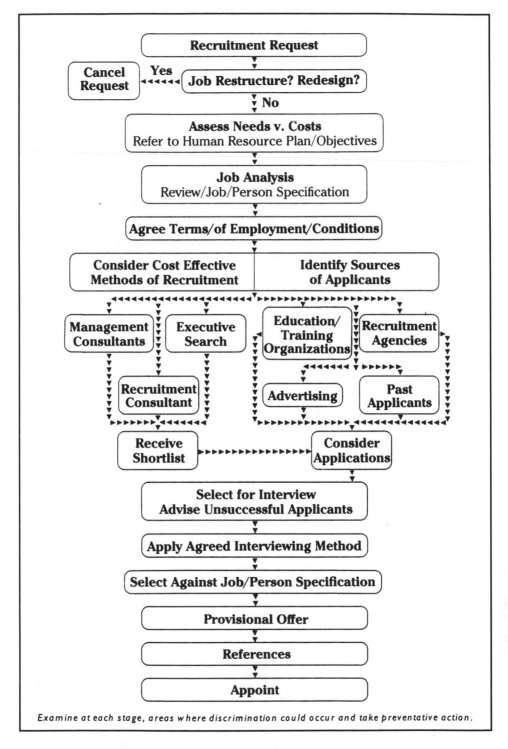

Figure 11.1   Recruitment checklist
(Reproduced courtesy of the Institute of Personnel Management)

continued *ad infinitum*. Keeping good people is almost invariably better than having to hire new ones and it is cheaper, too. Good practice means good hunting and you can then practise the finders keepers principle!

FURTHER READING

Courtis, J., *Interviews: Skills and Strategy*, Institute of Personnel Management, 1989

Courtis, J., *Recruiting for Profit*, Institute of Personnel Management, 1990.

Davey, D. Mackenzie, *How to be a Good Judge of Character*, Kogan Page, 1989

Higham, M., *The ABC of Interviewing*, Institute of Personnel Management, 1979

IPM, *The IPM Recruitment Code*, Institute of Personnel Management, 1990. Single copies are available free with an SAE from The Institute of Personnel Management, IPM House, Camp Road, Wimbledon, London SW19 4UX.

Plumbley, P., *Recruitment and Selection*, 2nd edition, Institute of Personnel Management, 1976

Ungerson, B. (ed.), *Recruitment Handbook*, 3rd edition, Gower, 1983.

12 Interviewing

John Courtis

For most managers, interviewing implies recruitment and selection interviewing but the same rules apply in other applications, such as appraisal, counselling and fact finding. The subject is massive and so is treated here on an exception basis with pointers to additional sources of specialist texts and advice.

We start from the premise that most interviews are unsatisfactory in some way, a premise supported by independent research over many years. Many interviews are abortive or unnecessary.

OBJECTIVES

It may seem trite to mention that you should be certain about your objectives before starting or even planning an interview but the point is often forgotten or taken for granted. For example, in hiring, few people stop to consider whether they are involved in a selection interview or just a recruitment ratification. Selection involves a qualitative filtering process in which you choose the best, or none, from a number of people interviewed. Recruitment, on the other hand, implies that you choose the first person who matches up to the minimum criteria, or perhaps all those who meet them.

There are secondary objectives which, although peripheral in many cases, are none the less important. For instance:

- your time management objectives;
- the public relations aspect of each meeting;
- house advertising, as an investment for the future;
- product and service advertising;
- research
- counselling (during internal selection processes).

If you do not identify your objectives clearly, you cannot plan to achieve them. You may also emerge from the interview without enough data to enable you to meet the objectives when you later realise what they are.

ABORT THE ABORTIVE

Several of the objectives outlined above demand that you do not run interviews which, in retrospect, prove to have been abortive. If you know they are abortive your interviewee probably does too so that not only have you wasted your time and the victim's; you have also damaged your own and your organization's reputation.

Better communication is the key. If there is an adequate exchange of information beforehand, some interviews will prove to be unnecessary. Others can be modified in content or objective to make them worthwhile. The simplest example is the person who is being interviewed for an inappropriate job, because details of the individual or the job have not reached employer and candidate respectively in a form which permits qualitative judgements by either or both. The defence which both sides usually offer for partial or non-disclosure is that they are afraid of 'putting off' the other side. This is at best shortsighted. It does not impress busy employers or busy candidates (usually the best ones) to find that time has been wasted for this reason. Worse, the chance to have a correctly planned interview which related more accurately to the individual and his or her potential within the organization has almost certainly been missed.

Even at 'recruitment' interviews it is still discourteous to interview people who do not fit the candidate specification or know that they could not or would not do the job as finally described to them. There is a tendency to dismiss this sort of error with the thought that 'It's only half an hour', conveniently ignoring the candidate's travel time, inconvenience, disappointment, and loss of earnings at a level where pride, money and time may all be in short supply. So, sometimes, is self-confidence. Your moral obligation to do the right thing is actually greater the wider the gap in seniority between interviewer and candidate.

TIME FLIES

Given the preceding fairly discouraging introduction, you may be wondering how it is possible to perform a good or worthwhile interview in the time normally allotted. The quick answer is that you cannot! Even in the sort of interview which is planned to take several hours (rather than dragging out to that length by the incompetence of the interviewer or the loquacity of the 'victim') it is entirely possible that the results will be incomplete, misleading, or just plain bad.

The secret is discipline: discipline about the conduct of the meeting and discipline about preparation. I have a theory that much of management consists of the avoidance of error, rather than dramatic flights of flair, fancy or invention. Nowhere is this more true than in interviewing. Proper research and preparation before the interview will make all the difference. Part of the selection process, for example, can be conducted on the telephone. Five minutes per candidate is enough to form a preliminary opinion about their merits, without the need to proceed further (except for a gracious written rejection later if both sides have not agreed that there is no point in going further).

PREPARATION

The environment may be the most important ingredient in the interview preparation. Certainly the difference between good and bad can change an interviewee's chance of communicating well quite considerably. A stress-free room, free of interruptions, threatening layout (large desk, uncomfortable guest chair), sun in eyes, draughts, excessive heat and noise nuisance, is firmly indicated.

Getting them there

We should not need to labour this point. However, you will have colleagues who are not prepared to be flexible about interview timing, either in respect of the time of day or the day of the week. They may also be thoughtless about the lead time necessary for someone in a worthwhile and demanding job to plan absences. (Where selection and recruitment is concerned, the following is worth considering: other things being equal, the best people are those who are still trying to honour their contracts with their present employers. Excluding the idiots who play hard to get on principle, the elusive are likely to be better than the all-too-available.)

As a final preparation you should:

- read their paperwork again.
- read again what you have sent them;
- smile;
- go out and greet them;
- tell them who you are;
- make sure they are who you think they are.

Tell them what you want to achieve during the meeting. (Call it a meeting, not an interview.) Make sure they are there for the purpose you think they are. Tell them the structure of the meeting. Now go ahead.

THE INTERVIEW PROPER

Reasonable readers might assume that this heading highlights a distinction between the main body of the interview and the peripheral matters previously covered. Not so. The alternative in the author's mind is the interview *improper*, which is unfortunately the norm in many organizations.

The caring interviewer – especially the recruiter – when approaching an interview, must remember that the interviewee has almost certainly been conditioned badly for the interview, in one of three ways:

- lack of experience;
- guidance from friend or counsellor who considers the candidate's objectives without regard to those of the recruiter/interviewer;
- lots of experience with bad interviewers (the interview improper).

According to the *Oxford English Dictionary*, the primary meanings of 'improper' are 'Inaccurate, wrong, not properly so called'. 'Wrong' will do for our purposes. The ways in which other interviews are wrong and yours can be right are varied but they all come back to the questions of objectives and control. The interviewer must run the meeting and concentrate on matters relevant to the objectives outlined earlier.

The alternative is anarchy and a wasted hour or more. For example, the sort of interview where the candidate takes charge and launches into a biography which duplicates the written material already exchanged (or is necessary because adequate written material has not been exchanged in advance) is wholly unproductive except to demonstrate the candidate's poor grasp of the objective. Given that he or she has been badly conditioned, it may be unfair to make an adverse judgement on this basis. The effective interviewer, by controlling and setting guidelines for the conduct of the meeting, does both sides a service.

This is less stressful for the candidate who desperately wants to recite a biography if the objectives are clearly specified. Something like this may be appropriate:

> I want to achieve three things during this meeting. First, to clear up any queries arising out of the paperwork we sent you, so that you can clearly understand the job and the company environment. Second, a brief review of your track record so that I can make sure that I have understood its relevance to the job. Third, I want to give you a chance to mention any experience or evidence of excellence that is not brought out in your CV.

It is useful at this stage to enquire whether the candidate has any timing constraints and to mention your own, if any. There are few things more damaging to an interview than one of the parties being under pressure on time, while the other is relaxed and could go on all day. Communication can be even worse when both have time problems and neither has disclosed them.

However, all interviews suffer from time pressures because no two people have the same idea of the right time to allocate. The solution is for the interviewer to make it very clear that the exchanges are on an exception reporting basis. If this is done, the candidate is forced to discipline the use of time and also is reminded that this is not going to be the sloppy norm experienced in other places. If he or she does not react to the message you have learned something else about them.

This economy of effort creates one trap. The quality and brevity of the information exchanges may improve, but the staccato rhythm is seductive and may tempt you, as interviewer, not to probe too deeply when an answer is superficially acceptable. This is exceptionally dangerous because the most important things in an interview, apart perhaps from body language, are the answers to supplementary questions.

Information volunteered by candidates may well be useful but is of their choice. Answers to your questions are more important because, if you are doing your work correctly, they are more relevant to your objectives. Supplementary questions are crucial because they refine or highlight key matters arising out of the other two.

For instance, there are many questions to which a candidate can give a stock answer which is largely under his or her control and is no more informative than the carefully polished words on a CV. Getting behind that stock answer to the unplanned spontaneous reaction can be much more informative.

'Why did you leave the So and So Co.?' is a classic and deeply boring question which usually attracts a well polished reply like 'There was a promotion bottleneck. My boss was only two years older and unlikely to move.'

You can tackle this in one of two ways. Either change the primary question, so that you are asking questions which previous interviewers have not asked and which therefore demand thought and unique answers, or use the probing supplementary.

In the case quoted, the alternative question might be 'Why did you leave the So and so Co. so quickly, when you appear to have been well paid and getting new experience?' This is quite sneaky, because there are at least two and possibly three implied criticisms which the interviewee must consider and rebut. Listen extremely carefully at this point because most people will omit to answer you on one or two of these. Note them. Come back to them, either by way of supplementary questions or a later approach from another angle. Anyone who actually covers all three points without getting tied in knots is probably quite bright.

You may want to try several possible supplementaries, arising from the earlier conduct of the interview. The obvious one is 'Why didn't you consider this when you joined them?' Because it is obvious it may be less informative than something more open-ended like 'Does that mean your priorities have changed since you joined them?' This gives you a chance to ask later what the priorities are now; quite important if you are trying to weed out job-hoppers.

Open-ended questions are almost invariably better than those requiring yes/no answers, except when you are trying to pin down a candidate of suspect credibility.

Questions of all kinds, as implied above, are more important than statements from either side. Even the nature of the candidates' questions can be more informative than their answers to bad questions. A pattern should emerge which will tell you whether the candidate is obsessed with detail or is a 'broad-brush' operator. Again, it is very important to listen and analyse these.

Apart from the heavy set piece question there are some very useful interjections which can be as useful as the formal question, e.g.:

- For instance?
- For example?
- How?
- Why was that?
- What, exactly?
- Can you be more specific?
- Tell me more.
- Can you explain that?
- I don't quite follow.

You probably have your own favourites. All are designed to provoke clarification or a fuller picture without interrupting the flow too much. Even 'Yes?' is both encouragement and reinforcement of this kind.

This is not the place for a detailed listing of all the possible 'good' questions. Instead, the general principle needs to be stressed. Questions are more important than statements, in both directions. The answers are even more important. If you think back over horrible interviews you have attended, it is almost certain that you have experienced the 'improper' interviewer who has devoted massive effort to the construction and issue of a very good question and sinks back exhausted and deaf the moment he asks it. Do not be like the 'improper' interviewer. Listen. Listen to the answers. Listen to their questions. Both are informative. Also if you do not listen to their questions carefully you may respond with your slightly irrelevant stock answer. The second-rate candidates will not notice or, if they notice, may not mind. The good ones will notice and mind. Even if you decide they are worth offering the job to, they will not accept because they have formed an unfavourable impression. This is so even if they will not be reporting to you in the job, but doubly true if you are the potential boss.

If you are surrounded by 'improper' interviewers who are very obviously unaware of these problems, there are three or four aids which may effect or influence a cure. Tape recording the meeting, overtly to permit later assessment, may aid self-awareness. Video recording and playback does the same thing more forcefully. A proprietary video training package by Melrose Films called *Listen* is very helpful on this point. So is the old Video Arts film *Manhunt* about the interview process as a whole. Finally, D. Mackenzie Davey wrote an excellent booklet for the British Institute of Management called *How to Interview*.

Tape recording your own sessions can also help. You will probably be unpleasantly surprised at first, both by your performance and by the number of non-sequiturs and other communication failures evident in the first few tapes, but this is the only way to learn discreetly, from self-example.

Replaying taped interviews will show you that abortive interviews are signalled very early in most cases. The candidate who comes to a meeting uncertain whether he or she is right for the job and vice versa is usually giving out warning signs, either in the nature of loaded questions, the absence of any questions, or a desire to hurry bits which should normally be taken seriously and slowly. For this reason the author nowadays goes immediately to the question of the candidate's interest in the job, without spending time on the candidate's relevance.

Other things being equal, unless you have a wide variety of jobs to fill, there is no point in interviewing in depth a candidate who is going to reject the job as soon as the nature of it is made clear. If this rejection can be identified early, both sides can save time and self-respect. The time saved can then, if appropriate, be devoted to exploring what the candidate can do which might be relevant to the organization's short term management development plans. Or you can both go home earlier.

BODY LANGUAGE

Reading a good book on body language is doubly important. There are several. Two are called: *Body Language*, (Fast, J, 1972, Pan Books, London; Pease, A, 1984, Sheldon Press, London) and Desmond Morris's books *The Naked Ape* and *Manwatching* both have relevant content.

You need this background for two reasons. First, it can help you interpret what the interviewee is thinking, if what they are saying or not saying is not the whole truth. Second, you can use the positions and signals described in the books to demonstrate sympathetic interest, or anything else you feel like, at times when you feel far from sympathetic or interested, but the good conduct of the interview demands that you be supportive. Conversely, if you want to get rid of a verbose candidate, body signals can help to reinforce other messages, without overt rudeness.

THE CLOSE

Getting rid of people on time is a tempting objective in some circumstances, but it must not be allowed to interfere with the correct disciplines for shutting down the meeting.

You must both know what you have agreed and what comes next. Your next action must be mentioned, with a time forecast. If the interviewee has to send you something – remind him/her and agree how soon it is needed. If you are not sure where they stand about the job, for heaven's sake ask them.

If you are uncertain about a job candidate's relevance, tell them why, so they have a chance to agree or clear the air. Even if it is disappointing, this is better than having them feel hard done by when an unexplained rejection arrives later. You may also find that some candidates drag themselves back into the running, on merit, at this point. Finally, ask them if they would accept the job if offered (also ask if there is anything else coming to the boil elsewhere). This gives a clearer picture than general interest queries. It also clarifies your lead time, if any.

INTERVIEWS AND THE LAW

This section is about some of the legal pitfalls which can occur in the badly run interview. The first, of course, is the possibility that someone inadvertently makes a verbal job offer at interview, which is then accepted. This is extremely rare and, unless the candidate is litigious and armed with a tape recorder, this is not a financial problem, just a goodwill and time waster.

The second, much more common, is that the interviewer asks questions or makes statements which are or could be misunderstood to be discriminatory. Given the nature of current equal opportunities legislation it is important, as pointed out earlier, that interviewers are briefed on what not to ask, or say, and that for every interview they make adequate notes which indicate clearly the reasons why the candidates meet or fall short of the organization's criteria. It is just as important that you record the reasons why Fred got the job as the reasons why Fiona did not. Tape recordings may help here in the training process. Even the most well intentioned manager can use words or phrases which in the mouth of someone with a desire to see the worst in everything can suggest a pattern of prejudice. If, for example, the use of photographs on application forms became discriminatory here as it is in at least one other country, interviewers who care about remembering which candidate was which would have to revert to a pen portrait of the candidate. When you have a spare hour, try writing such a description of a few strangers in a way that will permit instant recall without any potentially sexist or racist connotations. It is not easy.

THE SECONDARY OBJECTIVES

Interviews as PR

This is not as blatant as it may sound. Public relations in the better sense refers to your corporate communication with various audiences in and around the organization. Potential employees are an important part of several audiences. They may be, or may become, employees, shareholders, suppliers, customers, enemies or even advisers. The quality of your treatment of candidates, whether or not you know they are more than just members of the general public, can be very important to the organization's future, even in small ways. To take an extreme example, a candidate who has first-hand experience of being properly treated and well briefed about the organization is likely to be a powerful ally in any distant discussion arising from press misquotation. If the distant discussion includes a thoughtful MP who is going to vote about you the next day he or she is very likely to prefer a first-hand opinion to that of the press. All MPs know how the media misquote!

Interviews as advertising

Interviews often result from recruitment advertising. They can also replace future recruitment advertising, or product advertising. The warm interview with a good candidate who is of the right calibre for the organization but not quite right for the current vacancy should leave the door open for either side to renew contact in the future. If the briefing has conveyed a sense of excitement about the products and services of the organization, the candidates, their households and their present employers may be influenced as potential customers. Most sales staff would give a lot to have the attention of a prospect for an hour, half of which was to be spent discussing the excellence of the product. Good interviewing can be very effective marketing.

Interviews as sources

This does not refer to industrial espionage or illicit head hunting although, tactlessly handled, either might be suspected. In brief, if an interview goes well but both sides decide that there is not a match, there is a special professional bond between candidate and interviewer for a short while which sometimes makes it natural for the recruiter to ask if the candidate has ever worked with anyone who could and should do the job. It has to be left to the candidate to decide if there are any ethical constraints about such a contact but in most cases the new nominee is a past colleague rather than a current one or if current is known to be disaffected.

This also raises the question of the tow rope. It is not generally realised how many people move in groups rather than solo from company to company. Much publicized migrations, as in stock-brokers' specialist departments, are not significant by comparison with the key functional managers who pull one or more of their team along to the next outfit. Sometimes the initiative comes from above, sometimes from below, because the old place isn't fun any more without Fiona or Fred. Quite often, senior functional managers, perceiving other weaknesses in the new organization, will also recommend members of their peer group or even their ex-bosses. Much more of this happens than is evident from the appointments column. The tow rope is very powerful. Do not ignore the potential of this when team building.

Finally, when exploring referees other than the conventional ones, do ask about their personal merits and their relationship with the candidate. This is not for head hunting purposes – you need this to evaluate the later reference properly – but there may occasionally be a by-product which can be used without any twinge of conscience. The other bonus is that you find out how candidates talk about people close to them and can differentiate between the constructive and the negative attitudes. It is a useful part of your qualitative filter. (All appraisals tell you more about the author than the subject of the appraisal.)

OTHER KINDS OF INTERVIEW

Although we have concentrated on recruitment interviewing for examples so far, the other types are very important.

These include appraisal, counselling, fact finding, termination and warning (in the statutory context). Some are easier for the interviewing manager, some more difficult, but the basic disciplines remain the same. (Chapters 14 and 15 deal with appraisal and counselling in detail.) It is up to the individual manager to identify the extent to which each example differs from the norm and the need for special techniques or preparation.

The general rules which remain the same include:

- Remembering that the 'victim' always feels nervous, sometimes even threatened, although he may outrank you.
- Allowing for the difference in context between the different types of interview. This does not just refer to the objectives of each participant, but includes timing, the extent to which the meeting is voluntary, the desire for communication, the threat, as above, ignorance about the reasons for the meeting (very prevalent, even when the alleged agenda has been declared in advance), suspicion about the motives of the interviewer or the organization (not quite the same as the threat problem), and the extent to which the interviewer is dreading the meeting as much as or more than the victim!
- The need for preparation and for putting certain things in writing if they are to be remembered afterwards. This does not mean in typescript. It can be very effective to do a spontaneous handwritten note during the meeting to which the interviewee feels he or she has contributed. Indeed the content may well evolve naturally during the meeting. A photocopy for the interviewer and the original for the 'victim' (always this way – more courteous and more natural) suffices as an official but informal way of recording key points, whether one is explaining redundancy pay or listing points for personal improvement. In the latter case the use of the 'victim's' own words is appreciably more comforting.
- The need for communication, remembering always that communication is supposed to be a two-way process. Any alleged communication which is structured to flow only in one direction deprives the originator of a discrimi-

nating response. The feedback can amend or eliminate the need for the rest of the meeting. Always keep listening. Watch for non-verbal signals.

Appraisal

Here the key problem is to decide in advance the extent to which the objective of the meeting is compatible with the total disclosure sometimes mistakenly assumed to be implicit in an appraisal. There are some highly dangerous appraisal processes in which the corporate system requires that a document containing virtually all the victim's weaknesses is discussed with each subject. This is inimical to the achievement of the objective, in that it destroys or demotivates. The preferred position for appraisal disclosure (unless appraisal has to be combined with a statutory dismissal warning) is to concentrate on the curable and ignore the incurable. This raises a secondary problem – that of deciding what is and is not curable – which must be addressed. The knack here is to find a way of discussing the marginal points which you may suspect are incurable as if they were open to improvement, but without making it sound like the end of the world if they are not cured. The precise technique can only be decided in relation to specific faults in a specific context but, for example, suggesting that they are important for future career opportunities rather than crucial to current survival may get the message across without damage and with some chance that even an apparently insensitive employee may be interested in self-improvement.

A final thought on appraisal – people don't get worse at their jobs suddenly without good reason. If someone who was competent last year is substandard this year a change has taken place at work or at home which is creating problems. The appraisal meeting which ignores this is wholly wasted.

Counselling

This is often but not always a by-product of an appraisal system. It is less widespread than appraisal and rather more difficult. Ideally it should only be undertaken by someone with formal training. If this is not possible, someone relevant and sympathetic should be chosen. Allowing an untrained and even antagonistic boss to do it is not best practice. As with the pre-departure meeting, the choice of interviewer is the most important aspect of the preparation. The second aspect of the choice is that the interviewer must be given enough authority to help as a result of the counselling, which is seldom wholly one-sided. A good counselling interview will uncover faults in the organization, not just review the employee's past failings.

This point applies of course to all appraisal meetings and should be tattooed on all interviewers. Listen, record, react, keep promises.

Compulsory interviews

There is one outstanding respect in which most non-recruitment interviews differ from recruitment interviews. Most are compulsory for one side or other. This makes the climate quite sensitive. By comparison a recruitment interview is easier because, although one or both participants may be nervous (actually, in a sample of all interviews everywhere, *most* participants are probably nervous – and if they are not, they ought to be) in the recruitment interview one party actively wants a job and the other actively wants to hire someone. This predicates a better climate than one could forecast for many other meetings.

The compulsory interviews do of course include appraisal, but there are different degrees of compulsion about the fact finding meeting which may be research, fact gathering from a departing employee or just formalized data collection in normal operations. All require discipline but they are relatively non-threatening, and goodwill plus a willing and sensitive ear makes them effective. Only the pre-departure meeting is tricky, because there may be an immense amount to be learned and the employee doesn't necessarily see any valid reason for total disclosure. Equally, the interviewer, if too close to the problems, may not want to hear too much. Choice of a neutral and sympathetic interviewer is more important than trying to add technique to an unreceptive boss, who may well be the cause of the trouble anyway.

Firing people comes into the compulsory category, but need not always do so if the rule about listening is observed. If the organization has been communicating properly with its people, the meeting itself may be compulsory but the firing may not. In a substantial minority of cases the meeting may evolve into a resignation, request for redundancy, philosophical debate about how things are not working out or even an announcement of an impending event whose imminence (undisclosed) has been a factor in the performance failures which were causing the rift. The lovelorn can be transformed both by engagements *and* by the departure of an unsatisfactory partner. Better still, they sometimes want to change employers as part of the therapy.

When all else fails, listen – and keep quiet.

WHAT WE HAVE LEARNED

This has not been an encyclopaedic dissertation on every facet of every possible interview situation. Instead, you have a series of concepts, principles, thought-starters and horrid examples which should enable you to formulate your own policy and practice in the light of your unique knowledge of your own organization and indeed your own personal style.

There is no one right method of handling interviews or their preparation. What feels right for you is better than something which feels so alien that it impairs your performance, provided that you satisfy the basic guidelines given. You must satisfy them. Interview rules, especially in recruitment, are not made to be broken. If you want to break a rule, you must create an alternative discipline which satisfies the original objective. The best test has not yet been mentioned. It is very simple. If you were the candidate, would you be satisfied with what you and your colleagues are doing and not doing with each recruitment exercise? Even if you have not been a candidate for some time, it should be possible to answer this.

CHECKLIST OF KEY POINTS

1   Why are you doing this? i.e. what are your aims, desired results, possible 'product'?

2 When are you doing it?
3 Have you allocated enough time – soon enough, flexibly enough?
4 Have the others to be involved?
5 Who is responsible for the programme?
6 Where will you interview?
7 Is it an acceptable environment?
8 How will you do it?
9 Have you planned:
   - adequate exchange of data beforehand?
   - avoiding unnecessary meetings?
   - essential questions?
   - common post-interview report format?
   - quality control (could you meet BS5750..!)?
   - post-interview action and follow-up?
   - criteria by which selection is to be made?

10 Is everyone involved aware that interviews are like computers: Garbage In: Garbage Out?

FURTHER READING

Courtis, John, *Interviews: Skills and Strategy*, Institute of Personnel Management, 1989.

Courtis, John, *Recruiting for Profit*, Institute of Personnel Management, 1990.

Davey, D. Mackenzie, *How to Interview*, Professional Publishing, 1986.

Melrose Films, *Listen*, video training package.

Morris, Desmond, *The Naked Ape*, Pan, 1981 and *Manwatching*, Pan, 1978.

Video Arts, *Manhunt*

13 Developing your people

Cathy Stoddart

There is no chapter or section in this Handbook called 'Education and training' or 'How to choose the best courses for your staff'. This chapter is, however, entitled 'Developing your people' and although sending employees away from their place of work to attend courses is one way of developing parts of their competence, *it is only one way*.

The emphasis here is on the individual manager's responsibility for developing the people who report to him/her and less on what the personnel or training department can or should provide for those people. Considerable space is devoted to the 'small p' political issues and lobbying activities involved in gaining senior management support for training and development plans. The suggested route towards this support is by demonstrating how the implementation of such policies throughout an organization will contribute to the effective achievement of that organization's aims and objectives. This is as true for traditional manufacturing companies pursuing increased turnover, profitability or market share, as for service companies, non-profit making organizations, local authorities, community service bodies, charities or any other type of organization which is concerned to produce a quality product or service.

Obviously, it is much easier for a manager who has the support of senior management to implement effective policies and programmes for developing his/her own people. However, this chapter does set out to demonstrate that even without the resources of a training department or the wholehearted support of senior management, it is still possible to reap many benefits for the department and the organization from assessing training and development needs and taking action to meet them within one's own department.

THE POLITICAL ISSUES

An organization which sees its education and training programmes as its sole contribution to employee development would not see development as a political issue at all. It would be likely to view expenditure on apprenticeship schemes, induction courses or external refresher courses on technical matters in the same way that it views expenditure on the maintenance of its buildings, that is, as a recurring item which could be cut in the face of financial pressure.

However, an organization which sees education and training as one part of the organization's strategy for achieving its objectives will have another view. This organization may consciously group together training activities and the much wider development activities (described in a later part of this chapter headed 'Nuts and bolts') and describe them as Human Resource Development (HRD). Whether it explicitly labels its activities HRD or not, the organization which views training and development as an essential activity harnessing potential to achieve goals will not be so ready to cut its budget in times of financial difficulty. Seen in these terms, the HRD budget competes directly with that of other functions for scarce resources (even though it is distributed across many departments to be spent). Some companies are so committed to the importance of their HRD strategies as vital contributors to business success, that their reaction to financial 'hard times' is to *increase* the amount they spend on it.

Decisions about how much to spend and what types of HRD will be supported therefore become inextricably tied up with organizational politics and cannot be considered in isolation from the culture and traditions of the organization, its philosophy, and its aims.

Why bother to develop employees?

Many senior executives in business, commerce and public administration will put their hands on their hearts and agree that 'people are the most important asset in the organization'. They may even, in their business plans and strategy documents, make some reference to manpower and management resources. However, it is highly unlikely that there will be any links between business objectives and people development which are articulated in terms of performance. This is quite different from financial, production, sales and marketing, pricing, capital investment and other objectives which will probably have quite clear performance outcomes as targets. So, if HRD were to have specific outcomes or targets, what might they be?

Competence, Commitment and the Capacity for change (the Three Cs) can best be demonstrated by looking at specific goals linked to business objectives. One of these might perhaps be the introduction of information technology.

For example, one well known British manufacturing company recently decided to invest in an extremely expensive American system of computerized stock control. The board realised that not only would the hourly paid workforce need considerable training in the mechanics of using the new system, but also that a fundamental shift in attitudes was required throughout the production function if implementation of the system were to be successful. Supervisors, foremen, and managers were going to have to liaise more effectively within their own function, and communicate closely with other functions. So, along with specific training to give employees the knowledge and skills to use the new system, they also instituted 'interdepartmental problem groups' of foremen and middle managers. These groups examined both 'old chestnut' problems and anticipated new ones arising from the new system. They worked out for themselves the need for better communications and changes in attitude and had prior board commitment that

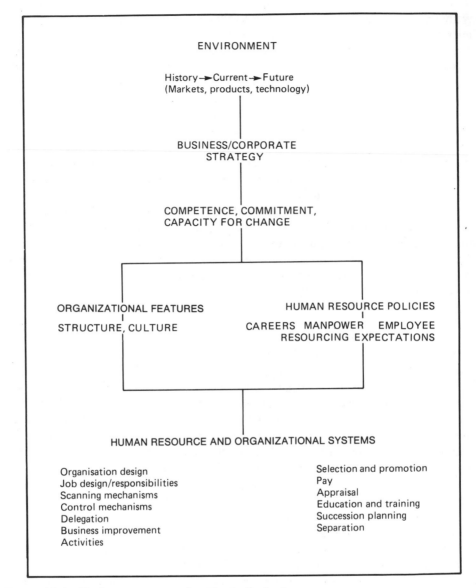

Figure 13.1   The human resource function in the business

(This illustrates the central importance and essential interdependence of the HRD function within a business.)

their problem group solutions would be implemented. Thus those managers took on 'ownership' of the problems and generated a commitment to their solutions.

This example is a good illustration of how HRD can contribute to the fostering of the Three Cs – Competence, Commitment and the Capacity for change (see Figure 13.1). Competition from other organizations is often a reason for bothering to develop employees. This may be in the form of intensified competition for the available recruits at any level – the brightest school leavers, the best qualified graduates, or the senior people with the most relevant experience. Increasingly, applicants are interested not only in salary and associated benefits, but also in what a prospective employer has to offer in terms of personal and career development, appraisal systems, and criteria for promotion. An organization might suddenly realise that, in spite of competitive benefits packages, it was not managing to attract and retain high calibre employees. This could be because there is no evidence of succession planning, the appraisal system is a mechanical procedure used principally for the airing of grievances, and criteria for promotion take little or no account of an employee's overall performance in a job. They rely solely on easily quantifiable achievements.

In this sort of case, the competition could be coming from an enormously wide range of organizations; the only similarity need be that they are seeking to recruit a comparable type of staff.

However, competition can also provide the motivation to undertake some systematic HRD if it is seen that a competitor is gaining some advantages through its HRD policies. For example, your company may begin losing market share to a competitor whose in-house seminars on how to get close to the customer are beginning to bear fruit. Or, the competitor's well established quality circles may have given way to 'zero-defect groups' which are now achieving their objectives. Of course, if your company has no mechanisms, either formal or informal, for finding out what competitors are doing on any front, then it is unlikely that it would know of such developments. A company which attached importance to 'scanning its environment' would, on the other hand, pick up these things quickly and be motivated into doing something itself.

Whose responsibility is it anyway?

Reality often falls far short of the ideal – in organizations as in all else. However, it is helpful to look at an ideal situation in order to assess what is, or what should be, the right answer to this question in any particular organization.

In an ideal world, the short answer to the responsibility question is that everyone in an organization is responsible to some degree for identifying and then articulating his/her own development needs and to a varying degree for identifying the development needs of others.

Stimulus for HRD activity will come from at least three directions (see Figure 13.2). It will come from the bottom where those closest to the manufacturer of the product or the delivery of the service are best placed to have innovative ideas for improvement, and to notice problems associated with existing procedures and practices.

Stimulus will also come from the top and cascade down through a management structure in which managers know that they have support in developing employee competence, commitment, and capacity for change. In this ideal world, the top stratum of management will have articulated clearly the organization's aims and philosophy so that no employee has any doubt about where the organization is heading and what values it holds most highly. In American and Japanese companies these intentions are often encapsulated in a very concise paper known as 'The Mission Statement'. This almost invariably includes statements summarizing the company's HRD aims and relating them to its strategic aims. As an example, one Japanese car maker describes its approach as follows:

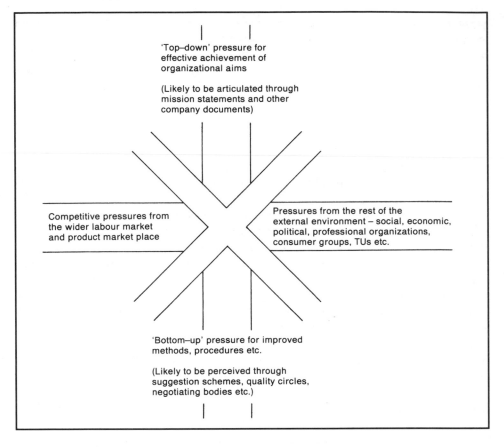

Figure 13.2　Pressures on an organization for effective HRD policies

BASIC EDUCATION PHILOSOPHY: to assist the company in its efforts to:

1　Offer the public superior products, thereby contributing to society through:

- research and development and creativity (good thinking, good products);
- marketing and after sales service (customer first policy).

2　Strengthen labour-management trust and promote a spirit of corporate involvement through:

- communications;
- teamwork;
- creativity, challenge, courage.

HUMAN RESOURCE DEVELOPMENT: employee education goals:

- development of personnel who can respond flexibly to their work;
- development of personnel who understand the company situation;
- development of creative personnel.

Statements such as these can leave no doubt in an individual manager's mind about the strength of commitment from above to positive policies for the development of human resources.

The third direction from which an organization can experience pressure for effective HRD policies is the external environment. The activities of competitors have already been mentioned, but in addition to these there are many other forces at work of which an organization sensitively tuned to its wider social, economic and political environment will be aware. For example, government exhortations to improve efficiency may be linked to grants from government agencies for training. Or customer tastes and preferences may be shifting towards those companies which provide 'the personal touch' as well as a reliable product or service.

So, in the ideal world, a departmental manager knows and accepts that the effective development of people at work is an important part of his/her job. This is fully recognized by senior managers, fellow line managers and functional specialists, as well as by subordinates. The role of the personnel, training or HRD department in this sort of company is likely to be that of a facilitator, enabler and specialist resource to be drawn on by departmental managers. Figure 13.3 breaks down the roles involved in an 'up and running' staff development programme to show the crucial role of line managers and also the enormity of the task facing them if they are lacking the clear support of the top management team.

In reality the situation may not look remotely like this. A manager who is already convinced of the benefits to his/her department and to the organization as a whole may well wonder how and where to start. If s/he detects little or no support, enthusiasm or resources from above, receives few positive signals from subordinates, and is unused to considering external factors in relation to his/her job, an indirect strategy is probably most likely to succeed:

- The first step might be to identify an operational problem within the department. Ideally, this should be one which is not totally specific to one department, but might be mirrored elsewhere in the organization.
- Propose a solution to this problem utilizing one or more of the elements suggested in the section called 'Nuts and bolts' below.
- The benefits of employee development are likely to be indirect as well as direct and these can then be demonstrated to appropriate senior managers as but small examples of what could be achieved with organization-wide programmes.

ASSESSING TRAINING AND DEVELOPMENT NEEDS

It is almost impossible to imagine an organization that has no reasons for continuing training and retraining. The only way in which it would be theoretically possible never to have a constant training need would be in an organization that could be cut off from change. This would mean that people in the organization never changed, never changed their jobs, never got promoted, never died. It would mean the organization produced the same product, subject to the same legislation, in the same market without ever making any technical adjustments or innovations.

Roles/actions	Top mgt team *	Managers	Staff	Specialist department **
Define policies	✓			Assist
Work within defined policies		✓	✓	✓
Allocate responsibilities	✓	✓		
Allocate resources	✓	✓		
Be committed	✓	✓	✓	✓
Encourage commitment amongst others	✓	✓	✓	✓
Clarify current and future priorities	✓	✓		
Analyse company needs	✓			Assist
Analyse departmental needs		✓	✓	Assist
Invest in staff development	✓			
Prepare training plans		✓		✓
Approve training plans	✓			
Prepare training programmes		✓		✓
Make and approve practical arrangements		✓		✓
Implement programmes		✓		✓
Coach others		✓	✓	✓
Participate in programmes	✓	✓	✓	✓
Check the results		✓		✓
Report on programmes		✓	✓	✓
Evaluate the total effort	✓	Assist		Assist
Brief and de-brief trainees	✓	✓		Assist

*   The 'top team' is deemed here to include the chief executive

**   The 'specialist department' here may be the personnel, training or HRD department. In any event, it will be the one coordinating activities

Figure 13.3   Breakdown of roles and actions required in a staff development programme

However, back in the real world, there are many situations, both internally and externally generated, which give rise to training or development needs. For example, an organization or department might be suffering from high staff turnover and low morale. One reason could be low pay. However, the problem might be more complex, stemming from lack of employee involvement and consequently lack of motivation to contribute more than their contracts require to the organization. If the first diagnosis is correct, a pay review should solve the problem. If the second is closer to the truth, a comprehensive training and development needs assessment is indicated.

It is clear from this small illustration that training and development needs are generated both from organizations themselves and also, via the jobs that they do, from individuals in their departments.

What training and development needs are generated by organizations?

Different environments, products, markets and customers mean that organizations have different expectations of their employees. Therefore, different training and development needs arise and different strategies or ways of dealing with them are appropriate.

The Prospect Centre has developed four models which illustrate the range of environments and appropriate HRD strategies. Companies of even moderate size may harbour more than one type in different parts of the organization. As change and uncertainty increase, companies need to increase the range of their response by adopting several strategies. Companies which adopt inappropriate stances can find their business strategies inadequately supported or even undermined.

As a first step, and to ascertain in which 'ball park' you are playing, it will help to decide which of these models is closest to your particular situation.

Ad hoc or unplanned maintenance

This strategy is, on its own, adequate for companies operating in essentially stable and predictable markets. The product/service is usually low-tech and is not subject to rapid change. The levels of knowledge, skill and competence required are relatively low. Any HRD needs which arise from time to time are easily identified because they spring from out-of-the-ordinary events or situations. They can be met on an ad hoc basis using whatever internal or external resources are available.

Planned maintenance

This model is best suited to a company operating in relatively stable markets. It can be assumed that it will operate successfully without too much change and that its competitive behaviour, its products/services, and its labour force will be much the same in three years' time as they are now. The company is responsive to some changes in consumer preferences without experiencing great competitive pressures. The product/service is essentially low-tech but may be complex and requiring considerable capital investment.

Companies which perform well according to this model have established programmes of new entrants' training, e.g. craft apprenticeships, graduate trainee schemes, induction courses etc. They commonly run upgrading courses (shop floor to supervision; supervision to management) and general management courses. They often have systems for manpower planning, career planning and management development. The purpose of these activities and systems is to keep the company in good shape. Ad hoc measures can also be taken in special circumstances.

A good system of planned maintenance HRD is not cheap. Money needs to be spent to ensure long term fitness but it is not seen as making a central contribution to survival or to vital changes in business strategies and objectives. It can therefore be, and usually is, cut in difficult times.

Business planning

This HRD model is needed by companies intending to change their business plans, or the strategies they use to achieve these plans, in order to achieve their goals. Such companies may be acting in response to important and foreseeable discontinuities in the market, in technologies, in products, in the political or social environment, or because management (often new management) have taken the decision to pursue a new range of business aims and objectives. This model is particularly appropriate when lead times are sufficiently long to be able to plan and implement the development of people as well as products and processes.

Formal off-the-job learning and a variety of job responsibilities have an important role to play in this model, as in 'planned maintenance'. The significant difference is that training and development activities are targeted towards change and innovation which will support identified business objectives. Typical activities include 'environmental scanning' and project teams, quality circles, innovation workshops – within and between functions.

Strategic capability

This model is particularly apt when environmental turbulence and uncertainty have become so pervasive that business success depends on the organization's ability to cope continuously with and manage effectively new, unfamiliar and surprising situations. For example, it is appropriate in high-tech companies which operate in fast moving, highly competitive markets with short new product development cycles.

Such companies must rely on the exploitation of the knowledge and creativity of a great diversity of talent within their whole workforce. Training and development activities need to go beyond those required for 'planned maintenance' by reinforcing the entrepreneurial, innovative culture in which learning and experimenting are part of everyday life. Typical activities help employees to accumulate a track record of positive achievement in novel and unpredictable circumstances. Activites may include secondments, sabbaticals, spinning off of products into little businesses and frequent changes of responsibility, as well as a vast array of other learning activities which are also associated with other models.

HRD in companies of this type is consciously embedded in day-to-day operational activities. Its costs are high but subject to considerable fluctuation. The non-budget element is likely to be much greater than in the previous model.

What training and development needs are generated within departments or functions?

The four models described above examine types of organizations in a 'macro' sense, in their wider environment. However, the manager who wants to undertake some staff development but is in an unsupported position needs to know where to make a start on the immediate, 'micro' level.

There is a variety of ways of approaching the analysis of training and development needs. Many of these, such as job analysis, task analysis and performance appraisal are well described elsewhere. They can also be very detailed, precise

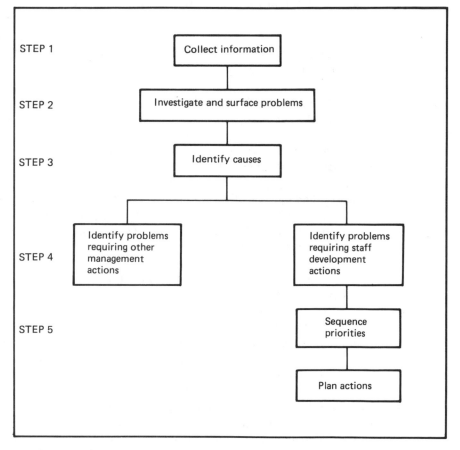

Figure 13.4   Five basic steps

(The systematic process is presented graphically here. It involves five basic steps.)

and consequently time-consuming in their application. Also, they tend to concentrate on the knowledge and skills components of jobs and tasks. However, if the subsequent training is then directed solely towards the acquisition of identified knowledge and skills, it does not help those being trained to develop their ability to manage or handle real work situations. A needs analysis which looks at the wider concept of 'job competence' (as in the Three Cs) is more likely to lead to a development plan which helps employees to manage situations in their jobs as opposed to simply carrying out instructions. 'Competence' therefore implies a capacity to use knowledge and skills for effective performance at work.

Five steps towards an analysis of training and development needs are shown in Figure 13.4 and might look like this:

Step 1 involves the usual methods of collecting information. Specifically:

- interviewing and discussing with key personnel both inside and outside the department or function;
- observing the work place, working conditions, processes and outcomes;

- examining records and other relevant written information, both internal and external.

At least two of these methods should be used to cross-check the accuracy of the information collected.

Step 2 involves comparing the function or department's performance with its objectives, targets and standards as specified (formally or informally) by the organization as a whole. Questions such as 'what is the key purpose of the department and in what respects is it not fulfilling that purpose effectively?' will help bring to the surface all sorts of problems.

Step 3 is crucial because the point in collecting information is really to identify the causes of problems faced by the company. Only then will management be able to direct or channel resources to solving such problems. Otherwise, the danger is that only the symptoms of problems are treated, not the actual problems themselves.

Causes may arise from some item or items that may be found to be inadequate or ineffective. They may also arise from a total absence of one or two items.

Step 4 takes account of the fact that although HRD is a highly significant factor, it is only one way to improve an organization's performance or effectiveness. The illustrative checklist in Figure 13.5 may help to demonstrate this. Those problems and causes which produce a 'possible' indication in this checklist require further analysis and investigation. For example, communication may be seen by a manager as a cause of some of his department's problems. If he sees this as his supervisor's inability to present and convey policies adequately to their subordinates, then some development activities might indeed be required. If, however, poor communication is the result of a lack of proper information channels, such as the availability of newspapers or staff circulars, then the problem should clearly be addressed by other management actions.

Having identified the problems and causes requiring training and development activities, a manager can then sequence them into groups under different areas (see Figure 13.6). These groupings assist the manager in identifying what types of activities to embark on, for whom, and towards what purpose.

Step 5 requires actions to be listed in order of priority according to where the need is most urgent. However, it should be borne in mind that there are often unexpected and indirect benefits from staff development measures, which can continue to accrue over a long time. Therefore a problem may be a long way down the list of priorities, but some of the benefits from instituting the solution may relate clearly to a problem much higher up the list.

Step 6 is a further step which will be compiled with the help of the next section of this chapter, 'Nuts and bolts', and also, where appropriate, with the help of the personnel, training or HRD department.

If the manager following this systematic process is not entirely without support and resources from within the organization, s/he must obviously at this stage

Inadequacy/ineffectiveness/absence of	Requiring staff development actions	Requiring other management actions
● Systems (e.g. production, distribution systems)	–	✓
● Resources (e.g. time, money, space, equipment, materials)	–	✓
● External environment (e.g. changes in working hours, employment laws, geographical location, economic/market conditions)	–	✓
● Communication	Possible	✓
● Procedures	Possible	✓
● Control	Possible	✓
● Planning	Possible	✓
● Knowledge and understanding	✓	–
● Skills	✓	–
● Attitudes (e.g. motivation, cooperation, discipline)	✓	–

Figure 13.5 The major causes of problems

(Check those parameters which are not meeting the department's objectives, targets and/or standards against the following major causes.)

Entry training	which involves new recruits and staff required to take on new jobs
Problem resolution	training to meet a shortfall or deficiency in job performance
Training for change	to prepare staff for jobs identified for the near future
Development	to equip staff for organisational changes in the future

Figure 13.6 Grouping the actions

consult with others to ensure that specific departmental plans fit in with any existing broad plan for the whole organization.

THE NUTS AND BOLTS OF TRAINING AND DEVELOPMENT

This section is intended to help the manager find the most appropriate and effective methods to implement his/her action plan. Ideally, such a departmental plan will be a reflection of the organization's overall staff development policy and so established methods will provide a good indicator as to the kinds of activities which best suit the organization's culture. In the absence of such a plan, the manager should begin by selecting the sorts of activities which are compatible with the prevailing culture and support any more adventurous moves later on with full consultation and discussion.

Training and development activities can be classified loosely according to whether they take place on or off the job and within or outside the organization. British managements traditionally favour off-the-job training methods, perhaps because these can be more readily quantified. That is not to say considerable on-the-job development does not go on in British organizations. Often activities listed here as falling within that category are simply not considered as such. They are often among the less expensive and less resource-intensive activities and yet can yield impressive and quantifiable benefits. For these reasons, more consideration is given to them here than to those off-the-job activities about which much has been written elsewhere.

Off-the-job training and development outside the organization

The course-providing industry is one which seems constantly to be expanding. The problem therefore is one of choice. Training is offered by a wide variety of institutions such as training organizations; consultancies; trade, industry and employer associations; plant and machinery suppliers; and publicly funded bodies such as government departments and training agencies.

These external resources must be used with care. Many of them can do a very good job, but others may not satisfy the organization's particular needs. At the very least when choosing a programme, it is important to see if what is being offered and expressed in terms of objectives and outcomes as well as methods actually fits the analysed training and development needs. It should also be remembered that however high the quality and/or the price tag of the external course or workshop, it cannot possibly do the total development job for any organization. There is always a need to reinforce a trainee's learning through thorough preparation and then debriefing, and also to supplement that learning with further training by applying it in the work place. That way, the knowledge and skills gained can be translated into job competence.

There are other, less obvious forms of off-the-job training and development outside the organization. These include periods of sabbatical study leave and secondments to other organizations. Secondments have been used in the UK to improve understanding of component manufacturing in assembly companies (and vice versa) and also for manufacturing companies to appreciate better the problems of the end user.

A large UK retailer also uses secondment as part of its personal development programme for senior managers. It seconds them for a year or more into charities or community enterprises which benefit from professional management expertise which they could not otherwise afford. The managers themselves benefit from the challenge of applying their competence in a very different environment.

Off-the-job training and development within the organization

Examples quoted here are in no particular order of priority. Whether or not they are selected for any particular department or organization will depend on the identified objectives for the training and development.

Subject workshops on specific issues

These can bring together all the personnel concerned with a particular issue or problem and focus their talents and energies on that issue. For example, a company in a highly competitive market might be concerned about keeping in touch with developments in its markets. The company could establish periodic 'competition workshops' whose purpose would be to provide information about competitors, create understanding about their people, plant systems and methods. This information could then be compared with the company's own, and ideas could be developed for beating the competition.

Senior management might be expected to participate in the first instance, but subsequently a wide range of employees (including supervisors and shop stewards) could be involved.

'By staff for staff' workshops/courses

These are used extensively by one well known American company in the highly competitive high-tech consumer goods market. This company's external environment and approach to staff development correspond closely to the 'strategic capability' model described earlier. They encourage staff members to prepare and give lectures, demonstrations or workshops on virtually any subject. These are advertised by the training department throughout the company. They begin in company time, but run over into personal time and are well attended. They accord with the company's general development policy of encouraging 'the habit of learning, the skills of learning and the desire to learn' amongst employees at all levels.

Quality circles and zero-defect groups

These can be used effectively to improve quality, to foster innovation and to increase employee involvement and commitment. However, they cannot simply be transplanted from the Japanese culture where they were born and grew up, to a completely alien one. Considerable preparation is needed through consultation and explanation. Also, specific training will be needed for circle participants and leaders in such skills as group work, statistical techniques, and presentation of recommendations. With considerable sensitivity to the prevailing culture, these circles and groups can make significant contributions.

Cross-functional project or problem groups

These can help in gaining the commitment of employees to, for example, the introduction of new technology affecting more than one functional area of the organization. To be effective, members of the groups need undertakings from more senior people that their proposals will receive full consideration.

Training departments in larger organizations

These may have the facilities and resources to provide tailor-made courses and workshops or even training programmes using high-tech facilities such as interactive video.

There is obviously more scope to ensure that the design of programmes closely mirrors the 'client' department's requirements when they are to be run in-house. However it is still important, as with external courses, to ensure that objectives are expressed in terms of job competence, and not simply knowledge and skills. That is not to denigrate 'pure' knowledge and skills programmes which may sometimes be needed when operational requirements mean that someone who is already competent in their job needs additional skills, for example, a foreign language or an ability to operate a new piece of equipment.

Open and distance learning

This does not fall squarely into any of the categories of activities since it may occur on or off the job and either inside the organization or in the employee's own time. In recent years open and distance learning materials have been produced which offer greater flexibility at lower unit costs than many traditional approaches. A survey of such materials, when considering the choice of development activities, might reveal that some of them support existing or proposed activities within the organization. Although the initial investment is large, there is at least one large British car manufacturer who speaks very enthusiastically about the benefits accruing from its open learning centre.

On-the-job development

Learning to do a job while actually carrying out the tasks involved used to be universally denigrated by trainers as 'sitting Mary next to Nelly'. If that were all that was involved, it might be an apt description. However, an approach to staff development which incorporates structured experience gained in handling different aspects of a job with planned inputs of knowledge and skills training, and aims at competence in job performance is a long way from the Mary and Nelly syndrome.

Work experience

This has been used for many years in traditional apprenticeship schemes although it could be argued that they have historically been too narrowly skill-based and have paid too little attention to competent job performance as an outcome.

Graduate entry schemes also often follow an off-the-job induction course with planned work experience in various departments.

The emphasis in modern youth training is away from education-led with some work experience, towards work-based learning with some education inputs.

Mentoring and coaching

These are ways of giving both organizational and individual support to someone's learning whilst they are in post. It can be as informal as a senior manager 'keeping a parental eye' on a recently appointed one who is not a direct subordinate. Alternatively, it can be used as a method of ensuring that someone in a technical or professional specialism gains and benefits from the right sort of work experience to progress to the next appropriate stage in their professional examinations. (See Chapter 16 on Mentoring.)

Another form of 'assisted' learning is the 'Meister' training used in Germany for supervisor and foreman training. These programmes are designed for people with similar background and although they include advanced technical knowledge, they also go beyond that. The programmes cover supervisory competence, commercial understanding and the ability to plan and carry out training of, and coaching for, those for whom the supervisor is responsible.

Planned job development

This can be seen as a staff development activity or as something that any good manager does anyway. The choice might depend on how receptive the senior manager being 'sold' these ideas was likely to be and whether they challenged the prevailing culture or not.

An example might be job rotation. People should not be left in the same job for too long, but given opportunities for acquiring wider experience. This is not merely a matter of sensible preparation for promotion, but also a useful way of bringing fresh minds to bear on old problems. Equally, a planned system of deputizing for absent colleagues (either on a similar or somewhat more senior level) could serve a dual purpose. The work of the person on holiday/overseas assignment/sabbatical would not just be left to pile up and the person 'standing in' would be adding to his/her personal development in a planned and anticipated way.

Finally personnel decisions about, for example, overseas postings or domestic relocations can be influenced as much by development criteria as say, promotion decisions are. It is all part of effective succession planning to ensure that personal development is a continuous process between promotional steps. A detailed and comprehensive database is of course an essential tool for a manager looking at these issues for his/her department.

Effective implementation of on-the-job development activities has been made much easier for managers in the field in the American 'strategic capability' company quoted earlier. That is because that company's training department has placed great emphasis on 'being close to the action'. Very few training officers are to be found anywhere near the training department. Instead, they are loosely attached to the various major functional departments of the company and are trained specifically to help departmental managers identify their training needs and plan suitable programmes within departments.

This is perhaps an extreme example of close cooperation between training and operating departments, but it serves to illustrate that appropriate expertise should be available to managers in companies big enough to have their own training departments. It is also clear from observing many other companies involved in this type of programme that any type of off- or on-the-job development programme needs meticulous planning and thorough training of any staff who will be used as trainers, mentors or coaches if it is to succeed.

CHECKLIST

Starter Questions:
1 Are business objectives and people development clearly linked in terms of performance?
2 Have you got mechanisms for looking at your company's competitive and wider environment?
3 Which of the four 'models' (see pp. 200–201) most closely fit your particular circumstances?
4 Do employees (management and staff) know whose responsibility it is to identify HRD needs and get them fulfilled?

Assessing training and development needs in five steps

1 Collect information.
2 Investigate and surface problems.
3 Identify causes.
4 Separate those problems requiring other management actions from those requiring staff development actions.
5 Sequence priorities and plan actions.

How to meet these needs

Off the job and outside the organization

1 Courses.
2 Sabbatical study leave.
3 Secondment.

Off the job within the organization

1 Subject workshops on specific issues.
2 'By staff for staff' workshops/courses.
3 Quality circles and zero-defect groups.
4 Cross-functional project or problem groups.
5 Training department facilities.
6 Open and distance learning.

On the job development

1 Work experience.
2 Mentoring and coaching.
3 Planned job development.

FURTHER READING

Rae, Leslie, *The Skills of Training*, Gower, 1983.

14 Making performance appraisal work

Andrew M. Stewart

A large part of your job as a manager involves getting other people to do things that you cannot do, either because you do not have time or you do not have the necessary knowledge or skills yourself. Performance appraisal is intended to help you plan and control the process of managing your people so that they do what you want well.

Although a great deal has been written and said about performance appraisal few people report that they are satisfied with the way it is done in their organization. This is perhaps because people have made a basically straightforward process too complicated.

The essence of performance appraisal is achieved when two people, the manager and the managed, sit down together about once a year to agree answers to the following questions:

- What did we set out to do during the last year?
- Did we do it?
- What are we going to do next?
- How will we know if we have done it?

This chapter offers some of the ways in which people have tried to answer those four questions.

THE PURPOSES OF PERFORMANCE APPRAISAL

People cannot learn unless you tell them how they are doing. Even this will not help much unless the feedback is both regular and frequent. Both successes and failures should be discussed. You should give feedback as soon as possible after the event. In the daily rush of getting things done you may well feel that you do not have time to do this. A formal performance appraisal scheme is supposed to make sure that even the most busy people get at least one chance a year to sit down with their manager to learn how they are doing, to correct their mistakes and to add new skills. Formal performance appraisal once a year is no substitute for daily contact and discussion with your staff about their work in the short term.

You will be reviewing past performance and planning to meet the needs of the future, so you are constantly preparing to manage change. You should be considering longer range targets, thus making positive and controlled growth for the organization more likely through the planned efforts of individuals. You will find that you and your subordinate have an opportunity to move back from daily fire fighting to considering courses of action which may reduce the need for constant short term action. Finally, you and your people are expensive. It makes sense to try to encourage everyone's best efforts.

A performance appraisal interview can be one of the most motivating events in an employee's year. If you handle it badly, it can be a disaster. There are usually four parties to an appraisal: the appraisee, the manager, the central planning and personnel departments and external bodies. The external bodies may include training boards, trade unions, and various groups set up to monitor or enforce equal opportunities legislation. The interests of the appraisee and the appraiser are the most important. Performance appraisal done mainly for planning or defence purposes is unlikely to encourage people to perform well.

Appraisal systems are used for three main purposes: remedial, maintenance, and development. You need a mix of all three in about equal proportions. The remedial part of the discussion is concerned with putting right things that are going wrong. If you do too much of this, then the appraisal interview can become a disciplinary interview, and the record form becomes a charge sheet.

The maintenance part of the discussion is concerned with encouraging the appraisee to continue to do those things he does well. If you over-emphasize this purpose, then the interview can become little more than a nod and a steady-as-you-go-message, without any depth or chance for your appraisee to raise new issues.

The development part of the discussion is concerned with what the appraisee needs to be aiming for next as a person. If there is too much emphasis on development, then you will find that you are spending too much time talking about the next job rather than the one currently in hand. You may even be seen as offering promises of future progress.

Above all, the appraisal interview is a time for you to listen. Your subordinate probably has a fairly accurate idea of how he is doing, and this is unlikely to disagree much with your view. In fact, your subordinate may well be tougher on himself than you would want to be.

VARIETIES OF SYSTEM

Many variations in appraisal systems have been tried. There is no single best method, but it is possible to list the main options so that you can select the ones that best fit your circumstances:

- Eligibility. Are all staff covered, or managers and salaried staff only?
- Employee access. Do employees see all of their form, some of their form, or none of it?
- Self-appraisal. Is this done at all, formally, or informally?
- Preparation for counselling. Is this offered at all, formally or informally?

- Is past performance only appraised, or is there a separate opportunity to discuss present performance?
- Measurement. Is this against performance targets or objectives, rating scales of performance, rating scales of personality, or are no measurement criteria specified?
- Rating scales. Are they used? How many divisions are offered on the scale?
- Target setting. Is there an opportunity to set specific and measurable targets for future performance?
- Training and development needs. Are these discussed for the present job, the next job, or for the longer term?
- Potential. Is this assessed at all? If so, is it on a one-dimensional scale, multidimensional, or by some form of narrative?
- Salary. Is discussion of this forbidden, compulsory, or optional?
- Frequency and regularity. How often do appraisals take place? Is there a set time of year which is the same for all, or are the interviews conducted on the anniversary of arrival in that post?
- Disputes. Are these resolved by appeal to manager's manager, personnel, union, or by no set procedure?
- Access. Who else may see the forms apart from the main people involved? What for?
- Storage. How are the forms kept and for how long? Do you need to comply with the provisions of the Data Protection Act?
- Use. Are the forms used for central planning, day-to-day management, coaching, internal selection, or any other reason?

The design of your system should reflect the answers you give to those questions. If your system is not working well, it may be that it is being used for purposes for which it was not originally designed.

Linking salary with performance appraisal

Should you link salary with performance appraisal at the interview? If salary is seen simply as compensation for work done, then the link with performance is weak. If salary is used as an incentive, to reward outstanding work and to encourage rising standards, then a link with performance seems clear.

The best way to manage this link is probably to have both performance and salary rated on the same scale, but separated by six months. In this way, everyone understands the system, but you have some freedom to vary the salary rating if your subordinate's work standard has changed significantly since the performance review. If salary review and performance appraisal occur at the same time you may feel tempted to drift the rating upwards in order to be able to give a satisfactory salary. This introduces distortions which have to be corrected later, usually upsetting everyone in the process.

WHO SHOULD DO IT?

Despite all the effort put into design and implementation, employee attitude surveys continue to show that few performance appraisal schemes are thought to work well. There are probably two reasons. The wrong people are doing the appraisals, and the organization is not serious in its support of them or the process.

The wrong people

Elliott Jaques has suggested that hierarchy is inherent in the nature of work. Jobs can be classified in terms of the target completion time of the longest task, project, or programme assigned to that job. This is called the time span, and is sometimes translated as 'how long before you are found out'. He has also shown that the nature of jobs changes suddenly at particular points in the time span range (3 months, 1 year, 2, 5, 10, 20, and 50 years). The change is quite like that which occurs to water at different temperatures. Water can be ice, water, or steam. The change is very clear, and happens suddenly at quite precise points on the temperature range, and yet the substance remains the same. It is merely in different states.

Just as different jobs have different time spans, so people have correspondingly different time frames within which they are most comfortable and competent to operate. People can develop and rise in organizations at different rates until they arrive at the time frame that is most appropriate for them, and in which they can operate in the mode which best suits them.

Appraisees are more likely to perceive the appraisal process as legitimate if their appraiser is working one level higher in time span terms, and is one category higher in time frame terms. In other words, a 5-year-job holder will find it hard to accept an appraisal unless their appraiser is occupying a 10-year-job, and is seen as personally capable of doing so. At a time when many organizations are reducing the number of layers in their structure, this form of analysis provides a rational, job-related basis for doing so. However, it can also leave a manager with a large number of subordinates to appraise.

The final responsibility and authority for the evaluative and judgemental content of the appraisal process should remain with the manager. The developmental aspects, however, can well be provided by a range of people. Self appraisal can be encouraged and developed, together with peer appraisal. If the appraisee has been engaged on several projects, the project leaders should be consulted. Upward appraisal by subordinates may be acceptable, and can be highly revealing, particularly of management style and perceived competence. Progress in, and any outcomes of, coaching or mentoring may generate further useful information. Where the appraisee has direct customer contact, the customers' input should be sought.

The manager who follows this approach has broadened the base on which an appraisal rests, and has delegated a good deal of the initial data gathering and some of the developmental discussion. He leaves himself with the task of understanding the various comments, turning them into a coherent whole, and discussing the overview and the evaluation with the appraisee.

In addition, a manager needs the skills and competencies to sustain the appraisal activity. Someone relatively unintelligent, socially inept, and untrained is not likely to deliver an effective appraisal. Further, a manager needs to be temperamentally suited to managing other people. There are many able and highly motivated people who are given management positions as a career reward for excellent technical work, despite the fact that they have little interest in managing, and would prefer not to have to deal with anything as vague and unpredictable as people. These people can find appraisal boring, unimportant, incomprehensible, or threatening. They will not conduct effective appraisals.

The organization

Even if the right person is asked to conduct the appraisal, the organization needs to play its part by providing efficient support systems, including paperwork, an appraisal procedure manual, and training in both content and the necessary interpersonal skills. A manager should not be permitted to conduct performance appraisals until he has completed the necessary training. Although many trainers are uncomfortable with this, evidence should be supplied that the training has been successful. Training without tested outcomes runs the risk of being neither effective nor taken seriously.

Most importantly, the organization culture should be overtly supportive of performance appraisal as part of its declared aim of taking human resource management seriously. The best evidence for this is when the managers' own rewards, both money and career, depend in part on their effectiveness at appraising and developing their people. If nothing that matters to managers is affected by how they appraise their people they will conclude, correctly, that the organization does not rate the importance of performance appraisal very highly. They will instead concentrate their attention and effort on those activities which do get noticed. This is why so many schemes fail.

PERFORMANCE CRITERIA

The criteria against which people are judged should be genuinely related to success or failure in the job. As far as possible, you should avoid subjectivity. It is also helpful if the criteria are easy to understand and administer, and they appear fair and relevant to employees.

There are two main measures in use in performance appraisal: personality and performance.

Personality measures are not much favoured nowadays. They are difficult to apply reliably. They depend heavily on the quality of the relationship between you and your subordinate. There is little that anyone can do easily if they are told their personality is deficient in some way. This can be highly demotivating and helps no one.

Performance measures have largely replaced personality measures. They have two main forms: rating scales and objectives.

Rating scales are generally printed on the form and are held to apply to all employees. They should be based on a thorough analysis of the skills and competencies relevant to your organization. They allow you to measure change in an employee over time. They also allow you to make comparisons between employees. This is useful if you want to use appraisal records for central planning of salaries, careers or succession. The main disadvantage of rating scales is that managers may not be using the same standards when they rate people on the scales, so the comparisons are not as fair as they might seem.

Objectives provide an individual performance measure, agreed between you and your employee. This gives you and your subordinate much more freedom to decide how you want to measure performance. This can also help motivate you and your people because you will have to discuss and understand the standards that you are using, whereas rating scales can be centrally imposed without a real discussion of standards. The main disadvantage of objectives is that no common yardstick may exist between different appraisers and appraisees, making cross-comparison very difficult.

It may be possible and desirable to combine rating scales and objectives in one system, thereby getting the best of both worlds. If you take this option, however, be sure to keep both sections brief, otherwise no one will want to fill the thing in!

Precision in measurement is important and desirable, but not at the expense of having a system which people are prepared to try to operate. If quantitative measure is possible and appropriate, then use it. On the other hand, a qualitative measure, the meaning of which is clear to you and your subordinate, is usually preferable to a quantitative measure which assesses with great accuracy something that does not matter much.

Examples of the various types of measure, in increasing order of precision, are:

- Personality: drive, loyalty, integrity.
- Performance: accuracy, clarity, analytical ability.
- Objectives: 'sell x items by y date to z customers'.

Each organization should seek out its own performance measures. An off-the-shelf prescription for the universal employee seems unlikely to be available for some time yet. You are much safer finding your own measures locally. Once you have found them, be prepared to change them as the needs of your people and the organization change. If you do not do this, you can find yourself appraising people against criteria which are no longer relevant to what you are trying to do.

SYSTEM DESIGN

Each of the four main groups of people involved in appraisal has different but overlapping purposes. These purposes all have implications for the way the system is designed.

The appraisee will want to make a contribution to the appraisal. This implies a face to face interview. They may need to sign the form to show that they agree with its contents – or have at least seen them. If they want long term guidance the system will need to provide the chance to discuss ambitions, training needs, and abilities which may not be evident in the present work. If they want to undertake some form of self-development, then you should provide copies of written objectives to which both of you can refer whenever you need to. There should also be further mini-appraisals during the year to check that self-development is actually happening. Many employees also find that a formal preparation for counselling form helps them to conduct their own self-appraisal before you meet, leading to a faster, better focused, and more constructive discussion.

The appraiser will want the employee to work to agreed goals and standards. This means that the system must make it possible to set and record a number of objectives and personal goals, with standards. These goals may need coordinating with those of other employees, so it must be possible to record the information in such a way that it can be shared. The preparation for counselling form should provide the appraiser with clues about the aspirations, unused skills, and constraints on performance perceived by the subordinate. There should also be a record of training needs and the extent to which they are being met. If money is being used as compensation, then you can communicate a salary increase at the interview, since pay and performance are not directly linked. If money is being used as an incentive, then you should conduct the salary review as a separate but related exercise.

Central planning and control may wish to conduct a manpower skills audit. If so, then there must be some common performance criteria across all employees. For manpower planning purposes the form may need to record additionally information about age, job history, mobility, and family circumstances. Succession planning will require the assessment of employee potential, as objectively as possible, together with judged suitability, aspirations and current performance. Salary planning may require an overall performance rating across all characteristics for the production of norms. The training function will need to know the overall picture of training needs to decide training priorities. Equity between employees can be checked by central monitoring of both quality and promptness of appraisals, and by a formal system for handling those who perform below standard.

Outside parties may have requirements which affect the design of your system. Local, industry or national codes of good practice may emphasise the need for job-relevant criteria, equity of treatment, and the handling of poor performers. Legislation concerning privacy and rights of access may require that employees be able to see the whole form, and that there be adequate safeguards against misleading interpretation, such as employee sign-off and a comment space. There will need to be a formal grievance procedure and a clear policy about who has access to appraisal information and for what purposes, together with location and duration of storage of records. There are particular requirements under the Protection of Data Act 1986 which may apply if you store any part of the information electronically.

DESIGNING THE FORMS

Because it is more complicated to approach appraisal system design in terms of the purposes of the various users, people often spend a great deal of time and effort designing the forms instead. The ideal appraisal form is sometimes said to be a blank piece of paper, so it may not be wise to spend too much time on elaborate forms. To keep the whole exercise as simple as possible, however, some suggestions may be helpful.

If individual objectives are to form the core of the process, then you need a blank piece of paper divided down the middle, with objectives on the left hand side and standards of performance on the right. You should be careful not to set too many objectives; nor should you try to cover the whole job. About half a dozen main objectives is enough. Anything more detailed than that is more suitable for day-to-day management rather than the overview of the year that performance appraisal is concerned with. Qualitative objectives, provided both parties understand them, can be just as useful as quantitative ones.

If narrative summaries are to be used, then the form will contain a list of key words, such as accuracy, speed, cash control, or timing. You will be asked to write a two-line summary of the employee's performance against each of these characteristics. This method has the advantage that it does apply common yardsticks across large groups of people, but does not ask for undue precision.

Rating scales will require that you rate the employee on each criterion, using a scale with a number of divisions. There is no point in offering more than five divisions. Scales with seven, nine or even thirteen points have been seen. Managers treat them as slightly vague five-point scales.

There are likely to be endless arguments about whether there should be an odd or an even number of points on the scale. Some people like a middle-point. Others regard a middle point as enabling a manager to avoid making up his mind. You can avoid the whole issue in this way: label the points on the scale, avoiding the word 'average', so that the first four are concerned with above the line performance, and only the fifth records work that is below standard. For example:

- Exceeds standards in all respects.
- Exceeds standards in most respects.
- Exceeds standards in some respects.
- Meets standards.
- Fails to meet standards.

In this case ratings are being made against the requirements of the job, not against colleagues. In addition, the scale can be described as a five-point scale, or as a four-point scale with an extra box for the unsatisfactory performer. You might also offer a 'not applicable' box for those cases where a particular measure is irrelevant to the job. Any overall rating should follow the separate rating scales. You could find it useful to consider a separate column to record immediate past performance. This emphasizes the fact that appraisal is supposed to be a review of the entire previous year, and allows any recent, marked changes in performance to be noted without distorting the way you judge the rest of the year's work.

Finally, keep reviewing your forms and system to make sure they are still relevant and helpful. Use the system: do not be used by it. If it does not help you to manage better, change it.

TRAINING

Appraisal training falls into three parts. First, obtain the managers' commitment. Second, train them in the formal systems and procedures. Third, train them in the necessary interview and interpersonal skills.

Commitment is best obtained by holding a series of meetings at which all those who will be affected by the system have a chance to hear what is being proposed and to argue about it. The purposes of the appraisal system must be very clear. You can negotiate about system design, but try to avoid getting bogged down in form design. The form should be the simplest possible that will support the purposes. This will win you quite a lot of friends.

Systems and procedures training should not take place until commitment has been obtained, otherwise much time will be spent trying to answer the question 'why' when the training is designed to answer the question 'what'. The training should tell managers why there is to be an appraisal system, what organizational improvements it is intended to produce, what actually happens in the interview, how the form is filled in, when, by whom, who receives the form, what happens to the information, and whose job it is to see that the actions agreed on the form are actually carried out. Special attention needs to be given to the grievance and poor performer procedures.

Skills training is only useful after successful completion of the first two stages; otherwise disruption is highly likely. Three approaches to training may be worth considering.

Role play is used automatically by many trainers. The main dangers are that people can always opt out by saying, correctly, that it is not real life. It can be useful, however, where attitude change is important. Trainees can be asked to play the part of someone whose attitude they need to understand, such as someone passed over for promotion. Role play can also help to unfreeze people by asking them to experiment with a new appraisal personality.

Real life counselling involves one participant counselling another about a genuine work or personal problem, under guidance, while the rest of the participants observe. This certainly lacks the artificiality of role play, but can get out of hand. Perhaps because of this risk it can be a better vehicle for learning counselling skills than the normal role play, where there are no real consequences.

Live appraisal of real tasks uses the following sequence:

- one person performs an appraisable activity while the rest of the small group observe;
- all prepare to appraise the volunteer, who prepares to be appraised;
- one person appraises while the rest observe;
- all prepare to appraise the appraisal, while the appraiser prepares to be appraised;
- one person then appraises the appraisal while the rest observe.

Repeat the module as often as necessary, and conclude with a general review. The exact nature of the starting task does not matter, so long as there is enough to appraise. Subsequent appraisals quickly become surprisingly real, and issues to do with objectives, standards and the basis of measurement will soon emerge. Rich feedback is essential, and a videotape can help a good deal as people will sometimes not believe that they have done or said what the observers say they did. Keep the focus on objective matters, such as who was talking most at various points of the interview, the amount of time devoted to extremes of performance versus the amount of time used to talk about the regular performance, the use of open and closed questions, and the amount of positive versus negative feedback offered.

If managers are reluctant to appraise or to be trained to do so, try offering training to their subordinates in being appraised. As soon as managers get to hear that their subordinates are likely to know more than they do about appraisal, there will be a queue outside the training manager's door.

Common issues needing attention in the skills training stage include: knowing your own biases, being prepared to discuss both good and poor performance in a straightforward manner, using open, closed or reflective questions, handling conflict, listening skills, and summarizing skills.

Common pitfalls met in appraisal, which therefore should be covered by the training, include: the halo effect, avoiding extremes of rating, talking too much, failing to support opinions with evidence, inadequate briefing of the appraisee, prejudging performance, not allowing enough time for the interview, not finding the right place for the interview, appraising on feelings rather than facts, overstating weaknesses or strengths, failing to take account of special circumstances, making false assumptions, and basing judgements on too short a time span. Training in these skills can have benefits well beyond the appraisal interview.

MONITORING AND CONTROL

All appraisal systems need monitoring. Particularly in the early stages of a new system you should be on the alert for two main kinds of problem: misunderstanding of terms, and misunderstanding the system.

Misunderstanding of terms may occur, particularly common ones such as objective, job description, man specification, training needs, development needs, counselling, personality, performance and behaviour. Trainers and management developers will be familiar with them but managers may not be, or may have developed their own peculiar definitions.

Misunderstanding the system will show up by forms going to the wrong place or being filled in late, inadequate coverage of certain employees or groups, peculiar use of rating scales, or partial completion of the forms.

Actions recommended on the appraisal forms should be followed up to see if anything is actually happening. The types of objectives being agreed can also be checked as part of this exercise. Predictions, particularly of potential, can be checked to see if they turned out to be correct in practice. Employee attitudes can be checked by means of a survey.

The following items have been found to be significant indicators of good interviews:

- I had a clear idea of his/her career path.
- He/she and I had the same idea about the direction of his/her career.
- My manager agreed with my rating.
- My rating came as no surprise to him/her.
- She/he accepted my rating of her/him.
- She/he fitted in with the rest of the work group.

- We wanted the same outcome from the interview.
- I could see him/her as my manager some day.

It made no difference to the effectiveness of the interview whether the manager had selected the employee for the job initially or not, nor whether the interview was conducted in the office or outside.

Any survey of employee opinions will raise their expectations. If you are not prepared to do anything differently as a result of what you find, do not start. There should be a policy about feedback of results, a method of feeding back locally useful results fast, and a commitment by top management to visible action if the results show a need for change.

IDENTIFYING POTENTIAL

Performance appraisal is designed to look backwards in order to look forwards. The best predictions of potential, using performance appraisal as the basis, are made when the next job is not very different from the previous one. The more different the new job is, the less likely is it that track record will be enough on its own. It would seem that performance appraisal is essential but insufficient as a predictor of future performance in a significantly different job.

There are many alternatives or supplements to performance appraisal as a means of identifying potential. These include assessment centres, psychological tests, assignments, secondments, peer and self-assessment, action learning programmes, career path appreciation, and so on. Ideally, any rating of potential will rest on more than one criterion or trait, more than one assessor, and more than one technique. In this way more reliable judgements may be reached in a difficult area.

If performance appraisal is to play a useful part in predicting potential, you should ensure that appraisal is on the basis of performance, not personality. The performance criteria should relate to success in the future job, not the present one. The appraising manager should know enough about the possible future job that he or she can actually make informed judgements. If you do not know much about the job, it is unlikely that you will be able to assess someone's suitability to do it.

Unsupported by other techniques, performance appraisal information can be seriously misleading as a predictor of potential. It can lead directly to appointing people to jobs just one level beyond their competence, since there is no information thus far in their careers that they are reaching their limit. You only find out by pushing them over it. This is neither kind nor efficient. However, the information yielded by a well designed and run performance appraisal system is a vital element in decisions about people's career potential.

PROBLEM PERFORMERS

People perform poorly for many reasons. Your first task is to discover which particular combination of reasons applies in the case in front of you. The problem may lie in a number of factors:

- *Intelligence.* Too little, too much, specific defects of judgement or memory.

- *Emotional stability.* Over-excitable, anxious, depressed, jealous, sexual problems, neurosis, psychosis, alcoholism, drug addiction.
- *Motivation to work.* Low motivation, low work standards, lack of organization, frustration, conflict.
- *Family situation.* Domestic crises, separation from family, social isolation from peer group, money worries.
- *Physical characteristics.* Illness, handicap, strength, age, endurance, build.
- *Work group.* Fragmented, over-cohesive, inappropriate leadership, wrong mix of personalities.
- *The organization.* Inappropriate standards, too little investment and management support, poor communication, span of control too large, responsibility without authority.
- *External influences.* Employment legislation, consumer pressure, health and safety legislation, changing social values, economic forces, change of location, trade union pressure.

Once you have found out what the causes of the problem may be, then you can use the appraisal system as part of the process of dismissal for unsatisfactory performance. Alternatively, and preferably, the system can be used to manage those people so that their performance improves and the problem no longer exists. Some of the options for action are:

- *Counselling.* Self-appraisal, preparation for counselling, some form of job climate questionnaire, vocational guidance, mid-career guidance, medical or psychological help, financial counselling.
- *Training and development.* As a reward and encouragement, not punishment; set up with precise, measurable objectives, careful monitoring and close follow-up.
- *Changing the job.* Physical layout, timing, induction, responsibility without authority, no feedback, late or distorted feedback, too many figurehead duties, little or no control over the job content, insufficient warning of changes, shared management of subordinates.
- *Termination.* This does not have to be rushed or without compassion; it can take account of financial arrangements, time off to look for a new job, vocational guidance, training in being interviewed, and an exit interview to try to ensure that all administrative loose ends are tied up and no residual resentments are unexpressed.

There is also an option to change jobs within the organization. Some appraisal schemes specifically exclude this possibility. In those systems your options are to help your subordinate improve his performance to a satisfactory standard, or to dismiss him. This runs the risk of sending away someone who could do a perfectly good job if he were in the right post. The idea is to avoid managers shuffling poor performers around the system instead of coping with the problem, but it seems likely to be wasteful to make a rigid rule that stops you trying someone out in a different role.

There are particular groups who perform badly simply because they are unhappy or confused. You might have this kind of problem with new graduates

If you do the following things in the order listed you can be fairly sure that nothing major will have been overlooked.

1   Agree a time, date and place for the appraisal well in advance.

2   Make sure the place is private and free from interruptions.

3   Set aside ample time — at least two hours.

4   Bring all relevant results and information about the appraisee's performance.

5   Ask the appraisee to review his/her performance point by point.

6   Ask the appraisee about any problems which might affect performance.

7   Ask the appraisee about the implications of any problems or events, and their effect on the individual, the team and the work.

8   Ask the appraisee what needs to be done by either of you to help improve performance.

9   The appraisee should ask about anything which she/he feels is affecting her/his performance.

10   Agree the key result areas.

11   The appraisee should suggest and agree standards of performance for the next review period.

12   You should suggest and agree standards of performance for the next review period.

13   Agree future action.

14   Make sure the record is complete and agreed or signed off.

15   Close with a firm date for the next interim review.

Figure 14.1   Checklist – performance appraisal sequence

who feel that their abilities and expectations are not being met by what you are asking them to do. If people do not get a proper induction into the organization they will almost certainly be uncertain and unhappy for a while, and their work may suffer permanently as a result of wrong conclusions drawn and poor attitudes developed through lack of early guidance.

Older employees might feel that they have reached their ceiling, or they might be experiencing difficulty with the increasing pace of change and the slower learning patterns that can occur with older people. People without clear career paths would appreciate information and options. People with a poor history in the organization need help to discover whether the problem is real and not merely a reputation which is following them around without any real backing.

The performance appraisal system should assist you to produce information, objectives and controls to assist with most of these situations, making the need to dismiss someone for poor performance rarer. The system should also help you to be more sure-footed when you do need to dismiss someone.

CONCLUSION AND CHECKLIST

Your performance appraisal system should help you to be a better manager, and should save you and your subordinates time. If it does not do this, sit down and analyse where the shortcomings are, and work on changing them. Remember the four questions:

- What did we set out to do last year?
- Did we do it?
- What are we going to do next?
- How will we know if we have done it?

Make sure that you can answer these questions. If you find that you are required to do much more than this, ask what is done with the results of the questions. If the answer is nothing, do not ask them. If the answer is of no benefit to you or your subordinates, question whether the performance appraisal interview is the right place to be asking them. Keep the system simple and direct. In this way you will make it more likely that managers will actually do their appraisals, and you stand a better chance of understanding the results. For a checklist on performance appraisal sequence, see Figure 14.1.

FURTHER READING

Boyatzis, R. E., *The Competent Manager*, Wiley, 1982

Handy, C. B., *Understanding Organizations*, 3rd edition, Penguin, 1987

Herriot, P. (ed.), *Assessment and Selection in Organizations*, Wiley, 1989

Jaques, E., 'In praise of hierarchy', *Harvard Business Review*, Jan–Feb. 1990, pp. 127–133.

Stewart, V. and Stewart, A., *Practical Performance Appraisal*, Gower, 1977.

Stewart, V. and Stewart, A., *Managing the Poor Performer*, Gower, 1982.

15 Counselling in the workplace

Mike Megranahan

The use of counselling and counselling skills in an employment context is growing as companies become increasingly aware of the benefits that can be gained, to both employee and employer, from these interactions. A trained employee represents a valuable asset which needs to be protected in the same way as plant and machinery. Councelling is one way of providing the company, as a whole, with the means of alleviating different problems which if not identified, discussed and resolved could erode the effectiveness of the person, not only as an asset in the organization, but as an individual.

Every person at one time or another is likely to experience a personal or job-related problem. Most people are unable to package problems neatly and confine them to specific areas and thereby avoid the effect that one may have on the other, e.g. home on work. If the employee perceives his manager or supervisor as potentially sympathetic and approachable, the opportunity to discuss the problem may be sufficient to help him see how it can be resolved. Any manager would be expected in the course of his job to undertake a number of formal and informal (or ad hoc) interactions with employees. The use of appropriate interactive skills in these situations should enable these contacts to be constructive, improve communication, and encourage trust.

This chapter attempts to demonstrate the differences between counselling and the use of counselling skills. It should also increase awareness of the respective uses of counselling and counselling skills, i.e. which should be used, when, how and by whom.

WHAT IS COUNSELLING?

Counselling may simply be described as a form of communication between two people. The person in the role of counsellor should be trained in counselling techniques; the person seeking counselling may need assistance with a particular area of concern. These elements set counselling apart as a form of communication. In addition, a number of important themes arising from different counselling strategies make counselling distinct from other forms of helping. For instance,

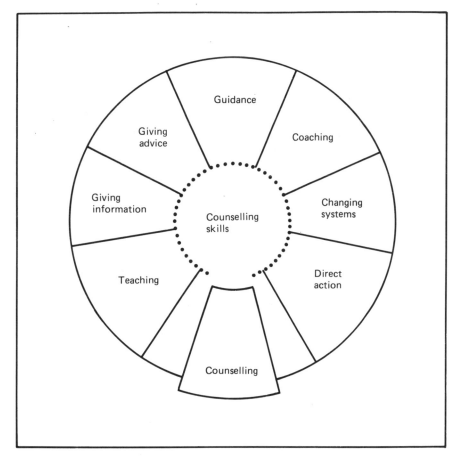

Figure 15.1   Helping interventions

(Taken from Megranahan, M. S, 'Counselling at work', *Journal of General Management*, Vol. 11, no. 1, Autumn 1985.)

counselling essentially adopts the premise that the person is the expert on their problem and the process of counselling is therefore used to:

- help the person talk about, explore and understand his/her thoughts and feelings, and work out what s/he might do before taking action; and further
- the person is helped to decide on his/her own solutions.

Other forms of helping

The need for counselling depends on the circumstances at the time; alternative strategies may be more appropriate and these may be enhanced through the application of counselling skills. The other forms of help which may be available to a person are summarized in Figure 15.1. Most can be readily identified with. We have all been in a position of giving or receiving most of these forms of interaction. In all these forms of assistance, the source needs to be perceived by the person to possess sufficient relevant expertise to justify contact. Where a person simply needs some information, for instance, counselling would be inappropriate, although counselling skills may help to establish and clarify the need for the information.

COUNSELLING SKILLS

Counselling skills may be applied in a variety of situations, forming an integral part of the manager's one-to-one interaction with employees. In addition to the use of the actual techniques of counselling skills, the manager needs to consider other important aspects. For instance, the manager needs to be consistent in the use of counselling skills across a range of formal and informal interactions with employees. He also needs to assess which situations merit the use of these skills: some situations may require more directive action.

Areas where counselling skills would be applicable

The manager, through knowledge of his employees, should be able to determine when counselling skills may be usefully employed and would therefore form a useful addition to his 'kit bag' of skills. Further, the organization provides the manager with the 'inbuilt' opportunity for him to demonstrate his approach to employees on a one-to-one basis through formal contacts. For instance:

- disciplinary interviews;
- appraisal interviews;
- coaching an employee;
- redundancy;
- pre-retirement;
- career development interviews.

Once employees become aware of a manager's style of interaction, e.g. enabling employees to communicate fully and in confidence, with a tangible end result, informal interactions may develop. These could include work- or home-related aspects which if confronted jointly by the manager and the employee at an early stage may avoid later deterioration of relationships and work performance. This mutual objective could help to identify ways in which the particular concern could be alleviated and may involve referral to a counselling resource. Examples of informal contacts are:

- ill health at home;
- mounting debt;
- feelings of isolation from work colleagues.

The employee may or may not be keen to volunteer thoughts, feelings or other information which he may perceive as potentially damaging to his situation if revealed to the manager. Therefore, if suspicion exists between a manager and an employee, communication is likely to be limited and interaction poor. Directive action in this case may lead the employee to further suppress and withhold information. This cycle could also develop between the manager and other employees resulting in poor working relationships and repercussions on aspects such as morale, attendance etc. Counselling skills, if used appropriately, could avoid this downward spiral.

What are counselling skills?

For counselling skills to be effective, the manager needs to have an awareness of his existing style of interaction and its subsequent impact on employees. Once this awareness has been developed, the manager may consciously make use of counselling skills to improve or refine interactions and therefore communication with others.

Appropriate verbal responses associated with counselling skills are insufficient if used in isolation. Consequently the following guidelines need to be drawn upon to identify and utilize those facets necessary to a positive outcome. The guidelines are applicable to many formal and informal contacts and are as important as the person's ability to use spoken techniques effectively.

PRELIMINARY PHASE

The physical setting for the interaction needs to be comfortable for both parties. Consider seating arrangements, e.g. do not have the employee facing direct sunlight, the room should be sound-proof, there should be no interruptions and the employee should have the sole attention of the manager. If background information is available or applicable then this should have been read and digested well in advance of the meeting.

INTRODUCTORY PHASE

The manager should attempt to establish an open atmosphere for the meeting. The initial contact with the employee is important – rapport needs to be established quickly since this can set the tone for the whole interaction. It may take longer to establish this aspect with some employees but it remains an essential element of future progress.

If defensive attitudes are detected in the employee then attempts should be made to overcome these, for example, by explaining the purpose, structure and objectives of the meeting.

WORKING PHASE

The discussion with the employee should be conducted without the use of unfamiliar jargon or technical terms. Confidence and trust need to be developed as a result of the interaction.

Effective listening is very important and the employee needs to be able to recognize that this is taking place. This requires 'reading' beyond the actual words that are spoken, attending to what is *not* said.

There should be empathic understanding of the employee's difficulty; this requires an understanding from the employee's point of view, to see and appreciate the feelings he has in his situation as he experiences it. Non-critical acceptance of the employee's difficulty is important.

Interruptions to the employee's flow of dialogue should be avoided. Be prepared for periods of silence and therefore avoid feelings of awkwardness. Opportunity should be given to the employee to express feelings and emotions; and as far as possible these should be reflected.

PLANNING PHASE

At the conclusion of the interaction, what was said and decided should be summarized and agreed upon:

- define the action he/she wants/needs to take;
- express this in concrete attainable goals;
- identify the strengths and resources he/she possesses;
- what resources and skills he/she may need to acquire;
- provision to provide support and encouragement.

Appropriate interview techniques and question style

The introductory, working and planning phases of the meeting need to be supported by an awareness of the use of both verbal and non-verbal responses by the manager. The employee needs to be encouraged to consider and express his concern fully. He will also be very conscious of the way in which the manager is responding to him, an aspect which needs to be remembered. Various techniques may be usefully applied during the interview to assist both the manager and employee to ensure that important aspects are covered. Some of the main techniques and associated question styles are shown in Figures 15.2 and 15.3. The latter needs careful forethought, since the types of questions asked will either block or elicit responses from the employee. In addition, the nature and form of the questions needs to be supported by the non-verbal actions of the manager (discussed later).

Non-verbal communication – an area for caution

If what every person said could be relied upon to be a true expression of their thoughts and feelings then the above would suffice. However, this is rarely the case and the person conducting the interview needs to be aware of other indicators during the interaction which may be contrary to the verbal communication.

Equally the person conducting the interview will be projecting a range of non-verbal communications to the employee and it is essential that these support the

TECHNIQUE	PURPOSE	QUESTION STYLE
Paraphrasing	This involves rephrasing what the person is saying in order to interpret and clarify factual information for both parties	As I understand it So what you're saying is ...
Reflecting feelings	This requires careful listening to detect feelings, accurate interpretation to put them into words and suitable responses. It is very useful for exploring attitudes and opinions in detail. Empathy is important for this technique to be used effectively	You feel that ...? It seems to you that ...?
Confrontation	This enables the person to identify inconsistencies, logical sequences etc.	What would happen if ...?
Silence	This indicates to the person that more is expected and it should be accompanied by various non-verbal signals	e.g. Hmm? Ah? Oh? Uhh?
Supportive statements	Used to encourage the person to continue talking. Non-directive in form	I see ... That's interesting
Mirror questions	An effective technique if used carefully. Simple rephrasing of the question tells the person that you would like to know more	'I don't like the job' 'You don't like the job?' 'No, it is too boring' 'It's boring?'
Identification questions	These can be used effectively to isolate specific facts and information	When did you first notice the pains?
Extension questions	If further clarification or explanation of a subject is needed then a fuller answer should be encouraged	How do you mean? How can you be sure? How do you know?

Figure 15.2   Examples of positive measures during a face to face interaction

type of questions asked. Very little could be achieved by inviting an employee to talk about their problem in a loud demanding voice and an aggressive posture.

Figure 15.4 illustrates the range of non-verbal communications which may encourage (or not) an employee to speak openly and freely.

Review

It would be beneficial to consider the use and outcome of the positive and negative aspects which may occur in a manager – employee interaction. Two approaches are described below: the first is directive in form and tends to disregard the principles of counselling skills. The second approach is non-directive and utilizes counselling skills. The position adopted by the person conducting the discussion determines which approach is adopted. The outcome for the individual is markedly different.

TECHNIQUE	PURPOSE OR OUTCOME	QUESTION STYLE
Multiple questions	This tends to lead to a confused response from the person. He is still trying to take in the questions, order the answers and recall the next question asked	Does your wife work? Can't you budget? Do you drive? Is it true that you're on holiday soon?
Trick questions	These may be used on the wrongful assumption that they may reveal some underlying aspects which have not yet emerged	Do you drink? When did you last see your doctor?
Leading questions	This type of question is suggestive in that it puts forward the right answer that the questioner expects from the person. Leading questions can take many forms.	You don't believe that ...? Isn't it true that ...?
Ambiguous questions	These tend to leave the person confused and the answer therefore of little value plus they interrupt the flow of interaction and make the person suspicious	What are you like with people? What about working with men?
'Why' questions	These should be avoided as far as possible since they may be perceived as threatening. They may also invoke justifications which prevent the actual causes being obtained	Why did you do that? Why have you asked to see me?

Figure 15.3   Examples of negative measures during a face to face interaction

A directive approach to the person's problem

In this approach the pattern of interaction between the manager in the helping role and the person seeking help begins after a statement of the problem by either the directive manager or the person. The former controls the discussion. The manager may be seen to encourage the person, to offer solutions to his problem by directing a series of leading questions. An example of this would be an employee whose difficulty is one of poor time keeping. The directive manager, after condemning the behaviour, may ask why the employee has this problem. This will often result in a non-committal reply. The next stage may be for the manager to use a number of leading questions, e.g. Do you oversleep? Have you been ill? Is your car not starting? Is it the children? and so on.

Not only does this process seldom lead to the discovery of the real problem; it suggests to the employee possible excuses which the supervisor – subordinate may find acceptable.

The main forms of remedy offered to the person in this directive situation, once a problem has been determined, are advice, warning, praise, and reassurance. All these actions emphasize the superior position of the person in the helping role and the dependent one of the employee. The manager assumes full understanding of the basic nature of the problem and both determines and attempts to introduce changes in attitude or behaviour which will remedy the conflict. An alternative action from the directive manager will be to make use of praise and reassurance in

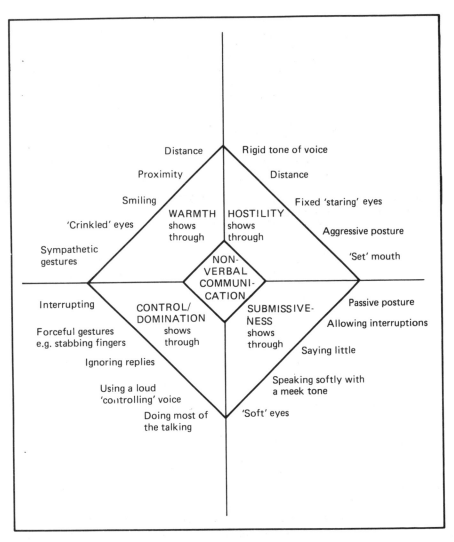

Figure 15.4   Non-verbal communication

(Non-verbal communication can, during the course of face to face interaction, provide valuable or detrimental projections which will be perceived by the employee: adapted from Mackay, I, *A guide to asking questions.*)

order to encourage the employee to overcome problems, or to realize that no problem really exists.

A non-directive approach to the person's problem

This approach is based on the belief in the person's ability to solve personal problems with the aid of a sympathetic listener. The role of the manager is one of understanding rather than passing judgement. There is no attempt to create a superior–subordinate relationship, positions are more or less equal. The non-directive manager assumes that the person is in the best position to know and understand the problem. An appropriate atmosphere needs to be created through a permissive and friendly presentation by the person in the counselling role, with actions and statements which exhibit continuing interest but not judgement. Silence may be used as an invitation for the employee to speak further. Attention is given both to the words spoken and the feelings behind the words. The intention is that, as the employee talks about the problem, the situation will become clearer and a truer picture will emerge of what lies behind the difficulty.

Once the employee has gained greater awareness, new plans, actions or attitudes may be developed. At this stage the counsellor may assist the employee to check that as many alternatives as possible (and their consequences) have been considered. At no time must an exploration of this kind expose any bias towards any of the alternatives. A review of the actions taken at a later time may be useful for some people but that choice remains with the employee.

Summary

These approaches to interaction with an employee give different outcomes. The non-directive approach can take longer and create more demands on the manager. However, the end result is that of an employee determining his or her own plan of action through a realisation that they have the resources to confront and resolve the problem facing them. Since the plan is self-determined it is more likely to be carried out. The manager should never attempt to take over the employee's problem.

Directive action may discourage an open, honest and frank discussion of an employee's problem, and advice offered (with the best of intentions) may not be adopted and acted upon. This aspect alone may eventually give rise to further conflict and anxiety between the employee and manager if the problem recurs.

There may be occasions when the two approaches merge, and not every problem requires the depth that the non-directive approach offers. It is important to consider which features either prevent or assist the employee to express his/her thoughts and feelings about different areas of concern and to ascertain as complete a picture as possible before deciding a future course of action.

IDENTIFYING PROBLEMS

The early identification of an employee's area of concern may save both the person and the company loss of considerable time, effort and resources. There are usually a number of indicators of underlying problems and it is the early detection of these which, if explored with caution and sensitivity, may provide an insight to more serious problem areas. Indicators of any kind will always need to be checked with the person concerned; a judgement on the basis of subjective assessment may be totally inaccurate and would not lead to the resolution of any problem that did exist.

How then can a manager begin to identify an employee with potential problems? A number of factors arising from the employee's behaviour manifested in inconsistent or poor work performance, irregular time keeping, scruffy dress, constant daydreaming etc may have been observed by the manager, prompting him to initiate contact with the employee to investigate. Alternatively the employee may not display any overt activity which may alert the manager to underlying problems. One example would be of an employee who regularly seeks information, perhaps not unusual in itself, but in practice it may be an attempt to initiate and sustain conversation. This type of behaviour is less likely to alert a manager to the potential difficulties being experienced by the employee, which in this instance take the form of firstly establishing contact, and secondly direct expression of the problem.

There may be a range of actions taken by an employee in order to 'sound you out' or to build up the courage to broach the area of concern. Personal experience and awareness of different employees should enable this form of activity to be recognized as potentially underpinning a problem area. Registering these flagging signals and thereby keeping communication open is not easy. However, to actively seek out flagging signals or potential indicators may lead to the misinterpretation of employee behaviour.

Examples of the range of indicators which may be observed by a manager and the types of underlying problems which may be their cause can be a useful guide. If any of the categories listed below are noted by a manager or supervisor over a period of time then these should be recorded and the employee invited to discuss these aspects in the context of employment-related issues, i.e. informally (as a work colleague) or formally (e.g. in a disciplinary interview). Where specific problem areas emerge concerning out-of-work issues or other serious aspects, e.g. alcoholism or where it is reasonable for the manager to suspect that other problems underpin the employee's behaviour, although the employee declines to reveal information supporting such concern, it may be beneficial for the manager and/or employee to have access to professional counselling resources. For the manager this would allow professional guidance on how to proceed with the employee, and for the employee recourse to an external help agency. Whether or not an employee takes up contact with these resources remains the employee's decision.

Potential indicators and their causes

Cause	Indicator
Marital – separation	Lack of concentration
– threatened separation	Irritability
Enforced change of residence	Indecisiveness
Loss, e.g. bereavement, material	Poor memory
Financial difficulties	Verbal attacks
Reduced social contact	Panic attacks
Role ambiguity at work	Slow in thinking/speech
Work overload/underload	Feeling tired
Poor work relationships	Lack of energy/apathy
Family illness	Poor judgement in work
Problems with children	Irregular attendance
Problems with parents	Inadequate time keeping
Alcohol/drug-related problems	Unacceptable appearance

Note: There are no direct correlations between one list and its opposite; indeed one cause may result in several different indicators. Further, another individual may not display the same indicators even where the cause is similar. There is no order of priority intended in either list; nor is either list exhaustive.

SHOULD MANAGERS COUNSEL?

Managers can make effective use of counselling skills to identify, through discussion with an employee, potential areas of concern in a more sensitive and thorough manner and this may enable the employee to find solutions. However, it is necessary for the manager to be trained in the professional use of counselling if he intends to take interaction with an employee further and therefore confront adequately the types of areas mentioned above. In both circumstances it is necessary for the person in the counselling role to first recognize and second work to, specific key factors:

- The counsellor needs to be aware of the limitations in his own personal areas of competence and experience. Attempts to go beyond such areas may have adverse affects on the outcome of manager – employee interaction.
- Unrealistic or unchangeable expectations on the part of the employee may give rise to problems (particularly if the counsellor is perceived to be part of the employing organization since this may encourage the employee to seek solutions through the manager rather than through his own efforts and insight).
- The counsellor needs to avoid encouraging feelings of dependency from the employee, the aim being that the employee should be independent.
- The ability to establish appropriate boundaries at the commencement of a counselling relationship is an important element, e.g. time spent in discussion, personal relationship boss v counsellor etc.
- The counsellor needs to be able to call upon a range of resources available for referral purposes and know at what stage these are appropriate, means of contact, fees, etc.
- There should be precise guidelines concerning confidentiality. The employee must be certain that information revealed during an interview will not be divulged and if it is considered necessary or beneficial to the employee to break confidentiality then this should occur with the person's knowledge and where possible approval. The person him or herself should also be encouraged to bring the matter out into the open. Managers may experience problems of dual loyalty.

Whilst suitably trained managers would be able to undertake the range of potential difficulties that arise in the course of a person's life to the depth required in counselling they may find it difficult to be totally effective due to role conflict problems originating from organizational factors, e.g. role ambiguity, dual loyalty, time etc. Added to which the employees's perception of a manager in the counselling role may not be conducive to the openness and honesty required before solutions can be sought. Managers not directly responsible for the employee or staff roles such as personnel or welfare would also be subject to these difficulties although possibly to a lesser extent.

INDEPENDENT COUNSELLING RESOURCES

An independent counselling resource would potentially overcome many of the problems originating from organizational factors. It could remain totally independent; meet the employee's expectations of total confidentiality, and not threaten future career progression or job security; achieve a non-judgemental environment; provide counselling for the potential range of employee's concerns including work-related problems; and it would be able to assess and develop a range of suitable referral resources.

The negative aspects from an employee's perspective might be that the counsellor would have little or no authority to institute organizational changes. Communication goes from the employee to the counsellor but external action comes from the manager to employee; therefore the value of the counselling resource depends on its ability to help an employee understand his own emotional problems and work out an effective solution to them, rather than implement changes on behalf of the employee. Employee-initiated solutions would be more likely to be adhered to and therefore enable them again to be fully productive not only in the work place but also at home.

Functions external to a counselling resource, e.g. line managers, personnel, trade unions etc. may draw upon its expertise in recognising the extent of their limitations and that common objectives are shared; those of a healthy, productive and happier employee and consequently organization.

One type of external counselling service which is increasing in acceptance is the Employee Assistance Programme (EAP). The EAP originated in the UK with the Employee Advisory Resource (EAR) in 1981. Since that time several other programmes have emerged.

The EAP provides every employee (and member of their family) within an organization with access to counselling 24 hours a day every day of the year. In this way the EAP is added to the benefits package and the employee can self-refer when they feel they want help and assistance.

THE OVERLAP OF COUNSELLING AND COUNSELLING SKILLS

We have discussed the use of counselling skills and the point at which counselling is more appropriate. The interrelationship of these aspects needs to be clarified to take into account the various permutations that may arise if an employee, for whatever reason, is not performing to the extent of his expected abilities. Figure 15.5 attempts to clarify these aspects and is based on the belief that work or personal-related problems may eventually affect a person's ability to maintain a fully productive position at work (or at home).

Once an employee becomes concerned about a particular area there are a number of ways in which the person may respond. The types of response depends on the person's own coping mechanisms (*vis-à-vis* the type of problem) and the knowledge of suitable and available resources. The resources reflected in Figure 15.5 are taken to be: managers who are able to use counselling skills appropriately to facilitate the emergence, identification and potential resolution of the problem; an independent counselling resource which may be in-house or external, referred to by the manager or contacted directly by the employee; a sympathetic friend or

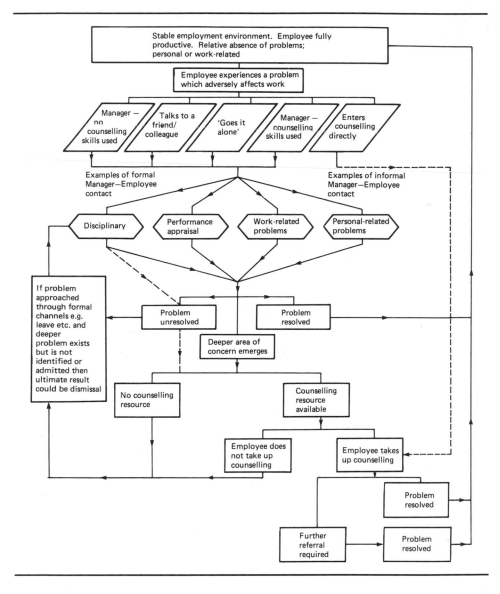

Figure 15.5   Interrelationship of counselling skills and counselling

colleague who can provide a shoulder to lean on; the person himself, who may be able to cope alone without any form of support; and lastly the manager who does not employ counselling skills, becomes aware of declining work performance, and initiates directive action such as suggesting leave, proposing training, or even implementing disciplinary action which if followed to its conclusion could result in dismissal.

In other areas of concern, counselling may combine effectively with the range of other helping strategies to resolve difficulties. Redundancy is an example where the loss of a job may have repercussions which require a variety of coping mechanisms to be supported by different helping strategies as shown below.

Financial planning Pension questions Statutory benefits	information giving and advice
CV compilation Application form filling	teaching and guidance
Interview training Job search activities	coaching
Personal problems Personal stress and anxiety	counselling

CONCLUSION

The benefits from the use of counselling and counselling skills cannot be easily translated into neat, tangible ratios. Many of the benefits are preventive which may appear in aspects such as reduced turnover (and associated recruitment costs) and absenteeism, and improved communication. These factors in turn would be reflected in improved productivity and quality, plus better morale and job satisfaction. The contribution of counselling to the working environment and employee wellbeing is an aspect which may be 'felt' by the whole organization but not easily measured. Counselling, it needs to be remembered, is distinct from counselling skills and the two should not be confused.

FURTHER READING

Kennedy, E., *Crisis Counselling. The essential guide for non-professional counsellors*, Gill and Macmillan, 1981
de Board, R., *Counselling People at Work*, Gower, 1983
Megranahan, M. S., *Counselling – A Practical Guide for Employers*, IPM, 1989
Nelson-Jones, R., *Practical Counselling Skills*, Holt, Rinehart & Winston, 1983
Reddy, M., *The Manager's Guide to Counselling at Work*, British Psychological Society, 1987

The Counselling at Work Division of the British Association for Counselling provides an information and support network for people who use counselling or counselling skills in work or work related settings. For further information please contact:
Dinah Wheeler
Secretary CAWD
82 Shepherds Hill
Harold Wood
Essex RM3 0NJ

CHECKLIST

Both the use of counselling skills and counselling share a number of basic principles. Both can be used with good effect to resolve conflicts, implement changes and facilitate decision making. There are clear guidelines for what counselling is and what it is not:

Counselling is	Counselling is not
• Counselling is thinking with another person	• Counselling is not thinking for another person
• Counselling is a process for solving problems	• Counselling is not speaking adages or cliches about what someone else ought to do
• Counselling is accepting another person's feelings as relevant data bearing on the problem at hand	• Counselling is not simply being sympathetic towards another's feelings
• Counselling is understanding human nature and realizing that people are alike in some ways and unique in others	• Counselling is not merely the application of techniques
• Counselling is assisting in changing things and developing confidence	• Counselling is not an ego trip for the counsellor
• Counselling is building self reliance by aiding someone else in making decisions and fulfilling commitments.	• Counselling is not being arbitrary or manipulative
	• Counselling is not just talking things over

16 Mentoring

David Clutterbuck and Helen Beech

> Mentoring is a process in which one person (the mentor) is responsible for overseeing the career and development of another person (the protégé) outside the normal manager/subordinate relationship.
>
> W. A. and M. M. Gray

WHAT IS MENTORING?

Think back to the most significant learning experiences of your career, the ones that really stretched you and forced you to grow. Was there someone more experienced, who challenged your assumptions, explored new ways of thinking with you, and opened up new career horizons? If so, you know what mentoring is about, because you have experienced it.

Mentoring is not new. Although it is often seen as a product of the 1980s, it actually began back in the days of apprenticeship to an older, experienced master craftsman. It was soon extended to management – indeed some people describe mentoring as a 'managerial apprenticeship'.

Mentoring takes place, informally, throughout the business world. The problem with these informal relationships, however, is that they can be highly arbitrary. The self-appointed mentor may choose a protégé for any number of personal reasons that have little to do with actual or potential performance. Moreover, many people who might particularly benefit from mentoring are left out. For example, in a study we conducted in 1987 of female managers and entrepreneurs in Britain, we found that the entrepreneurs were far less likely to have had mentors. In part, as a result, they were much more dissatisfied with career potential as an employee.

Formal mentoring attempts to focus this powerful development tool where it will have the most beneficial effect for both the company and the individuals involved. It can be a superb means of identifying and developing high flyers or of speeding and facilitating the induction of young people in general. Some also see it as a swifter path into middle and senior management for those subject to unfair discrimination.

Studies on mentoring began in the late 1960s when Ralph M. Stodgill referred to the mentor as 'an ambitious authority figure'. Ten years later Daniel Levinson called mentoring 'one of the most complex and developmentally important relationships a man can have in early adulthood.' Others have called the mentor a 'role model . . . a guide, tutor, coach and confidant'.

The price of mentoring should not be underestimated, however. If you are involved in a mentoring relationship either as mentor or protégé you will need to make an intense commitment of time and emotional resources for at least a year, more commonly two or three. It pays to prepare even a pilot mentoring scheme with great thoroughness, because once started, the process cannot easily be stopped without bringing into question the genuineness of the company's commitment to developing managerial talent.

A good mentoring relationship is one where mentor and protégé have mutual respect, recognise the need for personal development and have at least some idea of the outcome they wish to achieve. Many successful mentoring relationships blossom into strong friendships even though there may be a considerable age gap (typically 8–15 years) between the mentor and protégé.

Who can be a mentor? Pretty well anyone, who has experience which will be valuable to someone else in the organization. In most cases, however, formal mentoring relationships tend to be between a young person and someone at least two layers above and outside the immediate management line.

Why 'outside the management line'? After all, can't I be mentor to those who report to me? The answer is yes, you can, but formal mentoring relationships where the two people have to work so closely together are often fraught with problems.

Companies, which have attempted to use the immediate boss as a mentor, have usually found that there are significant conflicts between the two roles. For example, the high degree of trust required in a mentoring relationship is hard to maintain when the boss must impose discipline or allocate merit rises. Trafalgar House Construction, for example, appointed immediate bosses as mentors in year one of a formal programme, but switched to out-of-line relationships subsequently as the bosses found it difficult to reconcile the requirements of the two roles. BP Chemicals, which surveys protégés regularly about their experiences, found that they were unhappy about even having their boss's boss as a mentor. Mentoring between an individual and his or her immediate line boss works best on an informal basis, where friendship precedes the development of the line relationship.

In practice, there are normally four key parties to a mentoring relationship: the protégé, the mentor, the line manager and the training department (see Figure 16.1). All become involved in selecting appropriate learning activities. The mentor has to be very sensitive to the needs of the line manager, who can easily feel threatened by the relationship between the mentor and the protégé.

The number of protégés a mentor can have varies from one to as many as a dozen, depending upon the circumstances, but will usually be only one or two at a time. The range of employees covered is wide, too. Most commonly programmes cover:

- *Young graduate recruits* – for example, Cable and Wireless appoints mentors

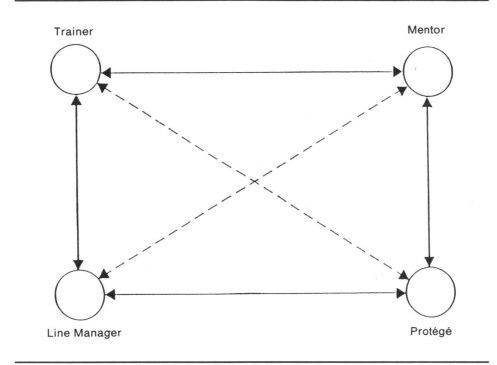

Figure 16.1   The mentoring quadrangle

from middle management for the two year duration of its graduate induction programme.

- *Young professionals seeking qualifications* – for example, some brewers, such as Bass, appoint technical mentors to assist employees studying for master brewer qualifications.
- *Junior managers into middle management* – for example, private hospital group AMI has a mentoring programme to assist potential high flyers into general management posts.
- *Middle managers aspiring to the board* – for example, Trafalgar House Construction's advanced management development programme appoints senior management mentors to assist middle managers through a four-year action learning MBA.
- *Disadvantaged groups* – some US companies use mentoring as a means of bringing women and racial minorities into the management structure. There are current proposals in the US to use mentoring to encourage the development of more black solicitors.

The concept of mentoring appeals partly because it makes use of existing networks and resources, and also because more of the onus of developing managerial talent can be handed back from the personnel department into the hands of experienced line managers, where it belongs. Mentoring is also a particularly efficient development tool because both mentor and protégé learn. Research suggests that people who have been mentored reach senior positions on average two years ahead of those who have not.

THE GROWTH OF MENTORING

Most of the early research into mentoring, during the 1970s, and early 1980s, was carried out in North America, where the number and variety of companies using the process was expanding rapidly. Although the growth is no longer explosive, a steady stream of US companies continue to adopt mentoring.

In the UK and Europe, most of the growth has occurred in the past five years. A recent study we carried out with The Industrial Society (late 1989) identifies 41 organizations with functioning mentoring programmes. Of these, 11 had begun within the past two years and 18 between two and five years before.

SELECTING THE MENTOR

So what qualities would you expect to look for in a good mentor? The word 'mentor' comes from Greek mythology. Before Ulysses left for his epic voyages, he entrusted the care and upbringing of his son to his old and learned friend Mentor.

Selecting a mentor is a critical task. Good mentors have empathy, relevant experience and are respected within the organization. They need to act as surrogate parents, combining authority and friendship, counsel and commitment.

In selecting a mentor, the company must bear in mind the manager's own stage of career and must have a clear sense of the qualities it is looking for. One of the key attributes of a good mentor is the ability to respond to an individual within a fairly unstructured programme. Although an excellent track record in developing other people is undeniably important, the mentor will also need excellent communication skills and a genuine interest in seeing young people advance. Every mentor who volunteers is worth a dozen press-ganged.

If you aim to become an effective mentor you may need to learn not to dazzle your protégé(s) with superior knowledge but encourage, enthuse and advise them. You must reassure the company you can both handle the workload and extend the hand of friendship beyond the usual business confines. You will also need a wide range of different managerial skills, and your rank should not be too much higher than the protégé's or the experience gap becomes a gulf.

The best mentors are often those with a sound and seasoned knowledge of the company, although an individual close to retirement may not have the necessary knowledge of the company's inner councils. At the other extreme, top management may acquire mentors from outside the company completely – for example, a trusted consultant. A successful mentor is also one with enough humility to learn from the younger manager.

As a mentor you must be able to recognise your protégé's ability and make it clear you believe in him. You should know when to let the protégé rely on you and when to force him to become more independent. If you create an open, candid atmosphere, the protégé can then assess his own skills and aspirations and discover his identity within the organization.

You can teach in many ways, but especially by challenging the protégé to apply theory to the real world and by holding problem-solving discussions. You may also play devil's advocate, encouraging the protégé to assert his opinions even in stressful conditions.

A good mentor will react to his protégé's problems and situations with practical help, making introductions and opening doors. He will also intervene should the protégé head off in a dangerous direction.

SELECTING THE PROTÉGÉ

How about protégés: is there any way of selecting them effectively? The criteria for choosing protégés changes from company to company, and the organization must clarify which particular group of employees it is orientating the programme towards. You should be prepared to modify the categories at a later date – for example, some schemes aimed initially at recent graduates have been widened to include promising non-graduate junior managers, who show similar potential to reach middle management.

You need to select protégés carefully, because including people who are not able to use the opportunity fully will waste a great deal of senior management time and demotivate those who feel they have been unjustly passed over. Many companies select upon track record, and recommendation reports from superiors rather than on the protégé's skill at self-promotion.

An effective protégé needs to be: intelligent; positive minded; flexible; self-aware; non-defensive; ambitious; conscientious; well organized; able to laugh at mistakes; a fast learner; have insight and sensitivity; strong interpersonal skills; and an eagerness to learn.

It is not essential for the mentor and protégé to have similar personalities or backgrounds. Indeed if a cultural readjustment is needed in the company, it may pay to avoid too close a match.

Whatever the criteria specified, they should always be drawn from one basic question: 'How much will this person gain from the mentoring relationship?'

WHAT DOES A TYPICAL MENTORING RELATIONSHIP LOOK LIKE?

Katherine Kram, assistant professor at Boston University's school of management, found mentoring relationships passed through four distinct stages. If you have already experienced mentoring, either as mentor, or protégé, or both, you will almost certainly recognize them.

The start of the relationship

During the first six months to a year, some protégés identify very strongly with their mentors. They hold an unrealistically ideal picture of these executives and draw a great deal of emotional support from the relationship. Others enter the programme with some suspicion, perhaps as to the older person's influence or standing. The mentor must go on to win the protégé's respect if the relationship is to succeed.

At this stage, the mentor is drawn to the protégé because of his willingness to learn and derives satisfaction from realizing he can speed the younger manager's progression. The protégé feels he is valued by the company and cared for by someone of note.

The middle period

This lasts two to five years and is the most rewarding and rich for both. The relationship is cultivated and trust and intimacy in the friendship grows. The mentor develops the protégé's managerial skills and reinforces his sense of competence, ability and self-worth. The younger person understands the business scenario better and knows how to control his work environment.

It is at this stage that the mentor gains an almost 'parental' pride in his protégé and having opened doors, receives a greater confidence in his own influence. The protégé now also has the skill to recognize the needs of the senior executive. The mutual confidence that develops between the two gives the protégé the ability to challenge the mentor's ideas and can be very productive.

By now the mentor and protégé have agreed a career path involving clearly defined horizontal or promotional moves – indeed the first of these may already have been taken. Review meetings rate success in achieving the objectives and discussions take place on strategies for further achievement. The mentor directs the protégé to additional sources of learning and challenges him to prove the successes he claims.

Dissolving the relationship

After two to five years the relationship begins to draw apart due to organizational changes and the growing independence of the protégé. Some protégés will feel anxiety and uncertainty, perhaps even betrayal, as the 'safety net' disappears. Others, fully prepared, enjoy the independence and ability to demonstrate their skills.

The mentor may still encourage his protégé, promote him at a distance and be kept informed of his progress. However some mentors take this too far and are unwilling to let go. The protégé will become frustrated and ultimately hostile if this continues and a company arbitrator may be necessary.

The protégé will have assumed more responsibility for his own training opportunities and experience will have taught him how to achieve his goals. In effect, the mentor has taught him all he knows.

Restarting the relationship

Mentor and protégé will usually continue to have some form of interaction after the relationship has ceased. Gratitude replaces the protégé's need and the two can now treat each other as equals, although there may be a period of uncertainty as they adapt to the new roles. In some cases this uncertainty may never be overcome and the protégé, scared he will fall into his former dependent role, behaves aggressively, and hostility replaces the former intimacy.

The mentor and protégé beginning a programme should be briefed on how the relationship is likely to develop. The company too should understand the stages of the mentoring relationship to provide support and head off any serious problems before they occur.

THE BENEFITS OF MENTORING

So far we have examined only the process of mentoring. But why should you – especially if you are an already overworked manager – put time and effort into such a complex relationship? The answer is that the rewards far outweigh the efforts, for the protégé, for your organization, and for you as mentor.

For the protégé

Mentoring gives the younger manager a whole range of business and managerial skills. He or she gains a higher profile, a feeling for the company culture and an 'insider guide' to internal politics. He learns the arts of self-preservation and self-publicity and along the way builds an invaluable sense of self-confidence and worth.

The mentor often becomes a role model to the protégé, a symbol of what can be achieved, helping him or her to focus aspirations and turn them into realistic objectives. He or she gives the protégé access to otherwise closed areas and an insight into successful management styles, revealing how power is gained and wielded. This crucial lesson on how to feel comfortable with power gives the young manager the kind of confidence when making major deals or taking calculated risks that business school theory can never match.

The mentor may advise on which jobs to take and when and how to prepare for each career step. He helps the protégé think through work and career issues, challenging wherever appropriate. The role involves a great deal of both coaching and counselling. If the relationship is successful the protégé is able openly to admit lack of understanding and expose sensitive problems to a non-judgemental and trusted source of advice.

The less gifted employee can also gain a great deal from mentoring. The mentor can help him understand how to work within his limitations, so that he draws increased job satisfaction and perceives challenges horizontally rather than vertically.

For the mentor

Grooming a promising young employee can be very stimulating for you. You often experience pride in your protégé and a renewed sense of purpose in seeing the values of the organization handed to a new generation.

As you have climbed the corporate ladder, you may often have missed out on new ideas, techniques and technology – for example, IT. Directing the learning experiences of the protégé also gives an excuse to devote time and open resources to developing your own knowledge – it is common for the protégé to educate the mentor as well.

Some mentors can also use their protégés as a means to accomplish at a distance what they cannot do from their more visible position. You can also ease your workload and gain fresh perspectives by delegating projects to 'past-protégé' managers.

Gaining a reputation for identifying and developing talent is frequently a career plus. Moreover, by grooming a protégé and identifying him as your successor, you may increase your own chances of promotion. Protégés, who subsequently outstrip their mentors, also prove to be useful allies in due course.

For the company

Companies with formal, long-standing mentoring programmes claim tangible increases in productivity and efficiency. Intangible benefits include improved staff morale, greater career satisfaction and easier recruitment and induction.

Assigning a mentor to new recruits helps overcome initial and often insurmountable culture shock. The protégés receive a clearer sense of their function and identify more quickly with the company's structure, aims and culture. This means employees become productive faster and are likely to stay with the company longer. (Pilkington, for example, reports an increased retention rate of graduate recruits within the first two years of employment from 69% to 95%.)

If necessary, the mentor can also help the protégé come to terms with slower than expected career progress, encouraging him to recognise and accept the longer term development plans. The mentor can help the protégé make the most of learning experiences inherent in his current role. Teaching the younger person also helps prevent the mentor from retiring mentally from his own job – typically he feels a constant need to improve, to clarify company aims and to keep up to date with new techniques.

The mentoring programme also ensures a stable corporate culture. Managerial skills, methods and values can be passed on to protégés accurately, decreasing the likelihood of friction. This degree of corporate stability is a key factor in long-term growth and survival. (Although in some cases it may be desirable to break the cultural mode. In these circumstances, it may be necessary to choose mentors who represent the new pattern of behaviours and values rather than the old.)

At lower levels in the organization the mentoring relationship may be less intense, but the potential benefits in terms of workforce co-operation and communication are considerable.

The protégé's unique ability to straddle several levels and communicate with both his own and his mentor's peer group, enriches the informal company networks. This tends to lead to more action, orientation, innovative learning and swifter adjustment to changing business needs.

Combined benefits

Our survey with The Industrial Society enabled us to quantify some of the benefits of mentoring for all three stakeholders. When we asked 'What are the main reasons for using mentoring?', the highest scores were, in order:

- to support a self-development programme;
- to induct more quickly;
- to increase retention of key staff;

- to improve the identification of potential.

When we asked about *achieved* benefits, however, the primary responses were, in order:

- to support a self-development programme;
- to increase retention of key staff;
- to build relationships.

We also asked what were the main benefits for mentors. Here, job enrichment was far and away the most important factor, although status, job interest for plateaued managers and career enhancement also received significant mention.

WHAT PROBLEMS CAN OCCUR?

'So where's the rub?' you may ask. 'After all, nothing's that good.' Mentoring is *not* a panacea for all management development problems. Whilst it is a powerful and often very successful development tool, it is not always appropriate, or superior to other forms of management training. It is a process best used alongside other, more traditional methods.

You have to monitor the mentoring programme very carefully and establish clear lines of communication, so difficulties can be rapidly recognized and resolved.

By assigning a mentor to a protégé in a different division, a company changes the nature of its informal structure. These close relationships can lead to an increase in company politics unless the company is vigilant.

Failure to make it clear to the protégé from the start that he or she is still primarily responsible to the line boss can cause serious power play problems. Because the mentor and protégé are adhering to an unusual system of loyalty, an invisible chain of command can emerge resulting in confusion and bitterness.

The protégé's line manager can be placed in a very difficult position. He may feel threatened or publicly undermined. In these circumstances he may resort to obstructing the programme, especially if he is resentful at his own lack of progress.

To combat this the mentoring relationship should combine openness with unintrusiveness. The protégé must not undertake extra work to please his mentor at the expense of the daily routines of his job, because this will cause friction with his boss and resentment among his 'unmentored' peers.

This danger of alienating failed candidates is a real one. Many of the disappointed will see it as a vote of 'no confidence' and the resulting lack of motivation among them can outweigh any of the programme's benefits. Some employees may feel that the real criteria for selection of protégés is an ability to impress or play at company politics, rather than who will benefit the most from the experience. Companies must provide scrupulously fair and public methods of selection to combat this.

To illustrate the point, one company started its scheme by inviting volunteers from junior management to apply. It received more than three applications for every place on the programme and eventually made the selection on the basis of two for each major location. Unsuccessful candidates were informed by letter that they had not been selected, and advised to talk to their local personnel officer about alternative ways of developing management skills. Only one made the contact, and she did so to hand in her notice!

Now this company makes sure everyone understands how protégés are selected and explains to unsuccessful candidates what they have to do to bring themselves to the top of the list next time. The personnel officer tells them face to face and provides and discusses the career-building options then and there.

Another concern is that the mentor may help perpetuate stereotypes if the ideas he passes down are obsolete or so vigorously imposed that the protégé forgets to think for himself. As a result the company can become entrenched in the past and unable to cope with rapid change. When giving advice you should stress it is just that. Having warned of potential problems, you should leave the protégé to make his own decisions.

Some mentors and protégés fail to establish the right kind of relationship. The mentor executive may be under too much pressure to develop the relationship fully for example. Either partner may expect too much. If the younger manager expects the mentor to transform his career, he may feel resentful or betrayed; equally, if the protégé does not develop as rapidly as you would like, you may also become very frustrated.

The protégé needs to be realistic. He should not expect the relationship to meet his every need nor to last indefinitely. Similarly you as a mentor must learn to let your protégé become independent. Some mentors must also learn the balance between exhibiting confidence in the protégé and burdening him or her with unbearable pressures.

You can damage the protégé's career if you have an insufficient understanding of the company or of the younger person's skills and if you push him in the wrong direction. If you fall out of favour with the company this may also have an adverse affect on the younger manager. Similarly the protégé may undermine *your* career if he fails on an important project. You may then feel obliged to withdraw to save your reputation, leaving the protégé to sink or swim on his own.

'Cross gender' mentoring relationships can be particularly problematic, as well as very rewarding. On the debit side, sexual tensions and gossip may halt a natural and necessary friendship. There may also be subtle pressures to adopt the established sexual roles. Most problems can be overcome, however, by keeping the relationship very open. Some mentors deflect this kind of criticism by having several protégés.

HOW OTHER COMPANIES TACKLE MENTORING

In the following pages we describe briefly the experiences of two companies, which have had formal mentoring programmes for several years. Their experience may be of value to you in deciding whether to institute a formal mentoring programme, or simply whether to seek informally the opportunity to become a mentor to people in your organization. If you would like access to further case study material, the European Mentoring Centre has a library on mentoring.

Case study

British Gas

When selecting mentors for its graduate training programme, British Gas looks for coaching, counselling and listening skills. Mentors are expected to have a genuine interest in the development of young people and the ability to act as role models. Regional functional managers select mentors from their senior management. Mentors are not usually a protégé's line manager, although this can occur because of a job rotation policy.

British Gas aims to provide a four-way link between mentor, protégé, line manager and the training department. The training department co-ordinates the graduate development programme and holds workshops. It educates non-mentoring managers about the aims of the programme to reduce friction and rumour. The trainers act as 'surrogate' mentors, for protégés whose relationships have broken down.

British Gas has had problems with its programme. Some line managers could not see the need for mentors, others regarded it as elitist and unfair. A few managers that were recruited as graduates resented the extra support given to new graduates that they never had, and if line managers proved to be more senior than the mentor, confidentiality and power play issues arose.

However the programme is deemed a success. Protégés form close bonds with each other, and with their mentors (who prove useful allies). Many mentors have offered to undertake the role again and some relationships carry on well beyond the conclusion of the formal programme.

The company is now considering extending graduate mentoring beyond the initial development period.

AMI Healthcare

AMI is a leading private healthcare provider in the UK, with 18 hospitals nationwide and over 4 000 staff. Its mentoring system was set up in 1986, specifically for senior managers on the company's executive development programme. Mentoring was seen as a natural step for a company that places strong emphasis on developing its own managers and giving them considerable autonomy, and involving senior management in all training and development activities.

Managers are selected for the executive development programme on performance and potential for enriching their role within the organization. To date three small groups of managers have been through the programme.

Mentors are normally chosen from the 20 executive hospital and corporate directors, and invited to participate. There are few rules governing who can mentor whom, but protégés are never mentored by their line bosses. When the programme began mentors were matched with protégés so that skill met with weakness, but personal incompatibilities proved troublesome. Now protégés are asked firstly if they would like a mentor (all seem to) and then to select one. There is sometimes a problem with too many protégés choosing the same mentor. Younger managers are then made aware of the other mentoring executives with relevant skills.

249

Initially mentors received a day's training involving an explanation of the concept of mentoring and some role playing, but now they can also discuss the highs and lows of mentoring with existing mentors.

Mentors are primarily expected to help their protégés achieve their programme objectives and this often means completing a project in an area new to the protégé, using the mentor's skills and ability to open doors. It is felt that if mentors and protégés have a clear joint objective at the beginning, the relationship will open up naturally. Mentors also help protégés draw up personal action plans, and act as sounding boards for new ideas. For a protégé promoted to a senior post, existing links with a mentor within the senior structure helps him to integrate more smoothly.

A 'pairing' is usually agreed four weeks before the programme commences and the couple are encouraged to meet informally beforehand. On the first day of the programme they discuss what it is they want the relationship to achieve. Objectives are presented to the programme group and also to the human resources department who can then monitor and stimulate. A review of these objectives is held during each programme when protégés give feedback to a group of mentors, protégés and human resources representatives. AMI tries to keep the whole system informal and driven by the mentors and protégés themselves.

Mentors enjoy the experience and the status it brings along with the practical help bright young managers can provide. The supply of mentors is to a certain extent self-perpetuating and of the first 14 managers on the programme, four, now in very senior positions are keen to keep the system going, and two have already acted as mentors.

Difficulties have in part been due to the relative unfamiliarity of mentoring in business life. An important aspect of the human resource department's role has been to create an atmosphere where managers can openly admit a relationship isn't working, without it being seen as an admission of failure. Experience has shown AMI that practical considerations such as geographical proximity and setting aside diary time is also important.

The mentoring system is evaluated at the end of the programme, checking how the relationship has worked and the quality of development projects completed by the protégés. AMI believes the acid test for success is a continual supply of would-be protégés and mentors, and this has so far been the case. Many relationships continue after the programme, partly because mentors help their former protégés progress their personal development plans.

In the future AMI may well encourage managers to look for mentors from outside as well as inside the company, which could offer all kinds of mutual benefits for the companies involved. AMI Healthcare feels mentoring has been well worth the effort and shall continue to use the process in future development programmes.

CHECKLIST FOR THOSE CONSIDERING MENTORING

1   Does the intended programme have clear objectives, understood and backed by the personnel function and top management?

2   How will the programme fit in with other methods of employee development?

3   Do we have a strategy to educate everyone (especially those not involved in the mentoring process) to demystify the scheme?

4   How will we ensure that the protégés' immediate line bosses are supported?

5   Do we have clear criteria for selecting mentors and protégés? Do mentors understand the time commitment involved? How shall we handle the issue of would-be mentors and protégés who are not suitable?

6   How shall we pair mentors and protégés?

7   Is there a carefully thought out training structure for both mentor and protégé?

8   How confidential should be what passes within the relationship?

9   How will we monitor and review?

10   How and when should we intervene in the relationship?

FURTHER READING

Clutterbuck, David, *Everyone Needs a Mentor*, 2nd edition, Institute of Personnel Management, 1991

Collins, N. W., *Professional Women and Their Mentors: a practical guide to mentoring for the woman who wants to get ahead*, Prentice-Hall, 1983

Phillips-Jones, L., *Mentors and Proteges*, Arbor House, 1982

Roche, G., 'Much ado about mentors', *Harvard Business Review*, Jan-Feb 1979

Zey, M. G., *The Mentor Connection*, Dow Jones Irwin, 1984

SOURCES OF ADVICE

The European Mentoring Centre,
Burnham House,
High Street,
Burnham,
Bucks., SL1 7J2.
Tel: 0628 662517.

17 Team building

Pauline Barrett

This chapter will explore the nature of teams, how to recognize them, how they are formed, why they are necessary, what they do and how they operate; it is about the realities of team life, the signs of a good team, and about ways of building teams from inside the unit or with help from outside.

It invites the manager, with some practical exercises, to pull everything out of the hat and to get the act together. The successful team may look as if it happened by magic but you can be sure that it did not. The winning team is the result of hard work and sound judgement and it is within any manager's grasp. Team building is challenging, exciting and rewarding; it is never dull and it is never ended.

WHY BUILD A TEAM?

Is team building just the flavour of the month? Is it really more than just good leadership? Does it have its own unique characteristics? I hope to be able to illustrate that there is something special about having a team (see Figure 17.1), and that a team building effort will give you a new base from which to leap to a higher level of success in both personal and business terms. If you have the feeling that 'things could be better round here' then you will find some ideas in the pages that follow.

The theoretical reasons for team building given in this chapter are supported by

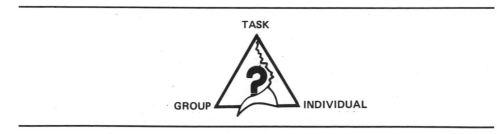

Figure 17.1   The mysterious 'team'

evidence from team leaders and their team members who have undertaken a team building exercise with outside help; the quotations come from participants who have engaged in team building events once, twice or three times. I will be considering team building both as an event aided by outside intervention, and as those management skills and practices which can be instituted by managers without outside assistance. In either event the task of building and maintaining the team belongs to the manager.

So why should you devote time and energy to team building? Perhaps you have worries about your work group, or you are under external pressures which are causing you a headache. Your group/team is not performing well and there is criticism from influential 'others'. You are aware that you have some square pegs in round holes, that internal tensions are getting in the way of progress, and that there are people out there gunning for you. Inside or out there are powerful individuals or groups who could help you into oblivion. There is plenty of evidence to show that the well-established team is in a strong position to survive when the weak go to the wall, so if you are under pressure from internal or external sources then this chapter will be of interest and use to you.

Why others bothered

The following quotations give a variety of reasons why other groups have taken the necessary steps to turn themselves into better teams. The reasons include the need for survival, members' unclear or conflicting goals, personal difficulties, or the pressing need for improved performance. Managers on team building exercises have said they did it because:

- We were not pulling together as a group, we needed improved morale and output.
- The senior managers were a group of individuals and rarely thought or acted as a group.
- A new management team was created by reorganization.
- We had rumblings of unrest between members, a lack of understanding of each other's burdens and no real sense of corporate direction.
- Ours was a new team and although individually able they were not working well enough as a team. To the outside world they did not have a team approach.
- To be effective in new markets we needed a team approach which matched aptitudes to needs.
- Team building was to build confidence in each other, to agree mutually acceptable objectives and ensure the best possible use of team members.

WHAT IS A TEAM?

Time and again the question 'What is a team?' ends up with answers in the realm of feelings and perceptions. When asked to explain 'teamness' both team members and team leaders fall back on what they *felt* rather than what they *did* to explain the need for team building. There is plenty of speculation about when a team is not a team, and many attempts at the ultimate definition, but for any work group it comes down to knowing that this work group feels and acts like a team.

To define the team it may be helpful first to say that a team is *not*:

- a collection of individuals who happen to have the same work place;
- a collection of individuals who happen to have the same director or line manager; or
- a collection of individuals who do the same job in the same department.

It is a group which shares, and says that it shares, a common purpose and recognizes that it needs the efforts of every one of its members to achieve this. A team is a team when it sees itself as a team, is going in the team direction, and has worked out its own team ways.

There is nothing in this definition which speaks of permanence, or the inability of members to be independent, or anything about living in each other's pockets. Teams do not need continual meetings or everyone involved in every decision. Teams do not diminish the leader, or the leader's authority. They do, however, banish hurt feelings over exclusion, and stifle that paranoia which has people going to meetings they have no need to attend for fear of missing out, or being overlooked. Teams do not do everything together; they are not a hunting pack; they are more like members of the relay team which passes the baton accurately and swiftly at exactly the right moment.

Why teams are necessary

The evidence is that teams are much more than the sum of the individual parts. The existence of a team is liberating and enabling. When a work group is a team the leader gains in confidence, each member sees his/her own contribution in a realistic light, and there is a release from the fears and mistrusts which are so often part of work life. Team building gives a new perspective on the leader, the members and the task in hand.

One team member lists the benefits of a quiet weekend in the country, where his group set about team building, as:

- Clearer recognition of mutual responsibility in establishing and fulfilling common objectives.
- A breakdown of some of the barriers of rivalry/jealousy which were a legacy of the previous structure.
- An improved climate for debate by the team of important (and less important) issues.
- Greater willingness to contribute/participate in discussion and mutual support.
- Reduced preoccupation with the risk of making a fool of oneself before fellow team members.
- Greater awareness of other team members' pressures and problems.

If you think your team has cracked all those problems of working life then go no further. If, however, you still think that your team has some distance to go then stay with these ideas and reflect upon your next steps to develop and build your team.

WHAT TEAMS DO

Teams *do* just what any work group does but they do it differently and more productively. They:

- plan;
- have agreed goals;
- make decisions;
- solve problems;
- succeed and fail;
- agree, or agree to differ and get on with the job;
- resolve conflict;
- consult inside the team and out;
- collect, sift and distribute information;
- use known, understood and effective communication channels;
- lose and gain members;
- meet the outside world;
- manage change.

Successful teams have seen themselves operating in the following ways:

- More planning, relating individual activities to the total objective.
- Less defensiveness in meetings or group discussions.
- Greater involvement in projects of individuals who had previously been consulted at too late a stage.
- Paying more attention to looking at short- and long-term objectives in meetings.
- Allowing greater reliance upon each other, sharing a common view of objectives.
- Achieving more in productivity, and in the confidence of outsiders.
- Adaptability to changing circumstances and pressures.

HOW CAN TEAMS BE DEVELOPED?

There are two areas of team building operation. There is team building as a routine activity of any manager, and there are team building events designed and facilitated by external agencies acting as catalysts. In each case the principles of building the team are the same, and many successful teams are built without any outside help. We will look at the necessary ingredients for any team building activity and relate the different methods of development, comparing and contrasting their strengths and weaknesses. There is a logical process to the practice of team building as shown in Figure 17.2.

The diagnosis

Before anything can be built there has to be an analysis of the present position, a collection of the facts. The groundwork has to be done to see the nature of the

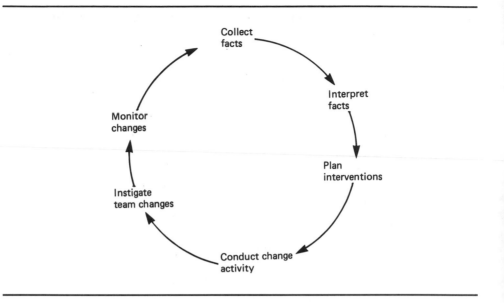

Figure 17.2   The process diagram for team building

foundation for the building. Often the diagnosis itself can carry a team forward most productively for they have not previously given their 'teamness' much thought.

This section includes an array of suggested exercises for you to carry out on your own team; they will begin the process of team building for you.

So ask yourself some stock-taking questions to measure the state of your team now.

The style of the team

This is the first area for diagnosis. Look at the 'THIS' or 'THIS' pictures in Figure 17.3. What are your conclusions about the state of your group?

If that gave you a few ideas but an inadequate picture try a descriptive exercise. Below is a list of adjectives which can be used to describe either the whole workplace, or a small group within it. Go through the list ticking those words which describe your team and then write a descriptive paragraph using those words.

Heavy	Interesting	Soft	Traditional
Innovative	Tired	Energetic	Colourful
Respected	Closed	Learned	Outdoors
Reflective	Driven	Harmless	Feeble
Despondent	Changeable	Nervous	Solid
Polished	Fun	Open	Gloomy
Rich	Experienced	Promising	Young
Driving	Pro-active	Sheltered	Genteel
Attacked	Pressurized	Muddled	Past it

Figure 17.3   A series of pictures for team analysis. Which pictures illustrate your team now?

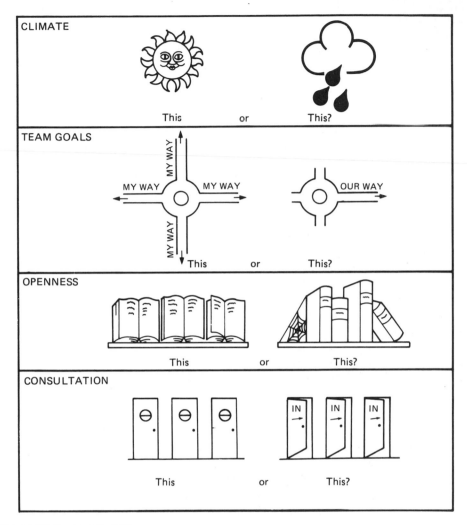

Figure 17.3   (concluded)

Narrow	Threatened	Inscrutable	Childish
Winning	Naive	Complex	Expanding
Dreary	Dynamic	Worthy	Worried
Distinguished	Jumpy	Fantastic	Competent
Trusting	Excitable	Confused	Belligerent
Patient	Losing	Anxious	Motivated
Supportive	Clueless	Treacherous	Threatened
Negative	Unhappy	Cheerful	Optimistic
Battling	Approachable	Reactive	Skilled
Nice	Divided	Organized	Creative
Boring	Practical	Talkative	Purposeful
Visionary	Academic	Businesslike	Influential

This is how you see your team. Read on to diagnose more.

The people in your team

These people are the lifeblood of your operation. Where has your team come from and what are you all like? The team building aspect of work life concerns itself not with the professional/technical competence of you all but with the match and mismatch of your styles and personalities. It is not about whether you have about you good engineers, accountants, lawyers or planners. It is about your separate and collective hopes and fears, your ambitions and past experiences. It is concerned with building team energy levels, team productivity, and the team's confidence in itself in the organization or the market place.

So where has your team come from? Did you inherit? Did you choose? Or have you a mixture? Think about each of your team members and answer the following questions:

- Was this person your choice?
- If so, on what grounds did you choose him/her?
- Did you make the right choice?
- On what have you based that judgement?
- If you did not choose this person what did you think when you found him/her in your team?
- Has s/he matched up to your expectations?
- Does this person perform his/her own role adequately? Or well?
- Has s/he grown in the job?
- Does s/he fit well into the slot s/he now occupies?
- Is s/he stretched?
- Is s/he happy?
- When did you last have a conversation that lasted longer than a few minutes, and what was it about?
- What are the development needs of this individual?
- Are you in danger of losing this person for any reason? If so what?
- Do you wish you could lose this person? Why?
- What are your plans for this individual's future?
- How does this person relate to all the others?
- Are you satisfied with performance in all areas?

For the total team answer these questions:

- Are they the right mix of abilities and interests for your needs?
- What is this mix that you need?
- Do they pull together?
- Are there easy and accepted ways of dealing with conflict and disagreement?
- Are there any misfits?
- Is your present team up to future demands, individually and collectively?
- Are you happy with your team leader position?
- Do all your team members come to you for help when necessary?

Your answers may indicate areas of concern or the need for team building; this diagnosis is the first step of the team building activity. You have already started if you have come up with some rueful thoughts about your present situation.

Current team issues

These form the focal point for your team building. Write down some of those aspects of your group which you know could be better, together with some of the things which would help you all to achieve more and, in hard times, to survive.

Whether you are working on your own to develop your team or using external help, this diagnosis of issues and needs is a vital step. It is important to realize and remember that in the field of human relationships many issues remain hidden while insidiously affecting the course and the outcome of any event. It is in this area that checklists or other instrumentation can be used to provide a common base from which team members can discuss the way they see things. They can identify their similarities and differences of view and feeling. There are useful books with diagnostic instruments, including the *Team Development Manual* by Mike Woodcock, published by Gower.

One team leader illustrated the extra value of an external agent when he heard the list of problems, needs and issues of his team. He said that none of these was a surprise to him but that now they had been 'named' they would have to be addressed.

Getting started

If you have thoughtfully and honestly answered the questions above you will know that there is always scope for improvement. For the manager who has a product or service which relies on individuals and the group working well, and who is wishing to improve the performance of the unit/organization then it is pretty certain that there is a team waiting to be built.

Asking the team members how they see the team is a good way to start. If you are serious about wanting to build your own team you could do a lot worse than find one, two, or all of your team members and show them the exercises on these pages. Taking them through these, preferably in a relaxed environment, could be your first step. Of course it is a risk; most of us have a work culture which is not open to the true expression of views, and which suppresses discontents until they develop into boiling cauldrons of frustration. It is these which the team can handle and the run-of-the-mill work group cannot.

If any of your own answers to the exercises give you cause for concern then start your team building by selected conversations to find out how the ground really lies. This may be quite tricky if your team is not used to this approach, and you may have to be reassuring about your motives for such uncharacteristic behaviour. You may also need to refer to other chapters in the book for tips on how to do it.

Working on team meetings is another good place to start your team building. Team meetings are often the only time when all team members come together and frequently they are deemed to be unsatisfactory for one reason or another. A recent comment was 'they're so boring'; many are worse: they are time wasters, battlegrounds, ego trips, and pointless. For the next exercise think back to your last team meeting and answer the following questions:

- Were you satisfied with the results?

- Did every group member make his/her contribution appropriately?
- Was it worth the time it took?
- Does everybody know what they should do now, and will they do it?
- Were there any undercurrents? If so, what were they about?
- Are you confident in the skill in the chairing role?
- Are you looking forward to the next meeting? And are the others?

Answers to those questions may give you some clues about making the team more productive and cohesive. If you would really like to build a team, type out those questions plus the next few and get each team member to answer them for discussion at your next team meeting. It is worth giving up an agenda item now and again to review how you are operating in your meetings. The additional questions could be:

- Did you have any difficulty in getting your ideas listened to?
- Were you happy with the agenda?
- Did you have enough information before the meeting?
- Were the environment and the timing right?
- What could have improved the meeting?

Team building tools

Whether team building is pursued as a routine activity within management, or as a special event with outside help, it is an art, a science and a skill. Working as a facilitator to other people's teams I find it difficult to explain what I do; and when I can explain, it sounds so much like common sense that it seems unlikely that everyone isn't doing it for themselves. But that view overlooks our management culture of keeping stiff upper lips, taking the medicine, not rocking the boat, and many more individual messages that are carried around in our heads.

You could already have done a great deal of team building if you have read the earlier pages and had a go. If you haven't, you might feel happier knowing a bit more of the theory. But eventually it isn't the theory that will build your team; it is the recognition of need and the determination to take on board something of the unknown.

The art of team building is to have an armoury of understanding about people, singly and in groups. Although a knowledge of the business/service and detailed work assists credibility, this is not what the team builder is there to develop. Indeed the art of team building is concerned with talking through needs, differences and individual contributions, and not about the details of the business. The closeness of the team builder to the balance sheets, market demands and production difficulties can often make it extremely difficult to achieve the amount of emotional detachment needed to help a team to achieve its deeper needs. In any team development there comes the moment when the team is ready to address itself fully to business plans and the future programme, but it is important that these details do not figure too much too early. In the team builder's art is the ability to see the team as a whole, and to release the energies of the members towards the solution of joint problems and away from the petty differences which can inhabit the work place. If the team builder is the manager then keeping the art going is harder, particularly when the manager may be threatened or uneasy about what is going on in the group.

The science of team building is the collection of the facts, and this is where the scientific approach can make its contribution. Building a team will entail the investigation not only of what has happened and what it is perceived will happen, but also of how people behave, and how they feel about what is happening. Within the walls of British institutions fact finding is well developed in areas which can be seen to be measurable. There is, however, less investigation into the underlying workings of the greatest industrial, commercial and service resource – people.

There are now plenty of theories and practical instruments which can measure personality, ability and performance; and these provide both valuable diagnostic information and a wealth of discussion material. But the team builder will always use diagnosis as a guide, data as a tool, and instrumentation as an additional asset. The scientific approach of listening intently, collecting facts and testing assumptions is the key to the enabling skills of the team builder.

Understanding team life, its characteristics and its dynamics, is an essential part of the team building process. In recent years much interesting work has been done on teams and a knowledge of this work and its application to your own group can help in the building of the team through understanding and planned development.

The great strength of a team lies in the differences between members, and yet these same differences can be the source of so much conflict and misunderstanding that strength is rapidly turned to weakness. The work of R. Meredith Belbin outlined in his book *Why Management Teams Succeed or Fail* brought into sharp relief the fact that people are different, and that those differences play a vital role in their working lives. For these differences are the result of psychological variations, and we are what we are. We are all familiar with the square peg in the round hole and Belbin's studies of how individuals make their unique contribution in groups, the characteristics of his eight team roles, and how people with very different (or very similar) ways of working will not work well together has opened the door for a new look at work groups.

One of the, now many, ways of mapping differences is the model which Charles Margerison and Dick McCann have developed in their Team Management Wheel. They have researched into the work that groups have to do to have a fully successful operating unit. From their research into the necessary work functions (Figure 17.4 (i)) and their analysis of personality, they have devised a comprehensive model (Figure 17.4 (ii)) of the work *preferences* of individuals. There is, in their model, a link between personal preferences for style of working and the function needs of the job. By using the identification of these preferences and building up a team profile it is possible to see how balanced and finely tuned the team is to tackle the task in hand. It also opens up discussion between team members of their own preferred way of working which has been previously misunderstood, ignored, or undervalued.

The Team Management Resource, built around the Team Management Wheel, is a computerized analysis of team members' preferences backed up by exercises which help the group to identify its preferences and assess performance. It is a useful tool for the selection and the creation of balanced teams and project

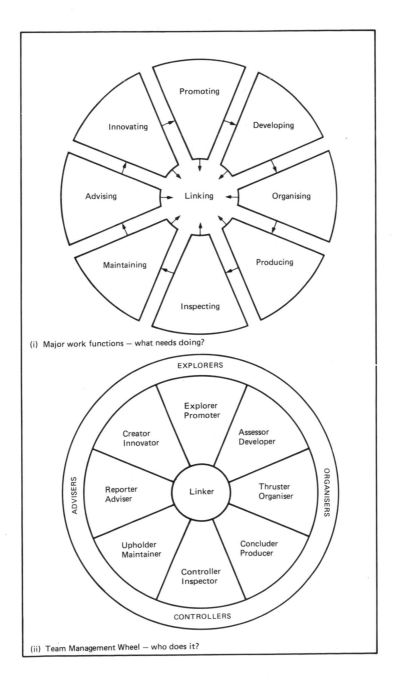

(i) Major work functions — what needs doing?

(ii) Team Management Wheel — who does it?

Figure 17.4   The Margerison/McCann team management resource

groups; but is also most productively used for already existing teams, offering them a tool for diagnosis and, perhaps even more valuably, a focus for discussion which can cover every area of the team's activity from individual relationships to work allocation.

A good team is a balanced team, but even the existing unbalanced team can better understand its difficulties and take steps to ease them by co-opting new members or redistributing tasks and responsibilities.

The skill of the team builder is that of the juggler. The juggler knows what the act is, knows the price of failure and against that balances the excitement of the risk and the likelihood of success. The juggler understands the environment and the essential resources, has many balls in the air, and plans strategies and practices to perfection. There aren't so many jugglers around these days and it seems there aren't enough team builders either. Practice and confidence in assessing situations and making interventions are the real skills for juggling and team building.

The practical skills which one sees a successful team using are nothing more or less than good management practices; the alarming thing is that so many work groups (not teams) do not achieve them. So the team builder's crucial skill is to open new doors, to unfreeze attitudes, and to reassure team leaders and members that this effort is one which will continue to pay off.

WHAT HAS TEAM BUILDING ACHIEVED?

It has to be said that not every work group is capable of being built into a great fighting force. Sometimes the ingredients are all wrong and the only thing to do is to go back to the drawing board. But going back to the drawing board can be a premature (and costly) business, and there are plenty of team leaders around who are amazed and delighted with the changes which have been wrought in an unlikely crew.

Teams which have consciously 'built' have been amazed at the improvements which they have brought about, and delighted with the unexpected results of their efforts. For those teams which have addressed themselves to the issue and have taken the path to team building, sometimes the accelerated one of external intervention, the changes have been felt in three main areas: the team leader, the individual members, and the work practices. These changes have in every case made a significant change to the organization. In some cases it has been an insurance policy for future survival. It has given the team the tools and the confidence to face often overwhelming odds in the cut and thrust of modern organizational life.

For team leaders

Once a team leader is considering team building seriously there is a very good chance that the outcome will be successful. Many managers will see no need for team building and many others would be so threatened by the whole idea that they would never start. If you have stayed this far you are probably interested in the benefits which others, team leaders and team members, have seen for the team leader:

- The team leader became stronger, more decisive and more effective.
- The leader changed his style, individuals took responsibility for the group and not just for themselves.
- There was an appreciation by the team leader that he needed to show positive interest in team members and their departments.
- It emphasized the leader's difficulty in being a leader.
- I was more able to speak 'directly' to the team. I have slowed down my thoughts/actions . . . as I have realized through getting to know them better that it is better for them to move one step at a time.
- Made more personal contact with some team members, felt that some (but not all) of the status and hierarchy had been got rid of.
- Greater commitment to the team and its objectives, great expectations had been generated, worried that they could not be fulfilled.

For individual team members

For the individual team members the benefits of team building have most frequently been about receiving information from colleagues on personal and sectional matters, about the unravelling of unsatisfactory relationships, the identification of further training needs, the challenge of colleagues' expectations, and frequently the growing confidence which comes from understanding self, others and the situation. The following quotes confirm:

- Individuals softened or amended their approach (although some did not). I felt I was able to be more tolerant of others and more free to approach superiors without feeling hidebound by hierarchy.
- Earlier problems with a particular colleague getting better, still disagree but we do debate the problems and listen to each other.
- Training needs were identified, some individuals had more confidence in colleagues and themselves and more issues were raised.
- One member realized that he did not fit in and could not make the grade so resigned.
- Less forthright and less confident members of the team subsequently blossomed into very effective managers and have revealed the potential that was stifled under the previous regime.
- I sensed a greater freedom and ability to communicate and to have dialogue with colleagues where previously I wouldn't have bothered.

For work practices

A team building event is often the first real look at collective responsibilities. It is a fresh look at the work group as a team and is a thorough reappraisal of the strengths, weaknesses and interactions of group members. And it can provide a new direction and drive which can cascade through other parts of the organization or institution.

For the team it can increase understanding, and acceptance, of their need for one another; it gives a new awareness of what makes other people tick, and it is an opportunity to sit back together and *think* of the issues facing the group.

Work practices are seen to have changed in various ways, including:

- Team meetings more structured and effective.
- Chairing of meetings better, minutes circulated promptly.
- Improvement in working to objectives, and in reviewing and evaluating individual and group inputs in a more professional manner.
- Communication more comprehensive and effective, even where the network is quite elaborate.
- Strong commitment to new goals.
- Greater autonomy for line managers but also more corporate management when called for.
- Greater use made of colleagues and working together at the top has affected work practices further down the line. Old dividing lines much more blurred.

In short, 'better results'.

ACTION FOR TEAM BUILDING

At this point it is appropriate to discuss the practice of team building using the external approach.

While there is an immense amount any manager can do to develop and maintain the team working strength of the group there can be a good case for outside intervention, and there are many consultants, facilitators, enablers, trainers and developers in the market place. There are instruments and packages, and there are people with skills. Some of them can really help you with your team building. In their book, *Organization Development through Teambuilding*, Woodcock and Francis give some advice on choosing a consultant. Every manager has a choice and there are ways of finding the contacts. The Association for Management Education and Development has a directory of consultants who engage in team building activities and will supply information. Acquiring a consultant, trainer or developer needs some care for it is your group (and maybe neck) that is at risk. However, after those words of caution, it has to be said that you can progress faster and further with professional help than without it.

It is possible to start in a small way on team building and to start today. Starting from inside or outside, with or without help, team building activities can be routine and gradual, or swift and accelerated. But before deciding about whether and how you should be proceeding to build a team you had better think about yourself, for there is no more exposed position than the one you hold. There are plenty of analogies about leaving the kitchen if you find the heat too much, but heading up a section, department or organization is more like the chill at the top of the mountain. It is extremely cold, the winds blow strongly and there are few people to share the view. Team building is a demanding activity; your team members may resist the idea that things could be improved and may need persuading; you may meet some defensive behaviour and be tempted to give up. But if you do decide to work along these principles you will be climbing the mountain in congenial company, and others will smooth the road. One team which had a particularly bad experience after its team building exercise has said that its members could not have coped without the new foundations which they had built.

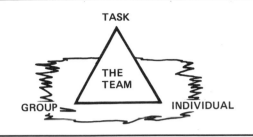

Figure 17.5   The team unites the task, the group and the individual

Another team leader wrote: 'Team building, like all sound structural engineering, should make sure foundations are right, that the structure has stability with flexibility, and also integrity.' Could you wish for more for your team?

Getting on with it

Collect the facts about your team; what does each member do, think, feel? What are the group dynamics and what needs improving? Which areas of the business are shaky? What is happening to the setting and the achieving of targets? Is all right with the group/team world?

Analyse the issues; those which everybody knows about and talks about, *and* those which everybody knows about and doesn't talk about. Take one or two which you have been ducking over the past months and find a route by which you can approach them with the people or person concerned.

Choose the route by looking ahead to your destination. Let yourself daydream a little to see your ideal team. Then come down to earth and imagine the small changes which would make such a difference to you, to the team members concerned, and to the climate of success in your group.

The reading list will give you lots of starting points. But your greatest asset and tool for success will be the realization that there is work to be done in the field of team development, and the determination to do it. Set yourself short targets which will indicate your success. Your journey will have no end; people and situations will be constantly changing, but it will be interesting and it will be productive.

Start now!

Open your own team building parcel (Figure 17.5) and discover for yourself that there is something new in there, that teambuilding is *not* a passing fancy but a positive way forward to the results which you want for yourself, your team and your organization.

CHECKLIST: A WINNING TEAM

And finally a checklist:
    Ask yourself whether, on the following criteria, yours is a winning team.

A winning team:

- Knows where it is going.
- Sets realistic targets.
- Uses all its resources in energetic and imaginative ways.
- Has a wide range of alternatives for action.
- Instigates coping strategies as needed.
- Monitors progress.
- Trusts its members to pursue their part of the common task.
- Has a confident yet realistic self-image.
- Handles its relationships with the outside world sensitively and assertively.

Does yours?

FURTHER READING

Adair, John, *Effective Teambuilding*, Gower, 1986

Belbin, R. Meredith, *Management Teams, why they succeed or fail*, Heinemann, 1981

Francis, Dave, and Young, Don, *Improving Work Groups*, University Associates, 1979

Hastings, Colin, Bixby, Peter, and Chaudhry Lawton, Rani, *The Superteam Solution*, Gower, 1986

Margerison, Charles and McCann, Dick, *How to lead a winning team*, MCB University Press, 1985

Margerison, Charles and McCann, Dick, *Team Management Resource*, Details from IMCB, Castle Street, Buckingham MK18 1BS

Patten, Thomas H., *Organizational Development Through Teambuilding*, John Wiley & Sons, 1981

Woodcock, Mike, *Team Development Manual*, Gower, 2nd edition 1988

Woodcock, Mike, and Francis, Dave, *Organization Development through Teambuilding*, Gower, 1981

18 Making the most of your support staff

Glenys Cater

So! It's 9.00am on your first day as a manager, and for the first time you have staff waiting for you to direct them and the department to success.

This would be so much easier if these people were robots who occasionally needed oiling or a spare part replaced, and could be ignored for the rest of the time. Well, in some ways people are like robots – only in the case of humans, the oil is replaced by your genuine interest in them and the spare parts by your making sure they have the correct tools, information and instructions to do their jobs properly. The difference is that people can't and shouldn't be ignored for most of the time.

The dictionary definition of 'support' is to prevent from giving way; back up; take their part; contribute to the success; or maintain the value of something. And all these are involved in the work of your support staff, and in your relationship with them, as this chapter will show.

Obviously, the success and the increase in the value of your department/ company is what you have been appointed to achieve. It follows, therefore, that building and maintaining a rapport with your support staff will be equally as valuable as any technical skills you may have. Be assured, if a department takes a dislike to a new boss, then his/her task will be well nigh impossible. Difficulties from surliness and non-cooperation to downright sabotage can be encountered. Whilst those will eventually be put right, it will probably be after you have left. Meanwhile it will reflect very badly on you. So it is important to get off to the right start.

START ON THE RIGHT LINES

As a first-time manager, you may have just one person as your support staff, or several. Amongst these will usually be someone with the job title of secretary or PA.

The top priority on your list on your first day is to make an ally of your secretary/ PA. So the first thing to do is to have a chat with her. You will need a fairly long chat eventually – but on your first day, a quick ten-minute chat will be sufficient to introduce yourself if she doesn't already know you, to give a brief outline of what you intend to do on your first day, and to arrange the time for the longer meeting.

The longer meetings should be repeated with every member of your support staff. On the first day all that is necessary is to get them together, tell them who you are, and ask who they are if you don't already know. Make sure to tell them that you will be having longer individual talks with them all during the course of the next week. The time-scale will, of course, depend on what your superiors may have planned for you, but, in any event, should take place as soon as possible.

The separate short preliminary talk with your secretary is indispensable, as it is with her you will be working most closely.

FIRST CHAT WITH YOUR SECRETARY

If time allows, this can also cover items suggested later for your longer talk, and the second talk dispensed with.

Tell her that you are relying on her for support. Give her some information on your background and previous experience. If you have had a chance to read her CV, comment on a few interesting items. Then arrange a time for the longer talk – and stick to it!

If you have any positive likes or dislikes in the way you would like things run, say so *now* in a tactful way.

LONGER INTRODUCTORY MEETINGS

The following list suggests topics you will need to discuss:

- How the filing system is to operate.
- How you would like the post to be dealt with.
- Which routine matters you would like your assistant/PA to deal with personally.

Make sure that you arrange a time to spend each day with your secretary/support staff to discuss ongoing matters. A good time is after the post has been opened and you have had a chance to look at it.

Your secretary/PA can be a very valuable asset. Do find out which parts of her job she likes most and which she likes least. Is there anything which she would like to do and which could fall within her scope? Has she any ideas which may improve the efficiency of the department, but hasn't till now been given a chance to implement? Her answers will provide you with much valuable information – about herself, and about the department. Do show that you are listening!

DAILY MEETINGS

A secretary, by definition of the word, is a confidant, one privy to a secret. So a good, experienced secretary will know that anything you discuss with her is not for general disclosure – unless it is information which you have told her is for general dispersal.

She is also an important link between you and the department. It follows that because she is in touch with the rest of the staff, you will be able to use her as a sounding board for ideas affecting the department. She can also give you information which may be useful about the rest of the staff. By this, I don't mean that she acts as a spy. She will be able to bring to your attention useful bits of information that can affect your thinking and the department's efficiency.

For example, if someone's work is not up to scratch or they are forgetful and make mistakes, it may be that they are having problems outside work. They may well discuss this with their peers, including your secretary, but would not think of discussing it with you. Your secretary will be able to act as a go-between in this way.

Instead of thinking that the person is no good, a friendly chat showing that you understand the problem and seeing if there is any way you can help should work wonders. Even if there is nothing you can do, just showing your concern for your staff will work wonders in their attitude to work.

YOUR RESPONSIBILITY TO YOUR STAFF

Your staff are your responsibility, and you 'carry the can' for what goes on in your department. Although this can seem daunting at first, it can have its advantages. Staff who see that their boss is willing to stand up for them are more often than not determined to see that he doesn't have to – it's all a matter of respect. This is a key word in the relationship between managers and support staff. Bosses who 'pass the buck' to their staff when things go wrong do not gain respect either from their subordinates or their superiors.

A boss who will support his team to his superiors and peers will gain respect from his staff who will see themselves as a united team, willing and able to achieve results. This type of team will be more willing to put themselves out or give extra when circumstances demand, than a team with a boss who constantly criticizes or blames them. In this case there will be an attitude of 'Why should we put ourselves out for him? He never does anything for us, and he blames us for things which were really his fault in the first place!'

Criticism and blame are difficult areas for the new manager, especially when they relate to the staff working most closely with him. Interestingly, many also experience awkwardness about praise. The guidelines are in fact quite simple. Always praise in public, if possible, and criticize in private, without fail. Praise should be wholehearted, and credit should be given. Criticism should be constructive and the person's good points should be noted. The talk should end on a high note if at all possible.

For example, 'You did a good job on the Frampton project last week, really excellent work. I liked the way you designed the background notes. That was your own idea, wasn't it? However, I think a little more attention to detail could have prevented the wrong date being put on those letters. Luckily in this case, you did spot it before they went out. It did cause a lot of extra work and expense, but I think you realize the problems which could have been caused if they had gone out, and you will be more careful in future. It was a good job you spotted the error and had the sense to report it straight away. It will remind us all to be more careful next time.'

THINGS WHICH ANNOY STAFF

There are a number of ways in which a manager can alienate his/her staff. Be warned.

Taking credit for their ideas

If any of your staff has a good idea which is implemented, *never* take credit for it yourself. Always give credit, preferably publicly in front of a superior, to the staff member whose idea it was. If you take the credit, the ideas will either stop coming or you will be by-passed so that the staff member can make sure that credit is given where it is due.

Passing the buck

If you have made a decision which later proves to be wrong, *never* in any way try to pass the buck to one of your staff. It won't go down well with your staff (who will start to question any of your decisions) and it won't go down well with your superiors. (They know that you are ultimately responsible for what happens in your department anyway.)

If you have asked your secretary to set something in motion in the department and it is queried, always back her up. One of the best bosses I ever had, when I asked him what I should do, said 'What would you do if I wasn't here? Make a decision on the facts to hand. If it's wrong I'll back you all the way in public. Privately I'll kick your . . . round the office. But we'll know where we stand. If it's the right decision, then you get all the credit!'

This boss used to take his turn cleaning the office refrigerator and making coffee. He didn't have to and neither did he lose any respect. Because we knew he would back us, then we backed him. When the chips were down we closed ranks and put in every ounce of effort.

Waitress service

Too many bosses employ highly trained secretaries and treat them as waitresses and odd job girls, expecting them to make tea, wash up, run personal errands (usually in their own time). Secretaries do make tea, coffee etc for their bosses. Usually it is more efficient that way. But it should never be taken for granted – this leads to resentment about doing it. And the secretary should always be thanked. (As I said earlier, my most respected bosses have never minded taking the odd turn at the tea and coffee making.)

Personal errands

If there is an absolute necessity for a member of your staff to do a personal errand for you, remember they are doing you a favour. If it is a business matter, then the errand should be done in company time. If it is not, then the staff member will have to do it in her own time. And do remember she may have planned to do other things during her lunchtime.

Always make sure that it is convenient and always thank her. Do not take it as a right. Such favours should be asked sparingly. Imagine how she feels hearing you say to someone, 'My secretary won't mind popping into Jones's to pick up the dry cleaning', when Jones's is half a mile in the other direction from the shop where she had planned to dash (in the pouring rain) to do a full week's shopping in her lunch hour. And this is made even worse by knowing that you will be sitting in the staff dining room in the dry all the while!

KEYS TO SUCCESS

This brings us to the three essential ingredients in a successful working relationship with your secretary/support staff: integrity, courtesy and respect. By proving your own integrity and showing courtesy to all staff you will earn their respect. And that respect makes all the difference between success and failure in running your department.

Integrity

Prove your integrity by doing as you would be done by. As we have already discussed giving credit where it is due, and not passing the buck will go a long way towards this. Also *never* criticize superiors or the company in front of junior staff.

Courtesy

It is just as easy to be pleasant and treat staff as humans than not. 'Please', 'thank you' and 'well done' do not take up much time but the time saved with willing cooperation is immeasurable.

I had a friend who once worked for the President of a large American company in New York. He was extremely rude to the point of clicking fingers, pointing and saying 'You, do this.' My friend did not like him or the job and one day, during a meeting with approximately thirty Vice-Presidents the following scene ensued:

President (to my friend): 'You, tea!'

My friend went out and prepared the tea (silver service, best china on tray) and walked back into the boardroom, luxuriously appointed with white shagpile carpet.

My friend announced 'Tea is served', and in a grand gesture threw the tray down onto the carpet. Result: thirty extremely amused (but trying not to show it) Vice-Presidents who themselves had previously suffered much; one very red-faced President who had lost all face; and one very satisfied friend, who by the time the President had regained sufficient breath to sack her, had long gone!

Nobody wants to work for a rude arrogant bully. How much easier it would have been simply to have said, 'Do you mind bringing us some tea?'

SUMMARY

Start with an open mind about your staff. Don't be prejudiced by the opinions of others (especially your predecessor, whose problems if any may have been of his own making).

Get them on your side, but don't try to be 'one of the boys/girls'.

Try to maintain an 'open door' policy. It's surprising how many good ideas your staff may come up with if they feel they can talk to you. You'll soon spot the time-wasters.

The rapport you build with your PA/secretary will help to keep you informed (but not in a spying way) of any staff problems affecting work. Remember this is information to enable you to help that person. Never gossip about your staff's personal problems.

Basically, 'do unto others as you would be done by'. Be courteous always. Show your integrity and win their respect.

And lastly, on that first day, remember: they are looking for someone they can get on with and they want a happy working relationship with the boss. You both want the same thing – so, no problem!

CHECKLIST OF KEY POINTS

- Get your secretary on your side from day one.
- Ask her advice.
- Delegate and give credit for ideas.
- Treat staff as people, and with as much care as valuable tools.
- Remember they may have useful ideas and different type of knowledge from you which may well be useful.
- Be prepared to listen to them.
- Always back them up when they are carrying out your instructions.

FURTHER READING

Adair, John, *The Action-Centred Leader*, Industrial Society

Attwood, Margaret, *Introduction to Personnel Management*, Pan

Morris, M. J., *The First Time Manager*, Kogan Page, 1988

Robinson, David, *Getting the Best out of People*, Kogan Page, 1988

19 Managing Communication

Krystyna Weinstein

Why do we discuss the issue of communication so much these days? Why do we become concerned when employee attitude surveys in companies tell us that staff get most of their information from the grapevine and rumour, that no-one tells them anything in time, that they don't recall what they have been told, or that they have little opportunity for 'upward' communication to tell management what they think?

WHY IS COMMUNICATION IMPORTANT?

Communication has been called the life-blood of an organization. Without it little would be achieved. So, until robots take over from us entirely at work, we will need to communicate with each other to get our individual jobs done. In a sense, then, communicating is sharing.

We also communicate with each other because using each other as a resource is the most effective way of running any organization. It has taken many managements many years to recognize that people who do the day-to-day tasks in a company are likely to know more about that work than anyone else. Involving them, and hearing what they have to say, is therefore pretty crucial.

But more importantly, communicating with people is recognizing their worth as human beings.

In a corporate setting, this means that we value people not merely as 'role people' but as 'whole people'. It is in everyone's interests that we all develop and make use of our varied skills, interests, and insights. Everyone, including the company, ultimately benefits.

Tom Watson, who built IBM into a highly successful global corporation believed that 'the basic philosophy, spirit and drive of an organization have far more to do with its relative achievements than do technological or economic resources, organizational structures, innovation and timing.'

So the quality of communication in an organization will affect staff motivation and job satisfaction, their sense of commitment and energy, their performance and

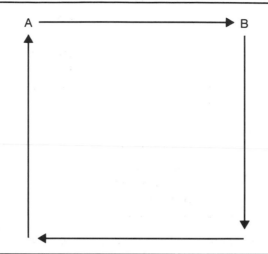

Figure 19.1   Real communication involves feedback

productivity. They will react to the 'climate' in the organization. And the main contributing factor to this is managers' values and styles.

A corporate philosophy that believes in openness and using all the human potential within its metaphorical four walls rests on, and must by definition be sustained by, good communications. Upward, downward, horizontal: everyone must be involved and be encouraged not only to communicate in all directions, but also to listen, and be prepared to get feedback.

SO, WHAT IS COMMUNICATION?

Communication is about conveying 'messages' to others: it is both a 'process' (how do I communicate) and a 'content' (what do I communicate) – though in fact they are often inseparable.

Two definitions encapsulate the simplest notions of communication:

1   'Communication is social interaction through messages'. The word 'interaction' focuses on a vital ingredient: the opportunity of feedback, without which there is no real communication. So, checking back, asking for clarification, feeding back one's own interpretations and understanding – only then are we truly communicating (see Figure 19.1). The alternative is a monologue.

This interaction involves three elements: the use of language (our prime, but not sole means of communicating with one another), our behaviour, and other 'symbols' (e.g. status symbols that also 'communicate').

The 'message' is the content – what we're trying to convey, and what we inadvertently convey.

2   'Communication is about creating shared meaning and understanding'. By communicating – interacting – we are creating an opportunity to share our view of something with others, and hear about their views. We are building a common understanding.

276

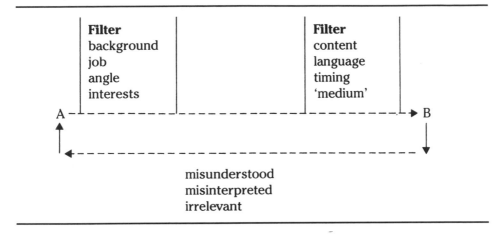

Figure 19.2 The impact of personal differences on communication

It gives us the opportunity to ensure that our words in particular, but our behaviour also, are not misunderstood or misinterpreted, as can so easily happen: a shrug of the shoulders, or the use of a word such as 'responsibility' – open to many interpretations.

WHY COMMUNICATION ISN'T SIMPLE

No organization is a gathering of homogeneous people. It is a mix of employees with different backgrounds and different levels of education. They bring to work different abilities and aspirations. Their past experiences differ, as do their present needs. Each performs a different job – exciting and demanding, or mundane and routine. Each plays a different role in the company, and views events and information from a different perspective and angle.

Each will therefore require slightly different information/communication, in different forms and at different times. One of a manager's main jobs is to understand and cater for these differences.

In other words, what starts out as a simple model becomes complicated with layers of potential confusion. (See Figure 19.2.)

This chapter sets out to unravel at least some of the intertwined strands of this complex 'ball of wool'.

A MANAGER'S JOB IS ABOUT COMMUNICATING

'It is by talking and listening that managers get most of their work done'.[1]

'Managers talk most of the time, and mostly face to face'.[2]

As these two quotes point out, communicating is a vital part of any manager's job. He or she is in fact at the hub of a communication network. (See Figure 19.3.)

Each of these contacts requires a differing form of communication. What a manager says to his/her boss, the language it is couched in, where and how it is conveyed, will differ from what he says to his subordinates, or other colleagues. The nuances are endless.

277

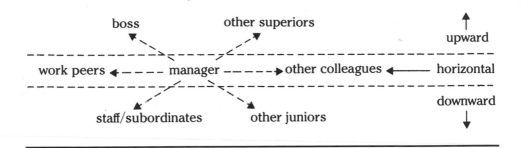

Figure 19.3   The manager as hub of a communication network

So, to perform the variety of roles that are required of a manager[3], he or she needs various communication skills: an ability to express him/herself clearly, be a good mixer, a good listener; to be aware, supportive, persuasive; above all to be fair and open, and be prepared to talk to everyone in this network. . . ie, to be able to manage the complex web of communications that surrounds him or her.

HOW CAN YOU MANAGE YOUR COMMUNICATIONS?

Communicating is about how we relate and interact, how we behave and speak. It is about what we say and to whom, how we say it, and how we convey it. (This includes what 'form' we use – the spoken or written word – and what 'medium' we use – a meeting or a memo.)

Journalists have long lived with a similar series of unstated 'questions' that they ask themselves when writing an everyday story with the right ingredients. These are: who, why, where, when, what – commonly known as the Five Ws.

These same Five Ws apply to all communications. If you, as a manager, bear them in mind, no matter what communication you're involved with, you will have a useful set of guidelines.

There is, however, a sixth W to remember: *how* (conveniently preceded by a silent 'W'!). Do I, for instance, communicate with my staff at a meeting, or by means of a memo? That choice is important, for as Marshall McLuhan said many years ago, 'the medium is the message' – or at least an important part of it. And what does my language and behaviour communicate?

Although this chapter will look at each of these Six Ws separately, in everyday life they are interlinked and inseparable: who you're communicating with determines what you will communicate, how and possibly even where.

Who you're communicating with

In everyday life, a conversation with our grandmother or our child will differ from one with a friend in a pub or winebar. The same is true in an organization.

The 'whos' in organizations will vary on a number of dimensions:

Who are they? What is their position in the organization? Are they senior managers, supervisors, clerks or secretaries? This will begin to tell us about their needs, their interests, their level of knowledge, the questions they may ask us, the detail we need to give them, the language to use with them. In other words, every bit of organizational information has to be 'translated' to suit their needs, to be made relevant to them in their work, or their position.

What is their role? Are they from sales, production, personnel, research, finance, advertising? Again, their needs will vary and will be geared to their specific roles, activities, and perspective – is it to produce more, save money, or ensure good working conditions?

Are they all from your own department? Then at least they probably all speak the same or similar internal language or jargon. But that is still no guarantee that they will be interested in the same detail or angle.

How many different 'whos' are you communicating with at any one particular time (e.g. at a meeting or when writing a report)? If many, you need to tell your story in different ways – while ensuring it is still the same story. So, maybe you run several separate meetings, or prepare additional separate written pieces.

Your awareness of people's differing needs, and being prepared to cater for them, is a powerful message to those you communicate with.

Why are we communicating?

'Why' is a vague question, not precise enough to elicit specific information. A more fruitful way is to ask: what has 'prompted' the need to communicate, and what 'outcome' am I seeking?

In organizations, any communication has a final purpose or 'outcome'. Something has to be done, or achieved, eg. a particular task has to be performed, to ensure delivery of an item. That outcome has itself usually been 'prompted' by something happening – or not. To continue our simple example, delays are being caused in another department.

Thus 'why we communicate' has two parts to it: a prompt, and a required outcome.

Between them, the prompt and outcome tell us what is the 'task' of our communication. Is it to teach, persuade, suggest, inform, motivate, establish good rapport with, and so on. Knowing what our task is, we can then decide 'how' best to go about it, ie, what 'medium' to use: a memo, a training session, a pep talk, or greater involvement in the work of the department. (See Figure 19.4.)

We should also remember that when we communicate with someone in our organization on a work issue, the main outcome is an organizational one. Managers who observe this are more likely to be fair in their interactions with others than managers who 'personalize' these organizational relationships.[4]

This is not to deny that we often have 'hidden agendas' when we communicate. The attractive man in the marketing department may be able to help me with my task, but I may also be interested in getting to know him better for other reasons! Nothing wrong in that. But I need to bear in mind that the organizational outcome

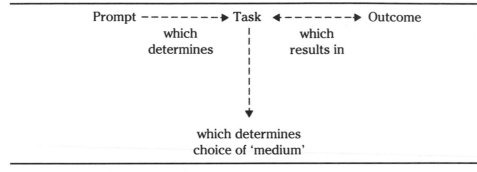

Figure 19.4 Why are we communicating?

is the one that dictates our communication, even when the marketing man has abandoned me for someone else.

Where will you communicate?

Where will you be communicating? In a one-to-one encounter, in a lecture hall, in your room, on the shop floor, at a meeting? Will the encounter be formal or informal? Will the other party to the interaction have notice of your 'communication'? Will they be prepared or caught unawares?

The answers to these questions will have implications not only for 'what' you can communicate, but also 'how' to communicate it. A personal reprimand on the shopfloor, or by memo, is less likely to achieve the desired effect than a face-to-face meeting in a quiet room. The 'task' gives us clues about where we can best communicate.

When will you communicate?

This is a perennial question for corporate communications. Rumour and the grapevine travel with an amazing speed and efficiency – with implications for managers. Get there first, or at least respond to them fast, and honestly. We come back to management style and philosophy.

Not having time is used as a frequent excuse for not communicating. Yet not-communicating is itself a powerful form of communication. It conveys messages about how unimportant the person not being communicated with is, how undervalued and mistrusted, and how important and scarce the information is ('information is power'). It also sends messages about the degree of commitment there is in the organization to 'open communication', in spite of all the protestations in corporate mission statements and Board pronouncements.

Consider the issue of a possible plant closure. Conveying and sharing this information earlier rather than later, in an open way, would lead to a greater understanding of the issue, and a commitment to explore and find the best solutions.

What am I communicating?

The 'what' of communication is about content. What is the subject matter, the detail, level, slant and angle? What is relevant, and what is my 'task'? The answers to these issues will be derived partially from asking the questions 'who' and 'why'.

There are essentially four categories of corporate communication:

- job or task related: without it, individual jobs and tasks would not get done;
- organizational/work related: relevant, but not immediately vital, and the result of a cross-fertilization of ideas, which sparks off thoughts, and leads to developments or changes;
- integrational: which involves people in the larger 'whole' of an organization, its values, vision and sense of purpose, and which adds a perspective and meaning to their work, and gives them a greater sense of commitment;
- housekeeping: less job-, and more people- and place-related: who has moved where, who has joined, how the canteen is being renovated, an office party.

Be clear about which category any particular communication falls into, for each of these four should be conveyed by different means. It is a strange (but authentic) organization that one day used a memo to communicate the introduction of a new computer system which would revolutionize everyone's work, and the next week used the same medium to ask employees not to throw orange peel into waste-paper bins.

So, to return to the four categories:

- the first type would involve face-to-face communication, or maybe memo;
- the second would occur at meetings, and through other two-way communications (eg. suggestions schemes), or focused and thought-provoking articles in a company newspaper;
- the third possibly through the well-written and thoughtful articles in a company newspaper but, crucially, backed up by everyday attitudes and behaviour, and further enhanced through training and other face-to-face communications, such as quality circles; and
- the last by noticeboard, or in a section in the company newspaper. (See 'What medium to use?' below.)

So, by thinking about, and carefully deciding, what to communicate to whom – provided you have assessed your recipient and his/her interests correctly – you are conveying your own understanding and sensitivity to your listener/recipient.

How shall I communicate?

Put simply: 'You can't not communicate.' Virtually everything we do, when in the company of others, communicates something to them.

So, just considering the questions posed in the five sections immediately preceding this, and creating the most appropriate 'communication', is a major step in the direction of good communications.

But there is obviously more to it than that. There are two further elements you need to consider: what 'medium' to use; and how you yourself come across to others.

What medium to use?

There are a number of different way of communicating:

Orally: one-to-one; small groups; committees; larger meetings; telephone; training sessions

In writing: letter; memo; note; report; research study; note on noticeboard; text on a computer screen

Visually: using a variety of visual materials when writing or speaking e.g. charts, diagrams, photographs, and film or video

You can thus vary your communication. But you need to ask a number of questions. How important is the information? Which is the best or most appropriate means for the task in hand? Should the recipient be given the opportunity to respond, or ask questions?

Can the information you want to convey be sufficiently simplified and clarified to be passed on by the written word? Or is it more complex, and therefore better conveyed orally, giving your recipients the chance to ask for clarification?[5]

It is not possible in a short space to discuss which medium is most appropriate for each occasion. But there is one simple test which will begin to help: ask yourself which you would prefer yourself, if you were in the position of being a listener/'receiver' of the 'item' you are planning to 'communicate'. If you have questions to ask, then the 'medium' you need to use is a two-way, face-to-face one, rather than a written one.

The catch, however, is that as a manager you are likely to be happier with the written word than some of the other people you deal with, and communicate with. Your own preference in this case should be carefully considered. Is your audience as literate as you?

If you opt for a face-to-face setting, you still have to decide whether a larger, more formal meeting is best, or a small discussion group. And that depends on whether the issue in hand is one which would benefit from a discussion, or whether it merely involves you imparting information.

Employee preferences

Employees are frequently asked how they prefer to 'hear' information. Figure 19.5 illustrates the result of one such typical survey. Most favoured were the various forms of face-to-face and two-way communications such as team briefings and regular, short departmental or section meetings – a method used successfully by Japanese firms here in the UK.

What also stands out from this and most other similar surveys, is that employees want their manager to be their prime source of information.

	Downward Communications			Upward Communications		
	Used %	Prefer %	Prefer as % of used	Used %	Prefer %	Prefer as % of used
Noticeboard	57	17	24	n/a	n/a	n/a
Informal conversations with your immediate boss	55	33	44	62	39	52
Internal memoranda/letters to staff	49	17	25	24	10	30
Grapevine/gossip	45	3	5	26	2	8
Department/group meetings	39	30	46	34	27	48
Company newspaper/house journal	39	13	23	n/a	n/a	n/a
Briefing groups/team briefings	36	27	48	30	26	54
Formal appraisals on how well you are doing	33	20	34	27	18	39
Newsheet	32	12	21	n/a	n/a	n/a
Pre-arranged meetings with your immediate boss	32	25	43	37	30	48
Conversations with more senior employees than yourself	32	19	36	29	18	38
Meetings with people from other departments/areas of company	29	18	35	n/a	n/a	n/a
Video	28	9	28	n/a	n/a	n/a
Trade union meetings	23	8	26	21	8	30
Employee version of annual report	21	13	26	n/a	n/a	n/a
Via employee representatives	15	8	34	20	11	30
Letters column in company newsletter	n/a	n/a	n/a	11	5	20
Via surveys of employee opinions	n/a	n/a	n/a	8	10	29
Some other method	3	1	19	2	1	38

Base: All respondents (1063)

Source: IMS

Figure 19.5   Table of communication media

The importance ... and the intention

The importance of the communication will to a large extent dictate the medium: in the example given earlier, announcing a new computer system by memo is clearly using a totally inappropriate medium. Something as important as a change in work practices must involve many meetings and discussion groups – as well as written information – with all concerned.

The 'intention' or task will also dictate the medium. It is not possible, for instance, to motivate individuals by writing to them. The issue is too complex, needing insights into what motivates them, and why they are demotivated. You can only find this out by having some form of two-way communication.

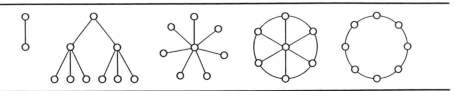

Figure 19.6   Varieties of channels of communication

The 'channel'

You also need to consider the 'channel' (see Figure 19.6): do you wish to communicate something to everyone? Will you do this by meeting people individually, or in a group? Or will you inform representatives, who then pass on the information? And if you chose the latter, will the information get distorted en route? And will it matter?

Spoken communication

Spoken communication – if well planned, sympathetically conducted, and if the number of people is kept small (no more than 10 people) – allows for discussion, sharing, and generally for productive communication, since people have the opportunity of contributing. Meetings (or team briefings) are an excellent means of discussing work procedures, introducing changes, or resolving other work-related issues. For personal and individual issues, face-to-face communication is the best, possibly preceded by a letter to alert the other person.

So, consider: will you be better able to convey your message, and is it more likely to be heard and understood, if it is presented by you in person, in a discussion group, in some written form, or visually – or by a combination of all of these? And if the subject matter merits a discussion, consider what type of gathering you think will be best.

Written material

Written material, being one-way, doesn't allow the recipient much opportunity to reply. Where a large amount of information has to be conveyed, the written form allows the reader to assimilate at his or her own pace. However, ask yourself whether your audience is as used to reading as you are; and if not, the shorter the message, and simpler the language, the better.

For quick communication of a straightforward, uncontroversial nature (and as a manager you need to decide whether this is the case), the memo or letter is the easiest and most direct.

HOW DO I COME ACROSS?

So far this chapter has looked at the 'mechanics' of how to communicate. But the other single most important element in any communication is yourself: the language you use; and your behaviour and body language.

Status . . . and subordinates

Whether we like it or not, another person's status frequently influences how we communicate, and particularly how we behave.

Plush office or open plan, great expanses of carpet or lino, which floor people inhabit, what they wear (dirty overalls or a dark pin-striped suit) influence how we behave – and in return how they behave towards us. Being told what a person 'does' also influences how we speak to them, involve them, and what we expect of them.

Being aware of this, and of how precisely any one of them influences you, is the first step to overcoming any 'distortions' that occur. 'Downward' communications (see Figure 19.2) are particularly prone to these distortions.

Clerks doing routine, mundane tasks, often feel their work has little or no significance. Behaviour towards them often reinforces this. Consequently they make errors and mistakes which bring down the wrath of those who depend on their work being done methodically. Yet a simple explanation to them of how their work is important because it is part of a chain and affects the work of many others could improve their standard of work, not to mention their motivation.

Inevitably, one such gesture is not enough, but it may be a beginning.

SEPARATION, DISTANCE . . . AND PERSPECTIVE

In most organizations communication is further complicated by separation and distance. Distance is not only geographic – at the other end of the country. It occurs much closer to home, in the same building, separated by floors. Being separated frequently means not meeting, not talking, not knowing, not understanding, and not communicating.

Distance may also mean working in a different department, ie. with a different perspective on the organization. Yet bringing together people from the various disciplines within a company may not only be vital to its continued productivity; it would also be 'integrational' and reinforce their sense of belonging, of being part of a coherent whole.

It is this growing realization that has resulted in many organizations creating quality circles, team briefings and suggestion schemes as part of their overall corporate communication strategies.

Suggestion schemes . . . by any other name

A structured two-way communication system. It has old-fashioned connotations, but is being revived, for it has the potential to tap into the accumulated knowledge and insights of employees, and gain their commitment and involvement.

It has been variously renamed as Brainwaves (British Airways), Winning Lines (British Rail), or Ideas Unlimited (BBC)

It requires a highly formalized system to:

- enable employees (individuals or teams) to spend the time on developing an idea; maybe the company can have a 'problems in search of a solution' file
- let them know exactly how to present ideas, and what criteria will be used to assess them
- inform them of the procedures by which their contribution will be accepted and assessed
- tell them who will assess the ideas, and how it will be done
- reward employees in a recognised way
- publicize the winners and their ideas, as well as others who also contributed
- market the idea widely, throughout the company, using all the various media available
- run the scheme efficiently, maybe even appointing someone to run it full-time

If well administered, it may become a stepping stone to gaining more employee commitment.

Note: When, in the 1980s Ford asked their hourly people to suggest easier ways of building one of their models, they received over 1 400 suggestions, and incorporated 500.

Team briefings

An idea used by over 500 organizations throughout the UK. It is a two-way communication system, though the impetus for holding briefings comes from managers. Their prime purpose is to communicate corporate policies and other information that staff need to be aware of.

Team briefings underline a basic element in a manager's job: to keep his or her staff informed of important issues within the company.

It is a 'cascading' system: senior managers inform those below them; they in turn brief their own managers; and finally section heads or their equivalent inform members of staff.

Briefings should be held regularly, no more than six weeks apart, in work time, for no more than 15 people at a time, for between 30–40 minutes. The manager gives his 'briefing' which is then followed by questions and answers.

Everyone in an organization must get the same information, although sometimes the slant of that information may differ, given the differing departmental perspectives, and the differing needs of employees at various levels and locations of an organization.

A manager needs to be well briefed him/herself first, with back-up written notes as help. He/She needs to be trained in listening and presentation skills; and needs to spend time working on anticipated questions, and the answers.

Quality circles

A Japanese 'invention' which has grown in popularity in the UK in the past few years.

The main aim is to bring together on a regular basis a group of people from different parts of an organization, and representing the same or different departments, to tackle a 'quality' issue for the organization. The questions quality circles ask are: 'how can we . . .' and 'what can be done to . . .'

The circle is given authority to call for information it needs, is able to question others, makes presentations, and offers recommendations.

The by-products of quality circles are at least as useful as the quality-related recommendations. Participants talk of feeling more involved in their work and in the company and its activities. They say their communication skills improve, and they develop more participative ways of working. Their self-confidence grows, and they find their opinion carries more weight with their colleagues. They also become aware that everyone has a different style and a different contribution to make at work, and to the business.

House magazines and newsletters

It is unlikely that a manager, on his or her own, will be required to produce a house magazine or newsletter. But they are a medium frequently used for conveying information.

They are excellent for 'integrational' material, possibly work-related ideas being shared, and certainly 'housekeeping' information (see 'What to communicate' above). But being a one-way form of communication they have their limitations, and are at their best when dealing with relatively straightforward 'information'. The question remains: is it simply 'management' generated and approved information, or can employee comments and dissatisfactions also be included? If the answer to the latter is 'no', their function is narrowed. Yet if they fail to publish controversial material, or what employees already 'know' (eg, the difficulties encountered on a new shop-floor production line; or the results of an employee survey with negative feedback) their credibility will be limited.

So, when creating such publications, managers need to decide what their 'task' is: to inform, persuade, or influence, and hence how the material is to be written and presented . . . and what material should be omitted, since it is best treated by 'oral' means.

Such publications are no substitute for real communication, which is two-way sharing and has more to do with attitudes and behaviour than information.

The Noticeboard . . . or Talking Board

An under-used medium. With the possibility of using eye-catching layout and design, and given the speed with which information can be placed there, added to, or changed . . . and its accessibility to all, it is a company's nearest equivalent to a daily newspaper, and a good sight cheaper. But its usefulness is – as is that of a newspaper – for conveying information of a non-controversial nature only.

Such a board needs a careful and well-arranged display of items, maybe differentiated by colours, and monitored daily for material that needs to be removed and/or updated. It can have allocated spaces for regular features, and could become a place for a 'letters to the editor'-style of communication, a talking board in fact (not dissimilar to graffiti!).

MANAGING YOURSELF . . . YOUR BEHAVIOUR

Our behaviour gives us away all the time: 'actions speak louder than words'. Old adages have a great deal of truth in them!

It follows that part of managing your communications is about managing yourself.

- 'An ear is as good as – or better than – any other communication channel.'
- 'A wise man encourages you to find out what you know for yourself.'
- 'Silence is golden.'
- 'If all else fails, try talking.'

These four quotes are not mutually exclusive, but are indispensable elements in how you communicate.

Listening . . . is communicating

Listening is a skill which is sorely neglected. Yet by listening to others we inform them that we think they are important. We are showing them that what they have to say is worth hearing, and that they are valuable. Listening can also take a lot of the effort – or drudgery – out of your own thinking. By listening you discover that others are already doing it for you!

Questioning . . . is communicating

Asking the right questions – not interrogative and accusing 'why' questions, but ones which open up a discussion, enable the other person(s) to reflect and analyse, and take initiative and responsibility – also send positive messages. Questions such as 'what would you do. . .' or 'how would you go about . . .' hands back to individuals their 'power' which is taken away from them when they are issued with instructions and orders.

. . . So is silence

Silence is another skill worth developing. Not the silence associated with 'not telling', but that associated with giving others the time and space – in any conversation and interaction – to reflect and decide what to do or say next. It is part and parcel of interacting with them creatively and positively. People who are given space and the encouragement to think will normally discover energy and commitment to work, and obviate the need for managerial interference.

Talking . . . establishing rapport

Managerial 'walkabouts', stopping to talk to staff, getting to know them as people and not simply as role fulfillers, discovering their strengths and what they can offer, how they think and what they value: these are all ingredients that go towards creating a 'communicating culture' in an organization. They are often more powerful than the 'communication initiatives' such as suggestion schemes and house magazines, that normally form part of a formal corporate communication strategy.

Body language . . . and tone of voice

Body language is our give-away. Most of us are not aware of our gestures, postures and quirks that tell the person we're interacting with whether we really are listening – while thinking we're giving that impression; whether we do feel confident and relaxed – in contrast to our brave verbal claims; whether we've heard what's actually being asked of us, and do intend to keep our promises.

Eye contact, a nod of the head, and the supportive 'aha' grunts as someone is speaking, not shuffling papers as someone is speaking, or looking at your watch . . . these are just some of the ways in which you can improve your own communication. By doing so, you signal to others that you mean what you say when you claim to want better communication and contact with them.

Similarly, tone of voice. More can be communicated this way than by the words that accompany it. A brusque 'That's interesting' communicates the listener's true state of mind.

Language . . . and words

When communicating, we tend to concentrate on the words. But they lay endless traps for us. Are we sure we are saying the 'right' thing? As one manager, anxious to assure his employees that the computers about to be installed in his office were nothing to be afraid of, reassured them 'There is no need to worry, since the computers can only do what you do'.

Language traps us in other ways. We use abbreviations, shorthand and jargon; or we indulge in long, abstract and increasingly imprecise words – on the principle that 'the weightier the word, the weightier the argument, and the more knowledgeable we appear.' This is a particular vice for writers, though speakers have been known to indulge in it. (See chapter 4, on Effective writing) Worst of all, though, we frequently fail to check that what we have said, or written, has been both heard and understood, i.e. we fail to get 'feedback'.

The words of Confucius uttered hundreds of years ago still make sense:

> If language is not correct, then what is said is not what is meant. If what is said is not what is meant, then what ought to be done remains undone.

THE IMPORTANCE OF FEEDBACK

We began this chapter by pointing out that interaction was an indispensable part of communication. This means giving and getting feedback: the person or persons you are communicating with must have the opportunity, and be encouraged, to respond. You must also listen to their responses, and be seen to be acting on them.

So, whenever you are communicating, consider which medium to use, for it is important and beneficial – for everyone – that there should be an opportunity for 'feedback' – whether in the form of agreement, disagreement, questions, other points of view, or clarification.

We frequently shun feedback because we are afraid of what we will hear. Yet from each such feedback we can learn something new, to apply in the future. As another old adage has it: 'there is no such thing as failure, only feedback.'

CHECKLIST OF KEYPOINTS

1 Remember: you can't NOT communicate.
2 Communicating is sharing.
3 Work through the Six Ws: who – why – where – when – what – (w) how.
4 Check your 'listener' has heard and understood.
5 Make sure there is a genuine opportunity for feedback.
6 Be aware that you communicate with language, behaviour and other symbols.
7 Listen yourself, ask questions, . . . and then talk.

NOTES

1 Rosemary Stewart has carried out extensive research into managers' jobs, and how they spend their time. In her highly readable book, *Managers and Their Jobs* (2nd edition, 1988), she states that:

> It is by talking and listening that managers get most of their work done. The amount of time that managers spend with others depends upon the job and its context, and the individual's inclination. The 160 managers in this study spent two-thirds of their time in conversation. Other studies have found an even higher proportion. . .

2 J. H. Horne and T. Lupton, 'The work activities of middle managers, *Journal of Management Studies*, Feb. 1965

> Managers talk most of the time, and mostly face to face. They seem not to be overwhelmed by paper or formal meetings. They swop information and advice and instructions, mostly through informal, face-to-face contact in their own offices . . . [this] calls for the ability to shape and utilise the person-to-person channels of communication, to influence, to persuade, to facilitate.

3 In his book, *The Nature of Managerial Work* (1973), Henry Mintzberg has listed ten roles that the average manager performs.

- six are active 'communication' roles:
  - three interpersonal roles: as a figure-head, representing his/her department; as a liaison with other departments; and as a leader of his own staff; and
  - three information roles: as a monitor, scanning for and receiving information; as a disseminator, passing on information; and as a spokesman for his department.

4   In this context, Alistair Mant, in his thought-provoking book *The Leaders we Deserve* (1983), has created a useful image. He talks of the 'binary' and 'ternary' manager. The binary manager tends to see relationships and communicating with another person in personal terms. A ternary manager sees that relationship, and any communication, as having an organizational/task outcome. By bearing this in mind, he or she can avoid becoming embroiled in highly personal and often emotional communication. For what may seem tough in personal terms becomes fair in organizational terms. (This in no way, of course, excuses thoughtlessness, inconsiderateness or other elements that creep in to destroy our communicating.)

5   Max Boisot, in a book full of insights – *Information and Organizations* (1987) – has added another useful dimension to the 'what' and the 'how'.

He has devised a method for classifying 'information' that we convey to others along two dimensions:

*   can it be coded easily (where one end of the continuum is highly structured and can be symbolically represented, eg, by numbers, and the other vague and full of intangible ideas); and,
*   can it be easily disseminated – by what means, and relevantly, to an appropriate audience.

So, if the information can be easily codified, in understandable language or numbers, the written word may be a means of transferring it to others. If, however, it is not easily codifiable, the sole means of conveying it to others may be face-to-face in a meeting, where there are opportunities for discussions and questions.

For example: motivating staff. This is a difficult, person-specific type of communication. Every one of us is motivated by something specific to ourselves and our needs, i.e. it is not 'information' that is easily codifiable. So, trying to motivate me in a large lecture on motivation may give me some intellectual insights, but will probably do little to actually motivate me. What I'd need is a face-to-face discussion, to uncover the reasons why I am feeling demotivated.

By contrast, sales figures are easily codifiable, will be widely understood, and thus lend themselves to being communicated by a process of dissemination such as a booklet, or even a lecture with slides.

FURTHER READING

Bland, Michael, and Jackson, Peter, *Effective Employee Communications* (Kogan Page, 1990)

Collard, Ron, 'The Quality Circle in Context', *Personnel Management*, Sept 1981

Drennan, David, 'Are you getting through?', *Management Today*, August 1989

Leeds, Dorothy, *Smart Questions for Successful Managers* (Piatkus, 1987)

McConville, James, and Wood, Andrew, *Suggestion Schemes* (Industrial Society, 1990)

MacKay, Ian, *A Guide to Listening* (BACIE, 1984)

Rogers, C. and Roethlisberger, F. J., 'Barriers and Gateways to Communication', *Harvard Business Review*, Nov. 1991.

'Team Briefing: practical steps in employee communication', *Industrial Relations Review and Report*, no. 361, Feb 1986

Weinstein, Krystyna, 'The communication syndrome', *Personnel Management*, June 1969

20 Making meetings work

John Gregory

Managers spend a great deal of time in meetings, often ineffectively and usually with a growing sense of frustration. This chapter looks at meetings and at why so many are ineffective, and suggests some steps to be taken to make them more effective. The chapter concludes with a simple seven-point guideline for the chairman and the meeting member.

GOOD MEETINGS MEAN MORE PROFIT

It is popular to grumble about meetings; indeed this pastime can become a dangerous obsession so that, in some organizations, the climate is such that managers find it very difficult to conduct effective meetings. Jokes and 'laws' about meetings proliferate and the well known video *Meetings bloody meetings*, although admirable, may have unwittingly contributed to the myth that meetings are a nuisance. Perhaps the typical management attitude to meetings is best summed up by a story told to me by a financial manager. He recounted the final act of a long and difficult meeting when after 2½ hours little had been achieved and the only decision that they were about to make was a time for the next meeting so that they could continue their fruitless endeavours. After much diary searching the chairman thought he had found a consensus and announced 'How about next Wednesday?' To which one of those present replied with a groan, 'Oh no not *Wednesday* – that ruins two weekends!'

So what is the message? It is that senior management should encourage and cultivate a 'good meetings climate' because in doing so they will improve:

- *Communication.* A business organization is by definition, two or more people engaged in commercial pursuit. Organizations cannot cohere or achieve goals without communicating and effective meetings play an essential part in this process.
- *Policy formulation and planning.* These activities require ideas, discussion and debate on key issues and on alternatives. They benefit from the collec-

tive wisdom of the management team and carefully considered proposals and options. This process can only take place in meetings.

- *Decision making.* Some decisions have to be made in formal meetings (or endorsed by them) because of constitutional or statutory requirements; for example Cabinet, council and boardroom decisions. But there are many circumstances in which the quality or durability of a decision will be enhanced if it is subjected to careful (and urgent!) consideration in a meeting at which those responsible for implementation or affected are present.

Better communication, better planning and improved decision making will have a positive effect on the bottom line and this is a justification for giving thought and energy to improving meetings.

Do we need a meeting?

If so many managers express the view that they spend too much time in meetings, perhaps they should not be there in the first place. It is undoubtedly the case that some meetings should never have been called so it is worth exercising the discipline of asking 'Do we need a meeting?' before setting one up. Figure 20.1 is a useful checklist which can be used to determine whether there is a need for a meeting.

A positive answer to one of the questions in the checklist suggests that a meeting is needed – but just by calling a meeting you don't communicate better, build teams, make good decisions or solve problems. Many meetings which undoubtedly should have been held fail. Let us now consider why this happens.

WHY DO MEETINGS FAIL?

Meetings can be broadly classified into formal and informal. The formal category embraces all those meetings that are required by some written constitution, Articles of Association or Statute. The conduct of formal meetings is usually governed by rules or custom and the membership controlled by election or some form of qualification.

By far the more frequent and managerially important meeting is the informal type which may be a regular or ad hoc problem solving type of meeting. Whatever the type the chances are that they fail from time to time or, in some cases, all the time! But why?

People problems

Since a meeting is a social group it is not surprising that they reflect the weaknesses and idiosyncracies of their members, for example:

- an incompetent chairman;
- an idle committee secretary;
- interpersonal conflict between members or departmental rivalries (the 'point scoring' syndrome);

Do the rules require a meeting?

So many formal meetings are required by statute or constitution and they have to be called and held in accordance with the rules. Although they often seem tedious and pointless, such meetings are consistent with open, democratic administration and provide some reassurance to those with an interest in the organisation concerned.

Is there a need to communicate?

How often do you hear the complaint 'nobody tells us anything'? When a business is proposing change there may be a strong case for holding briefing meetings in order that a positive attitude can be encouraged. The great advantage of a meeting over a written briefing is the two-way nature of the communication. So if you want to avoid rumour and distortion, you want to change attitudes or you want to take people with you, consider the case for a meeting or series of meetings.

Is there a need for team building?

Well conducted meetings can do much to build a good team. Leaders of the best sports teams, and winning generals, have recognised the benefits of the 'here's how we win' meeting and the same thing can work in business.

Do I need advice and guidance before making a decision?

It doesn't follow that if the answer is yes, a meeting is required since a few phone calls or a one-to-one discussion may achieve the desired result. However, collective advice reviewed and weighed in a meeting will often lead to a better decision. It has to be recognised, though, that some managers who are poor decision makers use meetings as a device for delaying or compromising when they would have been better to take speedy action.

Have we got a problem or crisis which can be better dealt with by a group solution?

Not quite the same as the last point because in this instance there is a crisis and a need for urgent action — but there are many circumstances in which a 'war cabinet' approach is needed. For example, an unexpected take-over bid, a lightning strike, a serious accident. The crisis may involve several departments or call for a range of specialist views or skills; the sooner they are all brought together in a meeting the better.

Figure 20.1   Checklist – do we need a meeting?

- an anti-meeting culture (the 'this is going to be a waste of time' syndrome);
- mistrust or envy by those outside the meeting (the 'what are they up to' syndrome);
- ill conceived membership – for example vertical or diagonal slice when a peer group is demanded.

Planning problems

The varied and awkward nature of human beings does not mean that meetings are always going to be difficult and ineffective provided someone gives some thought to the structure and content. More typically what happens is that there is:

- insufficient notice of a meeting or silly timing;
- no understanding of the aim: 'Why are we here?'
- no agenda or a badly structured agenda;
- poor paperwork: 'These figures don't add up!'

- a feeling that 'we've discussed all this before'.

Progress

It is a common complaint that after a meeting, even a productive meeting, nothing happens. For example there is no:

- record or minute circulated;
- action or follow-up on decisions taken;
- continuity between meetings;
- upward reporting.

It follows, therefore, that to achieve better meetings something has to be done to change managers' attitudes towards meetings and this can be achieved with attention to the three 'P's: people, planning and progress.

PEOPLE

It is worth giving attention to three 'people' factors; attitude, selection and training. Let me explain.

Attitude

Much damage is done because managers lack a positive approach to meetings. To encourage a positive view:

- *Avoid the word 'committee'.* Bureaucracy and inactivity are too closely associated with the word committee so where possible stop using it. Consider alternatives, using active descriptions such as working party, task force, and action group or using descriptions which emphasise efficiency or excellence like quality circle, profit improvement group etc.
- *Emphasize importance and urgency.* Senior managers have a key role to play in emphasizing the importance of the work done in meetings, and by encouraging their own staff to take a positive attitude by, for example, arriving at meetings on time, by preparing for meetings and by constructive contribution.

Selection

We rightly take time and care to recruit managers but rather less concern is shown when assembling a group to perform some managerial task. It seems that the 'least busy' or 'buggin's turn' principle is often applied. When forming a meeting group such matters as intellectual ability, experience, seniority, need for confidentiality, representational and personality factors all need to be considered. The group will have an aim similar to a manager's job description and there is, therefore, a case for preparing a 'group specification'. Obviously, in some circumstances, the group task preselects the group but there will be many occasions when members of a working party or task force should be carefully selected.

If care in picking members is important, the choice of chairman is often critical to the effectiveness of a meeting. There are occasions when seniority or status leave no room for consideration but when there is a choice, personality and skills such as listening, managing time, prioritizing, summing up, fairness, firmness, impartiality etc. must be taken into account.

Training

Once the importance of meetings is recognized the need for simple but effective training follows. There are short courses on effective meetings, training films and videos, and useful booklets. Any training aimed at improving the effectiveness of meetings will also help change the attitude to them. Don't overlook the special training needs of the chairman and of the secretary (preparing agendas, taking notes, writing action reports).

PLANNING

Once management attitudes are positive, the climate is right for effective meetings but this won't happen unless the chairman and the secretary give some thought to what they want to achieve and how they intend to set about it – in other words, planning. Specifically they will need to:

- time meetings to be cost effective and acceptable to the members;
- fix the location to be convenient and free of interruption and distraction;
- clarify their terms of reference or aim;
- plan and prepare an agenda. Some informal meetings may not need a written agenda as long as everyone knows why they are there and what is to be covered;
- consider the need for supporting papers which should be well written, up to date and accurate;
- consider the need for prior consultation and discussion on difficult issues in order to prepare the ground and save valuable time at the meeting.

In crises, meetings have to be called at short notice and little preparation is possible. In these circumstances the chairman's role becomes even more significant as does the post meeting progress of which more below.

PROGRESS

If I had to nominate one single factor which has contributed to the 'bad press' which meetings enjoy it would not be easy but post meeting inactivity would be high on my list. Nothing will have a greater potential for convincing managers that they are wasting their time if they can see no cause and effect relationship between the outcome of the meeting and subsequent action or if they are continually covering old ground. If something positive happens they will soon begin to change their attitudes to meetings. What needs to be done?

- *Circulate a record of the meeting.* Call them minutes if you like, but, if you are

For the chairman

1   Know your committee (terms, rules, members)

2   Prepare (compile agenda, plan meeting)

3   Consult before the meeting (i.e. prepare the ground)

4   Be firm but fair

5   Convey sense of urgency/importance

6   Listen

7   Seek consensus/agree the action

For the member

1   Prepare/know your facts; consult subordinates before the meeting

2   Don't be late

3   Accept the chair

4   Be constructive

5   Don't lose your cool

6   Question if in doubt

7   Fight your corner — but don't waste time

Figure 20.2   Checklists for better meetings

free of procedural requirements, it might be better to describe them as an 'Action and information report'. In any event it is a good thing to have an 'action column' in the record so that the names of those responsible for carrying out the agreed decisions can be noted. This puts the action manager on the spot and goes some way towards avoiding the 'I didn't realize I was supposed to do anything' reaction.

- *Take managerial action.* This means taking an interest in what happens post meeting – asking for a progress report and generally encouraging and prodding to ensure that matters are progressed.
- *Report post meeting progress.* Let those at the meeting and others know what has happened. This may encourage others and it will enhance the status of meetings.

CHECKLISTS OF SEVEN WAYS TO BETTER MEETINGS

Given that the priority is to produce a better meetings climate by encouraging a positive attitude there is much that the individual manager can do to improve his own performance in meetings be he the chairman or just a member. As a reminder and as a guide to better practice two checklists (Figure 20.2) are provided, one for the chairman and one for the member. Use these lists as a reminder. A bit more thought and some effort could do much to improve the effectiveness of your meetings.

FURTHER READING

Carnes, William, T., *Effective Meetings for Busy People – let's decide it and go home*, McGraw-Hill, 1983

Fletcher, Winston, *Meetings, Meetings: how to manipulate them and make them more fun*, Hodder, 1985

Janner, Greville, *How to Win Meetings*, Gower, 1991

Training Aids

Complete Communication, Training Package which includes a section on meetings, Melrose Film Productions, 1989

Impact at Meetings – with Greville Janner, videotape, Melrose Film Productions, 1990

Part III

MANAGING A SPECIALIST DEPARTMENT

Introduction: understanding specialist functions

Although it is often said that the manager is a generalist, in almost every case managers begin as specialists in one of the functions of the business. This can lead to a severe case of 'blinkerdom', with managers of specialist functions having little knowledge and even less understanding of what goes on in the other functions of the business. And what a shock to the system to be promoted to run one of these!

This section of the Handbook therefore offers the new manager, or the colleague in another department, the opportunity to look behind the scenes at the realities of managing a specialist department. Chapters cover Production, R & D, Distribution, Marketing, Sales, Personnel, Finance, and MIS, specialist departments found in most larger organizations. The writers in every case are experienced managers, well qualified to write about their speciality.

You will discover a common thread running through the chapters as each deals with the basic matters of planning, organizing, training, motivation, and control, but as specifically required by that function. Each chapter concludes with a checklist of the key points for the successful management of that department – a practical tool for the new manager.

21 Managing a Production Department

John Mapes

The job of managing a production department, at first glance, appears relatively straightforward. You have physical resources in the form of materials, labour and capital equipment which must be used to create products in sufficient quantities to meet customers' requirements. What makes this difficult is that customers' requirements include fast, reliable delivery, excellent quality and competitive prices. They also expect to be able to make changes in order quantities, delivery dates and product specifications at short notice. In addition to meeting all of these requirements, production managers must achieve good utilization of the physical resources for which they are responsible in order to ensure that unit production costs are kept as low as possible. Doing all of these things simultaneously represents a considerable challenge. Let us start by looking at the task faced by one production manager at the start of a typical working day.

A DAY IN THE LIFE

As Mike Roberts walks through the Assembly department back to his office there is much on his mind. At that morning's executive meeting the Managing Director has announced that their company has won a huge new order. The customer is one of the largest Japanese companies operating in Europe. As Production Manager, Mike knows that he should be pleased. The new order will mean greater job security and increased profits.

His concern is that his company might not be able to fulfil the requirements of the order. He knows that the existing production capacity is only just sufficient to cope with the existing workload. He will need to prepare a proposal for the purchase of additional machines and the recruitment of extra staff. Also, the existing production plan will need to be completely rescheduled. However, his main concern is whether his company is capable of meeting the stringent quality and delivery requirements set by the Japanese company. Existing quality control and inspection procedures will need to be completely revised.

Delivery on time, has always been one of the company's biggest problems. When

Mike took over as Production Manager 12 months ago, he made delivery performance his top priority. He has achieved substantial improvements, but only through personal intervention and the use of considerable amounts of overtime in the factory. The pricing of the Japanese order leaves little margin for error and he knows that he must find a less expensive solution to his delivery problems for the future. Looking back over the last 12 months Mike wonders whether the time that he has devoted to firefighting might not have been better spent on eliminating the causes of these problems permanently.

As he reaches his office his thoughts are interrupted by Les White, supervisor of the Packing department.

'Quality Control have rejected the whole of the Canadian order. If I have to repack the whole batch the costs will go through the roof and we'll miss the shipping date. Inspection claim that the printing is blurred but it looks all right to me. It certainly doesn't justify a late delivery. Can you sort them out?'

Mike makes no promises but agrees to look into it later that morning. As he goes through to his office, his secretary calls to him.

'Costing rang. They're very concerned about the adverse variances on labour costs last month. I've arranged a meeting for 11.30 am. Also, Spanndex want their next delivery brought forward three days. Production Planning thought that they should clear it with you before they agreed.'

Mike finally reaches his office and sits down. On his desk are four telephone messages, all marked urgent, and a computer printout of material shortages. It's going to be a long day. He reaches for the telephone to let his wife know that he will be late home for dinner yet again.

This scenario is fairly typical of the wide variety of problems which production managers have to deal with throughout their working day. If we look at the range of tasks that Mike is responsible for they fall into two distinct groups.

The first group are concerned with giving customers the service that they require. This includes delivering orders on time, ensuring that the goods are of the quality specified, responding rapidly to customer requests, and so on. The importance of these tasks cannot be over-emphasized. Talk to any group of dissatisfied customers and the discussion will nearly always centre on poor quality, late deliveries, long leadtimes and incorrect shipments. All of these are largely the responsibility of the production department. Getting these things wrong will rapidly lead to substantial losses in market share. Conversely, when these things are done well then market share can increase equally dramatically. This has been amply demonstrated by the Japanese for products ranging from motor cycles to televisions.

The second group of production management tasks concerns management of the resources required for production; materials, labour and capital equipment. Mike must ensure that there are sufficient of these to enable orders to be completed by the date agreed. He must also ensure that these resources are managed efficiently so that the desired level of customer service can be achieved at the minimum cost. For most companies the costs involved in the production and delivery of the finished product are about 80 per cent of total costs. Consequently, a small percentage change in production costs can cause a much larger percentage change in profits.

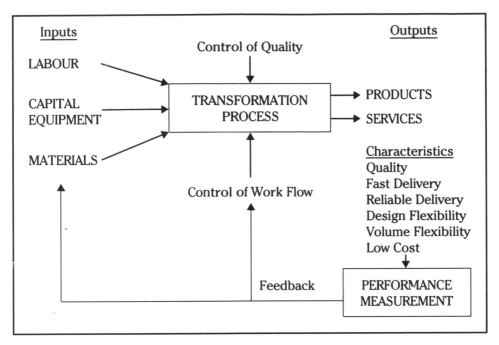

Figure 21.1 The operations management process

Obviously it is difficult to provide high quality and fast, reliable delivery without incurring additional costs. Fast delivery usually involves the expense of large stocks of finished goods; a product with a high quality specification is inevitably more expensive to produce than a product with a less stringent specification, and so on. The production manager must understand the trade-offs between the various factors and manage them accordingly.

The main elements of the production management task are summarized in Figure 21.1. It involves the management of all aspects of the transformation process whereby materials and facilities are converted into finished products. However, the production manager's job is not just to produce physical products but to do so to the customer's exact requirements as to delivery, quantity and quality. As customers often change their minds about these requirements at short notice, the production system must be capable of responding rapidly to changes while still achieving low production costs. Clearly this is a task of considerable complexity so how does one go about managing it?

An important first step is to gain an understanding of the key order-winning criteria for each product group. A list of possible order-winning criteria is included in Figure 21.1.

For each product group these criteria should be arranged in descending order of importance. For example, a customer ordering a large pressure vessel for a major construction project will not mind having to order well in advance so long as delivery is exactly on time. On the other hand, a supermarket chain will look for an ice-cream supplier capable of responding extremely rapidly to sudden increases in demand resulting from changes in the weather.

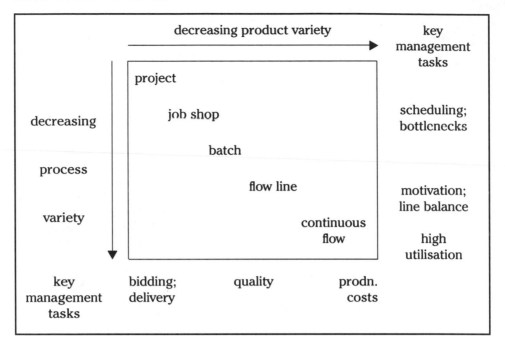

Figure 21.2   The product–process matrix

THE PRODUCT-PROCESS MATRIX

Apart from differences in order-winning criteria, what are the other factors that affect the nature of the production management task? One factor will be the variety of different products being manufactured within the same production unit. Clearly, if every order is for a unique product to the customer's exact specification this will present different management challenges to a production unit where there is a single, identical product produced continuously.

Another important factor is the variety of different routes which an order can follow during production. If every order requires exactly the same sequence of operations then monitoring the progress of orders is relatively straightforward. If every order requires a different set of operations in a different sequence then progress control is going to be rather more difficult.

One way of assessing the combined effect of product variety and process variety is to position each production unit on a product-process matrix like that shown in Figure 21.2.

Nearly all production units involve product-process combinations which place them on the diagonal of the matrix. Production units occupying the same position on the diagonal tend to face similar management challenges and to involve similar order-winning criteria. This enables production units to be classified into the following main groups.

Project

In a project-based organization every product will be unique, designed to meet each customer's exact requirements. An example of a project-based production system would be a civil engineering company specializing in bridge construction. Each contract won will be managed as a separate project. The key objectives will be to ensure that the bridge is built to the customer's specification, on time and within budget. Considerable emphasis will therefore be placed on monitoring the progress of a large number of inter-related activities with rapid corrective action being taken when problems are identified.

Job shop

A job-shop is frequently acting as a subcontractor to other companies, producing those items which it is not worthwhile to produce themselves. Orders are usually for small quantities to a design specified by the customer and there are relatively few repeat orders so that everything is made to order. One of the problems for job-shops is that the product mix is continually changing, causing fluctuating loads on the various work centres. In spite of this customers still expect reasonably rapid and reliable delivery. This is achieved through the use of general purpose machinery and a workforce with the skills and flexibility to switch from one type of work to another as the workload changes.

Batch

Batch production is used when a company has a range of standard products but none of them is required in sufficient volume to justify continuous production. Instead, batches of each product are made at intervals and placed in stock to meet demand until the next batch of that product is made. Provided items are in stock then a very rapid response to customer orders is possible. However, stockouts will nearly always lead to lost sales and will necessitate changes in the production schedule at short notice. Important features of the management task are therefore accurate forecasting of demand and careful production planning to ensure good capacity utilization and control of stocks. The aim is to ensure that there are few 'stockouts' while still keeping the total cost of production low.

Flow line

If a narrow range of products is being made in high volumes then the most cost-effective method of production is usually a flow line. The total production task is subdivided into a number of simpler operations which can be set up in a line. As each operation is completed the item is immediately passed on to the next stage. Because each operation is simple and repetitive, unskilled labour can be used or machines dedicated to that single operation can be developed. As items are passed down the line one at a time it is important that the line is carefully balanced so that there are no bottle-neck stages holding up the rest of the line. Also continuity of material supply is very important as shortage of any single item stops the whole line. One of the drawbacks of flow lines is that the work can be very monotonous. Motivating the workforce to maintain output and quality levels is therefore very important.

Continuous production

If a single, undifferentiated product is being produced in sufficiently high volume then continuous production might be possible. Examples of this include manufacture of basic chemicals, sugar refining and steel production. Because continuous production plant is dedicated to a single product it tends to be very efficient when operating at full capacity but highly inflexible. A major change in product specification may require the plant to be completely rebuilt.

Most products suitable for continuous production are commodity-type products for which the main order-winning criterion is price. Considerable emphasis must therefore be placed on minimizing production costs. As continuous production plant is usually highly capital-intensive it is important that it is operated at as close to full capacity as possible with minimum down-time.

From consideration of the position of a production unit on the product-process matrix and an analysis of order-winning criteria it should be possible to gain a clear idea of the key tasks for the manager of that production unit. The next step is to decide how the production unit should be managed in order that these tasks are successfully carried out.

PLANNING FOR PRODUCTION

An important part of this process will be the planning of production in order to ensure that promised delivery dates can be met and that the right quantities of resources in the form of labour, capital equipment and materials are available when required.

This will involve the assessment of the capacity of each work centre. Work must then be scheduled so that the load on each work centre does not exceed its capacity. Load and capacity are defined in the following way.

- *Capacity* is the maximum rate at which a production unit can produce output for a given set of operating conditions.
- *Load* is the amount of output which is required during a given time period, measured in the same units as capacity.

As capacity estimates are to be used for planning purposes it is important that they are realistic and achievable. This means that full account must be taken of production time lost due to tea breaks, machine maintenance, product changeovers, reject batches and so on. As most companies produce a variety of products, it is usual to measure capacity in terms of the total productive man-hours or machine hours available during a given period of time. Similarly load is based on the estimated man-hours or machine hours required to manufacture the planned quantity of each product. Work measurement techniques are available to ensure that these estimates are realistic.

If this is done, then a period by period comparison of load and capacity for each work centre should quickly reveal any major overloads and underloads. Figure 21.3 (a) shows a typical schedule for one work centre where there are some major mismatches between load and capacity.

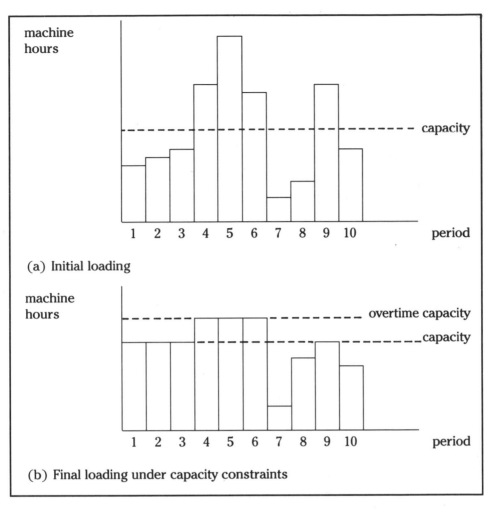

Figure 21.3   Load planning

However, in this case most of the problem can be dealt with by commencing some jobs a period or two early. This will still leave an overload in periods four, five and six which can be dealt with by overtime working. The final smoothed schedule would be as shown in Figure 21.3 (b).

Once this schedule has been prepared then it is easy to see the earliest time that additional work can be loaded onto this work centre. This helps to ensure that when new orders are received, realistic delivery promises are made to customers.

Also, work centres with insufficient capacity can be identified early. Action can then be taken to increase capacity by running an additional shift or buying extra machines.

MANAGING MATERIALS

In addition to ensuring that there is enough capacity in the form of labour and capital equipment to cope with the workload, it is also important to ensure that enough materials are available. Inventory is an important lubricant within the production system, enabling processes to continue operating even when there are delays and fluctuations elsewhere in the system.

Accountants classify stock into raw materials, work-in-process and finished goods. From a production point of view it is better to classify stock in terms of why it is there. The main reasons for holding stock are:

- to enable immediate delivery of finished goods to customers in spite of fluctuating and unpredictable demand;
- to protect against deliveries of items from suppliers which are either late or defective;
- to enable economic order sizes and production runs;
- to take advantage of favourable prices and bulk discounts;
- to provide a buffer between production stages so that a delay at one stage does not cause the next stage to stop.

Broadly, we have identified two kinds of inventory. Buffer stock provides protection against unplanned fluctuations of various kinds. Lot size stocks result from ordering or producing in quantities larger than necessary to meet immediate requirements in order to gain cost benefits.

Buffer stocks

Suppose that we receive a weekly delivery of fuel oil and average weekly usage is 800 litres. It might seem reasonable to top up the storage tank to 800 litres at each delivery as this will be sufficient to meet average usage between deliveries. In practice this would mean that whenever demand was higher than average or the delivery was late then a 'stockout' would occur. To protect ourselves against this we need a buffer stock in addition to the 800 litres. The smaller the desired risk of a 'stockout' the larger this buffer stock must be. The required buffer stock will also increase with the variability in usage between deliveries. Figure 21.4 shows a typical demand pattern and the buffer stock necessary to ensure only one 'stockout' on average every 2 years.

Computer packages are available which will calculate for each item the buffer stock necessary for a given stockout risk.

Lot size stocks

When a batch of items is to be manufactured on a machine then a certain amount of time is needed in order to set up the machine. This set-up time will be the same regardless of the number of items in the batch. It would therefore seem to make sense to manufacture in large batches so that the fixed set-up cost is shared amongst as many items as possible. However, when a large batch of items is made then they have to be stored until required, incurring stockholding costs. It is part of the production manager's job to decide on the lot size which will provide the best trade-off between set-up costs and stockholding costs.

The same principle applies when deciding how big an order to place with an outside supplier. The cost of raising an order is largely independent of the quantity

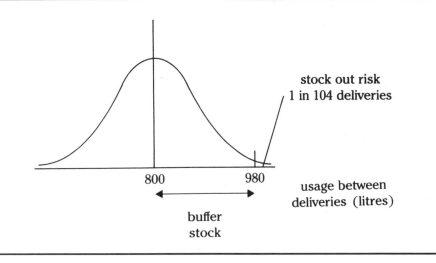

Figure 21.4   Buffer stock

being ordered but the benefit of spreading this cost across a large number of items has to be traded off against the cost of holding the items in stock until required. Also the effect of any bulk discounts must be taken into account.

Material Requirements Planning

Once a schedule of production has been decided upon together with policy on buffer stocks and batch quantities this must be converted into a detailed plan for the manufacture of the necessary components and sub-assemblies. Material Requirements Planning is one method of doing this. It is a computer-based system which takes the master production schedule of finished goods and 'explodes' it into the quantities of components needed to complete the master production schedule. Production orders are then released, timed to ensure that each batch of items is completed at the time that it is required for the next stage in the production process.

Just-in-time production

In the earlier discussion of safety stocks and order quantities, the problems which made them necessary – unreliable deliveries, long set-up times, etc – have been treated as unalterable facts of life. The consequence of this is high stock levels which are costly and make the organization slow to respond to market changes as existing stocks must be sold before the new items can be introduced. The Just-in-Time approach involves tackling the problems which make stockholding necessary. As these problems are eliminated, stock levels can be progressively reduced. Features of the Just-in-Time approach include the following:

- Emphasis on quality improvement so that less stock is needed to protect against defective materials.

313

- Deliveries from suppliers several times a day so that lot size stocks are much less.
- Set-up time reduction so that smaller batches become economic, reducing work-in-process.

Toyota Motor Company have been one of the leading exponents of Just-in-Time production. With the above improvements in place they have been able to introduce a very simple procedure for scheduling production called the kanban system.

Kanban is the Japanese word for 'card' and each small container of parts has an associated kanban. When a worker starts using a container of parts the kanban is removed and passed back to the previous stage. This is the signal for this stage to manufacture a replacement container of parts. As manufacture can only take place when a kanban is received, very strict control over work-in-process is achieved with parts only being produced when they are needed by the next stage in the process.

MANAGING QUALITY

Clearly another important aspect of production is ensuring that parts are produced to the specified quality. In the past this was seen as a policing exercise carried out by a quality control department operating independently of production. The thinking was that output was the primary concern of production sometimes at the expense of quality. The job of the quality control department was to inspect this output and reject any batches which were defective.

Since then there have been two major changes in our attitude towards quality, largely as a result of the success that Japanese companies have had in this area. The first change has been a recognition that quality means rather more to the customer than whether the product is within specification. Delivery on time, correct invoicing and after-sales service are all aspects of quality as far as the customer is concerned.

The second change has been a progressive transfer of responsibility for quality from the Quality Control department to the workers themselves. Doing it 'right first time' is much more cost-effective than trying to 'inspect quality in' afterwards.

Out of all this has come the concept of total quality management. The idea is that each individual in an organization should be able to identify three or four key measures of the quality of what they do. Then, by monitoring their performance on these key measures it should be possible to progressively improve performance on each of these measures. Applied across the whole of a company this should lead to continuous improvement in every aspect of quality performance. Applying total quality performance in the production department would involve the following steps:

1 Ask each group of individuals doing similar work to identify up to four measures of the quality of their work. For example, one group might identify three measures:

- % of defective items produced;

- % of batches completed on time;
- material wastage as a % of material used.

2 Help them to decide on target performance for each of these measures. This may be based on the best performance being achieved by other departments or other companies doing similar work. Alternatively it might be just a few per cent more than performance in the previous year. The important thing is that it should be an improvement on previous performance which is challenging but not impossible to achieve.
3 Help them to set up a procedure for measuring current performance and comparing it with target performance.
4 Inevitably there will be a gap between actual and target performance. Provide them with training in basic data collection so that they can identify the causes of poor performance and take action to eliminate them.

MANAGING THE WORKFORCE

The key to producing good quality products in the right quantity at the right time is to make better use of the operators who actually make the products. They are the real experts in what they do. If their knowledge and initiative can be more fully utilized then substantial benefits can be gained. A major part of the production manager's job is setting up systems and procedures which make it easier for the workforce to do a good job and motivating them to want to do so.

For many years financial incentive schemes which relate bonus to individual output have been used to motivate workers. Increasingly, such schemes are becoming less relevant to many organizations. This is partly because increasing automation has led to workers having less direct control of output. Also it is because most organizations recognize that output is not the only or even the most important measure of performance. Quality and adherence to schedule are usually more important than individual output in ensuring the efficient operation of the whole unit.

With or without a financial incentive scheme, the following basic principles will help to ensure a well-motivated and effective workforce.

- *Clearly stated working methods and quality standards.* Unless written procedures are clear, up-to-date and readily available then inefficient methods and poor quality are almost inevitable.
- *Training.* One of the biggest differences between companies achieving international standards of excellence and the rest is the amount of effort devoted to training. The best organizations provide training in not only doing the job itself but also in basic problem-solving so that everyone can contribute to improving performance.
- *Feedback on performance.* Even when there is no direct financial link, feedback on performance has a beneficial effect. Everyone likes to know how they are doing and how their performance compares with other people and other departments. People whose performance is below average try to improve. People whose performance is above average work harder to maintain their position. What is important is that the feedback should be simple, visual and

up-to-date. Aim to provide feedback on each week's performance the following Monday.

- *Increased responsibility and authority.* The traditional model of production management treated each worker as no more than a pair of hands. All of the decision-making and the application of judgement was carried out by managers or indirect workers such as quality control and maintenance staff. Not only did this make the operators' job dehumanized and monotonous, it was also inefficient, leading to high levels of indirect staff. By giving production operators responsibility for carrying out their own quality checks and routine maintenance, and involving them in performance improvement projects, their job is made more interesting and total costs can be reduced.
- *Recognition of good performance.* When an individual or group performs well, let them know that this has been noted and appreciated. Use news letters and house magazines to highlight exceptionally good performance.

THE ISSUES FOR MIKE ROBERTS

Now let us return to Mike Roberts. What actions can he take to improve his effectiveness as a production manager? First there would seem to be scope for greater delegation of day-to-day decisions. He should clarify the individual responsibilities of his staff so that they take more of the routine decisions themselves. Mike should only become involved when there is a conflict which must be resolved at his level. This should enable him to concentrate on longer-term issues.

In view of the Japanese order, the key issues currently seem to be increased output, increased on-time deliveries and reduced reject rates. He should therefore set very clear quantitative objectives for each of his staff and ask them to prepare plans for the achievement of these objectives within their area of responsibility. These should include proposals from the Production Control and Quality Control departments. Mike's task will then be to consolidate all of these proposals into a single plan and obtain approval from senior management.

He also needs to set up procedures for monitoring actual performance against target performance. This information should be the basis of regular group meetings with his staff in order to identify problems restricting performance and to allocate responsibility for the solution of these problems. In the longer-term he should explore ways of involving the workforce in this performance improvement process.

SUMMARY

Production is one of the most exciting and challenging areas of management. The most successful companies have been able to halve customer lead times and inventory levels and reduce defect rates to a few parts per million. This has not only enabled reductions in production costs of 30 per cent or more but has also been accompanied by improvements in customer service which have yielded dramatic increases in market share.

This has been achieved by focusing on the few performance measures that are really important and involving everyone in looking for ways of achieving improvements. The following checklist outlines the steps which are necessary to achieve similar results.

PRODUCTION MANAGEMENT CHECKLIST

1 Understand your customer's requirements. Identify key criteria for success and arrange them in descending order of importance.
2 Set quantitative performance targets for each of these key areas for the next 12 months.
3 Monitor performance for each key area and circulate the results to everyone in the department.
4 Involve everyone in the department in making suggestions for improvement.
5 Draw up action plans for improvement in each area.

FURTHER READING

Buffa, E. S., and Sarin, R. K., *Modern Production/Operations Management*, 8th edition, Wiley, 1987.

Goldratt, E. M., and Cox, J., *The Goal: Excellence in Manufacturing*, Creative Output, 1986.

Hayes, R. H., and Wheelwright, S. C., *Restoring our Competitive Edge: Competing Through Manufacturing*, Wiley, 1984.

Lockyer, K., Muhlemann, A., and Oakland, J., *Production and Operations Management*, 5th edition, Pitman, 1988.

Schonberger, R. J., *Japanese Manufacturing Techniques*, Collier Macmillan, 1982.

Schonberger, R. J., *World Class Manufacturing*, Collier Macmillan, 1986.

22 Managing R&D

Alan W. Pearson

For most organizations, change is a normal part of their activities. The introduction of new products and processes or the modification and extension of existing ones are vital to their survival. Such changes are frequently stimulated and made possible by developments in science and technology. This can be equally true for businesses which would not see themselves as being technically based, as the increasing attention being paid to innovation in services indicates. Here major changes are brought about through 'bought in' products, e.g. computers, smart cards, bar coding, etc. A prime need for such organizations is the ability to recognize which of an ever-increasing number and variety of developments is likely to be relevant to their needs and, more particularly, when they should commit themselves to changes which may require considerable capital investment, as well as investment in human resource development and redeployment.

Organizations which undertake research and development themselves will generally have a department specifically responsible for this activity and will employ professional staff across a range of disciplines. Their task is to ensure that the business remains competitive and is able to respond to threats and opportunities wherever they may arise. A well managed R&D function therefore makes a major contribution to the profitability of an organization. However, it is not a simple task to measure precisely the size of this contribution because of, for example, the lapse of time between the work carried out and the benefits received, the timing of implementation of results, the scale of production chosen, the direction and level of marketing expenditures, and the competitive response. The nature and strength of the organizational and communication links with other functional areas can have a considerable impact on the speed to market, a factor which is now being highlighted as a very important determinant of success, particularly when product lifecycles are shortening. Good project management is therefore demanded which embraces all people involved, irrespective of their functional base.

PLANNING

Planning in R&D is needed at a number of levels. First and foremost it is necessary to agree the total amount of resources to be allocated to the functional area and what form the financing arrangements should take. The former will largely determine the number of people who will be employed. The latter can have a big influence on the type of work which is undertaken and the way in which it is managed. Decisions about the total expenditure on R&D can be made in a number of ways with percentage of sales, and industry average being often quoted as major determining factors. The need to maintain a reasonably steady level over time is always emphasized, but unfortunately short term changes in profitability can and do have a significant impact, particularly when funding is dependent upon direct contributions from individual divisions and profit centres which see R&D as coming straight off their bottom line. This frequently has an effect on the longer term work and more innovative types of activity which may be perceived as less relevant to the organization's survival than the shorter term product and process improvement.

A major task for R&D managers – and one which becomes increasingly important as they move into more senior positions – is 'selling' the importance of the function to other senior managers within the organization. This is not always easy. Some see it as a distraction from their main responsibilities, requiring a great deal of effort, particularly at budget time. This is clearly not true, because it is a vital part of an R&D manager's job, and not just at director or senior levels, but across a much broader spectrum. It should also be seen as an ongoing process which is affected every time projects are started, accelerated or stopped, and whenever communication takes place with people from other functions and external customers of the business. It must also be recognized that blanket financing from corporate funds with little corporate control over directions does not necessarily lead to better innovations than does a good working relationship in which divisions and profit centres agree with R&D the financing for projects and areas of activity. In this case all the parties can mutually agree what is relevant to their needs in the long term as well as the short.

A way of opening up useful discussion on the overall level and direction of R&D is through the simple concept of relevance analysis. This can be portrayed as a matrix or in a tree format, as shown in Figure 22.1.

A top-down analysis identifies strategies to meet the organizational objectives. R&D activities or projects which support these strategies are then defined and planned, drawing upon the technology skills available. These may in turn draw upon the science base built up over many years. This might be seen as the 'market pull' approach. An analysis starting from the bottom can open up more possibilities by identifying how the science base can be built upon to the advantage of the organization, albeit in the longer term. This might be referred to as the 'technical push' approach. In practice a combination of market pull–technology push is likely to lead to maximum advantage to the organization, hence the need for strong and positive links between the 'customers' and the 'contractors'. Good communication on an ongoing basis, and not just at budgeting time is indicated.

Providing some slack in the system is also helpful, to allow individuals to pursue unusual ideas within agreed limits. Some innovative organizations state that they

319

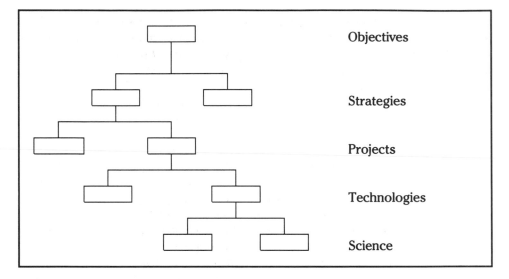

Figure 22.1   The relevance tree

encourage 'bootlegging' and that this practice has made important contributions to their profitability. The practice of building innovation into the objectives of senior managers, e.g. through analysing the percentage of current sales from products which were not part of the portfolio one, two, three etc. years ago is also recommended as a stimulus to encouraging a positive change mentality within an organization.

The next and very important stage for planning is at the project level. Good project management has been identified as a major contributor to success in many studies of innovation. When analysed in more detail this can be specified as setting clear objectives, identifying the key activities to be performed, gathering together team members, agreeing the tasks and roles for each person, building commitment to them, and ensuring that adequate resources are provided. Additional requirements are the need to openly discuss conflicts, challenge assumptions, and to be adaptive to changing circumstances caused by both technical and business factors. However, altering objectives and plans without due consideration of the consequences is not something to be encouraged.

The requirement for good resource planning is emphasized more as the R&D manager becomes responsible for a larger number and wider range of projects. Delays in progress and failure to achieve technical as well as business success are often caused by the lack of recognition at the outset of the demands made upon key resources by other projects which are going on in parallel or by new projects which might be introduced later. Much of the discussion about priorities which occurs at management meetings is caused by the lack of discussion of resource allocation at the evaluation and selection stage.

The very nature of R&D implies uncertainty, which inevitably means that short-term changes of priority at short notice may be necessary to cope with particular outcomes, but it is not uncommon to find some projects being given low priority for long periods for reasons which could have been identified at the outset. This situation tends to lead to a lowering of motivation and commitment, which might have been prevented by agreeing to postpone the project until resources required by the plan would be more likely to be available. An important responsibility of a project leader is therefore to check that the plan agreed by the team is feasible and of the senior R&D managers to make every effort to see that such agreements are honoured as far as this is possible. This is clearly easier when there is some slack in the system, a luxury which most R&D departments do not have.

CONTROL

Much has been written about the subject of control in R&D, often with the implication that it is either not possible or should not be attempted because of its potential negative effect upon innovation. The evidence from both research and practice suggests this is not true. Total freedom in research does not necessarily guarantee more innovative outputs. Obviously the type of work needs to be considered. Projects which are close to the marketplace do not necessarily produce more profit when people are allowed to make changes dictated by their most recent ideas, in fact just the opposite. More variety of inputs and ideas are usually better introduced at an early stage in the work when objectives have not been finally fixed, and substantial costs incurred.

Therefore an important question for R&D management is what degree of autonomy is likely to maximize motivation and performance. Here the research evidence suggests that there is more need for autonomy of means than of goals. That is, scientists and technologists are more likely to accept goals and directions, particularly if they have been involved in the discussions about them. They are less happy about accepting control over how they do the work, and of being constrained by rules which prevent them from tackling problems in the way they believe to be the best, based on their professional knowledge and expertise.

Most people find it unhelpful to be given formal responsibility for carrying through an activity but to have to submit to bureaucratic constraints such as getting authorization for small expenditures, or for transfer between, for example, accounting categories should the need be urgent enough. More experienced people may know how to do this unofficially, but this cannot be the right way to manage highly skilled and motivated people. Some flexibility is required. The evidence suggests that the extent of this flexibility must depend upon the type of project and the experience and motivation of the individual and the team, a point well brought out in the situational leadership literature.

If the principle of autonomy over means is accepted by the organization, the responsibility for monitoring progress towards the agreed goals falls in the first instance to the project manager, through to the group or section leader, division head, and finally to the R&D director. An effective way of managing this process starts with the preparation of realistic plans from which key decision points, stages or milestones can be derived.

These can be based on bar charts, networks or flow diagrams, the latter being most useful because they allow uncertainty to be represented, as shown in Figure 22.2.

The milestones should be based on technical performance parameters, allowing divergence from the agreed plan to be measured by the degree to which actual time and cost to agreed targets are met compared to the original estimates. This

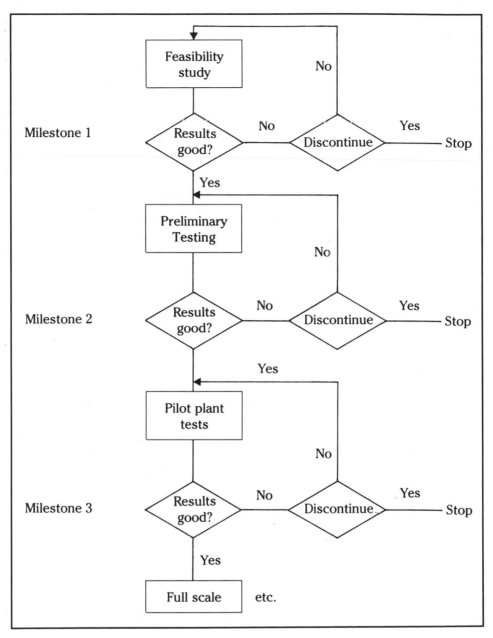

Figure 22.2   A simple flow chart

information can be portrayed using a very simple monitoring chart as shown in Figure 22.3. The numbers refer to the respective milestones as identified in the flow chart.

This approach to monitoring satisfies the need for autonomy because the means of achievement are left to those to whom the task has been delegated. Interference with this process should only occur when time and cost are overrunning, i.e.

		J	F	M	A	M	J	J	A	S	O	N	D
	Review time												
	J												
	F	1	1										
	M	2											
	A		2	2	2								
	M												
Calendar	J	3											
Time	J		3	3	3			3	3				
	A	4											
	S		4	4									
	O					4		4	4				
	N											4	4
	D												

Figure 22.3 Milestone monitoring chart

progress is not up to expectations. The point at which people outside the project, whether they are from R&D or from other functional areas – or even customers outside the business – need to intervene is clearly identifiable from the progress chart. In some cases, discussion about problems and possible solutions of a technical nature may be necessary. However, lack of progress may be due to other factors, for example, changes in priority, lack of resources, delays in authorization, and so on, in which case different actions may be required. From a management viewpoint considerable flexibility exists with this simple form of information system through the choice of distance between milestones and the frequency of review dates. The closer these are together the tighter is the control over day-to-day operations. Adjusting the intervals can therefore be used very successfully for performance development of individuals and of teams.

ORGANIZING

Many R&D establishments used to be organized on a functional or discipline basis, e.g. grouping together chemists, physicists, mathematicians, etc. In such situations recruitment, promotion and career development were essentially within the authority of an hierarchically-based vertical ladder. The project leader position was generally not a formal position, and not much activity occurred across disciplines. As projects required more inputs from different disciplines, some establishments redesigned their organizations to maintain a vertical orientation, but with groupings which embraced a number of disciplines. Others moved to what is generally known as the matrix form of structure, with the horizontal dimension being the direction in which project leaders linked with customers or users of R&D, drawing in people from different disciplines as and when required. This is illustrated in Figure 22.4.

Usually responsibility for recruitment, progression and career development remained with the discipline leaders, project leaders having little, if any, effect on the process. The usual argument was that the vertical groupings were responsible for maintaining the scientific and technical expertise and quality while the horizontal groupings were responsible for meeting time and cost targets on individual projects. Conflict over resource availabilities were often ironed out first between project leaders, and if not resolvable there, with the discipline heads. If no agreement could be reached at this point a higher level manager would be brought in. However, if this happened frequently it usually implied a failure of the structure to cope with the demands made upon it.

The need for intervention can be reduced if estimates of the requirements for key resources are monitored on a regular basis. If this is done, a diagram such as that shown in Figure 22.5 can be a useful guide for management decisions.

The gap shown is available to satisfy future and as yet unplanned demands, e.g. for new projects entering the portfolio. If this is seen to increase over time it may

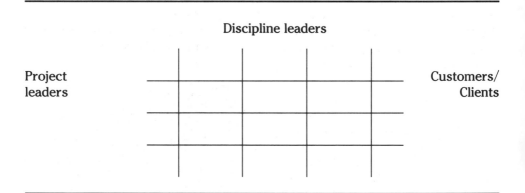

Figure 22.4   The matrix organizational form

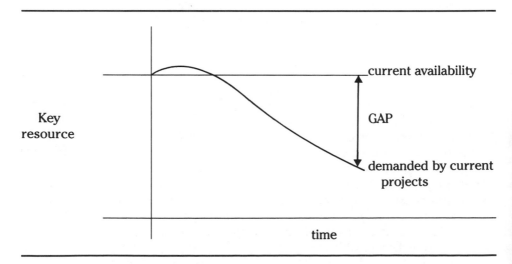

Figure 22.5   Resource loading diagram

indicate future underemployment of a particular resource, perhaps due to changing technical requirements. If the gap is closing, it almost certainly indicates a need to consider expanding the amount of this resource to meet future needs. Such increases cannot usually be made quickly and therefore the advance warning provided by a diagram of this type can be valuable.

Some organizations have found it difficult to operate with a matrix structure and placed more emphasis on the project dimension, effectively making this the dominant force. The debate as to which structure is more appropriate for which types of organization, or which of many hybrid forms might be more suitable, still goes on. Changes are often made from time to time, with unfortunately little attention being paid in many cases to specifically measuring the impacts. Research suggests that all of the structures have advantages and disadvantages, and a conclusion drawn is that the key to success is good project management within the chosen organizational form. This places much responsibility on individuals to set and agree objectives, build commitment, plan and control, manage resources, and all other actions described earlier. The project leader role is therefore becoming more important at all levels in an R&D establishment. Recent research suggests that in some organizations it is becoming a dominant career path, with the role of the project in providing challenges and professional growth becoming an important contributor to maintaining motivation and to effective performance.

There are, however, many different types of project in R&D. Some are short-term, some long-term, some small, some large. The membership of large teams might vary over the project lifecycle from idea to implementation. Management of the project will also be influenced by the extent of the uncertainty about both the goals or ends and the procedures or means by which these are most likely to be achieved. One way of characterizing projects is to use these two dimensions as the axes of an uncertainty map, as shown in Figure 22.6.

Quadrant 1 is one in which activity of an exploratory nature is best located. In

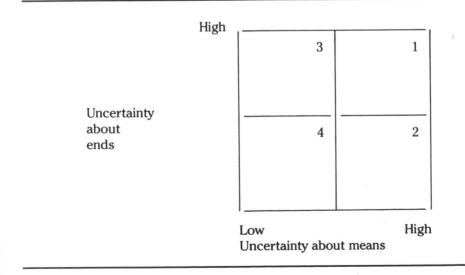

Figure 22.6   The uncertainty map

most organizations this would be described as programme rather than project work. Much of it will be undertaken by individuals, possibly those who will be seen as being on the scientific promotional ladder, as distinct from the management ladder.

Activity in Quadrant 2 is distinctly project oriented, with the ends or goals clearly specifiable but the means not so easily identified. Teams are likely to be the dominant mode of operation here, with strong leadership, perseverance, flexibility and open-mindedness being important contributors to success.

Quadrant 3 includes activities where the means are known, the science and technology exists, but the goals to which it might best be directed are not obvious. A creative imagination coupled to an awareness of potential opportunities and a desire to link techniques to markets are desirable attributes for the successful pursuit of activities in this quadrant. But they need to be associated with a recognition that variety is not always easy to handle, and that selecting and progressing a few alternatives quickly is more desirable than keeping too many options open for too long.

Quadrant 4 includes projects which are well defined in all respects. The ends and the means can both be specified. The need here is for clear identification of resource requirements, for good planning and control in the face of competition. Speed to completion is most important. To some these types of projects provide little motivation. They appear to be too easy and not really 'research'. For many organizations they are the lifeblood of the organization, and their successful completion is essential to survival.

Although this is a simple form of project analysis it does indicate that there can be a great variety of activities within research and development. It also suggests the value of considering together the people, project and environment fit. For example, innovators – particularly those with a strong individualistic streak – are likely to be most comfortable and productive in quadrant 1, while adaptors might perform best in quadrant 4.

MANAGEMENT DEVELOPMENT

In the past most people were recruited into research and development on the strength of their scientific and technical expertise. Increasing attention is now being paid to additional characteristics such as communication abilities, interpersonal skills, etc. The old dichotomy between scientists and managers is being less stressed, and more and more it is being accepted that good scientists can be and are good managers. However, many are not given the support to identify, develop and build up their inherent abilities in these directions. The old-fashioned approach to management development was to promote people to the point where they were seen to be incapable of managing and then to move them sideways or retire them earlier. At one time the so-called 'dual ladder' was seen as one way of coping with some of the problems of progression and rewards, but it is now generally seen to be a less than satisfactory solution. Most project leaders when they choose, or are chosen, to go on management development programmes make it clear that they wish they had been provided with the opportunity at an earlier stage in their careers.

They find value in many different aspects of training programmes, not least of which is the sharing of problems and potential solutions with people from other organizations, whom they find, often to their surprise, face similar situations. They want to know more about how R&D relates to the business interests, and how this can affect both the level and type of funding. They then want to know how they or their seniors, with their help, can obtain a better deal for themselves and for the organization as a whole. They want to know the constraints under which everyone operates, how good negotiating skills can lead to gains to all parties, that it is not necessarily a win or lose situation. They want to learn about how to handle relationships with other functions, particularly marketing. Managing interfaces is seen in most organizations as a problem area.

It is important for R&D people to know about the criteria used and the techniques available for project evaluation and selection and the methods and procedures for planning and monitoring which they can take advantage of for their own and their colleagues' benefit as well as the organization's. They want to know about the range of techniques for creative problem solving and for scenario generation, and when and how those should be used in practice. They want to know how to recognize when they should delegate and when they need to structure more closely the work of particular individuals and teams. They need to know how important it is to pay attention to managing at the macro as well as the micro level. Taking on management requires a reduction in the involvement in the technical work, and if this is not done all parties can suffer, the manager from pressure and the technical people from a feeling of interference. They also need to know of the importance of informal as well as formal communication and the potential value of adopting a 'walk around' management style.

The importance of teams and of team roles is an area which is well demonstrated by cases and class exercises, particularly those of an experiential nature. And in such exercises, personal characteristics and styles are readily identifiable. If these observations are backed up by analysis and discussion of personality characteristics derived from well established psychometric tests the value is considerably increased. Learning from experience is important for most people, but the evidence is that this can be accelerated by appropriate and continuing inputs from formal management development programmes starting early and continuing throughout an individual's career. The type of inputs needed will vary with the age, experience, organization and environment. Senior people usually demand more knowledge of areas such as scenario generation, managing change, negotiating and influencing. More junior managers benefit from information about planning and control procedures.

All managers should be aware of the potential value of formal management development programmes, not only for themselves but for their juniors and their seniors. The recent interest in quality management in R&D emphasizes this. Some organizations are now introducing training programmes for all personnel, including those in support positions, to get over the message loud and clear that everyone can and does have an influence on performance, and that even small changes can bring big rewards. The effect on motivation of such approaches cannot be over-estimated. There is no evidence that people's potential contribution to an organization goes off with age, but the issue of 'mature equals demotivated' is frequently aired at R&D seminars. If the concerns mature people express, the ideas they raise, the proposals for improvement they put forward are given a fair hearing, they will feel they can continue to make a significant contribution to the organization. If total quality management means doing the right things, doing things right and meeting customer needs better, one must draw on all available resources. In R&D the key resource is people.

SUMMARY AND CHECKLIST

Managing R&D effectively is a difficult task. It requires the application of good scientific and technical skills to a wide range of problem types. Size, uncertainty, and timescales are all important variables, but a common requirement of R&D management is that it should address the following issues:

- Relationships across the organization, taking into account economic, social, political and environmental as well as technical needs.
- Interfaces with other functional areas, and the reasons why some interfaces are difficult to manage.
- Sources of ideas, and the use of creativity and innovation problem solving techniques.
- Criteria for and relevance of formal methods to project evaluation and selection.
- Methods and procedures for project planning and control and in particular the generation of appropriate information for management purposes.
- The importance of providing autonomy of means and of managing the infrastructure well, not the detail of individual projects.
- Resource management, including the interrelationship between projects and the problems that are encountered by not taking these into account at the outset and at subsequent reviews.
- Organizational structure and in particular the value of focusing attention on the project, and on project leadership.
- The informal as well as formal structure, and the value of 'walk around' management and face-to-face communication.
- The use of measurement and feedback in performance development at individual, group and organizational level.
- The need to consider both effectiveness and efficiency when changes are contemplated in organizational structures and planning and control procedures.
- Developing an understanding by all people of the importance of interpersonal skills and roles in teams, so that effective project teams can be built quickly.
- The characteristics of different types of projects and the importance of matching people to activities where their skills are likely to be most appropriate.
- Identifying and understanding the management development needs of subordinates, peers and seniors, and how these might best be met through on-going training programmes.
- Drawing on all the energy within the R&D establishment by tapping into ideas and concerns whenever and wherever they arise, and following

through on them to show commitment to change and innovation wherever it is possible.

- Providing challenging assignments and encouraging professional growth.

FURTHER READING

Badawy, M. K. (1988) Managing Human Resources, *Research-Technology Management*, Sept–Oct. pp19–35

Farris, G. F. and Ellis, L. W. (1990) Managing Major Change in R&D, *Research-Technology Management*, Jan–Feb. pp33–37

Garden, A. M. (1990) Career orientations of software developers in a sample of high tech companies, *R&D Management*, Vol.20, No.4, pp337–352

Gratton, L. (1987) How can we predict management potential in research scientists? *R&D Management*, Vol.17, No.2, pp87–97

Gunz, H. P. (1980) Dual Ladders in Research: a Paradoxical Organizational Fix, *R&D Management*, vol. 10, No.3, pp113–118

Pearson, A. W. and Davies, G. B. (1981) Leadership styles and planning and monitoring techniques in R&D, *R&D Management*, Vol.11, No.3, pp111–116

Pearson, A. W. (1990) Planning and Control in Research and Development, *Omega*, Vol.18, No.6, pp573–581

Thamhain, H. J. and Wilemon, D., 1987. Building high performing engineering project teams, *IEEE Transactions on Engineering Management*, Vol.EM–34, No.3, August. pp 130–137

Tushman, M. L. and Moore, W. L. (Eds.) (1988) *Readings in the Management of Innovation*, 2nd Edn. Ballinger Publishing Co.

23 Managing a personnel department

Alan Cowling

Many of the skills required to manage a personnel department successfully are similar to those required to manage other functional departments. These include the ability to plan, organize, motivate and control the resources available in an effective manner. But in one special respect managing a personnel department is quite different from managing other departments. This is because of the unique nature of the personnel management process. A personnel manager is primarily concerned with the people in other managers' departments rather than his or her own department. This makes the task both challenging and difficult. Fortunately it can also be immensely worthwhile, offering the opportunity to make a significant contribution to the success of the business.

Management involves achieving results through people. Therefore all managers are to some extent personnel managers. But, as we know, not all managers are equally good at managing people. And even the best managers, busy controlling their own functional specialisms, or supervising major projects, require help and assistance. The primary task of the personnel department under the leadership of the personnel manager is to help other managers to manage their own people *better*.

People are a vital resource. After years of lip service to this principle, many organizations are now beginning to take it seriously. In the private sector the impetus has come from the need to achieve competitive advantage. The penny has now dropped. Competitive advantage can only be achieved by having a better trained and better led workforce than the competition. And in the public sector the impact of competitive tendering in local government, trust status in the health service, self management in schools, and similar initiatives have led to a re-appraisal of the significance of people as a resource, and a rise in the status of the personnel department.

In addition to helping managers to manage better, the personnel department also has a corporate responsibility. It is accountable to the board of directors and the chief executive for monitoring the utilization of people as a resource through-out the organization, as well as assisting in the formulation of personnel policy. Policy has to be put into practice, and so the day-to-day work of the personnel manager is the control of personnel management programmes.

THE FOUR PRINCIPAL ROLES OF A PERSONNEL DEPARTMENT

The personnel department then has four principal roles. These are:

1 Advising the board and chief executive on personnel policy.
2 Developing and managing personnel systems, programmes and services.
3 Providing expert advice to line management.
4 Monitoring the manner in which human resources are being managed through-out the organization.

These roles are now being strongly influenced by change. This influence will be even more important over the next decade. Economic change, technological change, social change, and political change are all affecting the management of people.

Managing a personnel department means not only managing a function which is changing, but also being an expert on organization change and development. This aspect of the work is now so important that newly appointed personnel managers, or personnel managers who qualified professionally some years ago, are well advised to update themselves by attending appropriate conferences and courses on organization change. Advice on this is available from the information departments of professional and managerial bodies. (See the end of this chapter for a list of further reading and relevant addresses.)

To reflect recent changes in emphasis, some personnel departments have adopted the title of 'Human Resources Department', and the training and development function has similarly adopted the term 'Human Resource Development' department. Properly speaking this change of name should signify a shift in focus from traditional concern with administration and a maintenance of the status quo to a more pro-active approach which makes a significant contribution to business strategy and performance. A new style HRM department should foster a partnership with line management in developing and motivating staff, and a commitment to organization change. The adoption of this new title, unfortunately, does not always reflect a full understanding or full commitment to new values, attitudes and the professional skills which are going to be required in the final decade of the twentieth century.

The four principal roles normally find expression in six areas of professional expertise, outlined below.

THE SIX KEY AREAS OF PROFESSIONAL EXPERTISE AND PRACTICE

The six key areas of professional expertise and practice in modern personnel departments are:

- organization and human resource planning;
- recruitment;
- human resource development;
- employee relations;

	Formulating Policy	Managing Programmes	Advice and Services	Monitoring and Feedback
Organization and Human Resource Planning				
Recruitment				
Human Resource Development				
Employee Relations				
Reward Systems				
Legal Compliance and Equal Opportunities				

Figure 23.1   The Personnel Management Grid

- reward systems; and
- legal compliance (including equal opportunities).

Managing a personnel department largely consists of managing activities in these six areas. A brief comment is therefore made on each of these areas of work below. There do, of course, exist other specialisms, depending on the nature of the organization, but these six are now the key areas.

THE PERSONNEL MANAGEMENT GRID

Combining the four principal roles of the personnel department with the six key areas of professional expertise and practice provides us with the Personnel Management Grid, illustrated in Figure 23.1. This grid provides a very practical framework for managing a personnel department. Each of the twenty-four cells represents aspects of work to be reviewed on a regular basis, and indicates where objectives should be set and monitored.

Organization and human resource planning

What used to be termed 'Manpower planning' is now more frequently referred to as 'Organization and human resource planning'. This reflects both the change already highlighted to treating employees as 'human resources' rather than simply 'labour' or 'manpower', and to the recently acquired significance of organization change and organization development.

Organization planning involves designing new and better ways of organizing people together at work, and facilitating the appropriate change processes. Recent examples include the trend to greater decentralization, reductions in the numbers of layers in the hierarchy, moves from mechanistic to organic structures, matrix structures, project management and developing new cultures and value systems. Organization structure and organization culture are today key issues in corporate strategy, and if a personnel manager wants to occupy a place at the 'top table', he or she must be familiar with the relevant concepts and practices.

Planning for human resources should commence with a hard look at both the demand and supply for staff. A newly appointed manager of the personnel and human resource development functions will probably find it easier to start with the supply side, which essentially amounts to an audit of the human resources available. This requires the following three stages:

Stage One: Ensuring that up to date and accurate records are available on the existing stock of employees. In any organization employing more than 100 people this means using a computerized personnel information system (CPIS for short). Any system must be able to provide instant basic information about individuals, as well as profiles and a collective analysis of cohorts of employees. For example, a CPIS system should be able to tell you how many people are eligible for retirement in the next five years, or how many employees possess professional qualifications.

Stage Two: Forecasting the future supply of manpower. This involves predicting the likely impact of retirement, ageing, labour wastage and absenteeism on the workforce. It also requires a hard look at the labour market to see where new recruits are going to come from. Even in times of high unemployment serious skills shortages pose a headache for many firms. And as soon as economic upturn takes place, the impact of demographic change, which means a shortage of young workers and school leavers, will create further problems. Human resource planning means coming up with constructive solutions to these problems, such as re-examining recruitment practices, reducing labour wastage and absenteeism, training for greater flexibility, and making greater use of part-time staff.

Stage Three: Forecasting the demand for manpower. Line management should be asked to predict their needs over the next few years. Look at any existing corporate plans to see what requirements for manpower have been built in. Examine the likely impact of new technology. Consider what new working practices are going to be required, and their implications for training and employee relations.

The outcome of these supply and demand exercises should provide a clear picture of where the organization is going, and the likely shortfalls unless remedial action is taken. This information provides an essential base for drawing up action programmes under the remaining five areas of professional expertise and practice, which we now examine.

Managing recruitment

Managing the supply of 'new blood' into the organization is a priority area for the personnel manager. The selection of staff has been dealt with elsewhere in this

Handbook (see Chapters 11 and 12), so only limited reference will be made here to selection methods.

For the manager of the personnel function, the management of recruitment starts with the manpower plans and the corporate strategy of the organization. Employing new staff is an expensive long-term investment. Recruitment should only take place if there are no suitable internal resources available, and if the need is supported by the human resource plan. As will be brought out later, effective retention policies should help to cut down the need for expensive recruitment.

Selection is the penultimate stage in the recruitment process, which begins with the establishment of the need for new recruits, and concludes with the induction of new employees. But selection cannot take place unless an adequate supply of potential recruits has been generated. Therefore managing recruitment requires a number of both long and short term measures. These include:

1   Ensuring that the company or organization has a good image as a place to work. It can take ten years to earn a good reputation as an employer and one year to lose it. Examine the reward packages and conditions of employment. Take steps to ensure that rewards match those of competitors, and that working conditions are attractive.
2   Examining the labour market from which your organization draws its staff. Where do your employees come from? Chart their locations. Look for new sources of recruits.
3   Examining your staff advertising procedures. Do your advertisements give you good value for money?
4   Examining your recruitment procedures. Are applicants dealt with promptly, courteously, and efficiently?
5   Examining your selection procedures, along the lines indicated in Chapters 11 and 12. Are they valid and cost-effective?

Managing human resource development

Achieving competitive advantage requires a skilled labour force, which is why human resource development (HRD) now commands so much attention. The modern personnel manager must actively manage the process of human resource development. It can no longer be left to an apprentice training officer and an education officer to simply administer their traditional programmes.

Managing HRD also commences with the manpower plan and corporate strategy. These should point out the skills required for the future. But HRD plays a bigger role in contributing to corporate plans than skill development. It also makes a major contribution to culture. Culture is based on values and attitudes. Appropriate values and attitudes need to be enhanced or changed in order to stimulate the kind of behaviour necessary to achieve quality products and service and hence competitive advantage. The ultimate goal of HRD is to achieve a 'Learning Organization'. This is an organization where learning new skills and attitudes and adapting to change is a natural and continuous process for all employees, resulting in a continuous process of self-renewal.

Line management is once again at the heart of this process. Management should become involved in human resource development as a natural part of managing and appraising people. (This was brought out in Chapters 13 and 14.) The personnel department facilitates this process both by the advice they give to line management and the support services provided by way of training and development programmes requested by line management or identified in the human resource plan.

Managing employee relations

Employee relations is concerned with the working relationships between different sections of the workforce, and aims to promote a high degree of trust and cooperation. It has the objective of uniting staff in the pursuit of organizational goals. It therefore means treating employees and their representatives with due respect and consideration.

The traditional approach to employee relations in the UK was termed 'industrial relations' or 'labour relations', and was based on a 'them and us' attitude, national collective bargaining, and bruising conflict with trade unions. Until a decade ago the greater part of a British personnel manager's time was spent on industrial relations matters. The strength of trade unions was frequently perceived as a threat to the success of the enterprise, and it was the primary task of the personnel manager to ensure that this threat was defused. Indeed, some personnel managers were appointed from the ranks of the trade unions, on the principle of 'poacher turned gamekeeper'. This approach was fostered by both traditional managers and trade unionists. Management frequently perceived workers as a potentially dangerous rabble. Trade union leaders saw management as the agents of capitalism, bent on exploiting the working classes. In this way, suspicion and mistrust became mutual and fed on itself. Regrettably, these attitudes can still be found in certain quarters of British society. But when managers blame the workers, they only really have themselves to blame. Poor industrial relations is the outcome of bad management.

Fortunately the situation is now much improved in many parts of the British economy, although national collective bargaining still predominates in the public sector. The 'them and us' philosophy has generally been replaced by a 'pluralist' frame of reference that recognises the legitimacy of the interests of different groups within work organizations; single union agreements have replaced the chaotic system of negotiating with five, ten or even more different trade unions simultaneously; and trade unions have taken a positive approach to flexible working practices and the reshaping of organizations.

But managing employee relations has a wider scope than managing relationships with trade unions. It includes such areas as consultation, communications, and conditions of employment. (Managing communications was looked at in Chapter 19.) At the heart of successful communications is the realization that communications must operate both upwards and across the organisation as well as downwards, and at the heart of successful consultation as well as negotiations lies the achievement of 'good faith'. Unless a high degree of honesty and good faith permeates employee relations there will be a return to suspicion and lack of cooperation. Managing employee relations requires a continuous monitoring of employee attitudes to ensure that good faith and confidence are being maintained.

Once again we come back to line management. Line managers are at the forefront of employee relations. And again, line management needs support, advice and assistance. The support comes from a good employee relations policy developed by the board on the advice of the personnel manager. The advice comes from the expertise of the personnel manager, and the assistance comes from the resources available to the personnel manager.

Managing rewards

To achieve competitive advantage, employees need to be motivated. They come to work seeking a range of rewards. These include money, status, recognition, self-fulfilment and companionship. Managing reward systems involves all of these.

Managing financial rewards requires a regular review of pay systems and procedures. This in turn requires a regular review of market rates of pay, to ensure that rates within the company remain competitive. This can be done by participating in pay surveys, subscribing to regular reports on the labour market, and by using your own employment department as a source of intelligence on pay. A policy decision of major significance concerns whether your organization aims to be a market leader on matters of pay, or to be an average or a below average payer. This significance arises from the sheer cost of employing people, which can make or break an organization, as well as the need to attract and retain suitable staff. But you must keep clearly in mind the fact that financial rewards are an investment as well as a cost, an argument which some accountants do not appear to understand. Good investment in people leads to quality products and services, and hence revenue and profits.

You also need to look internally at the fairness of your pay systems. Most employees have a strong sense of equity and justice about who gets what in the organization. This means that differentials should be based on job content and job performance as well as the external market. Job content can be established by job analysis and job evaluation. Job performance can be recognized in the pay-packet by linking pay to performance. This can be done through staff appraisal, a payment by results scheme, or a group bonus scheme.

Indirect benefits should be regularly reviewed. These benefits, which include pensions and holiday pay, are a form of deferred pay, and can add another thirty per cent to direct wage costs.

Finally, do not overlook the so called 'intrinsic' or psychological rewards that mean so much to many people. Individuals seek for recognition and a sense of achievement. Here again we come back to line management. Management development programmes must stress appropriate styles of leadership and the need to give recognition and opportunities for achievement to subordinates.

Managing legal compliance and equal opportunities

Employment today is covered by a mass of legislation. Personnel managers must be well versed in the relevant legislation and ensure appropriate levels of compliance. This includes the law as it applies to:

- *Contracts of employment*, affected both by Common Law and legislation such as the Employment Protection Acts.

- *Redundancy*, also affected by the latest Employment Protection legislation.
- *Disclosure of information and industrial relations*, affected by the Employment Protection Acts and Trade Union and Labour Relations legislation (and probably in the near future by EEC regulations).
- *Safe systems of work*, affected by the Factories Act and the Health and Safety at Work Act.
- *Equality of opportunity*, affected by Equal Pay, Sex Discrimination and Race Relations Acts.

Managing legal compliance requires the personnel manager to ensure that line management are trained in their basic responsibilities and that disciplinary procedures are kept under regular review. Sooner or later it will also require a knowledge of industrial tribunal procedures.

Managing equal opportunities should be seen in a more positive light than merely complying with the law. The provision of opportunities for employment and promotion to all sections of the community makes economic sense, because you are tapping the full range of potential available.

MANAGING RELATIONSHIPS WITH OTHER DEPARTMENTS

Because of its unique function and unusual power base, it is very important for the personnel manager to manage relationships with other departments with skill and diplomacy. The personnel function provides a service to other departments which impinges on what they may feel to be their own territorial rights, namely their own staff. This can lead to antagonism. At the same time, the personnel department acts as a monitor, checking on compliance with board policy on personnel matters, which may also cause some resentment. Because it does not directly produce anything, the personnel department may be treated as an overhead cost, a necessary evil, hindering the pursuit of results and profits. The personnel function frequently does not command the budget and resources available to line managers, and therefore lacks another basis for power. Finally, line management in the past have not always recognized the high degree of knowledge and professionalism required in a modern personnel department. They may think the personnel manager performs a job which a line manager could perform quite as well, and possibly with greater effectiveness.

A personnel manager must therefore earn the respect of line management, build up good relationships, and demonstrate a high level of competence. This takes time. Past personnel department practices such as imposing bureaucratic procedures and unwanted appraisal schemes must not be repeated. But to achieve this requires resources. Therefore a modern personnel manager must be able to demonstrate the case for resources using both marketing and financial language.

MAKING A CASE FOR RESOURCES

Making a case for resources has two aspects – the negative and the positive. The negative is pointing out what will happen if certain things are not done, and the positive is pointing out the benefits of doing the right things well. And this means putting a cost on its services, and a value on its benefits.

A wise personnel manager will go through the different services already outlined above, and put a cost and value on them. Thus with recruitment, the cost of recruiting staff should be calculated, covering aspects such as advertising, time spent on shortlisting, testing and interviewing. The results of even conservative costing may come as a shock – these things do not come cheap. Alongside the costs of recruitment you need to look at both the downside, i.e. the cost to the company of poor recruitment procedures leading to poor quality recruits, and the upside, the benefits of gaining good quality recruits. This can be linked to other costs, such as the cost of labour turnover and absenteeism and poorly performing staff.

Training is another area where costs and benefits can be beneficially calculated. Both on and off the job training can be costed, and the benefits of lifting standards to effective worker level and beyond can be calculated.

The best ally is senior line management. If they observe a proactive and helpful personnel department, a department where the staff get off their backsides and make the effort to link in with line management to help in achieving results, they will support the case for resources to do the job well.

MANAGING YOUR OWN DEPARTMENT

Too often the cobbler's children are badly shod. And too often personnel managers do not practise what they preach. Staff within a personnel department also require good organization, good training, good motivation and good leadership.

Depending on the size of the department, some specialization may be necessary. Typically these break down into the functional areas already discussed, such as recruitment, human resource development, employee relations, and so on. Remember however the need for career development, and do not leave staff too long in one specialization. Appraisal and development are as necessary in the personnel department as elsewhere.

The manner of organization within the personnel department should reflect, and indeed give a lead to the rest of the organization. As modern organizations change from being mechanistic, bureaucratic and hierarchical to being organic, proactive, and performance based, so the personnel department must also change in this direction. And as organizations become more decentralized, so the personnel department must become more decentralized, with personnel staff operating nearer to the coalface, rather than hiding in the head office. A modern personnel manager will practice MBWA – managing by walking about – and so will other staff in the personnel department. Managing a personnel department requires that you should be both seen and heard.

Many modern personnel departments, particularly in larger departments, contract out large areas of work. The aim is to keep overhead costs down to a minimum, and to 'buy in' consultancy services as appropriate. Thus the selection of senior managers up to shortlisting stage, or the running of tailor-made management development programmes are entrusted to consultants. The final competence therefore in our list has to be the management of consultancy services. Consultancy staff are not directly employed in the personnel department, but are part of the 'team' which have to be briefed and controlled. Personnel departments grow increasingly like Charles Handy's predicted organization structure of the future – the 'Shamrock' organization, employing a permanent core staff, but making considerable use of contract workers and outside consultants.

CHECKLIST FOR MANAGING A PERSONNEL DEPARTMENT

1   Clarify your role and decide your objectives on how you will:

- advise top management on formulating personnel policy;
- manage your personnel and training programmes;
- advise and support line management;
- monitor the effective use of human resources.

2   Develop and maintain competence in:

- Human Resource Planning;
- Recruitment and Selection;
- Human Resource Development;
- Employee Relations;
- Pay Policy and Rewards;
- Legal Compliance and Equal Opportunities.

3   Promote good relations with other departments.
4   Ensure you have adequate resources.
5   Manage your own staff well.

FURTHER READING

Bramham, J., *Human Resource Planning*, Institute of Personnel Management, 1989

Cowling, A. and Mailer, C., *Managing Human Resources*, 2nd Edition, Edward Arnold, 1990

Kenney, J. and Reid, M., *Training Interventions*, 2nd Edition, Institute of Personnel Management, 1989

Lewis, D., *Essentials of Employment Law*, Institute of Personnel Management, 1990

Williams, A., Dobson, P. and Walters, M., *Changing Culture*, Institute of Personnel Management, 1989

Some useful sources of information for personnel managers

The Institute of Manpower Studies, Mantell Building, University of Sussex, Falmer, Brighton BN1 9EF. (Telephone: 0273 686751)
The Institute of Personnel Management, IPM House, Camp Road, Wimbledon, London SW19 4UX. (Telephone: 081-946 9100)
The Institute of Training and Development, Marlow House, Institute Road, Marlow, Bucks. SL7 1BN (Telephone: 0628 890123)

24 Managing a marketing department

John Lidstone

The purpose of a business can be simply stated: *to create and keep customers.*
That is true whether you are a multinational company like Imperial Chemical
Industries, Shell or Unilever, or a small furnishing and fabrics retail shop in a
provincial town. And that statement sums up what marketing is all about.

It is the business of creating customers by looking at all your activities through
the consumer's eyes and supplying them with value satisfactions at a profit.
Customers don't buy products or services as such. They buy what these products
or services will do for them that they want done. Thus people do not buy an
insurance policy but 'peace of mind'; not a stout pair of walking shoes but
'comfortable feet during and after a long country hike'; not mechanical robots but
'beating Japanese competitors'; not a Rolls Royce motor car but a 'status symbol'.

Marketing is the management job of identifying, anticipating and satisfying
customer's requirements profitably.

How do we implement this successfully so that we stay in business? By planning
to produce and deliver the products and/or services that people want and value at
prices and in conditions that are more attractive than those offered by competitors
to a proportion of customers large enough to make those prices and conditions
possible.

STRATEGIC PLANNING AND THE MARKETING PROCESS

Most large corporations consist of three organizational levels: the corporate level,
the business level and the product level. Corporate headquarters is responsible
for designing a strategic plan to guide the whole enterprise into a profitable future.
Headquarters makes decisions on how much resource support to offer to each
business unit (division, subsidiary) as well as which new businesses to start. Each
business unit, in turn, must develop a plan to carry that business unit into a
profitable future, given the resources it has to work with from corporate headquarters. Finally, each product level (product line, brand) within a business unit
needs a plan for achieving targeted objectives in its particular product market.

These plans are then implemented at the various levels of the organization, results are monitored and necessary corrective actions are taken.

A key factor in the success a company enjoys as a result of its strategic planning is its *market positioning* strategy. A company can pursue one of three generic strategies within a market.

1 *Overall Cost Leadership*: Here, a company works hard to achieve the lowest costs of production and distribution, so that it can price lower than its competitors and win a large market share. Firms pursuing this strategy must be good at engineering, purchasing, manufacturing, and physical distribution. They tend to need less skill in marketing.

2 *Differentiation*: Here, a company concentrates on creating a highly differentiated product line and marketing programme so that it comes across as the class leader in its industry. Companies pursuing this strategy have major strengths in R & D, design, quality control, and marketing.

3 *Focus*: Here, a company focuses its effort on serving a few market segments well rather than going after the whole market. The company gets to know the needs of these segments and pursues either cost leadership, product differentiation or both within each segment.

Companies that pursue a clear strategy – one of the above – are most likely to perform well. Firms that do not pursue a clear strategy – 'middle-of-the-roaders' – do the worst. Middle-of-the-roaders try to be good on all strategic dimensions, but since each dimension requires a different and often inconsistent way of organizing the firm, these companies end up being not particularly excellent at anything.

Thus, a successful company is one that develops an appropriate strategy to reach its goals, builds an appropriate organizational structure to carry out this strategy, and equips the organization with effective systems of information, planning, control and reward to get the job done.

The key idea is that *strategy*, not structure, is the starting point. A company should first decide where it wants to go in the future, and then develop an organizational structure and systems to carry this out (see Figure 24.1).

COMPILING A MARKETING PLAN

A marketing plan should be one of a company's most important documents, for it should carry sufficient credibility to orchestrate the activities of all key departments and unite their energies in the achievement of a common goal. A plan should direct each department, advising it what part it needs to play (expressed qualitatively and quantitatively) to satisfy corporate – and shareholder – demands. A plan should also allocate the resources – people, finance, materials, etc. – which each department can use during the plan period.

That, then, is the purpose of a plan; but what should it say?

A plan should express the following questions:

- Where are we now? (*Situation analysis*)
- Where do we want to get to? (*Objective setting*)
- How will we get there? (*Strategy formulation*)

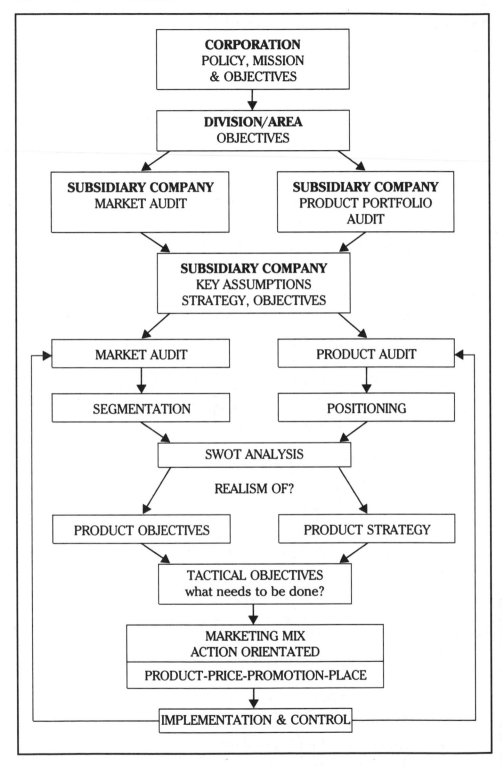

Figure 24.1   Planning framework

- How will we know when we've arrived? (*Control*)

To answer these questions, the planner must:

- Understand the needs of the company's customers and markets.
- Know the strengths and limitations of the company's resources.
- Decide the priorities for action (which opportunities will be met?)
- Allocate resources accordingly.
- Communicate these decisions throughout the company's management.
- Measure actual performance against the plan, and revise only if necessary.

The following areas will need to be considered and included in a final marketing plan.

Socio-political and economic environment. This will consist of extracts of key facts and assumptions from the company's guidelines. The extracts should be those factors that will have an impact upon product, that is, inflation, government attitude and plans, reimbursements, public opinion, and so on.
Market definition. A statement of the market definitions; that is, the main criteria for determining the chosen markets.
Historical review. A five year historical review of the performance of the markets, including major competitors, volume (units, procedures) and value.
Future developments. A summary of the major developments that are expected over the forecast period. This will include such things as product innovation, technological innovation, new competition, population trends, and so on, which would affect the market in which you are competing and/or the sales of your product.
Competitive analysis. This should include:

- A summary of the key elements from the company's competitive strengths and weaknesses analysis.
- A summary of the new products that you know will appear, including a description, expected impact on the market and estimated potential share.
- A summary of the current key competitive products, showing their strengths and weaknesses (product positioning), market share, historical promotion performance, and anticipated future actions.

Market segment evaluation. Outline the potential major segments that could provide you with an opportunity for future growth. This should show the definition, breakdown in units, value, competitors and key opportunity items.

A marketing plan could be compiled in the following stages:

Stage 1 – Formulate overall direction and goal. These are answers to the question 'what business are we in?' If the business is looked at in terms of customers, not products, a new orientation to the company can be developed. Needs and benefits, not functions or features, should be the focus. As the President of Revlon said – 'In the factory we make cosmetics but in the drug-store we sell hope'. It is too easy to become myopic and see only what the company makes; the danger is that as market needs change they are not recognized. Business definitions should be narrow enough to provide direction yet broad enough to allow the growth and response to changing market needs. The most productive approach is to define a business in terms of the needs it can satisfy and the segments of the market it can service. Thus, in order to be able to satisfy a market need and through this make a profit, a company needs to look critically at itself and identify:

- *its strengths* – what it is *good* at doing;
- *its weaknesses* – what it is *bad* at doing.

The plan can then concentrate on:

- Exploiting, perpetuating or extending strengths.
- Avoiding, minimizing or eradicating weaknesses.
- Converting weaknesses into strengths, e.g. by training.

Stage 2 – Identify the external opportunities. The aim here is to determine the market potential for own products in terms of needs that are not being fully satisfied. The needs of all segments should be considered. This stage of the process involves segmentation of the total market, and often indicates where market research should be directed.

Stage 3 – Identify the external threats. As well as identifying opportunities and threats from customers and prospects, it is also important to consider the threat to existing revenue and profit. This will come from competition, demand and other environmental factors. This stage of the process involves collecting data, the making of assumptions and production of forecasts for the business.

Stage 4 – Analyse internal strengths and weaknesses to produce marketing objectives and strategies. The marketing planning process is concerned with how the resources available to the company can be used to exploit the opportunity. Marketing goals must be realistic. This is achieved by analysing strengths and weaknesses and asking, 'Why should we be able to exploit the market opportunities we have identified?' Generating strategies is essentially a creative task. Ideally, the more alternatives that are generated the better. A good strategy will identify the main lines of business activity which will remain constant over the total planning period and provide the framework for tactical decision-making. Strategy aims to answer the question, 'What basic activities should we carry out?'

Stage 5 – Programme the marketing mix. Within the framework defined by the strategy this stage is concerned with determining the detailed programmes that attain the goals. The overall approach involves breaking down the marketing mix into:

- the product mix;
- the pricing mix;

- the pre-purchase promotion mix;
- the post-purchase performance mix.

This is followed by programming the activities of each mix, and integrating the separate programmes of each mix into the marketing plan.

Stage 6 – Communication and control. The elements of the communications mix are concerned with identifying and implementing the most appropriate communication activity between the company and its potential customers. It integrates the activities of personal selling with those of non-personal selling (Advertising, PR, Sales Promotion and Merchandising) and concerns decisions on the methods and types of sales effort required. Once the plan has been approved it can then be distributed. The final format of the plan must be such as to encourage revisions before senior management confirms its adoption.

Controls consist of bringing actual and desired results closer together. This is a four stage process involving:

- setting standards;
- collecting information;
- variance analysis; and
- corrective action.

Clearly, more people than the marketing manager and his immediate staff will be involved in the creation of a marketing plan. An analysis of probable participants and their roles is shown in Figure 24.2.

THE BENEFITS OF PLANNING

The skills and procedures that managers develop to deal with to-day's decisions are rarely adequate for making decisions about to-morrow. Marketing planning helps to develop the new skills and procedures that will be required.

1   Marketing planning helps ensure that the transition from to-day to to-morrow will be smooth and expected.
2   Planning for changed circumstances provides the single opportunity to gain significant advantage over competitors.
3   Marketing planning provides the vehicle for companies to communicate the changes that will be necessary and their effects in an open and non-threatening manner.
4   When planning for to-morrow, there is always a wider range of choice and this choice brings with it the increasing risk of mistakes. Marketing planning is concerned with both evaluating and seeking to reduce the available options to achieve the best chance of success and the least chance of error.
5   Marketing planning provides a method for handling the complexity involved in evaluating each market, establishing the nature of the changes and deciding on a profit potential.
6   In large companies, there is always competition for the limited resources of time and money. If re-active decisions have to be made, growth can become

Planning	Job Function	Responsibilities
Purpose and direction of all business activities	GENERAL MANAGER	Overall approval and control of organization. Reports to top management.
Purpose and direction division (broad strategy and general resource allocation)	COMMERCIAL DIRECTOR DIVISIONAL MANAGER	Approval and control of divisional performance.
Marketing and product portfolio information collected, analysed and projected.	MARKETING MANAGER GROUP PM	Evaluation and assigning of priorities. Controls planning and implementation of action plans.
Marketing and product information collected, analysed and projected. Determination of individual product strategies, tactical plans and control of progress.	PRODUCT MANAGER	Preparation of individual product plans. Monitoring of implementation, coordination of product related resources.
Management and direction to achieve company product sales targets.	SALES MANAGER	Implements and provides feedback on divisional plans in the field.
Individual sales activities to achieve sales target.	SALES REPRESENTATIVES	Achievement of sales targets and related customer contacts.

Figure 24.2   Contributors to the marketing plan

disorderly, and wasteful, resulting in loss of competitive advantage. A good marketing plan will prevent this type of disruption.

Marketing planning is a means of ensuring an orderly and profitable transition from to-day into the future. If as a manager you enjoy letting things happen, if things are good enough as they are, or if you like panic decisions, then marketing planning has no value. On the other hand, if you want to control your growth, improve your profits or increase your chances of the company's survival, then marketing planning is not an option, it is mandatory.

Above all such planning is not an activity carried out in isolation by an élite group of marketing brahmins. To be successful, it must determine activities and be recognised for what it is by the whole company. When completed it becomes the roadmap that guides everyone to implement the plan.

IMPLEMENTING AND CONTROLLING THE MARKETING PLAN

The sequel to all marketing planning is how to construct an effective implementation and control system to answer the final question: 'How will we know when we've arrived?' To answer this question quickly, top management need only refer to the section of your marketing plan in which you have included product profit and loss, summary of key objectives, plan assumptions and contingency plans. These items are covered in more detail in the following pages.

Product profit-and-loss statement (P&L)

This part of the marketing/product planning is concerned with the financial summaries of the individual steps and actions to be implemented in the planning year and beyond that for the total number of years covered by the long-range plan. Your product profit-and-loss statement provides the means by which you and your management colleagues can assess on an ongoing basis how much sales have been produced during the year and in each month. Figure 24.3 shows the generic form of a product P&L. If you produce individual product P&Ls, then each one should be included in your marketing/product plan.

Summary of key objectives/actions

Figure 24.4 enables you to summarize the objectives, strategy and key activities which have been included in previous sections of your plan. A chart similar to this one must be included in your product's plan.

Plan assumptions

As you are writing out your marketing plan and making forecasts, you are undoubtedly making certain assumptions; for example, we will get a price increase of 12% in January; we will be able to launch this new product by 1 July; raw material costs will be 4% over current level; and so on. These must now be stated so that top management are aware of them, and to allow for the preparation of contingency plans and re-forecasts if some of these assumptions prove not to be right or acceptable. Figure 24.5 shows a way of incorporating your key assumptions into your product plan.

Contingency planning

This is often called a 'What if' exercise. It involves you taking each one of the assumptions listed in Figure 24.5 and evaluating what would happen if that assumption proved to be incorrect and what actions you would need to take to pre-empt this from happening or lessening its negative impact. An example is shown in figure 24.6 to illustrate this process.

It is important that you also include your positive assumptions; that is, those

19...... PLAN & 19....../19...... FOR PRODUCT......

19...... Actual   19...... Update   19...... Plan   19......

DESCRIPTION

NET SALES
COST OF GOODS SOLD
GROSS MANUFACTURING MARGIN

OTHER CHARGES:
DISTRIBUTION MARGIN

DIRECT EXPENSES:
—INCREMENTAL:
  MARKETING ADMINISTRATION
  ADVERTISING
  DIRECT SELLING

  CONTRIBUTION

—ALLOCATED:
  MARKETING ADMINISTRATION
  ADVERTISING
  DIRECT SELLING
  R&D

MARGIN AFTER DIRECT EXPENSES

GENERAL & ADMINISTRATION

OPERATING INCOME
NON-OPERATING INCOME/ (EXP.)
TOTAL OPERATING INCOME

Figure 24.3   Plan for product profit-and-loss statement

assumptions which if they occurred would have a beneficial impact on sales and profits. For example, you could be assuming that the price increase allowed will be 5% but you know that there is a high probability of obtaining a 10% price increase. Would you then spend more in advertising or sales promotion?

Action timetable

To carry out the marketing plan for your product, you should bring together in a timetable the various actions that need to be taken by you in the next year. Figure 24.7 will help you list these key actions for the plan year. For each action listed you should note the related costs so that you have on hand a spending control document for your yearly budget.

Under the column 'Control methods' simply state how you will measure whether that action took place or not. For example, sales-force call rates may be measured

Objectives • Financial 5 years • Financial 1 year • Marketing 5 years • Marketing 1 year	
Product strategy • Position • Segment • Target market	
Promotion • Strategy • Mix • Spending	
Distribution strategy E.g. target outlets, stock policy, mix of business, support controls	
Pricing policy E.g. increases/ decreases, discounts, differential pricing	
Marketing research Programmes and costs, e.g. to confirm/clarify positioning options on (a), (b), (c), etc.	
Product testing Scope and nature	
Other strategies/ key actions	

Figure 24.4   Format for summarizing key objectives/actions

Item	Assumptions
1. *Financial:* • Product cost/margin • Pricing • Major contracts needed to meet forecasts, etc.	No increase in: • Bank interest • Company taxes • Inflation above forecast
2. *Raw materials* *manufacturing:* • Quality/availability	• No increases in prices • Will be available to meet production deadlines • Quality will not deteriorate
3. *Products:* • Registration/approval • Performance levels	• No newly discovered product problems
4. *Manufacturing:*	• No work stoppages, strikes, etc. • No major plant breakdown, e.g. power failures • No major packaging faults
5. *Legislation:* • Price control • Level of expenditure • Listing	• No increased product liability laws • No restrictions on promotional expenditure • No delisting of generic products in country x . . . y • No price restrictions
6. *Personnel:* • Marketing and sales force establishment	• No loss of sales force personnel • No loss of marketing support staff
7. *Market:* • Growth rate • New product launches impact • Level of spending trend	
8. *Competitive activity*	• No launch of new product identical to company's • No increase in sales force numbers, training or pay • No additional promotional expenditure: – sales cycles; – capture of major customer contracts held by . . . .
9. *Distribution*	• No loss of key distributors • No closure of major retail outlets • No increase in transport costs
10. *Company new product* *launch*	• Correct position • Segment right • Target market correct • Market size large enough • Product meeting need fully • Product benefits correct • Full support from distribution channels • Correct sales forecast • Environment has not changed unfavourably • Sales costs correct • ROI meeting plan • Manufacturing quality correct • Manufacturing meeting production targets • Sales force meeting sales targets
11. *Registration*	• That planned deadlines will be met
12. *Others*	

Figure 24.5 Plan assumptions

Example

Assumption	What if?	Probability of occurrence	Likely impact	Action
Advertising budget level at 9% of sales.	What if government restricts this to 5% of sales?	70%	Loss of brand awareness generated by media versus brand leaders.	Will increase sales force GP meeting budget by $75,000.
Price increase of 7% will be allowed in July.	What if we only obtained 5%?	50%	Will have $500,000 less revenues.	Will cut down on advertising by $100,000 and launch "new form" earlier to preserve net income as planned.

Figure 24.6   Example of contingency planning

by looking at sales-force call reports. Other control mechanisms could come from monthly budget reports, sales summaries, sample shipping reports, media insertion notices, advertising agency billing, and so on.

Performance feedback

Once the objectives have been set, the product strategies formulated, the marketing and promotional plans set in motion, you must ensure that there is a control process which will enable you to monitor the performance of your product and to identify any parts of your plan where corrective action may be needed. This means that you need to:

- Set standards of performance against which actual results can be measured; for example, annual, monthly, quarterly sales levels.
- Fix times for the regular review of your plan; for example, monthly.
- Compare results against standards and identify variances.
- Take corrective action to put the plan back on course or adapt the plan to meet changed circumstances.

Setting standards

The product plan contains specific, financial, marketing, sales, distribution and advertising objectives. These objectives provide the basis for the setting of standards in key areas: product sales in local currency/US dollars, sterling product sales in units, and product market shares.

ACTION PLAN FOR .... PLAN YEAR .... YEAR: ....
PRODUCT: ....

| ACTIVITY | TIMING | | | | | | | | | | | | CONTROL METHODS | REMARKS |
	J 1234	F 1234	M 1234	A 1234	M 1234	J 1234	J 1234	A 1234	S 1234	O 1234	N 1234	D 1234		
Sales force • Product briefings • Conferences • Selling schedules														
Advertising • Agency briefing (s) • Media • Mailing pieces														
Marketing research • Product • (a) • (b)														
Public relations • Symposia • Personal meetings • Exhibitions • Group meetings														
Sales aids • Literature • Samples • Give-aways														
Product plan updates • ....../...... (month)														
Internal reviews with: • (a) • (b) • (c)														

Figure 24.7   Format for action timetable

The first standard will be annual targets: what your product will produce in sales, profits and market share. This is known as the *absolute target*. It will tell you what has gone right or wrong but not *why*.

The second set of standards will be *moving standards*. These are the annual targets, divided into whatever is a sensible division of the year (eg. monthly/ quarterly/half-yearly targets). Here again, although these more frequent indicators of performance will forewarn of deviations from your product targets, they will not show why performance is varying.

There is a need for a third set of standards – *diagnostic standards* – which tell you what is causing variations and why, so that you can take appropriate corrective action; for example, reviewing sales call levels, distribution channels activities, level of acceptance in the field of your promotional message, sales disparity by geographical region, and so on.

Figure 24.8 is a marketing planning control system which shows how you can check the on-going performance of your product and apply appropriate actions.

Variance analysis

Variances are calculated by comparing actual results against pre-set standards. First, use cumulative totals so that individual monthly variations will tend to cancel each other out.

Second, moving annual totals (MATs) can be used by taking twelve months' performance up to and including the month in question. Because as each month is added the same month of the previous year is deducted, the trend in moving annual total will indicate present performance compared with the same period in the previous year.

Variance analysis can be done on what is called a 'Z chart', such as the one shown in Figure 24.9. This enables you to make comparisons on a single diagram of monthly performance against target, cumulative performance against target and via the moving annual total, the present year versus the previous year.

The benefit of a good control system and feedback mechanism is that it enables the manager to identify quickly product performance variances and the true reasons for them, and to react to changed circumstances. By controlling your plan you will then be in a position to report monthly and answer the following questions which may be raised by your top management:

- Are the plan objectives being met?
- What are the variances between budget and actual?
- What are the causes of these variances?
- What actions are being taken to correct them?
- Is a re-forecast/re-budget necessary?

These are the types of questions which are usually asked monthly, but especially at other update review periods. A manager is expected to know 'what is happening' with the product(s). The better your control system is, the more you will feel and appear to be in control of your product(s).

Type of control	Objective of control	Standards	How to measure performance	What to look for (examples)
1. Annual product plan control.	To examine if plan objectives are being achieved.	Sales quotas and market share financial targets.	Comparison of actual results against standards set in each area of performance.	Notable shortfall between standard and actual; failure of individual sales territories to achieve sales targets by buyer category.
2. Profitability control.	To examine if financial objectives are being met.	Profitability by product.	Comparison of actual results against standards.	Major shift in production mix; spending levels above plan levels; declining sales.
3. Efficiency control.	To evaluate and improve results of marketing expenditures.	Promotional deadlines. Distribution targets. Sales force activities.	Comparison of actual results against advertising plan; sales force (who called on/how many/call frequency/what done in each call).	Failure to meet deadlines or set standards in each area of promotion.

Figure 24.8   Product marketing plan control.

(a)

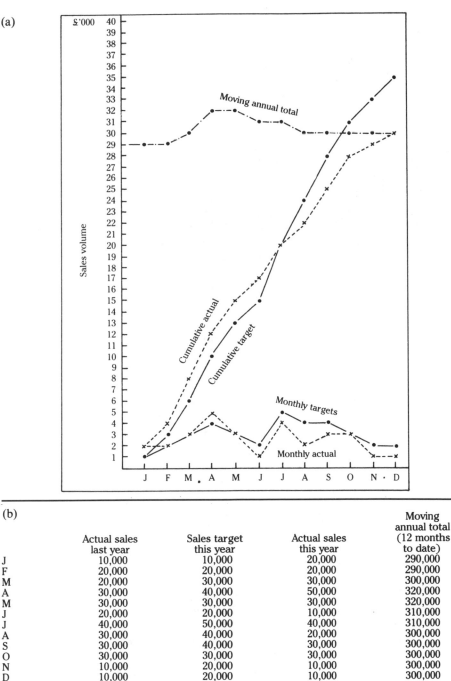

(b)

	Actual sales last year	Sales target this year	Actual sales this year	Moving annual total (12 months to date)
J	10,000	10,000	20,000	290,000
F	20,000	20,000	20,000	290,000
M	20,000	30,000	30,000	300,000
A	30,000	40,000	50,000	320,000
M	30,000	30,000	30,000	320,000
J	20,000	20,000	10,000	310,000
J	40,000	50,000	40,000	310,000
A	30,000	40,000	20,000	300,000
S	30,000	40,000	30,000	300,000
O	30,000	30,000	30,000	300,000
N	10,000	20,000	10,000	300,000
D	10,000	20,000	10,000	300,000
Total	280,000	350,000	300,000	

Figure 24.9 'Z chart': (Moving annual totals (MAT) are derived by taking 12 months' figures including latest month. Thus MAT for June covers period July last year to June this year. MAT for August is calculated by deducting August last year and adding August this year. Therefore if total rises, performance is better than last year.)

TRAINING AND DEVELOPMENT

In most companies the training and development of product and marketing managers is a haphazard affair. Some managers who have been appointed to their marketing jobs direct from the sales force – a familiar route in certain companies – take into their new roles the knowledge and skill of how to sell. They are then expected to learn how to tackle their new marketing role by 'sitting by Nellie'. The result depends upon whether 'Nellie' had any formal training or not. Another equally dangerous route in is that frequently taken by graduates with or without a Master's Degree of Business Administration (MBA).

Their entry, particularly in some large British and US multi-national corporations is a short stint in product management or, worse still, straight into corporate planning. And the result? They lack first-hand knowledge of selling, of sales management and, ironically, of marketing. The reason for the last-named deficiency is that too many MBAs are obtained by men and women *before* rather than after having had some business experience. Companies then compound the problem by failing to provide them with any basic marketing training – making the dangerous assumption that 'if you have an MBA, then marketing was surely part of your course'.

Added to this, if young men and women only stay in product management for one or two years, that is not long enough for the company to discover whether they can manage the marketing of a product or not. You need to stay in such a function for at least four years before you can claim a real track record. In the first year you either inherit someone else's mantle, or it is your first plan which good luck may smile on or misfortune maim. In year two, you have one year's trading experience to aid your analysis and decision-making. It is only then in the third year that most of the marketing variables to which I have already referred are neutralized and your planning stands or falls by your own marketing and management competence. Only in your fourth year in the same function can you prove by results whether you can repeat success – if you have achieved it – and not only that but improve on it or not. In one British industry sector I have analysed, in 70 companies, the average time spent by anyone in the product management job is 18 months.

So how should the training and development be tackled? First you need to analyse the levels of knowledge and skills the different marketing job functions require. Figure 24.10 is an example of such an analysis. The numbers from one to four indicate the level of training required. Because few companies have developed in-house marketing training programmes for their marketing personnel – not too surprising because unlike the sales force, the numbers in marketing may not justify the expenditure – you will have to look to external resources for help. The number of marketing training courses on offer from consultants, colleges and universities is legion, so you need to select a programme with care. Here are some guidelines to help you to make that selection:

1   Define your training needs by answering the questions in Figure 24.11. This personal training needs analysis – discussed with your management colleague to whom you report – enables you to assess the objectives and content of any

Marketing function	Marketing director or manager	Sales manager	Product or brand manager	Market research manager	Advertising and sales promotion manager	Salesman
Marketing research	2	3	3	1	3	3
Sales forecasting	2	1	1	2	3	4
New product development	1	3	1	3	3	4
Pricing	1	2	1	3	4	3
Packaging	2	3	1	3	3	4
Distribution	1	1	3	3	3	3
Selling	2	2	3	3	3	1
Advertising and sales promotion	2	3	1	3	1	3

Figure 24.10 Analysis of knowledge and skills levels for different marketing jobs

Source: HMSO, *Training for Marketing*, 1972.

Notes:
1 This is a prime area of work, and a high level of skill is demanded.
2 This is an area of work to be supervised and calls for sufficient skills to develop and control subordinates.
3 Enough knowledge is required to appreciate its function – an interrelating area of work.
4 Work related at a minor level, and knowledge is needed only to contribute suggestions and ideas if required.

Questions	Knowledge	Skills
1 What do I need to know and understand?		
2 What must I be able to do?		
3 What are the circumstances in which I must be able to do it?		
4 What standards must I reach to be able to do it?		

Figure 24.11 Training for marketing manager: personal needs analysis

course much more effectively. Above all it pinpoints what you are able to do at the end of the training.

2   Send for information about training courses. Check with the programme organizers the quality of the programme, in particular:

- Who will actually conduct the programme? What is his/her/their actual line experience and *above all are they trained trainers*?
- Which companies by name have used the programme?
- Ask for the names and telephone numbers of at least three people in positions similar to your own who have attended the course and to whom you can speak directly about it.

3   Choose the 'best' programme and attend it.
4   Decide what follow-up action is necessary. For example, you will probably need to review with your management what you learnt. If it represents a revolutionary change in policies to apply, then you have got to do some selling of ideas.
5   Perhaps the best form of training in marketing is to use a well-qualified marketing training specialist who brings to your training needs what I call a 'live ammunition' approach. This uses such tools as a computer-aided model in which all the stages of marketing a product are contained and then gets you to apply the techniques of marketing learnt through him and the model by using one of your own company's products for which you are responsible. (I have even seen a new product launched into Europe successfully using such a teaching method.)

Social skills training

There is, in addition to the acquisition of technical marketing skills, the need to be trained in the following social management skills:

- Making effective presentations.
- On-the-job coaching of the members of your team – if you have say a junior/ assistant product manager and a secretary.
- How to conduct meetings and the art of listening.
- How to negotiate – internally with other departments, externally with advertising agents and other bought-in services.
- Selling – don't forget that you are always selling, to the sales force your product strategy, to top management your case for say investment in a new product, to outsiders – so book yourself on to a once a year refresher course either run by your own company or on a good external one.

Finally remember that as a member of the management team your skill in achieving your marketing objectives will depend, as much as any other attribute, on how good you are as a trainer and developer of talent so that you can get results through other people. *In short: if you cannot train, you cannot manage a marketing function.*

MOTIVATION

Of all the skills required by managers, the one that is perhaps most widely misunderstood and so is practised with the least effectiveness is motivation. The main stumbling block that prevents managers getting the best results through people is a lack of knowledge and expertise in the whole subject of motivation and human behaviour.

Motivating factors

The factors that contribute to people experiencing job satisfaction and positive motivation are those centred on the job itself and the intrinsic possibilities provided to meet an individual's highest personal goals and the need for self-fulfilment. Positive steps taken by management to enrich these areas of potential job satisfaction are longer lasting in their effect upon individuals than the removal of sources of dissatisfaction.

Job satisfaction

Applying the lessons learnt from Herzberg and others (see John Adair's chapter on Leadership for more details), the ingredients for success – which sadly company managements are often too cowardly to implement – are these:

1   Make marketing jobs ones that have greater authority. Increase the job holder's accountability without constantly having to refer back. In one experiment in a division of Imperial Chemical Industries, it was found that the cost of complaints handling was markedly decreased when sales representatives could deal with them up to quite a reasonable sum of money. Likewise they were authorized to agree discounts with 5% discretion and never abused that responsibility.
2   Give a person a full job to do – not a Mickey Mouse one – so that real achievement is seen at key points in it. A Product Manager, for example, should be trained and competent to bring a product to launch – not be a paper pusher of mailing pieces.
3   Give more authority to an employee to do his or her job so that there is freedom to determine the tactics for achieving the overall objectives.
4   Increase the amount of information divulged to an employee. I recall the chairman of one of the UK's leading corporations saying with pride, 'I decide strategy and you get on with the day-to-day issues so there is no need for you to worry about the big picture'. On the contrary, it is by people knowing what the big picture is that they are better informed and motivated to play their part in making it happen.
5   Always have the courage to test marketing people to destruction, but build in a safety net. It is only when good people have been tested that they know what more they are capable of.
6   Introduce new and more difficult tasks not previously handled. But make sure that training is provided to equip individuals with the necessary skills and ability to handle them. And when they discharge those new tasks well, reward them if as a result financial benefit accrues to the company.

Continuing job satisfaction depends upon the extent to which an individual's needs are met in the day-to-day performance of his or her job. The motivating forces that will drive people on are those where there is the opportunity to exploit their talents, make decisions and exercise decision-making power, and where there is a sense of ownership of the outcomes of their efforts.

So the secret is to provide a motivational climate in which people's energies are released to the full in a constructive channelled direction.

CONCLUSION

In recent years there have been a number of attempts to identify the ingredients of corporate success. The authors of two books – one by Peters and Waterman *In Search of Excellence* and the other by Goldsmith and Clutterbuck, *The Winning Streak* – isolated what they believed were the key characteristics that respectively made forty-seven American and some twenty-six UK companies successful, successful that is at the time these two books were written.

Missing from these and other equally fascinating recipes are two ingredients that seem to me to be essential to sustain success year after year after year: the central importance of *marketing* as an all-pervading business philosophy; and, going hand in hand with it, how to make marketing happen successfully, not just once but again and again and again.

This chapter has attempted to address these issues, and offer guidelines for the management of the central concerns of the marketing department.

CHECKLIST OF KEY POINTS

Marketing is:

- a philosophy that should govern the attitudes, objectives and provide the driving force for everyone in a business, no matter what their job is;
- a key business function – the management job of identifying, anticipating and satisfying customer's requirements profitably. This is achieved by planning to produce and deliver the products and/or services that people want and value at prices and in conditions that are more attractive than those offered by competitors to a proportion of customers large enough to make those prices and conditions possible.

The acid test of a marketing plan is whether it provides answers to the following questions:

- Where are we now? (Analysis of the current situation)
- Where do we want to go? (Setting objectives for the future)
- How will we get there? (Setting out a plan of action)
- How will we know when we've arrived? (Establishing controls to monitor performance)

The keys to people management:

- Motivation: provide a motivational climate in which people's energies are released to the full in a constructive channelled direction.

- Training: As a member of the management team, your skill in achieving your marketing objectives will depend, as much as any other attribute, on how good you are as a trainer and developer of talent, so that you can get results through other people. *If you cannot train, you cannot manage a marketing function.*

FURTHER READING

Baker, Michael J. (editor), *The Marketing Book* The Chartered Institute of Marketing, William Heinemann 2nd edition 1991

Kotler, Philip, *Marketing Management*, Prentice-Hall 1980

Levitt, Theodore, *The Marketing Imagination*, The Free Press 1983

Lidstone, John, *Marketing Planning for the Pharmaceutical Industry*, Gower 1987

Lidstone, John, *Making Effective Presentations*, Gower 1985

Stapleton, John, *How to Prepare a Marketing Plan*, Gower, 4th edition 1989

Wilson, Mike, *The Management of Marketing*, Gower, 2nd edition 1990

25 Managing a sales force

M. T. Wilson

The strategy of marketing is concerned with arranging the resources of the company so that the needs of customers can be satisfied by presenting to them a product/price offering which when purchased provides a profit to the firm. This strategy is implemented through a number of tactical tools, some concerned with finding out what the needs are (marketing research), some with ensuring the product/price offering is correct (product development and testing), and some with presenting the offering to the customer. The sales function is a major tactic in this last area, while having a role to play in the first two.

The importance of the sales function cannot be over-emphasized in those companies where the bulk of the presentational effort is carried by the sales force. This covers most industrial and speciality markets and many consumer goods industries. In fact, it is not exaggerating far to say that in some markets – for example, office equipment and life insurance – the main difference between competing companies lies in the quality of their sales forces.

Moreover, the sales force can make valuable contributions in the definition of market segments and customer needs, and product development and rationalization. This is particularly true in industrial markets, where formal market research is less used. Obviously, since salesmen are not usually trained researchers, the information they collect has to be treated with care.

As sales management is a function (often the most important) within the marketing strategy, it is essential for the sales manager at least to be aware of the other tactics of marketing so that he can contribute to and benefit from them. These include:

1 New product development.
2 Distribution.
3 Sales forecasting.
4 Pricing.
5 Advertising and sales promotion.
6 Public relations.
7 Marketing planning and control (particularly the financial aspects).

In some companies the sales manager will directly control some of these; in others, they will be looked after by marketing staff. In every firm, the sales manager must integrate his activities with the rest of the marketing effort if the maximum value is to be gained from marketing expenditure.

The sales manager is the key man in developing a successful sales operation. He must do this by managing his team – not by doing their jobs for them. As a manager he is responsible for working through others to achieve economic objectives, but this process is hindered by the difficulties of dealing with geographically spread subordinates who spend most of their time with people other than their colleagues.

To do his job successfully, the sales manager must possess knowledge and skill in four major areas: selling, management, sales management and marketing. Only then can he claim to be a fully productive member of the executive team.

Sales management comprises five key elements – planning, organization, training, motivation and control. It is on these that this chapter concentrates.

HOW TO PLAN THE SALES OPERATION

The planning process is only one part of the basic and repetitive management activity necessary in any company seeking to grow. The firm must continuously answer three questions:

1 Where are we going? This is the objective-setting process.
2 How shall we get there? This is the planning process.
3 How shall we know if we are getting there? This is the control process.

These questions first appear at top management level and the answers constitute the corporate objectives, corporate plans and policies, and corporate control mechanisms. Typically they will result in a statement of the profit objectives of the company (usually expressed in terms of return on capital employed), a description of the business the company is in and its desired position in that industry, its plans and policies for each function of the company, and specific goals and targets to be met within set time-periods.

The whole process will then be repeated for each function of the company. Thus marketing, production, R and D, finance and so on, will each formulate its objectives, plans and controls. Within the marketing framework, the sales manager must specify his answers to the three questions in order to produce a format for his staff to work to. Each salesman may well be required to repeat the process with individual customers.

The sales manager's role in the continuum is obviously critical. If he fails to set clear objectives that are compatible within the hierarchy and does not initiate the appropriate action, the whole firm must suffer.

Setting sales objectives

The sales manager will commence by considering the marketing objectives, policies and strategies and control criteria. He will probably have a forecast of sales by revenue and volume, a forecast of gross profit required, perhaps an expense budget, a description of the product range available with additions and deletions, price structure, promotional support, etc.

Forecasting sales

In many firms the sales manager will be involved as a member of the marketing team in the definition of these items. The process will normally start with forecasting sales for the next period. This is the most critical prediction in the company as it will determine the production schedule, raw materials and finished stocks, promotional expenditure, etc. It is best to approach the forecast in two stages. First, what will sales be, assuming all variables in the situation are the same in the future as they have been in the past? Second, which variables will change and what will the impact be? Some of the variables will be internal factors which management decides to change; others will be external factors which are uncontrollable by the company but whose effect must be predicted.

Developing the sales plan

Having set the sales forecast and targets, the manager must now consider how they can be achieved. Obviously some thought will already have been given to the plan in formulating the objectives. After the plan is written it might well be necessary to reconsider the goals that were previously identified.

The sales manager has to consider five basic questions:

1 What is to be sold?
2 To whom?
3 At what price?
4 By what methods?
5 At what costs?

In some of these areas, notably the product range and pricing structure, he may well have limited influence; they are often controlled by the marketing planning department, through a brand or product management structure. In respect of all five he will certainly have to consider the inputs of other parts of the business. What stocks will be available from production, what money is available from finance, what advertising and sales promotion support is planned, etc.?

Deciding what is to be sold

In determining what the product range should be the sales manager can at least advise his marketing planning colleagues on the saleability of the various items in the range as well as new product requirements.

From a sales management viewpoint he will have to decide whether the full range should be sold to everybody. In some capital equipment markets, for example, where the distributor has to make a heavy investment in stock, it may not be in the interests of the company to supply dealers whose resources may not be adequate to finance the more costly products. Likewise, companies who have to make after-sales service arrangements may well decide not to sell products to customers who are geographically isolated.

To whom are the products to be sold

Next, the sales manager must consider the customers and prospects for his products. First, he will study the existing markets and decide whether business with them is likely to increase, decrease or remain static. This judgement will be based on a study of previous buying records.

By analysing customers in terms of their potential and actual purchasing of the various products he has to offer, he can identify the areas to be attacked. Prospective customers can be analysed in the same way.

Choosing the methods

Having identified from the product/market analysis the segments to be attacked, the sales manager can now consider the methods most likely to achieve the objectives set.

The first question to be answered is – what sort of service should the sales force provide in order to influence the buyer? For example, a crop-protection firm pondering how to increase sales to agricultural merchants will have to consider how the merchant will market the product to farmers. Perhaps the job of the sales force in this case will be to help the merchant develop his skills.

Such an analysis of the kind of sales effort needed will lead to identification of the appropriate sales methods. The complexity of seller/buyer relationships becomes rapidly obvious. It is only by such definition that the sales manager can develop the presentational approach that will enable him to succeed in the face of product/ price parity.

Having identified the nature of the sales method he can then consider the scale of effort required. He must calculate how many customers and prospects should be called on how often.

The customers are relatively easy to specify because obviously they are known by name to the company. The level of prospecting is more difficult to calculate; as in many companies potential customers cannot be identified by name. At least, however, the sales manager can indicate the characteristics of likely prospects. Such a profile can then be used by the sales force to select prospects to be called upon. Alternatively, the sales manager can plan simply to allow a certain percentage of time or calls for seeking new business, giving the salesmen the responsibility of using the time or calls wisely.

How often calls should be made is always difficult to assess. Obviously different categories of accounts will require different call frequencies. In some trades where there is an established buying pattern, usually little is gained by calling at a different frequency.

The support of the field force will also be covered by the sales manager's study of the methods required to achieve his objectives. Parts of the supplier/buyer relationship can often be more economically handled by techniques other than personal visiting by representatives. Telephone selling is one method that is successfully used to handle routine ordering, thus freeing the salesmen's costly time for more creative work.

Evaluating the costs of selling

The best approach is to look at the cost-effectiveness of the methods used and particularly to try to analyse the values gained for the costs incurred. For example, if the manager were concerned with the cost of generating prospects he could compare the cost per prospect from advertising, direct mail and cold canvassing. If he were analysing sales force activity, he might question what value was gained from 'courtesy calling' (i.e. routine visiting to check that the customer is satisfied with the products and service supplied). In such a case the manager might experiment by eliminating such calls in a test area and evaluating what, if anything, happened to the sales.

HOW TO ORGANIZE THE SALES FORCE

Many sales organizations have developed without objective analysis of their purpose or structure. Today they are out of date and unable to fulfil the purposes for which they were originally designed. This is because the traditional hierarchical structure is based upon conditions which no longer hold true in a great number of firms. Such organizations assume that there is a large number of relatively small, geographically separate and independent buying-points all with similar requirements, and that these can be serviced by a large number of geographically separated salesmen who can perform similar tasks and who represent the major promotional activity of the company.

Changes in buyer/seller relationships

The foregoing suppositions have been made obsolete by two fundamental changes in the buyer/seller relationship.

First, the buying power in many industries is no longer evenly distributed. In a large number of markets, a few big firms control the majority of the purchasing decisions. These oligopolies, developed largely through the processes of merger and acquisition, have resulted in a dramatic reduction in the numbers of independent outlets in the trades concerned. Thus, whilst sales organizations' structures have in many cases changed little, the number and type of customers with whom they deal have altered dramatically.

Second, the development of new marketing techniques has meant that some tasks traditionally performed by the sales force can be more economically or efficiently handled by other methods. The development of advertising and sales promotion in general, as well as the growing use of specific techniques such as telephone selling and contract ordering, have all had an impact on the nature and scale of the sales effort required. Furthermore, the reduction in sales force sizes and improvements in communications have in some cases obviated the need for regionally based management.

The prime objective of all salesmen is to gain business. From an organizational point of view, however, how they are to achieve their goals must be defined in order to identify what kind and quality of skills are required.

Matching the sales effort to customer requirements

Organizing the sales effort so that it matches the reality of the market place can alleviate such problems. First, the level and quantity of customer service must be defined and the personnel concerned identified.

Such an analysis will also begin to identify the work-loads of each level and suggest ways of grouping the various elements so that they can be better managed.

The sales force structure should also be scrutinized. A geographical split may be the most economical in that travel time is minimized. It may not, however, be the most effective. In one glass-container company it was seen that the prime service to be provided to the buyer was a technical knowledge of bottling as applied to the customer's particular industry. Thus the sales force was regrouped on an industry basis, changing the organization structure. Obviously there was some increase in travel costs because each industry group worked nationally but this was more than offset by the increase in sales.

At sales force level common groupings other than geographical are by industry, by customer size category, by buyer type (for example, purchasers and specifiers), or by service to be provided (for example, order taking and merchandising).

By conducting a customer service requirements analysis the sales manager can identify which organizational approach is appropriate.

The number of salesmen needed

The aim of building an organization is to give the appropriate level of service to each customer and the appropriate amount of work to each man. The only factor common to all salesmen is the number of working hours and this should be the starting point for a work-load analysis, which is the only really logical way of constructing a sales force. The amount of work per salesman can then be calculated by assessing the elements and the time taken on each. Typically, they include: prospecting, travelling, waiting, selling and report writing. If the number of actual and potential accounts to be visited and the frequency of visiting can be assessed, it is possible to calculate the number of salesmen needed as follows:

$$\frac{\text{Number of actual and potential customers} \times \text{Call frequency}}{\text{Average daily call rate} \times \text{Number of working days per year}}$$

TRAINING THE SALES TEAM

The art of selling is the presentation of product benefits in such a way that the buyer is persuaded that his needs will be satisfied. If the salesman is to be successful he must not only be knowledgeable about his product and his customer but also skilful in the presentation of this knowledge.

Induction training

When a new salesman joins a company he should be given some form of training. Too often, even when training is given, the whole time is devoted to company and product knowledge in the hope (usually unfulfilled) that the salesman will some-how pick up sales techniques in the field.

This initial training can be critical to the ultimate success of the new man as it will affect both his ability and morale. It must therefore be very carefully planned and skilfully executed.

The programme material will obviously vary from firm to firm, particularly in terms of the company and product knowledge to be taught.

There are, however, some basic areas of the sales job that should be included in most initial training courses, although with specific biases being given by different companies. Ten major elements should be covered.

1 *The marketing concept and the role of the sales force.* The salesman must understand fully the part he plays in the total effort of the company. Otherwise he will find it difficult to integrate his work with that of other departments.

2 *The nature of salesmanship.* It is essential that the salesman has a clear definition of what selling is, its role in society and the basic requirements of the sales job.

3 *Communications.* As selling depends on persuasive communication, the salesman must understand the inherent difficulties of interpersonal relationships and be given techniques for overcoming these problems. He must be skilled in other forms of communication, such as reporting and talking on the telephone.

4 *Preparation for selling.* This is normally a very weak area of sales skill and yet if a coherent, logical approach to the customer is to be adopted, it has to be structured in advance, and the technique for doing this has to be taught.

5 *Prospecting.* Every business depends to some extent on gaining new cus-tomers. This is probably the most difficult part of selling and the salesman should be taught a systematic approach to the finding of potential buyers. Having learnt how to look for new business, he will also be better motivated and less likely to avoid prospecting, as so often happens.

6 *Opening the sales.* Obtaining interviews with buyers and making the right impression in the early stages of the presentation are areas where skill is required. A casual approach will lead to failure to pass the receptionist or even when that is achieved, to curtailed, unsuccessful interviews.

7 *Making sales presentations.* To be effective as a persuader, the salesman must be skilled in oral presentation, visual aid handling and product demonstration. There is a body of techniques that can be learnt which will help the salesman to communicate convincingly.

8 *Handling objections.* Every sales interview is likely to produce customer objections on such topics as price, delivery, etc. Some of these can be prevented, others overcome. Certainly most objections can be predicted and the salesman trained in the answers to be given and the methods of expressing them.

9 *Closing the sale.* Again, this is normally a very weak area because the sales-man fears rejection. He therefore tends to avoid it by never asking for the order. If he never asks the buyer to buy, the buyer never has to refuse. Obviously the whole point of selling is to gain sales and the salesman can be encouraged to request orders more often and more persuasively by thorough training in proven closing techniques.

10 *Work organization.* The main emphasis of initial training is on improving the

quality of the salesman's skill. Due regard should also be paid to the quantity of selling so that the man knows how to utilize his very limited time to the maximum. He should be taught techniques of journey planning and day planning.

Concept of customer orientation

Throughout the initial training programme certain themes will have to be constantly emphasized as some of the basic concepts are hard to instil. One of the most fundamental of these is the philosophy of customer orientation. Without this approach, the salesman will find it hard to succeed and yet it is difficult to ensure that it will be practised.

Every salesman must recognize that buyers buy to satisfy needs, both rational and emotional. These needs are fulfilled by benefits of the product and these benefits are derived from product features.

Because of the difficulty of reversing the viewpoint in this way, successful training in this concept can be hard to achieve. It is helped if a product analysis is demonstrated and this technique is inculcated so that the salesmen analyse the needs, benefits and features of a situation before they commence selling.

Field training

The objective of field training is to ensure a continuous improvement in the salesman's performance. To achieve this goal there are five tasks that must be carried out by the manager:

1 Field performance must be assessed systematically against known standards.
2 Deficiencies must be identified and agreed and coaching given in the knowledge and skills necessary to correct the identified faults.
3 Guidance must be given on the self-training that is expected from the salesman.
4 Information should be collected about common faults that can be more economically or effectively corrected on a collective basis.
5 The effectiveness of the initial training should be assessed so that it can be improved in the future.

Sales meetings

The regular gatherings of the sales team create the other major opportunity for developing sales force performance. In all but the smallest sales forces, these are held at local level, where the regional, area or district manager meets with his salesmen. Where there are no intermediate supervisory levels between the national sales manager and the sales force these gatherings have to be held on a national basis. The objectives of such meetings should be:

1 To administer corporate training and development.
2 To inform and get feedback from the sales force.
3 To stimulate and if necessary rekindle the salesmen's enthusiasm and motivation.

4   To provide a meeting place and forum for all the salesmen.

HOW TO MOTIVATE THE SALES FORCE

The motivation of salesmen is probably the most common topic of conversation whenever sales managers meet. Every manager has his own pet theories on how to get the best out of his team. The reason why it is such a popular discussion point is because salesmen can be directly supervised only intermittently. It is therefore vital to success that they are deeply motivated to work on their own. Moreover, the sales job inevitably involves loneliness and certain customer contacts which can depress the morale of any but the most enthusiastic salesmen.

The nature of motivation

Because of the geographical separation and the wearing aspects of the job, it is vital for success that the sales manager possesses or develops the ability to motivate his men. In order to do so he needs a clear understanding of why people work and what they wish to gain from their work. Only then can he create an environment which will cause his staff to apply their full abilities to their jobs.

Incentives and disincentives

The basis of motivation is the provision of incentives which encourage salesmen to give of their best and the removal of disincentives which prevent them from devoting their whole energies to their work. Unfortunately, far too often, motivation is equated with incentives only, although it is common to find that the elimination of disincentives – for example, unfair treatment – is the more powerful influence.

It must also be recognised that virtually every incentive brings with it a disincentive, either for the same person or for his colleagues. For example, a competition may be a strong motivation for the winners; but it can be demoralizing for the losers, particularly if they believe that because of the poor construction of the contest they never had a real chance of winning.

The task of the manager is therefore to consider the needs of his team, both individually and as a group, and to arrange a balance of motivational influences that will encourage them to achieve the company's objectives. In essence, this is best done by ensuring that the individual's own goals in life are consistent with the aims of the firm. For example, there is little point recruiting people who are highly money-motivated into a company which offers security as its major satisfaction.

Although recognizing that everyone has his own individual need pattern, there are five motivational influences that the sales manager must fully understand. These are:

1   Remuneration.
2   Direct incentives.
3   Job satisfaction.
4   Security.
5   Status.

Remuneration

First, management should define the salary grades appropriate to the job level. This grade will represent the market value of the position as well as the worth of the job to the company. The bottom of the category will represent the remuneration of a man entering the position exhibiting minimum standards of performance, the upper limit being paid to a man who can achieve completely all the criteria of the job.

Second, the position of any individual within his grade should be determined by his performance against the job standards. An average performer would therefore be paid at the mid-point of the grade. Thus, the salary philosophy will reflect the two main elements of a logical payment structure: the degree of responsibiilty carried by the position, and the effectiveness with which the man discharges it.

Payment by results system

Such an approach to job grading and appraisal presupposes that the salesman will be remunerated at least in part by salary. Many sales forces are of course paid in addition, to some degree or another, according to results. In a relatively small number of companies the salesmen are paid entirely on commission. The choice of remuneration system – salary only, salary plus some form of commission, or commission only – will depend upon the desired mix of security and incentive.

Direct incentives

This term is used to cover the many systems of payment in cash or in kind other than basic remuneration. It includes fringe benefits, merchandise awards, point schemes and competitions. Apart from fringe benefits, such schemes do not usually make a significant difference to total earnings and their basic intention is motivational. Merchandise awards and competitive schemes are best used to focus short-term attention on particular aspects of the business. They are a tactical rather than a strategic motivational weapon. When employed in this way, they can be very effective to concentrate sales force attention on, for example, gaining new accounts, increasing sales of lower volume products, or even submitting call reports on time!

Job satisfaction

Direct incentives in either cash or kind are important elements in any motivational scheme. The so-called 'psychic wages' of the job however must be given at least equivalent priority. Salesmen spend more than half their waking life working. It is not surprising therefore that they seek fulfilment in the job as well as rewards for the job. It is an essential function of any manager to ensure that such satisfaction can be gained by the sales force from their work.

Security

The need for security is a very common, although seldom admitted, motive. The nature of the remuneration system and the relative importance of salary and commission will obviously affect job security and must be considered from this aspect.

However, the less obvious facets of security should not escape the sales manager's attention. In companies where insecurity is a constant feature of the environment morale tends to be low and, although there is often an appearance of frenetic action, achievement is usually very limited.

Status

The sales manager can help to improve the status of selling within the company and the market by ensuring that the job titles given carry as much prestige as possible. He should ensure, too, that the rest of the company realizes the importance of the function so that when a customer telephones and asks for one of the field force by name, the switchboard operator does not reply that as Mr. Smith is 'only one of our salesmen (or worse still, "travellers"), he is not in the office'. Likewise when the caller is eventually put through to the sales department, he should be greeted by someone who answers as 'Mr. Smith's secretary', although he/she can, of course, be 'secretary' to a number of other salesmen as well.

The salesman should be provided with the best possible equipment for his job. Well-printed visiting cards with his name in the middle, a well-made brief-case or sample case and good literature all contribute to his status in the eyes of his customers. His car is perhaps the most significant symbol of all, not only to his buyers but also to his family and friends.

HOW TO CONTROL THE SALES OPERATION

In order to control any activity, there must first be an objective and a plan. Unless it is known what is to be achieved and how, whether it is being achieved cannot be assessed. Conversely, there is little point in setting goals and defining actions unless there is an evaluation procedure.

For example, in one business equipment firm, the sales manager developed a system whereby he could analyse the monthly performance of every salesman under eighteen different categories of activity. Thus he could identify how many hours each man had spent on each facet of his job. He could ascertain for instance that salesman X spent seven and half hours on prospecting, salesman Y eight hours on report-writing. He obviously believed that control was constituted by the collection of detailed information. Such attitudes are common among sales management and part of the impact of computerization is that data suddenly becomes available in vast quantities, thus apparently giving even more minute control.

The concept of control

It must be realized that the collection of information, however accurate, up to date and detailed, in itself in no way constitutes control. This is for the very basic reason that there is little point in knowing what *has* happened unless there is a clear conception of what *should* have happened. Control can then be exercised by comparing actual performance with planned performance and deriving variances. It is on these variances that corrective action should be based. Control can be summarized therefore as:

$$A - S = \pm V$$

where A is the actual performance, S is the pre-set standard and V is the variance between the two.

To know that salesman X spent seven and half hours prospecting is meaningless by itself. However, if the standard for this activity is ten hours then there is a minus variance of two and half hours and it is this figure which should cause the manager to take corrective action. If, however, the standard were seven and half hours, as the actual performance is equivalent to the desired standard no managerial action is required. Only by adopting such a concept can management time be economically utilized.

Setting standards of field sales performance

To identify appropriate standards for control, the manager should ask two questions:

1 What constitutes success?
2 What affects the achievement of success?

Descriptive standards

In a sales operation success can usually be defined as the achievement of the sales targets. These serve as the prime standards of control. By themselves, however, they are insufficient. The achievement or otherwise of the annual sales target constitutes a descriptive standard. It measures what has happened but it is then usually far too late to redress the balance. Moreover, it does not indicate *why* the performance has been poor.

Diagnostic standards

Diagnostic standards, which help to identify why performance is varying from target, are defined by asking the second question: 'What affects the achievement of success?'

The manager must consider in the case of a particular salesman failing to achieve target what actions by the salesman himself should lead to the goals being met. Surprisingly, there are only four and these can be identified by the following questions:

1 What kind of people does he call upon?
2 How many does he call upon?
3 How often does he call?
4 What does he do while he is there?

How to set standards

One of the aims of setting standards is to control the sales activity at an early stage to prevent failure to achieve orders. This aspect of control can be further refined by evaluating planned performance against standard before the activity takes place. In fact it is only by assessing the intended action of the sales force that the sales manager can directly prevent failure. Obviously he must check his own plans to ensure that, if achieved, they reach the desired objectives. He can go further by assessing each salesman's activity plans before they are put into action. This is normally done by the submission of weekly calling plans on which each man identifies whom he is intending to visit, for what reason and when he last saw this customer (if applicable).

Variance production and analysis

Variances are produced by comparing actual results against the pre-set standards. However, this simple method may need refining as high variances can result which reflect the forecast error of the standards. For example, if the average daily call rate is set at eight, there is probably no cause for alarm if this varies between six and ten. Because so many of the standards are produced by averaging past performance it may well be necessary to process the actual results before comparing them against standard.

When the actual results are compared with the standards, variances will become apparent. These discrepancies may need more careful analysis before corrective action is taken. For example, in one firm it was known from past experience that most of the selling depended upon seeing the senior management of the customers, which could only be done by appointment. The results of some salesmen, however, were disappointing despite the fact that the percentage of calls by appointment was well up to the pre-set standard. But when performance against other standards was examined it was noted that their call rate was below par. Thus although the appointment to total call ratio was high, this was due to a smaller number of other calls rather than to an over-achievement of appointments. Furthermore, it was discovered that as they increased their number of appointments, their overall call rates decreased markedly.

What in fact was happening was that these men, in their enthusiasm to gain appointments, had not controlled the timing of such meetings. They had placed them in the middle of the mornings and afternoons, thereby limiting their ability to make other calls. The more experienced men systematically made appointments early in the morning, immediately before lunch, immediately after lunch or late afternoon, leaving mid-morning and mid-afternoon free to make cold calls which, although not as important, resulted in enough business to make their results superior. It would have been very easy to jump to the conclusion that the disappointing results of the less experienced men were due to a lack of sales skill. It was only by careful variance analysis that the real problem of appointment timing was identified.

Taking corrective action

Having identified the true nature of the variance, the sales manager has to decide whether it results from faulty standard setting or inadequate salesman performance. If the former, the standards will have to be modified. If the latter, the performance of the man will have to be improved, usually by some form of training or instruction. If the man is to improve he must be given specific targets to achieve within specific time periods, otherwise little or no change will result.

SUMMARY

Sales management is an important function within an organization and the sales manager is the key person in developing a successful sales operation. This is done by managing the sales force effectively, using the five elements of planning, organization, training, motivation and control with which this chapter has been concerned.

The following checklist offers an aide memoire to the busy manager.

CHECKLIST OF KEY POINTS

Planning:
1   Set sales objectives.
2   Forecast sales.

- What will sales be, assuming all variables remain the same as in the past?
- Which variables will change, and what will the impact be?

3   Develop the sales plan

- What is to be sold?
- To whom?
- At what price?
- By what methods?
- At what costs?

Organizing:
1   Customer service requirements analysis.
2   Determine organizational approach to match customer requirements.
3   Ensure optimal work-force numbers and work-loads.

Training:
1   Content:

- Product knowledge.
- Presentation skills.

- Customer orientation.

2 *Methods*:
- Induction training, covering the basic areas of the sales job.
- Field training, to ensure continuous improvement in performance.
- Sales meetings, on a regular basis, for developing sales force performance.

Motivation:
1 Understand why they work and what they wish to gain from their work.
2 Create the environment in which they can flourish.
3 Five motivational influences:

- Remuneration.
- Direct incentives.
- Job satisfaction.
- Security.
- Status.

Control:
1 Set standards of field sales performance.
2 Variance production and analysis.
3 Take timely corrective action.

FURTHER READING

Forsyth, P., *Running an Effective Sales Office*, Gower, Aldershot, 1980

Lidstone, J. B. J., *Motivating Your Sales Force*, Gower, Aldershot, 1978

Lidstone, J. B. J., *How to Recruit and Select Successful Salesmen*, 2nd edition, Gower, Aldershot, 1983

Lidstone, J. B. J., *Training Salesmen on the Job*, 2nd edition, Gower, Aldershot, 1986

Marketing Improvements Limited, *SalesPlanner*, Gower, Aldershot, 1988 (50 forms for systematic sales management, together with an explanatory book)

Melkman, A. V., *How to Handle Major Customers Profitably*, Gower, Aldershot, 1979

Strafford, John and Grant, Colin, *Effective Sales Management*, Heinemann, London, 1986

Wilson, M. T., *Managing a Sales Force*, 2nd edition, Gower, Aldershot, 1983

26 Managing distribution

Keith Newton

This chapter is written for the reader who is contemplating a career in distribution management in a company whose end product is not distribution but for whom distribution is a key activity. I hope it will also be read with interest by his colleagues, particularly his sales colleagues, and his immediate superior.

Distribution embraces everything required to physically move the company's products to its customers. The magnitude of the distribution task varies enormously from one company to another and your understanding of the relevance of the role of distribution manager to your career must stem from an assessment of the importance of the distribution function to your company.

In some companies distribution may simply be a minor function requiring sound management of a limited activity; maybe it will be of little interest to the reader except as a career broadening opportunity, perhaps an early chance to manage your own show and demonstrate your ability to manage other functions before returning to your planned career path. In other companies, distribution may be so expensive or so critical to the marketing and sales objectives that it offers career opportunities to Board level as either Distribution or Logistics Director.

There are, of course, companies whose *raison d'être* is distribution. Over the last twenty years they have been growing in size and sophistication and many of them are grappling with new kinds of growth to meet the ever more international and specialized needs of their customers. These companies do not use the title distribution manager; distribution is the name of their product rather than a description of managerial responsibility. Managers in distribution companies have titles like operations, sales, marketing and finance.

All companies who move a physical product from one point to another as part of the process of selling it to a customer are involved in distribution; they may be manufacturers, merchants or retailers. Any or all of the following factors can contribute to an assessment as to whether or not distribution is a key activity:

- *Cost.* Any company in which total cost of distribution is of the order of 10% of turnover should certainly be taking distribution management very seriously indeed.

- *Marketing edge.* Many companies use distribution as a marketing tool. In comparison to their competition they may give more reliable or faster availability, a fresher or wider range of products, show greater adaptability in responding to or stimulating new customer needs.
- *Risk.* There are many companies in which risk has a significant impact on the distribution process – the product may be inherently hazardous or may be prone to deterioration if incorrectly handled. For such companies, the risk of getting distribution severely wrong could put them out of business.

Finally, if distribution in your company is interesting to you, would you make a good distribution manager? Consider three points:

- The good distribution manager is a generalist not a specialist. The perfect distribution manager will know as much about the products as the buyer or manufacturing manager, as much about the customers' needs and perceptions as the sales and marketing managers.
- The good distribution manager is a team player not a *prima donna.* Because of his interface position his most significant contributions are usually made in conjunction with his colleagues.
- Any distribution manager needs broad shoulders. His team is often the last group who can rectify mistakes, his mistakes are almost always visible to the customer. He will also be blamed for the effects of foggy airports, jammed motorways and storms at sea. Rightly so: it is part of his task to set up a distribution structure that makes the impact of such events as invisible as possible to his customers.

HOW TO PLAN THE DISTRIBUTION OPERATION

Because distribution is an interface function, the distribution manager will only plan successfully if the whole organization is planning effectively. In particular, he must start with input from his Sales colleagues. The previous chapter described how the sales force must continuously answer the questions:

- Where are we going?
- How shall we get there?
- How shall we know if we are getting there?

So must the distribution department. The connection is that the input 'where are we going?' for the distribution department is the output 'how shall we get there?' from the sales force. At least this is true for the first round of shorter term planning, say for periods up to one year. For longer term planning, the distribution manager will also need to understand the long term plans of his colleagues in buying, manufacturing, marketing and even Research and Development.

I shall call shorter term planning, in response to an agreed sales plan, 'operations planning', and longer term planning 'strategic planning'.

Operations planning

For an established business, there is a fairly limited sales data requirement for operational planning purposes. Operations planning is essentially re-active and requires the sales force to provide forecasts of volume by product by destination phased over time together with any changes to service standards. The data are not necessarily as readily available as might be initially supposed. The units that salesmen naturally think in and discuss with their customers may be difficult to translate into units that relate to distribution. Sales territories may have little or no relationship to distribution channels. A great deal of the operations planning process is usually spent in translating the company's sales plan into meaningful distribution volume plans.

Typical sales forecast units might be money, individual item quantities or some standard equivalent sales unit by customer type or geographical area, but what are suitable units for planning the distribution function? There is no simple answer. One level of complexity arises from the wide variation of activities that can be embraced by the distribution function, for example:

- *Storage*: storage capacity cannot be derived directly from a sales plan without additional knowledge of buying or production planning.
- *Order processing*: requires knowledge of the number and complexity of orders to be processed not just total volumes sold.
- *Order picking*: requires a very detailed understanding of the ordering pattern. The same company might be shipping products in a mix of full pallets, full cases or individual packs. The picking labour content per pack sold can easily vary by a factor of 100.

A second level of complexity arises from the different methods that can be used to fulfil any one activity type, for example:

- *Transport*. One company may be using any mix of road, rail, sea or air with endless variations within them. Furthermore, these may be consistent e.g. customer A always gets supplied by road from depot X; variable with order, e.g. large orders direct ex-factory, small orders from depot X; at customer request, e.g. routine orders by sea, express orders by air.

The main goals of the operational planning exercise are:

- to ensure that facilities of all kinds are adequate to meet the requirements of the sales plan;
- to budget correctly for in-house and bought-in distribution services of all types.

In theory, to meet these goals, the work load and cost of every activity and every element of each activity has to be evaluated. In practice most of the time it is not necessary to rigorously go through every step of the procedure. In most companies, much of next year's plan can be extrapolated from last year. The distribution manager firstly needs to understand the sales plan sufficiently to identify the areas of significant change. This understanding usually comes more through discussion than looking at written plans. Secondly, he must understand his own operation well enough to know which changes may necessitate expanding existing resources or might give rise to opportunities for cost saving. Good communication and judgment are as much a part of the operations planning process as is the inevitable hard number crunching required to evaluate areas of significant change.

Strategic planning

Strategic planning as distinct from operations planning is essentially pro-active. Again the start point should come through or in conjunction with colleagues in sales and marketing. It is at this level that the distribution manager has the opportunity not only to plan his own future activities but also by offering alternative cost and service options to influence the future marketing plans of the organization.

The start point is knowledge of the actual or potential end-customers' service needs. Very few companies put enough resource into this; indeed many companies do not even realize that they don't know! Generally, I would not believe a company understands its service objectives unless it had conducted a fairly rigorous customer survey and investigated the significance of distribution performance from itself and its competitors to actual and potential customers. Factors which might be included in such a survey are:

- Speed of delivery.
- Order cut-off times.
- Reliability of delivery.
- A range of questions covering condition on arrival.
- Accuracy of invoicing.
- Response when things go wrong.

It is possible, with sales management's agreement, for the distribution department to organize their own survey along these lines. However, as we are trying to be pro-active, it is much more useful to combine such questions into a wider survey including questions on such factors as product quality, sales representative call frequency and price.

The advantage of the wider survey stems from the need to position calls for investment in improved distribution against more salesmen or a larger product development budget. Very few companies can take a market position in which they can afford to be 'the best' at everything and the important measures of distribution quality have to be balanced against price, product quality, innovation and all the other factors which add up to the customers' perception of service.

Having quantified customer service requirements, the next step is to devise a distribution strategy to meet them. Here we go through a similar round of thinking to the operational planning task but thinking much more widely because time is on our side:

- Do we open or close depots?
- Do we subcontract or bring activities in-house?
- Do we explore contractual possibilities with different types of carrier?

The first important question to ask at each step of this process is 'what is the critical factor which pushes up the cost or diminishes perceived service?'. We then go back to our colleagues to see whether a constraint can be broken to the total advantage of the company. Perhaps manufacturing can spend more and produce a robust product enabling savings in distribution.

The second important question is 'how much money need I spend in order to improve customers' perception of distribution?' Where opportunities are found, we then ask whether it is worthwhile in terms of profit on additional sales.

HOW TO ORGANIZE THE DISTRIBUTION DEPARTMENT

The range of functions embraced by the distribution manager varies considerably between companies. The full range is:

- Central stockholding.
- Picking and packing.
- Depot operations.
- Transport operations.
- Order processing.
- Customs & Excise.

In addition, a substantial distribution operation might well have its own support functions such as:

- Packaging design.
- Materials handling.
- Information technology.
- Safety and regulatory.
- Customer liaison.

There are no golden rules as to what should or should not be within the direct control of the distribution manager but to be effective he must have a superb two-way relationship with any of the above functions which are not under his direct control together with a clear functional responsibility for the totality of the service given.

One of the key changes in distribution thinking over the last decade has been a diminishing importance of line control of operations combined with increasing importance of control of systems, information and strategy. Before thinking about the organization of your department, you have to decide, function by function, which activities are best controlled directly and which are best sub-contracted either to a colleague within the company or to a third party specialist.

Some examples are:

Central stockholding

Many manufacturing companies have finished goods warehouses on the factory sites which merely form a buffer between the production lines and bulk shipping to distribution depots. Their day to day operation is probably best in the hands of the factory manager since most issues will be site rather than distribution specific. Labour supply, equipment maintenance, supervision and training may all benefit from being run as part of a larger local organization than as an outpost of the distribution department. In such a case, the distribution manager should devote his effort to his functional responsibility, ensuring that the warehouse is appropriately sized and is working to criteria which contribute appropriately to the total distribution function.

At the other extreme, the factory warehouse may be shipping direct to end customer in a high speed and volatile market. The bulk of day to day issues may centre round its interfaces with order processing and transport. In order to avoid continuous argument about who is damaging who's budget and to encourage a team approach to ensuring that customers' needs are met, such a warehouse might best be under the control of distribution management.

Distribution depots

Think of the potential benefits of using a professional sub-contractor:

- no capital;
- flexibility;
- specialist management;
- synergy with other users;
- free management time for more important activities.

It is actually quite rare to find a justification for in-house operation of distribution depots except where there are huge volumes of goods requiring unique handling techniques.

Packaging design

If packaging design is dominated by product presentation, customer appeal or manufacturing technology, then it should be under the control of the marketing or manufacturing departments. If, however, it is primarily there to facilitate safe handling and transport, it may well be best located in the distribution department.

General

There is not space here to consider all the organizational thinking but it is perhaps worth noting that some of the highest paid distribution or logistics managers are virtually one-man-bands. Their task is to ensure that other functions with line control are operating within a strategy and to standards of efficiency and effectiveness that fulfil and enhance the companies' goals.

TRAINING THE DISTRIBUTION TEAM

From the previous section on organization, we can see that there is no such thing as a distribution worker. The department may include warehouse staff, mechanical handling operators, administrators, computer specialists, drivers, freight buyers, sales liaison staff, analysts and specialists in customs and regulatory affairs.

Clearly, different job-specific training is required for all these categories but there are some general training requirements which are all too often overlooked.

Company awareness training

When any new employee joins the distribution department, he should be given some broad initial training to make him aware of the products he is handling, the market place to which they are being distributed, and any special characteristics of products or markets which influence the operation of the distribution department.

This training has two main objectives:

- To enhance job interest by providing a background of knowledge so that when he/she is told what to do in a specific job he/she can understand why.
- To engender a feeling of commitment. Many distribution workers are based in outposts of the company or are drivers out on the road. When, as will often happen, they are asked to 'pull out the stops', perhaps to correct errors of others, they must feel part of the whole team. They must feel that what is good for the company is good for their job security or career prospects.

Safety training

Many distribution departments have staff engaged in unskilled manual handling activities – stacking cases onto pallets, putting boxes away into racks, unpacking incoming goods, and so on. It is often deemed that no training is required. Such workplaces often have unnecessarily high accident rates. Among the most common are back injuries caused by incorrect lifting or general injuries brought about in falls caused by allowing spent packing materials to litter the workplace. It goes without saying that nobody should operate power handling equipment such as fork lift trucks without having successfully completed an approved training course. A busy warehouse is no place to learn how to put away a pallet, perhaps weighing a ton, fifteen feet or more above the ground.

Lost time is expensive, and a small investment in training in basic safe handling techniques and housekeeping is well worthwhile for both the employee and the employer.

Customer contact training

Many distribution departments have considerable direct contact with the customer. Delivery drivers may well have more face to face contact than sales representatives. Many manual and clerical workers regularly receive telephone calls enquiring or complaining about stock availability, delivery schedules or supply failures.

Anyone who has even occasional contact with customers should have basic training to ensure that the image of a caring, efficient supplier which the sales force is trying to build is not damaged by a disinterested or inaccurate response to a telephone enquiry or by a scruffy or uncooperative delivery driver.

Customer orientation

Everyone in distribution should be customer-oriented, not just those who have direct contact with the customer. The only purpose of anyone in the distribution organization, however far back down the chain of supply he may be, is to meet the needs of the customer.

Part of on-the-job training must be to give everyone time to meet and discuss problems with their customer: the next in line towards the end customer. Encouragement and facilitation of working groups at all levels to identify and solve problems adds to job interest and commitment as well as improving performance.

HOW TO MOTIVATE THE DISTRIBUTION DEPARTMENT

Motivation in a distribution department can be a real problem. It can be difficult to define clear motivational goals and even harder to motivate people towards fulfilling them.

A prime source of motivational difficulty is that performance is always viewed in terms of failure rather than success. The job of the distribution department is often seen by others as delivering everything required in perfect condition and on time in response to any demand put upon it by the sales force. You can never exceed this target; you can only do worse! This is exacerbated by the constant battering that distribution performance takes from external factors. Failure to distribute may be caused by colleagues, late supply from production or an over-enthusiastic salesman quoting an impossible lead time. Failure will also be caused by weather conditions affecting road, sea and air transport and by industrial action from third parties over whom one has no control (air traffic controllers, customs officers and dock workers are three groups which spring to mind).

A second problem stems from the conflict between accuracy and cost. Constant attempts to drive throughput up can lead to inaccuracies; incorrect order picking, missed deliveries, damaged goods or, worse, allowing vital back up operations such as stock checking to fall behind so that the whole operation can fall into disarray.

How should you respond to this challenge?

Remuneration

As a general rule I do not believe that direct performance related pay schemes work very well; they lead to

- cutting corners;
- disputes;
- large administrative departments setting and monitoring standards;
- inflexibility;
- exacerbation of the management versus men syndrome;
- disinterest in the problems of others.

In short, performance pay schemes are only suitable for the simplest of distribution operations where it is almost impossible to do anything wrong and where working faster really does mean working better.

I would rather put the cost of incentive schemes into a well-designed pay structure which ensures that distribution workers see themselves as comparably paid to people of similar skills within and outside the company and where breadth and depth of knowledge can be assessed and rewarded by promotion.

A good example would be to create two levels of warehouse worker, say the warehouse person and the senior warehouse person. At any one time, they might be doing exactly the same work but the senior warehouseman would have demonstrated his added worth to the company by:

- overall knowledge of his broader work environment;
- flexibility to change jobs;
- capability as a trainer;
- ability and readiness to identify and contribute to resolution of problems.

Promotion should never be a sinecure. It should be clear to all his colleagues that the senior warehouse person has earned and is continuing to merit his higher status and remuneration.

For senior distribution management, I do believe in performance related bonuses providing that bonus targets can be set against clear measurable goals which relate directly to the company's current performance objectives.

Combating demotivation

I have made it abundantly clear that there are ample opportunities for demotivation. The first and most important step towards motivation is to remove as much demotivation as possible.

In most companies, the main source of complaints to the distribution department is the sales force. Sales people are hypersensitive. Every one of them believes that today's delivery to one of his customers is the most important delivery the company has ever made! There is no point in trying to change this attitude. They wouldn't be much good as sales people if they didn't feel like that. Nevertheless, it can be totally demotivating to a transport manager if against all the odds he has struggled with bad weather or vehicle breakdowns to deliver ninety-nine out of a hundred orders and then gets ten minutes of abuse about the one failure. Here are some golden rules to minimize demotivation:

- Try to keep complaints away from those who do not deserve them. Field them yourself or in a complex environment set up a department of people who are trained and paid to deal with them.
- Never ignore complaints. Hidden among them will be important clues as to how you can really improve your operation.
- When things are going wrong, always tell the sales person before he/she tells you, especially before the customer responds.
- Make sure the sales force understand your problems but never explain a problem without offering at least one potential solution.
- Encourage and facilitate joint working teams to foresee problem areas and take pre-emptive action.
- Never make promises you cannot keep. If your delivery is stuck in traffic and

might arrive any time between two and four hours from now, do not say it might be there in two hours. Say it will be there in four hours. There is nothing you can do about it anyway, you may as well collect the credit for beating your promise as the blame for failure!

Motivation

However hard you try you will not stop demotivational noises filtering into your department. Whenever people are doing well and especially in the face of difficulties, it is up to you to ensure that enough compensating motivational feed-back is generated. Some ideas are:

- Tell them immediately.
- Make sure that others know.
- Small but tangible rewards for exceptional performance.
- Public recognition in department meetings.
- Departmental news-sheet.

Most importantly when praise comes in from customers and sales people, publicize it as widely as possible both to those who have contributed and to those who haven't. Take every opportunity to tell people that their efforts are appreciated and are contributing to the company's success. When appropriate encourage your non-distribution colleagues to come in and do the same.

HOW TO CONTROL THE DISTRIBUTION OPERATION

Control requires information but information does not necessarily give control. Good control information must satisfy the following criteria:

- It must relate to a specific activity of the department.
- It must be consistently measurable.
- It must be targetable.
- It must be presented in a manner which provokes positive use, to achieve improvements, rather than negative use, to attribute blame.

It is always easy to invent and implement measures of *what* is happening, orders picked per man hour, average order fill, percentage of deliveries made on time, etc. It is never easy to know what the achievement should be, why a target was not met or how to make things better in future. Making things better is the only justification for control information so, when deciding what information to collect, always start from here.

To know how to make things better you need to know which things are important and what better means. For this you require a full understanding of the company's goals.

Cutting cost may be a goal, but are we trying to reduce revenue expenditure such as labour or minimize capital investment in space and equipment? The two may be in conflict – make sure you measure the one that matters to your company this year.

Similarly, a goal of improved service may mean any or all of speed, accuracy of order fill, completeness of order fill, delivery by a deadline, delivery in a time slot, invoicing accuracy, quality of information on outstanding deliveries and so on. If you try to measure everything, you won't have time to use it. Try to pick on the important issues and put more effort into using measures to seek long term improvement than into measuring for the sake of it.

Whilst I would never believe that any organization which is not targeting and measuring key performance indicators is in control, I would equally never believe that a distribution department can be controlled through data alone. In comparison to many other activities, warehouse operations in particular require a great deal of good old fashioned man management. Workers are rarely tied like production line workers to a single work station and a work flow determined by the speed of a machine. Mistakes are often hard to spot until they reach the customer and cause dissatisfaction and cost of rectification. There is no substitute for time spent walking the floor and talking to the operatives.

Finally, the one thing that is always worth monitoring is mistakes. Whatever your goals, mistakes always irritate the customer or cost money, and often both. There is no point in simply counting mistakes. The source must be identified so that corrective action can be taken to avoid repetition. The source of a mistake can be difficult to identify; an order may be delivered late because of initial problems in manufacturing, buying, selling or distribution. It is unlikely that mistakes can be properly categorized without some mixed functional team going through them together. This may sound like a lot of work but if the same team are charged with improvement and discouraged from turning the exercise into merely targeting blame, it can lead not only to improved performance but also to improved motivation and a better understanding of every department's contribution to the success of the company as a whole.

CHECKLIST OF KEY POINTS

Do:

- Assess the importance of distribution to your company in categories of cost, marketing advantage and risk.
- Join as early and as much as possible in other managers' planning discussions, especially those of the sales force.
- Ask the customers about their perceptions of the different elements of service.
- Put effort into awareness training of the company's products, customers and markets for all levels of distribution employee.
- Ensure that anyone whose job involves any level of contact with customers is given proper contact training.
- Structure jobs into a system of remuneration which rewards knowledge, flexibility and quality of work.
- Encourage staff at all levels to join in quality improvement/cost reduction exercises with members of other functions.
- Put at least as much effort into building improvement as into measuring failure.

- Join the organizations catering for distribution managers and participate actively.

Don't

- Assume your boss/colleagues know the difficulties you overcome as well as the times you fail – tell them.
- Hang on to physical operations without good reason. Playing the subcontractor market often gives better service for money than hands-on control.
- Assume your only justification for change is reduced cost. The big money is in better service leading to more sales.
- Assume people will work safely at even the most menial tasks without proper safety training.
- Assume incentivised pay schemes make people work better or make people management easier.
- Let complaints get to people who are not paid to deal with them.
- Collect control information which doesn't lead to action.

TAKING IT FURTHER

Organizations

There are two invaluable organizations to help the distribution manager:

The Freight Transport Association (FTA)
Hermes House
St. Johns Road
Tunbridge Wells
Kent TN4 9UZ

The *FTA* is a national and regional organization representing over 13 000 operators and users of all modes of transport both domestically and internationally.

The Institute of Logistics and Distribution Management
Douglas House
Queens Square
Corby
Northants NN17 1PL

The ILDM is a professional institute offering training, publications and qualifications.

FURTHER READING

Christopher, Martin, *The Strategy of Distribution Management*, Gower, 1985
Gattorna, John (Ed), *Gower Handbook of Logistics and Distribution Management* 4th edition Gower, 1990

27 Managing a finance department

C. D. Verrall

One of the most important ingredients of management in making its efforts fully productive is a modern financial department. It is to the chief financial officer, more than to any other official, that the chief executive must turn for guidance in the direction, control, protection and financing of the business. To use the nautical analogy, the chief financial officer, or finance director, is not the captain of the ship – that is the task of the chief executive – but he is the navigator. He informs the captain how far he has come, where he is, what speed he is making, the influence of weather conditions, variations from course, dangerous reefs that lie ahead, and the course that should be set in order to reach the destination safely.

There is no place for reliance on luck in modern business. The successful business manager must know and use the instruments of guidance at his command; the executive who is best informed about his operations is in the best position to manage his business profitably.

Some of the most successful businesses in the world are in Japan. After its defeat in World War II, its industrial economy was rebuilt, mainly following advice from American consultants. There were three main factors for success that stood out in the lectures given to the leaders of Japanese industry. They were structure, responsibility and quality control. The Japanese have diligently and successfully applied these elements in their business activities and they are also some of the fundamental threads that are woven into the fabric of this chapter.

How the finance director applies these criteria, emphasizing the essential requirement of financial control over the business management process and the structures and principles required for this purpose, is described in the first section of this chapter.

FINANCIAL CONTROL

Good financial control is achieved and maintained by ensuring that decisions and actions are taken at the appropriate stages in the financial cycle. The cycle starts with the setting of objectives (see Figure 27.1).

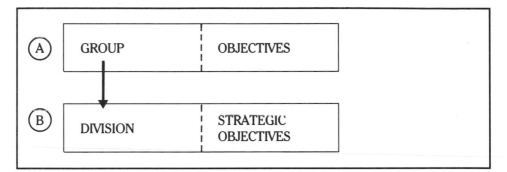

Figure 27.1   The beginning of the financial cycle

Group objectives

The basic financial objectives of the group should be ascertained by comparison with successful industrial organizations in similar fields and by reference to the perceptions of the Stock Exchange. The measurements should normally comprise a few simple ratios including, at least, those shown below.

1   Return on equity.
2   Gearing.
3   Average annual growth in earnings per share.

Division strategic objectives

Having established the group financial objectives, strategic objectives are calculated for each of the divisions.

1   Return on net operating assets.
2   Average annual growth in pre-tax profit.
3   Other.

The sum of these objectives should support, at least, the group financial objectives but need not necessarily be in the same form. For instance, it may be more suitable to use a return on net operating assets instead of a return on equity ratio to avoid problems of allocations of capital and reserves and to emphasize the importance of asset management. Other financial and non-financial objectives are also established according to management requirements.

Strategic plan

The strategic plan usually covers a three- or a five-year period, depending on the type of business, and uses a 'top-down' approach.
The principle characteristic of the plan are as follows:

1   Based on approved objectives.
2   Product line strategy.
3   New business strategy.
4   Problem identification.

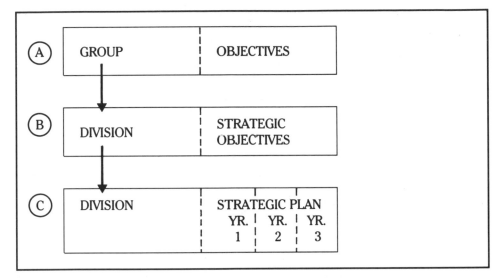

Figure 27.2   From group objectives to divisional plans

5   Consideration of alternatives.
6   Major programmes.
7   Critical milestones.
8   Resources required.
9   Functional plans.
10   Financial exhibits.
11   Various scenarios.
12   Action programmes.

It includes a narrative, placing early emphasis on product line and new business strategies, identifying principal problems for which corrective action must be developed. It is based on the consideration of alternatives and the reasons for the strategy chosen should be clearly given. Major programmes should be described and critical milestones identified. Broad indications and resources needed in terms of facilities, manpower, and finances should be demonstrated. Functional plans support the strategy and confirm the approved objectives.

The financial exhibits are calendarized by year and include various scenarios, reflecting the sensitivity of orders received, contract problems, etc. Changes between the years are analysed and explained.

Action programmes for each function showing responsibilities and planned completion dates are included. These are an important part of ensuring timely attainment of the financial and functional goals contained in the plan.

Individual plans prepared by the divisions are consolidated to form a 'group strategic plan.'

Organization

The group and the divisions must be organized to implement the approved strategy, reflected in organization charts and job descriptions. These define the

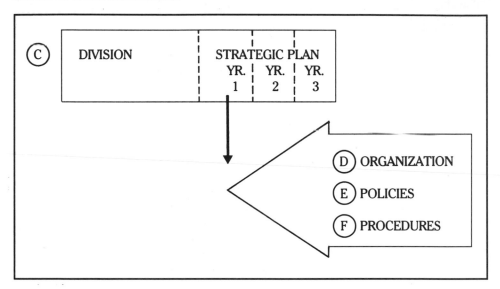

Figure 27.3   Organization, policies and procedures to implement the approved strategy

responsibilities and, therefore, following the rule of accountability and responsibility, the accounting system should be set up to measure them, as will be explained later.

1   Clear functional structure.
2   Clear-cut responsibility and authority.
3   Capable of contraction and expansion.
4   Separate staff and line organizations, and defined duties and responsibilities of each.
5   Precise job descriptions.

Policies

These are the written expression of purposes and the courses of action to be pursued to attain them in an orderly manner.

Procedures

These are written instructions detailing the way policies are to be implemented.

Operating plan

Following approval of the strategic plan, the first of the plan years forms the basis of the operating plan.

1   Detailed financial exhibits.
2   Based on the organization structure.
3   Covers operating and financial control.
4   Action programmes are updated.

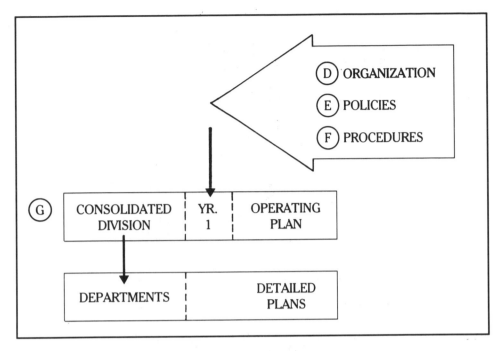

Figure 27.4   Plans and budgets, prepared 'bottom-up'

This is prepared 'bottom-up' together with subordinate functional plans which include a detailed set of financial exhibits, calendarized by months and based on the organizational structure of the divisions. Anticipated costs are taken into account as well as the continuing requirement for cost reduction. Typically, the exhibits will include profit and loss accounts, balance sheets, cash flows, departmental expenses and other supporting details that may be required. Any differences from the related annual figures in the strategic plan are analysed and explained. Suitable ratios and measurements are defined and included in the plan covering asset management, delivery times, quality, production efficiency and any critical measurable factor important in meeting plan objectives. The action plans included in the strategic plan are repeated and updated with assigned responsibilities and completion dates to ensure timely accomplishment.

Plans and budgets should not be imposed on managers; they must be closely involved in their preparation with a clear understanding of ownership. Any changes required during the review process must be with their agreement, otherwise how can the manager be held accountable?

Standards of performance

Measurement of the operating plan is achieved by establishing budgets and other yardsticks based on measured standards and quality tests; comparison with these standards measures the results which are recorded in management reports.

1 Budgets.
2 Production efficiency standards.

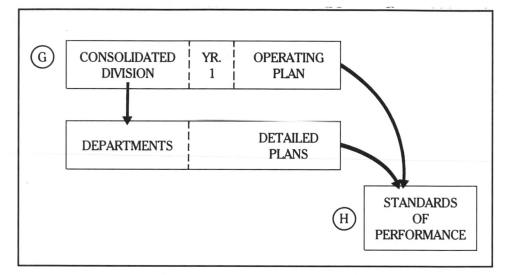

Figure 27.5   Measurement of the plans by using standards of performance

3   Purchasing standards.
4   Quality standards of design and manufacture, etc.
5   Other.

Records and reports

These involve the following main requirements:

1   Accounting records are established with the main objective of control.
2   Statutory requirements are important but secondary.
3   Chart of accounts.
4   Finance manual.
5   Principles of control – responsibility and accountability.
6   Formal list of reports.
7   Main management reporting requirements:

- multi-purpose;
- basis of exception reporting;
- for decision-making;
- timeliness;
- support by analytical comments.

8   Analytical studies:

- profitability of products, contracts, activities, etc;
- cost reductions;
- capital expenditures, investments and disposals;
- other.

The accounting records are maintained principally for purposes of control. The

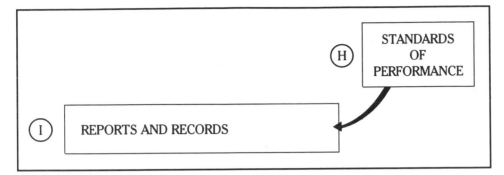

Figure 27.6   Report and records derived from standards and results

information should be readily convertible into reports required for statutory or regulatory purposes. A chart of accounts reflects the requirements of the reporting system and includes descriptions of the manner in which the accounts are used. The finance manual provides guidance and direction to the finance department in implementing financial policies.

Those responsible for the various phases of the operation are also responsible for preparing the related plans, therefore planning must be based on the organizational structure and on responsibility reporting. Responsibility reporting has three requirements:

- Functional definition.
- Assignment of responsibility.
- Accountability for results.

Report control ensures that the availability of information is published as widely as required and avoids duplication. Ad hoc reports resulting from information deficiency are eliminated.

Reports are reviewed periodically to ensure their adequacy. Wherever possible, existing reports are adapted to include additional requirements rather than issue a new report. In preparing reports there should be a definite purpose in mind, and the relationship of the data to that purpose should be absolutely clear. Reporting is a major part of the activity in the finance department and its scope very much depends on the management style of the company, size, nature of the business, etc. Generally, reporting of results takes place at the half year and year end for statutory purposes and, usually, monthly for management purposes. Other reports will depend on the needs of the business. Orders received, orders on hand and cash balances may require weekly or even daily reporting. In addition, special reports may be required to highlight continuing problem areas such as the cost of overtime or one-off analytical studies on the cost of engineering changes, high inventory levels, etc.

Facts and statistics should be translated into trends and relationships. The viewpoint must be that of the future – analyses of past results are of value only insofar as they indicate the proper course in the future.

The information must be timely. Facts which come too late to be acted upon are wasted effort and serve no useful purpose.

Remember that a business is not controlled by accounting data. People control the business, therefore the accounting reports should be so structured that they report on the basis of responsibility.

Internal control

To attain good internal control, the procedures must be subject to the two main principles shown below. This is most important to avoid problems involving transactions that are unauthorized or fraudulent.

1 Checks and balances.
2 Responsibilities clearly defined and determinable.

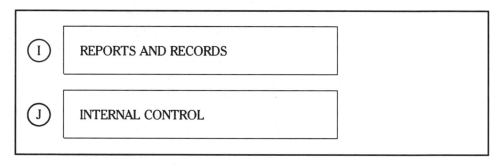

Figure 27.7   Reports and records are maintained for control purposes

Internal audit

Internal audit is only required in larger concerns. Smaller organizations depend on adequate internal controls.

1 Review of soundness, adequacy and application of controls.
2 Reports to management on compliance, quality and reliability of records and reports, accountability and safety of assets, loss minimization, etc.

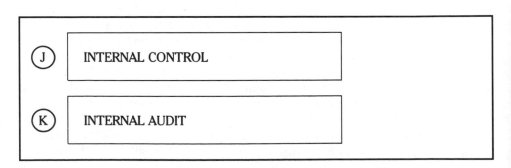

Figure 27.8   Control and Audit to review and report

The complete cycle is displayed in Figure 27.9.

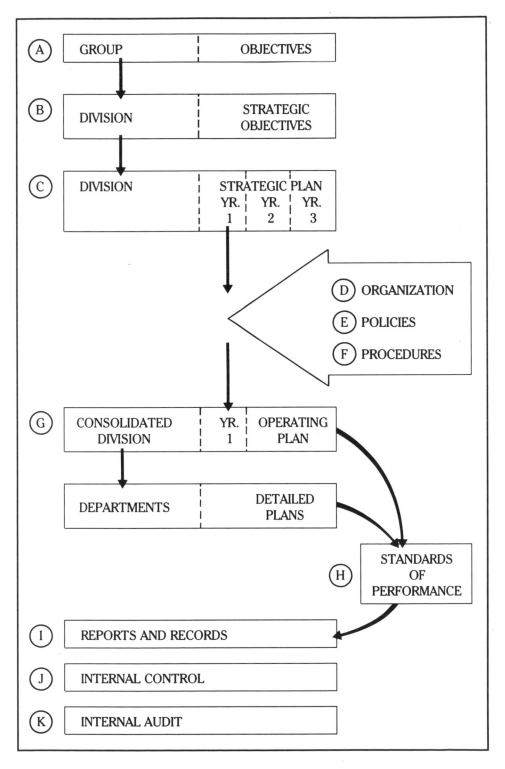

Figure 27.9   The financial cycle

THE ROLE OF THE FINANCE DEPARTMENT

The way in which the finance department becomes involved in this management process is described in the next section.

Accounting

A budgetary control and accounting system should be in place whereby, as described previously, the principles of responsibility and accountability are introduced. It follows, therefore, that approval to charge a certain department must be given by the person responsible for that department's budget, otherwise that person cannot be held accountable for any related adverse variance. Before an expense is incurred, the adequacy of the budget for that expense should be verified and, if not, permission to exceed the budget must be obtained first rather than justify unfavourable variances afterwards.

The accounting system should incorporate the necessary disciplines so that recording of accounting entries becomes routine. This means that lists of standard accounting entries with the names of those responsible for each must be prepared. To ensure speedy closing of the books at month or year end, timetables with defined responsibilities for each action should be published and followed. The objective is to reduce the possibility of omissions and errors and to secure on-time release of financial information.

Control over expenditure should operate on a pre-approval basis. Wherever possible, a purchase order should be generated and approved by the person responsible for the budget concerned before an item is ordered or an expense incurred.

Having established that all assets and liabilities are properly recorded, procedures should be followed to ensure prompt collection of amounts due to the company and that, wherever possible, liabilities are minimized.

A fixed asset register should be maintained and proper procedures followed to record gains and losses on disposals. Periodically, a fixed asset inventory should be taken. Ideally, department managers should be responsible for assets under their control.

If the nature of the business is contracting, good contract cost control is one of the most important factors contributing to success or failure of the business. Emphasis should be placed on comparison of regular estimates of cost to complete the contract made during the performance of the contract with those used to bid for the contract. Comparison with estimates made at different dates should reveal important reasons for variances relating to bidding procedures or contract cost controls requiring appropriate management action.

Financial planning and analysis

The finance department is responsible for the financial input to the strategic and operating plans and budgets. Coordination of the preparation of the plans is often the responsibility of the finance department.

The purpose of financial planning is to establish profit objectives for the plan period. It translates into financial terms all of the proposed activities of the company and allocates resources in such a way that equates short- and long-term objectives. It integrates the activities of various functions so that:

- The marketing department plans to sell the same products in the same quantities that manufacturing plans to produce.
- New designs coming out of engineering are properly integrated into marketing and manufacturing plans.
- Research and engineering have the requisite funds to maintain product development programmes.
- Personnel needs are capable of being met.
- Investment requirements are reasonable.

Plans are evolved from consideration of alternative courses of action based on sets of assumptions related to:

- Economic climate.
- Competitive strategy.
- Marketing posture.
- Changes in costs and prices.
- Probability of engineering and manufacturing difficulties.
- Introduction of new products.
- Capital expenditures.
- Rearrangement of facilities.
- Research and development programmes.

A narrative plan should be written, aimed at functional goals and their timing, supported by the assumptions used. The benefit of this is that written expression will assist later analysis and determination of reasons for variances, which may be due to foreseeable changes, lack of essential business intelligence sources, a poorly conceived plan or a poorly executed plan.

In addition to performance analysis, critical analysis of capital expenditure or disposal projects is also a feature of financial planning and analysis.

Cost accounting

The development of costs for decision-making is one of the finance department's most important roles because it is here that a significant opportunity is found to contribute to the profit of the company.

The type of cost system employed is determined by the product produced by the enterprise. Manufacture of standard products indicates the need for a standard cost system, non-standard products a job cost system. A brewer will use a process cost system and a contractor a contract cost system. These are just some examples of various systems available for different businesses.

Whatever system is used it should be chosen carefully to suit the needs of the business. There are a number of spin-off benefits derived from a cost system, apart from accumulating costs. For instance, in order to develop standard costs of a product a cost accountant is required to collect historic information on the purchase costs of component parts to enable the material cost standard to be calculated. An alert cost accountant will recognize that this gives him an opportunity to assess purchasing practices. Perhaps by buying in larger lots at less frequent intervals and having the supplier store the parts cost reductions may be achieved. Studies of various items in stock can yield valuable dividends. For instance, the question may be asked as to how many parts are there that have an identical function but are of only slightly different design? Standardization can yield valuable dividends. A cost accountant armed with information derived from his cost system can ask some awkward questions.

One of the largest investments made by business is in stock. Keeping it low but used efficiently, turning it over rapidly, weeding out by disposal in one way or another – all will keep the cost of finance and space down. It is the cost accountant who has all the information to study the dynamics of stock movement and the cost of production. He must use it to spearhead a continuing cost reduction programme.

Treasury

The raising of and conservation of funds employed in the business is the responsibility of the finance director. If the size of the business requires it, the operational aspects of treasury management will be in the hands of a treasurer who reports to the finance director. In smaller businesses, a separate function is not necessary. However it is structured, the following are usually the main activities:

- Raising of capital.
- Negotiating of loans or other financing arrangements.
- Opening of bank accounts and negotiating banking terms.
- Arranging bank transfers.
- Providing guidance on credit terms to be given to customers and accepted from suppliers.
- Establishment of special payment routines such as direct debiting, etc.
- Preparation of cash flow projections.
- Managing excess funds by placing on deposit, etc.
- Cash conservation activities.
- Hedging foreign exchange transactions.

Remember that cash is the life-blood of the business and should be protected accordingly. Many profitable companies have gone to the wall because they didn't watch the cash register. Actions should centre on conservation and accurate forecasting, for example:

- Continually examine forecasting methods and reasons for variances to seek improvements in forecasting and cash control
- Ensure that both trade debtors and other debit balances are regularly and thoroughly reviewed to maximize cash receipts. Review old balances and press for collection.
- Examine ways in which cash outflows are controlled. Payments should be made in such a way that maximum credit periods are taken.

Hedging foreign exchange transactions is a specialist subject requiring consider-

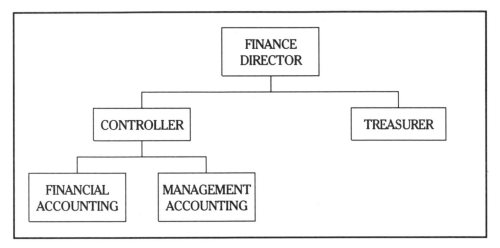

Figure 27.10   A simple structure for the finance department

able expertise, and technical guidance should be sought. In principle, any transaction involving foreign currency should be hedged. Foreign assets should be financed with the related foreign funds. Difficulties can be experienced with contracts priced in foreign currency, particularly during the time between the submission of a proposal, when the company is at risk, and the date of the award when it may or may not obtain the contract. However, banks have a variety of instruments to suit different situations, and if the expertise is not in-house the bank should always be consulted.

Don't forget to set off debit and credit balances within the same time-frame – it's cheaper!

THE FINANCE ORGANIZATION

The organization of the finance department to perform these tasks will depend on the size and nature of the business. Usually, the organization will, in its simplest form, look like the structure shown in Figure 27.10. In smaller organizations there is no need for a Controller.

Financial accounting covers the keeping of the books of account, in whatever form they may exist, and the preparation of monthly management accounts and statutory accounts.

Management accounting is responsible for financial planning and analysis and cost accounting.

Various permutations of this organization exist and quite often the finance department comprises three sections – financial accounting, financial planning and analysis, and cost accounting. They all work – it all depends on the style and specific needs of the finance director.

CHARACTERISTICS OF THE FINANCE STAFF

Having discussed their functions and the way they are organized to carry them out, let's look at their characteristics.

Their role is of a staff nature, supporting other executives and departments by supplying information to assist them in the performance of their duties. Initiative is required in determining their needs and the suitability of information requested. They should find out the purpose to which it will be put and judge its appropriateness. Very often functional executives will request financial data which they themselves will use in preparing studies. If these studies are of a financial nature, they should not be performed by other functions but by the finance department. This avoids incorrect treatment, inconsistencies and faulty conclusions. Inexpert studies of profitability of products, activities, customers, etc are lethal.

Other departmental staff may not come to the finance department when they require assistance. In order to encourage them to do so, the finance staff should anticipate their needs and problems and generally demonstrate their helpfulness.

They should understand the business they are in and the requirements of other departments, spending a lot of time studying their activities in order to determine ways in which they can be most useful. It is important to provide information in a form that others find easy to use but which may not necessarily be the way an accountant would prepare it. Anticipating and supplying the needs of other executives makes them dependent on the finance department.

Simplicity is the watchword. Finance staff should not provide data which others are left to interpret. The purpose of reports must be clearly defined in relation to the end use sought. To provide a report which then has to be reworked and reissued is time-wasting and costly.

Interpretation of reports, studies, analyses and trends must be followed up to ensure action. Unless chased, busy executives often concentrate on routine matters, but it is action that improves business performance, reduces costs and, therefore, improves profits.

They must act as advisers rather than critics. In that way they will be welcomed. The same applies to fairness and impartiality. Lack of these qualities can rapidly destroy their usefulness, and lose them their jobs.

As with any product – and information from the finance department is a product – it may require some selling. This, like most other products, depends on quality. Nothing can destroy the usefulness of finance staff more than the production of inaccurate or incomplete information. Checking and quality control is vital.

In a cost-conscious world, finance staff must be aware of the cost of their product. Continuous examination of ways to improve the way their job is performed is essential, with the emphasis on reducing cost. Studies which are interesting but which do nothing to further the profitability of the enterprise yield nothing.

Finance people are not noted for their presentation and communication skills. Simplicity in preparing displays and charts, comprehensible to the reader, enables speedy decision-making and enhances their usefulness.

STAFFING THE FINANCE DEPARTMENT

It is obvious that the size and complexity of the business will determine staff requirements in terms of numbers and skills, so these comments can only be of a general nature.

These days, where the availability of computer power covers a wide range, from personal computers to large main-frame machines, clerical labour required in a business can be managed down to very low levels. It is vital, therefore, that computer programmes are designed with close involvement of finance personnel who should very clearly define their requirements.

One of the first and most important judgements a finance director must make relates to the financial information base. The objective must be to ensure the integrity of the numbers, that financial information is prepared rapidly, in a form that can be readily used, and is accurate. Not until then can reliable decisions be made from subsequent analysis.

Basically, therefore, staffing considerations of the finance department should be to ensure that the information system provides timely, accurate information with a minimum of clerical labour.

Emphasis should be placed on recruiting skilled financial analysts. Employing a large army of clerks to break down costs into a myriad of parts does not control costs and serves no useful purpose. Cost must always be weighed against the potential financial benefit to be derived. Where, for instance, petty cash is used for expenditure under a specified limit and total amounts are immaterial, why waste time in breaking it down into smaller parts?

RECRUITING AND TRAINING

There are three types of person to be recruited into the finance department. Firstly, there is the accountant type – reliable with the numbers, well-disciplined and fully *au fait* with accounting principles. The source for this person is the profession or, at a lower level, directly from universities with a business administration degree. Secondly, there is the analyst with skills in financial or cost analysis who should have a degree from a good business school and some appropriate post-graduate experience. Thirdly, there is the treasury person with a background in banking, preferably in commercial operations. Of course, if the background is of sufficiently high standard, the easiest place to look is in competitors' offices.

Once on board, having identified in the job interview that the applicant has the appropriate skills, it is important that those skills are properly used. It used to be common, and probably still is in some organizations, for the finance department to be run by a finance director or chief accountant who did all the interesting and exciting tasks, with a group of clerks reporting to him – his arms and legs – who did all the menial and boring jobs. If the finance department is run in this way, the following will occur:

- Nobody will be trained to succeed the finance director or to substitute for him during holidays or illness.
- No one of any calibre will be attracted to the department if there is no interesting and stimulating work to do.
- Morale will be non-existent.
- The performance of the department will be of low quality.

The message is – '*delegate* – but don't *abdicate*'. Sensible delegation separates the good managers from the bad.

It is not enough to recruit someone who will then have to learn on the job. It is important that the employee is not only clearly instructed and trained, but also has a full understanding on what happens in the rest of the finance department and the company. A period of rotation through other departments is very valuable. Regular refresher courses from within the organization or by the professional bodies enables the employee to keep up with 'state-of-the-art' developments and, if carefully selected, can be very useful.

COMMUNICATIONS

If the finance staff is to mould into a team, regular staff meetings must be held. The staff may comprise a Scottish chartered accountant with a degree from Glasgow University as chief accountant, someone who gained experience on the shop floor of British Steel as the manager of the cost department, a graduate from the University of Aston as financial planning and analysis manager, and a treasurer who came from American Express. Each one will gain immeasurably by being exposed to discussions of problems and plans relating to other sections of the department. This can best be achieved by holding regular meetings of the department managers, usually on a weekly basis at a time convenient to all the participants and when all are most likely to be in the office. At these meetings matters concerning the department, progress on action plans, etc. are discussed.

In addition, and particularly for larger organizations, periodic seminars can be most useful. At these seminars, senior members of the finance staff are informed on the performance and progress made by the company and by the finance department in its programme to improve its operations, systems, etc.

Communication pulls a team together, improves its morale and makes an efficient finance department.

SUMMARY

The business ocean is littered with wrecks, many the result of faulty navigation. In the first paragraph of this chapter the finance director was likened to the navigator, with the responsibility for ensuring that the corporate vessel passes safely through what could become treacherous waters. A safe passage requires appropriate instruments of guidance and a competent crew skilled in their application. The successful finance director will have made sure they are available.

CHECKLIST OF KEY POINTS

1   Ensure integrity of the numbers with timely, meaningful financial reporting based on responsibility.

2   The financial function does not end with the production of figures. The accountant is in the best position to analyse them and to suggest courses of action.

3   Forecasts of profit and cash should be prepared regularly with comparable analysis aimed at highlighting trends, always seeking ways to improve their accuracy.

4   Set tough but attainable financial objectives, identifying the means for their attainment and regularly tracking progress through reporting. Chart alternative

courses in the event of unforeseen difficulties so that 'crash' changes are avoided at a time of crisis.

5   Use initiative in selecting analytical tasks. Trends in margins and expense levels, product profitability studies, and analysis of high cost elements are all fertile areas for study. Get close to the business, understand its dynamics and look for opportunities to improve profitability.

6   Develop and improve systems with the objective of minimizing clerical effort so that limited staff resources are directed towards financial planning and analysis.

7   Ensure the availability of adequate financial resources at all times with particular attention to gearing, avoiding the pitfall of placing too much reliance on bank facilities, such as overdrafts, repayable on demand.

8   Maintain good relationships with bankers, keeping them informed of developments within the company. In difficult times nothing is worse than a nervous banker; bankers get nervous if they don't know what's going on.

9   Never lose sight of the need to keep the costs of the finance function as low as possible and always be looking for ways to improve its efficiency.

10   Select good people and provide career progression wherever possible. Keep them informed and develop a good spirit. A finance director is only as good as his or her team.

FURTHER READING

Dickey, R. I., Ed. *Accountant's Cost Handbook*, Ronald Press

Gabor, A., *The Man Who Discovered Quality*, Times Books, 1990

Peters, T. J. and Waterman, R. H. Jnr., *In Search Of Excellence*, Harper and Row, 1982

Sizer, J., *An Insight Into Management Accounting*, Penguin Books, 1979

Welsch, G. A., *Budgeting, Profit Planning and Control*, Prentice-Hall

28 Managing the MIS department

J. Garvin

Management decision-making is often complex and involves a considerable amount of uncertainty. Information is needed to reduce this uncertainty and it is the function of the MIS department to provide that information in a cost-effective way. It is useful at this point to differentiate between *data* and *information*. Although these two terms are often used interchangeably they can be more precisely defined to illustrate a fundamental difference.

Data refers to collections of facts and figures, which for processing purposes are organized into structures and groups, and form the *input* to a management information system (MIS).
Information is data that have been processed into a form that is meaningful to the recipient, and is of real or perceived value in supporting decision-making. It thus forms the *output* from a management information system.

Computerized management information systems are capable of producing vast amounts of indigestible data which hinder rather than help managers in making quick, effective decisions. It is important, therefore, that MIS designers clearly understand the use that will be made of the output to be produced, and specify the form of presentation appropriately.

INFORMATION NEEDS OF MANAGERS

Most of the information required by managers is to help them *plan* and *control* the activities for which they are responsible, but the nature of this information differs depending on their position within the organization hierarchy.

Strategic (or Top) management makes long term decisions regarding overall organizational objectives. Consequently, planning information predominates, based on external information and summarized internal information.

Tactical (or Middle) management implements policies set by top management, requiring decisions with a time scale of months rather than years. Their information needs are more evenly balanced between planning and control, external and internal, and summarized vs. detail information.

Operational (or Lower) management deals mainly with day-to-day decisions, so they require mostly internal information of a detailed nature, for control purposes.

The reasons why managers do not use MIS output reports can be reduced to:

- *Relevance* The information supplied is not thought to be relevant to the user's area of responsibility.
- *Accuracy* The output is perceived as being insufficiently accurate.
- *Timeliness* Information received too late to be of value.
- *Ease of use* The time and effort required to extract the required information exceeds the benefit to be gained from it.
- *Detail* Insufficient or too much detail renders the information useless for the intended purpose.
- *Comprehensibility* Information not understood.

Most, if not all, of these problems can be overcome by proper consultation with users at the *analysis* stage, continued liaison at the *design* stage, careful customer testing and education at the *implementation* stage, and ongoing monitoring and review during the *operation* stage.

Utility value of information

This is the value of information to the organization in terms of the benefits it is able to generate. The *net utility value* is the amount by which the utility value exceeds the costs required to produce it.

HARDWARE AND SOFTWARE

Hardwear

Hardware is the name given to the physical components of a computer system. There are four basic components involved in data handling, as shown in Figure 28.1.

Classification of hardware

Computers can be classified according to size, speed, and storage capability into one of three categories:

1 *Mainframes and supercomputers.* These are the largest and most expensive and can process millions of instructions per second.
2 *Minicomputers.* These are smaller and cheaper than mainframes, but are powerful enough to satisfy the needs of most small to medium sized businesses.
3 *Microcomputers.* The smallest computers, such as desk-top and personal

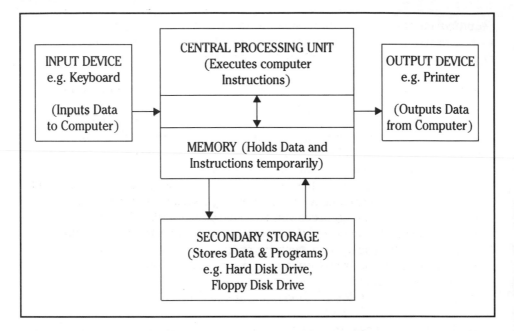

Figure 28.1   The four basic components involved in data handling

computers (PCs), fall into this category, and are so inexpensive and powerful that they have become widely used in all kinds of organizations. They are typically operated by only one user at a time, unlike the two larger types of machine which can be accessed by more than one user at the same time.

MIS departments are usually concerned with the effective operation of mainframe and minicomputers on which data are processed centrally, but the proliferation of personal computers independently of central control has created new problems. Many organizations have responded by creating an *Information centre* within the MIS department to provide users with support in operating their own equipment involving:

- Setting *standards* for PC hardware and software.
- Providing *training* and *support* to users for standard hardware and software.
- Giving *advice* to users on suitable software to meet their needs.
- Controlling *access* to corporate data.
- Providing *technical assistance* when required.
- Applying *cost control* criteria to applications.
- Ensuring *data security* and *integrity* to comply with the Data Protection Act.

Software

Computer software are the sets of instructions that enable computers to turn data into information. Software may be packaged and sold for general use, or written specially for a specific client.

Classification of software

There are two general types of software, *horizontal* and *vertical.*

Horizontal Software is not developed for one specific task but provides a 'shell' within which the user develops specific applications, often using 'menus' or lists from which options can be selected. The most common of these are *spreadsheets, database managers* and *word processing* packages, with *'integrated packages'* which combine the capabilities of all three also becoming widely used.

Vertical Software is software that is developed for specific tasks, e.g. stock control systems for inventory management, accounting systems covering accounts payable and receivable and general ledger requirements, planning and scheduling systems for production control purposes, etc. Such software can be produced 'in house' by the MIS Department with its own programming capabilities, or contracted out to a specialist software company or consultancy.

CENTRALIZATION vs DECENTRALIZATION

In centralized computing, all input, processing, and output is carried out in the MIS Department on a central computer. In a decentralized system, terminals are placed in various locations away from the main computer and are linked to it to provide access. In a *distributed data processing* system the actual processing is dispersed to user locations where microcomputers can be operated independently, or linked via a *network* to enable data to be passed between them. The decision on the degree of decentralization to be adopted in an organization is a difficult one which requires careful consideration, and must take into account the organization's future requirements as well as those of the present.

THE USER AS A CUSTOMER

The MIS Department should adopt a policy of regarding users as 'customers' whose needs are paramount. Thus the quality of service provided should be regularly assessed from the customers' viewpoint, and improved as necessary.

CHARGING OUT

If MIS and computing costs are treated as a corporate overhead, users tend to view such services as 'free' and see increasing computerization as a way of reducing their own costs – even when applications are of dubious utility. By 'charging out' the costs involved, such undesirable applications are eliminated, users expect higher standards of service, and greater efficiency in the use of MIS department resources is encouraged.

MIS MATURITY IN ORGANIZATIONS

Since management information systems are continually being developed and expanded in most organizations, there is a continuum along which they progress with time. A number of stages can be identified which indicate the level of maturity reached:

Stage 1 Introduction of *transactional processing* systems for routine data processing (payroll, stock control, bills of material, etc) with summary reports for management use.

Stage 2 Development of *management information systems* within functional areas to aid control, mainly by the analysis of historical data. Manual integration between such applications, e.g. by transfer of data on 'floppy' disks.

Stage 3 Automated integration of functional data into corporate MIS for control purposes. Development of *decision support systems* incorporating probability theory, modelling and simulation techniques, with 'what if?' capabilities to assist in planning within functional areas.

Stage 4 Introduction of *external* (i.e. environmental) data to develop MIS's capable of supporting decision-making at the strategic level. Overall management planning becomes increasingly dependent on such systems.

Stage 5 Extension to a totally integrated MIS application portfolio including knowledge-based and expert systems capable of dealing with uncertainty in non-repetitive decision-making at the highest level. As well as involving the user in the decision process, such systems can search for optimum solutions, and explain how solutions have been reached.

Most organizations will have reached Stages Two, Three or Four, and when planning future developments should take account of their current status and the next logical stage as indicated above.

Now that we have completed a review of the general scenario in which management information systems are developed and used, we can turn our attention to the *planning, organizing* and *controlling* of the MIS department itself, with the objective of optimizing its effectiveness and efficiency in pursuit of the overall corporate objectives of the organization.

PLANNING IN THE MIS DEPARTMENT

It is essential that the overall corporate objectives of the organization, and the policies required to achieve them, have been established before planning of the MIS strategy commences. Once the goals and objectives for each functional area have been set, attention can be directed towards identifying the information required to ensure that they will be achieved.

Identifying user needs

The information needs of user departments can be established by means of *interviews* and *questionnaires*. It is preferable for the MIS manager to hold interviews individually with managers of user departments, at least initially. Group discussions can be dominated by individuals with strong personalities, sometimes inhibiting others with a worthwhile contribution to make.

Once basic requirements have been established, the MIS manager, in conjunction with specialist staff from his/her own department, can begin to draw up a plan to satisfy these needs. In doing so, the need to integrate the various requirements as far as possible with common data flows, data bases, and output reports should be uppermost in his mind. As the plan comes together, further discussions with users will be necessary to ensure agreement on the proposals.

A 'top-down' approach to systems design which starts with the major functions or objectives, and then breaks them down into increasing levels of detail until the lowest level is reached, is useful here. When combined with a *modular* approach where the overall system is made up of modules or blocks, a particularly robust and flexible system results, which is more easily modified and developed to meet future requirements. The advantage at this stage is that the major building blocks for a system can be quickly decided upon, giving a much better basis on which to estimate the time and resources required to be allocated to them.

Preparation of the master plan

The final product of the planning stage should be a *master plan* which shows the activities to be carried out in the MIS department over the next year, and estimates of the resulting workload. It may be desirable to extend the horizon to two or even three years if several projects of long duration are involved, in which case the proposals should be classed as *firm* for one year and *tentative* beyond that. The *master plan* is built up from:

- a systems development plan, and
- an operations plan.

The systems development plan

This is best drawn up in Gantt chart form (see page 418) to show the planned *start, duration* and *finish* times for each project to be undertaken, or in the case of large projects, for each module involved. It is a 'high-level' view showing:

- the order in which projects will be tackled;
- the start and finish times for the *major phases* (ie. analysis, design and implementation) of each project, or module;
- an estimate of the resources required in each time period for each project, e.g. number of analysts, programmers, etc;
- a total for each resource over all projects in each time period.

Although analysts and programmers carry the bulk of the load involved in new projects, some data preparation, data base updating, and computer operations are usually involved at the testing and implementation stages and this must be included.

The operations plan

Of equal importance to the development of new systems is the running and routine maintenance of current systems. Although the work load falls mainly on staff involved in data preparation, data base maintenance and computer operation, there is some involvement by systems analysts in answering queries and investigating problems, and by programmers correcting coding errors. As this is impossible to forecast in detail, it is sufficient to allocate a proportion of analysts' and programmers' time to maintenance of this kind, (typically 10–20%).

The load per time period on each resource due to the systems currently operating, less any it has been agreed should be phased out, plus those planned for implementation (from the systems development plan) with adjustments to allow for anticipated growth or decline in throughput, constitutes the final operations plan.

Finalizing the master plan

Some 'fine tuning' of schedules and iteration between stages is inevitably required to even out the workload on the department when the systems development and operations plans are combined. All such changes need to be discussed with the managers or departments which will be affected, and the approval of management at the highest level obtained, so that the final plan is universally understood and accepted. This ensures that the resources required to meet the plan are committed to, and that the problem of constantly changing priorities, which is so wasteful of resources in the MIS department, is minimized.

It is also important that all members of the MIS department itself are actively involved in the preparation of these plans, particularly in estimating the times required for completion of activities in which they will be involved. This increases awareness and commitment, and reduces the likelihood of projects running late.

ORGANIZING THE MIS DEPARTMENT

Organization structure

The detailed structure of the MIS organization depends very much on its size and complexity, and the exact nature of its responsibilities. Generally, however, there are two distinct divisions within the department which are concerned with (a) *systems development* and (b) *operations*.

Systems development includes all systems analysis, programming, PC information centre activities and personnel who are mainly involved in the design and development of new MIS applications, and the improvement of those currently in use.

Operations deals with the day-to-day running of current management information systems and involves the data preparation, database maintenance and security, and computer operations activities.

Allocation of responsibilities

As with the organization of any department, the responsibilities associated with each job title must be clearly defined and set out in a proper job description. It is the responsibility of the MIS manager to ensure that there are no 'loose ends' in this respect, nor any overlapping of responsibilities which might lead to conflict.

Having identified the general responsibilities associated with each job, the specific responsibilities involved with achievement of the *master plan* for the year ahead can now be allocated to individuals or groups of individuals.

Sometimes it may be preferable to leave the short term allocation of work between analysts or programmers to a senior analyst or senior programmer. This gives greater flexibility in use of resources, but the responsibility for keeping on schedule and within budget for specific projects then passes to the supervisor concerned.

Measuring capacity

To ensure that capacity is adequate to fulfil commitments, it is necessary to have some unit of measurement for each resource.

Data preparation and manual data input capacities can be measured in 'key depressions per minute' per operator. Standards exist for competent, trained operators and input rates can be recorded by much of the equipment used. Computers can log the time required to run individual jobs, and averages over a number of runs can be used for planning purposes. With experience, reliable estimates of the run time for future work can be made, based on the amount of input, processing and output involved. Capacity depends on the number of shifts operated, the hours available per shift, and the utilization achieved.

For programming, estimating the workload and measuring the capacity are much more difficult. In general, it is probably adequate to estimate workload in man hours or man weeks for direct comparison with resources available.

Similarly, an analyst's workload is measured in man hours or man weeks which makes for easy comparison with capacity. As with any form of estimating, accuracy improves with experience, particularly when actual times are regularly compared with estimates, and differences analysed.

Scheduling workload

By breaking down the *master plan* into commitments against each resource and specifying in greater detail what is involved, a work schedule can be extracted for each individual or group of individuals, as appropriate. By regular monitoring of progress against this schedule (at least once per week), deviations can be noted at an early stage, and corrective action taken as necessary. (See the section – Controlling the MIS department – for more detail).

Allocation of work

For analysts in particular, it is best to assign individuals to work in particular functional areas. One analyst may deal with all the accounting systems for

413

instance, another with production and inventory control systems, etc. This can work very well as individuals build up detailed knowledge about specific areas and are recognized as the authority in particular fields.

Too much specialization, however, can be dangerous, particularly when someone leaves. By assigning analysts to assist on large projects in areas which are not their speciality, their experience grows. This is particularly valuable as applications develop across functional boundaries. Rotation between jobs can also be useful in stimulating new interest, and bringing fresh insight to an established area.

Experienced programmers are best allocated the most difficult work on new projects, the less experienced attending to more routine modification work and 'debugging'. Similarly, tests and initial runs of new systems on the computer are best carried out by the more senior and experienced operators, until all the problems have been ironed out.

Staff training

Owing to the rate at which technology in computing develops, it is difficult to keep up to date. It is important, therefore, to set time aside for attendance at training courses and conferences for all personnel. Since most of the staff in this area will be computer specialists, it is desirable that they should undergo training in general business disciplines as well. Secondment to user departments within the organization for a few months could be an investment that pays handsome dividends.

Motivation

An efficient, well run department which sets clear goals for its members, monitors performance carefully, and rewards good performance with personal development and a clear career path, should not experience problems with motivation. High levels of achievement, especially in 'leading-edge' MIS applications, are the most effective motivators of all.

PROJECT PLANNING AND CONTROL

Because major projects on new MIS applications form such a sizeable proportion of the department workload, and involve so much interaction with other departments, this section will deal exclusively with the problem of planning and controlling them.

Stages of a project

These are best illustrated by means of a flowchart, as shown in Figure 28.2.

Stage 1 – The feasibility study. This entails a fairly brief study of the problem, normally by a systems analyst, to determine if the proposal is (a) technically feasible, (b) economically desirable. The output is a brief report summarizing the findings, and includes estimates of the cost of a suitable system and the anticipated benefits both tangible (i.e. costed) and intangible (cannot be costed).

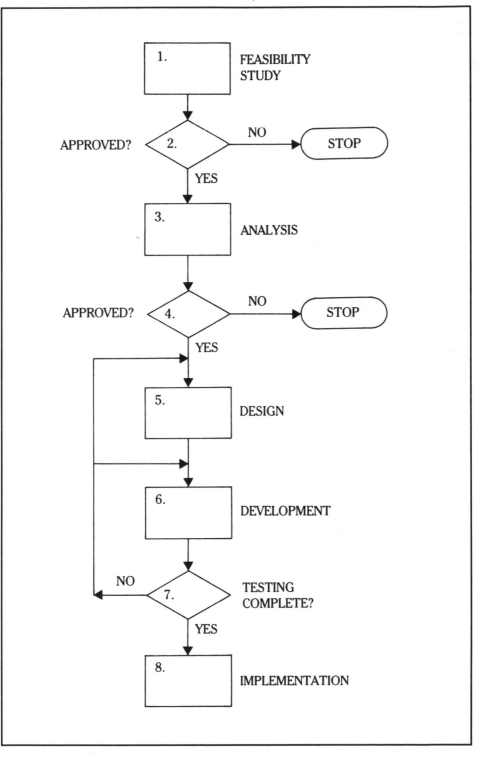

Figure 28.2 Flowchart showing stages of a project

Stage 2 – Management approval. Depending on the scale and costs of the project, management approval may be required at different levels, e.g. full Board approval for major projects over £100 000. If approval is given, the project proceeds, otherwise it stops.

Stage 3 – The analysis stage This involves a full-blown analysis of the problem, of the present system, and of the requirements of the customer in terms of output. Detailed analysis of costs and benefits are included in the report to management produced from this stage.

Stage 4 – Management approval In the light of the much more detailed analysis of the proposal and its costs and benefits, management once again must give it the stamp of approval for it to proceed, otherwise the project is halted.

Stage 5 – Systems design This involves the analyst in designing the output, determining what input (s) and processing will be required, and evaluating alternatives in terms of hardware and software. More than one solution may be possible and choices to be made in discussion with the various parties involved. A prototype or model may even be produced to help the user or client clarify exact requirements. The ultimate output is a detailed design specification which passes to the next stage.

Stage 6 – Development The principal activities here are *programming* and *testing*. *Programming* involves coding the instructions required to comply with the specification supplied by the analyst.

Testing takes place in three stages:

- Program (or unit) testing of individual programs.
- System testing to ensure that all the programs work together.

Both these stages are carried out by the programmer using test data which is specially produced to test for likely errors.

- Volume or customer testing. Real data are used in this case in large volumes which can reveal errors not shown up by test data. The test should be organized by the analyst in conjunction with the 'customer' who should satisfy himself that all is in order, and sign his name to that effect.

Stage 7 – Testing Completed Only when all testing has been completed and the customer has confirmed that he is satisfied with the output, can the implementation commence.

Stage 8 – Implementation This involves *education* and *training* of users and issue of a user manual, creation or conversion of *files* where required, and introduction of additional *hardware* that may be necessary. When all is in place the *system conversion* takes place, i.e. the new system is put into operation. This can be done in a number of ways:

- *Direct conversion* – the old system is replaced by the new one in one step.

- *Phased conversion* – the old system is replaced by the new one in a series of steps.
- *Pilot conversion* – the entire system is adopted by some of the users until it has been proved, then it is universally introduced.
- *Parallel conversion* – both the old and the new systems are operated simultaneously for some time until the old one can safely be dispensed with.

The most appropriate method to use depends on a number of factors including the cost of each alternative and the risk associated with it. Thorough testing at the development stage diminishes the risk considerably, and is normally considerably less expensive than parallel running which it can render unnecessary.

During system conversion, full support is required from the MIS department to deal with any teething troubles, but this can be reduced once the system has settled down.

Planning the project

Although the project should appear on the MIS department *master plan*, the level of detail is not sufficient for proper monitoring purposes. At the analysis stage of the project, however, a very detailed plan is produced, normally in Gantt chart form, showing what is involved right through to implementation (See figure 28.3). It is this plan that is used for monitoring progress.

Project controller

Except for minor projects which can be satisfactorily controlled by the MIS department, all others should have a project controller appointed from the user area who assumes responsibility for the overall project. This gives ownership of the system and its project to the user, who has a vested interest in achieving success and can ensure that adequate time and resources are devoted to the project by the customer.

For really large systems which involve several functional areas, it is usual to appoint a *steering committee* made up of senior managers from each of the areas involved. This committee assumes overall responsibility, and is the body to whom the project controller reports.

Control of the project

The project controller monitors progress regularly, usually calling weekly meetings for this purpose, and reports to the steering committee less frequently, e.g. monthly, or at significant milestones in the plan. The MIS manager, or the analyst involved, would attend the weekly meetings to report progress by the department. The MIS manager may well be a member of the steering committee. Minutes should be issued highlighting deviations from plan, decisions made, actions required, etc, so that concerted action is taken when necessary. Monitoring of costs is also an important part of the project controller's responsibilities.

Project: **STOCK CONTROL SYSTEM** Prepared by: A. N. OTHER Date: 12/12/1990

ACTIVITY SCHEDULE

	ACTIVITY	1991 1	2	3	4	5	6	7	8	9	10	11	12	1992 1	2	3	4	5
1	PRELIM. DESIGN	▪	▪															
2	MAIN SYST. DESIGN		▪	▪														
3	SYSTEM SPEC.				▪	▪	▪											
4	WRITING USERS' MANUAL							▪	▪									
5	TRAINING USERS									▪	▪							
6	SYSTEM TEST										▪	▪						
7	CUSTOMER TEST											▪	▪					
8	IMPLEMENTATION												▪	▪				
	TOTAL SYSTEMS ANALYSTS (1–8)	¼	¼	½	½	1	1	1	1	½	1	1	1	½				
1	CODING PROGRAMS						▪	▪	▪									
2	TEST/MOD. PROGRAMS									▪	▪	▪	▪					
	TOTAL PROGRAMMERS (1–2)						1	2	2	1	¼	¼	¼					

Figure 28.3(a) Project plan – Gantt chart showing activity schedules

STOCK CONTROL SYSTEM

Project:

Prepared by: A. N. OTHER

Date: 12/12/1990

RESOURCE SCHEDULE

RESOURCE		MONTH	1991 1	2	3	4	5	6	7	8	9	10	11	12	1992 1	2	3	4	5
ANALYSTS	PROJECT		¼	¼	½	½	1	1	1	1	½	1	1	1	½				
	MAINT.														½	½	½		
PROGRAMMERS	PROJECT							1	2	2	1	¼	¼	¼					
	MAINT.														¼	¼	¼		
TRAINING STAFF										½	1	1	½	½					
LINE STAFF										½	1	2	1	2	1				
COMPUTER TIME (HRS)	TESTING									2	8	2	4						
	PARALLEL RUN												5	5	5				
DATA PREP. STAFF									¼	¼	½	½	½	¼	¼				

Figure 28.3(b) Project plan – summary resource schedule

419

CONTROLLING THE MIS DEPARTMENT

As with planning, there are two main aspects of control, namely, (a) control of systems development, and (b) control of operations.

Control of systems development

A regular departmental meeting can be held, say once a week, to review progress against the master plan. Each systems analyst should report on the projects for which he is responsible, highlighting milestones passed and any particular problems encountered. These reports should be brief summaries only (detailed reporting on major projects has been dealt with in the previous section), serving as a vehicle for keeping everyone informed about the overall progress of the department.

An informal atmosphere can encourage a free exchange of ideas, promote a group approach to problem solving, and reduce the feeling of isolation that can affect someone working on their own most of the time. The MIS manager can use this opportunity to adjust resources and priorities when necessary to achieve targets, and to decide what actions are required to overcome any problems.

Progress by the programming team can often be adequately reported by a senior programmer or supervisor for all projects. An additional summary of programming modifications completed, in hand, and outstanding will help to complete the picture.

Control of operations

Operations need to be monitored on a day-to-day basis by a supervisor or senior operator, who can report to the weekly meeting using summary measures, e.g. 'down' time on the computer, actual operating hours, throughput trends, etc, and highlight any exceptional problems which require attention.

The outcome of the weekly meeting should be a clear understanding by everyone of the current status of the projects with which they are involved, the action(s) they need to take over the next week to remain on target, and impending problems that they need to address. A formal written report of the proceedings is desirable, circulated to senior management as well as internally in the department, to keep everyone informed.

Auditing management information systems

Besides the financial auditing of their affairs required by law, many organizations carry out regular quality audits and management audits. It is good practice, though not often applied, to carry out audits of management information systems. Once a system has been implemented long enough to have settled down, a detailed review should be carried out to check that:

- performance is satisfactory;
- output is being used as intended;

- costed benefits are being realized;
- running costs are in line with estimates.

Any deficiencies can then be addressed quickly to ensure that the effectiveness and efficiency of the system are maximized, and that payback periods are not exceeded. In addition, on a yearly basis, all management information systems currently in operation should be reviewed to ensure that:

- they are still required;
- they are being fully used;
- the value of benefits is brought up-to-date;
- the running costs are correct.

As a result of this audit, decisions can be made to phase out uneconomic systems, eliminate unused reports (or some copies of them), and to consider re-designing systems which are becoming outdated.

The costed benefits of individual systems can be totalled and compared with the costs of operation of the MIS department, to ensure that it is effective as a service organization. A 'profit' can be a considerable morale booster, a 'loss' can focus minds on the need to improve the value of the service provided.

Security

One of the most important aspects of control is ensuring the security and integrity of data. In particular the Data Protection Act of 1984 imposes certain legal obligations on the processors of personal data (i.e. data relating to living individuals) in that such data must be accurate, up-to-date, and protected from loss or unauthorized access. Since these requirements apply equally to much of the data processed which is not of a personal nature, there is a need to ensure that:

1   Computer hardware is safeguarded by restricting access to it, and by protecting it from possible fire and other hazards.
2   Back-up copies of programs and data bases are safely held in secure locations separate from the normal processing area.
3   Input data are subject to validity checks by the computer where possible, and manual input is reduced to a minimum by the use of data capture techniques employing badges, bar codes, etc.
4   Access via remote terminals is controlled by means of access codes allocated to specific individuals and changed frequently, and such access is logged by the computer where sensitive data are involved.
5   Distribution of output is controlled, and terminals and microcomputers are positioned so that screens are not visible to casual passers-by.

The loss of all or a significant part of its computerized management information can be a disaster to any organization, so considerable effort should be expended to safeguard it, and to prepare contingency plans to deal with such an emergency.

SUMMARY

The responsibility of the MIS department is to provide information to management in a cost-effective way. This means providing the right information to the right people at the right time in the right form, at an acceptable cost.

In this chapter, I have tried to show how this can be achieved. Many of the activities are particularly difficult to carry out, but with care and attention to detail, plus a willingness to learn from past mistakes, the techniques described in this chapter can be most effective.

The end result, a management information systems department which is seen to be effective, and a valuable resource in enabling all levels of management to achieve their objectives, is worth all the effort involved.

CHECKLIST OF KEY POINTS

There is a need for:

- Correct identification of user needs.
- Careful, detailed planning.
- Effective control of the use of resources.
- Regular liaison within the department, and with other departments.
- Continued feedback to assist control.
- Emphasis on cost justification of all activities.

FURTHER READING

ACCA, *Systems Analysis and Design*, ACCA (Accountancy) Study Text 2.7, BPP Publishing, 1987

Edwards, Ward and Bytheway, *The Essence of Information Systems*, Prentice Hall, 1991

Ahituv and Neumann, *Principles of Information Systems for Management*, W. C. Brown, 1986

Capron and Duffy, *Using Microcomputers – a complete introduction*, Benjamin/ Cummings Publishing Company, 1989

Szymanski, Szymanski, Morris and Pulschen, *Introduction to Computers and Information Systems*, Merrill Publishing Company, 1988

Part IV
MANAGING THE BUSINESS

Introduction: understanding the business

Last but not least, you need to understand the business. There are enormous differences between industries and between individual businesses within an industry, but there are also skills and knowledge held in common. The secret of success as a manager is to broaden your skills and knowledge base to include something of all these, instead of sticking narrowly to your technical specialism, accounting, production, marketing etc, which earned you your promotion to management. Great managers are generalists.

Understanding the business provides answers to such fundamental questions as: why are we here? what do we think we are doing? what should we be doing? how do we do it? If you feel these questions are perhaps a little metaphysical for a manager, consider how even the great seat-of-the-pants operators can also come unstuck. Prevention *is* better than cure.

In Part IV we offer ways of thinking about these matters as well as guidelines for developing your own business skills. It begins with an introduction to accounting, written to dispel the non-accountant's bafflement. A chapter on the whole process of project management, from project concept to post-completion audit, applies to every function of management, but may perhaps be seen to add a production viewpoint.

Three techniques chapters follow in areas which are crucial to the business: creativity and innovation (and not just for new product development); decision making and problem solving; and negotiating.

29 Financial information and management

William P. Rees

A number of surveys have suggested that accounting information is probably the most influential source of information for investment analysts. One such study, by Arnold and Mozier, reported that the income statement was ranked first, the balance sheet second, half yearly results were third, and the source and application of funds was fifth. (Direct contact with company personnel was ranked fourth whilst many of the remaining twelve categories were accounting based.) This dominance of accounting information as inputs into the decisions of these specialists rather encourages accountants whose faith in their product can be sorely tested by the awareness of its subjectivity and irrationality. Many have rejected the usefulness of accounting data after examining the difficulties of producing meaningful financial reports. However, the converse of the sceptics' rejection of accounting information is the arguably more dangerous reliance that the uninitiated may place on the apparent numeric exactitude of accounting statements, coupled with a reverential awe of the alchemy employed by the fiscal wizards who produce them.

It is the purpose of this chapter to give those uninitiated in the use of accounting information a balanced view of the reliability of the information produced by accountants, to convince them that a knowledge of the detailed methods of accountancy is unnecessary to its understanding, to explain and illustrate the techniques of financial interpretation, and to show how accounting information is used in management decision making. Throughout, the level of technical explanation is elementary, whereas a relatively sophisticated discussion of the implications is considered important to business managers. Jargon is kept to a minimum but the occasional technical term cannot be avoided. This chapter can usefully be read in conjunction with Charles Verrall's description of the organizational necessities of financial management in Chapter 27.

The chapter is divided into four sections. In the first the process used by accountants to distil measures of income and wealth from a vast array of transactions is examined. The explicit focus is on the formal reporting system for the preparation of published accounts but in most organizations the same principles are employed for the internal reporting system. The second section examines the accounting statements of two competing organizations to illustrate the information that can be extracted from these data and the degree of reliance that can be placed on them. The later part of this section concentrates on the technique of ratio analysis. The third section drops the emphasis on external reporting and considers the managerial uses of accounting data, either for evaluating decisions or for monitoring progress. Although in many instances the accounting system will be part of this managerial process the information used is less formal or prescribed. The final section concludes the discussion.

THE ACCOUNTING PROCESS

Accounting attempts to measure two interrelated concepts; income and wealth. It should be emphasized that as concepts these are not directly observable phenomena. Consequently a set of rules has become generally accepted or enforced to try to impose some measure of standardization on the assessment of these two ephemera. This is best illustrated by an example, focusing on one of the many transactions which might make up the activities of an organization.

In this example a contract for the sale of a 'stegdiw' is won in month 1, and the raw material is immediately ordered and received. In month 2 the supplier is paid £500 in full settlement and the labour force completes and is paid for £500 worth of work. The 'stegdiw' is delivered in month 3, and full payment of £1 500 is received in month 4. In addition monthly overheads of £150 are incurred and an asset costing £2 400 with an expected life of 24 months is being utilized.

The transactions involved, together with the conventional accounting representation of these transactions, are shown in Figure 29.1.

Whilst this is a naive example it does illustrate most of the problems involved in accounting.

- Notice that there is no correlation between profit and cash flows. In the long run there is a usual but not necessary link. This difference, or time lag, has been the downfall of many a profitable and expanding company.
- The income is taken to profit and loss account not when the order is received, nor when cash payment is made, but (usually) when the product is delivered.
- Expenses are taken to the profit and loss account, either when incurred, in the case of general expenses, or when the revenue for the product they have created is accounted for. Thus expenses are matched to the relevant income.

   This point is especially significant in the case of the depreciation charge for the asset purchased. The expense is gradually accounted for over the expected life of the asset. This means that the balance sheet figure representing fixed assets is simply that proportion of the cost of the asset which has not yet been written off as an expense, even though it is often thought of as an estimate of the asset's value. Strictly speaking depreciation costs incurred in producing the asset should be added to the stock value in a similar manner to the labour costs.

- There is no necessary link between accounting measures of income and wealth and the underlying economic values. The asset values in the balance

	Month 1	Month 2	Month 3	Month 4
CASH FLOWS				
Purchases		(500)		
Labour		(500)		
Payment				1500
Overheads	(150)	(150)	(150)	(150)
	(150)	(1150)	(150)	1350
PROFIT AND LOSS				
Sales			1500	
Labour		(500)		
Purchases	(500)			
Stock adj.	500	500	1000	
Gross profit			500	—
Overheads	(150)	(150)	(150)	(150)
Depreciation	(100)	(100)	(100)	(100)
Net profit	(250)	(250)	250	(250)
BALANCE SHEET				
Fixed assets	2300	2200	2100	2000
Stock	500	1000		
Debtors			1500	
Bank	(150)	(1300)	(1450)	(100)
Creditors	(500)			
	2150	1900	2150	1900
Opening capital	2400	2150	1900	2150
Profit/loss	(250)	(250)	250	(250)
Closing capital	2150	1900	2150	1900

Figure 29.1   Example accounting transaction

sheet are neither an assessment of the realizable value nor the replacement cost of the asset. Even if they were, the value of the firm as a whole may well be very different from the value of its constituent parts. In our example a valuation of the firm would have recognized the impact of the contract when it was won, not as it was completed.

This dichotomy between accounting and economic values can be shown by example if we accept stock market capitalization of a company's shares as their economic value and compare this with the accounting measure of shareholders' equity (see Figure 29.2). It can be seen that the accounting measure of value is very different from the market's. More crucially the relationship between the two is unstable.

- Because there is a difference between the date at which inputs are purchased, notably fixed assets and stock, the date at which they are used in the production process, and the date at which the product is sold, the original

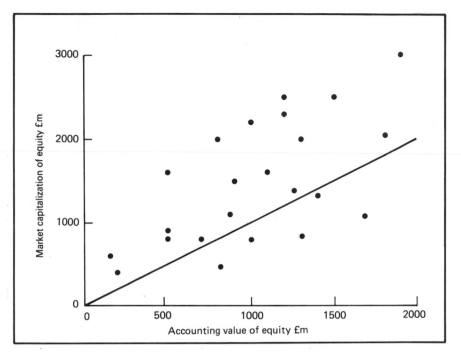

Figure 29.2   Accounting value of equity *vs* stock market capitalization

(The data refer to a cross-section of companies from the FT 100. Companies whose accounting value is equal to the market capitalization would lie on the line shown.)

measure of the cost of these expenses is no longer accurate. This is due to the change in the purchasing power of sterling due to general price level inflation; and the change in the value of these costs in relation to other items. Both these factors will tend to distort and, in the case of productive as opposed to financial companies, usually overstate any traditional accounting measure of income. Furthermore, if assets or liabilities are held which are measured in monetary amounts, such as debtors, creditors, loans, and bank balances, a company can incur a holding gain or loss during inflationary times. This element of income is not measured by traditional accounting systems.

- When accounts are prepared for any company there will be a great many transactions in various stages of completion at the accounting date and many more that will have been completed during the period under review. The sheer magnitude of the task involved in collating and valuing the myriad transactions presents a serious practical problem in measurement for the accountant and the degree of subjectivity involved complicates the auditor's task of verification.

We can see that accounting tries to measure income and wealth by applying a set of procedures. For the UK these are laid down in the Companies Acts, by the Stock Exchange for quoted companies, and in Statements of Standard Accounting Practice prepared by the accounting profession. These requirements attempt to standardize a vast range of accounting practices but they must leave room for sufficient flexibility to accommodate differing circumstances. It is this scope for subjectivity which periodically excites a considerable degree of criticism of (creative) accounting practices. Whilst there is some truth in the complaints the alternative of a more regimented system may lead to less meaningful accounting statements and will certainly impose some costs on the firm and its shareholders. Whilst the detail is uninteresting there are certain general conventions which would bear examination.

- The accruals (or matching) convention. This refers to the attempt to account for expenses in the same period in which related revenues are treated and results in profit measurement differing from cash flows.
- The prudence convention. This governs the timing of the realization of income, and hence expenses, in the accounts. As prospective losses are more readily allowed than future profits a pessimistic bias is reflected in the accounts.
- The consistency convention. Given the choices available from a wide spectrum of accounting practices it is desirable that a company should be restrained from switching between alternatives to suit its own convenience.
- The going concern convention. This assumes that the company will persist for the foreseeable future and that the value of assets on liquidation is thereby not normally relevant.

Further to those specified, a number of implicit but not necessarily trivial conventions apply. First we measure and aggregate diverse items in monetary amounts though the value of money is not stable. Second, we define and report on an entity but the specification of that entity can be problematical when groups of companies are involved. Finally we define and report on a specified period of time and it is the attempt to allocate transactions to particular periods that creates many of our problems.

It is interesting to speculate why these conventions and the multiplicity of more detailed rules have come into being. We have seen that they fail to produce measures that are consistent with economic reality, that they fail to cope with the distorting effects of inflation and that flexibility in the accounting rules, together with the subjectivity required in applying them, allows considerable scope for 'creative accounting'. This does not sound like a strong recommendation. However, the source of these conventions lies not in any deep and consistent theory, but in a pragmatic trade-off between economic relevance and practicality. These accounting rules were adopted as standard practice because they were, rather more flexibly, general practice. As such they represent the distillation of experience.

Many times in the last twenty-five years, commentators have suggested that accounting measurement is flawed and that alternative financial statements are required. Yet no alternative has yet proved viable and analysts still pay more regard to accounting information than to other variables. If one is aware of the shortcomings of accounting statements and knows what to trust and how far to trust it, such statements contain a vast range of useful data relevant to many decisions. That is not to say that improved methods of accounting for inflation, or alternatives to income measurement-based statements, could not perform much the same, or even complementary functions. But it is conventional historic cost statements which are currently understood and utilized, though not necessarily at the same time, by the business world for external reporting and within an organization for decision making and control procedures.

UNDERSTANDING ACCOUNTING INFORMATION

It can be seen from the preceding section that accounting is not only an imprecise language, but it is not always sure what it is trying to say, let alone how to say it. Under these circumstances the value of the accounting numbers comes not from their absolute value but from the comparison with others. The problem here is to find valid comparisons. The measurement difficulties and the instability of any bias mean that the performance for one company in any year cannot easily be compared with the results of a different company or year. To give some insight into the information that can be drawn from accounting statements, this section will describe and compare the accounts of two typical companies.

A further difficulty is the mass of data presented and the awkwardness involved in making comparisons between organizations of differing size. Both of these problems can be countered to some extent by the use of ratio analysis which concentrates the information contained in accounting statements into summary statistics and in doing so attempts to standardize the ratio for size.

The accounting statements

The exhibits here are simplified and adjusted data from two large quoted companies operating across a diversified range of activities (see Figure 29.3). The accounts are prepared for the group as a whole with subsidiaries (at least 50 per cent owned) 'consolidated' into the totals. Other partly owned companies, associated companies or investments are accounted for by a variety of methods which only take account of the relevant proportion of the investment.

According to the accounting profession's discussion document, *The Corporate Report*, 'Financial position statements (balance sheets) should be concerned with disclosing the amount and sources of capital employed and an appropriate analysis of its disposition'. (This document has been superseded by a number of more recent discussion papers produced by the various bodies which make up the British accounting profession. However *The Corporate Report* still represents the typical view of the objectives and meaning of accounting statements.) The format shown here is prescribed by the Companies Act of 1985 *et al* and most categories would be supported by notes to the accounts expanding on the detailed composition of the entries or their method of computation. It is by far the easiest way to think of a balance sheet as a list of the values of the assets and liabilities of a company with the net difference represented by the shareholders' investment in a company. We already know this to be a naive approach as the valuations attached to each category have little to do with their cost of replacement or their disposable value. Furthermore, even if the individual asset and liability values were accurate the value of the company as a whole could be very different from the component parts. However, bearing in mind the limitations of the valuations used, we can

CONSOLIDATED BALANCE SHEETS (£m)	Alpha		Beta	
	1991	1990	1991	1990
Capital employed:				
Fixed assets				
Tangible	122.2	114.7	158.5	135.0
Investments	27.8	25.0	50.0	39.7
	150.0	139.7	208.5	174.7
Current assets				
Stock (inventory)	94.2	84.3	62.8	68.3
Debtors (accounts receivable)	111.7	100.2	49.7	54.3
Investments	3.3	12.3	0.7	0.0
Cash	16.7	11.0	21.0	18.2
	225.9	207.8	134.2	140.8
Creditors due within one year	−153.3	−142.5	−120.8	−126.2
Net current assets	72.6	65.3	13.4	14.6
Total assets less current liabilities	222.6	205.0	221.9	189.3
Creditors due after one year	−69.9	−80.3	−89.5	−79.0
Provisions for liabilities and charges	−5.2	−3.5	−1.2	−0.5
	147.5	121.2	131.2	109.8
Financed by:				
Capital and reserves				
Called up share capital	22.2	22.0	11.0	11.0
Share premium account	69.0	68.5	18.5	18.5
Revaluation reserves	22.7	10.0	72.2	48.3
Profit and loss account (retained profit)	27.5	14.7	4.3	9.0
Shareholders' funds (equity)	141.4	115.2	106.0	86.8
Minority interests	6.1	6.0	25.2	23.0
	147.5	121.2	131.2	109.8

NOTES TO THE ACCOUNTS (£m)	Alpha		Beta	
	1991	1990	1991	1990
Creditors payable within one year				
Loans and overdrafts	42.7	45.2	32.0	38.4
Trade creditors	60.8	54.3	29.8	27.0
Other creditors	23.5	23.0	31.7	33.2
Taxation and social security	17.7	12.7	16.0	16.3
Bills of exchange	2.3	3.3	7.0	7.3
Proposed dividends	6.3	4.0	4.3	4.0
	153.3	142.5	120.8	126.2
Creditors payable after one year				
Loans	67.0	75.0	88.5	77.8
Taxation	1.7	1.5	0.5	0.7
Other	1.2	3.8	0.5	0.5
	69.9	80.3	89.5	79.0
Provisions				
Pensions	2.6	3.5	0.0	0.0
Taxation	2.6	0.0	1.2	0.5
	5.2	3.5	1.2	0.5

Figure 29.3 The balance sheet

(*Note*. There would be many further notes to the accounts relating to other items, giving further detail or explanations, but as these are not necessary for this explanation they have been omitted for the sake of clarity.)

examine the individual items to discover what deductions can be drawn from the information contained therein.

The assets of the companies suggest that whilst Beta has slightly less invested in assets (208.5 + 134.2 = 342.7 as opposed to 150.0 + 225.9 = 375.9) it apparently has a much higher percentage in fixed assets than Alpha (100*208.5/342.7 = 61% against 100*150.0/375.9 = 39%). The fixed assets are either tangible, such as plant or property, or intangible, usually investments in other companies. The distinction between fixed and current rests on the intention to maintain fixed assets as part of the company's strategy for earning future profits whilst current assets either rise as part of the trading cycle or are incidental stores of surplus funds such as short term investments.

Overall growth in assets is much the same for both organizations at around 8 per cent but whilst growth is a natural objective for management it ties up capital and is therefore only beneficial if productive. Note, however, that in Beta's case fixed assets apparently increased by £33.8m whilst current assets fell by £6.6m. We will see that this growth may be illusory. Fixed assets are originally valued at cost and for most assets this cost is gradually written off as depreciation. However at the same time inflation may well be increasing the net value of the asset and the unexpired cost becomes increasingly outdated as a surrogate measure of value. Both Alpha and Beta have tried to adjust for this by revaluing property, in Alpha's case by £22.7m and Beta's by £72.2m (see revaluation reserves). This practice would be outlawed under the accounting regime of most other western countries. The amount of this uprating which occurred in the year under review accounts for much of Beta's fixed asset increase. Thus the difference in asset structure could be explained, either by differing enthusiasm for revaluation, or genuine differences in asset structure.

The liabilities of the companies are not readily identifiable from the balance sheets as they are revealed as summary statistics elaborated on in notes to the accounts. From the notes it can clearly be seen that a large section of creditors comprises sources of finance. Even using a narrow definition of finance, loans and overdrafts amount to £109.7m in Alpha's case and £120.5m for Beta (loans and overdrafts payable within one year plus loans payable after one year). The remaining creditors are either short term debts due for expenses incurred, trade and other creditors, demands upon the profits of the company, not yet discharged (tax and dividends) or bills of exchange.

Provisions represent distant liabilities which are expected to fall due in the foreseeable future as a result of the current activities of the company though there is no present legal obligation.

The finance provided by the shareholders is divided into four sections. The nominal value of the shares sold is 'called up share capital' and any excess over the nominal value charged for those shares is 'share premium'. There is no effective difference between these two and together they represent the funds invested into the firm by shareholders. The 'revaluation reserve' has already been discussed and represents the write-up of assets, normally property, though as no profit has yet been realized this adjustment is not taken through the profit and loss account. The 'profit and loss account' is the residual value of all profits earned on behalf of the shareholders which has not yet been distributed to them in the form

Consolidated profit and loss accounts (£m)	Alpha		Beta	
	1991	1990	1991	1990
Turnover	581.2	328.2	394.7	392.8
Operating expenses	521.7	291.2	352.9	357.3
Operating profit	59.5	37.0	41.8	35.5
Share of associated companies' profits	1.5	1.3	7.8	11.0
Investment income	4.0	3.3	2.7	3.2
Finance costs	−14.7	−10.5	−14.2	−14.3
Profit on ordinary activities before taxation	50.3	31.1	38.1	35.4
Taxation	−14.0	−9.0	−11.0	−9.3
Minority interests	−1.0	−0.5	−2.3	−2.8
Extraordinary items	−4.3	−2.2	−0.5	−1.8
Dividends	−11.5	−7.5	−4.8	−4.0
Retained profit	19.5	11.9	19.5	17.5

Figure 29.4   The profit and loss account

of dividends. Minority interests represent the shares of subsidiaries not owned by the group.

The profit and loss account (or income statement) should, according to *The Corporate Report*, 'be concerned with the measurement of performance although they may also be used in the measurement of capital maintenance and income distributability'. Here we will consider only the performance measurement aspect of income statements. From the example accounts (Figure 29.4) it can be seen that Alpha's turnover has soared by 77 per cent whilst Beta's was relatively stable. In both cases some allowance should be made for the effects of inflation. In the example, no breakdown of the operating costs is given but Company Law does require firms to provide a simple analysis, and the management's internal accounts would be very much more detailed. The operating profit percentage earned by Alpha has dropped slightly (10.2 per cent from 11.3 per cent). Meantime Beta's margin rose (10.6 per cent from 9.0 per cent), leaving them with a modest increase in income. The remaining costs and revenues allocated to this period are not dissimilar apart from the higher income earned by Beta's greater investment in associated companies (classified as fixed asset investment on the balance sheet) and the considerably higher proportion of income paid out by Alpha as dividends.

Flow of funds statements (statements of source and application of funds) 'should be concerned with distinguishing between funds generated or released by different means and the uses to which such funds are put' (*The Corporate Report*). Whilst these statements are the third main financial statement, and could be extremely informative, the methods of computation and presentation are not yet sufficiently standardized to make them readily accessible to the non-specialist. The accounting profession is currently struggling with improvements to the prescribed method of preparing this accounting statement. They are not dealt with further.

Ratio analysis

Ratio analysis is a technique which has built up something of a mystique and yet it is a simple attempt to produce summary statistics to save time in the perusal of a large number of accounting statements and to facilitate comparability by standardizing the results for size.

Thus our two companies have reported profits on ordinary activities in 1991 of £50.3m and £38.1m respectively. Yet these results are not comparable because of the different scale of the two operations. It would be possible to standardize the results using a number of different scaling factors, for example turnover, capital, or employees.

	Profit margin	Return on capital	Profit per employee
Alpha	50.3*100/581.2 = 8.65%	50.3*100/147.5 = 34.1%	50.3m/10,050 = £5005/emp
Beta	38.1*100/394.7 = 9.65%	38.1*100/131.2 = 29.0%	38.1m/15,453 = £2466/emp

Which of the many scaling factors to use and which of the multitudinous possible combinations of ratios to compute rather depends on the focus of the study in hand, but some general guidance can be given.

Various studies by British and American academics which analysed comprehensive sets of ratios for large samples of industrial or commercial firms have shown that many of these ratios are substitutes rather than complementary. Once a different aspect of corporate performance has been identified most of the pertinent information can be derived from one or two ratios. Thus five ratios may well contain about 80% of the information available from a set of 40 or more. The five main characteristics, or factors, which are examined in more detail below, are profitability, financial leverage, working capital position, asset turnover, and liquidity. It must be emphasized that whilst these categories were distinctive in the study it does not follow that they are universally applicable or necessarily significant. For instance whilst the inventory/current assets ratio was found to contain most of the available information about short term liquidity, liquidity is not necessarily a useful indicator for an analysis of efficiency. Nevertheless the five ratios indicated above would form a good starting point for a general review of corporate performance.

As with other accounting data, ratios must find a point of comparison. The ratio statistic in itself is uninformative and supposed benchmarks, such as a working capital ratio of 1.5, are misleading. A convenient way of obtaining both a time series and cross-sectional perspective would be to lay out the statistics as follows:

	1986	1987	1988	1989	1990	1991
Sales growth %						
Gamma (examined company)	12.2	15.5	18.9	23.0	17.2	25.3
Delta (competitor 1)	14.7	15.9	19.7	21.8	22.0	20.8
Epsilon (competitor 2)	17.5	18.5	20.1	23.4	18.2	17.0
Industry average	15.1	16.2	18.5	20.0	18.2	16.2

Thus this example shows the industry and three of its constituents making a substantial recovery during the second half of the decade, tailing off in the 1990s for all of the series save for Gamma. Some caution should be employed when contrasting different industries or firms from different countries as accounting practices can result in considerable variation. For example the return on equity of British firms often appears to be slightly higher than their American rivals and considerably above that of continental competitors even when the reality is the reverse.

It seems necessary to compare corporate performance with the closest competitors directly as industry groupings cover such a wide range of products and organizational sizes.

When using ratio analysis or attempting to interpret accounting statements it must be left to the individual's experience of the industry, coupled with the information that can be drawn from time series or cross-sectional trends, to arrive at informed conclusions.

One exception where a more general approach has become accepted is in the use of Z scores to try to predict corporate bankruptcy. This statistic is an amalgam of various ratios which have been found to have a significant relationship with impending failure. Thus commercial organizations publish the Z score trends for companies in comparison with sector averages. It should be noted that some commentators are sceptical of this approach and more subjective attempts to identify corporate difficulties or managerial incompetence have been suggested.

The key ratios identified are now examined and explained using the sample accounts for illustrative purposes. Alternative specifications of these ratios are often used.

Profitability:

> Alpha 25.3% (17.2%) Beta 20.8% (22.0%)

Return on capital is profit before interest and taxation, expressed as a percentage of total capital employed, e.g.

$$100*(59.5 + 1.5 + 4.0)/(147.5 + 42.7 + 67.0) = 25.3\%$$

As such this is a crucial ratio which measures a company's efficiency in earning a return on capital employed. In the example used, Beta's return suffered a marginal decline due largely to the revaluation of capital invested in fixed assets whereas Alpha showed a marked improvement due to the remarkable increase in reported profits. Further evidence on these trends would be informative.

However, this ratio, using the final accounting computations of capital and profit, incorporates and exaggerates any measurement errors involved. In inflationary times profit is often overstated and capital understated.

Financial leverage (gearing):

> Alpha 60.8% (65.1%) Beta 61.7% (65.2%)

A complex ratio calculated as total liabilities expressed as a percentage of total assets, e.g.

$$100*(153.3 + 69.9 + 5.2)/(150.0 + 225.9) = 60.8\%$$

The higher the proportion of relatively cheap capital in the form of liabilities the greater the average return shareholders can expect, but the risk of large fluctuations in that return also increases. It is a moot point as to whether leverage is beneficial or not, even when there are apparently tax advantages. This ratio is heavily dependent on the dubious valuation of shareholders' equity in the balance sheet and is more reliable when the stock market valuation of equity is used.

The competitors here show little difference though both have slightly increased their reliance on equity capital.

Working capital position:

$$\text{Alpha } 0.60 \ (0.60) \text{ Beta } 0.39 \ (0.45)$$

This ratio is calculated as current assets divided by total assets e.g.

$$225.9/(225.9 + 150.0) = 0.60$$

and illustrates the relative importance of flexible and liquid current assets compared to long term assets. A high level of current assets does imply the possibility of inefficient asset management. The fall in Beta's ratio is due to the revaluation, but there is still a substantial difference between our two competitors.

Liquidity:

$$\text{Alpha } 0.42 \ (0.41) \text{ Beta } 0.47 \ (0.49)$$

A slightly unusual method of computation is used here as inventory is divided by current assets e.g.

$$94.2/225.9 = 0.42$$

However, the influence of current liabilities was examined in the leverage ratio and the statistic used here was influential in research studies. Our example shows Beta with a marginally higher proportion of relatively illiquid stock but there is little evidence of any unhappy trends.

Asset turnover:

$$\text{Alpha } 1.55 \ (0.94) \text{ Beta } 1.15 \ (1.25)$$

This statistic measures how effectively an organization uses its assets to produce output and is calculated as turnover divided by total assets, e.g.

$$581.2/(150.0 + 225.9) = 1.55$$

Beta maintains a fairly stable level of output per unit of assets though there appears to be a marginal decline. However, the increase in assets is largely accounted for by the revaluations which pushed up the reserve by £23.9m. Alpha again shows a startling increase in asset turnover. Something is going on!

The ratios examined are not definitive and many alternatives are available but they are illustrative of the techniques that can be used to elicit information from formal accounting statements.

ACCOUNTING INFORMATION AND MANAGERIAL DECISION MAKING

The information produced by the accounting system is not only of importance to outsiders via the medium of financial reports. Management use accounting data to evaluate current performance to establish whether or not corporate objectives are being met, to assess the contribution that alternative decisions are likely to make towards reaching those objectives, and to monitor the progress of previous decisions. This managerial decision making process and the role of accounting information is best illustrated diagramatically as shown in Figure 29.5.

The two areas that we will focus on here are the decision making process and monitoring the effects of the decision via the budgetary control process. Brief mention is also made of the technique of financial modelling which is a valuable aid to both of these functions.

Managerial decision making

Although accounts are a measure of past events, they are important for what they tell us about the future. The presumption is that the results and trends identified by the accounting statements of the last few years can be suitably modified by management's appreciation of changing circumstances to give a useful forecast of the future. This is important as business decisions should primarily be evaluated by their effect on 'the future differential cash flows' of the company:

Future, as we cannot affect past cash flows though we must live with their consequences.
Differential, because it is the expected change induced by a decision when compared to the next best alternative that should be the focus of the decision making process.
Cash flows, as it is cash receipts and expenditure which affect a company's ability to invest in alternative projects to earn interest or income. Thus the effect of a decision on the profit is only incidental to the cash flows generated.

Long term decisions require consideration of the timing of the cash flows generated by the decision. Early receipts can be reinvested to earn further returns whilst later receipts are still tied up in the project. Under these circumstances the differential cash flows, both income and expenditure, must be 'discounted' by an appropriate interest rate to adjust the cash flows to a uniform measure. This is a 'net present value' computation and any manager concerned with long term decisions should be familiar with the techniques involved. The detail is beyond the scope of this chapter but a simple example is worthwhile. In this example the early investment in productive equipment and working capital creates an immediate net cash outflow. The first year is also negative followed by a build-up of net receipts before the returns on the product start to decline. A terminal cash outflow is created by taxation residues and cessation cost. The discounting rate, here 15 per

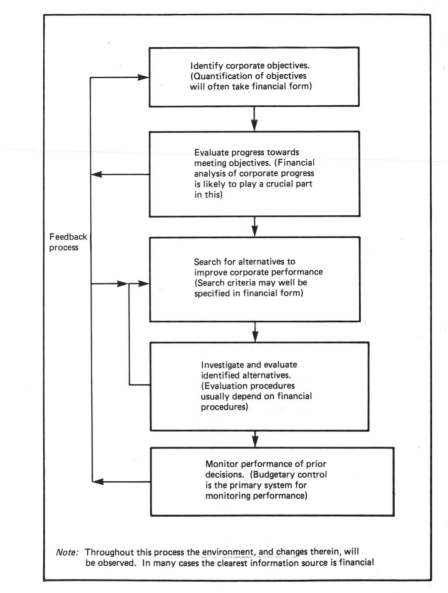

Figure 29.5   The role of accounting information in the decision making process

cent, depends on the risk of the project and not on the actual cost of the particular source of capital utilized. This technique can be applied to any decision which is expected to alter the cash flows of a company, be it increasing sales revenue, disposing of assets, or reducing expenditure. The effects of inflation and tax can be confusing and are best dealt with by estimating after tax actual cash flows and discounting by the after tax actual, as opposed to real, cost of capital appropriate to a project of this risk.

In the example in Figure 29.6 it can be seen that the net cash flows resulting from the decision to invest are positive. After adjustment for the timing of the cash

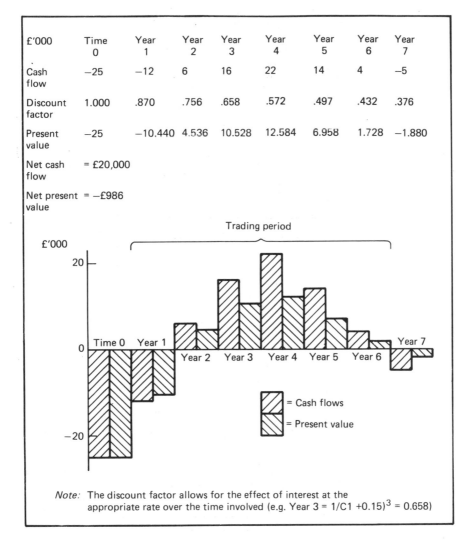

£'000	Time 0	Year 1	Year 2	Year 3	Year 4	Year 5	Year 6	Year 7
Cash flow	−25	−12	6	16	22	14	4	−5
Discount factor	1.000	.870	.756	.658	.572	.497	.432	.376
Present value	−25	−10.440	4.536	10.528	12.584	6.958	1.728	−1.880
Net cash flow	= £20,000							
Net present value	= −£986							

Note: The discount factor allows for the effect of interest at the appropriate rate over the time involved (e.g. Year 3 = $1/C1 +0.15)^3$ = 0.658)

Figure 29.6 Actual and discounted cash flows for project evaluation

flows, however, a negative net present value is calculated indicating that the project should not proceed. The reported accounting profit could be expected to average £3333 per year with higher profits in the years where sales peak. It would appear that profitability of a long term decision is not a suitable assessment criterion.

It is also apparent that management must be concerned with financing decisions but it is assumed that anyone involved in this is likely to be familiar with the contents of this chapter and therefore beyond its purview. Suffice it to say that whilst financing decisions might affect the value of a company they are insignificant in comparison to investment decisions where the viability of a company is determined. Good products will find good finance but poor products cannot be saved by efficient financing.

Short term decisions often drop the emphasis on cash flows in order to focus on the contribution to profit of a particular decision. This is an approximation as it is still the cash flows that are crucial, but where the timing differences are minimal the contribution towards profit is an acceptable compromise. The essential requirement is to separate out the costs and revenues that affect contribution from those that are fixed costs for the purposes of the decision under review. Many costs appearing as relevant to a product on traditional accounting statements are, in fact, beyond the influence of the decision maker and are therefore irrelevant to the decision. As a general rule those costs which require arbitrary allocation to distinct products or are unaffected by the volume of output of a product should be ignored in short term decision making. Examples are depreciation charges, administration and overhead expenses, production costs unaffected by volume, even that proportion of production wages that is fixed in the short term. All costs are variable in the long term and most are at least sticky if not fixed in the short term. It should also be noted that just because a cost is allocated by the accounting system on the basis of some output measure does not mean that it is a variable cost.

When variable costs and revenues have been separated from the irrelevant clutter of accounting statements, decisions can be based on the maximization of contribution towards fixed costs and profit. The example here is based on a pricing and advertising decision for a product whose fixed costs are thought to be £5000 per month and variable costs £15 per unit. Alternative prices under consideration are £18, £20, £22 and £24 for which demand figures are estimated at 3000, 2000, 1500 and 1000 respectively. The demand could be increased by 20 per cent by an advertising campaign costing £1000.

It can be seen from Figure 29.7 that the option of selling at £22 each, supported by the advertising campaign, is the preferred decision. The graph includes the fixed cost element for illustrative purposes but it is apparent that the same decision would be arrived at whether the fixed costs were £0, £5000 or £50,000 assuming that the costs are genuinely fixed and the option of closing down is not available.

Two points arise from the above example. First, the graphical presentation is unnecessary as the result can easily be calculated but the presentational benefits and the ease with which changes in expectations can be evaluated make the graph useful. Second, the decision was arrived at after considering the total contribution which requires incorporation of the effects on demand of the alternatives.

Thus the traditional approach of pricing at cost plus a mark up is deficient where demand depends on price and can lead to ridiculous decisions. In one example an engineering firm allocated expected costs across its work force and priced its product using labour costs plus a mark-up. A decline in demand led to an upgrading of the costs to be borne by each labour hour and a consequent increase in prices. This is not usually recommended when demand is falling.

Financial modelling

Financial modelling is a use of accounting data that is closely related to the internal decision making of a company. A computer-based replication of the accounting statements is produced, usually utilizing 'spreadsheet' software. The relationships between inputs, outputs, costs and revenues are carefully specified

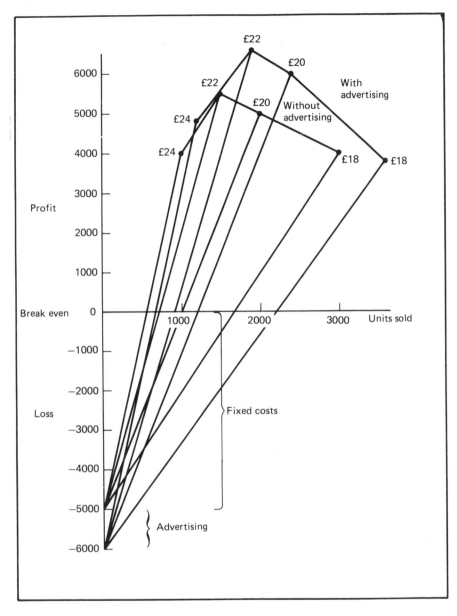

Figure 29.7   Graphical representation of contribution analysis

and the forecasts and decision variables obtained from management. The expected results from this complex set of interrelationships are then produced, allowing management to investigate readily the effect of changes in forecasts, decision variables, and the environment, and react accordingly. Whilst it will normally require a financial specialist to produce a sensible computer-based model, once it is completed, non-specialists should be able to alter parameters such as prices, costs, product mix, growth and inflation forecasts, and tax regulations, and immediately examine the results occasioned by such alterations.

Budgetary control

Accounting information is used for control as well as for decision making. Not only can the information feedback enable corrective action when necessary but the process of reviewing the outcome of earlier decisions may help to improve subsequent ones. It may also identify areas where individuals have been over optimistic in their claims. However it is difficult to provide more than a very brief and general insight into budgetary control systems. These systems are usually unique, being designed with a particular firm or set of circumstances in mind, and a meaningful explanation would fill this chapter. However an overview may well be of help and it is apparent that the budgetary control system is one of the key methods used by management to try to ensure that the decisions previously made are being carried out effectively and are having the desired result. Significant deviation from budget should instigate an investigation and remedial action, whilst providing feedback to the decision makers. The budgetary system is also sometimes seen as part of the (de) motivational process and it probably represents the non-financial specialist's most common brush with accounting data. Budget statements are usually produced by the financial accounting system and as such are similar in appearance and concept, though often only show a subsection of the full results. The clearest difference from normal accounts is the three categories of information reported: the results for the period; the intended results for the period; and the variance between the two.

Some crucial points need to be borne in mind when dealing with budget statements either as perpetrator or victim.

The reporting entity is often a subsection of the company and this resents troublesome allocations. Costs applicable to the whole organization are allocated to budget centres, often on arbitrary bases, and as these are beyond the control of the centre manager they are irrelevant to the budgetary and decision making process. The inputs and outputs of goods and services by the centre require pricing if the profit or loss is to be computed, yet when this is not an arm's-length transaction the transfer price used can often be misleading.

The responsibility for the results of a budget centre should be matched by the power to affect those results. Thus a cost centre manager can often affect the volume but not always the price of the costs; profit centre managers may find aspects of the revenue generating process beyond their control, and investment centre managers would often have to live with the actions of their predecessors.

The budgetary regime which is designed to induce a congruence of goals and coordination within the organization can often promote sub-optimal behaviour by managers. There is many an apocryphal story, but in general short term remedies to meet budget constraints can have a damaging long term effect, though cunning operators will ensure that they are long gone before the problem is realized.

The setting of budget targets can be a useful short term planning process and provides a motivational tool but this will not come cheap. If a budget is set easily it has probably been done improperly. It is essential that the managers who will have to meet budgets have been consulted about, and preferably have agreed to, their targets. It is also necessary to ensure coordination between the budgets of different centres and this can be aided by the use of financial models as previously discussed.

It is apparent that budgets are not popular but that they are essential both as an aid to planning and as an early warning system when those plans start to fail.

CONCLUSION

In one brief chapter it is impossible to give more than a flavour of the accounting process and its uses. However, it will be apparent to most managers or investors that financial data provide some of the most important sources of information available, the misreading of which can be fatal for a company's progress or a manager's career prospects. It is hoped that this chapter has illustrated that ignorance of accounting systems does not preclude a general understanding of accounting reports. Perhaps the most subtle insight is the required balance between unfounded faith in the numeric exactitude of accounting and sceptical rejection of its relevance to decision making.

Some examples of the uses of financial information have been alluded to. Although rather more experience would be required before one would feel confident applying these techniques perhaps the reader will have a greater understanding when subjected to them. Indeed there may be opportunity to point out to the perpetrators some errors in their ways.

CHECKLIST OF KEY POINTS

1   Whatever its failings financial information is pervasive in business. This suggests that it is seen as being useful by management practitioners and that a working knowledge is essential for career development.
2   There is no single correct set of accounting results. Financial statements are a product of the choice of accounting methods, a number of subjective decisions, and the underlying transactions.
3   If managers are aware of the limitations of financial statements, a considerable amount of valuable information can be derived from them. Ratio analysis is one technique which is often utilized to this end.
4   When analysing long term decisions it is advisable to take account of the timing of cash flows. It is the future differential cash flows, discounted by an appropriate cost of capital, which are relevant.
5   Short term decisions concentrate on marginal costs and revenues. The interrelationships between prices, demand and costs are difficult to estimate but are fundamental to effective decision making.
6   Financial information can play a valuable role in budgetary control. Such systems are often pervasive within the firm and it is advisable to understand their motivational and social impact as well as their controlling and feedback role.

FURTHER READING

Arnold, J. and Hope, A., *Accounting for Management Decisions*, 2nd edn, Prentice Hall, 1991

Arnold, J. and Mozier, P., 'A Survey of the Methods used by UK Investment Analysts to Appraise Investments in Ordinary Shares', *Accounting & Business Research*, Autumn, 1984

Rees, W., *Financial Analysis*, Prentice Hall, 1990

Walton, P. and Bond, M., *Corporate Reports: Their Interpretation and Use in Business*, Hutchinson, 1986

30 Project management

John Lewington

Projects are the main mechanism used by management for coping with the introduction of new systems, products and processes, and any changes outside the normal day-to-day operations of the organization. Projects inevitably bring about change to some facet of the organization and often all of the skills embodied in this book will be necessary to complete a project successfully. A project may be as small as the implementation of a word processing system, or as large as the building and equipping of a new factory. Large organizations will have highly developed bureaucratic systems of project submission, appraisal, presentation, approval and resourcing. Small organizations with short communication chains will often have very simple decision making processes and informal systems of project appraisal.

This chapter will define the main phases of project management and show how a manager may tackle each phase in a professional manner (see Figure 30.1). All projects involve elements of risk. The level of risk can be very high if the size of the project is large in relation to the size of the organization carrying it out. Successful projects should enhance a company's profitability, market position and self-esteem. However, projects often fail through poor appraisal of potential problems, inadequate organization, lack of technical expertise and under-funding.

Good project management systems should embody the following aims:

- Ensure that the organization reacts to environmental pressures and changes in a rational manner.
- Accurately estimate the resources required to complete the project successfully, and ensure that no resource needs are hidden or forgotten.
- Fully appraise the total expenditure of resources in terms of the economic and organizational benefits.
- Implement the project through a coordinated plan on a time scale appropriate to resources availability and organizational needs.
- Develop the organization's current systems and resources to be able to cope with the changes that the project will bring.

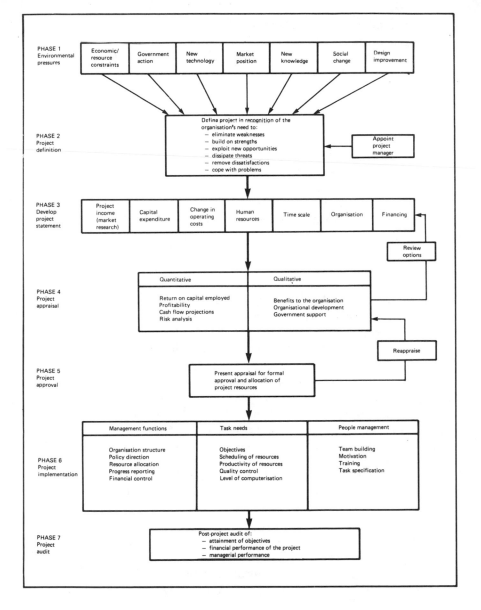

Figure 30.1   The main phases of project management

(This diagram provides an overview of the main phases and components of project management.)

ENVIRONMENTAL PRESSURES

The main skills in this phase of project management are perceptual. Change must be seen as possible or necessary due to internal or external opportunities. The ability of the organization to respond to environmental stimuli will depend on a number of factors such as:

- attitude of mind of management to change;
- internal politics and management's perception of the relative importance of the problem or opportunity;
- organization's size and structure;
- bureaucratic complexity and internal inertia in launching new ideas;
- perceived threats/risks of the change.

Small organizations may be quick to perceive new opportunities, but will sometimes lack the financial resources to exploit fully the environmental change. Large organizations will have the resources, but internal politics, bureaucratic systems and organizational inertia may stifle innovation. Most projects will be appraised on their economic justification. The stronger the economic justification, the more likely the project is to be raised to reality. The four main areas likely to generate new projects are:

- increased productivity;
- resource constraints;
- new products, services and markets;
- government action.

Increased productivity

Some projects may present obvious advantages and indisputable need through clear economic viability. Cost savings through increases in resource (labour, materials, space, equipment) productivity are vital to the survival of any organization. The application of new knowledge and technology will provide the driving forces for change. Replacement of old facilities should also provide the opportunity to improve methods and implement new systems.

Resource constraints

Many projects are forced upon management through shortages of labour, raw materials, space and equipment. Successful products and services may outgrow their operational resource provisions. Therefore, projects are devised to provide additional capacity, the cost of which must be balanced by cost savings and additional revenue generation. Other projects will be developed to cope with physical shortages of raw materials and office/factory space that are constraining operations.

New products, services and markets

The introduction of new products, services and markets will generate projects which define the resources, timing and expenditures involved in the venture. The organization will need to assess the impact of the new product on existing products in determining the possible viability of the project. The expenditures on R and D, new facilities and market launch must be matched by future forecasts of sales revenues.

Government action

New legislation often initiates new projects in order that an organization's facilities and systems comply with government requirements. It is unlikely that these projects will generate cost savings or additional revenues. Therefore, organizations may use the project as a mechanism for controlling and minimizing costs.

PROJECT DEFINITION

Projects must be accurately defined as the research involved in the development of a project statement may involve substantial investment of resources. Therefore, a project may be categorized under one of the following headings:

- Cost savings.
- New products and services.
- Replacement of plant, vehicles and buildings.
- Product research and development.
- Exploration for mineral reserves.
- Expansion of product/service capacity.
- Marketing campaign to increase sales.
- Organizational development/training programme to enhance an organization's human resources.
- Environmental, health and safety enhancements.

All of the above categories would be expected to produce long term economic benefits, except for environmental projects which might be necessary to comply with legislation.

The initial sponsors of the project must clearly define its aims and objectives. This will require intense discussions about the 'fit' of the project with existing policies, resources and skills of the organization. If the project is beyond the scope of the organization's current skills, then it may be necessary to employ consultants or approach specialists to frame the project appropriately. The rationales and hypotheses should be submitted to senior management for formal approval before starting the next project phase.

DEVELOPING A PROJECT STATEMENT

When an idea, concept or suggestion seems worth considering then the approval of senior management will generally be sought. The data collection will involve considerable time in the compilation of a large project statement. Therefore, a presentation of the objectives, rationales and potential benefits may be necessary before starting the study. The technical and business research involved in this phase may involve several of the following activities in order to make accurate estimates of expenditures and revenues:

- Market research – estimates of selling price, market share, market size, selling costs.
- Technical research – experimental products and model plants.

- Patent surveys and searches.
- Development of synthetic time and work standards.
- Preliminary negotiations with government, local government and unions.
- Computer simulations to aid the design of systems.

In many projects with a long gestation period and high technological uncertainty these estimates will be little more than guesstimates or 'ball park' figures. A diagram of the main cost factors that can arise is given in Figure 30.2. From Figure 30.1 you will see that there are a number of areas to be considered in this phase to ensure that a comprehensive project statement is compiled.

Project income

Most projects will stand or fall on their ability to increase the organization's net income, either through new revenue generation or cost reduction. The increase in 'cash flow' will be the sole justification for the capital expenditure. Any of the following sources of income generation may be used individually or in combination to justify the project's capital expenditures:

- Sales revenue from new products or services (or royalties).
- Release of capital through disposals of existing assets.
- Increase in revenue from expansion of capacity.
- Reduction in costs of existing operations.
- Government grants and special contracts.

Capital expenditure

Every project statement will contain a listing of the capital expenditures (long term assets) necessary. A wide variety of funding methods (see Financing, page 454 may be feasible/desirable for different facets of the project depending upon the size of the expenditure, corporate policy and attitude to risk. Expenditures may be categorized according to their economic life in order to make some forecasts of depreciation.

There is always a tendency to *underestimate* capital expenditure on projects. This is particularly true of long term projects where the problems of delays, inflation, technical change and new factors (e.g. pollution control) may surface as the project progresses. Therefore, the inclusion of a 'contingency allowance' to cover unforeseen eventualities and problems may be justified. The main areas of project expenditure can be stated as follows:

- Land and buildings.
- Plant and equipment.
- Tooling and storage facilities.
- Working capital.
- Vehicles and materials handling equipment.
- Computers (hardware and software) and telecommunications networks.

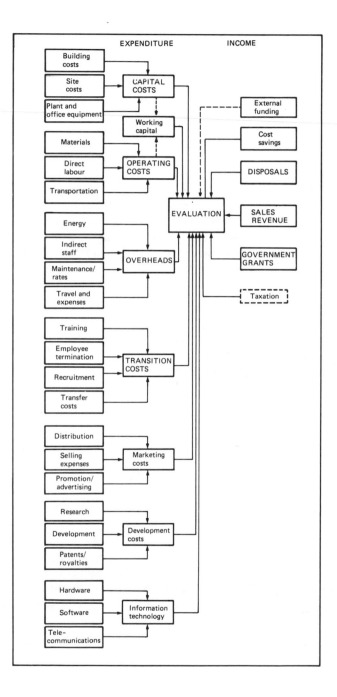

Figure 30.2   Factors of income and expenditure for project statements

Changes in operating costs

Most projects will result in some changes in operating costs. The main focus of a project may be cost savings in materials or labour through increasing capital investment. The result of this is a higher risk situation in terms of changes in the level of activity.

Productivity increase projects can be focused upon the following areas:

- Improved material utilization.
- Increased labour productivity.
- Overhead reduction or faster absorption.
- Reduction in telecommunications or energy costs.
- Reduction in sales or distribution costs.
- Improved information systems and decision making.

Human resources

A project may require special technological or managerial skills to be completed successfully. These skills may be in short supply. Therefore, the utilization of these skills will either be expensive in terms of their actual or opportunity (internal to the organization) costs. The creators, innovators and entrepreneurs who will be crucial to the success of the project must be coordinated and scheduled carefully. The project manager must consider the task needs in selecting and blending an effective team to solve potential problems. The 'real' cost of the man hours that will be required for the project must be accurately assessed.

Time scale

Some consideration must be given to an outline plan of the main activities to establish an overall duration for the project. There may be a tendency to *underestimate* the time scale in order to encourage project selection. Judgements about time scale are always partly subjective and there is always senior management pressure to reduce the total time scale of the project to a minimum. This will encourage the 'crashing' of activities, that is, the pouring in of resources to reduce activity time scale. Conversely, the delay and late completion of activities will have harmful effects on a project. If the cumulative loss of benefits (financial) and the overall cost of the project on different time scales are considered together, then the sum of loss of benefits and project cost may provide an optimal time scale (see Figure 30.3). Ultimately, product life cycles and other environmental stimuli (competition) may have the most profound effects on management's perception of an appropriate time scale. If it is feasible, some consideration should be given to phasing the project in such a way that the first phase will generate funding for subsequent phases.

Organization

A preliminary assessment of organizational problems must be made. The way in which a project is organized and operated after completion will have cost impli-

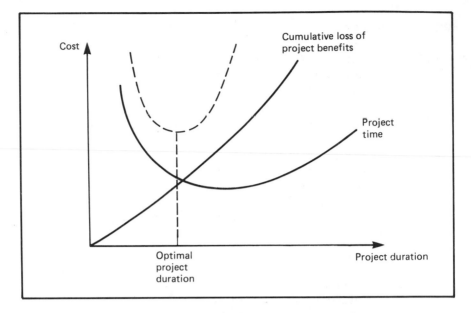

Figure 30.3 . Total cost of project

cations in terms of expenditure and revenue. The person appointed as project manager will have to answer several key organizational questions:

- How should the personnel be organized in order to maximize communication, motivation and task completion?
- Should the whole project be handed over to a sub-contractor on a turnkey basis?
- What sort of organization will be required to operate the new system in order to plan for training and staffing?
- What information and computer systems will be of benefit to the project team?

Financing

Most projects will be financed internally using current cash flow or borrowing capacity. However, large and/or high risk projects may require alternative funding strategies. One of the following alternatives may be used to reduce the impact of adverse risks on your organization:

- Venture capital funding.
- Joint projects in the form of partnerships or consortia.
- Royalty and licensing agreements.
- Locating to obtain government employment grants and subsidies.
- Leasing and renting buildings and equipment.

Once these issues have been decided the project is ready for appraisal. The estimates, guesstimates and 'ball park' figures will form the basic budget for the project. Some updating, review and changes will undoubtedly occur from feedback during the appraisal.

PROJECT APPRAISAL

In this phase management are concerned with appraising the information and rationales put forward in the project statement. Several alternative options should be appraised to allow for choice. However, this is not always practicable. The appraisal may result in feedback on management's attitude to facets of the project which will result in revisions of the project statement and reappraisal. As the project statement may have been gathered from a wide variety of sources the information must be screened for consistency.

Surveys reveal that great emphasis is placed on the quantitative factors in project appraisal. However, it should be remembered that these are only *estimates* and *forecasts*. In addition the qualitative factors expressed in the objectives, rationales and non-quantifiable benefits should fit with current strategies and business policies. Therefore, the main objectives of this phase are as follows:

- To determine whether the project meets the organization's criteria for financial return on the investment.
- To ensure that the estimates present an accurate/practical/realistic view of the project.
- To appraise the risks in relation to the economic returns.
- To determine the fit and effects of the project on the organization's future strategies and policies.

Project appraisal may require considerable management accounting and computing skills; you should therefore consult Further Reading at the end of the chapter for the detail behind these techniques.

Profitability

Most projects will be undertaken because they promise to improve the economic position (wealth) of the sponsoring organization. One problem in selecting projects is to define an appropriate rate of return for any given risk. Many organizations ignore this problem and set one rate of return for all projects. Deciding on an appropriate rate of return can be affected by many factors such as the organization's cost of capital, returns from other similar projects, or returns from other investments outside the organization. Other factors such as inflation, current interest rates and taxation may have some bearing on the figure. Profitability criteria can be expressed in a number of ways, but payback period and rate of return on investment predominate.

Payback period

This is the time taken to repay the investment out of the cash flow from the investment.

Payback period (years)	1	3	5	7
Projects	Computers	Vehicles	Property	Government

The payback method is very easy to understand and is very widely used by all sorts of organizations.

Rate of return on investment

This is expressed as a percentage rate per annum.

Generally, organizations set a minimum rate (sometimes called cut-off rate) of return to be obtained from their projects.

Minimum rates of return (%)	10	20	30	40
Projects	Government Property	Vehicles		Computers Pharmaceuticals

Several techniques are used for assessing rate of return, all of which give different answers. Some employ formulae (accounting rate of return); others attempt to forecast cash flows then apply discount factors (discounted cash flow DCF). There are two kinds of DCF technique: net present value (NPV) and internal rate of return (IRR). Net present value utilizes the organization's minimum rate of return and determines the result on a 'go' – 'no go' basis. Internal rate of return attempts to determine the exact compound rate of return for the project over its entire life. The result is then compared with the minimum rate of return. Both techniques lend themselves more to computer models of sensitivity than manual calculations.

Projects not meeting the organization's criteria for profitability will rarely be progressed. If a project makes good basic business sense then it might be recycled through the statement and appraisal phases for investment trimming and re-thinking.

Cash flow projections

Expenditures, forecasts of income and time scale projections should be combined into a cash flow projection. This will provide management with an overall view of cash commitments and the rate at which loans might be paid off. Using a spreadsheet will enable a model of project cash flows to be developed. This will allow management to appraise the effects of inflation and taxation.

Risk analysis

A spreadsheet cash flow model will greatly ease the burden of examining the risk aspects of the project. The relative significance of the investment decision is dictated by the size of the investment in relation to an organization's net assets. Failure of a small project can be absorbed, but failure of a large project could be disastrous. Therefore, risk analysis should make management aware of the 'down-side' risks which might evolve under certain environmental conditions.

One technique of risk appraisal is *sensitivity analysis*. The approach is to take each main factor in the project (e.g. sales income, materials cost) and vary it by + 10 per cent and − 10 per cent, one at a time. This should give some indication of the most sensitive variables which will provide a concentration of attention. This awareness of potential problem areas may result in some reorganization of the project or hedging of risks.

Another method is to examine the project through a variety of scenarios. This may provide some insights into how the project should be managed in different environments.

Generally, risk should be related to reward. If a project has high risks then a high rate of return should be expected. However, most organizations have one rate of return for all types of projects. This rate of return is set relatively high on the basis that those projects which work out will pay for those which fail.

Benefits to the organization

In project appraisal the decision making process will undoubtedly be affected by some qualitative factors which cannot be expressed in economic terms. In cases where accurate estimating of costs and revenues is difficult then these may be the most important decision making variables. Any one or a combination of the following factors may be used to provide project justification:

- Improvement of product/service market position.
- Stronger cost structure of products or services.
- Security of employment for the work force.
- Release of non-productive assets.
- Improvements in the organization's financial structure.
- Implementation of new technology to meet competition.
- Establish technological lead over the competition.
- Establish a position in a high growth market.
- Development of new products or services.
- Comply with health and safety regulations.
- Improve corporate image.
- Develop new skills and expertise in the work force.
- Improve managerial control and decision making.

Organizational development

Projects may be the catalyst for organizational development. They may provide many new directions to the organization's task systems, a focus for change, learning, conflict resolution and a new set of working relationships.

Government support

In most industrialized countries the government plays a significant role in providing financial support for high risk and economically marginal projects. This support may be through taxation relief, direct loans, grants or contracts. Intangible government support may make funding easier to obtain or provide an opening in export markets. The effect of government funding is to reduce risk and provide a market for products and services. In return the government will require job creation and stability of employment for a specific region.

PROJECT APPROVAL

In this phase the project statements and appraisals should be combined into one summary document for presentation to senior management. In large organizations this will involve the completion of standardized forms covering the factors to be considered by their specific type of organization and business. The summary report may be accompanied by a presentation, 'selling' the project to senior management.

The report and/or presentation should contain the following elements:

- Main objectives of the project.
- Main rationales supporting the project.
- Models, pictures and outline designs of new products or services.
- Market information – strategy, size, share, pricing, promotion and advertising.
- Proposals for the organization and staffing of the new system.
- Outline of information systems and data processing support networks.
- Product/service cost data.
- List/summary of main capital expenditures.
- Profitability statements.
- Cash flow forecasts.
- Financing proposals.
- Potential risks and environmental problems.

If the project is not approved then senior management should provide their reasons for rejection. This might then involve further research and appraisal before re-submission.

PROJECT IMPLEMENTATION

The implementation phase involves the planning, scheduling and coordination of a wide variety of resources. The physical activities must be paralleled by the development of appropriate human resources to implement and operate the new system. The integration of activities will involve the mobilization of resources on both an internal and external basis. The organization of the project must evolve around clear lines of responsibility and communication married to an integrated set of activities with a time phased plan.

Task objectives

In general, the aim is to minimize project duration. However, while this may be an important consideration in many projects it is not the sole criterion. Projects may be implemented using one or more of the following objectives as a guide to planning:

- Minimize total project duration.
- Minimize the total systems cost of the project.
- Minimize cost for a given project duration.
- Provide an even (steady) loading on scarce resources.
- Minimize time for a given project cost.
- Maximize the use of available resources.

Organization structure

Project management requires both a vertical and horizontal flow of work which cannot be achieved through rigid formal authority. Three basic structures exist for managing projects. However, none provides a perfect solution and each has its strengths and weaknesses.

Functional structure

Where projects are confined to one specific function (e.g. production, marketing) in the organization then this approach may be appropriate. Where projects cut across functions, control becomes difficult.

Project structure

Teams of specialists are formed to carry out a specific project. Responsibility and lines of communication are very clear in this type of organization. However, the costs of maintaining this type of structure in a multi-project environment can be very high.

Matrix structure

In this structure the project manager maintains a team against a background of functional activities. This structure promotes learning and a strong technical base, but may sometimes evoke a conflict of priorities with functional managers.

Policy direction and resource allocation

Projects often create new operating systems, but managers have to maintain the existing systems. This will cause conflict between the project manager and functional managers if priorities are not clearly stated by senior management. Resource requirements should be identified, related to tasks, and provision made to ensure that the resources will be available at the required time.

Financial control and progress reporting

Most organizations will operate their main controls through the finance department. The simplest way is to plot a cumulative forecast of expenditure and then monitor the actual expenditure against it. The purpose of this is to highlight possible overspending before it gets out of control. Expenditure forecasts are generally broken down into spent (bills paid), committed (orders placed), and to be committed. Written reports and occasional presentations will be required on some projects.

Scheduling of resources

The scheduling of resources will be accomplished using a network to link activities logically (Figure 30.4). Organizations use a variety of names for this approach; critical path method (CPM) or analysis (CPA), precedence network or pro- gramme evaluation and review technique (PERT). Once the network has been drawn logically relating the completion of activities then a bar chart can be drawn or produced from a computer package (Figure 30.5).

First, management must make a decision on the detail in which they plan to schedule each task. The basic information required on each task is:

- a brief description of the task;
- a time duration of the task;
- a responsibility for the task;
- a list of tasks that must be complete before the task can start.

An arrow is used to represent a task in the project and this is most commonly known as an 'activity'. The activity is bounded at each end by a circle commonly known as an 'event' (or node). An example of a single activity such as 'write report' is shown in Figure 30.6. The length and orientation of the arrow is *not* related to the duration of the task. However, the arrow does point in the direction of the time flow for the task. After the activity 'write report', the next task may be 'typing' and this is represented as shown in Figure 30.7.

The numbers at the tail and head of the arrow are called 'event' numbers. Therefore, activity 1–2 is 'write report'. If the report were a long one then it might be worth commencing typing before it was completely finished. However, for this example we will assume that typing cannot start until the writing is finished. The cover of the report could be designed whilst the report is being written; and such concurrent (or parallel) activities are represented as shown in Figure 30.8.

Once the report and cover are ready then they may be printed, bound and distributed. Figure 30.9 shows the complete sequence. The dashed arrow con- necting event five and event six is a 'dummy' activity with zero time duration and it is used to maintain proper logical order and unique numbering (for computer input purposes) within the network diagram.

The network is not only a plan, but is also a communication device for ensuring that all departments understand how their contribution fits into the whole picture. A main network may have to be broken down into a series of sub-networks to be used within individual departments.

Even small projects justify the drawing of a network and construction of a simple bar chart. Larger projects will justify the use of computers for control and updat- ing purposes. If computers are to be used then schedules of resources associated with each activity may also be required. If activities are delayed or get ahead of

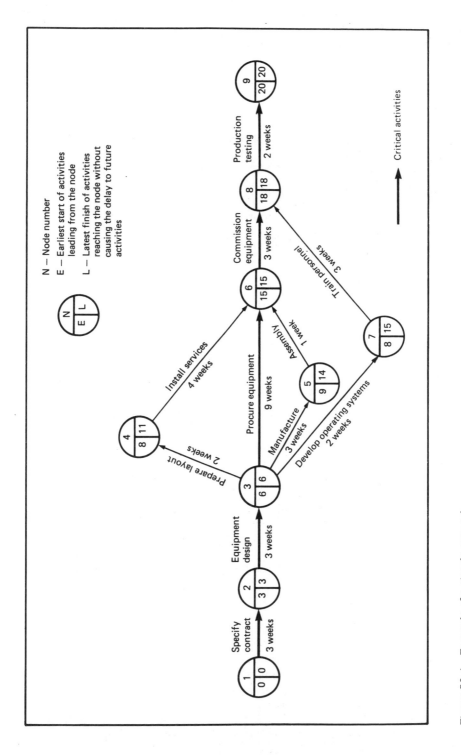

Figure 30.4 Example of a simple network

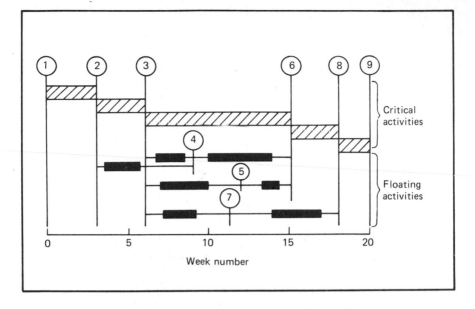

Figure 30.5   Example of a simple bar chart

schedule then the impact on later activities can clearly be seen. A wide variety of commercially manufactured aids for displaying projects and plans is also available.

Some activities will have to be completed to an exact time schedule; these are called the 'critical path' activities and set the shortest time in which the project can be completed. Activities not on the critical path will have some free time referred to as 'activity float'. This means that management will have some limited discretion on the start and finish of non-critical activities. This discretion may be used to level demands on scarce resources.

Level of computerization

The level of computerization depends very much on the size of organization and systems available. The advent of microcomputers allied to low cost packages means that it is now economical to set up even a small network on a computer. The increased power of microcomputers allows for hundreds of activities to be handled and a wide variety of sophisticated features made available to the project manager.

Principally, these features are:

- calculation of start, finish and float times for all activities;
- development of bar charts for each activity;
- preparation of activity schedules by individual manager responsibility;
- production of calendar and milestone charts;
- sorting of reports according to need;
- incorporation of public holidays;
- tracking of multiple (5+) resource demands and cost per activity;
- modelling and 'what if?' facilities that provide trade-offs between manpower, cost and time; and the levelling of resource demands.

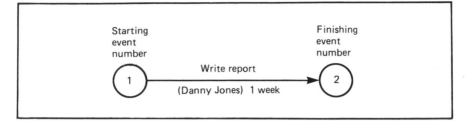

Figure 30.6   Example of a single activity network.

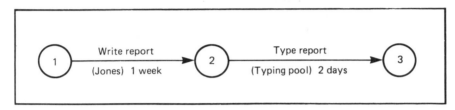

Figure 30.7   Two-activity network

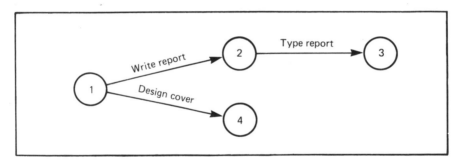

Figure 30.8   Example of how concurrent activities are represented

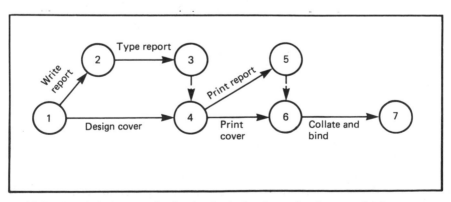

Figure 30.9   A complete network, showing logical order and unique numbering

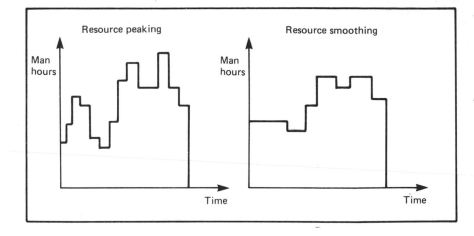

Figure 30.10   An example of resource smoothing

The use of other computer packages such as spreadsheets and databases should provide further modelling and control facilities for larger projects.

Productivity of resources

The use of computer models and packages will enable the project manager to devise schemes and schedules of implementation for any of the six task objectives stated earlier in this section. Therefore, by using computer packages to update and reschedule resources the trade-off between project completion, resource costs and resource productivity can be constantly updated.

One of the greatest problems facing the project manager is that of resource peaking (see Figure 30.10). Therefore, the manager may attempt to 'smooth' or 'level' resource requirement over a period of time.

Quality control

This may present substantial problems particularly on large projects involving complex sub-contractor interrelationships. Therefore, the quality of work must be constantly monitored by designers, surveyors and architects. The information and reports should be stored using a database computer package for cross-referencing. This will enable project management to keep comprehensive control and records of all quality control reports. Quality circles can be set up to provide a constant dialogue on quality problems and project progress.

People management

Many aspects of personnel management are effectively dealt with in other chapters of this book. However, it is very easy to forget about human resource development when the task aspects (getting things finished) appear to predominate. But individuals and groups must be *motivated* to achieve project objectives. In technically complex projects there may be a high element of *training* taking place both formally and informally. Therefore, it is necessary to build effective *teams* capable of supporting and assisting each other (see Chapter 17 for team building). This involves good communications, mutual respect, and an ability to resolve conflict effectively. There is no such thing as delegation in the management of a project. Every activity must have an owner who is committed to resolving problems so that the task is completed successfully.

AUDITING PROJECT PERFORMANCE

To improve future performance it is not unusual to carry out a post-project audit. The main focus of an audit should be on the accuracy of the project statement, the adequacy of the project appraisal process, and finally the effectiveness of the implementation. All large projects should probably be audited one year after full implementation. Smaller projects may be sampled and appropriate examples of good and bad results examined. The results of the audit may assist management in formulating an effective organizational development programme aimed at greater effectiveness in project management for the future. The main areas of examination are listed below.

Objectives

Has the project achieved its objectives in terms of performance, resolving problems, exploiting opportunities and provided an appropriate return on investment?

Project statement

How accurate were the forecasts of costs, expenditure, income and time scale? Could/should more accurate estimates have been prepared?

Appraisal

Did the appraisal process properly consider all of the practical alternatives, risks and organizational implications? Were effective strategies developed for coping with potential problems and reorganization?

Implementation

This will undoubtedly come in for the greatest scrutiny in the following areas:

- Planning and scheduling of resources.
- Procedures for contracting and tendering.
- Labour, materials and equipment utilization.
- Adequacy of financial control mechanisms.
- Progress reporting and communication systems.
- Analysis of delays and lost time.
- Organization structures and personnel policies.

Use of the checklist

The checklist that follows is designed as an *aide memoire* for the busy manager and should be used in conjunction with Figures 30.1 and 30.2 to ensure the rounded consideration of a project. Most large organizations will have their own systems, procedures and project peculiarities; and it may be useful to develop an internal checklist of factors for your own organization's environment.

PROJECT MANAGEMENT CHECKLIST

Environmental pressures

1 Does the organization have sensing mechanisms and communication channels in order to:

- spot market changes;
- recognize new business/service opportunities;
- adopt new technology and systems;
- reduce costs and be more competitive;
- incorporate employee suggestions;
- resolve customer problems;
- respond to social change.

2 Who is responsible for project initiation?
3 How are potential projects formulated for project definition?

Project definition

1 Can the project be adequately categorized (i.e. R and D, cost saving, replacement, expansion etc)?
2 Which person/group/department/committee is responsible for defining the terms of reference/objectives/constraints of the project?
3 Is the potential project consistent with the current policies of the organization?
4 Is it likely that top management will support the project?
5 Are the technical expertise/skills requirements within the scope of the organization or should consultants be employed?

Developing a project statement

1 Has the project been approved in principle by senior management?
2 Have the rationales/objectives/constraints/importance of the project been adequately defined for costing and estimating purposes?
3 Can the income/sources of revenue for the project be adequately defined/guesstimated/forecast?
4 Have all of the following items of expenditure been properly considered?

- land, new buildings and site facilities (roads etc);
- machines, office equipment and computers (hardware and software);

- training costs for completion of the project and implementation of the new system;
- employee recruitment and termination;
- relocation of employees and facilities;
- research and development costs;
- marketing and sales.

5 What changes in annual operating costs will occur after the project is completed?

- materials and staffing;
- transportation, distribution and energy costs;
- rates, building and equipment maintenance;
- computing and telecommunications costs;
- staff travel and expenses;
- marketing and sales.

6 Will any specialist scarce human resources be required to complete the project successfully?
7 Does the estimated time scale for the project conflict with the required completion date? If so, how can the two be reconciled?
8 Will a special organization structure be needed to complete the project?
9 Will a new organization structure be required after the completion of the project?
10 Can the project be financed internally? If not, where will the external financing come from?
11 Can appropriate measures of profitability be calculated from the information available?

Project appraisal – quantitative

1 Does the project meet the organization's criteria for profitability in terms of payback and/or return on investment?
2 Will the project/investment enhance the long term profitability and security of the organization?
3 Will the cash flow projections for the project affect other projects and/or the normal operational requirements of the organization? If yes, how can this problem be coped with?
4 Will the project involve cost savings and stronger market position?
5 Can any limits of accuracy be placed upon the market size, market share and product life?
6 Will inflation have a significant impact on the larger items of expenditure?
7 Can the relative risks be assessed in quantitative terms through 'sensitivity analysis'?

Project approval

1 At what level in the organization can the project be approved (department manager/area manager/managing director/board)?

2 Are you satisfied that the project statement represents the 'best' solution to the problem?

3 If the project cannot be approved in present form what areas need changing to make the project viable?

4 Are the contingencies for cost overruns sufficient on large items of expenditure?

5 Can resources be allocated in step with the current time scale for the project?

6 Is the project too large/risky for the present organization? If so, should a partner/venture capital be found to form the project as a separate venture?

Project implementation

1 Has an appropriate balance been defined between resources–time scale–projected expenditure?

2 Have responsibilities/organization structures been defined to ensure successful completion of the project?

3 Has senior management provided appropriate policies for the conduct of the project?

4 What progress reporting will be required in terms of frequency/detail/format/expenditure?

5 What financial controls should be implemented to ensure successful completion of the project?

6 What mechanisms exist for coping with cost overruns and expenditures not originally forecast?

7 Have the main task activities been clearly defined and responsibilities allocated?

8 Are the milestone dates and activity completion times clear to the whole team?

9 Is the scheduling/rescheduling of resources and activities complex enough to justify computerization?

10 Do the current plans maximize the productivity of project resources?

11 Who is responsible for controlling/monitoring the quality of the work completed?

12 What processes are planned into the organization structure for developing the project team and/or the team to operate the new system?

13 What incentives exist to encourage the team/contractor to complete the project on time?

14 What training will be required for the project team members and/or the people operating the new system?

15 Have appropriate task specifications been prepared for individual members of the project team?

Project audit

1 Is the project sufficiently important to warrant an audit? If so, how long should elapse before an audit is meaningful?

2 To what extent has the project achieved its objectives?

3 Did the project attain its financial performance objectives in terms of return/ project budget?
4 Was management of the project effective and were resources used efficiently?
5 What can be learned to improve future projects?

FURTHER READING

General

Harrison, F. L., *Advanced Project Management*, Gower, 1985

Lock, D. (ed.), *Project Management Handbook*, Gower, 1987

Meredith, J. and Mantel, S. S., *Project Management: A Managerial Approach*, Wiley, 1985

Stallworthy, E. A. and Kharbanda, O. P., *Total Project Management: From Concept to Completion*, Gower, 1983

Project definitions and statements

Bright, J., *Research, Development and Technological Innovation*, Irvin, 1964

Twiss, B., *Managing Technological Innovation*, Longman, 2nd edition, 1982

Project appraisal

Franks, J. R. and Scholefield, H. H., *Corporate Financial Management*, Gower, 1979

Souder, W. E., *Project Selection and Economic Appraisal*, Van Nostrand Reinhold, 1983

UNESCO, *Project Evaluation*, HMSO, 1985

Project implementation

Dinsmore, P. C., *Human Factors in Project Management*, American Management Association, 1986

Hoare, H. R., *Project Management using Network Analysis*, McGraw-Hill, 1973

Lockyer, K. G., *Critical Path Analysis*, Pitman, 1966

Project auditing

Turner, W. S., *Project Auditing Methodology*, North-Holland, 1980

31 Decision making and problem solving

Peter Walker

The fortunes of large corporations depend on the quality of decisions made by their management. Despite this, many managers have little formal training in decision making and little understanding of how they finally arrived at a decision and made a choice.

Certainly, literature is available on many specific techniques which can aid decision making, but to be useful these techniques must be applied within an overall framework. The purpose of this chapter is to look at such an overall framework which may be used to make any decision.

Effective decision making will often require inputs from problem solving and contingency planning and hence these processes are also discussed. Because creativity is required in all the other processes it is also referred to.

DECISION MAKING, PROBLEM SOLVING, CONTINGENCY PLANNING AND CREATIVITY

The purpose of decision making is to make the best possible choice, based on sound information. However, if the information is either inaccurate or incomplete, the decision may fail. The purpose of problem solving and contingency planning is to improve the quality of information being processed.

Problem solving looks at the past with the purpose of understanding the causes of any problem that needs correcting. Contingency planning looks to the future with the purpose of anticipating future problems.

Problem solving, when required, must precede decision making because the decision must be based on the best understanding of the past and present situation. In contrast, contingency planning will be conducted after a decision has been made in order to refine or improve the chosen course of action before implementation.

Thus decision making can be seen as the process of bridging from the past to the future when the manager wants to change the present (see Figure 31.1).

470

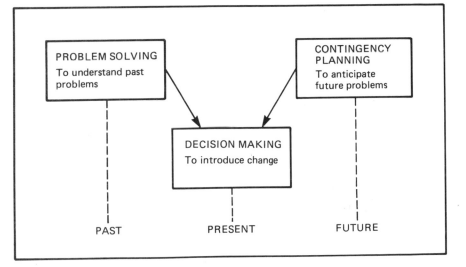

Figure 31.1   Relationship of decision making with problem solving and contingency planning

(The causes of past problems and an understanding of possible future problems are information necessary for an effective decision.)

CREATIVITY

Applied creativity is essential to each of the three processes outlined above. For example, creativity will be needed in problem solving to develop possible causes of problems. It may also be needed in decision making to develop new alternatives or solutions from which to choose. In contingency planning, creativity will be used to develop ideas about future problems which could occur and possible reasons for those problems.

There are several techniques to enhance creativity, of which brainstorming is the best known. However, one thing which is common to these techniques is that judgement is suspended while the new ideas are being generated. In other words, we should not try to both create and evaluate an idea simultaneously. Rather we should create first and evaluate second.

This is illustrated in Figure 31.2 where a concern is used to focus on creative generation of possible approaches to resolving that concern. Next, an analytical approach is used to select and implement the best approach to reach a solution. A simple example of this could be the situation in which you need to establish a rapid transport link between two towns. As a result of creative thinking the following 'possible approaches' might be generated:

- scheduled airlines;
- private helicopter;
- private car;
- carrier company;
- railway transport.

Evaluation of these ideas is delayed until after they have all been generated, when

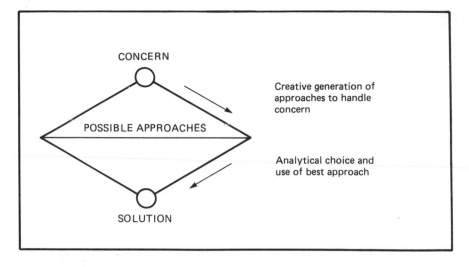

Figure 31.2   Separation of creativity and analysis

criteria such as cost, time, reliability etc can be used to evaluate them and a detailed schedule established for the chosen means of transport.

Each of the processes of problem solving, decision making and contingency planning use this two-step approach where ideas are first generated and then analysed and it is this separation of creativity and analysis which helps to make the process so effective.

Where the phrase 'brainstorm ideas' is used in this chapter it means 'creatively generate new ideas without stopping to criticize or evaluate at this stage'.

PROBLEM SOLVING

The purpose of problem solving is to discover what caused a current situation, so that this knowledge may be used to decide how to handle it. If the causes are already fully understood, or there is no desire for change, there is no need for problem solving.

The formal use of problem solving is badly neglected for the simple reason that many managers fail to recognize that their problems require analysis. Rather, when something goes wrong they make an assumption about the cause and then act upon that assumption without checking it. If the assumption is correct then all is well, but too often the hoped-for improvement fails to occur and this triggers another idea on problem cause which is once again acted upon. In this way time, effort and resources may be wasted while the problem continues.

The definition of a problem

We have a problem when 'an object or a system has a defect and the cause of that defect is unknown'. In turn a defect can be defined as a deviation in performance from the required standard (see Figure 31.3). The first step in problem solving is to write down a problem statement. This is particularly important in group problem solving when agreement on the statement ensures a common under-

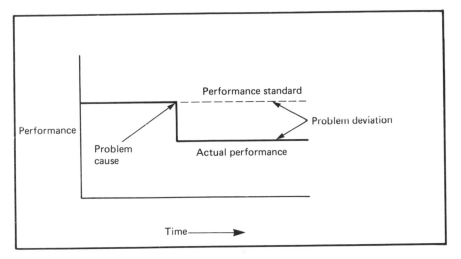

Figure 31.3   Deviation diagram

(*Note*: The deviation could be a step function as shown or a gradual deterioration.)

standing of the problem. A good problem statement will be a short sentence which specifies the object and its defect.

Thus, for example, if the floor in part of the factory becomes particularly dirty and the reason for this is unknown, then the problem statement could simply be: 'Floor in area B gets dirty'. Note that the required standard is that the floor should be 'clean'.

A common mistake is to phrase the problem statement in terms of the expected solution. Thus an incorrect problem statement would be: 'How to clean the floor in area B'.

Use of the incorrect problem statement will focus people's thinking on solutions about how to clean the floor while at the same time tending to exclude the types of solutions aimed at preventing the floor becoming dirty in the first place. Certainly the group will give little thought to *why* the floor is getting dirty.

Getting to the root cause

Often problem solving will not stop when the immediate cause of the problem has been uncovered. Rather the cause of the immediate problem can become the focus of further problem solving to uncover the cause of the cause.

For example, the initial problem might be 'sales revenue below target'. Investigation shows the cause of this to be poor sales of product X. In turn, poor sales of product X are caused by a salesman leaving the company as the result of bad supervision. This can be illustrated in Figure 31.4.

Of course we can go further than 'bad supervision' and ask what caused the supervisor to perform poorly. The point at which we stop and cut the cause–effect chain is when we reach a cause where we can take effective action. For instance, if only one supervisor is performing badly we may choose to replace him while if a number of supervisors were inadequate we might need to go back further and find out why.

473

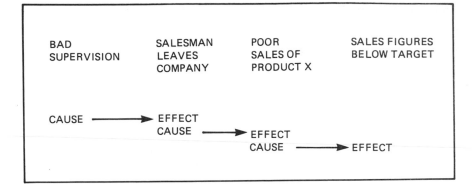

Figure 31.4   Cause/effect staircase

Methods of problem solving

Brainstorming

Used on its own this is the simplest technique for generating ideas on the cause of a problem. Here the problem solving group simply generates a list of possible causes which are written down without criticism by the group leader for all to see. Ideas from one person trigger other ideas from group members. In this way a very comprehensive list of possible causes can be generated which significantly increases the possibility that the true cause will be recognized.

The weakness of this approach is that it offers no way to test the ideas that are generated, and also there is no segregation of causes from causes-of-causes.

In the previous example, brainstorming would show 'bad supervision' and 'salesman leaves company' both as causes of 'below sales target' rather than 'bad supervision' as the cause of 'salesman leaving'. However, it is possible to reorganize the brainstormed list after it has been generated to identify causes-of-causes.

The Ishikawa diagram

Sometimes called the 'Fishbone' or 'Cause and effect' diagram this is widely used in the quality circles movement.

It provides a simple way to structure brainstorming of problem causes in a manner which has a good visual impact and also segregates each level of cause from the preceding one, by introducing a branch in the diagram between each effect and its cause. It is common to start the diagram by assuming that all causes can be included under the headings of manpower, methods, machines and materials. This is illustrated in Figure 31.5. The Ishikawa diagram also has the weakness that it offers no way to test the ideas that are generated.

Difference analysis

This provides an analytical approach to problem solving which has a number of advantages compared with simple brainstorming and Ishikawa diagrams. It provides a structured method for collecting information which:

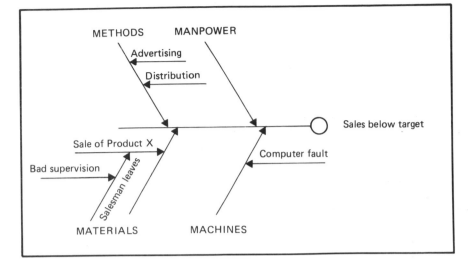

Figure 31.5 Partially completed Ishikawa diagram

- narrows the area within which the problem cause may lie and hence provides a focus for brainstorming possible causes;
- helps identify missing information which may be important;
- aids the process of disproving possible causes which are in fact incorrect.

However, while the method has significant advantages over other problem solving techniques, it is also more difficult to use and requires practice to become proficient. Working with a skilled consultant or attending a training course are probably the simplest ways to acquire the skill and get feedback on how to improve.

The principle behind difference analysis is however quite simple. If an object has a defect, then by definition it is not performing to the expected standard. The reason you believe the expected standard to be 'expected' or 'reasonable' is because somewhere, at some time, you have seen the problem object or something similar to the problem object meet the expected standard or a similar standard.

If you have a new and unique object that has never performed to the required standard then it is important to ask if the standard is reasonable and realistic. If you decide the standard is reasonable, the judgement will be based on your experience of the most similar object and situation you know. Thus if you have two identical objects in identical situations, then by definition they must behave in an identical manner.

Hence the statement 'this object has a fault' means that it must in some way be *different* from a similar object without a fault, and further the difference provides us with a clue about why the fault exists.

Putting it another way, this means that when we are looking for the cause of a problem we can eliminate from consideration all those features of the faulty object which are identical with objects not having the fault.

This is exactly what the service engineer does when repairing faulty equipment. If when he looks at the faulty equipment he can see anything which is different from

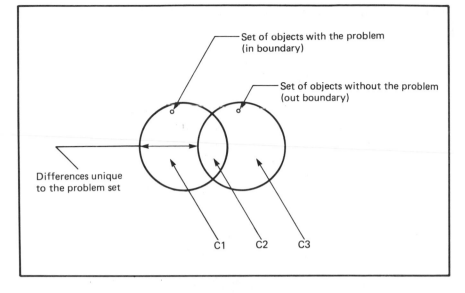

Figure 31.6   Differences unique to the problem set lead us to problem cause

(C1 is a change that acts on a difference unique to the problem set, while C2 is a change acting on features common to both problem and non-problem sets and C3 is a change which acts on differences unique to the non-problem set. Here C1 is the only change which *may* be the cause of the problem because it is the only change acting on something which is *different* about those objects which exhibit the problem.)

the way he knows good equipment to be then he will focus on that difference in looking for the cause of the fault.

The principle is obvious in the case of the service engineer, and when we are problem solving in a familiar situation we instinctively use the technique. We have a clear mental image of a non-defective object which we use to identify (and hence examine) differences which exist in the defective object compared to the non-defective object.

The principle may be illustrated by the following example. A hotel has purchased new cups and saucers. After a while the hotel manager notices that the new cups are getting chipped more frequently than the old ones used to, and also more frequently than the new saucers.

To learn more about the chipping he may compare the new cups with the old cups. Also he may compare the new cups with the new saucers. Dependent upon this comparison he may identify a number of things which are unique or different about the new cups, i.e. shape and decoration. Using 'shape and decoration' as a focus for further examination he may find that the new shape results in the cups knocking together in the dishwasher and hence chipping. Here a *change* (i.e. the dishwasher action) has acted on a *difference* (the cup shape) to cause the *problem effect* (cup chipping).

This is illustrated in Figure 31.6 where the 'set of objects with the problem' are the new cups and the 'set of objects without the problem' can be taken as the old cups. Then one of the 'differences unique to the problem set' is the new cup shape. Because the dishwasher action affects or acts upon the *difference* (i.e. the new cup shape) it may be the cause of the problem. Note that it is irrelevant whether or not the dishwasher action also affects features common to objects without the problem.

As a shorthand, we will talk about objects within the problem set as being 'in boundary' while any object not having the problem is 'out boundary', or outside the boundary of the problem set.

It will be clear from the above example that the technique of difference analysis is most obvious and easy to apply when we have very similar objects 'in boundary' compared to objects 'out boundary'. This is because the number of differences will be small and hence they should lead us quickly to the cause of the problem.

Thus the 'old cups' are probably a more useful 'out boundary' set than the 'new saucers' and both are clearly more useful than knives or forks, both of which are valid 'out boundary' sets but too far removed from the problem set (i.e. too many differences) to be really useful.

However, even when a close 'out boundary' set cannot be found, the method can be remarkably successful if systematic questioning is used to uncover the differences.

When looking for useful 'out boundary' sets look for the element of surprise. If you are surprised that the old cups chip less often than the new, then they are likely to be useful in the difference analysis. Because you are less surprised that the knives or forks don't chip then they are likely to be less useful.

Good questioning skills are crucial in the effective use of difference analysis. Rudyard Kipling summed it up in the following verse:

> I keep six honest serving men
> (They taught me all I knew);
> Their names are What and Why and When
> And How and Where and Who.

In order to uncover all the differences between the 'in boundary' problem and the 'out boundary' situation where the problem does not exist, questions must be asked systematically to cover all aspects of the case.

A common sequence in which to ask the questions is as follows:

- What – what is the object with which we are having difficulty?
      – what is the defect?
- Where – where is the object when the difficulty is first seen?
      – where on the object is the defect?
- When – when (time and date) does the problem occur?
      – when in the object's life cycle does the problem occur?
- How much – how much of the object is affected by the problem?
      – is there a pattern to the defects?

The full set of questions which must be asked is shown on the problem solving worksheet Figure 31.7. To explore the problem in sufficient depth, follow-up questions should also be asked to each of the questions shown.

For example, if we ask 'where are the chipped cups first seen?' the answer may be 'preparation area'. This leads us into the follow-up question of 'where in the preparation area are the chipped cups seen?' By narrowing down the area in which

PROBLEM SOLVING WORKSHEET			PROBLEM STATEMENT: *New cups chipping*	
	In boundary	Out boundary	What is different in the boundary?	Have any changes occurred related to these differences?
What object	What is the object with which you expect to have a similar difficulty? *New cups*	With what other objects would you expect to have a similar problem, but are not? *Old cups* *New saucers*	Is there any feature which is common to the objects in boundary, which is in no way true of objects outside the boundary? *Shape* *Decoration*	*New shape and decoration on cups introduced one month ago*
What problem	What problem is occurring that should not be occurring? *Chipping*	What other problems might you expect to have with the object but have not? *Large cracks*	What is peculiar about the problem in boundary which doesn't apply to problems outside boundary?	
Where	Where geographically is the object when the problem is seen? *Preparation area for laying tables*	Where geographically might the problem be expected to occur but is not seen? *Laid tables*	Is there anything peculiar to the place in boundary which doesn't relate to other places outside boundary? *Washing and storage*	
	Where is the problem seen on the object? *Rim*	Where on the object might the problem be expected to occur but is not seen? *Handle* *Base*	Is there anything peculiar to the part of the object in boundary which doesn't relate to other parts outside boundary? *Thinnest part*	
When	When do these problems occur in calendar or clock time (not relative to events)? *Last month*	When might they occur but do not? *Before this*	Is there anything happening during the time in boundary which doesn't apply to any other stages outside boundary? *New cups introduced*	*Introduced one month ago*
	Within what stages (parts) of the life cycle do these problems occur? *After washing*	Within what stages might you have expected the problem but have not found it? *After evening clear up* *Before dishwasher loading*	What is peculiar about stages in boundary which doesn't apply to any other stages outside boundary? *Dishwasher action* *Dishwasher loading procedure*	*Dishwasher action* *Dishwasher loading procedure*
How much	How much of the object is affected by the problem? *10% of all new cups* *One or two chips per cup*	How much of the object might you expect to be affected but is not? *100% of all new cups* *Multiple chips*	What is peculiar to the affected area in boundary which does not apply to areas outside boundary?	
	How frequently do the problems occur? *One or two per day*	How frequently might the problems occur but do not? *Weekends only*	What is significant about the frequency in boundary which wouldn't apply to other frequencies outside boundary?	
	What is the trend of these occurrences? *Level at one or two per day*	What trend might normally have been expected but does not occur? *Varies with people on shift*	Is there anything significant about the trend in boundary which wouldn't apply to other trends outside boundary?	

Figure 31.7 Problem solving worksheet

(A partially completed worksheet illustrating its use on the problem of the chipping cups. *Note:* Everything changes with time. This means that any time differences (like dishwasher action) are automatically repeated in the changes column.)

the problem is known to exist we eliminate equipment, personnel etc not used in this more narrowly defined area.

At some point the follow-up questions will become so detailed that we don't have the requested information. If we still lack sufficient information to determine problem cause, then the follow-up questions point to the additional information required. When we have sufficient information, the 'differences' column will lead to a solution.

As we saw earlier the problem cause must be a 'change' acting on a 'difference'. Hence we can first identify 'changes' to the 'differences' and then identify which of those changes could be the problem cause. In practice people often find it helpful to simply use the 'differences' and 'changes' columns as a focus for brainstorming possible causes.

If we have an object that has always been defective, or defective over the time period that information has been available to us, then the 'changes' column will not help us and we must brainstorm problem cause from the 'differences' column only.

Disproving possible causes

Following brainstorming there will often be a significant list of possible problem causes with only one of them being the true or correct cause.

Typically people only try to verify theories about cause by checking to see if they can cause the problem in the defective objects. This is only half the story. Another key test is to see if the theory can also explain why the problem does not occur in all those objects in 'out boundary'.

For example, our theory may be that high humidity has caused the sudden outbreak of rusting on metal parts in stores. A key question to ask is, 'how does the high humidity theory also explain why other metal parts in stores are free from rust?'

In general most people try to prove their theories correct by looking for supporting evidence which can only make the theory more probable. However, if you look for evidence to prove your theory wrong but cannot disprove it, then there is a good chance you may be correct.

The method of trying to disprove possible causes is as follows. Each of the possible causes from the brainstormed list is examined in turn against the 'in boundary' and the 'out boundary' information. For each piece of 'in boundary' information we ask 'can the cause explain why we see that this problem exists in this way?' and for the 'out boundary' information we ask 'can this cause explain why this problem does not exist in this situation?' Any possible cause which cannot explain all the facts may be rejected, leaving perhaps one or two possible causes to be checked out through actual test.

Separation of individual problems is necessary in difference analysis because it is an analytical process designed to link a specific cause to a specific problem. This can be contrasted with simple brainstorming or Ishikawa diagrams which may link a number of causes to a generalized problem.

For example, if you have an ongoing reject rate of 5 per cent in a production process (due to machine tolerances) which suddenly jumps to a total of 12 per cent (caused by a batch of faulty materials) then you have two problems.

Thus if you brainstormed the general problem of 12 per cent reject rate, both 'machine tolerances' and 'faulty materials' could appear on the list and be seen to contribute to the overall problem.

However, with difference analysis the problems of 5 per cent reject and 7 per cent reject should be treated separately or the information on one problem will blur the information on the other, i.e. it is more difficult to link the start of the 7 per cent problem to the receipt of the faulty materials, when our information also shows rejects occurring (due to the 5 per cent problem) before the faulty material was received.

While a simple problem may not require completion of a formal worksheet as shown in Figure 31.7, it is always worth checking what we believe to be problem cause by mentally checking if it explains all the 'in boundary' and 'out boundary' information we can think of.

DECISION MAKING

To be successful a decision must have:

- Rational quality – to the extent that there is a difference between the available choices it will be important that the alternative offering the most benefit is chosen.
- Commitment to implement – to the extent that the commitment of the people involved is necessary for effective implementation, it will be important to gain that commitment.

When choosing who to involve in a decision, you should consider who can contribute to requirements for quality and commitment. Although most managers give overriding consideration to achieving a high quality decision, more decisions probably fail through lack of a real commitment to follow them through and make them work.

The decision making process described here is ideal for use individually or with a group. Because it offers a clear and logical approach to selecting a high quality alternative while actively involving the group in the decision making process it is also excellent as a means of gaining group commitment.

Every decision will contain three elements:

- objectives – or the things we wish to achieve as a result of the decision;
- alternatives – or the choices available to us;
- risks – or the uncertainty that a particular alternative will actually deliver the objectives we want or has unplanned side effects.

The ideal decision maker will be someone who clearly identifies his objectives, creatively generates new choices or ways of meeting those objectives, and is prepared to make choices involving risk where the benefit/risk pay-off of a choice makes it the most appropriate solution.

However, our flesh and blood manager frequently behaves very differently from the ideal model. Typically he adopts an approach which may be called incremental analysis in which he moves a minimum distance from the existing situation when change is required.

First he may have no clear idea of his objectives. Rather he finds that something has gone wrong and he simply wishes to get out of trouble or make some improvement. Thus he is looking for an acceptable rather than the best solution.

Next he may have spent little time creatively generating new approaches with the result that the choices available to him only represent small changes to the existing situation.

Finally, he may not be working in an environment in which risk taking is encouraged. Too many people may have an investment in the current situation and be unwilling to exchange it for the uncertain future associated with a significantly different approach.

The process for decision making discussed helps to overcome these difficulties because it is structured in the following way. It starts with a discussion of the objectives (rather than an argument over the alternatives). By doing this we can:

- improve understanding of what an ideal solution could achieve;
- generate commitment to more than a minimum solution;
- avoid the politics of 'hidden objectives' because every individual knows that an undeclared objective will not be available to give weight to his choice at a later stage.

Following agreement on the objectives, a brainstorming session can take place to creatively generate new solutions or choices if this appears appropriate (i.e. existing choices appear lacking in some respect). The brainstorming can be creative and avoid criticism because it is understood that evaluation against objectives is the next step.

After alternatives have been generated they are scored against each objective in turn with the purpose of finding the maximum overall benefit (achievement of objectives). This avoids the 'information overload' and fruitless argument that can result from a direct overall comparison of alternatives against each other.

Having identified the alternative which offers the best overall benefit we then evaluate that alternative for risks. What are the unknowns and what could go wrong if that choice were adopted? If the alternative offering the best benefit also has significant risk, then other alternatives must be evaluated and the one offering the best risk/benefit pay-off chosen. This allows an open discussion on the level of risk people are prepared to accept.

Decision level

Decisions can occur at three levels and it is important to be clear at what level you are acting.

Decisions you can make are those decisions where you have the authority to act.

Decisions you can recommend are those decisions where you can only recommend to the person having the authority to act.

Decisions you must accept are those decisions made by others which will not be changed by any recommendation of yours. Here you can only make subsidiary decisions on how to come to terms with a situation which will not change.

If we try to act at too high a level then time is wasted in planning a decision that will not be acted upon. If we act at too low a level then we may be accepting unnecessary constraints which result in a sub-optimum choice.

The decision statement

The decision making process should start with a single-sentence decision statement to specify the decision to be made. Care should be taken to ensure that the decision level is correct and that there are no unnecessary modifiers. Take for example the decision statement, 'Buy a new car for my wife'. Is the word 'new' an unnecessary modifier and would you consider a second hand car? Do you really

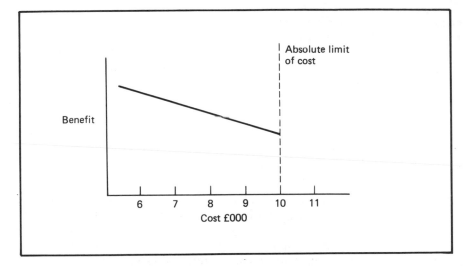

Figure 31.8 A benefit graph for car cost

(Within a defined limit there is a relationship between cost and benefit. Beyond this limit the graph is discontinuous and no effective decision can be made.)

have the power to act or will your wife be unhappy if you choose a car for her, without her involvement?

Decision objectives

The extent to which an alternative meets an objective is the benefit that the alternative provides. In addition some objectives may have limits which must not be violated or the decision will have failed.

For example, if you can raise a maximum of £10 000 to buy a car but you would like to buy as cheaply as possible, then the benefit graph would look as in Figure 31.8.

By breaking the cost requirement into two parts it can be described as follows: essential objective – cost not to exceed £10 000; and desirable objective – cost to be as low as possible. However, not every requirement will have an essential and desirable objective within it.

For example, we order from a supplier a shipment of goods, but our plant is shut down until 10 August and our customer contract will be cancelled if the goods are not available by 20 August. Between 10–20 August it makes no difference when the goods are received. In this case we only need specify an essential objective, i.e. delivery must be between 10–20 August.

Note that if it were an advantage to have the goods early then there would also be a desirable objective – 'Goods delivered as soon as possible after 10 August'.

An example of a desirable only objective could be the plant colour scheme, i.e. – colour scheme liked by staff and promotes effective work practice. While it is possible to imagine a colour scheme so grotesque that people stop working or leave the company it is so unlikely that an essential objective need not be framed in these terms.

Setting objectives

The first step is to brainstorm all the possible objectives and examine them to ensure that all aspects of the decision are covered. Next examine the objectives for overlap and combine any objectives which are saying the same thing in different ways. Next, separate the objectives into those which are essential and those which are desirable.

Essential objectives should then be worded so that the limit is clear and measurable, because it will be important to know if an essential objective has been violated and that choice is a 'no go'.

Desirable objectives should be worded so that it is clear how alternatives can be measured against those objectives.

The achievement of some objectives will be more important than that of others and it will be necessary to weight the objectives so that the final choice will be focused on satisfying the most important objectives.

The method of weighting desirable objectives is chosen for two practical considerations:

- People are much better at making comparative than absolute judgements. For example few people have 'perfect pitch' and can tell you the frequency of a musical note. However most people can tell if one note is higher or lower than another.
- The ability to discriminate is limited and the weighting scale used must be comparable with our ability to use that scale. A scale of 1–10 appears practical and convenient.

In order to weight the desirable objectives, first identify the most important desirable objective and 'benchmark' it with a weighting of 10. Each of the other desirable objectives is then compared with the benchmark and given a weighting from 1–10 dependent upon how important it is seen compared with the benchmark.

It is quite acceptable to have two or more objectives with the same weighting. Be careful not to finish up with a large number of low weighted objectives which in total outweigh a single high weighted objective which is in fact more important.

Below is an example of what our objectives might be if we were considering a job offer.

Essential objectives
   Salary greater than £25 000
   House move not necessary

Desirable objectives	Wt
Offers interesting work	10
Salary as high as possible	8
Opportunities for advancement	4

Objective	Job 1	Job 2	Job 3	Job 4
Salary as high as possible	Salary offer £23 500 Score N/A	Salary offer £26 000 Score 6	Salary offer £27 500 Score 8	Salary offer £30 000 Score 10

Figure 31.9   Evaluating job offers

Note that if you only have one job offer then you are faced with a binary decision so that you can either accept or refuse that offer. Your decision will depend upon how well your present job and the offer compare against the objectives.

Observe also how the essential objectives are clearly measurable, allowing a determination of whether an alternative meets the requirements and is a 'go' or 'no go'.

Generating alternatives

In some situations the alternatives are fixed and there is no need to pursue new, or attempt to improve existing ones. Choosing a new car might be an example where you are limited by what is available on the market within your price range, and generating additional alternatives will not be possible.

If none of the alternatives available meets your needs very well this is an indication that you should look for new ideas. Even if existing alternatives are satisfactory this should not blind you to the possibility of an even better alternative.

Brainstorming or other creativity techniques may be used to generate new alternatives, using your objectives as a focus for creating the new ideas.

Evaluating alternatives

Once alternative solutions have been identified they must be evaluated against the objectives to determine which one offers the most benefit. First, any alternative which fails to meet an essential objective can be eliminated. Second, all the alternatives should be scored against each objective in turn.

Say for example you have received four job offers and were evaluating the salary objective, then the evaluation might be as in Figure 31.9. Note that the job offering £23 500 has been eliminated because it does not achieve the minimum requirement of £25 000.

Note also that the score need not have a simple relationship to salary, i.e. because of current debts, house mortgage or other reasons, a salary of £27 500 might be much more valuable than a salary of £26 000, while a salary of £30 000 might be only marginally more useful than £27 500. The question the score should be answering is what does this (salary) mean to me? What is it worth?

Also be careful to ensure that what you measure is what you want. For example, if one job also offers a car, will you give that a cash value and add it to salary? If

Objectives	Job 2	Job 3	Job 4
Highest salary possible	Salary: £26 000 Score 6	Salary: £27 500 Score 8	Salary: £30 000 Score 10
Objective wt 8	Weighted score: 48	Weighted score: 64	Weighted score: 80

Figure 31.10   Weighted scores for salaries in each job

another job involves a long journey to work will you deduct travel costs to determine net salary?

Once the alternatives have been scored for an objective the weighted scores are calculated as a product of the objective weighting and the alternative score. Thus, where the salary objective has a weighting of 8 we get weighted scores for salaries in each job as in Figure 31.10.

By summing up the weighted scores that an alternative has for each of the objectives we come up with an overall score which represents the 'benefit' delivered by that alternative.

The alternative with the highest score is then the 'best initial choice'. This is illustrated in the case study which follows, 'Choosing an office copier' and the worksheet in Figure 31.11 which shows the Premiere copy machine being the initial choice with a score of 180.

Risks

When we make a decision, our initial choice is based on what we think is most likely to happen if the alternatives were implemented. However, making any choice involves some risk. The choice we make might not work out the way we expect, or its introduction may have unplanned side effects. Thus we have to make a final decision based on the benefits and the risks of the alternatives.

We all take some risks, and will for example cross a road without concern despite the risk of death associated with a car accident. When crossing the road the high seriousness of an accident is offset by the low probability of its occurrence.

As traffic builds up, accident probability increases and we delay crossing for a while. At the other extreme, people will risk a high probability loss (of cash) in a fruit machine because the seriousness of that loss is low.

Hence the size of a risk (and our willingness to accept it) is a function of probability (of occurrence) and seriousness (if it does occur).

When evaluating risk the elements of probability and seriousness may be conveniently evaluated on a three-point scale of high, medium and low. Risks with high probability and seriousness will be most significant, while those with a low probability or low seriousness will be the least significant. If the initial choice also has little risk then clearly it is the one to adopt.

DECISION MAKING WORKSHEET

Decision statement: Choose an office copier

OBJECTIVES		Zenith MK 1		Premiere		Alpha Copy King	
Essential		Info.	Go/No	Info.	Go/No	Info.	Go/No
Delivery by 1 June		Ex stock	Go	Promised 30 May	Go	Immediate delivery	Go
Plain paper, judged acceptable by user for customer use		Yes	Go	Yes	Go	Zinc oxide paper	No Go
Down time 2 days maximum		Contract available	Go	Contract available	Go		Go
Desirable	Wt.	Info.	Sc.	Wt. Sc.	Info.	Sc.	Wt. Sc.	Info.	Sc.	Wt. Sc.
Lowest cost	10	£2800	10	100	£3200	8	80			
Minimum down time	8	Replacement service	7	56	Good repair service	10	80			
Reduction capability	2	No	0	0	3 reductions	10	20			
INITIAL CHOICE (TOTAL)				156			180			
RISKS			Pr. Se.		Pr. Se.		Pr. Se.			
Probability/ Seriousness				Initial choice	Missed delivery date M H					
					Dealer bankrupt M H					
FINAL CHOICE		Best overall choice								

Figure 31.11 A convenient format for information when making a decision

However, if the initial choice has significantly more benefit than the others but also has substantial risk, then the final choice is more difficult. Here we need to ask two questions: is this a level of risk I would be prepared to accept in any circumstances? and is this a level of risk which is justified by the superior benefits of this alternative?

If the risks associated with the first initial choice are too great then the next alternative must be evaluated, and so on.

Some people are temperamentally greater risk takers than others and there is no correct degree of risk to accept. Thus risk cannot be subtracted from benefit in a mathematical sense to arrive at the best overall choice. Rather the final choice is a matter of judgement.

While an effective manager may be a high risk taker he will also work to reduce risk to a minimum in a given situation and only take risks to achieve worthwhile benefits.

An example of where risks may rule out an alternative is given in the case study which follows. In Figure 31.11 it can be seen that the Alpha Copy King has been eliminated because it does not use plain paper. The Premiere is the initial choice because it offers the best overall benefit (i.e. a score of 180). However the Premiere also has risks of missed delivery and bankrupt dealer which are both seen as medium probability with a high seriousness and which are not outweighted by its marginal advantage. Hence the Zenith Mk1 offers the best overall choice.

Case study – choosing an office copier

Imagine you have just opened a branch office and need to purchase a small copier which is essential to the operation. While cost is a major consideration you will have to pay what it takes to get one. The essential requirements are that it can be installed by 1 June, it must use plain paper and produce copies of a quality you believe can be sent to customers.

You require a minimum down time for repairs and it is essential that the copier is never unavailable for more than two days. Any down time will disrupt office routine to some extent.

While a reduction capability would be nice to have it would not be used very often; other special features are unnecessary as volume will be small. The following copy machines have been examined.

Zenith Mk1

This uses plain paper and is available ex stock at a price of £2 800. You have examined the copy quality and feel it is perfectly suitable to send to customers. From your past experience it is a reliable machine. However the manufacturer's service organization can only offer you a next day repair service. However they have an excellent and reliable loan scheme which offers an immediate replacement machine if any repair exceeds 48 hours. This is a basic machine and offers no special features such as reduction capability.

The Premiere

This machine is new on the market and you are very impressed with the performance of the demonstration model which produces really first class plain paper
copies. Because it is new, delivery is a problem and the dealer was very reluctant
to commit to a 30 May delivery date. It will be repaired by an independent service
organization who can offer an excellent eight-hour repair time. However, you
happen to know the service organization is in financial difficulty and if it went
bankrupt your repair contract with them would lapse. The machine has a number
of features including three different reduction settings and looks good value at
£3 200.

The Alpha Copy King

This produces clear, easily readable copies and at £1 600 it is by far the cheapest
machine. The manufacturer has its own repair organization and offers a 'guaran-
teed next day' repair service. Unfortunately the copier uses a special zinc oxide
paper which is not of a quality suitable to send to customers. Immediate delivery is
available.

CONTINGENCY PLANNING

When a choice is made the implementation of that choice can be seen as an action
plan. Contingency planning is the process of protecting a plan against what might
go wrong in future.

Without a plan, nothing can go wrong and hence contingency planning can only
start once a plan has been developed (this is in contrast to problem solving which
should occur first to provide the information needed to make a plan). Contingency
planning may be needed because there is a weakness in a new plan or to protect an
existing plan where the situation is changing. It can be seen as a number of
brainstorming steps designed to uncover possible future problems which then
become the focus of subsidiary plans to either prevent those problems occurring
or to reduce their effects. Steps in contingency planning are as follows:

1　List all the steps in the plan and identify key areas which include unknowns or
which are particularly critical to plan success.
2　Using 1 as a focus, brainstorm possible problems and then identify those on
your list having a high seriousness and high probability of occurrence.
3　Using 2 as a focus, brainstorm possible causes of major problems and identify
causes with a high probability of occurrence.
4　Develop plans aimed at preventing problem causes identified in step 3 and
which have a high probability of occurrence.
5　Using 2 as a focus identify problems still likely to occur (despite steps 3 and 4)
and list the negative effects that would happen.
6　Develop plans to handle serious negative effects identified in 5. Ensure a
warning mechanism if those effects could start suddenly or unexpectedly.

Because people are anxious for their plans to succeed, they often fail to examine them critically and hence miss flaws which could easily have been corrected. In the same way it is easy to be defensive about criticism of a plan rather than thinking how we can use the information to our advantage.

In contrast Napoleon is said to have mentally rehearsed every battle he fought weeks before the event. He would go over his own tactics, visualizing the enemy defences, their reaction and the terrain.

In the same way we can significantly increase the success of our own plans by mentally rehearsing them both to eliminate possible problems and to prepare our defence should these problems arise.

CHECKLIST

1 *Decide what to work on first:*

- List all the issues you face on a sheet of paper.
- Prioritize list on the basis of seriousness and urgency of each issue.
- Work first on most important issue.

2 *Determine if problem solving, decision making, or contingency planning, is required:*

- If something has gone wrong, use problem solving as necessary to understand root causes.
- If you need to take action to resolve a current problem or capture a current opportunity, and root cause is already known, use decision making.
- If you are concerned that something may go wrong in future, use contingency planning to protect your plans.

3 *If problem solving is required:*

- Specify the problem as a deviation between actual and expected performance.
- Collect 'in boundary' and 'out boundary' data about the problem.
- Test possible causes against the data and through experiment.
- Confirm root cause.

4 *If decision making is required:*

- Specify the overall purpose with a one line decision statement.
- List objectives, separate 'essential' and 'desirable' objectives, and give a weighting to those that are desirable.
- Evaluate possible alternatives against the objectives.
- Check best alternatives for associated risks.
- Make the best overall choice.

5 *If contingency planning is required:*

- Imagine the plan in action.

- List all the possible problems which could occur.
- Develop preventative and protective actions to prevent problems occurring and to reduce the impact if they do still occur.
- Establish measurements and monitor plan for problem occurrence.

FURTHER READING

Adair, John, *Management Decision Making*, Gower, 1985

Buzan, Tony, *Use Your Head*, BBC Publications, 1974

Kepner, Charles H. and Tregoe, Benjamin B., *The Rational Manager*, McGraw-Hill, 1965

Prince, George M., *The Practice of Creativity*, Macmillan, 1972

Simon, H. A., *The New Science of Decision Making*, Harper & Row, 1960

Yetton, P. W. and Vroom, V. H., *Leadership and Decision Making*, University of Pittsburgh Press, 1973

32 Negotiating

Bill Scott

This chapter is in three parts. The first describes a style of negotiating designed to produce the greatest area of agreement in the joint interest of both parties. This is a pattern of negotiating in which the parties work together, creatively, *towards agreement*. The second pattern is one in which each party is concerned more with its own advantage than with the joint advantage. Goodwill and agreement are still important, but the overriding consideration is that which is *to independent advantage*. Third, when goodwill is not important, negotiations can sometimes deteriorate into a pattern of *fighting*.

NEGOTIATING TOWARDS AGREEMENT

When the parties are concerned to work together creatively towards agreement the key activities are exploration of each other's position, and creative recognition of what is in their joint interests.

Those phases of exploration and creativity, however, hinge on having first created a suitable climate and on having some procedure which helps the parties to work together. There is no cause for heavy use of negotiating tactics but there is a need for effective preparation.

The sequence in this section will therefore be:

- Creating the climate.
- Opening procedure.
- Sequence in negotiations.
- Exploration.
- Creativity.
- Subsequent phases.
- Preparation.

Creating the climate

Negotiators usually operate best when the climate is brisk and businesslike. When negotiating towards agreement, they need a climate which is also cordial and cooperative.

The pace of a negotiation, be it brisk or lethargic, is set very early. Within seconds of the parties coming together, during the rituals of meeting and greeting, a pace is established which is durable. It should be a brisk pace – briskness established by the pace at which the parties are moving about and by the speed at which they are communicating.

The cordial character is established in an ice breaking phase. As the parties first meet and interact with one another, they need to adjust and to build their regard before getting into possibly controversial areas. The ice breaking, therefore, needs to be a period in which they focus on neutral topics – the football, the weather, the journey and so on.

The ice breaking is an essential preliminary, so important that it deserves possibly 5 per cent of the prospective negotiating time: a couple of minutes even at the outset of short negotiations; a preliminary dinner and evening out before protracted negotiations.

The brisk and cordial character is thus very soon established. The development of the busineslike and cooperative characteristics comes as the parties sit down and move towards business. Timing and the form of first remarks at the negotiating table should provide the right atmosphere: timing, by an immediate statement so that there is no long gap as members get seated; and the form of the opening remarks focusing on the business, towards agreement.

The cooperative character can be set too at this early stage. This depends on effectiveness in handling the opening procedure.

Opening procedure

There is nothing more likely to produce a cooperative atmosphere than the immediate question, on sitting down: 'Well gentlemen, can we first agree on procedure?'

Note that the word 'agree' is used at the outset. Note that the question is one which will most certainly produce the answer 'Yes'. Also, note that the two parties both establish the 'agree' mood from the outset.

There are four procedural items which should be explored and agreed in this opening stage – the four 'P's: pace, purpose, plan and personalities. The *pace* is the speed at which the parties need to move together. There needs to be harmony on this pace if parties are to work together effectively. There will not be such harmony if one believes that there is a whole afternoon available whereas the other has another engagement in half an hour.

The *purpose* is the reason why the parties are meeting. If one party thinks that the meeting is purely exploratory, while the other believes the purpose is to achieve a final settlement, then the parties are going to be working at cross-purposes.

Even when the purpose has been established in preliminary communication, it is still important at the outset to refresh the consciousness of that purpose. And to take the chance to emphasize that both parties *agree* on that purpose.

The *plan* should be in the form of a short agenda – some four main stages through which the meeting should move.

These first three 'P's – pace, purpose and plan – should be agreed at the outset of every negotiation. The fourth 'P' in the opening procedural stage is *personalities*: the introduction of members who do not know one another, their backgrounds, what they can contribute to the meeting. Skilfully used, this opening procedure has great advantages:

- The meeting can proceed with both parties recognizing joint objectives and a joint means of moving forward.
- The plan gives a framework for control of the remainder of the meeting.
- The mood of agreement can be quickly stated and established.
- The groundwork is set for a smooth and cooperative entry into the later stages of the negotiation.

There is a consistent sequence in these later stages of any negotiation. The sequence is:

- Exploration.
- Creativity.
- Shaping the deal.
- Bidding.
- Bargaining.
- Settling.
- Ratifying.

These phases are – or should be – found in any negotiation, even though they may sometimes become mixed and muddled. The importance of each phase varies a lot, however.

In negotiating towards agreement, the key phases are those of exploration and creativity.

Exploration

When two parties come together, each has its own distinctive view of the aims and possibilities for the negotiation. If the parties want to work together to bake the biggest possible cake, it is imperative that each should:

- recognize what both see in the same way;
- recognize and respect what others see in a different way; and be clear about the way in which their own interests are distinctive.

From such recognition can spring the creative spark of what is then most in their joint interests.

To achieve that recognition each party should independently make a broad statement of its own position, and give opportunity for the other to seek clarification. Then get a comparable 'broad picture' of the other party's position, and clarify that.

Each opening statement needs to cover:

- our understanding – the broad area within which we believe the negotiation will take place;

- our interests – what we would like to achieve through the negotiation;
- our priorities – what are the most important aspects for us;
- our contribution – the way in which we can help to our joint advantage;
- our attitudes – the consequence of our previous dealing with the other party; their reputation as it has come to us; any special hopes or fears which we may have for collaboration.

Characteristic of the opening statement are the following points:

- The opening statements of each party should be independent. Each should state its own position, and not attempt at this stage to state the joint interests of the two parties.
- They should not attempt to make assumptions about the position or interests of the other party. (The making of this assumption serves only to irritate, to confuse and to introduce disharmony.)
- The statements should be general, not detailed, not yet quantitative.
- The statements should be brief. Each should give the other party an opportunity to come into the discussion quickly, both so that the parties can quickly interact and so that others do not get a sense of being overwhelmed by either the duration or the complexity of an opening statement. Keep it short.

As one party makes its opening statement, the other party needs to listen, clarify and summarize.

Listen. Do not waste energy by thinking up counter-arguments.

Clarify. If in any doubt, question to get clear what he is trying to say. But note: question for clarification. Do not question for justification – that forces the other negotiator on to the defensive and runs counter to the creative climate being sought.

Summarize. Feed back the key points of what you understand him to be saying, so that he can check.

Having got clear the view of one party then comes the time for the other party to offer its own opening statement, and for first party's corresponding response – listen, clarify, summarize.

For really creative negotiations, there is a need for these opening exchanges to be carried through frankly in an environment of mutual trust and respect. For these reasons great attention has been paid to creating a positive climate and to underlining agreement and preparing minds in the opening process.

Skilled negotiators are skilled at giving and getting information. They are also conscious that some other parties will seek to exploit them. They therefore look out for danger signals which would suggest a need to change strategy.

If in the ice breaking, the other party insists on probing about business matters ('How's trade? cash flow? quality?') beware. Probably he is simply an unskilled negotiator, but possibly he is aggressive, seeking information that he can later use aggressively. If he is highly assertive in the phase of proposing and agreeing procedure – then again we must beware. An amber light is flashing.

494

If he is excessively anxious that we should be the first to make an opening statement, or in challenging that opening statement: then a further amber light is shown – indeed, this is virtually a red light.

Given a succession of amber lights, or just one red light, then the skilled negotiator will be prepared to change his strategy. He should seek a recess, even though it is still an early stage of the negotiation, reconsider the other party's behaviour and decide whether he needs to change to either of the strategies in later sections of this chapter.

But skilled negotiators practising this characteristic style of negotiating towards agreement can normally produce a positive response.

There is thus a great need for negotiators to develop the skills of creating a cooperative climate, of agreeing procedure, and of openness in the exploratory phase.

Creativity

Agreement-oriented negotiators now have a unique opportunity to achieve something to joint advantage, something bigger than either party could get when negotiating to independent advantage. This is the moment to be seeking together to bake the biggest possible cake.

To achieve that creativity they need first to be imaginative. Later they must impose the forces of reality, but the most productive of ideas may not be seen unless the parties are prepared to range as far as the borderline between reality and fantasy. Be imaginative.

Scandinavian negotiators have a special phrase to launch into this phase. Having summarized the respective positions of the parties as discussed in their opening statements, they say 'All right then – what are the creative possibilities?'

In looking for those creative possibilities there are a few guidelines:

- The pattern of generating the ideas must be broad in its sweep, and interdependent.
- It must be broad because immediately the parties focus on one suggestion (either criticizing or exploring in depth), their minds cannot revert to broad and imaginative thinking.
- It must be interdependent, not only to sustain the cooperation between them but also because each fresh suggestion can kindle a new spark in the imagination of the other. The parties have great potential to be creative together.

This process on recognizing creative possibilities should generate a number of different ideas. There then comes the need to form a bridge between the world in which the parties have been thinking imaginatively and the world of reality in which their performance must be measured by business criteria. They must decide which of their imaginative ideas offer realistic possibilities. They must then assess and agree on the action needed to turn possibility to mutual advantage.

Subsequent stages

The critical periods of negotiations towards agreement are the exploratory and creative phases. From them springs the recognition of mutual interest. There is, of course, need for the later realities to be foreseen, for agreement on the commercial conditions, and for the establishment of realistic plans to implement decisions. Given however the creative atmosphere, then views and possibilities for these commercial and planning discussions can be developed in a similarly open atmosphere.

The approach – 'Let us now explore together' – can be sustained through these later stages without the need to get into the tough bidding and bargaining encountered (and to be further discussed) in the context of other strategies.

However, before starting any negotiations, each party must arrive at the negotiating table well prepared.

Preparation

For any form of negotiation, the negotiator must have done his homework beforehand. He must know the facts, the figures, the arguments.

He needs also to have prepared in two other respects. First preparing for the procedure. He should think through the pace, purpose and plan which he will suggest for the meeting. And having thought them through, it is advisable to jot down the headlines of pace, purpose and plan on a postcard, to serve as a reminder during the meeting.

Second, he needs to have prepared his opening statement: his understanding of the matter for discussion, his interests, priorities, contribution, attitudes; and again, to jot the headlines on a postcard.

It is important, when negotiating towards agreement, not to overprepare. The negotiator who has built a detailed framework of prices, deliveries and so on in his preparations is so mentally committed to those preparations that he obscures the possibilities for being creative in any wider sense.

To summarize, when their strategy is negotiating towards agreement, the parties must first create a climate which is brisk, businesslike, cordial and cooperative. They must then establish and agree on a procedure helping them to work together effectively. From the opening procedural discussion they move into important exploratory and creative phases, and thereafter should be able to sustain the high cooperation already established. This must be founded on effective preparation by each party before the event.

NEGOTIATING TO INDEPENDENT ADVANTAGE

Different skills are needed when the negotiator is concerned with gaining special advantage for his party. In some ways these skills mirror those needed when negotiating towards agreement; in other ways, new and different skills are needed.

In particular bidding and bargaining become the crux of the negotiation. Early moves set the framework, and a different form of preparation is needed. The sequence of this section will therefore be:

- Opening moves.

- Bidding.
- Bargaining.
- Preparation.

Opening moves

The negotiator working to independent advantage must approach the negotiation with a difference of attitude. No longer is his concern to work creatively together with the other party. Rather it is to establish the best deal in the interests of his own side.

Assuming however that the deal will need the other party's cooperation to be implemented, or that there will in due course be a need to negotiate some other deal with the same party, it is important that goodwill should be sustained. Aggressive tactics and power struggles should be avoided.

The negotiator's attitude should not be that he will work towards the other party's disadvantage. His attitude must be to find the best way to divide the cake to give satisfaction to both parties. If he likes icing more than fruit, and the other party likes fruit more than icing – there is no problem. Both sides can 'win'. The skilled negotiator thus works towards influencing the other party to value the fruit more than the icing.

The opening moves will again establish the climate for the meeting. Because of the concern for sustaining goodwill it is again important that the climate should be brisk, businesslike, cordial and cooperative; and it is again important that procedure should be agreed at the outset.

Exploration now takes a different form. It becomes necessary quickly to identify the shape of the deal, rather than to look creatively for some new shape. In this process, both parties become more concerned with 'what our party wants'.

The response to the other party needs to be one of probing, to find out which issues or which ingredients are important to the others. Are they, for example, more concerned about price than delivery, quality, terms of settlement?

It is important in these exploratory stages to keep the dialogue on a broad front. If the move to discussion of a particular item (such as price) is taken too soon or too deeply, it is likely to lead to a premature conflict and also to erode some of the most effective possibilities for later bargaining.

Bidding

In negotiating to independent advantage, the guideline to bidding is to start with that which is the highest defensible. (For buyers, the corresponding phrase is of course 'lowest defensible offer'.)

The opening bid needs to be 'the highest' because:

- The opening bid sets a limit beyond which the party cannot aspire. Having once made it, no higher bid can reasonably be put at a later stage.
- The first bid influences others in their valuation of our offer.
- A high bid gives scope for manoeuvre during the later bargaining phases. It gives something in reserve with which to trade.

- The opening bid has a real influence on the final settlement level. The higher the level of aspiration, the greater the prospective achievement.

The opening bid needs to be high. At the same time it must be defensible. Putting forward a bid which cannot be defended does positive damage to the negotiating process. It is found to be offensive by the other party; and if it cannot be defended when challenged in subsequent bargaining, there is soon a loss of face, a loss of credibility, a forced retreat.

The content of the bid of course usually needs to cover a range of issues. The components of the opening bid in a commercial negotiation will not simply be price, but a combination of price, delivery, payment terms, quality specification and a dozen other items.

The 'highest defensible bid' is not an absolute figure; it is a figure which is relevant to the particular circumstances. It is specifically a figure which relates to the way in which others are operating. If they are pressing to their independent advantage, then we must open with a high bid; but if faced with a lot of competition, the bid must be tailored to the level at which it will at least enable us to be invited to continue the negotiations. If we have established cordial relationships with others, possibly over a long period of time, then we shall know the style in which they will operate and the degree of cooperation we can expect – we know the level at which it is prudent for us to make our bid.

On each individual item the opening bid needs to be the highest defensible. We are certain, when negotiating to independent advantage, to be pushed by others to compromise on one or two issues. We cannot be sure which until the bargaining process is under way; we must aspire high on all issues and keep room to manoeuvre.

The manner in which the bid is stated is important. It should be put firmly – without reservations, without hesitations – so that it may carry the conviction of a conscientious negotiating party.

It should be put clearly so that the other party recognizes precisely what is being asked. The creation of a visual aid, i.e. taking a sheet of paper and writing figures on it, within the sight of the other party, whilst one is stating the bid – this is powerful reinforcement.

It should be put without apology or comment. There is no need to apologize for anything that can be defended. There is no need to comment since the other party can be expected to raise questions on matters which concern it. And voluntary comment (before others ask for it) simply makes them aware of concern about issues which they might never have considered.

Those then are three guidelines to the way in which a bid should be presented: firmly, clearly , without comment.

In responding to bids by the other party there is a need to distinguish between clarification and justification.

The competent negotiator first ensures that he knows what the other party is bidding. Precisely. He asks any questions which are needed to ensure that he gets the picture clear. He makes sure, in the process, that the other party recognizes that these are questions for clarification and not demands to justify. And once satisfied, he summarizes his understanding of the other party's bid, as a check on the effectiveness of communication between them.

The first party should at this stage deflect questions which demand that he justifies his position. He has put a bid and he has a perfect right to know what the other is prepared to offer in return.

Bargaining

The first two steps in the bargaining process should be: get it clear; and assess the situation. It is vital to establish a clear picture of other party's requirements at the outset. We should have got a clear picture of *what* he is bidding already. Now we need to know *why*.

The need is increasingly to build an understanding of what will give him satisfaction and of how to trade to advantage whilst giving him that satisfaction.

We must discover what for him are essentials and what else is desirable but not essential, and what aspects of his bid are really of fringe interest only – where he could readily give.

To achieve this clarity, the guidelines are:

- Check every item of his bid. Enquire why. Ask how important the item is and how much flexibility he could introduce.
- Never speculate on his opinions or on his motives. A speculation only irritates. Moreover it is often misconceived – it is out of our frame of reference, not his, and confuses the negotiations between the pair of us. Never put words into his mouth.
- Note his answers without comment. Reserve our position. Avoid deep diving or premature diving into any issue. Keep it on a broad front.

Assuming significant differences between the parties there are now three options for the negotiator: he can accept; he can reject; or he can carry on negotiating. If he decides on the latter he must be prepared for the next round. His options at this stage are:

- to make a new offer;
- to seek a new offer from the other party;
- to change the shape of the deal (vary the quantity or the quality or the use of third parties); or
- to embark on give-and-take bargaining.

The steps for preparing for that give-and-take are first to issue identification – list the issues in the package. Then prepare the bargaining position:

- An essential conditions list – those issues on which it is impossible to concede anything.
- A concessions list – those issues on which concession is conceivable. For each such issue, a progression stepped from that minimum which could be offered (against counterconcessions from the other party) in the next round of bargaining, to that ultimate limit which might be forced in successive rounds.

During the bargaining stages, each successive negotiation meeting should be opened with a new round of climate formation and with agreement on procedure. Each round should be concluded with the establishment of some means of resolving outstanding difficulties.

In between, the negotiations should be conducted laterally rather than vertically. That is to say, the aim should be to reach agreement in principle on a broad front, then to tackle more detailed negotiations, still on a broad front. A sequence of several successive moves across the broad front; not a succession of narrow penetrations.

When the time comes for compromise, neither party will readily 'lose face'. Neither party will readily concede on one issue without having some corresponding concession on another. It is thus important to solve difficulties on a broad front or, at the least, two at a time; not simply one at a time.

For example, when the parties have been exploring a difference between them in price and when they are reaching the stage of preparedness to make concessions, it is helpful to both parties if one of them interjects a comment such as 'Well, just before we finish that discussion on price, could we at the same time tie in this question about (e.g, the shipping risk) and who is to be responsible for that?'

And so sustaining goodwill and sustaining efforts to keep a cooperative climate even through tough bargaining – the negotiation should move towards settlement to independent advantage.

Preparation

As ever, preparation is of critical importance, and the general pattern of preparation should repeat that previously described, with one important difference. This is the need to be more specific during preparation processes. Whereas in creative negotiations it is important to keep one's preparations general and to preserve flexibility, in more divisive negotiations the negotiator needs to be protected from exploitation. He needs to have considered his bids at an early stage. There is this constant dichotomy between the need for flexibility and the need for precise preparations. The one is the enemy of the other. The choice should reflect the strategic situation which will be referred to at the end of this chapter.

To summarize: bidding and bargaining are the key phases in negotiating to independent advantage. It is a type of negotiation needing distinctive attitudes and skills. Bidding and bargaining become more important than exploration. Climate formation and procedural development remain important. So does preparation though it takes a slightly different form.

FIGHTING

Warfare is not a commendable form of negotiation. Nevertheless, negotiators do become involved in confrontations in which the aim has to be to 'win' – or, at any rate, to ensure that they do not 'lose' at the hands of an aggressive party.

This section will review:

- the use of fighting methods;
- the pattern of a fighting negotiation;

- fighting tactics;
- counter-measures.

The use of fighting methods

The fighter's aim is to win and to make the other party the loser. This is a dangerous attitude to negotiations. It puts goodwill at risk; it obscures the possibility of creative cooperation; it naturally provokes the other party to fight back, causing delay and putting at risk the fighter's chances of success. Even when the fighter batters an 'opponent' into submission, he is not likely to find the deal implemented energetically.

The means which the fighter uses are powerful. Both by his personal behaviour and by the negotiating tactics which he uses, he seeks to reinforce the power of his position. His methods include:

- a constant search for gain at every opportunity;
- at each successive stage in the process of negotiating, he wants fresh advantage;
- any withdrawals must be deliberate, tactical withdrawals, designed only to promote greater advance;
- power methods; high in terms of the pace, size and forcefulness of demands, low in readiness to listen or to yield;
- task-centred, concern for his special advantage, not concerned with other party's pride or dignity nor with their feelings. Forcing them to 'accept or else'.

The pattern of a fighting negotiation

The central concern of the fighting negotiator is to win. This winning takes place in the fighting phase of the negotiation – a special version of the bargaining phase. A special version at which he is expert and best able to use his personal characteristics. Quickly he leads the negotiation to the point at which his form of bargaining becomes the dominant activity.

This leaves little time or interest for the early stages of negotiating; little time to get on the same wavelength as other party, or to agree on a plan; little time to explore mutual interests. Even issue identification is hastened and the negotiation quickly becomes focused on his first chosen issue.

The pattern of the negotiation is then 'vertical', deep diving on the first selected issue. He aspires high and pushes until he 'wins' on that and each successive issue.

Fighting tactics

He knows a lot of tactics and manoeuvres, and regularly uses a number. He has his own repertoire, and admires (and tries to emulate) tactics which have been used 'against' him by other negotiators. Here are some of them:

1 *Probing from the start.* The fighter enters the negotiating room, shakes hands

and wishes us 'Good morning' and immediately starts probing. Probing about our business situation, probing about the product or service in which he is interested, probing even about one's personal situation.

The advantages he seeks are in getting information, in building a picture about other party and especially in recognizing weaknesses and vulnerabilities. Additionally, he establishes a power position – a pattern of aggressive leadership.

2   *Get/give.* He is concerned to get something before he will give anything; to get a small concession before he will give a small concession; to get a big concession before he will give a big concession; to get information before he will give information; to get the other party's bid before he will give his own bid; to get the power of being the first to make an opening statement.

Get/give tactics used by skilled negotiators can have positive commercial advantages in the short term. They may well gain ground during the early stages of a negotiation; but in the long run, they lead to delay and deadlock (neither party being willing always to give before it gets).

3   *Showing emotion* (anger, for example). Loud and emotional statements, possibly banging the table: the form of eye-contact, posture, gesture and voice, all displaying emotions.

4   *Good guy/bad guy.* This is a tactic for use by a team of two negotiators. One takes the role of the 'bad guy'; being aggressive, making excessive demands, dominating, uncooperative. He holds the stage for a long time whilst his colleague remains quiet. When he has softened up the 'opposition' with his tactics, the 'good guy' takes over the lead role constructively offering solutions, quietly trying to reach a mutual understanding.

The tactic parallels the archetypal method by which prisoners of war are cross-examined; the prisoner first ruthlessly interrogated by a tough investigator, then offered the sympathy of a different personality to whom – with luck – he would open up.

5   *Poker-faced.* Giving away nothing by expression, tone, posture or gesture. An important part of the fighting negotiator's armoury.

6   *Managing the minutes.* Taking responsibility at the end of each session for production of the record. Slanting interpretations of what has been agreed always to his advantage. Readiness to include the odd item 'which ought to have been agreed' even if there was insufficient time to include it in the discussion – provided, of course, that the odd item is favourable.

7   *Getting upstairs.* When unable to come to an agreement with the other negotiator, taking steps to contact his boss, or boss's boss's boss.

8   *PR.* Many fights are conducted by negotiators acting on behalf of other groupings. For example, the union negotiator representing the work force; the government negotiator representing his country. It is here important for the group which is represented to be kept informed and influenced so that they continue to give their backing to the negotiator. His ability at public relations is thus an important part of the fighter's armoury.

9   *Forcing moves.* There are, of course, yet other moves which some negotiators use – bribery, sex, blackmail, bugging. Most negotiators would see such devices as rankly unethical; but people negotiating very important deals are at risk and need to be on their guard.

Counter-measures

Counters to those who fight are in two forms: long term and short term measures. In the long term, where there is expectation of repeated rounds of negotiations, for example in labour negotiations, there is a need for the development of attitudes, skills and relationships.

This development takes place best when the parties can come together at a place remote from their normal battlefield, and at a time during the off-season for fighting. Especially fruitful is the practice, which has been well developed in Scandinavia, of holding joint working seminars for two or three days. The product of such seminars is not only the development of relationships but the planning of subsequent joint activities.

That is a long term approach. In the short term, meaures to counter the fighter fall into three categories:

- Head him off.
- Control the battlefield.
- Cope with his tactics.

The most satisfying way of coping with him is of course to head off the fight before it develops. If this is to be achieved it must be done in the critical opening seconds and minutes:

- Deflect his opening questions.
- Preserve a neutral ice breaking period.
- Do not be drawn by his probing questions.
- Do not let him assert leadership.
- Do not let him dominate the early moments – what is being talked about, when to stand and when to sit, the seating arrangements.

We are able to control the skirmishing if we can somehow control the battlefield. In negotiating terms, this 'control of the battlefield' is control of the procedures of negotiating. Guidelines are:

- Seek form and plan for the proceedings.
- Seek opening discussion of purpose, plan and pace.
- Keep bringing him back to the agreed plan.
- Keep things fluid. Use the 'broad front' approach.
- Seek for compromise. He will be impervious either to searches for creative resolution of differences, or to sensitive attempts to influence him. His metier is that of compromise. If his position is that he is asking £120 and ours is that it is only worth £100, then settlement is likely to be at the

compromise point of £110. Bargain slowly until you get him down to at most £110.

Above all, keep control of the process – keep control of what is being negotiated and in which sequence – keep to the plan. It will irritate him. He much prefers to be able to run free, but do not worry. A caged fighter cannot do as much damage as one on the loose. To cope with some of the fighter's tactics: when he is using the 'get/give' tactic, we must not give too easily, for if we give before we get, he will regard this as a sign of weakness. He will want to get yet more and will change the tactic into 'get/get/give/' and soon will be aspiring even higher to 'get/get/get'.

We must not give in. We must trade scrap of information for scrap of information, scrap of readiness for scrap of readiness, scrap of concession for scrap of concession.

The only counter to displays of anger is to suspend negotiations, either temporarily or permanently. The human brain is such that emotions (such as anger) are handled in one part of it, rational thinking in another part. Once the brain becomes focused on emotive thinking, then the rational part is cut off. The angry party cannot receive rational messages and it is no use other party trying to instil them. So the counter is to suspend operations.

It does not matter if first party's anger is simply a display rather than real anger. Second party has no way of being sure about the matter. First party has behaved in ways which are not acceptable and second party should immediately suspend.

The 'good guy/bad guy' tactic is difficult to recognize and difficult to counter. But, of course, if it has been recognized in one round of negotiating then the negotiator will be alert for it during later rounds and must hope either to be able to ignore the bad guy or to separate the two 'opponents'.

The counter to 'getting upstairs' is to state strong objection to the tactic and then to arrange for our own boss to come and make it clear that theirs was a losing tactic.

Formality is, inevitably, a device used to try to bring order to such negotiations. However, the fighting negotiator becomes expert in framing and fighting for a rule book which is to his advantage. He is expert not only in drafting and amending rules but in interpreting and manipulating them. The effective negotiator from the other side therefore is forced to build his own corresponding expertise.

Preparation is, as ever, of critical importance for effectiveness in negotiating. When faced with a fight it is imperative to be well prepared procedurally and imperative also to have precise objectives, targets and prepared concession lists. There is special need to prepare options ('scenarios' in the current jargon), alternative approaches which could enable both parties to move forward whilst minimizing loss of face.

The counter to his competence at public relations is to develop equal competence and to ensure that the relevant public is suitably influenced.

In meeting with a fighting 'opponent' then, the negotiator is operating in a world of power. He needs skill to control the battlefield and to prevent his being exploited.

But that is a short term approach. The longer term interest demands that he should work for some joint development of attitudes, skills and relationships with the other party.

SUMMARY

This chapter has been concerned with three distinct forms of negotiation: first, in which two parties seek to move foward cooperatively to create the best possible deal in their joint interests; second, in which both parties aim to preserve goodwill whilst at the same time trying to maximize their independent advantage; third and finally, with fights in which continuing goodwill is not treated as being important.

The choice amongst these approaches to negotiating will depend on a number of strategic issues:

- The extent to which the parties will need to come together again from time to time.
- The respective strength of the parties in the market place.
- The character and quality of their negotiators.
- The time scale and the importance of the prospective deal.

These strategic issues are considered at greater length in the last two books given in the section on Further reading (below).

CHECKLIST OF NEGOTIATING SKILLS

We suggest that readers make two or three copies of this checklist. Fill in one copy, drawing a profile of your own skills – what you're good at, what you're not at all good at, and what lies in between. With a different coloured pen, put in another profile, on the same copy: a realistic ambition of the skill level to which you might develop.

Get a couple of knowledgeable colleagues to use the other copies, and then discuss with you their views of your actual and potential skills.

On this basis, decide what skills you need to develop. For each skill desired, set down on a separate sheet the specific steps you could take to improve your performance. Make a diary note for three months ahead, to check your new effectiveness against the targets you set yourself.

	10	9	8	7	6	5	4	3	2	1
Preparation										
Climate formation										
Planning & control of agenda										
Exploration										
Presentation of views										
Listening skills										
Using creative tactics										
Personal impact										
Choosing bids										
Presenting bids										
Assessing others' needs										
Helping others get satisfaction										
Sustaining goodwill										
Bargaining to advantage										
Using fighting tactics										
Employing countermeasures										
Controlling the negotiating process										

FURTHER READING

Karrass, C. L., *Give and Take*, World Publishing Co., 1974. A good treatment of the tactics used by American negotiators

March, P. D. V., *Contract Negotiation Handbook*, Gower, 2nd edition, 1984. Excellent treatment of negotiating strategy of general interest. Preceded by a mathematical/economic analysis of bidding – also excellent, but demanding a reader with mathematical talents

Scott, Bill, *The Skills of Negotiating*, Gower, 1981. A highly readable expansion of his ideas by the author of this chapter of the Handbook

33 Innovation and Intrapreneurship

Pauric McGowan

Nothing is more dangerous than an idea, when it's the only one you've got.

E. Charter

The environment in which commercial enterprises currently operate is character-ized by intensive competition and change. That change which many organizations experience may often be radical and unexpected; it may be caused by the actions of a competitor, by developments in technology, changes in fashion and tastes, or trends in the economy in which the organization is operating.

An imaginative and innovative response is needed to deal with these challenges not just from the management of the enterprise but from its employees as well.

How ready and able the organization is though to make that response is the focus of this chapter.

Specifically we'll consider:

- why one organization is more innovative than another;
- what is involved in generating an environment for internal entrepreneurship, known as intrapreneurial activity;
- where to look for some innovative ideas; and
- some simple, though tried and tested, techniques to stimulate innovative thinking for solving difficult and thorny problems.

As a consequence it is hoped that managers will:

- see how they might become more innovative and intrapreneurial them-selves;
- have increased knowledge of and skill in managing innovation and innovative people in their enterprise;
- have a greater understanding and appreciation of the importance of encour-aging employees who demonstrate an aptitude for innovative activity; and
- demonstrate a greater sense of commitment and determination to building an innovative environment in their enterprise.

DEFINITIONS

In the introduction above a number of possibly unfamiliar terms were used which must be explained further before we continue, specifically entrepreneurship and intrapreneurship and innovation. Arising from these terms we need to get a picture of who the intrapreneur is and what he does, what innovative tasks might be and what sort of process is involved to implement them.

Entrepreneurship and intrapreneurship

Entrepreneurship is an activity which involves creative thinking, innovation, organization and planning skills. It is reflected in psychological characteristics and behavioural activities of individuals. The practice of entrepreneurship usually refers to owner managers starting or developing their own small businesses. Increasingly though it is recognized that entrepreneurship has an important role to play in the continued growth and development of well established professionally managed enterprises. The increasingly popular term for the practice of entrepreneurship within an enterprise is 'intrapreneurship'.

The intrapreneur

The intrapreneur then is one:

- who demonstrates an ability to think creatively, and to innovate, to organize and plan actions through to implementation;
- who prefers to work within the relative security of a large organization but who thrives in circumstances of persistent, sometimes radical, change;
- who, if given the opportunity, will be the very initiator of the process for change.

In the current highly competitive business environment both the management and employees of the enterprise need to be intrapreneurial.

This is an issue which is developed further below where we discuss factors which determine why one business enterprise is more innovative than another.

What is an innovative idea?

If a company fails to plot the market appeal of its existing product lines and to prepare for the timely launch of new additional products before those existing lines go into decline, it will seriously compromise its market position, its profitability, its potential for growth and perhaps therefore its very existence. So the first definition that comes to mind for an innovative idea must be the identification and development of new product ideas.

However the generation of innovative ideas is equally critical where:

- a new method of production is needed to improve efficiency or a new source of raw material is required to increase competitiveness; or
- new sources of capital need to be identified; or

- a new structure is required to be introduced into the organization to give improved opportunity to talented people or to enhance the systems of communications in existence throughout the organization; or
- new types of skilled labour need to be identified and introduced into the organization alongside the introduction of new, perhaps more complex, technology.

Indeed the generation of innovative ideas is critical in all areas of activity in the enterprise where problems exist and innovative solutions are required to resolve them.

The intrapreneurial act

The intrapreneurial act involves the introduction of a new idea into some situation or circumstance leading to change. The resultant change may be radical and rapid, with a course of development which may be difficult to predict accurately.

The introduction of any new idea then brings with it varying levels of uncertainty and risk. It raises the possibility of resistance to the introduction of new ideas from less intrapreneurial employees within the enterprise and even from some interests outside it.

The practice of intrapreneurship therefore is not likely to be a constant activity conducted every minute of every day. It will rather be a carefully calculated response to opportunities and challenges as they arise.

In the meantime, at a purely operational level the enterprise needs to be organized and run for optimum efficiency and at minimum costs.

The need for tight control for efficiency and a more relaxed environment for intrapreneurial activity however gives rise to potential conflict. It requires a particularly intrapreneurial management flair to balance the two; a point addressed below.

The process of innovation and intrapreneurship

This is a creative activity then where the emphasis is more on the implementation of a creative thought or idea. It is an apparently never-ending process which starts with the identification of an opportunity or a need to be met or problem to be solved.

The process tends towards a conclusion when a decision is made to implement a particular idea from the many that might have been identified and considered, and action is taken to do so.

Figure 33.1 represents very simply the main action areas in the process to identify and implement the best idea, opportunity or solution to a problem.

FACTORS WHICH WILL DETERMINE INNOVATIVENESS

An enterprise's degree of success as a creative and innovative operation depends on a number of factors, for example:

- The quality of the people employed by the enterprise and their aptitude for such activity both at management and employee level.

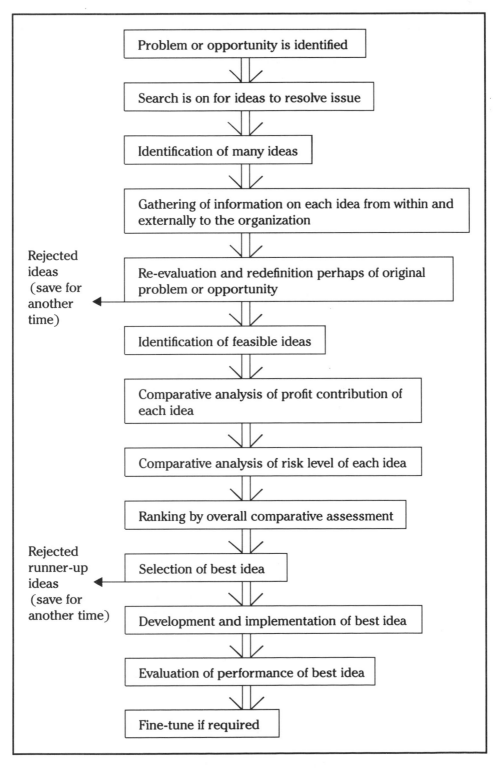

Figure 33.1   The process of innovation and intrapreneurship

- The environment within the enterprise, whether or not it is conducive to such activity and attractive to such people who demonstrate a potential for it.
- The imaginative and efficient application of the process of innovation in developing the new idea.
- The enterprise's record for innovative output as reflected in the quantity and quality of ideas generated by its creative people.
- The effectiveness of screening the ideas for adoption and commercial exploitation; the enterprise's success rate in picking winners.

So is your enterprise innovative? To get some idea consider the following questions. (The list is not exhaustive.)

- Do you or have you ever sought to identify intrapreneurial people in your organization and to give them responsibility and authority to develop their talent?
- What degree of importance do you attach to identifying intrapreneurial people within your enterprise?
- Would you consider the environment within your organization to be supportive of innovative and intrapreneurial activity and attractive to people with an aptitude for such activity?
- Have any/many of your particularly talented and intrapreneurial employees left your company to go on to bigger and better things in the companies of your competitors? If so, do you know why?
- How many innovative ideas have emerged from your organization in the past three years? What were they and who were the contributors? Were they successful?

The management of innovation and intrapreneurship

The management of the process of innovation and intrapreneurship is represented very simply in Figure 33.2. It gives an overview of the broad issues involved.

In the first instance there is the need to ensure that the environment within the organization is such as to encourage intrapreneurial activity, one that is capable of attracting innovative people into the company and keeping them in it. Four key factors in successfully generating such an environment are considered: the style of management in the enterprise, the employees themselves, the organization's structures and the systems of communications within it.

Possible sources of new ideas are considered next followed finally by the management of the new idea, chosen from many, through to implementation.

Each issue is developed in the following sections.

GENERATING AN INNOVATIVE AND INTRAPRENEURIAL ENVIRONMENT

The successful generation of an innovative and intrapreneurial environment within any organization depends, to a great degree, on the style of management practised

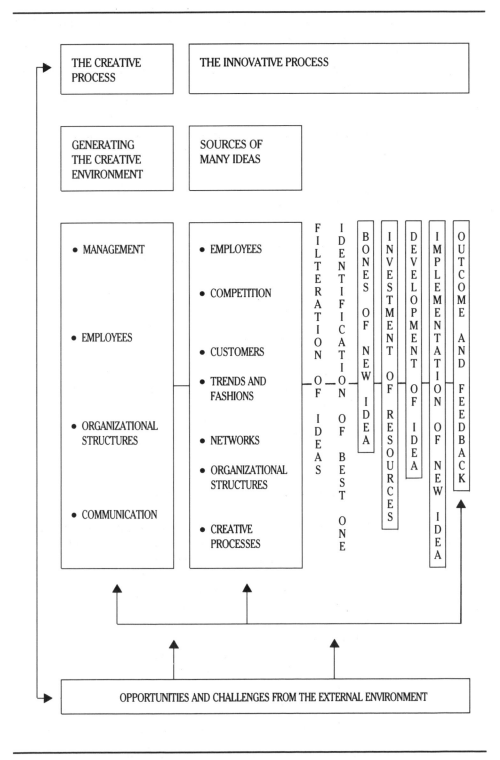

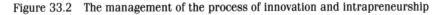

Figure 33.2   The management of the process of innovation and intrapreneurship

within the enterprise, the organization structures and the systems of communications that exist within it.

At the end of the day success in generating an environment conducive to intrapreneurial activity will depend on how information rich that environment is, or how readily and totally accessible the information, particularly technical, is available throughout the enterprise, not just in any one section of it. The four issues raised above have a significant bearing on the determination of the richness of that information flow.

Management styles

The management style adopted by the manager of any enterprise will clearly have an influence on the environment within it for innovative activity.

Always at the forefront of any manager's mind, however intrapreneurial he himself wishes to be, is the need to maintain the enterprise as commercially successful. Operational arrangements must be efficiently controlled if targets are to be met. The facts are that innovation and change activity can be highly disruptive to the enterprise's operations.

Where the enterprise is geared essentially for efficiency the potential for innovative activity is reduced. On the other hand, too much freedom, in the interests of encouraging the innovative spirit, may be wasteful and lead to grand solutions to the wrong problems.

Herein lies a particular management dilemma. A sensitive entrepreneurial management style is essential to striking the right balance between organization for efficiency and freedom for creative and innovative activity to exploit an opportunity.

Note also that for a manager to give employees freedom to act entrepreneurially in pursuit of solutions to thorny problems or ways to exploit new opportunities, he must give to them responsibility and authority to get on with the work.

Some of the key attributes of the intrapreneurial manager which arise from the above points are given in a checklist in Figure 33.3. Review the list and ask yourself:

- As a manager can you identify with any/many of the attributes listed?
- What attributes do you not identify with, why don't you, and what steps will you take to change the situation?
- Can you strike the right balance between control and efficiency and freedom for intrapreneurial activity amongst your organization's innovative employees?
- Can you give a lead to the more innovative employees without appearing to be overly interfering?
- Is your management style such that you are comfortable with delegating responsibility and authority to your innovative employees? or
- Do you perhaps feel that as manager it is your responsibility to identify new ideas in the organization or to suggest imaginative solutions to problems and your employees simply to implement your decisions?

- Disatisfied with the status quo and seeks to foster an environment within the enterprise equally as dissatisfied with it.

- Feels decidedly vulnerable in such circumstances.

- Sees in change and new ideas or new ways of thinking, both opportunity and risk (he seeks to exploit the former and to calculate the latter).

- Has faith in himself, in what he's doing and in an ultimately successful outcome.

- Demonstrates great personal stability therefore in times of change and radical, often unpredictable, instability.

- Can visualize how things can be.

- Can see value in the vision and intrapreneurial talent of others.

- Has courage and confidence in his own judgement of himself and of others.

- Is action oriented and seeks to focus intrapreneurial activity within the enterprise on the needs of that enterprise.

- Sees innovation and intrapreneurship in the enterprise as a desirable resource that can be managed within the enterprise and not as some random accidental occurrence or a threat to progress.

- Can motivate people, harnessing their potential in an imaginative way.

- Is authoritative in a sensitive way, a successful communicator and negotiator.

Figure 33.3 The typical attributes and style of the intrapreneurial manager – a checklist

The type of relationship that might exist between the intrapreneurial manager and those of his employees who are just as innovative and intrapreneurial in their attitude is demonstrated in the simple continuum in Figure 33.4.

Intrapreneurially mature employees need freedom to behave innovatively. The likely management response might be to delegate responsibility without completely abandoning control and ultimate directive authority.

There will always of course be employees who are highly dependent on management for direction, supervision and control.

Review the diagram and consider if there is a particular employee or group of employees in your enterprise who demonstrate an aptitude for intrapreneurial behaviour. To what extent might it be worthwhile acting as a mentor to such a

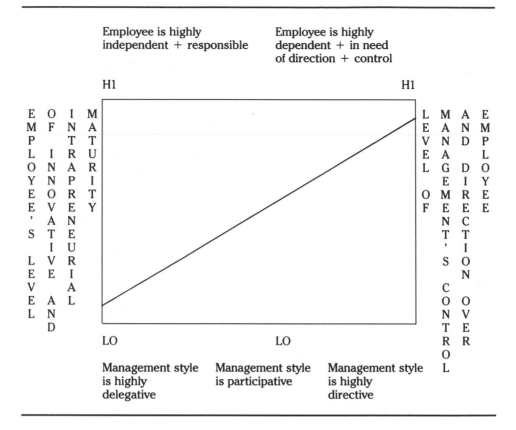

Employee is highly
independent + responsible

Employee is highly
dependent + in need
of direction + control

Hl   Hl

E O I M   L M A E
M F N A   E A N M
P   T T   V N D P
L I R U   E A   L
O N A R   L G D O
Y N P I   E I Y
E O R T   O M R E
E V E Y   F E E E
' A N   N C
S T E   T T
  I U   ' I
L V R   S O
E E I   N
V   A   C
E A L   O O
L N   N V
  D   T E
                    R R
                    O
LO   LO   L

Management style   Management style   Management style
is highly   is participative   is highly
delegative   directive

Figure 33.4   The appropriate management style of the intrapreneurial manager and his relationship with his intrapreneurial employee

person or group of people to bring them on in terms of their role and activity in the enterprise?

INTRAPRENEURIAL EMPLOYEES

There will be employees at every level of the enterprise who have innovative ability and will want an opportunity to act intrapreneurially.

These people in particular are a significant resource to the enterprise. They can be a significant influence on other less intrapreneurial employees, encouraging them and giving them different perspectives on the possible solutions to problems old and new. They can also contribute to the establishment and development of an environment which is conducive to greater innovative activity. Their dissatisfaction with the status quo can be a real force behind the constant striving in the enterprise for new and better solutions to problems or ways of opening up new opportunities.

The challenge to the management throughout an enterprise is:

- to identify those innovative people;

- to give them scope to use their talents;
- to place them in the organization structure where they can be the most influential; and
- to protect them on those occasions when things get particularly tough and uncomfortable for them.

With respect to this last point it is worth noting that intrapreneurs, as the introducers of new things, as initiators of change, often attract adverse responses from colleagues in the enterprise at all levels.

As mentioned above, managers have a responsibility, in recognizing the value of the intrapreneurs' contribution to the enterprise, also to appreciate some of the difficulties they might encounter in their relations with colleagues. Management must be prepared to move to protect them from particularly negative or destructive responses. This is a dimension of the mentoring activity mentioned above and also addressed in chapter eighteen written by David Clutterbuck.

As an aid to identifying who the typical intrapreneur is consider the attributes listed in Figure 33.5.

Ask yourself:

- Can you identify the intrapreneurial employees in your enterprise?
- Have you considered mentoring any particular one or group of intrapreneurial employees?
- Have you considered introducing training and development programmes in the area of innovative practice in order to deliberately encourage greater intrapreneurial activity in the enterprise?
- Do you seek to recruit intrapreneurial people into the enterprise as a policy?
- Do you seek to maintain an environment in the enterprise which encourages intrapreneurial people to remain and doesn't so constrain them as to drive them away from it?

ORGANIZATIONAL STRUCTURE

Very simply the structure of any enterprise defines the relationships that exist between management and employees, between management themselves and between employees themselves.

The structure of any enterprise usually has a formal aspect which reflects the hierarchical relations and channels of communication that exist within it. But there will also be an informal aspect which reflects the unplanned associations and friendships that have emerged throughout the enterprise over time.

Both types of relationships, the formal and informal, assist management in its decision making by defining responsibilities and corresponding levels of authority.

Where the management structure for example is such that sole responsibility and authority for initiating new ideas and for identifying the solutions to problems is retained at the top of the enterprise by senior management, it might be said to be highly centralized, highly directive and excessively control oriented.

The scope for independent intrapreneurial initiative at any other level in the enterprise is limited, bordering on the nonexistent. The likely outcome is an exodus of talented people from the enterprise in search of a more accommodating organizational environment.

- Actively seeks and prefers freedom of action. Flexibility is important to him/her. Resists the influences of traditional beliefs or prevailing value systems, is essentially open-minded.

- Is relatively detached as a personality (perhaps as a consequence of the above points), requiring sensitive management to encourage his/her participation.

- Is a critical evaluator of existing ideas and things, but learns to manipulate, resolving problems from within the system.

- Is sensitive, therefore, to problems – seeking redefinition and originality, implying a fluency of thinking.

- Is a divergent thinker, seeking possible alternative solutions and rejecting, therefore, the first answer as a matter of course.

- Is a good, almost dramatic, communicator, adept at getting others to agree to own private vision.

- Is a persuasive, effective negotiator.

- Is strong on presentations with perhaps a record of lectures, demonstrations or even publications.

- Is essentially self-contained and self-confident.

- Is adventurous/curious/resourceful/speculative in nature.

- Is a moderate risk taker.

- May sometimes be irrational, is certainly a complex character.

- Enjoys his/her work and is committed to it, gets hands dirty.

- Is responsive to opportunities to develop, especially into unplanned areas.

- Is particularly appreciative of recognition and peer interest and wishes to prosper within the organization.

- Is sensitive to criticism and is creatively impotent in an environment which is constrictive, highly organized or ignorant of the value of such activity.

Figure 33.5   The typical attributes of the intrapreneurial employee – a checklist

To generate a creative and innovative environment, an intrapreneurial environment, in the enterprise requires that it adopts a structure which:

- allows the intrapreneur flexibility and freedom to work in the area of greatest interest to him and where he can be most fruitful; (This has implications for mobility *across* the organizational structure.)
- facilitates contact and greater interaction between all intrapreneurial people across the enterprise, particularly on an informal basis, thus allowing a greater cross-fertilization of ideas;
- encourages an open communication system throughout all levels of the organization to ensure an optimum flow of information between intrapreneurial people themselves and management;
- provides scope for real recognition and appreciation of the efforts of intrapreneurial people in the enterprise in terms of both monetary reward but particularly professional advancement;
- ensures an easy identification and access to that person who is responsible for and has authority to make sure an idea is taken up and its potential explored without any demoralizing delay.

An appropriate structure is needed within the enterprise to address that difficult management dilemma of organization for efficiency and accommodating enough freedom for creativity and innovation.

One type of structure which offers scope for a balance between the two is a matrix structure. (See Figure 33.6.) This structure is based on the establishment of project teams formed for specific purposes or to address particular problems.

These teams traditionally draw their membership from across the functional divisions of the enterprise (ie marketing, accounting, personnel and production) or wherever the talent required is to be found in the enterprise, particularly innovative and intrapreneurial. They are, therefore, multi-disciplinary and offer a team-based approach to problem solving.

In addition a matrix structure allows for greater project management control and an opportunity to define 'what has to be done' as far as a specific project is concerned. Creative and innovative activity will have some focus as a consequence.

It also offers an opportunity for the creative person to 'detach' him/herself from the current problem and to become involved in other project teams for a while.

The approach has one main drawback which needs to be recognized. There is often confusion of loyalty for team members to their project group on the one hand and their functional or specialist group on the other. Senior management have a role to play in resolving this confusion and ensuring a full commitment of team members to the project in hand until its completion.

SYSTEMS OF COMMUNICATION

The successful generation of an organizational environment which is supportive of intrapreneurial activity within the enterprise will depend heavily on the effectiveness of the systems of communication, within it. This in turn will depend on how effectively barriers existing in the system have been identified and removed.

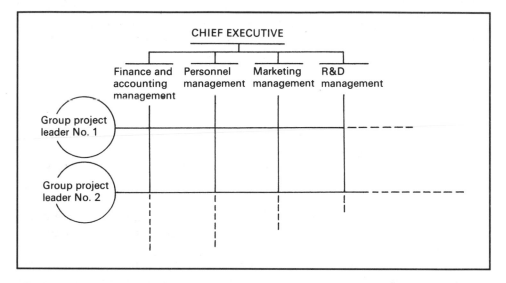

Figure 33.6   A matrix structure

- Separates the functional areas from the production or project areas.
- When a new production idea is identified, a suitable team is established drawing the requisite skills from each of the functional areas.
- Main advantage: rapid response to change, substantial personal involvement and interest generated.
- Main disadvantage: breaks principle of unity of command. (Any one person has two bosses.) Requires, therefore, careful planning and introduction to ensure people understand the system and to minimise conflicts.

It is worth emphasizing that the richness of the information in the enterprise and its flow throughout it will be a key determinant of just how entrepreneurial that enterprise can be.

The richness of the information in the organization will very much be determined by the quality and currency of knowledge and education of the staff in the organization, their skills in interacting with each other, in working in teams and in interacting with developments in the environment outside the organization in terms of keeping abreast of new techniques, best management practices and so on.

The flow of the 'rich information' will, to a large extent, be determined by the structures existing in the organization itself, the people working in it, and the style of management adopted to encourage the flow.

In the first instance, therefore, management needs to take stock of how information is communicated through the system to key personnel who have the skill, the imagination and the motivation to act upon it. Failure by management to identify and remove barriers to open communication will undermine the enterprise's efforts to encourage intrapreneurial activity.

Figure 33.7 lists some of those major barriers which you might look for in your audit. Consider the list and ask yourself:

- Are your innovative employees able to keep up to date in terms of current technical knowledge and best management practice?

- The intrapreneur's fear of being perceived as stupid, irresponsible or wrong. This may be based on a personal anxiety about revealing plans, especially unplanned or outlandish ones which as yet have no immediately definable focus.

- Self-censorship by the intrapreneur because of fear of early criticism of his/her own ideas. As a consequence, ideas are not revealed to associates for assessment but rather bottled up and left unexploited. A loss to the organization.

- Feelings of futility on the part of the intrapreneur in the face of management indifference or ignorance of his contribution. 'Nobody else cares so why should I?'

- A sense of inertia experienced by everybody in the organization about mentioning ideas because time is short and the organization's structures are geared to efficiency, not creativity. The very size of the organization itself may be a barrier to open communications.

- A sense of suspicion on the part of intrapreneurs about sharing their ideas with colleagues and management. This may be due to misplaced rivalry and internal competition or just an inability to communicate their ideas in terms that operating people can understand.

- Inability of operational people and management to understand the technicalities/language being used with respect to the project idea.

Figure 33.7   Barriers to effective communication

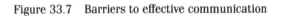

- What provision does the company make to ensure that they do in terms of training programmes undertaken and conferences attended?
- Is the rich information available to the enterprise shared throughout it?
- Is it easy for an employee to come forward with a new idea without fear of ridicule, criticism or prospect of being considered a fool and not promotable material?
- Do intrapreneurial employees who bring innovative ideas forward receive a sympathetic hearing from management and encouragement to continue being intrapreneurial?
- Is it possible that many innovative ideas are lost to the enterprise because management don't have the time, due to other pressures, to appreciate the value of the contributions of their intrapreneurial employees?
- Is the structure of the enterprise itself such that the intrapreneurial employee is unable to present his innovative ideas *direct* to management, to those who ultimately have the authority to decide?
- What barriers exist to the current flow of information and what steps need to be taken to remove them and to encourage a greater information flow?

FINDING NEW IDEAS

The sourcing of new ideas which contribute to the exploitation of new opportunities or to the imaginative resolution of difficult problems is of critical importance therefore to the progress of an enterprise. It is an activity that can be and ought to be conducted in a fairly deliberate systematic way.

A number of the main sources to research for innovative ideas are the following:

The enterprise's current product line and production processes.

Almost all 'new' ideas are developments of ideas already in existence. The development of new products therefore from those already in the enterprise's product portfolio or its existing production processes is a possible source of new innovative ideas. On the other hand a redefinition of an existing product or process may suggest itself for other uses and lead to its introduction to wholly new markets or market segments.

It is in this sort of area that the enterprise stands to make its greatest return on its investment in generating a creative environment and for encouraging intrapreneurial activity amongst its personnel.

The creative talent of such people will allow them to analyse and redefine the fundamental aspects of an existing product or process and to see in them possibilities which would otherwise have been missed by the casual, less intrapreneurially practised observer.

The enterprise's customer

If the enterprise places the customer at the centre of its activities, they become a particularly relevant source of ideas for ongoing development.

Suggestion systems, point of sale interviews and group discussions are ways of canvassing customers for their views on the enterprise's total service to them and in particular how they might be changed for the better.

The company's own people in the market place (sales executives, company representatives, service engineers, delivery personnel) are a ready source of feedback on customers' ideas, criticisms and suggestions. Indeed they are often a fertile source of ideas for product improvement, on gaps in the market, or new sources of raw materials at the right price which neither the enterprise itself nor its competition have yet appreciated.

The competition

The enterprise's competition will always be a keen source of innovative ideas and as close a watch as is legitimately possible must be kept on them and their research and development activity.

The introduction of a new product, the penetration of a new market, the improved sourcing of raw materials, the development of an improved structure within the enterprise, all to ensure an even more effective business and customer focus, need to be identified quickly and evaluated. Steps then may need to be taken by the enterprise to evaluate these initiatives, and to produce a response which is better. (The management of an enterprise must remember of course that the competition is ever watchful too.)

Trends and fashions

The environment outside the enterprise must be one of the most fertile sources of innovative ideas. Although beyond the influence of the enterprise, this external environment is constantly sending signals: information on trends, changes in fashion and tastes, details, however embryonic, of new technologies or best management practice.

There will be those, practised in intrapreneurial activity, who will have the vision to perceive the potential in these changes, with the courage to act upon them. Others, less practised, will simply fail to recognise them until it is too late.

Networks

There are numerous contacts and opportunities for networking outside the enterprise which may offer access to new ideas. The thoughtful intrapreneur will seek to develop these networking opportunities and to bring his skill to bear in determining the likely potential of each.

Likely sources for networking might include, for example:

- Universities and Polytechnics (especially where there exists a track record for research in both the technical and management areas and a bridging between academia and industry).
- Consumer groups.
- Development agencies (Central government funded but established usually on a regional basis to support enterprise development).
- Suppliers.
- Banks and financial institutions (especially where they have units dedicated to assisting new venture development).
- Membership of professional bodies and social clubs.
- Visits to exhibitions, conferences and foreign markets.

BENEFIT ANALYSIS

Encouraging intrapreneurs to think and behave innovatively cannot be done effectively on a 'stop-start' basis. It must be a continuous activity.

As with the athelete running a race, he cannot expect to perform at an optimum level without many hours of often painstaking practice and exercise beforehand.

Similarly with people within the enterprise with an aptitude for intrapreneurial and innovative ability, they need to be regularly involved in the detail and excitement of resolving the difficult problems and exploiting the promising opportunity or idea. Only with constant practice will they perfect their intrapreneurial skills and ultimately increase their effectiveness within the enterprise.

The importance of the multi-disciplinary team has been addressed above. Through such teams more people within the enterprise can be encouraged to develop these intrapreneurial skills. Additionally, the contribution of a number of innovative people from different backgrounds guarantees a greater diversity of input and a greater prospect as a consequence of the best possible solution, from the many, being identified.

One tried and tested approach to stimulating innovative thinking amongst a team is outlined below. It is a practical exercise which you are encouraged to undertake.

Benefit analysis – the background to the exercise; defining 'benefits'

Consumers buy a company's products because those products offer them benefits which they want and for which they are prepared to pay a price. For example, additional benefits which might be sought by the owner of a BMW motor car in addition to mobility might be reliability, safety, prestige and an image of being successful.

Your company's products or services offer benefits to your customers which will determine:

- in what ways your product differs from your nearest competitors;
- what additional benefits might yet be offered to the customer which are not currently available;
- how the product might be effectively promoted; and ultimately
- what price might appropriately be charged.

So let's look at the exercise. It seeks to help the company to identify its unique selling proposition and in what ways that advantage might be maintained over the competition.

A step-by-step approach

The intrapreneurial manager should bring together a group of about six or eight 'informed' people involved with a given product or service of the enterprise, namely:

- company personnel who interact with customers such as company representatives, delivery or sales personnel,
- customers, both actual and potential, of the company.

The group should be asked to identify a chairperson immediately to conduct proceedings. The person most immediately involved with the product should *not* take the chair. This product/service manager should play an essentially supportive role to the proceedings responding to queries put to him by group members. Enough time should be set aside for the exercise, between an hour or an hour and a half is suggested, and no disturbances should be allowed during the exercise. A flipchart should be kept handy for recording the contribution of members.

Step 1: Identify the product or service by name; be sure everyone in the group is clear.

Step 2: The group should list *all* the possible benefits sought by customers who buy this product or service; identify as many as possible.

(Note: the focus of this step is to identify all possible benefits customers buying this product might want and is not solely on the benefits currently being provided by the enterprise itself.)

Step 3: The chairperson should attempt to seek a consensus amongst group members as to the relative importance of the benefits listed in step two.

Step 4: From the prioritized list in Step Three the Chairperson should now ask the product or service manager:

- to identify those benefits sought by customers which the company is currently providing;
- to identify those benefits which the company is *not* currently providing;
- to identify those benefits which the company's closest (in comparison terms) competitor is currently providing his customers;
- to identify those benefits which the company's closest competitor is currently providing which the company itself is not.

The whole exercise may be clearly and systematically presented using the format in Figure 33.8.

The exercise will raise many additional important issues so long as:

- the product/service manager cooperates with the group members and does not direct the group's work
- he avoids exaggerations, half truths and/or hopeful aspirations in his responses;
- he is prepared to learn from the exercise even if the lessons are not always what he likes to hear; and
- he's ready to take action.

CONCLUSION

Once a manager in any enterprise decides that 'at last' the enterprise has finally 'made it', he is in deep trouble. The enterprise that would seek to stand still in the face of the increasing competition and the constant change which characterizes the new entrepreneurial age is much like King Canute of old, ordering back the advancing tide.

It is the intrapreneurial enterprise, the one which fosters dissatisfaction with the status quo, which is practised in intrapreneurial and innovative activity and organized to accommodate the intrapreneurial employee within it, that is likely to achieve continued growth.

These and other issues which distinguish the intrapreneurial and innovative enterprise from those less so have been considered in this chapter. Issues such as the appropriate management style for encouraging and directing the intrapreneurial effort in the enterprise were discussed, as were the characteristics of intrapreneurial employees and the importance of their contribution to the growth-oriented enterprise.

We also considered the appropriate structures and communication systems for the intrapreneurial enterprise to ensure continued intrapreneurial and innovative effort. In addition to a practical exercise in innovative thinking, the sourcing of new

BENEFIT ANALYSIS EXERCISE

NAME OF PRODUCT/SERVICE _____

NO.	WHAT BENEFITS DO CONSUMERS WANT FROM THIS PRODUCT/SERVICE?	Benefits being provided currently by company's product	Benefits not being provided yet by company's product	Benefits being provided by products of company's nearest rival	Benefits being provided by nearest rival's product and not yet provided by company's product

Figure 33.8   Format for conducting the benefit analysis exercise

ideas from amongst the enterprise's current product portfolio, its customers, its competition, its external environment and its networks were also considered and evaluated in the chapter.

Now review the contents and answer the many questions posed at the end of each section. Note the lessons to be learnt from your answers and what gaps remain to be filled in your commitment to building an innovative environment in your enterprise. Then take action!

CHECKLIST ON INNOVATION AND INTRAPRENEURSHIP

- Is your organization in an environment which is subject to intense competition and constant change?
- Is your competition just a little too often more successful in identifying and developing new ideas in the face of this same intense competition and change, than your company?
- Do you ever wonder how come your competition is so effective in adopting new technologies or in responding so swiftly to changes in fashion or trends in the economy?
- How many successful innovative ideas have emerged from your enterprise in the past two or three years?
- Is the environment within your organization supportive of innovative activity and attractive to people who are good at identifying and developing new ideas?
- Do you feel that, as manager, it is your responsibility to identify new ideas in the enterprise or to suggest solutions to problems and your employees' responsibility to implement your decisions?
- Do you know and appreciate how important a resource your innovative employees are to the success and growth of your enterprise?
- Can you identify innovative employees in your enterprise or do you recruit innovative people?
- Do you maintain an environment within the enterprise which encourages such people to remain and doesn't so constrain them as to drive them away from it?
- Is your management style such that you are comfortable with delegating responsibility and authority to your innovative employees to use their creative talents in identifying imaginative solutions to problems?
- What barriers exist in the flow of up-to-date information throughout the enterprise, so critical to the prospects of effective innovative activity within it?
- Is your enterprise organized for optimum efficiency and control or is there scope in the structure for innovative people to behave intrapreneurially in pursuit of better solutions to difficult problems?

This chapter seeks to help you answer these questions.

FURTHER READING

Drucker, P. F., *Innovation and Entrepreneurship*, Pan Business Books, 1985

Nolan, V., *The Innovator's handbook, the skills of innovative management*, Sphere Books Ltd, 1987

Majaro, S., *The Creative Gap, Managing ideas for profit*, Longman, 1988

Pinochet III., G., *Intrapreneuring, Why you don't have to leave the corporation to become an entrepreneur*, Harper and Row, 1985

Index